See God with Open Eyes

Om. Here in this city of Brahman is an abode, a small lotus [of the heart]; within it is a small space. What exists within that space [Atman] should be sought.

Chandogya Upanishad, 8:1:1

Tad vishnoh paramam padam sada pashyanti surayah.

Rig Veda 1:22:20

Sages always see the all-pervading Supreme Lord Vishnu.

Ramakrishna in samadhi during a kirtan in Calcutta, 21 September 1879.

See God with Open Eyes

Open Eyes

Meditation on Ramakrishna

Swami Chetanananda

Vedanta Society of St Louis

Library of Congress Cataloging-in-Publication Data

Names: Chetanananda, Swami, author.
Title: See God with open eyes : meditation on Ramakrishna / Swami
    Chetanananda.
Description: First edition. | St. Louis, MO : Vedanta Society of St Louis,
    2018. | Includes bibliographical references and index.
Identifiers: LCCN 2018038933| ISBN 9780916356095 (hardcover : alk. paper) |
    ISBN 9780916356101 (pbk. : alk. paper)
Subjects: LCSH: Ramakrishna, 1836-1886. | Meditation--Hinduism. | Religious
    life--Hinduism. | Ramakrishna Mission.
Classification: LCC BL1280.292.R36 C465 2018 | DDC 294.5/55--dc23
LC record available at https://lccn.loc.gov/2018038933

FIRST EDITION 2018

Cover painting by Swami Tadatmananda
Cover design by Diane Marshall
Printed in Canada

*Those who wish to learn in greater detail about the
teachings contained in this book may write to*:

Vedanta Society of St. Louis
205 S. Skinker Blvd.
St. Louis, MO 63105, U.S.A.

www.vedantastl.org

Contents

Illustrations

Introduction

See God with Open Eyes: Meditation on Ramakrishna[*] — this title raises several questions: Does God have a form? Can we see God as we see other objects and beings in this world? Can we hear or touch God? Ramakrishna answered these questions with his words and through his life — and many of those answers are collected in this book.

Apart from the mystics and illumined souls, many people doubt the existence of God and think that it is impossible to see God with their eyes open. The doubters' misgivings will be dispelled only if they practise spiritual disciplines according to the guidance of an illumined teacher.

Many mystics of different religions have testified that they have seen God and heard God's command. Moses heard the voice of God from within a burning bush, "I am that I am." Later he received the Ten Commandments from God on Mount Sinai. Saint Teresa of Avila saw Jesus and talked to Him.

God watches every being. A disciple of a Sufi saint experienced this. The saint wanted to test his disciples' spiritual progress. In the morning, he gave a chicken to each one of them and asked them to slash its throat in a secluded place where no one could see this. Most of the disciples returned after following their teacher's order, but one disciple did not return. In the evening, he finally returned with the live chicken and told the teacher: "I saw that God was watching me, so I could not find any secluded place in which to kill the chicken."

*See God with Open Eyes: Meditation on Ramakrishna is based on the author's Bengali book Dhyanaloke Sri Ramakrishna.

Shortly after Ramakrishna passed away, he appeared to Holy Mother. On 16 August 1886, the Master's body was cremated and his ashes were brought in an urn to the Cossipore garden house. That evening Holy Mother began to remove her jewellery, following the custom of Hindu widows. As she was about to take off her bracelets Ramakrishna appeared before her, looking as he did before he was stricken with cancer. Holding her hand, he said: "Am I dead, that you are acting like a widow? I have just moved from one room to another." She did not take off the bracelets, and instead wore them as long as she lived.[1]

Swami Vivekananda wrote in the *Rule Book of Belur Monastery*: "The Lord has not yet given up the Ramakrishna form. Some see Him in that form even now and receive instructions from Him, and all can see Him if they so desire. This form will last until He comes again in another gross body. Though He is not visible to all, that He is in this Order and guiding it is a fact of everybody's experience."[2] In fact, if one sees an Incarnation of God it is the same as seeing God. Jesus also said: "Whoever has seen me has seen the Father" (John, 14:9).

Someone once asked Swami Brahmananda, "Can one see Ramakrishna even now?"

The swami replied: "Yes, Swamiji saw the Master many times. We also see him from time to time."[3]

It is mentioned in the life of Swami Vivekananda that in 1894 at a dinner in Detroit, some vindictive people added poison to his coffee. When Swamiji was about to drink it, he saw Ramakrishna standing by his side, saying, "Don't drink. That is poison."

The Vedanta scriptures such as the Upanishads and the Bhagavad Gita emphasize that Brahman or the Atman cannot be perceived through our eyes or through any of the other senses. The Shvetashvatara Upanishad says: "His form is not an object of vision; no one beholds Him with the eyes. They who, through pure intellect and the Knowledge of Unity based upon reflection, realize Him as abiding in the heart become immortal" (4:20). The Mundaka Upanishad says: "Brahman is not grasped by the eye, nor by speech, nor by the other senses, nor by penance or good works. A man becomes pure through serenity of intellect; thereupon, in meditation, he beholds Him who is without parts" (3:1:8). In the Gita, before showing Arjuna his Universal Form, Krishna said to him: "With these eyes of yours you cannot see Me. I give you a divine eye; behold, now, My sovereign yoga-power" (11:8).

These statements from the scriptures tell us that we cannot see Brahman or God with human eyes; we need divine eyes, or spiritual eyes.

Scientists use telescopes to see planets that are beyond our perception; they also use microscopes to see minute things that our eyes cannot see. There is no doubt about this because it is a scientific truth. Similarly, we need spiritual eyes to see the unseen God, and this divine sight develops through meditation and other spiritual practices. The *Guru Gita* says: "Salutations to the Guru who with the collyrium stick of knowledge has opened the eyes of one blinded by the disease of ignorance."

On 24 August 1882, M. asked Ramakrishna: "When one sees God, does one see Him with these eyes?"

The Master replied: "God cannot be seen with these physical eyes. In the course of spiritual discipline one gets a *premer sharir*, love body, endowed with *premer cakshu*, love eyes, *premer karna*, love ears, and so on. One sees God with those 'love eyes.' One hears the voice of God with those 'love ears.'

"But this is not possible without intense love of God. One sees nothing but God everywhere when one loves Him with great intensity. It is like a person with jaundice, who sees everything yellow. Then one feels, 'I am verily He.'"[4]

On another occasion, Ramakrishna said: "One cannot see God if one has even the slightest trace of worldliness. Matchsticks, if damp, won't strike fire though you rub a thousand of them against the matchbox. You only waste a heap of sticks. The mind soaked in worldliness is such a damp matchstick. Once Sri Radha said to her friends that she saw Krishna everywhere, both within and without. The friends answered: 'Why, we don't see Him at all. Are you delirious?' Radha said, 'Friends, paint your eyes with the collyrium of divine love [*anurag-anjan*], and then you will see Him.'"[5]

Ramakrishna went to the Brahmo Samaj and found the members meditating with their eyes closed. He told Vijay Goswami, a Brahmo leader: "There was a time when I too would meditate on God with my eyes closed. Then I said to myself: 'Does God exist only when I think of Him with my eyes closed? Doesn't He exist when I look around with my eyes open?' Now, when I look around with my eyes open, I see that God dwells in all beings. He is the Indwelling Spirit of all — men, animals and other living beings, trees and plants, sun and moon, land and water."[6]

The goal of this book is to train our eyes to see God in all. *Sarvabhute brahmadarshan* — seeing or experiencing Brahman in every being and everything is the culmination of Vedantic experience. The Chandogya Upanishad tells us, "*Sarvam khalu idam brahma* — Truly, all this [the visible universe] is Brahman."

As a scientist experiments to test his or her hypotheses, so Rama-krishna tested and verified his visions. Swami Vijnanananda recalled: "When the Master was blessed for the first time with the vision of the Divine Mother, he thought, 'If this vision of mine is true, then let this big stone [which was in front of the nahabat] jump up thrice.' Immediately, the stone did in fact jump thrice. Whatever he thought came to pass. Seeing this, the Master was fully convinced of the genuineness of his vision."[7]

Ramakrishna always encouraged his devotees to see God with open eyes, as He pervades everything and every being. His nephew Ramlal said: "If anyone would meditate or close his eyes while repeating his mantra inside the Kali temple, the Master would tell him: 'What are you doing? You are seated here in front of the living Mother. Look at Her to your heart's content. Practise those spiritual disciplines elsewhere, where you cannot get this direct experience. Suppose you have gone home to visit your mother. Would you sit before her with closed eyes and repeat her name?'"[8]

Ramakrishna: A beacon in the turbulent ocean of maya

Ramakrishna is now in the abode of meditation and not in the domain of name and form. The purpose of this book is to enable readers to reach Ramakrishna, the Divine Incarnation of this age, through various meth-ods of meditation: such as meditation on his blissful form, omniscient mind, divine qualities, exalted lila, and unselfish service.

In addition, meditation can be focussed on the places that he sancti-fied, how he taught meditation and prayer, or on the magnitude of his life and message.

With the advent of each avatar, a new scripture evolves, such as the *Tripitakas* of Buddha, the New Testament of Jesus, and the Koran of Muhammad. *Sri Sri Ramakrishna Lilaprasanga* (*Sri Ramakrishna and His Divine Play*) and *Sri Sri Ramakrishna Kathamrita* (*The Gospel of Sri Rama-krishna*) are the Ramakrishna scriptures. In *See God with Open Eyes: Medi-tation on Ramakrishna*, the authentic history of these last two scriptures is recorded. There are some incidents and quotes that have been cited more than once in this book. I could not avoid these repetitions because remov-ing them would disrupt the flow of thought in each context, and the ideas they illustrate would not be fully presented.

The purpose of the scriptures is to make the unknown known. Once a brahmachari asked M., the recorder of *The Gospel of Sri Ramakrishna*, "What was unique about the advent of Sri Ramakrishna?"

M. replied: "The Master came to prove that God exists. He realized God in many ways — with form and without form. He also made it possible for his intimate disciples to experience God. If those who have never met the Master focus their thoughts on him, he will graciously appear to them. He told his disciples: 'Those who think of me inherit my treasures, as children inherit their parents' wealth.' The Master's riches include knowledge, devotion, discrimination, renunciation, love, peace, mahabhava, samadhi, and so on."[9]

God is truly a mystery to us because God is hidden. This world is God's playground and we are God's playmates. God loves to play the game of "Hide and Seek" with us. Christ said: "Ask, and ye shall receive; seek, and ye shall find; knock, and it shall be opened unto you".[10] If we sincerely seek, we shall find God. The merciful Lord responds when His children sincerely and wholeheartedly call for help. It is meditation that connects us with God and makes our lives peaceful and blissful.

Meditation: A healing balm for the mind

Ramakrishna answers these questions: How should we meditate? Where should we meditate? On whom should we meditate? When should we meditate? What shall we achieve from meditation?

The mind is of two kinds: pure and impure. Peace and bliss are experienced in the pure mind, which cannot be bought in the market. The mind becomes pure when it is free from sense objects; it becomes impure when it is absorbed with sense objects. We wash our dirty clothes by putting them in the washing machine, adding detergent, and turning on the machine. It churns and washes dirt off the clothes automatically. Similarly, mantra and meditation churn the mind and clean it by removing lust, anger, greed, jealousy, ego, and attachment. The whole mystery of spiritual life lies in this cleansing process of the mind. Christ said: "Blessed are the pure in heart for they shall see God."

The primary result of meditation is experiencing God as a living presence in our heart, which brings joy and peace of mind. God is so near to us but we do not see Him. We see everything through our eyes, but we do not see our own eyes. Once in Pasadena, Swami Vivekananda asked an American teenager named Ralph, "Can you see your own eyes?" Ralph answered, "No, except in a mirror." "God is like that," Swamiji told him. "He is as close as your own eyes. He is your own, even though you can't see him."[11] Swamiji meant that we need a clean mind-mirror in which God is reflected all the time.

There is no end to the human imagination. Some think that meditation is nothing but imagination. We imagine so many things but are they all real? Swami Turiyananda answered: "One's imagination [of the truth] ripens into realization. Today's imagination becomes tomorrow's realization. But one should hold onto the truth firmly. If one imagines in the beginning then realization may follow; otherwise it will not. The Atman is first to be heard of, then reflected on, and finally meditated upon. Afterwards, when It is experienced, that is known as realization."[12]

Meditation is the science of calming the mind and attaining spiritual enlightenment. Various teachers worldwide have developed methods to still the restless mind. Equanimity of the mind is called yoga. Patanjali, the founder of yoga psychology, taught that one can control and calm the mind by repeated practice and nonattachment. In fact, practice makes a person perfect. Suppose I want to meditate for sixty minutes, but I fail to focus the mind for fifty-nine minutes. At least I connected my mind with God for one minute: that experience will stay with me forever. It is as if someone brought sixty grains of sugar and dropped one grain on my tongue but took away fifty-nine grains. The experience of that one grain of sugar convinced me that sugar tastes sweet. Thus I shall never doubt the taste of sugar in my whole life. Another example: A mason tried to break a piece of stone by hammering it for fifty-nine times, but failed. However, he succeeded in breaking it on the sixtieth stroke. Did those fifty-nine strokes go in vain? Thus our spiritual journey is a series of ups and downs. Without struggle, there is no victory.

Meditation and other spiritual practices strengthen and calm the mind, develop will-power, and enhance the power of discrimination. Ramakrishna repeatedly said that lust and gold are maya and that attachment to them is responsible for human misery. Devotion and meditation act like a healing balm to the distressed mind.

Ramakrishna: The avatar of the present age

In this present age, Ramakrishna's life and teachings are very effective not only for seekers of God but for others as well. Ramakrishna is now the ideal of innumerable people both in the East and the West. It is the nature of a lover to want to know all of the minute details concerning the beloved; and the more we know, the more our love increases. When love dawns, meditation becomes easy. *See God with Open Eyes: Meditation on Sri Ramakrishna* will enable readers to visualize various facets of the Master and learn many new minute details of his life. This will enhance the intensity of their meditation and help them develop more faith, hope, and love, which are indispensable in human life.

When God takes a human form, we want to see how that avatar lives, acts, talks, walks, laughs, cries, eats, and sleeps like other human beings. When we study the lives of Rama, Krishna, Buddha, and Jesus, we observe their overwhelming divine aspects and supernatural power, but learn very little about their human aspects. We do not see them laughing, crying, and joking like other human beings; but in the Ramakrishna literature we can see the Master crying bitterly for God and his devotees, laughing heartily during conversations, making jokes with his disciples, and also merging into samadhi. Ramakrishna was never a dry monk. As human beings, this human aspect brings us closer to him, and we feel he is one of us and our very own. What shall we do with a God who is seated on a throne in heaven? We need that avatar who will be our eternal companion in our day-to-day life.

This book depicts how lovers of God can establish and deepen their relationship with Ramakrishna through prayer and meditation, and that strong bond makes them feel safe, secure, and saved. Finally, Ramakrishna's heavenly smile during samadhi is an instance of how this joyless world can be transformed into a mansion of mirth.

○　　　○　　　○

I wish to express my gratitude to my proofreaders, my typesetter, my designer, and those who corrected the manuscript on the computer. I also gratefully acknowledge the help that I received from my editors: Kim Saccio-Kent, a freelance editor in San Francisco; Pravrajika Shuddhatmaprana, a nun of the Vedanta Society of Southern California; Linda Prugh, an English teacher in Kansas City; Janice Thorup, a former adjunct professor of writing at Washington University, St. Louis; Chris Lovato, professor, University of British Columbia, Vancouver. Margy Olmstead, a devotee in Tucson, Arizona, made the index.

In conclusion, I must mention what induced me to undertake this project: During meditation with closed eyes, I try to think "*Aham Brahmasmi* — I am Brahman." Again, when I serve human beings with opened eyes, I try to think "*Tattwamasi* — thou art that, or you are Brahman." Both are the great Vedic dictums (*maha-vakya*) indicating that "I" and "you" are the same. This experience of oneness — unity in diversity — is the culmination of Vedantic wisdom taught by Sri Ramakrishna. Only this nondual experience can bring eternal peace and bliss to humanity.

1

Meditation on Ramakrishna's Form

D oes God have a form, or is God formless? This is an eternal dilemma. According to Judaism, Christianity, and Islam, God has no form, but is endowed with qualities such as omniscience, omnipotence, omnipresence, mercy, and power.

According to Nondualistic Vedanta, Brahman is the ultimate reality, the One without a second. It is Existence-Consciousness-Bliss Absolute. It is beyond name and form, devoid of qualities, without beginning or end. It is the unchanging Truth, beyond space, time, and causation. Nonetheless, this vast, infinite Brahman manifests Itself as the universe and individual beings through Its inscrutable power of maya. Thus the one becomes many. When Brahman is associated with maya, Brahman is called God, or *Ishwara*.

According to Dualistic Vedanta, God or Ishwara has a form. God is the creator, sustainer, and destroyer of the universe. God is omniscient, omnipotent, omnipresent, all-powerful, merciful, the bestower of the results of action, and so on.

Are God with form and without form different? Sri Ramakrishna answered this question:

> God with form and God without form are not two different beings. He who is with form is also without form. To a devotee God manifests Himself in various forms. Just think of a shoreless ocean — an infinite expanse of water — no land visible in any direction; only here and there are visible blocks of ice formed by intense cold. Similarly, under the cooling influence, so to say, of the deep devotion of His worshipper, the Infinite

15

Ramakrishna, photographed while in samadhi at Dakshineswar in early 1884.

reduces Himself into the Finite and appears before him as a Being with form. Again, as on the appearance of the sun, the ice melts away, so on the appearance of knowledge, God with form melts away into the formless.

Fire itself has no definite shape but in glowing embers it assumes certain forms. The formless fire is then endowed with forms. Similarly, the formless God sometimes invests Himself with definite forms.

God is one, but many are His aspects. As one master of the house appears in various aspects, being father to one, brother to another, and husband to a third, so One God is described and called in various ways according to the particular aspect in which He appears to His particular worshipper.[1]

Atheists do not believe in God, while agnostics doubt the existence of God. The German philosopher Friedrich Nietzsche declared, "God is dead." Neale Donald Walsch, an American author, wrote: "We need a new God. The old God isn't working anymore."[2] Millions and millions of people think that God does not exist because we do not see God. In this present age, Ramakrishna demonstrated religion to believers as well as to unbelievers such as atheists, agnostics, sceptics, and materialists.

This storm of confusion about God reminds me of an Indian folktale:

A young king asked his minister to answer three questions within three days: 1. Does God exist? 2. If He does exist, in what direction does He look? 3. What can He do?

The minister could not answer the king's questions. When his young servant saw his master depressed, he asked the minister the reason for his sadness. Learning the reason, the servant said: "Sir, I know the answers to those questions. Please take me to the king." Curious, the minister went to the king's court the next day with his servant. The young servant said to the king: "I shall answer those questions, but I have two conditions. First, you will have to come down from the throne and I shall sit there. Second, you will have to ask those questions with folded hands from the floor." The king agreed.

When the king asked, "Does God exist?" the servant replied, "Please bring a glass of milk and put it on the table." When that was done, the servant asked, "O king, is there any butter in the milk?"

"Yes."

"Can you see it?"

"No. But if the milk is churned, butter will float on the surface."

"That is your answer to the first question. If you practise spiritual discipline under the instruction of a real guru, you will see God." The king was satisfied with the answer.

The king then asked the second question: "In what direction does God look?" The servant asked for a candle to be lit and then asked, "In what direction does the light go?"

"In all directions," answered the king. The servant replied, "So God looks all directions." Again, the king accepted the answer.

Finally, the king asked the third question: "What can God do?" The servant replied: "O king, I am a servant of your minister; now I am on the throne and you are on the floor. Just see what God can do."

Doubt is a horrible disease of the mind. An illumined teacher always tries to remove the doubts of his or her disciples. In 1925, two young scientists came to Calcutta to visit Swami Saradananda in Udbodhan House. One of them asked him, "Does God exist?"

"Yes," replied the swami.

The scientist asked, "What is the proof?"

"The words of the rishis [seers of truth]. After experiencing God, they proclaimed that God exists."

"There is a possibility that they made mistakes."

"Is it possible that all sages have made mistakes?"

"I won't believe without experiencing God myself."

"Very well," said the swami. "Is it possible that you will believe anything only when you see it yourself? Suppose you have never been to England. You will have to learn about England from those who have visited it. Although you have not seen it, you can't deny the existence of England. Likewise, God exists: you will have to trust the judgement of those who have seen Him. After seeing God, Ramakrishna said: 'I have seen God. You can also see Him through spiritual disciplines and longing.' In this scientific age, the Master came to dispel doubt by demonstrating religion." The young scientists were convinced by Saradananda's words.[3]

It is not possible for ordinary human beings to comprehend the Infinite God, so God descends to this earth from time to time as an avatar. At that time, we can love and serve God, talk to God, touch God, and establish a relationship with God. That God incarnates as human is not a myth, but a fact. The founders of all world religions testify to this. Ramakrishna said: "The avatar or saviour is the messenger of God. He is like the viceroy of a mighty monarch. As when there is some disturbance in a far-off province, the king sends his viceroy to quell it, so whenever there is prevalence of irreligion in any part of the world, God sends His avatar for its destruction."[4]

Some of the disciples of Ramakrishna were brought up with a western education and they tested their guru from various angles for many years. He always encouraged his disciples to challenge him and not to follow him blindly. "Test me as the money-changers test coins," he would say. "Before you decide to accept a guru, watch him by day and by night." The disciples and devotees witnessed how their guru manifested before them as different forms of gods and goddesses. Ramakrishna appeared as Kali, Shiva, Rama, Sita, Krishna, Radha, Vishnu, Christ, Chaitanya, and many other forms. This convinced the disciples that the Master was an embodiment of all gods and goddesses.

After studying the various forms of Ramakrishna we have come to the conclusion that he was the infinite Lord who took a human form so that we can easily attain him. He himself said: "Who can comprehend everything about God? It is not given to man to know any aspect of God, great or small. And what need is there to know everything about God? It is enough if we only realize Him. And we see God Himself if we but see His Incarnation. Suppose a person goes to the Ganges and touches its water. He will then say, 'Yes, I have seen and touched the Ganges.' To say this, it is not necessary for him to touch the whole length of the river from Hardwar to Gangasagar."[5]

Similarly, if one's mind thinks of any part of Ramakrishna's body, that is akin to perceiving an avatar, or an incarnation of the infinite Lord. One can meditate on any form of Ramakrishna that one prefers. According to Patanjali, "One can meditate on anything that appeals to one as good." However, it is wise to practise meditation according to the instruction of one's guru. But what does one gain from meditation? Ramakrishna answered: "As children inherit the wealth of their parents, so those who meditate on me will inherit my treasures."[6] His treasures are discrimination, renunciation, knowledge, devotion, unselfish love, and samadhi.

There are two things that make Ramakrishna unique as an incarnation: his photographs and his gospel, which came from M.'s personal diary. We have to imagine how other incarnations of God looked, but for Ramakrishna we have three photographs that were taken during his lifetime. Moreover, they were taken when he was in samadhi. We have read many times how the scriptures describe samadhi, but seeing a person in that state is quite different. This is the first time in the religious history of the world that the joy of samadhi has been photographed. These pictures help his devotees in their meditation.

Sometimes we gaze at a picture of Ramakrishna and think: "Will our lives end having only seen a picture of the Master? Shall we have no realization?" But we must remember, we can bring the picture to life through our imagination, and this can lead us to realization. We can meditate on the entire form of Ramakrishna or on various parts of his body, connecting them with various episodes in his life. This method generates more fervour and concentration in the mind of the meditator. Here are a few incidents and stories in connection with Sri Ramakrishna's body that we can use for meditation.

O **Ramakrishna's feet**: The Master's feet remind us of the feet of Vishnu that are worshipped in Gaya, where Ramakrishna's father, Kshudiram, had the vision of the Lord telling him that He wanted to be born as his son. The infinite Lord took a finite form and entered the womb of his mother, Chandramani. We can imagine how Ramakrishna walked on the paths and in the meadows of Kamarpukur, travelled to Calcutta on foot, and strolled in the temple garden of Dakshineswar.

One day Manomohan Mitra, a devotee, came to Dakshineswar. When the Master saw him, he drew up his feet and sat cross-legged. Manomohan was hurt. He said: "Sir, please extend them as before. If you don't I shall cut them off and carry them to my home so that the devotees may worship your blessed feet."[7] The Master smiled and allowed the devotee to touch his feet.

Once another devotee, Kalipada Ghosh, accompanied the Master from Dakshineswar to Calcutta by boat. In the middle of the Ganges, Kalipada grabbed the Master's feet and said: "Sir, I am a wicked man and a drunkard. You are an ocean of mercy. Kindly save a ruffian such as I, who is devoid of disciplines and righteousness."

The Master asked, "What do you want?"

"When I leave this world," replied Kalipada, "I shall see darkness all around, and that terrible darkness will fill me with horror. My wife, children, and other relatives won't be able to help me then. At that terrible time you will be my only saviour. You will have to take me, holding a lamp with your left hand and me with your right hand. I shall always be with you then. You will have to fulfill this prayer of mine."

With his heart full of compassion, the Master said: "All right, all right. Your prayer will be fulfilled. My goodness! You have brought me to the middle of the Ganges and have created such a scene!"[8]

One early afternoon Rakhal arrived from Calcutta and found the Master alone, resting on his bed. Ramakrishna asked Rakhal to sit on the bed and massage his feet. At first Rakhal was reluctant, but the Master insisted, saying: "Look, there is a tangible result from serving a holy man." Soon after he began massaging the Master's feet, he saw the Divine Mother, in the form of a girl aged seven or eight, circumambulating the Master's bed a few times and then enter into his body. This vision overwhelmed Rakhal. The Master then said to him with a smile: "Did you see the result of serving a holy man?"[9]

○ **Ramakrishna's hands:** We can visualize the Master inside the Kali temple waving the oil lamp and fanning the Divine Mother during the vesper service or holding a bit of cotton near the nostrils of the image of Kali to determine whether the Mother was breathing. Some other extraordinary events also took place within the Kali temple.

During Ramakrishna's sadhana his longing for the vision of Kali became so unbearable that he took the sword that hung on the wall and was about to end his life with it — only to fall into deep samadhi. In another incident, the Master slapped Rani Rasmani when he read her mind and discovered that she was thinking of a lawsuit while a devotional song was being sung.

On several occasions, the Master used his ring finger to write a mantra on his disciples' tongues.

One day when Narendra came to Dakshineswar, the Master touched his chest with the palm of his hand and the world disappeared from Narendra's mind.

When Chandramani was dying at the bakul-tala ghat, the Master held her feet with his hands and said with tearful eyes, "Mother, you don't know whom you carried in your womb."

Once, while in a state of ecstasy, Ramakrishna had a vision of Jagannath and tried to embrace Him, but at that moment he fell and broke his arm.

○ **Ramakrishna's chest:** The Master once described how he felt a terrible pain in his chest when a devotee tried to give him money:

> Mahendra Pal of Sinthi once gave Ramlal five rupees. Ramlal told me about it after he had gone. I asked him what the gift was for, and Ramlal said that it was meant for me. I thought it might enable me to pay off some of my debt for milk. That night I went to bed and, if you will believe me, I suddenly woke up with a pain. I felt as if a cat were scratching inside my chest. I at once went to Ramlal and asked him: "For whom did Mahendra give this money? Was it for your aunt?" "No," said Ramlal, "it is meant for you." I said to him, "Go and return the money at once, or I shall have no peace of mind." Ramlal returned the money early in the morning and I felt relieved.[10]

○ **Ramakrishna's back**: The Master's experience of oneness with all creation was made manifest in his own body. Saradananda wrote:

One day the Master was in an ecstatic mood as he stood on the spacious ghat of the main porch looking at the Ganges. Two boats were anchored there, and the boatmen were quarreling with each other. Gradually their quarrel grew intense, and the stronger man slapped the weaker one sharply on his back. At this the Master cried out loudly in pain. The sound of his distressed cry reached Hriday inside the Kali temple. He hurriedly ran to the ghat and saw that the Master's back was red and swollen. Impatient with anger, Hriday asked repeatedly: "Uncle, show me the person who hit you. I will chop off his head." When the Master regained his composure, he told Hriday what had happened. Hriday was dumbfounded by this and asked himself, "How is this possible?"[11]

O **Ramakrishna's collar bone**: When the Master was suffering from cancer at Cossipore, his body became so emaciated that it was hard to recognize him. One day Niranjan was attending the Master and observed his sunken eyes and prominent collar bone. Realizing that he was sad, the Master told Niranjan: "Look, I am now in such a state that whoever sees me in this condition will attain liberation in this life by the grace of the Divine Mother. But know for certain that it will shorten my life." Upon hearing this, Niranjan became more vigilant about protecting the Master. He sat at the gate day and night with a turban on his head and a stick in his hand like a gatekeeper to prevent outsiders from visiting the Master. Niranjan sometimes had to deter people, but he accepted this as an unpleasant duty necessary to protect the Master's life.[12]

O **Ramakrishna's throat**: The Master had a wonderful and musical voice; many people were moved when they heard him sing. Yet it was his throat that became affected by cancer. Swami Saradananda recorded:

> One day in Shyampukur he had an incredible vision. He saw his subtle body come out of his gross body and move around the room. He noticed some wounds on the back of its throat and was wondering how those wounds came to be, when the Divine Mother explained it to him: People who had committed various sins had become pure by touching him, thereby transferring their sins to his body and causing those wounds. At Dakshineswar the Master sometimes told us that he would not hesitate to be born millions of times and suffer for the good of humanity.[13]

At Cossipore, the following incident occurred:

Gopal used to wash the Master's cancerous sore daily with a special solution of margosa leaves boiled in water, which is considered to be antiseptic. One day when Gopal touched the sore, the Master cried out with pain. Gopal said sadly: "Sir, what can I do? If I wash your throat, you will get pain, so let me not do it." "No, no, you go on washing it. Look, I have no more pain," the Master replied. He then withdrew his mind from that spot, and Gopal was able to wash the area carefully. All the while the Master remained silent and cheerful as if Gopal were washing someone else's wound.[14]

O Ramakrishna's face: One can meditate on every aspect of the Master's face. The Holy Mother said that she had never seen the Master gloomy. He was a man of bliss and he shared it with others. His skin was so soft and sensitive that he could not be shaved with a razor. The barber would simply trim his hair and beard with scissors.

Innumerable teachings, including those from *The Gospel of Sri Ramakrishna*, came from the lips of the Master. But he always said that it was the Divine Mother who spoke through him. Not a single untruth ever came from those lips. Swami Vivekananda once said: "For the first time I found a man who dared to say that he saw God, that religion was a reality. He criticized no one. For years I lived with that man, but never did I hear those lips utter one word of condemnation for any sect."[15]

The Master would brush his teeth every morning with a twig and also scrape his tongue. One day while he was in samadhi he fell down and chipped one of his upper front teeth.

Sometimes we wonder: Do our prayers reach the Master's ears? Once Hazra also asked, "Does God listen to our prayer?" The Master answered: "Certainly. I can assure you of that a hundred times. But the prayer must be genuine and earnest."[16]

The Master's eyes were extremely bright and penetrating, compassionate and loving. During his days of sadhana he would cry so intensely for the Divine Mother that the ground of the Panchavati would become soaked with his tears. In later days someone asked him, "How can we attain God?" Ramakrishna replied, "Can you weep for Him every day?" His eyes saw God in everything and every being. In spite of all our imperfections and shortcomings, we hope the Master will always cast his glance of grace on us so that we can see him and attain the goal of human life.

Long after the Master's passing away, a disciple asked Holy Mother, "Does the Master really partake of the food that you offer him?" She replied: "Yes, he does. A light comes out of his eyes and draws up the food. His ambrosial touch replenishes it again, so there is no decrease."[17]

Let us conclude our meditation with this prayer: "O Ramakrishna, sweet is thy life story! Sweet indeed is thy holy name! Sweet too are thy forms, thy words, and thy songs! In fact, what concerning thee is devoid of sweetness?"[18]

2

Meditation on Ramakrishna's Mind

What is necessary for practising meditation? A pure mind. We don't meditate with our bodies or senses. We meditate with a concentrated, one-pointed mind. What is this mind? What does it do? Where does it dwell? Happiness and misery, bondage and liberation are all in the mind. It is very important to understand the mind. We see our bodies and experience the function of our senses, but the mind is incomprehensible to us. At the same time, we think with the mind; we are human, so we are capable of thought. Ramakrishna said, "He who is aware of his conscious self is a man." This awareness is the awakened living mind.

According to Vedanta, mind-intellect-memory-ego originated from the sattvic aspects of the five *tanmatras*, or rudimentary elements: space, air, fire, water, and earth. The four "inner instruments" originated from sattva, so they are pure and transparent. The mind thinks in pairs of opposites. The intellect makes decisions. Memory, or chitta, remembers. The ego establishes relationships of "I" and "mine." When pure consciousness is reflected on these inner instruments, it becomes the *jivatma*, or the individual self. It then functions in the human body as the doer and enjoyer.

Some people think that the mind and intellect are conscious, but they are produced from maya, which is insentient matter. The rays of the sun may fall on a stone and a mirror, but it is reflected only in the mirror. When the sun is reflected in a mirror, it looks luminous, and children can play with the reflected light. The mirror does not generate its own light

Ramakrishna's mind merged in the Infinite watching a flock of *sada bak* (snow white egrets) against dark rain clouds in Kamarpukur. He was then six or seven years old. (*Photo illustration by Diane Marshall.*)

but instead reflects the light of the sun. Similarly, the human mind functions by means of the consciousness of the Atman.

"Desire, determination, doubt, faith, lack of faith, steadfastness, lack of steadfastness, shame, intelligence, and fear — all this is truly the mind."[1] The mind functions in the waking and dreaming states, but dissolves in ignorance during deep sleep, which proves that the mind is not real because it does not exist in all three states. This moving and unmoving world are perceived by the mind. When the mind becomes functionless (that is, without thought waves, or *vrittis*) it does not perceive duality. The mind is the product of maya; when maya ceases to exist for a person, the dualistic world vanishes. In the *Maniratnamala*, Shankara writes: "Who has conquered the world? The person who has conquered the mind."

The Atman, which reigns in the human body, and dwells in the heart like a king. The mind is the Prime Minister and the sense organs are the workers. The king appoints the minister to administer his kingdom. The minister collects information from his workers and presents it to the king. This is the way the human system functions. The king (the Atman) silently observes everything without becoming involved.

The position of the mind in the human body is inscrutable. Sometimes the mind is inside, sometimes outside, sometimes near, and sometimes far away. Where does the mind dwell? In this respect, schools of philosophy have different viewpoints. According to the *Naiyayikas* (logicians), the mind is located in the head. The organs of knowledge are in the head, and the mind also is an organ of knowledge — in fact, it is the gate of all knowledge. The Nyaya school posits that the mind is eternal and formless. Because it is formless, it was not created. It does not expand or contract.

According to Sankhya philosophy, the mind is not eternal: it is a created object. The mind exists until a *jiva* (individual soul) attains liberation. The Chandogya Upanishad testifies that the mind has a form — were this not so, it could not connect with other objects. The sage Uddalaka told Svetaketu that the mind is made of food. Therefore, according to Sankhya the mind has a form. It is destructible, but not so easily. Because it originated from primordial nature, the mind dwells in each human body; it cannot be destroyed without liberation.

According to the Yoga school of Patanjali, "Concentration may be attained by fixing the mind upon the Inner Light, which is beyond sorrow" (Yoga Sutra, 1.36). There is an eight-petalled lotus in the heart chakra that is the dwelling place of the mind. When one meditates on the effulgent light of the Supreme there, one's mind becomes luminous.

It is truly a wonder how deeply our ancient sages and the authors of the scriptures thought. They realized the transcendental truth and left their experiences for us.

According to Tantra and Purana, the position of the mind is between the eyebrows. This is called the *ajna-chakra*. When the mind is concentrated here, it thinks, the nerves of the brain begin to vibrate, and our eyes, ears, and other sense organs begin to function.

However, Vedic teachers hold different opinions regarding the location of the mind: some think it is in the brain and some in the heart. Vidyaranya Muni says in *Panchadashi*: "The mind, the ruler of the ten organs of sense and action, is situated within the lotus of the heart."[2]

Ramakrishna gave a wonderful solution to the problem of where the mind dwells, saying: "The seat of the mind is between the eyebrows [*ajna chakra*]." When he was asked, "Where should we meditate?" He answered: "The heart is a splendid place. Meditate on God there." We meditate with our minds. During meditation, the mind becomes calm and rests in the heart, or merges into samadhi, stopping the thought waves. When we are working, the mind stays in the brain and through its willpower commands the senses to function. We understand from Ramakrishna's words that the mind's resting place is in the heart and its office in the head. In addition, the mind can go inside or outside of the body, or anywhere else. The minds of worldly people move in the lower sensual plane, whereas the yogi's pure mind travels in a higher spiritual realm.

The mind of an ordinary person jumps around like a mad elephant. The minds of most people are busy with lust and gold. Ramakrishna described how the mind of the spiritual aspirant rises into the higher realm:

> There is much similarity between the seven "planes" described in the Vedanta and the six "centres" of Yoga. The first three planes of the Vedas may be compared to the first three Yogic centres, namely, Muladhara, Swadhisthana, and Manipura. With ordinary people the mind dwells in these three planes, at the organs of evacuation and generation and at the navel. When the mind ascends to the fourth plane, the centre designated in Yoga as Anahata, it sees the individual soul as a flame. Besides, it sees light. At this the aspirant cries: "Ah! What is this? Ah! What is this?"
>
> When the mind rises to the fifth plane, the aspirant wants to hear only about God. This is the Vishuddha centre of Yoga. The sixth plane and the centre known by the yogi as Ajna are one and the same. When the mind rises there, the aspirant sees God. But still there is a barrier between God and the devotee. It is like the barrier of glass in a lantern, which keeps

one from touching the light. King Janaka used to give instruction about Brahmajnana from the fifth plane. Sometimes he dwelt on the fifth plane, and sometimes on the sixth.

After passing the six centres the aspirant arrives at the seventh plane. Reaching it, the mind merges in Brahman. The individual soul and the Supreme Soul become one. The aspirant goes into samadhi. His consciousness of the body disappears. He loses the knowledge of the outer world. He does not see the manifold anymore. His reasoning comes to a stop.[3]

Ramakrishna's mind

We generally meditate on Ramakrishna's form and lila (divine play). Very few people meditate on Ramakrishna's mind. Our minds are impure, limited, and full of desires and doubts, whereas Ramakrishna's mind was pure, cosmic, and free from desires and doubts. So it is almost impossible to comprehend Ramakrishna's mind.

We do not stop at seeing the external form of a person whom we love; we want to see his or her inner qualities. Otherwise, we could not know that person fully. In *Sri Ramakrishna and His Divine Play*, Swami Saradananda minutely analyzed various aspects of Ramakrishna's mind, which will be the object of our reflection and meditation. Observing the constitution, movements, and actions of the Master's divine mind, we shall be able to rectify the shortcomings of our minds during meditation. The Master reassured us, saying: "I cast the mould, you put your mind into it and shape yourselves accordingly."[4]

1. His desireless mind: There is no end to human desires. They come one after another. The desire for money replaces the desire for lust, and again that desire is replaced by the desire for name and fame. These three desires — name and fame, wealth, and procreation — have thoroughly bound human beings. In contrast, the Master's mind was free from desires. He cautioned the devotees to be careful about worldly desires: "Is it so easy to take refuge in God? Inscrutable are the workings of Mahamaya, the great enchantress! Does She free anyone so easily? A person who has no relatives, She entangles in this world with a pet cat. That poor person collects fish and milk from here and there and says: 'What can I do? The cat won't eat anything but fish and milk.'"[5]

2. His incredible memory: The Master could remember anything that he heard even once. He had a fantastic memory. During his boyhood, after watching a *yatra* (an outdoor play) about Rama or Krishna, he would teach the lines for different roles from the plays to his friends, and they would perform the entire play in Manik-raja's mango orchard. The village farmers were amazed when they attended that play, and they wondered how it was possible to memorize the dialogue and songs just by hearing the play once.

Nowadays singers put a music book in front of them and sing the songs. Ramakrishna learned 182 songs just by hearing each one once. Once M. related an incident to the Master that he had told to Pandit Padmalochan, but the Master corrected M., saying that he had said that to Bamandas of Ulo. At Shyampukur, the Master asked one of the devotees to sing a song by the great devotee Ramprasad that begins with the lines "Who is there that can understand what Mother Kali is? Even the six philosophies are powerless to reveal Her." While listening to the song, from time to time the Master explained the gist of the song's words to Dr. Sarkar in a low voice. When the singer sang the last line as, "But while my heart has understood, alas! my mind has not," the Master interrupted him, saying, "That is incorrect; please reverse the words. It ought to be, 'But while my mind has understood, alas! my heart has not.' While trying to know Him, the mind easily understands that it cannot comprehend the beginningless and endless God. But the heart is reluctant to admit this; it constantly feels that it can realize God."[6]

3. His resolute mind: The Master always kept his word. He never deviated from truth. When he was nine years old, he promised Dhani, the blacksmith woman who was his godmother, that he would receive alms from her first during the sacred thread ceremony rather than his own mother, which was the custom. He kept his promise during that initiation, going against the wishes of his family members, and defying social customs and traditions.

During his early years, he said, "I do not want to pursue a bread-winning education." He stopped going to school. When he was 17, his elder brother took him to Calcutta and tried to give him a standard education, but failed to interest him in it.

4. His brave mind: There was an inn at the southeast corner of Kamarpukur village that belonged to the Laha family. On the way to Puri, many monks and pilgrims would stop there to rest for a few days. It was said that itinerant monks sometimes kidnapped young boys, so the village boys always stayed away from the monks. But young Gadadhar (Ramakrishna) fearlessly served those monks by bringing them wood for cooking and water to drink. Those monks taught him devotional songs and shared their food with him.

Much later, during his sadhana, Ramakrishna would practise meditation in the deep jungle of the Panchavati at Dakshineswar, which was infested with snakes and known to be haunted. With the intent of stopping him from going there, Ramakrishna's nephew Hriday would throw stones around him to try to frighten him, but Ramakrishna was not deterred.

When Ramakrishna was in Kamarpukur, he would go to the cremation grounds near Bhuti's canal and Budhui Moral at night to meditate. In the dead hours of night, his brother Rameswar would go there in search of him and loudly call for him. Ramakrishna would shout back from a distance to warn him: "All right, brother, I'm coming. But don't come any nearer — the spirits might harm you."[7]

5. His fun-loving mind: Some people think that a monk or a holy person should be grave and serious. But the Master was a humorous and joyful person, as this story shows:

> Many uneducated people of the village could not read the Ramayana or the Mahabharata. In order to hear the epics they would invite a brahmin or an educated man of their community to their homes to read and explain the texts to them. When the reader arrived, people would wash his feet, offer him tobacco in a new hubble-bubble [water pipe], and give him a good seat or a new mat to sit on for the reading. Thus honoured, it would sometimes happen that the reader became puffed up with pride. The sharp-witted Gadadhar observed how such a reader would haughtily occupy an elevated platform in front of the audience and express his own superiority by reciting the verses using an affected tone and making various odd gestures. Later, the fun-loving Gadadhar would amuse people by mimicking egotistical readers amidst peals of laughter.[8]

The Master could laugh loudly and enjoyed making others laugh. One could write a book on his humour. In many places in *The Gospel of Sri Ramakrishna* we find "All laugh" and "Laughter." The Master's face wore a blissful sweet smile.

6. His natural characteristics: Swami Saradananda wrote the following:

> By studying stories of the Master's early life we understand the kind of mind he had when he began his spiritual disciplines. He accomplished whatever he set out to do; he never forgot anything he heard; he shunned forcefully and immediately any obstacle that prevented him from reaching his goal. We see that he performed all actions in this world by placing his firm faith in God, in himself, and in the innate divine nature of all people. He could not accept any idea tinged with even the slightest

narrowness, nor could he bear any low, impure thoughts. Purity, love, and compassion guided him always in every respect. We realize that this aspirant's mind could not be deceived by its own thoughts, nor could it be deceived by others. Keeping before us the characteristics of the Master's mind, we shall be able to comprehend the uniqueness of his life as a spiritual aspirant.[9]

7. His devout mind: Ramakrishna's father, Kshudiram, was absolutely truthful and a devout brahmin. During his childhood Gadadhar observed how his father strictly observed his food practices and brahminical customs, and how he was devoted to worship and spiritual disciplines. After his father's death, Gadadhar was invested with the sacred thread and began to worship their family deity with great sincerity. When the Dakshineswar temple was dedicated, Gadadhar ate puffed rice instead of partaking of the prasad of the temple because it belonged to a non-brahmin. Afterwards, he used Ganges water to cook his own food. Only later did he begin to eat the cooked prasad of the Divine Mother. Observance of strict food habits and steadfast disciplines enhances devotion in spiritual life. In the *Gospel*, Ramakrishna eulogized the steadfast devotion of the gopis and of Hanuman.

8. His faith-filled mind: Ramakrishna had the faith of a little child. According to the scriptures, if a person meditates under an amalaki tree with a particular wish, that wish comes true. With that faith, the Master began to practise meditation under the amalaki tree near the Panchavati after removing his cloth and sacred thread. He told Hriday: "One should meditate by becoming free from all ties. From their very birth, human beings are tied with eight fetters: hatred, shame, family status, good conduct, fear, fame, pride of caste, and ego."[10] Our minds oscillate between faith and doubt, so it is hard for us to comprehend the Master's steadfastly guileless mind. He said:

> Ah, what a state of mind I passed through! One day something bit me while I was sitting in the grass. I was afraid it might have been a snake, and I didn't know what to do. I had heard that if a snake bites you again immediately after its first bite, it takes back its own venom. At once I set out to discover the hole so that I might let the snake bite me again. While I was searching, a man said to me, "What are you doing?" After listening to my story, he said, "But the snake must bite in the very same place it has bitten before." Thereupon I went away. Perhaps I had been bitten by a scorpion or some other insect.
>
> I had heard from Ramlal that the autumn chill was good for one's

health. Ramlal had quoted a verse to support it. One day, as I was returning from Calcutta in a carriage, I stuck my head out of the window so
that I might get all the chill. Then I fell ill. (*All laugh.*)[11]

As we contemplate these stories of the Master, sometimes we are
struck with wonder and sometimes with mirth. To create faith in the
devotees' minds, the Master narrated many of his life experiences and
parables.

9. His independent mind: Ramakrishna never flattered anybody to
get a job as a priest; instead, he was selected because he made a beautiful image of Shiva. When Mathur, the owner of the Kali temple, saw
Ramakrishna's image of Shiva, he requested Ramkumar to prevail upon
his brother to accept a position as priest in the temple. However, Ramkumar knew the nature of his brother: No one could force him to do
anything. At that time Hriday came to Dakshineswar for a job. One day,
Mathur called for Ramakrishna, but Ramakrishna already knew what
was in Mathur's mind. He told Hriday: "I have no desire to be tied down
to a job for life. In particular, if I agree to perform worship here, I'll be put
in charge of the goddess's ornaments. This worries me. It is not possible
for me to accept that responsibility. However, if you were to take responsibility for the ornaments, I would then have no objection to performing
the worship."[12]

When Mathur heard of Ramakrishna's intention, he agreed to his proposal. Ramkumar was also happy. However, the Master could not perform the worship for long. When he was in a god-intoxicated mood, he
could not work. Mathur then appointed Hriday to be a priest of the Kali
temple.

Jadu Mallick, a wealthy devotee, heard that the Master had a problem
eating the late lunch from the Kali temple, so he engaged a cook named
Sudhamukhi for him. After three days, the Master said in a humorous
Bengali couplet: "Sudhamukhi's cooking — no more, no more. When I
eat, I cry." He realized that he would lose his freedom if he continued
accepting this service from Jadu, because whenever Jadu called for him,
he would be obligated to comply. So he released Jadu's cook.

10. His poetic mind: There is no rule that says a person becomes a poet
only by writing poems. The Sanskrit word for "poet," *kavi*, also means
seer of truth or the creator of something wonderful. Rabindranath Tagore
addressed Emperor Shajahan as "Emperor of poets" because he was the
creator of the Taj Mahal, a wonder of the world. Achintya Sengupta, a
famous Bengali novelist, wrote a book titled *Kavi Ramakrishna* in which

he described Ramakrishna's poetic characteristics. For example, Sengupta writes that the Master's sense of beauty was unparalleled and that his creative and artistic abilities manifested in his conversation, singing, dancing, painting and so on.

Swami Vivekananda said: "With a view to teaching the highest truths to the world, the creator created the rishis of the Upanishads, who were poets transcending the ordinary human minds." In this perspective, Ramakrishna was a rishi-poet. Undoubtedly, Ramakrishna's words represent the new Upanishads.[13]

11. His student mind: It is said that only a good student can be a good teacher. Ramakrishna was a great learner. Although he had only a rudimentary school education, from his elder brother he learned how to read Chandi and to perform the worship of Kali and other deities at Dakshineswar. Before he began to worship Mother Kali, however, he took initiation in the Shakti tradition from Kenaram Bhattacharya. During Ramakrishna's sadhana, he took initiation into Tantra from Bhairavi Brahmani and into Vedanta from Tota Puri. In addition, he continuously learned from nature, from his surroundings, and from both good and bad people. One of his famous sayings is, "Friend, as long as I live, so long do I learn." Ramakrishna's main teacher was the Divine Mother. Failing to understand his own divine mood, he prayed to the Divine Mother: "What is happening to me? Am I on the right track?" He supplicated the Divine Mother with a longing heart: "Mother, I don't understand. Why am I in this situation? Please make me do what I am supposed to do and teach me what I am supposed to learn. Hold me close to You all the time."[14]

12. His guileless mind: There was no deceit or "theft in the chamber of the heart" in Ramakrishna. His body, mouth, and mind worked in harmony. He told his disciples: "Whatever one should renounce or accept, one should do it with body, mind, and speech equally. Only then will a spiritual aspirant be worthy of God-realization."[15]

During his sadhana, he observed three main obstacles to God-realization: lust, money, and vanity. The moment his mind determined every woman to be the Divine Mother, his body and senses immediately accepted this one hundred percent. As soon as he realized that the Divine Mother dwells in all women in the world, his lust for women disappeared. Recognizing that attachment for money is an obstacle, he held a rupee in one hand and a lump of clay in the other, and then saying, "money is clay and clay is money," he threw both into the Ganges. From then on he could never touch money. To get rid of vanity, he cleaned the open sewer drain at the house of the sweeper Rasik and washed the toilet at the Kali temple, wiping it with his long hair. He thus destroyed his pride in being a brahmin. The Master taught through his life and not merely through words.

13. His self-controlled mind: Swami Saradananda described how Ramakrishna tested his self-control:

> One day while Sarada was massaging the Master's feet, she asked him, "How do you look upon me?" The Master replied: "The same Mother who is in the temple, the same Mother who gave birth to this body and is now living in the nahabat, that same Mother is now rubbing my feet. Truly, I always see you as a form of the blissful Divine Mother."
>
> One night as he watched Sarada lying asleep beside him, the Master began to discriminate, addressing his own mind: "Oh, my mind, this is the body of a woman. Men look on it as an object of great enjoyment and they always lust after it. But if one possesses this body, one must remain confined within the flesh; one can't realize God. Oh, my mind, let there be no theft [hypocrisy] in your inner chamber. Don't be thinking one thing [inwardly] and pretending another outwardly! Be frank! Do you want this woman's body, or do you want God? If you want the body, here it is in front of you. Enjoy it." Discriminating in this way, the Master was about to touch Sarada's body when his mind suddenly recoiled and lost itself so deeply in samadhi that he did not regain normal consciousness all night. The next morning after considerable difficulty he was brought back to the conscious plane when the Lord's name was repeated in his ear.[16]

14. His divine mind: Our minds are out of control, drunk on worldly intoxicants. When we sit for meditation, our minds become restless like a restless monkey that has been stung by hornets. We are not the masters of our minds, but rather the slaves. The Master was the master of his mind. Whatever orders he gave his mind, it obeyed. Later the Master told his disciples how his mind and body functioned during meditation:

> There is an image of Bhairav [Shiva] in meditation on the parapet of the natmandir in front of the Kali temple. While going to the temple to meditate, I would point to that image and tell my mind, "You must meditate on the Mother like that motionless statue." No sooner did I sit down to meditate than I would hear clattering sounds in all of my joints, beginning in my legs. It was as if someone inside me were turning keys to lock me up, joint by joint. I was powerless to move my body or change my posture, even slightly. I couldn't stop meditating, or leave the temple, or do anything else I wanted. I was forced to sit in that posture until my joints began clattering again and were unlocked, this time beginning at my neck and ending in my legs.[17]

15. His dynamic mind: The scriptures say that the goddess of fortune helps an active person. A man with a lazy and unfocussed mind cannot complete a project after starting it. He blames everyone, even the gods, for his failure. Swami Saradananda wrote:

> The Master's energetic mind could not leave any work half done. This characteristic of his was as manifest in the subtle realm of the spirit as it was in the gross material realm. Because of this natural proclivity, if his mind became filled with an idea, he could not rest until he had explored it to its ultimate limit. Studying this aspect of his nature some readers may ask: "But is this good? Is it beneficial for a person to pursue any idea that arises at any time and become its puppet?" Although the Master's nature did not lead him astray, his behaviour in this respect should not be followed by most people. Positive and negative thoughts constantly arise in weak human minds. It is not prudent for ordinary people to have such faith in themselves so as to believe that only good thoughts will arise in their minds. Therefore, it should be everyone's duty to harness powerful ideas with the rein of self-control.[18]

16. His mind as the guru: In this ocean of worldly enjoyment, our minds harass us continuously and we gasp for a little relief. Swami Saradananda described how the Master's mind would guide him like a guru:

> A spiritual aspirant becomes pure by controlling the mind completely through constant practice of detachment and self-control. The Master used to say that one's very mind then becomes one's guru. Whatever thought waves arise in a pure mind lead the aspirant quickly to the goal rather than leading him astray. It is therefore to be understood that within the first four years of his sadhana, the Master's ever-pure mind acted as his guru to guide him and help him to realize God. We have heard from the Master that at that time his mind not only taught him what to do and what not to do, but at times it would also manifest itself as a separate person who would emerge from his own body and appear before him. That person would encourage him to practise sadhana and threaten him with punishment if he did not dive deep into meditation. That person would also explain to him why he should practise a particular ritual, and would tell him what the result would be. During meditation he would see a young monk holding a sharp trident emerge from his body and say to him, "If you do not meditate on your Chosen Deity, shunning other thoughts, I will pierce your chest with this trident!" On another occasion he saw that young monk emerge to kill the pleasure-loving *papa-purusha* [an evil being] when it emerged from his body.[19]

17. His clairvoyant mind: Ordinary yogis develop the occult power of clairvoyance by practising *samyama* (concentration, meditation, and samadhi). However, the Master was an avatar, so all those occult powers were always present in him.

During Durga Puja in 1885, the Master was staying at Shyampukur for treatment. During the sandhi puja, he went into samadhi for half an hour. Then he said to his disciples: "A luminous path opened from this place to Surendra's house. I saw the presence of the Divine Mother in the image; She had been evoked by Surendra's devotion. A ray of light beamed forth from Her third eye! Rows of lamps were lit before the Goddess in the worship hall. In the courtyard Surendra was crying piteously, 'Mother, Mother!' All of you, go to his house right now. When he sees you he will regain his peace of mind."[20]

Immediately Swamiji and other devotees went to Surendra's house. They were amazed when Surendra told him that the Master's vision during samadhi was consistent with the actual events.

18. His one-pointed mind: A candle is made with white paraffin. The manufacturer adds dye to the melted paraffin and makes candles of different colours. Similarly, the Master's mind would take the colour of a particular mood. At that time if anyone would speak on a different topic, he would experience pain. Swami Saradananda wrote:

> Whenever a spiritual mood arose in the Master's one-pointed mind, he would become absorbed in it for some time. That mood would fully occupy his mind, eradicating all else and transforming his body into a suitable instrument for its manifestation. We heard that he possessed this nature from childhood; while we visited Dakshineswar regularly we also witnessed this phenomenon. We observed that when his mind was absorbed in a particular mood — which arose from listening to a song or in some other manner — he felt an excruciating pain if someone sang a song or spoke in a different mood. Evidently, he experienced pain because his thought waves were suddenly obstructed from flowing towards that particular goal. When a current of thought flows forcefully toward a particular object, the great sage Patanjali called that mental state *savikalpa samadhi*; the devotional scriptures describe it as *bhava samadhi*. From childhood, the Master's mind was accustomed to remaining in that type of samadhi.[21]

19. His powerful mind: The Master's mind was so powerful that it would even affect his body. This is an amazing phenomenon. For example, when he was practising *dasya bhava* (the servant attitude towards God) and took upon himself the mood of Hanuman, his tail bone lengthened about an inch. Again, when he was practising *madhura bhava* (Radha's attitude towards Krishna), the functions of his body changed. Saradananda recorded: " He was so absorbed in thinking of himself as a woman that he could not think of himself as a man even in dreams. His body and senses functioned naturally like those of a woman. We heard from the Master that during this time, every month drops of blood would ooze from the pores near his *swadhisthana chakra* for three days, like a woman's monthly cycle. "[22]

A similar phenomenon occurred in the life of St. Francis of Assisi. While meditating on Christ, the stigmata (the wounds from Christ's crucifixion on his hands, feet, and side) appeared on his body.

20. His noble mind: The Master's mind was as vast as space and as deep as the ocean. He disliked narrowness and bigotry. Saradananda wrote:

> He was not very fond of anyone who was narrow-minded or dull-witted. We all heard him say: "You should be a devotee of God, but does that mean you should be a fool?" Or "Don't be bigoted and narrow-minded; that is not the attitude of this place. The attitude of this place is, I shall enjoy food prepared in various ways — in a plain soup, a hot dish, or a sour dish." He considered a bigoted intellect to be monotonous and hackneyed. If a disciple could not enjoy a particular attitude of God, he scolded him or her, saying, "You are too narrow-minded." Undoubtedly motivated by this liberal and universal attitude, Sri Ramakrishna practised the modes of sadhana in all faiths and discovered this great truth: "As many faiths, so many paths."[23]

Once Girish Ghosh expressed a wish to write a drama that denounced the Kartabhaja sect of the Vaishnava tradition. But the Master forbade him, saying, "It is also a path."

21. His omniscient mind: According to Vedanta, if one knows Brahman, that person knows everything, just as, if one knows gold, one knows all modifications of gold — rings, necklaces, bracelets, and so on. The cosmic mind of the Master traveled in the realm of ideas. He was all-knowing and aware of what others were thinking. Saradananda wrote:

> The most amazing thing we observed in the Master was his ability to travel freely in the realm of ideas. He could understand all ideas, great or small. He knew what was in the mind of a child, a youth, or an old person. He could grasp the thoughts of the worldly and the holy, of the followers of knowledge and of devotion, of men and women. He could see how far they had advanced in spiritual life and what methods they had used to do so, as well as the kind of spiritual disciplines they needed at present to make further progress along the path they had adopted. He guided each person in a way that was appropriate for his or her condition. It seemed to us that the Master had experienced in his life the entire range of mental states of the past, present, and future; and he remembered precisely

what happened when each one of those states appeared and disappeared in his mind. So when a person described his thoughts to the Master, he could understand them by comparing with his own experiences; and he then instructed that person accordingly.[24]

22. His all-renouncing mind: We would have to cover our faces in shame if we tried to compare our deceitful minds with the Master's pure mind. Our minds are crooked and two-faced, and we have not learned to free ourselves from worldly desires. Regarding the Master's all-renouncing mind, Saradananda wrote:

> The Master said that no worldly object or relationship obstructed his journey to the experience of nirvikalpa samadhi according to Vedanta. At the outset of his spiritual path he had renounced all desires for enjoyment in exchange for the vision of the Divine Mother. He prayed: "Mother, here is Thy knowledge and here is Thy ignorance; here is Thy righteousness and here is Thy unrighteousness; here is Thy good and here is Thy evil; here is Thy virtue and here is Thy vice; here is Thy fame and here is Thy infamy. Grant me only pure love for Thee. Do Thou reveal Thyself to me." With this, he sincerely renounced all desires within his mind, because of his pure love for the Mother. Ah, can we experience — or even imagine — that kind of one-pointed love? Sometimes we say to God, "Lord, I offer everything to you"; and in the next moment in everyday life we take possession of everything and reject God, and calculate our own profit and loss. We consider public opinion before we perform any action. We run around restlessly. As we dream about the future we sometimes sink in boundless misery and the next moment float in excitement. And we are convinced that although we may not be able to overturn the whole world ourselves, at least we can have some effect on it. However, the Master's mind was not deceptive, as is ours. When he said, "Mother, please take back the things you gave me," immediately his mind stopped casting covetous looks at them."[25]

23. His truthful mind: We recite the peace mantra of the Rig Veda, "May my mind be one with my speech and may my speech be one with my mind" — but our honest hearts tell us that prayer is merely on our lips. The Master's life was established in truth and his mind and speech were united. He said, "Religion is to unite the mind and speech." Saradananda described Ramakrishna's steadfast devotion to truth:

> Even though the Master offered the Divine Mother righteousness-unrighteousness, virtue-vice, good-evil, fame-infamy, and everything else pertaining to the body and mind, he could not say, 'Mother, take

Thy truth and take Thy untruth.' The Master himself once told us the reason for this. He said that if he renounced truthfulness in that way, how could he hold onto the truth that he had offered everything to the Divine Mother? What steadfast love for truth did we witness in the Master, even though he had offered everything to the Mother! When he said that he would go to a place on a particular day, invariably he went there at the proper time. If he said that he would accept something from a certain person, he could not take it from anyone else. When he said that he would not eat a particular thing or do a certain action anymore, from that day on he could not eat that food or do that thing. The Master used to say: "One who has steadfast love for truth attains the God of truth. The Divine Mother never allows the words of one who adheres to truth to become untrue."[26]

24. His vivacious mind: The minds of some people are dull, listless, and unexcitable. But the Master's mind was always full of enthusiasm. It was like a dry match that catches fire instantly. He would experience spiritual awakening even from a trivial conversation or song. Our minds break down even over petty matters; we become nonplussed and see no way out. The Master loved the robber's brave attitude; he did not care for faint-heartedness. To make their minds forceful and resolute, the Master said to his disciples:

> Why do you say, "I shall realize God in the next life, if not in this?" You should not have that kind of lukewarm devotion. "By His grace I will realize Him in this life and right now" — one should maintain such determination and faith. How can it be possible otherwise? In Kamarpukur when the peasants go to market to buy bullocks for their ploughs they touch the animals' tails first. Some bullocks do not react and meekly lie down on the ground. The peasants recognize that these are without mettle and no good. They select only those bullocks that show spirit and frisk about when their tails are touched. Lukewarm devotion is no good. Strengthen your determination and say with conviction, "I must realize God right now." Only then will you succeed.[27]

Swamiji described Ramakrishna's mastery over the mind: "It is no great matter to control external material powers by some means and to perform miracles. But I have never seen a greater miracle than the way that 'mad brahmin' would handle human minds like a lump of clay. He would pound those minds, beat them into shape, develop them, and then with a mere touch he would cast them into a new mould, with new thoughts."[28]

25. His discriminating mind: The first step in practising Vedanta is discrimination between the real and the unreal. This is possible only if a person has a sharp intellect and a pure mind. The Master used homely examples to describe his unusual method of discrimination, which left an indelible mark on his disciples' minds:

> Listen, one should discriminate between the real and the unreal. Always endowed with discrimination, one should talk to one's mind in this manner: "You, mind, are eager to enjoy various objects — to eat this thing, to put on that thing, and so on. You see, potatoes, vegetables, rice, lentils, and so on are produced from five elements,* and again sandesh, rasagolla, and other delicious sweets are made from the same. The same five elements that made a beautiful female body, consisting of bones, flesh, blood, and marrow, made your body as well — and also all bodies of men, cows, goats, sheep, and so on. Why do you crave such things and even die for them? They cannot help you to attain God." If the mind is still not convinced, enjoy something a couple of times with discrimination, and then renounce it. For example, your mind is inordinately desirous of eating rasagolla, and you are helpless to bring it under control. All your powers of discrimination are ineffective. So buy some rasagollas, put them into your mouth, and tell your mind while you are chewing them: Mind, this is called 'rasagolla'. It consists of modifications of the five elements, the same as potatoes and vegetables. When it is eaten, the body transforms it into blood, flesh, faeces, and urine. It is sweet as long as it is in the mouth, but after it goes down the throat, you won't remember its taste. And if you eat too much, you will be sick. Still you are so greedy for it! Shame on you! Fie on you! Now you have eaten rasagolla; don't hanker after it anymore. (*Pointing to the would-be monastics*): One should use this process of discrimination when enjoying ordinary things, and then renounce them. But this method does not apply to serious things; one becomes entangled as soon as one indulges in them. That is why one should drive serious worldly desires away from the mind by using discrimination and seeing the fault in them."[29]

26. His detached mind: The scriptures say that the mind of a knower of Brahman is not affected by pleasant and unpleasant, good and evil, happiness and misery, praise and blame. Such a person's mind is saturated with the Atman, so there is no feeling of happiness and misery. The Master said: "Two persons live inside me — a devotee and the Mother. The devotee has cancer in the throat, but the Mother is free from it." The Master would experience pain when his mind came down to the physical plane. He lived in a body, but in reality, he was beyond the body.

Once when he was in bhava samadhi, a chunk of live charcoal fell on his body and he did not feel it. At Janbazar in Calcutta, Mathur's priest

*Ether, air, fire, water, and earth.

Chandra Haldar once kicked him, but he did not feel any humiliation or pain. There are many such examples in his life. His advice was: "Let the pain and misery know each other; O my mind, dwell in bliss."

When an avatar becomes incarnate in this world, he or she behaves like a human being. The mind of an avatar has feelings; the avatar is not like a piece of wood or stone. The Master cried when loved ones died, including his nephew Akshay, his mother, and his devotee Adhar. But that temporary grief did not overwhelm him. In addition, shame, hatred, and fear could never arise in the Master's mind, as it was always filled with love, compassion, and forgiveness. This is a characteristic of the mind of an avatar.

27. His simple mind: Regarding the simplicity of the Master's mind, M. gave this example:

> Once the Master ate at Keshab Sen's house, though Keshab was not a brahmin. He forbade us to tell anyone about it, lest the temple officials refuse to let him enter the Kali temple. The next day, however, when the temple manager was passing by, the Master told him: "Yesterday I went to Keshab's house and he gave me a sumptuous feast. I don't know whether the food was served by a washerman or a barber. Will it harm me?" Smiling, the manager replied: "No, sir, it is all right. Nothing can pollute you." The Master was simple like a child.[30]

Saradananda wrote:

> The Master told us many times that he visited each holy place with a specific spiritual mood in mind. He said: "I expected to find everyone in Varanasi absorbed in samadhi, meditating on Shiva twenty-four hours a day, and everyone in Vrindaban wild with ecstatic joy in the company of Krishna. But when I went to those places, I found them to be different." The Master's extraordinary and simple mind accepted and believed everything like a five-year-old boy. Since childhood, we have learned to look upon people and things with critical eyes. How can our crooked minds have that kind of faith? When we find people who believe anything without question, we consider them foolish and dull-witted. We heard from the Master for the first time: "Look, people become guileless and open-minded as a result of many austerities and various sadhanas. One cannot attain God without simplicity. He reveals His true nature to a person who is simple and believing." Again, lest one think that one must be stupid in order to become honest and believing, the Master said: "Be a devotee. But does that mean you should be a fool?"[31]

28. His wonderful mind: According to the scriptures, all the desires of a knower of Brahman are fulfilled. Saradananda wrote:

At this time in Cossipore the Master was suffering from a terrible cancer. Swami Vivekananda and some of us tearfully asked the Master to apply his mental powers to freeing himself from disease for our sakes, but he could not make such an effort. He said that although he tried to do this, he could not create a strong resolve in his mind at all. He told us: "I could by no means bring this mind back from Satchidananda and put it in this cage of flesh and bone. I have always considered this body to be trifling and contemptible, and have offered my mind to the Divine Mother forever. Now, my children, how can I bring it back from Her and put it on the body?"[30]

The disciples could not fathom how the Master's wondrous mind would roam in higher realms. Once the Master expressed a boyish eagerness to see a couple of things through a microscope, so the devotees decided that they would borrow one and show it to the Master that afternoon. Dr. Bipin Bihari Ghosh brought a microscope to Balaram's house to show the Master. Saradananda wrote:

> The Master got up and went to the microscope but returned without looking through it. When he was asked why, he said, "The mind is now in such a high plane that I can by no means bring it down to a lower plane to see things." We waited quite a while to see if the Master's mind would come down. But that day the Master's mind did not return from that exalted spiritual plane, so he could not see anything through the microscope. Bipin showed it to some of us and finally left with the instrument."[32]

M. recorded how the Master's mind would travel in the infinite Brahman and the finite world simultaneously:

> When the Master was going to Vidyasagar's house he asked me: "My shirt is unbuttoned. Will that offend Vidyasagar?" I assured him: "Oh, no! Don't be anxious about it. Nothing about you will be offensive."
> What a wonderful person the Master was! A few minutes earlier in the carriage he had been in samadhi, and when he alighted he was still absorbed in that mood, so his steps were faltering. But still he was quite aware of social formalities, such as the condition of his clothes. What a fantastic mind he had! At that time two opposite ideas were harmonized in his behaviour. On the one hand his mind had transcended the world and was merged in God, and on the other he was inquiring about human affairs. This should be the ideal: "True to the kindred points of heaven and earth." This we find in the lives of the avatars [incarnations]. The avatar brings the message of the Infinite to the finite world.[33]

A bright, transparent crystal has no colour. However, when one puts a red, blue, or yellow flower near it, one sees that particular colour in that crystal. There is no colour in Brahman or the Atman. All colours are in the realm of Prakriti, or maya, which has three gunas (qualities). One becomes many when the colours of the three gunas are superimposed on the Atman. Prakriti has adorned herself with many colours and thus enchanted human beings. God plays with the power of maya, creating multiple colours and enacting the *Doljatra* or *Holi* play (festival of colours).

The Shvetashvatara Upanishad says: "He, the One and Undifferentiated, who by the manifold application of His powers produces, in the beginning, different objects for a hidden purpose, and in the end withdraws the universe into Himself, is indeed the self-luminous [Supreme Self]. May He endow us with clear intellect" (4:1).

What is this power? Why did God create variety and diversity? This is God's power of maya. With this power, God created variety to enjoy His own lila. God remains hidden during creation and preservation, but at the time of dissolution God absorbs the creation within Himself. Again, at the dawn of creation, God begins to create variety as He did in the previous cycle. Human beings pray for a pure intellect to understand this divine mystery.

It is not possible for human beings to measure the mind of Ramakrishna because our minds are impure, finite, and limited, whereas Ramakrishna's mind was pure, infinite, and unlimited. During the waking state, Ramakrishna would be aware of this universe and the beings within it, but they would dissolve during samadhi. When Ramakrishna touched Swamiji's chest, the world vanished from the latter's mind; when Ramakrishna touched him again, the world returned. What great power the Master had! That is why the Upanishad referred to God as "the great magician."

On 19 September 1884, Ramakrishna said to Radhika Goswami: "A man had a tub of dye. Such was its wonderful property that people could dye their clothes any colour they wanted by merely dipping them in it. A clever man said to the owner of the tub, 'Dye my cloth the colour of your dye-stuff.'"[34]

Now we will have to be a little clever and pray to him: "Master, please dye our minds the way you have dyed yours."

This is the meditation on Ramakrishna's mind.

3

Meditation on Ramakrishna's Divine Qualities

Brahman does not have any form or qualities, but Ishwara (God) has both. Ishwara is the reflected consciousness of Brahman on cosmic maya. God enacts his divine play through the three gunas of Prakriti, or maya. All creation originates from the three gunas — sattva, rajas, and tamas. Sattva-guna is stainless, luminous, and free from evil. It binds human beings to this life through attachment to happiness and knowledge. *Rajo-guna* is the essence of passion born of hankering and attachment. It binds through attachment to action. Tamo-guna is born of the ignorance that deludes all embodied beings. It binds through inadvertence, indolence, and sleep. God functions through the power of maya, but maya cannot bind God. God has full control over maya, as a snake has full control over its poison. With the power of maya, God creates, preserves, and destroys. This universe is God's playground and all beings are God's playmates.

We do not see maya because it is very subtle, but we observe actions that originate from maya. The goal of human life is to transcend the three gunas of maya and become free from their bonds. In the last part of the fourteenth chapter of the Gita, Krishna describes the person who has transcended the gunas. Good and bad are all in the domain of maya. One must transcend the gunas through the gunas. Conquer tamas with rajas and rajas with sattva. Ramakrishna said that all three gunas are robbers. Tamo-robber says, "Kill this man." Rajo-robber says, "Don't kill this man but bind him." Sattva-robber waits for an opportunity and then releases the man. All three gunas are necessary in human life. If there were no

Hamsa means swan and also a soul. A swan lives in water but it shakes off water as soon as it is on the ground. Ramakrishna was known as paramahamsa, a great soul, an all-renouncing monk.

tamo-guna, people would not be able to sleep, and thence they would become mad. Without rajo-guna, there would be no activity and people would starve. And without sattva-guna, people would not enjoy peace and bliss.

In the thirteenth chapter of Book Eleven of the Bhagavata, Krishna describes these three gunas in detail. These gunas belong to Prakriti and not to the Atman. Sattva-guna lifts the human mind upward; rajas and tamas drive the mind downward. If sattva-guna increases, one attains devotion. How does one increase sattva-guna? Krishna suggested ten methods:

1. Study the scriptures, such as the Upanishads, Gita, and Bhagavata.
2. Drink and bathe in the holy water of the Ganges and Yamuna.
3. Associate with holy people.
4. Live in a holy place.
5. Practise meditation in the early morning and in the evening.
6. Perform unselfish actions.
7. Take initiation from a guru.
8. Meditate on God.
9. Repeat Om or the Ishta-mantra.
10. Purify the body and mind.

There is a saying: Whatever one sincerely visualizes will come to pass. Ramakrishna said: "If you meditate on an ideal, you will acquire its nature. If you think of God day and night, you will acquire the nature of God. A salt doll went into the ocean to measure its depth. It became one with the ocean."[1]

There are many ways one can meditate on God, such as meditation on the form, mind, qualities, lila, and message. When God incarnates as a human avatar, people get joy by meditating on him in many ways, just as one gets joy by thinking of one's beloved. Valmiki wrote the Ramayana while meditating on Rama's life and message; Vyasa wrote the Bhagavata while meditating on Krishna; and M. recorded the *Kathamrita* (*Gospel*) by meditating on Ramakrishna.

Most people meditate on the form of God or an avatar, because it is physical and thus easy to do. Meditation on a quality is subtle and more difficult. Meditation differs according to the gunas: For example, meditation on an enemy is tamasic, meditation on lust and gold is rajasic, and meditation on God is sattvic. In tamasic meditation, the mind becomes full of jealousy and anger, and one contemplates taking revenge against an enemy. In rajasic meditation, the mind thinks of sex, money, and name and fame. In sattvic meditation, the mind thinks of God, and thus one becomes free from the bondage of maya and attains bliss.

Ramakrishna glorified the sattva-guna. If you have the quality of sattva, you will attain God quickly. However, although the sattva-guna shows the way to reach God, it cannot give you Self-knowledge. All three gunas are thieves that rob human beings of their Self-knowledge. Sattva-guna preserves, rajo-guna creates, and tamo-guna destroys. Sattva-guna saves human beings from rajas and tamas. It is the last upper step of the ladder before one reaches the roof. In the state of sattva, one cannot bear disturbances; however, in that state one is protected from lust and anger.

On 7 March 1885, Ramakrishna described his true nature to M.: "There is no outsider here. The other day, when Harish was with me, I saw Satchidananda come out of this sheath. It said, 'I incarnate Myself in every age.' I thought that I myself was saying these words out of mere fancy. I kept quiet and watched the fullest manifestation of Satchidananda; but this time the Divine Power is manifested through the glory of sattva."[2]

According to Vedanta, the person who has a preponderance of sattva is Ishwara or God. He is the repository of all goodness and has full control over maya. Shvetashvatara Upanishad says: "The power of maya belongs to the Lord Himself and is hidden in its gunas" (1:3). One cannot realize Brahman without transcending the gunas. Krishna explained how to transcend the gunas: "This divine maya of mine consisting of the gunas is hard to overcome. But those who take refuge in me alone transcend this maya" (Gita, 7:14).

In his vesper hymn, Swami Vivekananda reveals Ramakrishna's true nature: he is the breaker of the world's bondages; stainless, even though he has assumed human form; attributeless, yet full of attributes. While free from gunas, the avatar plays with the gunas. According to Vedanta, one can meditate on Saguna Brahman (God with attributes) with the mind and describe him with speech, but not Nirguna Brahman (God without attributes). But Vidyaranya Muni, a great teacher of Vedanta, holds a different view. In the *Panchadashi* he says that if one posits that Brahman is beyond speech and mind and so cannot be meditated upon, then there can be no knowledge of Brahman" (9:56). But this is against the teachings of the scriptures. There is a long discussion on this subject in the *Panchadashi*. The bottom line is that the uninterrupted flow of the thought "I am Brahman (aham brahmasmi)" is meditation on Brahman.

God adorned the bodies of human beings with beauty and their minds with noble qualities, so our minds rush to objects that we see as beautiful. This is natural. Beauty is one of God's splendors, so people adore it. Once Hafez, a Sufi saint, was charmed by the beautiful face of a courtesan. Noticing his intent gaze, she asked, "Hafez, you are a holy person. Why are you casting a lustful look at a woman?"

Hafez replied: "Look, I have no lust in my mind. Your exquisite beauty reminds me of the Creator. I don't know how much more beautiful He is than you."

Physical beauty is very transient, but the inner beauty of the gunas — purity, nonattachment, devotion — is long lasting. In this world, people try hard to preserve their physical beauty. They use make-up and even have cosmetic surgery to maintain a youthful appearance, but still they cannot avoid aging. This body is made from five elements (earth, water, fire, air and space) and in the end it will return to those elements.

What about the quality of one's character? When a great man leaves this world, people glorify his noble qualities. He commands love and respect from all. In the Bhagavad Gita, Krishna mentioned 26 divine qualities, such as fearlessness, purity of heart, self-control and sacrifice; nonviolence, truth, and freedom from anger; renunciation, compassion, non-covetousness, gentleness, modesty, courage, forgiveness, and fortitude (16:1-3). Those who are endowed with these divine qualities are worshipped by people as God.

We refer to Brahman as *Satchidananda*: *Sat* (existence), *chit* (consciousness), and *ananda* (bliss). These are the essence of Brahman, not Its qualities. God is the repository of infinite divine qualities. Although there is no end to God's qualities, Jiva Goswami, a follower of Chaitanya, listed 39 of them in his famous book *Bhagavat-Sandarva*. These are taken from the Bhagavata (1:16:26-28). They include truthfulness, cleanliness, compassion, renunciation, contentment, simplicity, self-control, knowledge, divine power, strength, courage, memory, freedom, skill, beauty, patience, modesty, talent, steadiness, faith, fame, and humility. While meditating on Ramakrishna's divine qualities, one will witness how the qualities mentioned in the scriptures manifested in his life.

One should adore the person who displays these divine qualities. Ramakrishna used to say: "Look, God is displeased if one doesn't pay respect to an honourable person. They have become great by His power. It is He who has made them great, so by neglecting them, one neglects God."[3]

Ramakrishna is God in human form. When we gaze upon his photo, we can meditate on his form and qualities. This meditation will help us to have the vision of our Chosen Ideal. Meditation may not change one's physical body, but it does change one's mind. The cruel king Ashoka became a virtuous king, and the murderous robber Ratnakar became the sage Valmiki by meditating on divine qualities. Meditation on divine qualities makes a person divine. Meditation on divine qualities is higher than meditation on form, and meditation on the Atman is higher than meditation on qualities.

It is certain that our divine nature will awaken if we meditate on Ramakrishna's divine qualities. Now the question is: How shall we meditate on his divine qualities? Swami Vijnanananda said:

> What is the purpose of prayer to Ramakrishna and repeating his name? Thus one can imbibe his divine qualities. He attains the quality of a person on whom he deeply meditates. It is in the Gita: "A person is made of his faith. One is whatever his faith is" (17:3).
>
> The first quality of God is his lordliness. Meditating on God we develop full control over the senses. We must be lord of ourselves. Second, all actions take effect by the mere wish of God. Similarly, we must turn our wishes into action. Third, God's infinite unconditional love. We must love all like Him. Thus he who has imbibed as much as God's quality, his meditation has been developed to that proportion.[4]

In the scriptures, various characteristics of God have been described. We should try to meditate on the qualities of Ramakrishna accordingly. The Vayu Purana lists various aspects of God: He is endowed with knowledge, renunciation, power, truthfulness, forgiveness, compassion, fortitude, power of creation, preservation, and destruction, and so on. Some scriptures have cited six characteristics of God: *aishwarya*, supernatural power or splendour; *virya*, virility; *yasha*, fame; *shri*, beauty and wealth; *jnana*, knowledge; and *vairagya*, renunciation. We shall try to explain how these six signs manifested in Ramakrishna's life.

1. *Aishwarya*, or splendour, supernatural power. The word *aishwarya* also refers to money, gold, palatial house, luxury car, and so on. Of course, Ramakrishna did not have material wealth. He inherited a mud hut with a thatched roof in Kamarpukur. He lived with his brother in a tiny apartment in Calcutta for a few years and then lived in the Dakshineswar temple garden for thirty years. The temple authorities took care of his food and lodging. He despised worldly wealth. Standing on the Chandni ghat one day, he took a lump of clay in one hand and one silver rupee in the other, considered both, and then threw them into the Ganges, saying, "Money is clay and clay is money." Thus he got rid of the desire for wealth forever. He once told his nephew Ramlal, "If I knew the world was real, I would cover Kamarpukur with gold."

Once the Master had a desire to listen to Keshab Sen give a lecture.

The event was arranged at the Chandni ghat of Dakshineswar and all sat on the platform and steps. Ramakrishna mentioned the lecture:

> One day Keshab and his party came to the temple garden at Dakshineswar. I told them I wanted to hear how they lectured. A meeting was arranged in the paved courtyard above the bathing-ghat on the Ganges, where Keshab gave a talk. He spoke very well. I went into a trance. After the lecture I said to Keshab, "Why do you so often say such things as: 'O God, what beautiful flowers Thou hast made! O God, Thou hast created the heavens, the stars, and the ocean!' and so on?" Those who love splendour themselves are fond of dwelling on God's splendour.
>
> Once a thief stole the jewels from the images in the temple of Radha-kanta. Mathur Babu entered the temple and said to the Deity: "What a shame, O God! You couldn't save Your own ornaments." "The idea!" I said to Mathur. "Does He who has Lakshmi for His handmaid and attendant ever lack any splendour? Those jewels may be precious to you, but to God they are no better than lumps of clay. Shame on you! You shouldn't have spoken so meanly. What riches can you give to God to magnify His glory?"[5]

When he heard the Master's words, Keshab firmly understood that the best wealth to attain is God-realization. Ordinary people want material wealth from God, but they do not want God. That wealth is God's magical splendour, but real wealth is God's divinity, lordship, control over creation, supernatural power, indomitable will, and so on.

Ramakrishna said: "You will achieve everything just by thinking of me. He who thinks of me will attain my wealth, as children inherit their parents' wealth. My wealth is: knowledge, devotion, discrimination, renunciation, pure love, and samadhi."[6]

2. *Virya*, or vigour. This word has many connotations, such as heroism, prowess, power, strength, invincibility, valour, and manliness. Ramakrishna was strong in the physical, mental and spiritual planes. If he had not possessed physical strength, he could not have practised so much austerity in his life. To test his strength of character, Mathur took him to some prostitutes; however, he saw them all as manifestations of the Divine Mother. Vaishnavcharan also took him to the Kachibagan ashrama, where some male and female Vaishnavas practised left-handed Tantra. Observing his self-control and purity, those women declared that Paramahamsadeva (Ramakrishna) was established in his vow of brahmacharya. Moreover, he attained success in the practice of Virabhava (heroic mode) according to Tantra.

Observing the Master's unconventional worship, the Dakshineswar temple manager told the guard not to allow him to enter the Kali temple, and reported this to Mathur, the owner. When the Master was about to enter the temple to perform the ritual, the guard tried to stop him. The Master pushed him aside, entered the temple, and began the worship. The guard rushed to the office and reported this to the manager, who informed Mathur what had happened. Mathur sent a message, "Don't say anything to the Master."

According to the Ramayana, the physical strength of a kshatriya is nothing compared to the spiritual power of a brahmin. Ramakrishna was endowed with the power of Brahman, and with that power he admonished people without fear. Once Rani Rasmani, the founder of the temple, was thinking of a lawsuit while listening to the Master sing. He immediately slapped her face. Similarly, when Jaya Mukherji, a devotee, was repeating the mantra absentmindedly, the Master slapped his face. When we consider our own insincerity, we feel that we deserve many slaps from the Master. It is said that person only can punish who loves.

Once the middle-aged Master challenged his young disciple Hariprasanna to wrestle in his room at Dakshineswar. Hariprasanna recalled:

> One day I went in the afternoon to visit the Master at Dakshineswar. Many devotees were seated in his room. He did not say anything to me, nor did I ask him anything. Then one by one the devotees took their leave, and suddenly I found myself alone with him. The Master was looking at me intently. I thought it was time for me to depart, so I prostrated before him. As I stood up to go, he asked: "Can you wrestle? Come, let me see how well you wrestle!" With these words he stood up, ready to grapple with me. I was surprised at this challenge. I thought to myself, "What kind of holy man is this?" But I replied, "Yes, of course I can wrestle." Sri Ramakrishna came closer, smiling. He caught hold of my arms and began to shove me, but I was a strong, muscular young man and I pushed him back to the wall. He was still smiling and holding me with a strong grip. Gradually I felt a sort of electric current coming out of his hands and entering into me. That touch made me completely helpless. I lost all my physical strength. I went into ecstasy, and the hair of my body stood on end. Releasing me, the Master said with a smile, "Well, you are the winner." With those words, he sat down on his cot again.[7]

M. described a vivid scene of the Master's steady and self-possessed movement in the *Gospel*:

> It was late in the evening. M. found the Master pacing alone in the nat-mandir in front of the Kali temple. A lamp was burning in the temple on either side of the image of the Divine Mother. The single lamp in the

spacious natmandir blended light and darkness into a kind of mystic twilight, in which the figure of the Master could be dimly seen.

M. bowed down low before him and took his leave. He had gone as far as the main gate of the temple garden when he suddenly remembered something and came back to Sri Ramakrishna, who was still in the natmandir. In the dim light the Master, all alone, was pacing the hall, rejoicing in the Self — as the lion lives and roams alone in the forest.

Master (*to M.*): "What makes you come back?"

M.: "Perhaps the house you asked me to go to belongs to a rich man. They may not let me in."

Master: "Oh, no! Why should you think that? Just mention *my name.* Say that you want to see me; then someone will take you to me."[8]

There is a beautiful prayer in the Shukla Yajur Veda Samhita about virya: "O Lord, Thou art the embodiment of infinite energy; do Thou fill me with energy. Thou art the embodiment of infinite valour; do Thou endow me with valour. Thou art the embodiment of infinite strength; do Thou bestow strength upon me."

3. *Yasha*, or fame. Fame spreads through various ways, especially from acts of charity and sacrifice, or from heroism and courage. In this world, we glorify famous people. When a person is endowed with many noble qualities, they manifest in the person's life and they spread that person's fame. The scripture says: that person lives whose fame and achievements live on after death. Again, a person who has no fame or achievements may be alive but yet is dead. In this world, life, wealth, youth, and beauty are very transient. But the person who has fame is remembered even after his or her death.

Ramakrishna was born in a poor family, had no formal education, and took a job as a temple priest. How could such a person have attained name and fame? It is said: He who wants, does not get; and he who does not want, gets. Ramakrishna never wanted name and fame: to a spiritual aspirant, these are subtle bondages. Ordinary people cannot digest name and fame; they become puffed up with pride and fall from their spiritual journey. Mathur tested the Master by engaging beautiful girls, offering him plenty of wealth, and worshipping him like a God; yet he found that the Master was egoless and was not attracted by anything. Then Mathur said to the Master, "Father, you are God."

Manomohan Mitra wrote:

One day I went to Dakshineswar and saw the Master talking to the devotees in the Panchavati. About the same time Keshab reached there with some of his followers. Sri Ramakrishna was delighted to see Keshab.

They talked for some time. Then Keshab said to the Master: "Sir, if you permit, I want to make your message known to the public. It will definitely do people good and bring peace to the world."

Sri Ramakrishna replied in an ecstatic mood: "It is not the time to spread the message of this place [i.e., his message] through lectures and newspapers. The power and ideas that are within this body will automatically spread all around in the course of time. Hundreds of Himalayas will not be able to suppress that power." As the Master said this his eyes were wide open and his face emitted a wonderful glow. All were quiet. Then the Master went into samadhi.[9]

Another scene for meditation on this subject was narrated by Swami Premananda: "One night I was sleeping in the Master's room. At dead of night I woke up and found him pacing from one end of his room to the other, saying: 'Mother, I do not want this. Do not bring me honour from men. Don't, Mother, don't. I spit on it!' Saying this, he paced back and forth like a madman. I was filled with wonder. I thought: How strange! People are so eager for name and fame, and he is pleading with the Mother not to give it to him!"[10]

Most people are beggars for name and fame. The Master demonstrated that the goal of human life is to realize God — and to attain God, one must shun the subtle bondage of name and fame. Ramakrishna, who shunned name and fame, is now known all over the world. He is worshipped by millions of people, and his life and message are spreading very fast. The Guru Gita says: "My lord is the lord of the world, and my guru is the guru of the world."

4. *Shri* or beauty. *Shri* has many connotations, such as elegance, splendour, prosperity, money, and wealth. The person who has no *shri* is ugly and poor. That is why we put *Shri (Sri)* before a name such as Sri Ram, Sri Krishna, Sri Ramakrishna, and Sri Saradadevi. We see youthful beauty in the images of Hindu gods and goddesses. When we talk about God, we use words such as *satyam, shivam,* and *sundaram* — truth, auspiciousness, and beauty.

Once a devotee said to Swami Vijnanananda, "Swami, when we see the Master's picture, we don't feel that he had a majestic personality, but we see that in Swamiji's picture." Swami Vijnanananda replied:

No, don't say that. The Master was an extraordinary and wonderful person. I noticed that a wave of spiritual power played on the Master's body all the time. On one hand, a little power in the brain makes an ordinary person a famous chemist or physicist or politician. On the other, a tremendous spiritual current flowed in every centre of the Master's body. What terrific power he had!

Once the Master told me, pointing to his own picture: "Look, I dwell in this picture. Meditate on me."

All the forms of gods and goddesses are within Sri Ramakrishna's form. His photograph symbolizes the piercing of the six centres of the kundalini. When I look at his luminous form, it seems to me that the Master is immersed in the blissful ocean of Satchidananda transcending the six centres of the kundalini. I see many wonderful things in the Master's picture. Sri Ramakrishna manifests himself to those people who are pure in heart.[11]

Ramakrishna's physical beauty helps a devotee to meditate on his form. He himself described his own beauty: "At that time [1869] my beauty became manifest in such a way that people would stare at me. My face and chest were always crimson, and a lustre would emanate from my body. Because people stared at me, I would cover myself with a thick *chadar* [shawl]. I would pray to the Divine Mother, 'Take away my external beauty, O Mother, and give me inner beauty.' I used to pass my hand over the body and slap it again and again, saying, 'Go within, go within.' After some days my skin turned pale, as you see it now."[12]

Holy Mother described the Master's beauty, and his joyfulness:

His complexion was like the colour of gold — like that of *harital* [a yellow orpiment]. It blended with the colour of the gold amulet which he wore on his arm. When I rubbed him with oil I could clearly see a lustre coming out of his entire body. People looked at him wonderstruck when he went with slow, steady steps to the Ganges to take his bath. And when he came out of his room at the temple, people stood in line and said to one another, "Ah, there he goes!"

It also happened at Kamarpukur. Men and women looked at him with mouths agape whenever he chanced to come out of his house. One day he went for a walk in the direction of the canal known as Bhutir Khal. The women who had gone there to fetch water stared at him and said, "There goes the Master!" The Master was annoyed at this and said to Hriday, "Well, Hridu, please put a veil over my head at once." The Master was fairly stout. I never saw the Master sad. He was joyous in the company of everyone, whether a boy of five or an old man. I never saw him morose.[13]

Someone asked the Master's niece Lakshmi: "What was the condition of the Master's body during samadhi?" She answered: "During samadhi, the Master's body became motionless. Tears trickled from his eyes, and sometimes both sides of his abdomen would tremble a little.

His appearance was then extremely beautiful and one could see a halo around him."[14]

Once Swami Adbhutananda said to a devotee: "Look, some days you see something and it instantly penetrates the mind. I saw the Master in samadhi many times, but one day I saw him in a beautiful and unique form. His complexion had changed and his face radiated fearlessness and compassion. Even now I cannot forget that form of the Master."[15]

All three photographs of Ramakrishna were taken when he was in samadhi, in other words, when he was one with God. Before these photographs were made, there was no known record of a photo being taken of a person merged in nirvikalpa samadhi. It is said that beauty is in the eyes of the beholder. Some worldly people may not like Ramakrishna's divine form, but because of his divine qualities, his pictures are now worshipped by millions of people all over the world. Form and quality are interconnected. When we see Ramakrishna's form, his divine qualities manifest in our minds. As we meditate on the Master's qualities, our own qualities become divine.

5. *Jnana*, or knowledge. Here knowledge indicates understanding of the sense objects, grasp of the scriptures, awareness of the truth, realization of God, and knowledge of the Self. Ramakrishna used to say: "Knowledge of oneness is true and knowledge of many is ignorance." According to Vedanta, a person who knows Brahman is omniscient. If a person knows gold, he or she knows all modifications of gold, such as rings, necklaces, and bracelets.

Ramakrishna did not attain knowledge by going to school; the Divine Mother endowed him with all learning. Later, he adorned himself with a garland of scriptures around his neck and danced. He used to say: "If you want to know in one sentence, come to me; and if you want to know in a thousand words, go to Keshab Chandra Sen." Another time a person asked Ramakrishna, "Sir, give me knowledge in one sentence." He answered, "This world is not real; Brahman alone is real."

Knowledge or learning is a special quality. God is omniscient: God knows everything and everyone, collectively and individually. Ramakrishna taught his gospel from his own realization and illumined intellect. Keshab Sen, Vidyasagar, Padmalochan, Gauri Pandit, Shashadhar, and other great scholars were spellbound when they heard his spiritual talks. The Master said: "Getting a ray of light from the goddess of learning, a man becomes so powerful that before him big scholars seem mere earthworms."[16] The Divine Mother spoke through the Master's mouth, so he could impart the knowledge of Brahman simply by a wish or a touch.

The following are some examples of how the Master's knowledge manifested from the beginning of his life.

When Ramakrishna was a boy of 9 or 10 years old, many distinguished scholars were invited on the occasion of a *shrāddha* ceremony (rites for the manes) held by the Laha family. There was a debate among them on a scriptural subject and an exciting argument was going on. The young Ramakrishna listened to them attentively and then asked a well-known scholar, "Can't the problem be solved in this way?" He then offered a solution. Dumbfounded, the scholar placed Ramakrishna's solution before the other scholars and they all praised his sharp intellect.

Another picture for meditation: In Dakshineswar, one foot of the Krishna image in the Vishnu temple was broken. After some debate, scholars concluded that a broken image cannot be worshipped, so it should be immersed in the Ganges and a new image should be installed. When the Master was asked for his opinion on this matter, he replied: "If any one of the Rani's sons-in-law were to break a leg, would she forsake him and put someone else in his place? Wouldn't she rather have him treated by a doctor? Let it be the same in this case. Mend the image and worship it as before. Why should the image be discarded?"[17] All were amazed. This illustrates the Master's strong common sense and his feeling that God is one's very own.

The Master would become nervous if he had any scholarly visitor, and he would pray to all the pictures of gods and goddesses in his room. It was wonderful to watch his childlike behaviour. Once he heard that Mr. Cook, an American evangelist, was coming to Dakshineswar by steamer with Keshab. Ramakrishna became so nervous that he had to frequently go to the pine grove to answer the call of nature. Finally, he boarded the steamer and charmed everyone there with an illuminating talk. When everyone praised him later, he replied: "You see, I was completely unaware of it."[18] The Divine Mother spoke through him.

Another day the Master became very nervous when Pandit Shasha-dhar visited Dakshineswar. He said:

> Look, there is no book-learning here. I'm an unlettered man. I was terribly afraid when I heard that the pandit was coming to see me. You see, I'm not even aware of my clothing. I was extremely nervous that I might say something improper. I prayed to the Divine Mother: "Look after me, Mother. I don't know any scriptures except You. Please protect me." I told some people around me: "You all be present when the pandit arrives. I shall feel confident if I see you near me." When the pandit arrived, I was not entirely rid of my nervousness; I kept looking at him

and listening to his words. Suddenly, the Mother revealed Shashadhar's inner self to me. I saw that scriptural erudition was of no avail without discrimination and renunciation. Then I felt a current rush towards my head, and the last trace of fear vanished from my mind. I was completely overwhelmed. My face turned upward and out of my mouth came an incessant torrent of words. The more I talked, the more I felt that a fresh supply was coming from within, just as when a man in Kamarpukur measures paddy, another person pushes forward a fresh supply. I was entirely unaware of what I was saying. When I regained a little consciousness, I found the pandit in tears, completely overwhelmed.[19]

Reflecting on these incidents, one can see how the Divine Mother adorned the Master with divine wisdom. Millions of people all over the world are eager to hear the message of the person who said "I am an unlettered man."

6. *Vairagya*, or renunciation. This term implies nonattachment to worldly objects, disgust for sense enjoyment, self-abnegation, sacrifice, and so on. Some consider renunciation to be something negative. But renunciation has two aspects — negation and affirmation — such as detachment regarding worldly objects and attachment to God. The dark or selfish aspect of love is enjoyment, and the bright or unselfish aspect of love is renunciation. Renunciation does not mean that one must go to the forest or hide in a cave, giving up friends and relatives, and everything else, or even that one must shun luxury and lead a plain life. According to Hinduism, true renunciation means having the firm conviction that the world is not real. True renunciation is not being attached to anything in this world. Patanjali says: "Attaining Self-knowledge, one ceases to desire any objects made by the gunas — that is the highest renunciation" (1:16). As gold and diamond jewellery enhance a person's beauty, so intense dispassion and renunciation increase the beauty and glory of a holy person.

Swami Vivekananda called Ramakrishna the "king among renunciants." We marvel when we hear stories of the Master's renunciation. After he renounced money, he could not even touch it for the rest of his life. To test the Master, Swamiji once secretly put a coin under his mattress. When the Master sat on his cot, he jumped up, saying, "My body is burning!" His hand would bend if it touched any coin and his breathing would stop. The Master used to say: "A bird and a monk do not save." He demonstrated that a monk should not save anything for the future.

Holy Mother described a wonderful scene of the Master's renunciation:

Renunciation alone was his splendour. We utter his name and eat and enjoy things because he renounced all. People think that his devotees also must be very great, as he was a man of such complete renunciation. Ah, me! One day he came to my room in the nahabat. He had no spices in his small bag. He used to chew them now and then. I gave him some to chew there and also handed to him a small amount packed in paper to take to his room. He then left, but instead of going to his room, he went straight to the embankment of the Ganges. He did not see the way, nor was he conscious of it. He kept repeating, "Mother, shall I drown myself?" I became restless with agony. The river was full to the brim. I was then a young woman and would not leave my room, and I could not see anyone around. Whom could I send to him? At last I found a brahmin belonging to the Kali temple coming in the direction of my room. Through him I called Hriday, who was then eating his meal. He left his plate, ran to the Master, caught hold of him, and brought him back to his room. A moment more and he would have fallen into the Ganges. Because I put some spices in his hand he could not find his way. A holy man must not lay things by. His renunciation was one hundred percent.[20]

One day the Master overheard Mathur consulting with Hriday about turning over an estate to the Master. This angered him. He scolded Mathur, saying, "Rascal, do you want to make me a worldly householder?" On another occasion, Lakshminarayan Marwari saw that the Master's bedsheet was not clean. To make sure that his needs could be met, he decided to invest ten thousand rupees in the Master's name, so he could be supported by the interest. As soon as the Master heard this, he fell unconscious. When he recovered, he told Lakshminarayan: "If you utter such words again, you had better not come here. It is impossible for me to touch money. It is also impossible for me to keep it near me."[21]

Another time, Mahendra Kaviraj of Sinthi gave five rupees to Ramlal for the Master, without the Master's knowledge. When Ramlal told him about the money that night, the Master thought it could be used to clear the debt for his milk. He later said: "I had slept only a little while when I suddenly woke up writhing with pain, as if a cat were scratching my chest. I went to Ramlal and said to him, 'Go at once and return the money.' Ramlal gave it back the next day."[22]

As we visualize these incidents, we glimpse the Master's renunciation. It is amazing how these six qualities of God manifested in the Master's life at different times and under different circumstances.

God is infinite, as are God's qualities

Although some scriptures specify six important attributes of God, God's divine qualities are limitless. Some additional divine qualities of

Ramakrishna are mentioned here so that devotees can absorb those qualities and visualize them during meditation.

O Purity. There may be stains on the moon, but there is no stain in Ramakrishna's character. In fact, he was such a blazing embodiment of purity that impure beings could not bear his presence. The Master and Rakhal once went to see Gopal-ma in Kamarhati. She was delighted to see them. After serving lunch to them, she arranged a bed in a room upstairs for them to rest. The Master was lying down, with Rakhal sleeping next to him, when two ghosts appeared and said: "Why are you here? Please leave this place. The sight of you causes us unbearable pain." They could not bear the Master's divine presence. The Master woke up Rakhal and they left. (In December 1970, the present author had an opportunity to take pictures of Gopal-ma's room and the house, but later the house was torn down.)

Regarding Ramakrishna's purity, Swami Brahmananda once said: "One day the son of a public woman came to Dakshineswar. The Master was sleeping in his room. The man entered and touched his feet. The Master at once jumped up as if someone had thrown fire on him. He said: 'Tell me frankly all the sins you have committed. If you cannot, then go to the Ganges and say them out loud. You will be freed from them.' But the man was ill-fated and could not do so."[23]

In the beginning, Mathur considered the Master's samadhi to be a mental disease — and he thought the cause of that disease was the Master's unbroken chastity. One day, without asking the Master, Mathur took him to Mechuabazar, a red-light district in Calcutta, and sent him to the room of Lakshmi-bai and other prostitutes. When the Master saw them, he cried out "Mother, Mother" and merged into samadhi. The women were afraid. They began to fan him and begged his forgiveness. Embarrassed, Mathur brought the Master back to Dakshineswar.

On another occasion, the Master went to the temple to perform the vesper service. When he returned to his room, he saw a beautiful young woman with large eyes seated on his bed. He recalled: "In order to test me and also to cure my madness, they brought a prostitute into my room. She was beautiful to look at, with pretty eyes. I cried, 'O Mother! O Mother!' and rushed out of the room. I ran to Haladhari and said to him, 'Brother, come and see who has entered my room!' I told Haladhari and everyone else about this woman."[24]

There was no theft (hypocrisy) in the chamber of the Master's heart and his mind and speech were united. He even tested himself by sleeping in the same bed with his wife for eight months when she first arrived in

Dakshineswar, but he never broke his celibacy. Later, Holy Mother moved into the nahabat. One midnight the Master's disciple Jogin could not find him in his room. He suspected that the Master had gone to the nahabat to be with his wife, and left the room to investigate. Just then he saw the Master coming from the Panchavati. When the Master saw Jogin near the nahabat, he understood Jogin's doubt and told him, "You must examine a sadhu by day and by night before believing in him."[25] Incidents such as these are unique in the lives of saints. They are wonderful scenes for meditation.

O **Steadfastness in truth.** Truth is God. The Master used to say that one must hold to the truth in order to realize God. Truthfulness is the austerity of the kaliyuga. Tulasidas said: "Call Tulasidas a liar if God is not attained by practising truthfulness and obedience, and maintaining a filial attitude towards women."

The Divine Mother never allowed the Master to speak a single untruth. When we read the Master's stories and teachings in the *Gospel* and the *Divine Play*, we should have no doubt of their veracity. In addition, the Master was extremely displeased if people did not keep their word. Vidyasagar was a great scholar, but when he did not keep his word, the Master said to M.: "Why doesn't Vidyasagar keep his word? Vidyasagar said he would come here and visit me. But he hasn't kept his word."[26]

Swami Brahmananda gave this eyewitness account:

Oh, how deep was the Master's devotion to truth! If he happened to say that he would not eat any more food, he could not eat more, even if he was hungry. Once he said that he would go to visit Jadu Mallick [*whose garden house was adjacent to the Dakshineswar temple garden*] but later forgot all about it. I also did not remind him. After supper he suddenly remembered the appointment. It was quite late at night, but he had to go. I accompanied him with a lantern in my hand. When we reached the house we found it closed and all apparently asleep. The Master pushed back the doors of the living room a little, placed his foot inside the room, and then left."[27]

One day the Master went to Shambhu Mallick's garden house and talked to him about spiritual life. Shambhu had a charitable dispensary there. From time to time the Master suffered from stomach trouble, so Shambhu suggested that he take a little opium every day and asked him to get some from him before he returned to the Kali temple. The Master agreed. However, the Master left after their discussion, forgetting about the opium. On the way back to the temple, he remembered it and returned to the garden house. By this time Shambhu had entered the inner apartment. The supervisor of the dispensary gave the Master some opium and he began to walk back to the Kali temple. As he was walking, he became confused and could not find the way, though he saw Shambhu's garden behind him clearly. This was a strange phenomenon: He felt as if someone were pulling his legs back toward the garden house. When this had happened a few times, it struck him: "Oh, Shambhu told me, 'Please take the opium from me.' But instead I took it from his supervisor without telling him; for that reason the Mother is not allowing me to move on. The supervisor had no right to give it to me without Shambhu's permission, and I should have taken it from Shambhu as he suggested. My action was wrong on two counts, falsehood and theft. Because of that the Mother is turning me around and keeping me from returning to the temple." With that thought he went to Shambhu's dispensary, but he could not find the supervisor, who had gone to eat. So he threw the opium packet through a window, calling loudly, "Hello, here I am returning your opium." Then he started towards Rasmani's garden. This time he did not have any dizzy spells; he saw the road clearly and reached the temple garden.

The Master said: "I have completely surrendered myself to the Mother, so She is holding my hand all the time. She never allows me to take a false step."[28]

These stories about the Master sound like fairy tales to us. However, the more we meditate on his love for truth, the more we shall also develop love for truth.

○ **Simplicity.** Ramakrishna used to say that a person cannot have simplicity without having undertaken many austerities in previous lives. Without simplicity one cannot readily have faith in God and attain God's grace. If a person calls on God with a simple heart, God is revealed to that person and listens to his or her prayers. Simplicity is a sign of one's last birth. God is easily available to that person who is simple. Those people whose minds are infected with deceit and impurity cannot speak fully and with an open heart. Their tongues are sweet but their minds are vicious — and this is how they deal with others. According to Vedanta, this world of maya is a mixture of truth and untruth. Nonetheless, Ramakrishna's mind and speech were united and there was no discrepancy between his words and his actions.

M. described this incident:

Once the Master ate at Keshab Sen's house, though Keshab was not a brahmin. He forbade us to tell anyone about it, lest the temple officials refuse to let him enter the Kali temple. The next day, however, when the temple manager was passing by, the Master told him: "Yesterday I went to Keshab's house and he gave me a sumptuous feast. I don't know whether the food was served by a washerman or a barber. Will it harm me?" Smiling, the manager replied: "No, sir, it is all right. Nothing can pollute you." The Master was as simple as a child.[29]

Children are simple because their minds are not cluttered with double dealing, worldliness, and selfishness. The Master was as simple as a child. This filled his disciples and devotees with awe, but most of the temple workers considered him to be foolish and mad.

If a person is lustful, he or she hides it out of shame; otherwise that person would face public humiliation. The Master had nothing to hide in any circumstance. During his sadhana, he experienced lust, which he described to the devotees at Devendra's house on 6 April 1885: "Is it an easy matter to get rid of lust? I myself felt a queer sensation in my heart six months after I had begun my spiritual practice. Then I threw myself on the ground under a tree and wept bitterly. I said to the Divine Mother, 'Mother, if it comes to that, I shall certainly cut my throat with a knife!'"[30] How many people could speak so candidly?

Lust is a great obstacle in spiritual life. Generally, people feel shy to talk about it. When one of Ramakrishna's young disciples was suffering from lust, Ramakrishna offered this advice without hiding anything:

"Look, lust doesn't completely go away even when one realizes God. As long as the body lasts, a little lust remains even after God-vision — but it can't raise its head. Do you think I am free from it? At one time I believed that I had conquered lust. Then one day when I was seated in the Panchavati, I suddenly had such an onrush of lust that it was hard for me to maintain control! Immediately I began crying, rubbing my face in the dust, and saying to the Divine Mother: 'I have made a big mistake, Mother. I shall never again think that I have conquered lust.' Only then did it subside. Do you know, you boys are now passing through a flood tide of adolescence? You can't stop it. Can an embankment or a breakwater stop a tidal wave? The overflowing water breaks through and rushes forward, and then the water stands as high as a bamboo over the paddy fields. There is a saying, 'Mental sin is not considered to be a sin in this kaliyuga.' If a bad thought happens to arise once or twice in the mind, why should you go on brooding about it? Sometimes those feelings come and go. They are natural to the body; consider them to be physical functions like the call of nature. Do people worry when they have an urge for the call of nature? Similarly, consider those feelings to be insignificant, trifling, and worthless, and don't think of them anymore. Pray to God intensely, chant His name, and meditate on Him. Don't pay any heed to whether those feelings come or go. Gradually, they will come under control." It was as if the Master had become a youth while talking to that young man.[31]

The Master's solution to this vital problem overwhelms us with its simplicity and teaches us how to counteract this obstacle in spiritual life.

There was a pond in Rani Rasmani's Janbazar estate. Rani divided the property among her four daughters so that there would be no friction among them. One day Jagadamba, Mathur's wife, bathed in her sister's pond and collected some watercress. The Master, who happened to be passing, saw her do this. Immediately there was a great commotion in his mind: "It is very wrong for Jagadamba to take something that belongs to another in this way. Does she not know that taking something without asking first is theft? Why does she crave what belongs to another?" As he was thinking this, he saw the daughter who owned that pond. The Master immediately reported everything to her. Listening to the story and seeing the Master's serious mood because of Jagadamba's "heinous" act, she could hardly control her laughter. However, she feigned indignation and exclaimed, "That was very wrong of her, Father!" Meanwhile, Jagadamba arrived. When she learned why her elder sister was merry, Jagadamba jokingly reproached him: "Father, is it proper for you to expose me in this way? I took that watercress secretly so that she might not see it. And now you have embarrassed me by reporting my theft to her." Then the sisters could no longer control themselves and began to laugh. "I don't know your worldly ways," the Master told Jagadamba. "But when property has been divided, it is not good to take anything without the owner's knowledge. So I informed your sister. Now let her decide." Both sisters continued laughing, thinking how simple and naïve the Father was.[32] This is a scene for meditation on the Master's honesty and simplicity: we see the two sisters laughing near the pond and the Master's bewildered expression.

O **Humility.** According to Vedanta, people function in this world by means of "I" and "mine." If there were no "I and my", the world would vanish from the human mind. Ramakrishna's "I," or ego, died forever. He could not utter the word "I" and "my"; in lieu of those words, he used "here" and "this place." He used to swear, "Upon my word, I don't feel vanity even in the slightest degree."[33]

Regarding the Master's humility, Girish Ghosh commented: "This time the Lord has come to conquer the world through prostrations. In his incarnation as Rama, he conquered by bow and arrow; as Krishna, it was the flute; as Chaitanya, the Name. But the weapon of his powerful Incarnation this time is the salutation."[34] The Master humbled Girish by prostrating before him. At that time westernized young people, such as the Brahmos, considered the practice of bowing down in respect to others to be mere superstition and beneath one's dignity. The Master narrated how Keshab Sen was changed by coming in contact with him:

> I visited him at his house in Coolootola Street. Hriday was with me. We were shown into the room where Keshab was working. He was writing something. After a long while he put aside his pen, got off his chair, and sat on the floor with us. But he didn't salute us or show us respect in any other way.
>
> He used to come here now and then. One day in a spiritual mood I said to him: "One should not sit before a sadhu with one leg over the other. That increases one's rajas." As soon as he and his friends would arrive, I would salute them before they bowed to me. Thus they gradually learnt to salute a holy man, touching the ground with their foreheads."[35]

The Master said that the ego originates from tamas. The ego is like a mound on which water does not accumulate. One cannot realize God if there is a slightest amount of ego. "I and my" are the offshoots of ignorance. All problems cease when the "I" dies.

With a view to uprooting caste superiority and hatred, the Master cleaned the toilet and drain in the temple garden at night and swept the street with a broom. In addition, M. mentioned: "The Master himself told us that once he cleaned the open drain of the sweeper Rasik's house with his own hair while praying with tears in his eyes, 'Mother, destroy my pride in being a brahmin.'"[36]

One day the Master was walking in the flower garden at Dakshineswar when Dr. Kailash Basu came to visit. He thought that the Master was a gardener and asked him to pick some jasmine flowers for him. The Master immediately obeyed. Later when the Master was suffering from cancer in Cossipore, Ram Datta consulted Dr. Basu about the Master's illness. Dr. Basu had heard Ram describe the greatness of his guru, and he said: "Look, Ram, you people try to make a mountain out of a molehill. If you find a little goodness in a man, you won't rest until you have given him a big title such as 'paramahamsa' or 'avatar.' I wouldn't mind humiliating this kind of paramahamsa or avatar by twisting his ears." When Ram protested, Dr. Basu apologized for his comment. However, he went with Ram to Cossipore. No sooner had Ram and Dr. Basu entered the room, than the Master saluted the doctor and asked: "Hello, doctor, will you examine my disease first or twist my ears?" Dr. Basu was startled. He realized that this paramahamsa was the all-knowing God. No one else had been present when he talked with Ram. How did Ramakrishna know what he had said? Dr. Kailash Basu humbly replied to the Master: "Sir, please forgive the offence of this wretched person. I made a mistake uttering slurs about you without knowing you. Please don't embarrass me further." He examined the Master with love and respect and became his lifelong devotee. His ego had been crushed. Later, he would never leave home without bowing down to a picture of the Master.[37]

The Master demonstrated how one should be humble. He swept the paths of the temple complex, and he carried away the leaf-plates on which the beggars had eaten. He prayed to the Divine Mother: "I don't want any name and fame, or any praise or respect from people. Please destroy my ego completely. Make me the lowest of the lowly and humble."

The scriptures say that to a knower of Brahman honour and dishonour are equal. The Master demonstrated that. Once he went to attend an evening prayer meeting of the Sadharan Brahmo Samaj, where Narendra was a singer. As soon as the Master arrived, there was a commotion in the hall. The speaker did not receive the Master, but instead he ordered the gas light to be turned off to disperse the crowd. There was a huge uproar in that dark hall as the Master stood there in samadhi. Narendra rushed to the Master and slowly took him out through a back door. He was pained by how the Brahmos had humiliated the Master, and he reprimanded the Master for coming there without an invitation. But the Master was totally unconcerned.

These anecdotes offer more scenes for our meditation.

O *Shraddhā*, or faith. Shraddha turns into faith as love deepens into prema (intense love). Shraddha is not a mechanical belief in or acceptance of the words of a holy person or book. Rather it is an affirmative and reverent attitude towards supersensuous truths. The word *shraddha* has many meanings, such as cordiality, respect, love, confidence, faith, steadfastness, intense sincerity, and inner strength. Shraddha is a wonderful asset, and it is a virtue in human life. The Gita says: "A person is made of his faith. One is whatever his faith is" (17:3). Our scriptures glorify shraddha and faith. Shraddha is important not only in spiritual matters, but also in one's personal, family, and social life. According to Vedanta, shraddha is faith in the truths of Vedanta as taught by the guru. The devotional scriptures also mentioned nine steps of supreme love, the first step being shraddha. Patanjali wrote in the Yoga-sutras: "For illumination a yogi needs shraddha or passion, energy, collectedness, absorption, and discrimination" (1:20). He who is full of faith obtains knowledge.

Spiritual life is not possible for a person who is devoid of shraddha and faith.

Ramakrishna developed these two divine qualities intensely during his period of sadhana and as a guru. He attained success quickly with their help when he practised Tantra, Vedanta, and other sadhanas. It is unprecedented how the Master attained success in sixty-four branches of Tantra sadhana in such a short time. Similarly, he attained nirvikalpa samadhi in only three days! Indeed, the Master completed many different and difficult sadhanas, a feat that is beyond our comprehension.

Once a monk wanted to go to Uttarkashi in order to practise austerity. He sought advice from an elderly disciple of Holy Mother, who said: "Look, before you go for tapasya, please read the second part of the *Ramakrishna Lilaprasanga* [Sadhak-bhava — Ramakrishna as a spiritual aspirant]. There you will notice how the Master's shraddhā, faith, and sincerity helped him attain perfection so quickly. First meditate on the Master's austerity and then go to Uttarkashi."

Ramakrishna's dazzling life of austerity is a vivid example for us to follow. Observing his faith and sincerity, Bhairavi Brahmani arranged to build a Panchamundi (a Tantric place of worship) under the bel tree at Dakshineswar. The Master recalled:

> During the day, the Brahmani would travel to various places far away from the temple and collect rare articles prescribed by Tantra. At nightfall, she would set up the ritual either under the bel tree or under the Panchavati, then call me to worship the Divine Mother with those articles, advising me to be absorbed in japa and meditation. But I could seldom do japa after worship because my mind was so absorbed that I would merge into samadhi while turning the rosary. I would truly experience the result of that rite, as described by the scriptures. Thus, I had vision after vision and innumerable wonderful spiritual experiences.[38]

This was the outcome of his shraddha and faith.

A Vedanta monk named Tota Puri came to Dakshineswar. As soon as he saw Ramakrishna, he recognized him to be a qualified candidate for sannyasa. Whenever the Master accepted anyone as his guru, he unhesitatingly surrendered to that person, and with absolute faith followed the instructions he was given. Whatever Tota instructed him to do, he carried out exactly as he was told. After performing the viraja homa, Tota asked the Master to concentrate on the nondual Brahman. Ramakrishna related:

> I almost lost hope of reaching nirvikalpa samadhi. I opened my eyes and told the Naked One: "No, it can't be done. I cannot raise my mind to the

unconditioned state and force it to be absorbed in the Atman." Irritated, the Naked One said sharply: "What do you mean — can't be done? It must be done!" Then he looked around the hut and found a bit of broken glass. He picked it up and stuck its needle-sharp point between my eyebrows and said, "Fix the mind here." I sat down to meditate again, firmly determined. As soon as the form of the Divine Mother appeared in my mind, I used my discrimination as a sword of knowledge and with it mentally cut that form in two. Then all distinctions disappeared from my mind, and it swiftly soared beyond the realm of name and form. I lost myself in samadhi."[39]

We can imagine the Master's love and faith in his gurus and how they helped him to attain his goal. We can visualize the dark nights at the Panchavati and the Panchamundi where he practised his sadhanas in solitude as the Ganges flowed nearby with a murmuring sound. During our meditation, we love to see the image of our Chosen Ideal in his surroundings.

The Master narrated two examples of his childlike faith:

Ah, what a state of mind I passed through! One day something bit me while I was sitting in the grass. I was afraid it might have been a snake, and I didn't know what to do. I had heard that if a snake bites you again immediately after its first bite, it takes back its own venom. At once I set out to discover the hole so that I might let the snake bite me again. While I was searching, a man said to me, "What are you doing?" After listening to my story, he said, "But the snake must bite in the very same place it has bitten before." Thereupon I went away. Perhaps I had been stung by a scorpion or some other insect.

I had heard from Ramlal that the autumn chill was good for one's health. Ramlal had quoted a verse to support it. One day, as I was returning from Calcutta in a carriage, I stuck my head out of the window so that I might get all the chill. Then I fell ill."[40]

We read various stories and parables of the Master on the pages of his *Gospel*, and all of these can be the objects of meditation. For example, one could meditate on the following: the milkmaid who walked on the river, chanting the name of Rama, while her guru fell into the water; Narada, who rolled over the diagram of hell drawn by Vishnu on the floor and thus completed the period of suffering in hell that he was fated to endure; the guru who continually received curd from a pot that Krishna had given to his poor disciple; Vyasa, who ate milk and curd and then said to Yamuna, "If I did not eat anything, O Yamuna, make a dry path for me so that I can cross walking through you."

Swami Vivekananda was skeptical about those stories. One day he referred to the devotees' belief as "blind faith." The Master told him: "Well, can you explain what you mean by 'blind faith?' Faith is always blind. Has faith eyes? Either simply say 'faith,' or say 'knowledge.' What do you mean by classifying faith — one kind having eyes, the other being blind?" Swami Vivekananda said later: "In fact I was embarrassed when explaining the meaning of blind faith to the Master that day. I could not find any meaning in that expression. After understanding that the Master's words were true, I never again used that phrase."[41]

O **Devotion and longing.** Before practising meditation, one should know the object of meditation well. For example, before meditating on Ramakrishna, one should know to some extent who Ramakrishna is. Without knowing a person, we cannot establish a relationship with him or her. If we want to love a person, we must know him or her. Thus love and knowledge go together. Stories of Ramakrishna's love and longing for God will strengthen our meditation, and we shall be able to detect our shortcomings.

Narada defined bhakti as follows: "Devotion is the surrender of all activities to God and extreme anguish if He is forgotten." Intense longing thus leads to devotion. The scriptures say that one cannot attain devotion without giving up worldly enjoyment. Swami Krishnananda wrote:

Love is the basic element of human life. This love makes a person attached to sense enjoyment, and again it makes him renounce the sense enjoyment, friends and family, and it makes a loving devotee. In fact, love, attachment, and passion are wonderful, but if they are diverted towards a bad place or a bad person, they will produce bad results. You love your guru, scriptures, knowledge, good action, Mother Annapurna, Radha-Krishna — that love will give you good results. Whereas you love to drink, visit prostitutes, steal another's money, criticize holy people, or mix with evil company — that love will give you bad results. So there is no fault to love; the problem is the application of love."[42]

God reveals Himself or Herself to those who have devotion and longing. Sometimes we wonder how we can love God, whom we have not seen. Ramakrishna said to the devotees: If you have yearning, you will get holy company. Yearning is a sign of God-vision as the golden glow in the morning sky indicates sunrise. Cry to God with a longing heart, secretly and in solitude, then his grace will dawn on you. You will get his vision and a taste for repeating his name. Your kundalini will also be awakened, and God will definitely answer your prayer.

How does devotion manifest through the three gunas? Ramakrishna answered this question:

Sattvic bhakti is known to God alone. It makes no outward display. A man with such devotion loves privacy. Perhaps he meditates inside the mosquito net, where nobody sees him. When this kind of devotion is awakened, one hasn't long to wait for the vision of God. The appearance of the dawn in the east shows that the sun will rise before long.

A man with rajasic bhakti feels like making a display of his devotion before others. He worships the Deity with "sixteen ingredients," enters the temple wearing a silk cloth, and puts around his neck a string of rudrāksha beads interspersed here and there with beads of gold and ruby.

A man with tamasic bhakti shows the courage and boisterousness of a highway robber. A highway robber goes on his expedition openly, shouting, "Kill! Plunder!" He isn't afraid even of eight police inspectors. The devotee with tamasic bhakti also shouts like a madman: "Hara! Hara! Vyom! Vyom! Victory to Kali!" He has great strength of mind and burning faith.[43]

We glibly say, "I love you." Is love such a trifling thing? We are disheartened when we hear the signs of true love of God according to the Master: "First, it makes one forget the world. So intense is one's love of God that one becomes unconscious of outer things. Second, one has no feeling of 'my-ness' toward the body, which is so dear to man. One wholly gets rid of the feeling that the body is the soul."[44] When the Master meditated under the Panchavati, sometimes a snake would crawl over his knees, or a bird would sit on his head and peck in his hair looking for food. These are scenes for meditation.

Some other scenes of the Master's longing come to mind. Facing the sun as it set over the Ganges, the Master would rub his face on the grass near the Panchavati and cry: "Mother, another day is gone in vain. Still Thou art not revealed unto me." His face would bleed and the green grass would turn red. The village women who came to fetch water from the bakul-tala ghat would see the Master crying and ask the temple officials to help him. But they would refuse, considering this to be a sign of the Master's madness.

The Master had his first vision of the Divine Mother through the intensity of his longing. This he described to his disciples, and Swami Saradananda reported it in the *Lilaprasanga*:

There was an unbearable pain in my heart because I could not have a vision of Mother. Just as a man wrings out a towel with all his strength to get the water out of it, so I felt as if my heart were being wrung out. I began to think I should never see Mother. I was dying of despair. In my agony, I asked myself: "What's the use of living this life?" Suddenly my eyes fell on the sword that hangs in the Mother's shrine. I decided to end my life then and there. Like a madman, I ran to the sword and seized it. Then I had a marvelous vision of the Mother and fell down unconscious. Afterwards what happened in the external world, or how that day and the next passed, I don't know. But within me there was a steady flow of undiluted bliss that I had never before experienced, and I felt the immediate presence of the Divine Mother.[45]

There are three signs of God's grace — intense self-effort, longing, and untiring endeavour — which were evident in the Master's life. These are wonderful themes for our meditation.

O **Forgiveness and forbearance.** The scriptures say that the beauty and greatness of a strong person is forgiveness. The Master explained the mystery of the three "sa-s": "There is no higher quality than forbearance. He who forbears, survives; and he who does not, perishes. In the Bengali alphabet no other letter occurs in three different forms except sa — ś, sh, s — this means forbear, forbear, forbear. Everyone should cultivate forbearance. A blacksmith's anvil remains immovable under the countless blows of his heavy hammer, so everyone should endure with a firm determination all that is said or done by others."[46]

Forbearance and forgiveness are interconnected. Without these two qualities human life would become unbearable. The Master said: "If there is any strained relation with anybody, one should try to communicate with that person and ease the relationship. If your humble efforts fail, don't think about that person anymore. Take refuge in God and think of God. It is not necessary to focus on petty squabbles that distract your mind from God. The mind is supposed to be offered to God. Why should one misuse it by thinking of others?"[47]

The scriptures say that there is nothing more praiseworthy than forgiveness. Chandra Haldar, a priest of the Kalighat temple, was very jealous of Mathur's love and respect for the Master. He thought that the Master had cast a spell on Mathur Babu and hypnotized him. Swami Saradananda wrote:

Early one evening the Master was lying on the floor in ecstasy at the Janbazar house. No one else was in the room. The Master was coming down from samadhi and slowly becoming aware of the external world. At that time Chandra Haldar, the family priest, arrived. Seeing the Master alone in that condition, he thought his time had come. He approached him, looked around, and shaking the Master's body several times, demanded: "Hey, tell me how you captured Mathur Babu? Don't pretend you can't talk! How did you hypnotize him? Speak up!" Despite this kind of repeated insistence, the Master did not say anything because at that moment he had no power to speak. This made Chandra extremely angry. "So you won't tell me, you scoundrel!" he cried. He kicked the Master violently and left the room in disgust. The humble Master said nothing of this incident, knowing that if Mathur learned of it he would be furious and might punish the brahmin priest severely. Soon after this, Chandra incurred Mathur's anger by committing an offence and was dismissed. Then one day in the course of conversation the Master told Mathur what had happened. To this, Mathur said in anger and agony, "Father, if I had known that then, he would have been killed."[48]

The Master accepted this humiliation because he was an avatar; in contrast, when we get a little criticism, we flare up in anger and start a war of words. If we meditate on this scene, we shall develop forgiveness and forbearance.

M. described two other scenes that demonstrate forbearance and forgiveness in the Master. One day the Master went to attend the Brahmo festival at Nandan-bagan. The owner of the house had passed away and his sons arranged the festival. They gave a cold reception to the Master, but he did not mind. When it was time for dinner, no one called the Master. Rakhal angrily said: "Sir, let us leave here and go to Dakshineswar."

Master (*with a smile*): "Keep quiet! The carriage hire is three rupees and two annas. Who will pay that? Stubbornness won't get us anywhere. You haven't a penny, and you are making these empty threats! Besides, where shall we find food at this late hour of the night?"[49]

Finally, with great difficulty, a place was found for him to eat in a dusty corner where people kept their shoes. A woman served him some curry, but the Master could not eat it. He ate a luchi with salt and took some sweets. It would have been inauspicious for the household if a holy man had left without taking some food. Although the young hosts had not shown him proper respect, the all-forgiving Master showered his grace on them nonetheless.

M. narrated another example of the Master's forgiveness:

Rani Rasmani and Mathur recognized the Master's divinity. But Trailokya, Mathur's son, and others could not understand him. Once at the Dakshineswar kuthi [mansion], Trailokya arranged a party and some women singers were also invited. He invited the Master and requested him to sing a song. The Master said: 'I have come here to listen to their songs. It is not necessary for me to sing at this party.' However, the Master sang and those women sang also. When the Master was about to leave, they offered him some refreshments but he refused. Trailokya, however, sent some food to the Master's room through a servant.[50]

Nonetheless, it is said that patience has a limit. There came a day when the Master could no longer bear his nephew Hriday's harsh words and humiliation, so he was about to jump into the Ganges, but he stopped; and at another time, he wanted to move to Varanasi. Finally, he said to Hriday: "You bear with my words and I shall bear with yours. Then only we can live together. Otherwise, the temple manager may have to be called for settling our disputes."[51]

Another interesting scene for meditation occurred in front of the Star Theatre in Calcutta. The Master once went to see a play that ended late at night. Girish had arranged supper for the Master with hot luchis, curry, and sweets. As the Master was preparing to return to Dakshineswar, Girish, who was drunk, demanded, "You be my son." Ramakrishna said: "Why should I be your son? I shall be your Ishta [Chosen Deity]." Girish insisted and the Master said again: "I shall be your Ishta. My father was extremely pure. Why should I be your son?" Intoxicated, Girish began to use filthy words against him. The devotees were enraged and ready to punish Girish, but the Master stopped them and laughingly remarked: "What kind of devotee is this? What does he say?" Girish continued to abuse the Master, and the devotees then escorted the Master to the carriage. Girish followed the Master and lay down on the dirty and muddy street as he bowed down in front of the carriage. The Master left for Dakshineswar.

All of the devotees suggested that the Master should not see Girish again. However, the next day Ram Datta came to Dakshineswar and heard the whole story. He said that Girish did not do anything wrong: human beings worship God with whatever has been given them. As the snake Kaliya worshipped Krishna with his poison, so Girish worshipped the Master with his rude language. Immediately the Master took Ram's carriage and went to Girish's house. Girish approached him with tears in his eyes and fell at his feet. Only when the Master said, "All right, all right," did he finally get up. This is a wonderful illustration of forgiveness.

O **Sense of humour.** God is Satchidananda — existence, consciousness, and bliss. If God was not blissful, it is doubtful whether people would call upon God. When God incarnates as an avatar, people are drawn to him to enjoy his company. However, we don't hear uproarious laughter with other avatars as we do with the Master. The scriptures do not describe Rama, Krishna, Buddha, or Jesus as laughing loudly. When we read *The*

Gospel of Sri Ramakrishna, however, we find several places that say "all laugh" or "laughter." The face of the Master in samadhi seems to indicate that he was unable to contain his joy.

We see Jesus portrayed in the Bible as an embodiment of sadness. But the Master was a great humorist and a blissful man. In this joyless world, he laughed and made others laugh. This was one of his special qualities. He prayed to the Divine Mother, "Mother, don't make me a dry monk; allow me to enjoy the fun in life."[52] However, anything that he said in humour had a hidden significance. For example, he once said: "I don't give the youngsters a pure vegetarian diet: now and then I give them a little water smelling of fish. Otherwise, why should they come?"[53]

This world was Ramakrishna's mansion of mirth. There are many funny scenes in the Master's life that make us laugh and dispel our gloom. Suresh Chandra Datta wrote: "One day the Master assumed the mood of a woman. He wore his *dhoti* [a man's cloth] like a sari, and showed me how a woman charms a man. He pretended to be a housewife and began to serve food to an imaginary husband. When the husband refused to eat any more, the wife said, 'Please have another piece of sandesh and another piece of jilipi.' As the wife fed her husband, she let him know what she wanted: 'My neighbour friend got a seven-string necklace yesterday. I wish I could have one like that.'"[54]

Suresh was dumbfounded as he watched the Master enact the role of a worldly-minded wife, perfect to the last detail, as she gestured with her hands, glanced at her husband, and wheedled a necklace out of him.

Truly, the Master was a king among actors. His acting was precise in whatever role he would act, be it a man or a woman, because he was both Purusha and Prakriti in the same body. In the *Gospel*, M. described a wonderful scene:

> Sri Ramakrishna was in the happiest mood with his young and pure-souled devotees. He was seated on the small couch and was doing funny imitations of a kirtani [a woman singer]. The devotees laughed heartily. The kirtani is dressed lavishly and covered with ornaments. She sings standing on the floor, a coloured kerchief in her hand. Now and then she coughs to draw people's attention and blows her nose, raising her nose-ring. When a respectable gentleman enters the room she welcomes him with appropriate words, still continuing her song. Now and then she pulls her sari from her arms to show off her jewels.
>
> The devotees were convulsed with laughter at this mimicry by Sri Ramakrishna. Paltu rolled on the ground. Pointing to him, the Master said to M.: "Look at that child! He is rolling with laughter." He said to

Paltu with a smile: "Don't report this to your father, or he will lose the little respect he has for me. You see, he is an 'Englishman.'"[55]

There is no need to comment on that description. However, a person should not misunderstand: the Master was not a mere entertainer; his humour and mimicry were connected with spiritual life. His smile radiated a wave of the blissful ocean of Satchidananda, and that wave would push the devotees closer to its shore.

Ordinary people cannot absorb serious spiritual talk for a long time; they begin to gasp for air and feel uncomfortable. That is why the Master would tell humorous stories in between offering spiritual advice, and thus would relax them. M. recorded how the Master portrayed phony aspirants:

Master (*to the devotees*): "There are people who indulge in all kinds of gossip at the time of their daily devotions. As you know, one is not permitted to talk then; so they make all kinds of signs, keeping their lips closed. In order to say, 'Bring this,' 'Bring that,' they make sounds like 'Huh,' 'Uhuh.' All such things they do! (*Laughter.*)

"Again, there are some who bargain for fish while telling their beads. As they count the rosary, with a finger they point out the fish, indicating, 'That one, please.' They reserve all their business for that time! (*Laughter.*)

"There are women who come to the Ganges for their bath and, instead of thinking of God, gossip about no end of things. 'What jewels did you offer at the time of your son's marriage?' — 'Has so-and-so returned from her father-in-law's house?' — 'So-and-so is seriously ill.' — 'So-and-so went to see the bride; we hope that they will offer a magnificent dowry and that there will be a great feast.' — 'Harish always nags at me; he can't stay away from me even an hour.' — 'My child, I couldn't come to see you all these days; I was so busy with the betrothal of so-and-so's daughter.'

"You see, they have come to bathe in the holy river, and yet they indulge in all sorts of worldly talk."

The Master began to look intently at the younger Naren and went into samadhi. Did he see God Himself in the pure-souled devotee?

The devotees silently watched the figure of Sri Ramakrishna motionless in samadhi. A few minutes before there had been so much laughter in the room; now there was deep silence, as if no one were there. The Master sat with folded hands as in his photograph.[56]

Here is another wonderful theme for meditation: the Master's humour brought peace to belligerent groups. Sometimes we quarrel due to differences of opinion and we stop talking. One example of the Master's peacemaking concerned the Brahmos. Keshab had arranged his 13-year-old daughter's marriage to a member of the royal family of Coochbehar, which was contrary to the Brahmo Samaj rule against child marriage. As a result, there was a schism between people who were loyal to Keshab and those who were loyal to Shivanath and Vijay. The latter group started the Sadharan Brahmo Samaj. During a boat trip, the Master used humour to ease the relationship between Keshab and Vijay. M. recorded the incident:

> Master (*to Keshab*): "Look here. There is Vijay. Your quarrel seems like the fight between Siva and Rama. Siva was Rama's guru. Though they fought with each other, yet they soon came to terms. But the grimaces of the ghosts, the followers of Siva, and the gibberish of the monkeys, the followers of Rama, would not come to an end! (*Loud laughter.*) Such quarrels take place even among one's own kith and kin. Didn't Rama fight with His own sons, Lava and Kusa? Again, you must have noticed how a mother and daughter, living together and having the same spiritual end in view, observe their religious fast separately on Tuesdays, each on her own account — as if the welfare of the mother were different from the welfare of the daughter. But what benefits the one benefits the other. In like manner, you have a religious society, and Vijay thinks he must have one too. (*Laughter.*) But I think all these are necessary. While Sri Krishna, Himself God Incarnate, played with the gopis at Vrindaban, trouble-makers like Jatila and Kutila appeared on the scene. You may ask why. The answer is that the play does not develop without trouble-makers. (*All laugh.*) There is no fun without Jatila and Kutila. (*Loud laughter.*)
>
> Ramanuja upheld the doctrine of Qualified Non-dualism. But his guru was a pure non-dualist. They disagreed with each other and refuted each other's arguments. That always happens. Still, to the teacher the disciple is his own.[57]

O Saviour of the fallen and destroyer of sin. One of the special characteristics of an avatar is that he manifests compassion and forgiveness. He takes the sins of the sinners upon himself and frees them from the results of their bad karma. An ordinary person can relieve another person of a heavy weight by carrying it, but an ordinary person cannot take on another person's sin and bad karma. Only an avatar or a great soul possesses that redeeming power.

It is well known that the Master took Girish's power of attorney. As Jesus needed Mary Magdalene to prove himself to be a saviour, so Mary needed Jesus to remove her sins. Similarly, Ramakrishna proved himself to be a saviour by absorbing Girish's sins, and by doing so he suffered from cancer. This is the lila of God and the devotees. We can imagine the

Master seated on his small cot in Dakshineswar facing east and Girish seated on the floor with folded hands in the following exchange.

Girish: "Sir, what shall I do from now on?"
Master: "Do just what you are doing now. Hold on to God with one hand and to the world with the other. Eventually, when one side [the world] falls to pieces, whatever is ordained to happen will happen. At a minimum, think of God in the morning and evening."

Girish remained speechless as there was a storm in his mind. He felt suffocated at the mere thought of being bound forever to a particular vow or to a rule.

Finding Girish silent, the Master read his mind and said, "Well, if you cannot do that, then remember God before you eat and before you sleep." But still Girish remained silent. Then the Master said: "So you are unwilling to agree even to this. All right. Give me your power of attorney."[58]

This is the culmination of self-surrender. Girish, giving his power of attorney to Ramakrishna, is an example of how God removes the sins of sinners. This offer of the power of attorney has not expired. Even now, if a wayward person gives his or her power of attorney to the Master with heart and soul, the Master will accept it.

The Master said: "I am a destroyer of action and the French colony." There is a deep inner meaning to these words. During the Master's lifetime, India was under the rule of the British, French, and Portuguese. If anyone did anything wrong in British India and took refuge in the French colony, the British could not punish that person. Similarly, if anyone commits a heinous act and takes refuge in the Master, he will protect that person.

In Shyampukur, during the Master's illness, he said to Dr. Sarkar: "There is a river called the *Karmanasa* [destroyer of duties]. It is very dangerous to dive into that river. If a man plunges into its waters he cannot perform any more action. It puts an end to his duties."[59] The Master indirectly indicated that he was that Karmanasa river. He has the power to erase people's bad karma. The Master not only made Girish and Kalipada free from sin, but he also transformed many courtesans, such as Binodini and Banabiharini, who worked as actresses in Girish's theatre.

Swami Premananda said:

One day the ladies of Balaram Babu's family were sitting before the Master in his room when a prostitute named Ramani passed along the road nearby. The Master called to her and asked, "Why don't you come nowadays?" The ladies were scandalized to hear the Master talking with a prostitute.

Shortly afterwards the Master took them to visit the shrines. When they reached the Kali temple the Master said to the Divine Mother: "Mother, Thou indeed hast become the prostitute Ramani. Thou hast become both the prostitute and the chaste woman!" The ladies understood that they were wrong in despising Ramani, and that the Master spoke with her, knowing her to be the Mother Herself. They should not be so proud of their chastity, for it was all due to the Mother's will.[60]

The Master saw the Divine Mother in all women. He described one of his visions: "One day when I was meditating, seated in the Kali temple, I could not bring the Mother's form to my mind at all. Then I saw that She had appeared in the form of Ramani, a prostitute who came to bathe at the Dakshineswar ghat, and was peeping from behind the water pot before the image. I laughed and said: 'O Mother, you have a desire to become Ramani today! All right. Accept my worship today in this form.' Thus, She made me understand: 'I am also the prostitute. There is none other than Me.'"[61]

There is no end to the divine qualities of Ramakrishna. In the eleventh chapter of the Gita, Krishna described his divine manifestations. Finally, he said: "Know that in all cases whatever in existence is powerful, glorious, and beautiful issues from but a spark of my splendour" (11:41).

In this chapter, we briefly discussed some of Ramakrishna's divine qualities. Some of his other qualities manifest vividly in front of our eyes, such as his compassion and affection for the poor and lowly, his unselfishness, appreciation of other's virtues, skill in action, not finding fault in others, excellent human behaviour, service to humanity, patience, steadfastness, firmness, bravery, outspokenness, wonderful skill in conversation, honesty, uprightness, elegant demeanour, mastery in singing and dancing, scientific outlook, sharp intelligence, strong common sense, and above all his love for humanity.

The more we discuss Ramakrishna's divine qualities and reflect upon them, the more we see his greatness. Being incapable of expressing the infinite glory of God, Pushpadanta declared in his hymn on Shiva:

O Giver of boons, how poor is my ill-developed mind, subject to afflictions, and how boundless Your divinity — eternal and possessing infinite virtues. Though terror–stricken because of this, I am inspired by my devotion to offer this hymnal garland at Your feet. O Lord, if the blue mountain be the ink, the ocean the ink pot, the biggest branch of the celestial tree the pen, and the earth the writing-leaf, and if by taking this, the goddess of Learning writes forever, even then the limit of Your glory can never be reached.[62]

Meditation on Ramakrishna's Lila

We cannot see Krishna, Buddha, Jesus, or Ramakrishna with our physical eyes, but God gave us an inner eye with which to visualize their *lila* (divine play). Meditation opens the inner eye, known as the "third eye," the "mental eye," or the "eye of knowledge."

There are various kinds of meditation, such as meditation on God's form, divine qualities, divine message, or divine play. The infinite God takes a finite human form and plays in this world like one of us so that we can feel His presence and glimpse God's infinite nature. In connection with meditation on the lila, I gave this example to a devout Catholic woman:

> If you want to feel the presence of God quickly, practise meditation on the *lila*, or divine play, of God-men. Close your eyes and mentally visualize Christ walking through the street. The multitude is following him. He enters the house of Simon. Mary Magdalene, a fallen woman, washes the feet of Jesus with her tears and then wipes them dry with her long hair. She opens an alabaster box and anoints his feet with scented ointment. The compassionate Christ blesses Mary, putting his hands on her head. This is a small episode in Christ's life. Try to visualize these scenes, one after another. Go slowly. Don't move to the next scene until the first scene has taken a luminous form in your mind. After visualizing the entire episode, look at your clock. You will see that you have lived with Christ for twenty minutes, forgetting space, time, and causation. This is called meditation on the divine play of the Lord.[1]

There is no end to the human imagination. We can choose various episodes from the avatars' lives and meditate on their glories, which will illumine our hearts. Avatars are the light of the world. Those who follow them will not be trapped by maya's darkness, or ignorance. It is the nature of a lamp to light all around and thus remove darkness. Ramakrishna, the avatar of this age, lit the lamp of dharma and wisdom to remove the dense darkness of delusion. Referring to Ramakrishna, Vivekananda wrote:

> India has lost her life-force again and again, so the Divine Lord has re-peatedly revived her by manifesting Himself. Before this present degen-eration, no veil of darkness had ever enveloped the holy land of India so deeply as this last dismal night, which is now merely a remnant — it is almost gone.
>
> During this current spiritual renaissance, the new avatar of the age, endowed with tremendous divine power, will gather together the divid-ed and scattered religious ideals, practise and realize them in his own life, and rediscover the knowledge that was lost. He is the embodiment of all religious ideals and the support of all branches of learning.
>
> So at the dawn of this momentous epoch, the message of the harmony of religions has been proclaimed. This new religion of the age will benefit the whole world, but most especially India. Bhagavan Sri Ramakrishna, the founder of this new religion, is the reconstructed manifestation of the earlier founders of religions.[2]

Avatars take a human form but in reality are formless

On this earth, the infinite God becomes finite, taking a form despite being formless, and embracing qualities while being devoid of qualities, in order to enjoy the play as a human being. God's human play is sweet and also intriguing. The avatar behaves like a human being, so it is diffi-cult to recognize him. Like other humans, the avatar undergoes hunger and thirst, disease and grief, fear and anger. For example, Ramachandra was grief-stricken at losing Sita and, angry at the ocean because it would not allow a bridge to be built to Sri Lanka (where Ravana had taken Sita); he intended to shoot an arrow into the ocean. As a cowherd boy in Gokula, Krishna grazed his cows, carried his friend Sudama on his back, and danced with the gopis. He stole butter and curd, then hid himself from his foster mother, Yashoda. The child Gadadhar (later Ramakrishna) ate puffed rice and jilipi for breakfast, swam with his friends in the Hal-darpukur, acted in a children's yatra [play], and entered Durgadas Pyne's house in disguise as a poor weaver woman. It is wonderful to envision an avatar's lila. Thus we can enjoy Ramakrishna's lila through hundreds of episodes, just as the Christians watch Passion Plays.

Above: Ramakrishna's early lila: Kamarpukur, his parental home, where he lived 17 years.
Below: Ramakrishna's middle lila: After living in Calcutta for 3 years, he moved to the Dakshineswar temple garden where he lived for 30 years.

Above: Ramakrishna's last lila: Shyampukur house, where he lived nearly 3 months.
Below: Cossipore garden house, where he lived nearly 9 months.

Regarding the necessity of Ramakrishna's advent as a human being, Vivekananda said:

> In order that a nation may rise, it must have a high ideal. Now, that ideal is, of course, the abstract Brahman. But as you all cannot be inspired by an abstract ideal, you must have a personal ideal. You have got that, in the person of Sri Ramakrishna. The reason why other personages cannot be our ideal now is that their days are gone; and in order that Vedanta may come to everyone, there must be a person who is in sympathy with the present generation. This is fulfilled in Sri Ramakrishna.[3]

Biographers of avatars record their important life stories, their extraordinary sadhana and achievements, and their miracles and messages, but they usually do not record their daily routine, the tiny incidents in their lives, their likes and dislikes, or their informal dealings and conversations with friends and families. As a result, we do not get a full picture of avatars such as Christ and Ramachandra. Swami Vivekananda said to his disciple Nivedita: "As I grow older I find that I look more and more for greatness in *little* things. I want to know what a great man eats and wears, and how he speaks to his servants."[4]

The details of Ramakrishna's life and message have been recorded in *Sri Ramakrishna and His Divine Play* and *The Gospel of Sri Ramakrishna*. We become close to the avatars when we learn about the tiny and insignificant incidents in their lives; and we become impressed seeing their human aspects. In this chapter we shall explore Ramakrishna's daily personal life, his relationships with his own people, his love for and concern about other people, his day-to-day environment, and insignificant incidents that are often hidden. We shall see Ramakrishna angrily punishing hypocrites; mourning the death of his dearest ones; and tendering love and affection to his parents, brothers, sisters, and other relatives. We shall see him suffering from dysentery and cancer, and again merging in blissful samadhi transcending the body idea. We shall see him singing, dancing, laughing, joking, scolding his disciples, and showering them with his love.

When we observe all this, we feel that Ramakrishna is not a god sitting in heaven but a human being like us moving about on earth.

Difficulty in recognizing an avatar

To a lover, every detail of his or her beloved's life is important, because it brings more familiarity, affection, and joy. As human beings, we can easily understand the human aspects of an avatar. Satchidananda (God) descends to this earth as a human being, an avatar, becoming God in human form. In the biblical tradition, there is a reference to a ladder that connects heaven and earth, which is known as "Jacob's ladder." Romain Rolland compared Ramakrishna's life to that ladder: "In the life of Ramakrishna, the Man-God, I am about to relate the life of this Jacob's ladder, whereon the twofold unbroken line of the Divine in man ascends and descends between heaven and earth."[5] So while holding onto Ramakrishna, we can move in both the earthly and divine planes. It is difficult to comprehend the infinite God because our minds are impure and limited. Regarding the Cosmic God, there is a mantra in the Mundaka Upanishad (2:1:4): "The heavens are His head; the sun and moon, His eyes; the quarters, His ears; the revealed Vedas, His speech; the wind is His breath; the universe, His heart. From His feet is produced the earth. He is, indeed, the inner Self of all beings."

When we recite mantras such as this, we feel dizzy thinking of the Infinite God. How can we love a Cosmic God who has the sun as one eye and the moon as the other? It is frightening to imagine such a being — so we turn our minds to Ramachandra, Krishna, Buddha, Jesus, Chaitanya, Ramakrishna, and other great teachers of the world. When God comes as a human being, we can understand God to some extent; we can establish a relationship with God through love and emotion.

It is truly difficult to recognize an avatar if the avatar hides his glory and power. Ramakrishna tried to disguise his divine nature by taking birth in a poor family and having little formal education. This did not work out. Then he tried to hide by accepting the lowly position of a temple priest. That did not work out either: a blazing fire cannot be hidden underneath a basket. Mathur, the owner of the Kali temple, tried to test the young priest Ramakrishna in several ways. When he offered Ramakrishna money and an estate, Ramakrishna angrily chased Mathur away with a stick, saying, "Rascal, you want to make me a worldly man?"

Mathur then tried to tempt him with beautiful women, but that also failed; instead he learned that Ramakrishna was completely free from lust and desire for wealth. Finally, he adored Ramakrishna as a god but found that Ramakrishna had no desire for name and fame. He was free from ego. After testing him in various ways, Mathur became convinced that Ramakrishna was not an ordinary man, and that outside and inside, he was nothing but God. Mathur finally took refuge in Ramakrishna, saying, "Father, there is nothing inside you but God."

The avatar knows his own divine nature. Once Ramakrishna said to M.: "Have you heard of a tree called the 'achina' [literally, 'unrecognizable']?"

M.: "No, sir." Master: "There is a tree called by that name. But nobody knows what it is."[6]

Ramakrishna repeatedly declared that one cannot see God without God's grace. If God does not reveal Himself, no one can recognize God. On 22 October 1885, Ramakrishna said to Dr. Sarkar: "There is a river called 'Karmanasha' [destroyer of duties]. It is very dangerous to dive into that river. If a man plunges into its waters he cannot perform any more action. It puts an end to his duties."[7]

On another occasion, he said: "I am the destroyer of karma. I am the French colony." At that time India was divided among three colonial powers: British, French, and Portuguese. If a man did something wrong in British India, he could take shelter in the French colony where the British had no jurisdiction. "I am the French colony" means that whatever sinful actions one does, one need only take shelter in Ramakrishna to be free from fear and punishment. No worldly rules can bind such a person. Only a saviour has the power to save and eradicate people's past karma.[8]

It is extremely difficult to catch a glimpse of Ramakrishna's divine nature. When he was in a normal state, he maintained the conviction that all beings from the lowest to the highest are God; moreover, he had the attitude that he was a servant to all beings. Truly, at that time he considered himself to be lower than the lowest, humbler than the humblest, and he would take the dust of the feet of anyone whom he encountered. However, when he ascended to a higher state, his demeanour and behaviour with others took a different form. Becoming like the mythical wish-fulfilling tree, he would ask a devotee, "What do you want?" as if he were ready to use his superhuman power to fulfill the devotee's desire immediately.[9]

Ramakrishna tried to live in Dakshineswar incognito. He did not wear an ochre cloth, rosary, or any marks on his forehead. He looked like a most ordinary person. In the 1870s, Keshab Chandra Sen was writing about Ramakrishna in his newspapers and magazines, and had made the people in Calcutta aware of him. Yogin-ma's grandmother read about the Master in the newspaper and went to Dakshineswar to meet him. Strangely enough, upon arriving there, the first person she encountered was Ramakrishna himself, but she did not know who he was, since there was nothing unusual about his dress or appearance. Addressing the Master, she asked, "Could you tell me where Ramakrishna Paramahamsa is and how I can see him?"

The Master replied: "What do I know about him? Some people call him 'Paramahamsa,' some call him 'Young Priest,' and others call him 'Gadadhar Chattopadhyay.' Please ask someone else to help you find him."[10]

Girish saw his life changing under the influence of Sri Ramakrishna, yet he could not fathom the nature of this great soul. One day he asked the Master, "Who are you, sir?" Sri Ramakrishna replied: "Some say I am Ramprasad [a poet-saint of Bengal], others that I am Raja Ramakrishna. I simply live here."[11]

Harinath (later Swami Turiyananda) was studying Vedanta and trying to realize Brahman through his own efforts when he met the Master at Balaram's house in Calcutta. He heard the Master say, "Nothing can be achieved — neither knowledge, nor devotion, nor vision — without God's grace." Harinath felt as if these words had been directed to him, for he had been straining every nerve to attain illumination by his own efforts. After a short while, the Master regained his normal consciousness and began to sing a song based on the *Uttara Rama Charitam*, where Hanuman tells the sons of Rama:

> O Kusa and Lava, why are you so proud?
> If I had not let myself be captured,
> Could you have captured me?

While Ramakrishna sang, tears rolled down his face, literally wetting the ground. Harinath later remarked: "I was deeply moved. That very day the Master deeply imprinted on my mind the fact that one cannot attain God through self-effort, by performing sadhana. Only if God reveals Himself is it possible to attain Him."[12]

Ramakrishna's love for his parents

The parents of an avatar are not ordinary human beings. Ramakrishna's father, Kshudiram, was a great devotee of God and a votary of truth; his mother, Chandramani, was a simple, pure, and deeply religious woman. When Chandramani was pregnant with Ramakrishna and began having labour pains, Kshudiram told her: "Please wait. Let me finish the worship of Raghuvir." According to the Hindu custom, when a child is born, there cannot be any worship of the deity in the house for three days. Chandramani gave birth to Ramakrishna the next morning. Kshudiram's steadfast devotion to his Ishta (Chosen Deity) overwhelms us. The Master absorbed his father's virtuous practices and steadfast devotion.

The Master also had deep love for his mother. Towards the end of her life, Chandramani came to live in Dakshineswar. Lakshmi, the Master's niece, recalled:

> All through his life the Master had stomach trouble. When Grandma [*Ramakrishna's mother*] was living in Dakshineswar, the Master would salute

her every morning. Grandma was a large woman and very beautiful, but she was also old-fashioned and very shy. Even before her youngest son [*Ramakrishna*] she would cover her face with a veil. When he came she would ask him, "How is your stomach?" The Master would reply, "Not very good." Grandma would then advise: "Don't take the prasad of Mother Kali. [*It was very spicy food.*] As long as your stomach is not all right your wife will cook plain soup and rice for you. Please eat only that."

Sometimes the Master would get tired of eating invalid's food every day and would ask his mother to cook one or two dishes and season them as she used to do in Kamarpukur. So occasionally Grandma cooked for him and the Master enjoyed it.

The Master used to encourage women to cook. "It is a good occupation for the mind," he would say. "Sita was a good cook, and so were Draupadi and Parvati. Mother Lakshmi [*the goddess of fortune*] would Herself cook and feed others."

After the death of her two older sons, Grandma became somewhat quiet and withdrawn. Furthermore, she would not eat her lunch until she had heard the noon whistle of the Alambazar Jute Mill. As soon as it sounded she would exclaim: "Oh! There is the whistle of heaven. That is the signal to offer food to Lakshmi and Narayana." A problem would arise on Sundays, however, when the jute mill was closed. No whistle was blown at noon, and consequently she would not eat. This worried the Master very much, and he would lament: "Oh dear! My old mother will refuse her food today and she will be weak." Brother Hriday would say to the Master: "Don't be anxious, Uncle. When Grandma is hungry she will eat of her own accord." But the Master would reply: "Oh no. I am her son. It is my duty to look after my old mother." With much coaxing the Master would persuade his mother to eat the prasad of Krishna.

One day Brother Hriday blew through a pipe to make a high-pitched sound. He then said to Grandma: "There, Grandma, did you hear the whistle of heaven? Now, please eat your food." But Grandma laughed and said: "Oh, no. You made the sound with your pipe." Everyone laughed.

When Chandramani died on 13 February 1877, the Master wept. Later, M. pointed to the bakul-tala ghat of Dakshineswar, and said: "Just before Chandramani passed away, her body was brought here. She was lying on a rope cot. Two legs of the cot were in the Ganges and the other two legs were on the cement ghat. Holding his mother's feet, the Master said tearfully: 'Mother, who are you who carried me in your womb?' He meant that she was not an ordinary mother."[13]

According to the Hindu custom, a sannyasin has no right to perform *shrāddha* (funeral rites), so the Master's nephew Ramlal performed this duty. Seeing the Master crying for his departed mother, Hriday said, "Uncle, you are a monk, so why are you crying for your mother?"

The Master replied: "Rascal, I have become a monk. That does not mean I am a heartless animal."[14] However, after his mother's passing away, one day Holy Mother carried the food tray for the Master. He told her, "Please wait, let me go to the Panchavati and cry for my mother." Afterwards he ate his meal. No one can repay the debt owed to one's mother. As the Master could not perform the shrāddha ceremony for his deceased mother, he tearfully performed *tarpan* (a sacrament in which water is offered) for her.

Ramakrishna at Kamarpukur and Jayrambati

When we visit Ramakrishna's cottage in Kamarpukur, we wonder how the Infinite God could live in such a small place. It is a thatched hut with a mud floor and mud walls — only 12'10" long and 8'10" wide. There is one door and one window. During the evening when an oil lamp was lit in his room, Ramakrishna would sit under a mosquito curtain and become one with the Infinite. At night, he would tell stories about God to Sarada Devi and share his spiritual experiences. Later, the Master said to Holy Mother, "Hello, look after the cottage of Kamarpukur." This cottage was the centre of the Master's early lila.

Generally during the rainy season, the Master would leave Dakshineswar to stay in Kamarpukur because at that time the Ganges water would become muddy and salty, which upset his stomach. Mathur would send sufficient money for the Master's needs. Sitting on the veranda of the Yogi Shiva temple in Kamarpukur, the Master would talk to the villagers, inquire after their families, and inspire them with spiritual talks. He probably answered the call of nature near Bhuti's canal and took his bath in the Haldarpukur. In the morning, his breakfast was puffed rice and jilipis, and at noon and night he would eat the prasad cooked for Raghuvir. His sister-in-law Shakambhari and Holy Mother would also serve him some of his favourite dishes.

While in Kamarpukur, Ramakrishna visited relatives and friends in Jayrambati, Sihar, Shyambazar, Vishnupur, and other villages. Swami Subodhananda related an incident which took place in Jayrambati: "One night in Jayrambati, the Master went to bed after supper. Afterwards Holy Mother had her supper and finished the housework. When she entered the Master's room, she found a blazing light shining on the bed, but the bed was empty. She stood there the entire night with folded hands. At daybreak the Master emerged from the light and bowed down to Holy Mother, saying: 'You have appeared in this form — very good.'"[15]

Ramakrishna in Calcutta

In 1850, Ramakrishna's elder brother, Ramkumar, opened a Sanskrit school in the Jhamapukur area of Calcutta. He rented an apartment with a tiled roof in a slum on Bechu Chatterjee Street and brought the Master there in 1852. The Master lived there for three years. As he was averse to pursuing a bread-winning education, Ramkumar engaged him to perform rituals in the homes of some of his clients. After performing the worship, the Master would receive some fruits and sweets, which he tied in a thin towel. On the way home he would sit in the shop of Nakur Bostom, a neighbour from Kamarpukur. Nakur was a devout Vaishnava and was very fond of the Master. This shop was located close to M.'s house. Nakur later told M.: "Whenever the local people requested the young Master to sing some devotional songs, he would sing forgetting everything. Meanwhile, some young kids would unfold the Master's towel and eat those offered articles. But the Master would not get upset at all. He would smile and carry the towel home."[16] Every afternoon the Master would sit in front of the Thanthania Kali temple, which still exists as it was (although the slum is no longer there).

The human mind is the fastest vehicle in the world. With the mind, one can visit any place in the world in a single moment. M. described an incident that took place one day when he was with the Master:

> One day a man was showing pictures through a magic lantern on a sidewalk in Calcutta. He was shouting, "Come, see Haridwar; see Badrika" — two famous holy places in the Himalayas. The Master was curious to see that show. He peeped into the box and seeing Badri Narayan, the deity of the Badri temple, he went into samadhi. After a while when he regained outer consciousness, he asked a devotee, "Please give this man something." The devotee paid six pice to that man. When the Master heard the amount the devotee had given, he said: "What! This man showed us Badri Narayan, and you have given so little! He should be given one rupee."
>
> The Master was not a human being. Wherever his mind was focussed he would experience God. His mind was like a dry matchstick, which could ignite by the slightest friction. Minds soaked in worldliness are like damp matchsticks. One may rub them a thousand times against the matchbox, but still they won't ignite.[17]

Ramakrishna was not a dry monk; he enjoyed witnessing the fun and frivolities of the world. He went to the zoo and museum, and even went to see a circus. M. recorded:

> One winter a circus company came to Calcutta. We bought tickets for the cheapest seats [half a rupee] and went to see it with the Master. Sitting on

a bench in the upper gallery, the Master said: "Ha! This is a good place. I can see the show well from here." Like a child, he could not contain his joy. There were exhibitions of various feats. A horse raced around a circular track over which large iron rings were hung at intervals. The circus rider, an Englishwoman, stood on one foot on the horse's back, and as the horse passed under the rings, she jumped through them, always alighting on one foot on the horse's back. The horse raced around the entire circle, and the woman never missed the horse or lost her balance. When the circus was over the Master and the devotees stood outside in the field near the carriage. Since it was a cold night he covered his body with his green shawl.

The Master then said to me: "Did you see how that Englishwoman stood on one foot on her horse, while it ran like lightning? How difficult a feat that must be! She must have practised a long time. The slightest carelessness and she would break her arms or legs; she might even be killed. One faces the same difficulty leading the life of a householder. A few succeed in it through the grace of God and as a result of their spiritual practice.[18]

Ramakrishna at Dakshineswar

Dakshineswar, where the Master lived for 30 years, is the playground of an avatar — an important holy place. In Dakshineswar Ramakrishna practised various sadhanas, taught his devotees and disciples, and enacted his main divine play.

M. said: "Every particle of dust of the Panchavati is holy and vibrant because it was touched by the feet of God. The trees, plants, and vines of Dakshineswar are gods, ancient rishis, and devotees who are still seeing and enjoying the divine play of God. Truly, they are witnesses of the avatar's lila."[19]

Every year millions of people visit Dakshineswar and try to visualize the events of Ramakrishna's divine play. Over the years, many things have changed there, but the spiritual environment of the temple garden still lifts the minds of visitors to a higher plane. Every spot of the Dakshineswar temple garden is connected with the Master. Pilgrims make those spots live through meditation, prayer, worship, longing, and tears. None can deny the glory of Dakshineswar, as it is connected with an avatar. Although more than 130 years have gone by since Ramakrishna's passing away, still we feel his presence there.

Ramakrishna's room is situated in the northwest corner of the temple complex. His room is 21 feet long from east to west, and 19 feet wide from north to south. There were two images in his room, one of

Buddha and one of Ramlala. There were 17 pictures on the walls: Gopal and Radha; Radha; Durga; Krishna-Kali; Ram-Sita; Kali of Kalighat; Buddha; Gauranga, Nityananda, and their devotees; Tara; Brahma; Vishnu; Gayatri; Dhruva; Prahlad; Ramchandra and Guhaka; Ramachandra and Krishna; and Jesus rescuing Peter.

There were two cots in Ramakrishna's room — one for sleeping and the other for sitting. Both of them are still there. Old photos show that there were two bricks below each leg of the big cot and one brick below each leg of the small cot to protect the cots from water when the floor was washed. There was no other furniture in his room except a stool and a wooden cabinet, where he would keep prasad, sweets, and fruits. For the devotees, there were a mat, a carpet, a palm-leaf fan, and a tumbler for drinking water. There was also a big jar containing Ganges water in the northwest corner. Below the small cot there was a door mat, which he used to rub his feet on before sitting on the cot. There was a trunk in which he kept his clothing (especially his winter clothes). There was a hubble-bubble and smoking supplies in the southwest corner of the room; a knife for cutting twigs (which he used for cleaning his teeth) was on the brick of the southwest leg of the big cot. There was a wooden frame hanging from the ceiling over his two cots to hold a mosquito net. Dakshineswar was infested with mosquitos, so he used to meditate under this net.

Every day a maidservant or a devotee would sweep the red cement floor with a broom and then wash it with water. Every evening the maid, Vrinda, would light an oil lamp in the Master's room and burn incense powder to drive away the mosquitos. Then she would close the doors and windows so that the mosquitos could not get in. During his first visit, M. saw the Master seated in this smoky room.

At midnight, the Master would walk on the bank of the Ganges. Sometimes he would watch the high tide of the Ganges from the semi-circular western veranda of his room. He had tremendous faith in the purifying power of the Ganges. He would say: "Ganges water is Brahman." He advised his disciples to drink Ganges water if they had any bad thoughts. He himself would bathe in the Ganges and drink its water. If any worldly person entered his room, he would ask his attendant to sprinkle Ganges water where that person had been.

In the northwest corner of the temple garden, there were some pine trees and bushes where the Master would go to answer the call of nature. His attendant would then fill a jug with water from the goose pond and help the Master wash. He would wash his clothes, hands, and feet at the southern ghat of the goose pond, which was east of the Panchavati. Early in the morning he brushed his teeth with a fresh twig and scraped his tongue.

According to records from 1858, Rasmani allotted six dhotis (cloths that men wear) a year for the Master. At the beginning of his stay in Dakshineswar, the Master did not eat the temple prasad, so he would receive an allotment of one pound of rice, a few ounces of lentils, two banana leaves, two ounces of tobacco, and five pounds of firewood for cooking. His monthly salary was five rupees; this was later raised to seven rupees.

Every day Ramakrishna wore two dhotis, which had thin red borders. The devotees supplied him with shirts made from cheap fabric. A set of clothes that he wore when he visited Calcutta was kept in his trunk.

There is no record of Ramakrishna's weight or height. In 1951, while making the marble image of Ramakrishna for Kamarpukur, Swami Nirvanananda informed the sculptor that the Master's height was 5'9¼". The swami made this calculation on the basis of the length of a coat that Ramakrishna wore that is now at Belur Math. The Master is wearing this coat in the photograph that was taken at a studio in Radhabazar, Calcutta, in 1881. By measuring the coat and calculating the relation of the coat to the figure, Swami Nirvanananda established Ramakrishna's height.

As far as we know, Ramakrishna was in fairly good health, or he could not have practised so many austerities over a period of 12 years. Occasionally he suffered from dysentery, fever, a cold, and cough. He finally succumbed to throat cancer, from taking upon himself others' sins.

Sometimes Ramakrishna would go for a walk in the gardens of Jadu Mallick and Shambhu Mallick, which were within walking distance of the temple garden. He always kept in touch with neighbours and inquired about their welfare. When Holy Mother was going to Kamarpukur, the Master advised her to keep good relations with the neighbours and inquire about their families. M. recalled: "When the Master visited Jadu Mallick's garden, the caretaker would fan him. The Master once went into samadhi as he witnessed that man's devotion. One day the caretaker invited the Master to lunch, and he accepted. The Master went there accompanied by Rakhal Maharaj, me, and a young brahmin boy from Orissa [M.'s cook]. Perhaps he would not have accepted an invitation from a rich man."[20] This proves that despite merging into samadhi often, the Master maintained social formalities.

No one knew when Ramakrishna would enter into samadhi, so he always needed someone to stay near him. Once while he was in an ecstatic mood, he tried to embrace Jagannath, but he fell and broke his hand. The

Divine Mother had told him, "Do thou remain in bhava (divine mood)" in the relative world, but the Master would forget this. He himself said: "Now and then I forget Her command and suffer. Once I broke my teeth because I didn't remain in bhava."[21]

M. said, "While listening to the temple music [*rasun chauki*] being played at the nahabat, the Master would go into samadhi....The Master would also merge into samadhi when he saw someone closing an umbrella. It reminded him of withdrawing the mind from the world and giving it to God."[22]

"It was a winter morning, and the Master was sitting near the east door of his room, wrapped in his moleskin shawl. He looked at the sun and suddenly went into samadhi. His eyes stopped blinking and he lost all consciousness of the outer world. After a long time he came down to the plane of the sense world."[23] The Master's samadhi reminded M. of this passage from the Gayatri mantra: *Om tat savitur varenyam bhargo devasya dhimahi* — I meditate on the luminous One who dwells in the solar region.

Ramakrishna was in samadhi during a kirtan at Natabar Goswami's house in Phului-Shyambazar, as well as at the Harisabha in Jorasanko. He went into samadhi off and on and became one with God. All three photographs of Ramakrishna were taken while he was in samadhi. Worshipping his picture is the same as worshipping God. We find many references to samadhi in the *Gospel of Ramakrishna*, which we do not find in the life of other avatars.

Swami Ambikananda recalled:

The Master told my mother, "You put on jewellery like the Mother in the temple." So my mother followed the Master's command. Once while he was in ecstasy, my mother visited him. Hearing the sound of her bangles, the Master was startled and cried out: "Ooh! So much noise!" Because of this sound, the person who had gone to the other world might not be able to return to this body from there. The fine connection could be torn like a thin wire. From then on, my mother would tie her bangles tightly to her hand so that they could not make any noise.[24]

The Master could not sleep more than two or three hours at night. Out of an abundance of sattva, he would remain in a divine mood. Now and then he would walk alone in the dead hours of night in the temple garden. Sometimes he would ask the night watchman, "Hello, could you chant Ram's name a little?" In the early hours of the morning he would pace back and forth in his room and chant the names of gods and goddesses. At that time, he could see the obstacles to his disciples' spiritual progress and would help them accordingly. While going to the Panchavati at 3 o'clock in the morning, he would call his niece Lakshmi and her aunt (Holy Mother) to get up and practise japa and meditation.

The Master never said any untruth, but he sometimes said some harsh truths to his devotees for their good. Swami Adbhutananda recalled:

> One day the Master told Jadu Babu: "You have saved so much for this world. What have you acquired for the next?"
>
> Jadu Babu replied: "Young priest, you are the one who will take care of the other world for me. You will save me at the moment of death, and I am waiting until then. If you don't grant me liberation, your name 'deliverer of the fallen' will be marred — so you cannot forget me at my death."
>
> You see, although Jadu Mallick had plenty of money, he couldn't give up the desire for more. Another time the Master told him, "Jadu, you have saved so much money, yet still you want more."
>
> Jadu Babu replied: "That desire will not go. You cannot give up the desire for God. In the same way, we worldly people cannot give up our desire for money. Why should I renounce money? You renounce all the things of the world and yearn for God, while I am a beggar asking for more and more of His riches. Doesn't worldly wealth also belong to Him?"
>
> Master was very pleased to hear this line of argument. "If you maintain this attitude, you have no need to worry. But tell me, Jadu, are you saying this sincerely?"
>
> Then Jadu Babu replied, "Young priest, you know that I cannot hide anything from you."[25]

Ramakrishna spent 14 years in the room on the northwest corner of the Dakshineswar temple courtyard. During this period, he came in contact with many pandits, distinguished people, wealthy people, and devotees, and he received all of them cordially. He talked to them about God, and about human problems as well. These conversations and teachings were recorded by different chroniclers, including in the *Gospel* by M.

The Master tried to hide his real divine nature but could not always succeed. He disclosed his true divine nature to his disciples on many occasions. For example, on 15 March 1886 at the Cossipore garden house the Master said: "There are two in this [body]. One is the Divine Mother and the other is Her devotee. It is the devotee who broke his arm, and it is the devotee who is now ill."[26]

As a husband and guru

People marry for happiness and peace, companionship and security, and of course some want children and an extended family. An ideal marriage requires mutual love and respect. Married life becomes easy and smooth if spouses have a common goal and a similar nature. Otherwise, constant friction and bickering, mistrust and selfishness between two souls make married life a hell. Ramakrishna and Sarada Devi were married for 27 years, and they demonstrated an ideal marriage without a physical relationship. There is no record that they ever quarreled. A few times they did have a difference of opinion, but they resolved this immediately through conversation. The following incidents show how they interacted at those times and how much love they had for each other:

> Devotees often brought sweets and fruits for the Master. Holy Mother would set aside some for him and distribute the rest to the devotees. One day Holy Mother distributed all the sweets. No rules or laws can bind a mother's heart. One day the Master expressed his disapproval, asking her, "How can you successfully run a household, if you give away things like this?" Holy Mother said, "All right," and abruptly left the room. Greatly distressed, Ramakrishna said to Ramlal: "Go at once and placate your aunt. If she gets angry then all my spirituality will come to naught."
>
> Sometimes so many devotees came to Dakshineswar that there was not enough food in stock to feed them all. Holy Mother had some difficulty cooking for large groups of people. One day she asked Senior Gopal to buy a large quantity of vegetables from the market. When the Master saw this, he asked Holy Mother, "Why did you ask for so many vegetables?" "I have to feed many people," she replied.
>
> The Master objected: "The temple authorities are supposed to supply the groceries. It is not good to spend so much money. Moreover, if you cook for long hours, you will get sick from the heat. You will not have to cook so many dishes anymore. I shall not eat them." The Master did not eat any of the dishes that she made with those vegetables. Holy Mother wept bitterly, and Ramakrishna consoled her: "Look, I admonished you because you suffer when you cook so many dishes over the fire twice a day! I have decided that I will not ask you to cook particular dishes anymore. I shall eat what chance may bring. If you have any desire to cook something for me, please do. Don't ask me about it."[27]

In March 1872, Sarada Devi visited Dakshineswar for the first time. She had two fears: first, that her husband had become mad; and second, that he might reject her because he had taken sannyasa. However, as Sarada alighted from the boat, she heard the Master say to Hriday: "O Hriday, this is her first visit. I hope the hour is auspicious." The Master's first words, laden with tenderness, encouraged Sarada to go straight to his room. Her companions waited outside. As soon as the Master saw Sarada, he said: "So you have come. Very good. I am very happy." He then told someone, "Spread a mat for her on the floor." Sarada and her father sat on the mat.

When the Master heard that she was ill, he expressed his concern. In an apologetic tone, he said: "You have come so late. Alas, my Mathur is no longer alive to look after you. With his death I feel as if I have lost my right arm." After that welcoming conversation, Sarada wanted to go to the nahabat (concert tower), where her mother-in-law was staying. The Master said: "Oh no, stay in my room. It will be inconvenient for the physician to see you there."

One can imagine what was going on in Sarada's mind while lying in her husband's room. She was relieved to find that her husband was not insane. He seemed normal and rational, loving and affectionate. His cordial welcome eased her anxiety and uncertainty, and she was convinced that her godlike husband would not renounce her.

In the early days of Holy Mother's living in Dakshineswar, a maid would stay with her in the nahabat at night. One night there was torrential rain and the maid could not come, so the Master asked Holy Mother to sleep in his room so she would not have to be alone. When she arrived, the Master asked: "Where is your jewellery? Bring it here." Holy Mother replied: "I can't go back now. It will be all right." This little incident shows the love and concern that Ramakrishna had for his wife, although most of the time he was in an ecstatic state.

It seems that the Master saw Holy Mother from three angles: He gave advice to Sarada as a disciple; he allowed her to serve him as a devoted wife; and he worshipped her as the veritable Divine Mother of the Universe. Holy Mother also served and worshipped Ramakrishna as her husband, guru, and Ishta [Chosen Deity].

As a guru, Ramakrishna loved his disciples and trained them so that they could carry on his mission, but he was a great taskmaster. M. related this incident:

> The Master scolded Swamiji twice: first at Dakshineswar and second at Cossipore. When Swamiji first began visiting Dakshineswar, he frequently criticized Kali. Finally the Master said gravely, "Don't come here anymore." Despite this scolding, Swamiji did not become upset. He immediately began preparing a smoke for the Master. Later in Cossipore the Master scolded Swamiji when he said something about the views of Tantra. The Master said, "I have seen that those who practise those esoteric sadhanas in the name of religion go astray."[28]

Narendra was a handsome young man with beautiful curly hair. One day the Master ruffled his hair and said, "My child, we have not come to this world for enjoyment." Swami Shuddhananda, a disciple of Viveka-nanda, recalled:

> Swami Vivekananda was then Narendranath; he was visiting Rama-krishna regularly at Dakshineswar. Pointing to Narendra's well-combed curly hair, the Master teased him about his foppishness. Narendra was also unsparing; he pointed out to the Master his varnished shoes, hub-ble-bubble, mattress, bolster, and so on. Then the Master told him, "Look here, the amount of austerity I practised for God-realization, if you can do one-sixteenth of that, I shall arrange for you to sleep on a costly bed-stead putting mattress upon mattress."
>
> Swamiji practised severe austerity in his life; and then when he re-turned from the West, his Western disciples presented him with a spring bed and mattress [which are still preserved in his room]. While lying on that Western mattress and remembering those words of the Master, Swa-miji would tell that incident to his disciples with tears.[29]

Ramakrishna's food preferences and other habits

We feel the Master to be like us when we see him eating his favourite foods, talking to the devotees, dealing with human problems, walking, or sleeping. He practised and taught humanity, "First God and then the world." Problems begin when we reverse this. Ramakrishna lived in this world for 50 years, completely dependent on God. Rasmani and Mathur provided his food and shelter, and they met all of his needs for most of his adult life. Even when he could not continue his active service as a priest, the temple authorities sent his food to his room. For breakfast, he received a little butter and a piece of rock candy from the Krishna tem-ple, and sweets and fruits from the Kali temple. For lunch he ate cooked prasad from the Kali temple; for supper he had a few luchis, sweets, and farina pudding, which were also the prasad of Mother Kali. Some nights when he was hungry he ate sweets and fruits, or Holy Mother would make halwa (a thick farina pudding) for him. He advised his disciples to eat heavily during lunch but sparingly for supper, as one cannot practise sadhana if one eats too much at night.

Sometimes the oily and spicy prasad would upset his stomach, or lunch would not reach his room till 1 or 2 p.m. The Master once said:

> Jadu Mallick noticed the late hours of my meals and arranged for a cook [a woman named Sudhamukhi]. He gave me one rupee for a month's expenses. That embarrassed me. I had to run to him whenever he sent for me. It would have been quite a different thing if I had gone to him of my own accord....After the attainment of my exalted state, I noticed how things were around me and said to the Divine Mother, "O Mother,

please change the direction of my mind right now, so that I may not have to flatter rich people, who serve with a motive." Sudhamukhi's cooking no more — no more. When I eat, I cry.[30]

The Master was a free soul, so it was not possible for him to become entangled with any kind of obligation.

Later Holy Mother took over responsibility for the Master's meals. She knew what food was suitable for the Master, and she saw to it that he ate regularly before noon. Once Holy Mother left for Kamarpukur to attend Ramlal's marriage. Swami Saradananda wrote in the *Divine Play*:

> The Master (*pointing to Balaram*): "Well, can you tell me why I married? What is the purpose of having a wife? I cannot even take care of the cloth on my body — it just drops off. Why then do I have a wife?"
> Balaram smiled and kept quiet.
> The Master: "Oh, I understand (*taking a little curry from the plate and showing it to Balaram*) — for this reason I married. Otherwise, who else would cook for me with such care? (*Balaram and the other devotees laughed.*) Truly speaking, who else would look after my food? They all left today — (*seeing that the devotees did not understand who had left*) along with Ramlal's aunt. Ramlal is going to be married, so everyone left for Kamarpukur today. I watched her departure impassively. It was truly as if someone else had left. Then I grew anxious when I thought about who would cook for me. You see, some kinds of food do not agree with my stomach, nor am I always conscious enough to eat. She (*the Holy Mother*) knows what kind of food suits me and makes various preparations accordingly. So I asked myself, who will cook for me?"[31]

Ramakrishna smoked a hubble-bubble a few times a day and after lunch chewed a betel roll that Holy Mother prepared for him. When he went to Calcutta, his attendant would carry his towel and his spice bag, which contained fennel seeds, cardamom, caraway, cloves, and cubeb. Sometimes to bring the mind back from samadhi, the Master would express a desire, such as "I shall eat bitter squash curry (*sukto*)." "I shall drink water." "I shall smoke a hubble-bubble."

Once at Dakshineswar the Master gave a betel roll to Swami Akhandananda, who was very austere and did not take such things. The Master said: "Chew it. It is good to chew a couple of betel rolls after meals. It removes bad breath."[32] Swami Premananda recalled:

> Sometimes the Master would entertain us by imitating a dancing girl, placing one hand on his waist and moving his other hand about. Again, through humour, tales, and parables, he would explain to us the most intricate philosophies, which were confusing even to scholars. His

wonderful skill in teaching left a deep impression in our hearts forever. The Master was adept in explaining supreme spiritual truths in simple, sweet language.

We saw how lovingly the Master would receive the devotees at Dakshineswar. He would ask, "Do you want to chew a betel roll?" If the devotee said, "No," he would then ask, "Would you like to smoke tobacco?" He took care of the devotees in so many ways.[33]

The Master's bath

The Master would bathe in the Ganges at the Chandni ghat, but if he had a cold he would bathe with a bucket of water heated by the sun. He had a separate dhoti that he wore when bathing. Either he or someone else would rub oil on his body before his bath. We do not have any record that he ever used soap, but he once told the Holy Mother to rub his body with *basan* (lentil powder), which cleanses the body. The body is the temple of God, so the Master always kept it clean. Once the Master went to hear a spiritual discourse and the speaker remarked: "Those who chant Rama's name become free from dirt." The Master had the faith of a child. He immediately asked, "Then why is there dirt on my body?" Krishnakishore then explained, "The inner impurities go away and not the external dirt."[34]

How the Master's hair and beard were trimmed

During his second visit to the Master (28 February 1882), M. saw that the Master was about to have his beard trimmed on the southeast veranda of his room. The Master's skin was so soft and sensitive that he could not be shaved with a razor. The barber would simply trim his hair and beard with a pair of scissors. M. later recalled: "When we first saw the Master, his beard had begun to turn grey. The barber would trim his hair and beard when they became long....Before the barber started, the Master would tell him: 'Please wait. Let me think about God.' Thus he withdrew his mind from the body before having his hair and beard trimmed."

Swami Ambikananda said: "When the Master was at the Cossipore garden house suffering from cancer, his beard grew long. For this reason the doctor could not see or touch his throat properly, so he suggested shaving that area. The Master asked Latu to bring scissors and told him, 'I shall give you a signal when I have withdrawn my mind from the body, and then you trim my beard.' After seeing the signal, Latu began to trim it with a pair of dull scissors, but the Master did not feel anything at all."[35]

Many years later the Master's barber came to visit Belur Math and met Swami Shivananda. He said to him, "I could not recognize

Paramahamsadeva; I only cut his hair and beard." Swami Pavitrananda was present at the time. He told the present author that after Mahapurush Maharaj heard the barber say this, he joyfully told his attendant: "Look, this man was the Master's barber. He is very fortunate. Give him money, a cloth, and feed him nicely." By touching the divine body of the avatar, that illiterate barber became blessed.[36]

The Master in different moods

According to Vedanta, this world is a mixture of truth and untruth. In human interactions, people mix truth and untruth. For example, we cannot publicly express many things that we think because our minds are not 100 percent pure. If everybody expressed what they truly thought then social and family life would fall apart. We function in our day-to-day life by expressing some truths, some twisted truths, and some untruths. This kind of life was not possible for Ramakrishna because his life was established in truth. He himself said, "The Divine Mother never allowed a single untruth to pass through my lips." He also said, "Religion is to unite the mind and speech."

To maintain our social fabric, we disregard many things. Ramakrishna could not do this. In our scriptures it is written: *"Satyam bruyāt, priyam bruyāt, na bruyāt satyamāpriyam"* — which means "Speak the truth, speak the pleasant truth, but do not speak an unpleasant truth." However, if you love a person, you may need to speak an unpleasant truth for that person's good. The Master sometimes told unpleasant truths and even slapped a few people for their own welfare. He himself admitted this:

> In that state of god-intoxication, I used to speak out my mind to all. I was no respecter of persons. Even to men of position I was not afraid to speak the truth.... I went with Captain to see Raja Sourindra Tagore. As soon as I met him, I said, "I can't address you as 'Raja', or by any such title, for I should be telling a lie."
>
> One day, in that state of divine intoxication, I went to the bathing-ghat on the Ganges at Baranagore. There I saw Jaya Mukherji repeating the name of God; but his mind was on something else. I went up and slapped him twice on the cheeks.
>
> At one time Rani Rasmani was staying in the temple garden. She came to the shrine of the Divine Mother, as she frequently did when I worshipped Kali, and asked me to sing a song or two. On this occasion, while I was singing, I noticed she was sorting the flowers for worship absent-mindedly. At once I slapped her on the cheeks. She became quite embarrassed and sat there with folded hands.
>
> Alarmed at this state of mind, I said to my cousin Haladhari: "Just see

my nature! How can I get rid of it?" After praying to the Divine Mother for some time with great yearning, I was able to shake off this habit.[37]

Like any other embodied being, an avatar experiences happiness and misery, honour and dishonour. Sometimes they are affected and sometimes not depending upon the state of the mind at that time. One day Hriday was scolding the Master, and he absorbed this rage by chewing cubeb. On another occasion, when Hriday's scolding became unbearable the Master went to the Ganges intending to jump in.[38]

Sometimes the Master would become angry, as would any ordinary human being. M. said: "One day Hriday went to buy some hay for some business affair. He told the temple manager that his uncle would perform the worship that day. When the Master found that the Mother's worship was not being done, he hurriedly went to the temple and performed the worship with the help of Ramlal. When Hriday returned, the Master beat him. Hriday understood his mistake and said, 'Uncle, beat me more.' Then the Master said: 'Look, when I am angry, you keep quiet. And when you are angry, I shall keep quiet.'"[39]

In family life, it is natural to have a little friction and difference of opinion. When we wash cups, plates, and saucers in the sink, it makes some noise; however, that does not mean we should break them. Anger is fire. The Master demonstrated how to extinguish that fire.

Krishna declared in the Gita that lust and anger are two terrible enemies of human beings. Day and night do not stay together, so with God and worldly desire. As Ramakrishna faced anger, so he also faced lust. He said:

> Look, lust does not completely go away even when one realizes God. As long as the body lasts, a little lust remains even after God-vision — but it cannot raise its head. Do you think I am free from it? At one time I believed that I had conquered lust. Then one day when I was seated in the Panchavati, I suddenly had such an onrush of lust that it was hard for me to maintain control! Immediately I began crying, rubbing my face in the dust, and saying to the Divine Mother: "I have made a big mistake, Mother. I shall never again think that I have conquered lust." Only then did it subside.[40]

The Master was the embodiment of purity. He said, "I have never enjoyed a woman, even in a dream." He encouraged his devotees to overcome lust by sharing his own experiences. As long as one has a body, one might feel lust — but one can transcend this by focussing the mind on God.

The Master always helped those who were sincere and sought his guidance. Sometimes we marvel at how skillful the Master was in using examples in his teachings. M. said: "One day the Master said to Thakur-dada (Narayandas Bandyopadhyay, a storyteller of Baranagore): 'Your teeth are not set properly. Now and then please come to Dakshineswar. I shall grind your teeth and set them properly.' The Master meant that Thakur-dada's spiritual practices were not being done properly, and he would gladly make adjustments to them, just as an expert dentist fixes someone's dentures."[41]

Ramakrishna lived in two planes — divine and human. In the former, he was not affected by disease, suffering, or grief. But when he was in the human plane, he experienced grief or pain as we do. When God becomes human, he or she acts accordingly.

The Master was very fond of Keshab Sen, the leader of the Brahmo Samaj. When Keshab died at the age of 45, the Master wept and remained in bed for three days, covering himself with a chadar. He said, "My brain is boiling like hot water." Keshab's son visited Dakshineswar soon after, and the Master embraced him and wept. When our dearest ones die, we cry, and so did the Master. M. said: "When the news of Adhar Sen's death reached the Master, I was in his room. He immediately went into samadhi. Regaining normal consciousness, he wept and said to the Divine Mother: 'Mother, you asked me to stay in the world with the devotees, cherishing devotion. Now look, how much pain I have.'"[42]

Last days of Ramakrishna

At the end of his life, Ramakrishna suffered from throat cancer. But he used to say: "Let the affliction and the body take care of themselves. O my mind, you dwell in bliss." The cause of his suffering was absorbing others' sins. Because of his cancer, he consumed only milk, thin farina pudding, and other liquids. As a result his body became emaciated, and at the end he was practically skin and bones. Once Swami Niranjanananda was looking intently at his emaciated guru in the light of a kerosene lantern and feeling sad. Knowing what he was thinking, the Master said to him: "Niranjan, look, I am now in such a state that whoever will see me in this condition will be a *jivanmukta* (liberated-in-life) by the grace of the Divine Mother. But know for certain, if many people see this body, my life will end quickly."[43] When he heard these words, Niranjan took a bamboo stick and sat at the entrance to the Master's room, acting as a gatekeeper to prevent newcomers and other people from seeing the Master. He wanted his guru to live as long as possible.

M. recalled: "The Master suffered from throat cancer for more than ten months. He had terrible hemorrhage from his wound, but the devotees served him wholeheartedly. Holding the doctor's hand, he plaintively said, 'Please cure my disease.' But as soon as he felt a little better, he would talk about God. Finally he said, 'The Divine Mother will not keep this body anymore.'…The entire report of the Master's illness is in my diary. I recorded the amount of blood from each hemorrhage, the intensity of his pain, what he ate, and other things. Every day I carried that report to Dr. Mahendralal Sarkar."[44]

M. recorded details of the Master's illness in his diary, but not everything was published in *The Gospel of Sri Ramakrishna*. The last entry was on 24 April 1886. The previous day (23 April 1886) was Good Friday. M. carefully described what happened on that day, including the following incident: It was evening. A lamp was lighted in the Master's room. Amrita Basu, a Brahmo devotee, came in. A garland of jasmine lay in front of the Master on a plantain-leaf. There was perfect silence in the room. A great yogi seemed to be silently communing with God. Every now and then the Master lifted the garland a little, as if he wanted to put it around his neck.

Amrita (*tenderly*): "Shall I put it around your neck?"

Sri Ramakrishna accepted the garland.[45]

At the Master's instruction, M. arrived the next day (24 April 1886) with his wife, who was grief-stricken over the death of her son. M. recorded:

> That day the Master several times allowed M.'s wife the privilege of waiting on him. Her welfare seemed to occupy his attention a great deal. In the evening the Holy Mother came to the Master's room to feed him. M.'s wife accompanied her with a lamp. The Master tenderly asked her many questions about her household. He requested her to come again to the garden house and spend a few days with the Holy Mother, not forgetting to ask her to bring her baby daughter. When the Master had finished his meal M.'s wife removed the plates. He chatted with her a few minutes. [This is a wonderful scene for meditation.]
>
> About nine o'clock in the evening Sri Ramakrishna was seated in his room with the devotees. He had a garland of flowers around his neck. He told M. that he had requested his wife to spend a few days at the garden house with the Holy Mother. His kindness touched M.'s heart. M. was fanning him. The Master took the garland from his neck and said something to himself. Then in a very benign mood he gave the garland to M.[46]

Here M.'s entries in the *Gospel* during the Master's lifetime end. The human aspect of Ramakrishna revealed through such incidents is very moving. Despite his terminal disease, he was thinking of others' welfare. We see that the Master assuaged the grief of M.'s wife and also blessed the recorder of his gospel with a garland.

It is not known why M. did not publish the entries from his diary through the last days of the Master. Swami Saradananda also did not write about the Master's last days at Cossipore. When he was requested to complete *Sri Ramakrishna and His Divine Play*, he humbly said: "Perhaps it will never be completed. I am not getting inspiration from within. The Master made me write whatever he wanted."[47]

Human desires are insatiable. We are hungry to know more about our beloved Master, but at the same time we are unable to fathom God's will. We will remain ever grateful to M. and Swami Saradananda for what they gave us about the Master. Moreover, the problem of our discontent to learn more about Ramakrishna was answered by the Master himself in the following conversation.

> Sri Ramakrishna said about his intimate devotees, "All of you are part of this place [*meaning himself*]."
> M: "That I have understood. But I am not fully satisfied."
> Master: "You will never be fully satisfied."
> M: "Sir, the amount of longing I had at the beginning still remains. I don't have full contentment."
> Master: "None can have full contentment in God [because He is infinite]."[48]

God is infinite, and so is God's lila. The discussion of this topic is unending. It is beyond human imagination to fathom why and how the Infinite God descends to this earth and acts like a human being — laughing and crying, singing and dancing, suffering from hunger and thirst, disease and death. We shall never fully understand the Infinite Ramakrishna, but if we are pure, simple, and sincere, one day he will have mercy on us and reveal himself. *Nānya panthāh* — there is no other way. Among innumerable episodes of Ramakrishna's human lila (*nara-lila*), a few have been presented in this chapter that will surely be helpful for our meditation.

5

Meditation on Ramakrishna's Service to Humanity

What do we need for spiritual life? An illumined soul tells us to practise these five things: *sevā*, service to others; *swadhyāya*, study of spiritual books; *sādhanā*, practice of spiritual disciplines; *satya*, speaking the truth; and *samyama*, self-control. Service to others (karma-yoga) comes first because it purifies the mind. The pure mind becomes one-pointed by means of upāsanā (bhakti-yoga), and the one-pointed mind leads (jnana-yoga) to God-realization. A mystic saint of India said: "*Sevā, bandi, aur adhinatā, aise mili raghurāi* — Service, worship, and humility are three important disciplines for God-realization."

The word "service" has many connotations: occupation, work, employment, waiting upon, nursing, assisting, helping, worshipping, perforance of duties, exertion made for others, serving the guru or God, and so on. According to the dualistic tradition of Vedanta, there are five attitudes through which one can establish a relationship with God, and one of them is that of the servant. A devotee thinks: "Lord, you are the Master and I am your servant." One of the main obstacles of spiritual life is the ego, and the servant attitude keeps the ego down. The Ishta-mantra of Mira Bai, a renowned mystic of medieval India, was "*Chākor rākho ji* — O Krishna, make me your servant." The gopis of Vrindaban considered themselves to be *ashulka-dāsikā*, or unpaid maidservants, and prayed: "Lord, we want to serve you and love you without any expectation." This unselfish love makes God vulnerable and subject to the beck and call of devotees.

Sixteen monastic disciples of Sri Ramakrishna. Left to right, standing: Adbhutananda, Yogananda, Abhedananda, Trigunatitananda, Turiyananda, Vijnanananda, Ramakrishnananda, Niranjanananda. Seated in center: Brahmananda, Vivekananda. Seated on ground: Shivananda, Saradananda, Subodhananda, Akhandananda, Premananda, Advaitananda.

Photo illustration by Diane Marshall, adding seven direct disciples to the group photo taken at Alambazar Monastery, 1896.

The ancient scriptures and saints of India emphasized that service to others is vital in every stage of human life. During the convocation of the Vedic period, gurus advised their disciples: "Serve and adore your mother, father, teacher, and guest as God. Perform those deeds which are faultless."[1] Krishna said in the Gita: "Learn the knowledge of Brahman by prostration, by inquiry, and by service."[2] Regarding the attainment of devotion, Chaitanya mentioned five disciplines: seeking out holy company, serving God, studying the Bhagavata, repeating God's name, and living in the holy place of Vraja. Service is considered to be a kind of meditation. Rupa Goswami stated in the *Bhakti-rasāmrita-sindhu* that meditation is deep thinking of the form, qualities, lila of God, as well as performing service to God. According to the Vaishnava scriptures, worshipping Vishnu is the highest form of devotion, and serving the devotees of Vishnu is higher than that. Krishna said, "O Partha, those who are my devotees are not truly the highest devotees; those who are my devotees' devotees are real devotees." So in the Vaishnava scriptures, it is the greatest sin to humiliate, criticize, or physically assault a devotee of God because devotees carry God in their hearts. In other words, when one attacks a devotee one is attacking God.

A true devotee carries God in his or her heart, so the devotee's body is a temple of God. It is mentioned in the *Gospel*: "This earth is the largest thing we see anywhere around us. But larger than the earth is the ocean, and larger than the ocean is the sky. But Vishnu, the Godhead, has covered earth, sky, and the nether world with one of His feet. And that foot of Vishnu is enshrined in the sadhu's heart. Therefore the heart of a holy man is the greatest of all."[3]

In front of the Krishna temple at Dakshineswar, while listening to the Bhagavata, Ramakrishna once saw in a vision that a beam of light, like a cord, came from Krishna's feet and touched the Bhagavata and then entered the Master's chest, connecting all three. This convinced him that God, the devotee, and the scriptures are in reality one and the same though they appear to be distinct entities. The Master used to say, "The Bhagavata, the devotee, and God — these three are one and the One manifests as three."

In the Mahabharata we learn that during the *Rajasuya* sacrifice, Krishna washed the feet of the kings. During the last supper, Jesus washed the feet of his disciples. Thus these incarnations of God humbled themselves. Regarding Ramakrishna's humility, Girish remarked: "This time the Lord has come to conquer the world through prostrations. In His incarnation as Krishna it was the flute; as Chaitanya, the Name. But the weapon of His powerful Incarnation this time is the salutation."[4]

Human beings learn through seeing, hearing, and experiencing. Regarding meditation on Ramakrishna's service to people, we shall observe how the embodied God set an example for all of us by serving his relatives, disciples, and devotees. Service brings fondness among human beings, and it prompts divine beings to offer boons. It melts people's cruel hearts and tames even ferocious animals. The power of service is phenomenal. Mutual service brings peace and harmony in family life and eradicates quarrelling, ill-feeling, and selfishness.

Meditation on the activities of the avatars raises the mind to a higher plane. Generally, people meditate on the divine form, qualities, and lila; but one can also meditate on the life and actions of an avatar. In the Ramayana, we see Ramachandra eating fruit that Shabari had tasted and establishing friendship with the monkey chief, Sugriva, by embracing him. In the Bhagavata, we see Krishna carrying Sudama on his shoulders, grazing the cows, and playing the flute on the bank of the Yamuna. In the Bible, we see Jesus serving bread and wine to his disciples. Visualizing these actions of the avatars is a kind of dynamic meditation that quickly connects our minds with the *Ishta* (Chosen Deity).

Ramakrishna's service to his relatives and family deities

Ramakrishna lost his father, Kshudiram, when he was seven years old and that created a vacuum in his mind. To fill that gap, he began to walk alone in the cremation ground near Bhuti's canal and in Manik-raja's mango orchard. He became very serious and thoughtful. He was fond of solitude. He briefly went to primary school and learned to read and write. He loved to listen to the stories from the Puranas and watch the open-air *Yatra* (drama) performances. His hobby was making clay images of gods and goddesses.

At the age of eight, he began to spend time with the itinerant monks who would temporarily stay in the Lahas' roadside inn in Kamarpukur. The young Ramakrishna began to observe how the monks stoked the *dhuni* (sacred fire) in the morning and evening and sat around it, absorbed in meditation; how they offered to their Chosen Deities the simple food they had obtained by begging, and joyfully partook of the prasad; how they endured severe illness without a murmur, solely depending on God; and how they were reluctant to disturb anyone even with their pressing needs. He began to help the monks by performing small services such as collecting wood for cooking, fetching drinking water, and other errands. The monks were pleased with the handsome boy. They taught him prayers and devotional songs, gave him spiritual instruction, and enjoyed sharing with him the food they had collected as alms.

One day Gadadhar appeared before his mother with his body smeared with ashes; another day he appeared with a mark on his forehead. Once he tore his own cloth into pieces and made a *kaupin* (loincloth), wearing it like a monk. Upon returning home he said, "Look, Mother, how the monks have dressed me." This is a scene to be meditated upon.

When Ramakrishna was about to complete his ninth year, his brother Ramkumar began to arrange his *upanayana* (sacred thread ceremony). This initiation is essential for a brahmin boy and indicates that he is now able to perform rituals. Their family was poor, and to earn money Ramakrishna's two brothers were performing worship and other rituals in different homes. Ramakrishna took responsibility for worshiping their family deities — Raghuvir, Rameswar Shiva, and Mother Shitala. He also helped his mother with the household work. This young boy's sense of responsibility is amazing.

Ramakrishna recalled his boyhood experience of service:

> During my boyhood, God manifested Himself in me. I was then eleven years old. One day, while I was walking across a paddy field, I saw something. Later on, I came to know from people that I had been unconscious, and my body totally motionless. Since that day, I have been an altogether different man. I began to see another person within me. When I used to conduct the worship in the temple, my hand, instead of going toward the Deity, would very often come toward my head, and I would put flowers there. A young man who was then staying with me did not dare approach me. He would say: " I see a light on your face. I am afraid to come very near you."[5]

In 1849, Ramkumar's wife Sarvajaya died while giving birth to a baby boy. Chandramani raised her newborn grandson, Akshay. Ramakrishna was then 13 years old. His mother was busy with the cooking and other household work, so Ramakrishna looked after his baby nephew Akshay. In 1852, Ramakrishna left for Calcutta to help Ramkumar perform rituals for his clients.

Ramkumar was overworked: in addition to managing a Sanskrit school in Calcutta, he was performing daily worship in private homes. He engaged Ramakrishna to perform this worship service for some of his clients. Their family was poor, so Ramakrishna came to Calcutta to assist his elder brother and contribute to the family income. In 1855, Ramkumar accepted responsibility for conducting the dedication ceremony of the Dakshineswar Kali temple that had been established by Rani Rasmani.

He then moved from Calcutta to Dakshineswar and became the temple priest. Soon afterward, Ramakrishna joined him there and became the priest of the Krishna temple. He took initiation from Kenaram Bhattacharya and learned Kali worship from his brother. Within a year Ramkumar died and Ramakrishna became the priest of the Kali temple, with his nephew Hriday as his assistant.

A new chapter of Ramakrishna's life began, and he dedicated himself to serving the Divine Mother. He made beautiful garlands with flowers that he picked from the garden himself, decorated the image and altar, sang songs in his melodious voice, and prayed wholeheartedly for a divine vision. Ramakrishna's mode of worship is a wonderful object for our meditation. Saradananda wrote:

> We heard from the Master that after the regular service was completed he would continue his worship of Her by singing devotional songs of Ramprasad and other mystics. His heart filled with emotion as he sang those songs with exuberant devotion. He thought: "Ramprasad and other devotees had the vision of the Divine Mother. One can definitely see Her. Why can't I?" He would often exclaim piteously: "Mother, You showed Yourself to Ramprasad. Why won't You show Yourself to me? I don't want wealth, friends and family, or objects of enjoyment. Please reveal Yourself to me." Thus he would pray, as tears streamed from his eyes and flooded his chest. This would somewhat lighten the burden of his heart. Then prompted by burning faith and heartened with hope, he would again try to please the goddess with songs.
>
> Thus the Master spent his days in worship, meditation, and devotional singing; and day by day his love and longing increased. From that point on he began spending more time performing worship and serving the goddess than was regularly allotted. While performing worship, he sometimes placed a flower on his head, according to the prescribed rule, and then he would meditate for two hours, sitting still as a log. After offering food to the goddess, he might spend a long time thinking that the Mother was eating the food. On some mornings he would spend several hours picking flowers, making garlands, and decorating the goddess. Or for a long period he would remain engaged in performing the vesper service with exuberant devotion. Sometimes in the afternoon he would sing for the Divine Mother and become so absorbed and overwhelmed with devotion that he would be unaware that the time for the vesper service had passed. Although he was reminded again and again, no one could induce him to conduct the vesper service. Thus, the worship continued for some time.[6]

During the vesper service, Ramakrishna would wave the fan for such a long time that the musicians' hands ached and Hriday had to take the fan from him. Observing this kind of unconventional worship, the temple officials concluded that the Master had become mad. They complained about him to Rasmani and Mathur. One day Mathur secretly observed the Master's worship and reported to Rasmani: "We have got a wonderful worshipper. It seems the goddess will be awakened very soon."

Saradananda described Ramakrishna's performance of rituals in great detail:

Previously, during worship and meditation the Master would see the Mother's hands, or Her shining delicate feet, or Her beautiful, loving, and smiling face. But now — even when it was not the time for worship and meditation — the Master would see the complete form of the luminous Divine Mother smiling, talking, accompanying him, and guiding him by saying, "Do this; don't do that."

Earlier in his sadhana, while offering food to the Mother, the Master would see a flashing ray of light emanate from the Mother's eyes, touch the offered food articles, gather their essence, and then withdraw back into Her eyes. But now as soon as he offered food, and sometimes even before that, he would see the Mother Herself seated to eat the food, the lustre of Her body pervading the whole temple. Hriday told us that one day he went to the shrine and watched as the Master took a hibiscus flower and a bel leaf in his hand to offer at the feet of the Mother. He held them and meditated, but then he suddenly cried out: "Wait, wait! Let me say the mantra first, and then You can eat." He then offered food to the Mother before finishing the ritual.

During worship and meditation the Master used to see the living presence of the Mother in the temple's stone image of Her; now he could not see that stone image at all. In its place was the living Mother, the embodiment of consciousness, Her hands bestowing boons and fearlessness. Later, he described what happened: "I put my hand near the Mother's nostrils and felt that She was actually breathing. At night I watched carefully, but in the lamplight I could never see Her shadow on the temple wall. From my room I would hear Mother running upstairs, as merry as a little girl, with Her anklets jingling. I would rush outside to see if this was true. And there She would be standing on the veranda of the second floor of the temple, with Her hair blowing in the breeze. Sometimes She would look towards Calcutta and sometimes towards the Ganges."[7]

Hriday left an eyewitness account of the Master's worship service:

When one entered the Kali temple in those days one could perceive an ineffable divine presence and feel an eerie sensation, even when Uncle wasn't there — and much more so when he was. I couldn't resist the temptation of seeing how he acted when he was performing the worship. As long as I was actually watching him, my heart was full of reverence and devotion.

I saw Uncle taking hibiscus flowers and bel leaves in his hand, touching first his head, then his chest, then all over his body and even his feet, and finally offering those at the feet of the Divine Mother.

I saw Uncle's chest and eyes become red, like those of a drunkard. He'd get up reeling from the worshipper's seat, climb onto the altar, and caress the Divine Mother, chucking Her affectionately under the chin. He'd sing, laugh, joke, and talk with Her. Sometimes he'd catch hold of Her hands and dance!

I saw how when he was offering cooked food to the Divine Mother, he'd suddenly get up, take a morsel of rice and curry from the plate in his hand, touch the Mother's mouth with it, and say: 'Eat it, Mother. Do eat it!' Then maybe he'd say: "You want me to eat it, and then You'll eat some afterwards? All right, I'm eating it now." Then he'd take some of it himself and put the rest to Her lips again, saying: "I've had some. Now You eat."

One day Uncle saw a cat at the time of the food offering. It had come into the temple, mewing. He fed it with the food that was to be offered to the Divine Mother. "Will You take it, Mother?" he said to the cat.

Some nights I saw that when Uncle put the Divine Mother to bed he would sometimes ask: "Mother, do You want me to lie down next to You? All right, I'm lying down." Saying so, he would lie down for some time on the Divine Mother's silver bedstead.

Again I saw that while Uncle performed worship he was so deeply absorbed in meditation that he had not the slightest outer consciousness for a long time.

Every morning when he arose, Uncle would pick flowers to make garlands for the Divine Mother. At those times I noticed him talking with someone unseen, laughing, coaxing, and joking.

I further saw that at night Uncle did not sleep at all. Whenever I awoke I found him in an exalted mood, talking, singing, or immersed in meditation in the Panchavati.[8]

This faithful description of Ramakrishna's mode of worship rouses longing in our hearts. We visualize how the Master served the Divine Mother. After his vision of the Divine Mother, the Master could no longer continue the worship service as he was carried away by a spiritual tempest. He gradually became absorbed in sadhana of the different paths of Hinduism, including Tantra, Vaishnava, Shakta, and Vedanta. He planted five trees — ashwatha, banyan, ashoka, vilva, and amalaki — to form the Panchavati grove as a place to perform his sadhana, and he built a fence around it.

While practising the servant attitude to God, the Master uprooted his ego and as a result, for the rest of his life he could not say "I" and "mine." Although he was a high-caste brahmin and a temple priest, he cleaned the privy for the Kali temple. M. said: "The Master himself told us that once he cleaned the open drain of Rasik's house with his own hair while praying with tears in his eyes, 'Mother, destroy my pride in being a brahmin.'"[9] Rasik was the sweeper for the temple complex.

M. presented another eye-witness account: "One day I saw the Master sweeping the path next to the northern veranda with a broom. He told me, 'Mother walks here; that is why I am cleaning this path.'"[10]

These are different scenes for meditation.

During his sadhana as a confidante of Radha, the Master dressed like a woman. During that period, he attended Durga Puja at Mathur's Jan Bazar house in Calcutta. Jagadamba, Mathur's wife, accompanied the Master to the shrine during the vesper and he fanned the Divine Mother with a chamara. We love to visualize the scene, with Swami Saradananda's description:

> Suddenly, Mathur's eyes fell on the women, and he saw a stranger, adorned with gorgeous clothes and ornaments, standing next to his wife, fanning the Divine Mother. Despite looking again and again, he could not recognize her. He thought that she might be a friend of his wife, or the wife of a wealthy man who had perhaps come at her invitation.
>
> After a while, Mathur went to the inner apartment and by the by asked his wife, "During vespers, who was standing next to you, fanning the Deity?" Jagadamba replied with a smile: "What! You did not recognize him? It was the Father, in an ecstatic mood, who was fanning. It is quite understandable that you did not recognize him—when the Father is dressed like a woman, it is hard to recognize him as a man." Dumbfounded, Mathur said: "This is why I say that even in trifling matters no one can know the Father if he doesn't allow himself to be known. Look, I live with the Father twenty-four hours a day, and still I did not recognize him!"[11]

Ramakrishna had great love for his mother, Chandramani, and he served her till she passed away. Chandramani moved from Kamarpukur to Dakshineswar sometime before 1864. After her second son, Rameswar, passed away, she decided to stay with her youngest son on the bank of the Ganges. Ramakrishna's niece Lakshmi recalled:

> Grandma would not eat her lunch until she had heard the noon whistle of the Alambazar Jute Mill. As soon as it sounded she would exclaim: "Oh! There is the whistle of heaven. That is the signal to offer food to Lakshmi and Narayana." A problem would arise on Sundays, however, when the

jute mill was closed. No whistle was blown at noon, and consequently she would not eat. This worried the Master very much, and he would lament: "Oh dear! My old mother will refuse her food today and she will be weak." Brother Hriday would say to the Master: "Don't be anxious, Uncle. When Grandma is hungry she will eat of her own accord." But the Master would reply: "Oh no. I am her son. It is my duty to look after my old mother." With much coaxing the Master would persuade his mother to eat the prasad of Krishna.[12]

Ramakrishna's nephew Akshay became the priest of the Krishna temple. In 1869, Rameswar arranged Akshay's marriage, but within a few months Akshay developed a fever. Rameswar had him treated, and he recovered, but soon after Akshay returned to Dakshineswar, his fever returned. Ramakrishna then predicted he would not survive. Hriday became extremely anxious upon hearing this. He called in good doctors and tried his utmost to cure Akshay's disease. But the illness gradually became worse, and he suffered for a month. When the Master saw that Akshay's last moment had arrived, he went to his bedside and told him: "Akshay, say, 'Ganga, Narayana, Om Rama.'"[13] Akshay repeated that mantra three times, and then passed away.

Birth and death are not in human hands, and even avatars grieve when their loved ones pass away. Ramakrishna said:

Akshay died before my very eyes, and I felt nothing at the time. I stood there and watched how a man dies. It was as if there were a sword in a sheath, and the sword was suddenly drawn out of the sheath. The sword remained the same as before. Nothing had happened to it. And the sheath lay there, empty. When I saw that, I felt great joy. I laughed and sang and danced. They took Akshay's body away and burned it and came back. But the next day as I stood there (*pointing to the southeastern veranda of his room*), I felt as though a wet towel were being wrung inside my heart. That was how I suffered for Akshay. "O Mother," I thought, "this body of mine has no relation even to the cloth that enfolds it; how can it feel so much for a nephew? And if I feel so much pain, what agony must householders suffer! Is that what You are teaching me, Mother?"

But, you know, those who hold on to the Lord do not lose themselves in grief. After experiencing a few blows, they soon regain control over themselves. But people of poor calibre become very restless and are completely lost. Have you not seen the plight of small fishing boats when steamers pass through the Ganges? It seems as if they are about to sink and cannot survive. A boat may even turn upside down. But the large thousand-ton barges soon regain their balance after having a few jolts. Similarly, everyone will have to encounter a few jolts in this life.[14]

This theme for meditation brings great comfort to us when we lose our dearest ones.

Before Akshay's passing away, Ramakrishna went to Vrindaban on a pilgrimage with Mathur and his family. He was so fascinated with the playground of Krishna that he wanted to live there permanently, but his love for his mother brought him back to Dakshineswar. The Master said: "I forgot everything when I went to Vraja. I thought that I would never return to Dakshineswar. But after a few days I remembered my mother, and I realized that she would suffer and grieve for me. Who would look after her and serve her in her advanced age? When this thought arose in my mind, I could no longer stay there."[15]

Chandramani died on 13 February 1877. When she passed away the Master wept. Later, pointing to the bakul-talá ghat of Dakshineswar, M. said: "Just before Chandramani passed away, her body was brought here. She was lying on a rope cot. Two legs of the cot were in the Ganges and the other two legs were on the cement ghat. Holding his mother's feet, the Master said tearfully: 'Mother, who are you that carried me in your womb?' He meant that she was not an ordinary mother."[16]

According to the Hindu custom, a sannyasin has no right to perform *shráddha* (funeral rites), so the Master's nephew Ramlal performed this duty. Seeing the Master crying for his departed mother, Hriday said: "Uncle, you are a monk. Why are you crying for your mother?" The Master replied: "Rascal, I have become a monk — that does not mean I am a heartless animal."[17] One day after his mother's passing away, Holy Mother carried a tray of food to the Master. He told her, "Please wait, let me go to the Panchavati and cry for my mother." Afterwards he took his food. No one can repay one's debt to one's mother. As the Master could not perform the shráddha ceremony for his deceased mother, he offered *tarpan* (a water offering) to his mother through his tears.

Service to our parents is extremely important, because they have brought us to this world so that we can use our lives for God-realization. The Master told his disciples:

> Look, my children, parents are the greatest gurus in this world. As long as they are alive, one should serve them to one's utmost ability; when they die, one should perform the shráddha ceremony as far as one is able. One who is poor and has no means to perform the shráddha ceremony for parents should go to the forest and weep for their memory, thus repaying the debt to them. One may disobey one's parents without incurring any sin only for the sake of God. Although his father forbade it, Prahlada did not stop repeating the name of Krishna. Dhruva disobeyed

his mother and went into the forest to practise austerities. But in performing these actions, neither of them incurred any sin.[18]

Although he had become a monk, Ramakrishna performed his duty to his wife. He taught Holy Mother various sadhanas and took care of her needs. During the Shodashi worship, when he formally worshipped her as the Divine Mother, he offered the results of his sadhanas to her, so that she would not have to practise too many austerities to attain them. He asked Holy Mother, "Please look after the Calcutta people" (referring to worldly people who are suffering from misery and entrapped by maya).

The religion of this age is to love and serve people. The gopis attained Krishna by those two methods. Ramakrishna left his inexhaustible spiritual treasures to humanity and taught us to love God and serve human beings as God. He came to make religion easy. He said: "I have cooked the food, you need only enjoy the meal"; "I cast the mould, you put your mind into it and shape yourselves accordingly"; and "If you can't do anything, give me your power of attorney." Nonetheless, he also said: "Give up all desires one by one, and only then will you succeed"; "Be like a cast-off leaf before a gale"; "Renounce lust and gold, and call on God"; and "I have done sixteen parts, you do one-sixteenth of that."[19]

Serving the monks

Rani Rasmani's Kali temple had a good reputation among the monastic community because there they would be given food and shelter, a water pot, and a blanket. Once Ramakrishna had a desire to serve the monks. He said:

> Once a desire arose in my mind to supply aspirants of all sects with whatever they needed for their sadhanas. If all their needs were met, they could then practise sadhana without anxiety, and I would watch them joyfully. When I told this to Mathur, he said: "That's no problem, Father. I'll arrange everything right now. You distribute everything as you wish." Arrangements had already been made to give rice, lentils, flour, and so on to mendicants regularly from the temple store. Now Mathur made additional provisions for water pots, blankets, seats for meditation, and even marijuana and hemp for those who used them and wine for Tantric aspirants.
>
> At that time many Tantric aspirants who came would arrange a Chakra, a holy circle in which they would perform rituals as a group. I supplied them with peeled ginger, onion, puffed rice, and fried gram — ingredients used in their rituals — and observed how they used these articles in their worship and prayers to the Divine Mother. On many occasions

they made me join their holy circle, and sometimes invited me to lead the group. They would always ask me to drink the consecrated wine, but when they found that I was incapable of taking it because I got intoxicated while merely chanting the Mother's name, they did not ask me anymore. However, because it was the custom to drink wine in the holy circle, I'd put a drop on my finger and mark my forehead with it, or smell it, or at the most sprinkle a drop on my tongue, then pour the wine in their glasses. I noticed that after drinking wine, some of them would concentrate on the Divine Mother and call on Her passionately. Some of them, however, would drink greedily and become drunk instead of calling on the Divine Mother. One day I saw them become excessively drunk, so I stopped supplying wine to them.[20]

Ramakrishna found much joy in serving holy people. Later, when his own devotees arrived, he would tell them about his guru Tota Puri's wonderful life and sadhana. Regarding the Master's service of monks, M. said:

> The Master told me this story, which took place during his early years at Dakshineswar when he was twenty-five years old. Before the arrival of Tota Puri, various monks visited the Master. One of these monks lived for a time in the Panchavati and served Gopala [the child Krishna]. The Master used to visit him and listen to his teachings. According to tradition, one should serve the guru for three days. The Master served the monk by bringing him water, food, and so on for three days and then stopped going to him.
>
> The monk asked, "Why are you not visiting me anymore?"
>
> The Master replied, "I decided to serve you for three days and now that time is up."[21]

M. described another incident, which took place on 29 September 1884:

> A sadhu was staying at the Panchavati. But he was a hot-tempered man; he scolded and cursed everyone. He came to the Master's room wearing wooden sandals and asked the Master, "Can I get fire here? Do you have some tobacco?" Sri Ramakrishna saluted him and said, "Yes, sir." Tobacco was supplied. The Master stayed standing with folded hands as long as he remained in the room.
>
> When he had left, Bhavanath said to the Master with a laugh, "What great respect you showed the sadhu!"
>
> Master (smiling): "You see, he too is Narayana, though full of tamas. This is the way one should please people who have an excess of tamas. Besides, he is a sadhu."[22]

Serving God in the poor

In 1868, Ramakrishna went on a pilgrimage with Mathur and his family. Their first stop was Vaidyanath in Bihar. Swami Saradananda described the Master's reaction when he encountered the poverty-stricken people there:

> On the way to Varanasi and Vrindaban, the party stopped for a few days at Deoghar to visit the famous temple of Vaidyanath Shiva. The Master was overcome with compassion when he saw the miserable condition of the poverty-stricken people in a nearby village. He said to Mathur: "You are a steward of Mother's estate. Give each of these poor people one piece of cloth, and one good meal, and also some oil for their heads." At first Mathur was reluctant. He said: "Father, this pilgrimage is going to cost a great deal, and there are many people here. If I give them what you ask, I may find myself short of money later. What do you think I ought to do?" The Father paid no heed to that excuse. Overwhelmed with compassion, he shed tears at the sight of the villagers' abject misery and cried in anguish: "You wretch! I'm not going to Varanasi. I'm staying here with these people. They have no one to care for them. I won't leave them." Like an obstinate child, he left Mathur's company and sat with the poor villagers. Seeing such compassion in the Father, Mathur had cloth brought from Calcutta and fulfilled his other requests as well. The Father was pleased by the villagers' happiness. He then took leave of them and joyfully left for Varanasi with Mathur. We heard that at another time the Master went with Mathur to a village near Ranaghat, in his estate, where he had similar feelings of compassion for the pitiable condition of those villagers and made Mathur do what he had done near Deoghar.[23]

Ramakrishna may have appeared to be simply a salaried priest of the Kali temple, of which Mathur was the owner, but in reality, the Master was the son of the Divine Mother and Mathur was a custodian of Her wealth. In the domain of the Divine Mother, Her son has the right to give orders to the Mother's manager of Her wealth.

Serve human beings as God: Practical Vedanta

Once in 1884 at Dakshineswar, Ramakrishna was talking with Narendra and other devotees on various topics, both spiritual and humorous. By the by, the topic of Vaishnava dharma arose and someone mentioned what Chaitanya told Sanatan Goswami: "*Jive dayā nāme ruchi vaishnav sevan, Ihā vinā dharma nāi shuna Sanātan.* — Listen, O Sanatan, there is no other dharma than practising compassion for all living beings, loving God's name, and serving devotees." Swami Saradananda recorded the

Master's commentary and how Swami Vivekananda found the seed of Practical Vedanta there:

> The Master explained: "This religion advises its followers to practise these three salient disciplines sincerely: love of God's name, compassion for all living beings, and service of devotees. God and His name are identical. Knowing the Name and the possessor of the Name to be the same, the devotee should always chant His name with love. Knowing God and His devotees, Krishna and the Vaishnavas, to be the same, one should respect, worship, and make obeisance to monks and devotees. Understanding that this world belongs to Krishna, one should show compassion for all beings." As he said, "compassion for all beings," he suddenly went into samadhi. After a while he came down to a semiecstatic state and said: "Compassion for all beings? How foolish to speak of compassion! Human beings are as insignificant as worms crawling on the earth — and they are to show compassion to others? That's absurd. It must not be compassion, but service to all. Recognize all as manifestations of God and serve them as such."
>
> Everyone heard the Master's words, but no one except Narendra understood their significance. When the Master came to the normal plane of consciousness, Narendra left the room and said to some of his friends: "What a wonderful light I saw today in those words of the Master! How beautifully did he reconcile the simple, sweet, and refreshing ideal of devotion with the knowledge of Vedanta, which people believe to be dry, difficult, and heartless! For so long we've heard that anyone who wants to attain nondual knowledge must retire to the forest, shunning family and friends completely and forcibly uprooting love, devotion, and other sweet sentiments from the heart, driving them away forever. If aspirants who strive to attain that knowledge consider this world and all people within it to be impediments to their spiritual path, they will develop hatred towards them and go astray. But what the Master said today in his ecstatic mood is clear: One can bring Vedanta from the forest to the home and practise it in daily life. Let people continue with whatever they are doing; there's no harm in this. People must first believe and understand that God has manifested Himself before them as the world and its creatures. Whomever people come in contact with in every moment of their lives, whomever they treat with love, respect, and compassion — they all are parts of God, God Himself. If people consider every human being to be God, how can they consider themselves to be superior to others and harbour anger, hatred, and arrogance — or even compassion — towards them? Their minds will become pure as they serve all beings as God, and soon they will experience themselves as parts of the blissful God — by nature pure, illumined, and free.

"The Master's words also shed a special light on the path of devotion. As long as an aspirant can't see God in every being, it isn't possible to attain true and supreme devotion. When true devotees serve human beings as Shiva or Narayana, they see God in others and are soon blessed with supreme devotion. The followers of karma yoga and raja yoga will also find great light in the Master's words. Embodied beings cannot remain without activity for even a moment, so their duty is to perform every action as service to God within human beings; thus they will soon reach the goal. If it's the will of God, I shall proclaim to the world at large the noble truth that I've heard today. I shall preach this wonderful message to all — the wise and the ignorant, the rich and the poor, the brahmin and the pariah."[24]

This message is extremely significant in the philosophy of the Ramakrishna Mission's philanthropic activities — "Serve human beings as God." It is the basis of Practical Vedanta in daily life, which Vivekananda introduced in the activities of the Ramakrishna Mission. Moreover, this was the philosophical basis of his karma yoga. When you meditate with closed eyes, think: "*Aham Brahmasmi* — I am Brahman." And when you see people with open eyes, think: "*Tattwamasi* — You are Brahman." The same Brahman pervades all beings; this knowledge is the culmination of Vedantic experience.

The sage Vyasa said: "*Paropakārāya Punyāya, Pāpāya Para Peedanam* — Helping others is virtue; hurting others is sin." Serving or doing good to others may be a great virtue, but this does not always bring peace and happiness. Jagadamba, Mathur's wife, was suffering from blood dysentery and was in a critical condition. When the doctors lost hope, Mathur fervently requested the Master to cure her disease. Out of compassion, the Master said in an ecstatic mood, "Your wife will recover." She was cured, but the Master took her disease upon himself and suffered for six months from dysentery and other complaints. Later he contracted cancer after taking upon himself the sins of Girish Ghosh. Swami Saradananda mentioned another incident:

Once a man suffering from leucoderma came and plaintively implored the Master to pass his hand over his leucoderma and thus cure his disease. The Master said compassionately: "Well, I don't know anything; but because you ask me I will pass my hand over you. If the Divine Mother wills it, you will be cured." He then passed his hand over the man's skin. For the rest of that day the Master's hand hurt so terribly that he restlessly prayed to the Divine Mother, "I will never do such a thing again, Mother." Later the Master told us, "That man's disease was cured, but his suffering passed over to this (*pointing to his own body*)."[25]

Ramakrishna demonstrated through his life how to serve human beings as God. Saradananda wrote:

> Although the Master's body became exhausted from the strain involved in teaching, his enthusiasm for this did not waver. Whenever a competent spiritual aspirant arrived, he knew this deep in his heart. Immediately overwhelmed with divine power, he would give instructions to the aspirant and with a touch start him or her on the spiritual path. The newcomer's spiritual mood would call forth a similar mood in the Master, subduing his other moods for a while. The Master could then use his divine vision to see how far that aspirant had proceeded on the path towards perfection, and why that person could go no further. Next the Master removed all obstacles and established the aspirant in a higher spiritual realm. Until the last moment of his life, the Master served all human beings as God, initiated them into the divine knowledge of the Fearless One, and fulfilled the spiritual longings that had been driving them birth after birth. This, according to the scriptures, is the greatest gift to humankind.[26]

Devotee abuse: A sin according to the Vaishnava tradition

According to the Vaishnava scriptures, it is a great sin to humiliate, criticize, or abuse a devotee of God physically or mentally because devotees carry God in their hearts. Ramakrishna could not bear any criticism or disrespectful behaviour towards devotees or to any other person. Swami Premananda recalled: "Once Prankrishna Mukhopadhyay, whom the Master called 'the fat brahmin,' criticized Naren. The Master was very displeased with him because to him Naren was Lord Shiva himself, one of the seven sages, the jewel in his crown. This fat brahmin had criticized his Naren! After some days Prankrishna sent some fruit to the Master at Dakshineswar. The Master immediately returned the fruit to him because he had criticized Naren. The fat brahmin rushed to Dakshineswar, panting all the way, fell at the Master's feet, and apologized. The Master then forgave him."[27]

The Master would sometimes make jokes regarding Balaram's miserliness, but he would not tolerate anybody criticizing Balaram. Once Golap-ma made a critical remark about Balaram's miserliness and the Master immediately silenced her, saying: "It is not to bring a few rasagollas amounting to eight annas for me. Balaram has to maintain several establishments at Cuttack, Kothar, Puri in Orissa, and also in Calcutta and Vrindaban. He spends money for the worship service of the deities of those places. Shame! You are criticizing him! He is staying in Calcutta so that he can have my company."[28] Then to give Golap-ma a lesson, the Master stopped talking to her and forbade the devotees to visit her. Swami Turiyananda recalled:

Once Sri Ramakrishna was very angry with a lady devotee [Golap-ma]. He asked all of us not to go to her house or eat her food. He also asked her not to come to Dakshineswar. Given this serious injunction, who would dare visit her house? Nevertheless, one day Swamiji said to Swami Shivananda, "Come, let us go for a walk." In the course of the walk they came upon the lady's house and Swamiji asked her for something to eat. The lady was beside herself with joy and fed him heartily. Afterwards Swamiji went to Sri Ramakrishna and told him what he had done. The Master said: "Well, I forbade you and yet you went there and ate!" Swamiji replied: "Well, what harm was there? I have also invited her to come here."[29]

We observe how the great teachers teach, and we learn from them. However, in this case the Master was moved by the large-heartedness of his main disciple.

One should not hurt others. Rude behaviour is a great obstacle to spiritual life. Some monks develop a spiritual ego and think that they are greater than householders. Once a wise monk told a young monk, "You are a householder." This proud young monk replied, "No, I am a monk." The wise monk said, "Do you know who is *grihastha* — a householder? The person who lives in the *griha* [literally, house], that is, the body, he is a householder. If you live in the body, you are a householder. A real monk lives in the Atman transcending the body idea."

The Master once gave a lesson on humility to Swami Adbhutananda, which he beautifully described:

Once a devotee at Dakshineswar was behaving badly, and I found it impossible to check my irritation. I scolded him and he felt very hurt. The Master knew how the devotee had suffered, and when the devotee had gone he said to me: "It is not good to speak harshly to those who come here. They are tormented with worldly problems. If they come here and then are scolded for their shortcomings, where will they go? In the presence of holy company never use harsh words with anyone, and never say anything to cause pain to another."

Do you know what he told me next? "Tomorrow, visit this man and speak to him in such a way that he will forget what you said to him today." So the next day I visited him. My pride was humbled. I spoke to him very sweetly. When I returned, however, the Master asked, "Did you offer him salutations from me?"

Amazed at his words, I said that I had not. Then he said, "Go to him again and offer him my salutations."

So again I went to that man and conveyed the Master's salutations. At this the devotee burst into tears. I was moved to see him weeping. When I returned this time the Master said, "Now your misdeed is pardoned."[30]

Serving the disciples and devotees

The scriptures say that *jivanmuktas* (liberated souls) will not be born again. Those who love and serve them will receive their virtues; and those who hate and criticize them will receive the results of their bad karma. Holy Mother, Hriday, and the disciples and devotees served the Master with food, nursing, and personal service, as most of the time he was in a god-intoxicated state. But the Master also served the devotees and disciples in many ways.

According to the Bhagavata, one can serve others in four ways. First, one can serve others physically with all of one's energy. Second, one can offer financial help; but the Master did not have any money, so he served with his spiritual wealth. Third, one can serve with one's intellect: The Master had a luminous intellect full of wisdom that he shared with his followers. Fourth, one can inspire others through speech: The Master spent the last part of his life continually teaching others.

Swami Premananda described the Master's way of service: "We saw how lovingly the Master would receive the devotees at Dakshineswar. He would ask, 'Do you want to chew a betel roll?' If the devotee said, 'No,' he would then ask, 'Would you like to smoke tobacco?' He took care of the devotees in so many ways."[31]

Many devotees would come to Ramakrishna at Dakshineswar and stay the night. For them he kept mats, carpets, mosquito curtains, pillows, and *chumki* water pots for drinking water, as well as sweets and fruits that had been offered at the temple. For young disciples who would come secretly without informing their parents, the Master arranged to pay their return carriage fare. While they were there, he taught them how to pray. He demonstrated this by lying on the floor, thrashing about, and crying like a child having a tantrum. He transmitted power into young Hariprasanna by wrestling with him. If the disciples could not come to Dakshineswar, he would put together packages of temple prasad and send these to devotees in Calcutta through his nephew Ramlal, or he would take them himself.

One night Purna was studying alone in his room at home when he suddenly noticed M. standing outside near his window. He immediately came out and M. whispered to him: "The Master is waiting for you at the junction of Shyampukur Street and Cornwallis Street [now Bidhan Sarani]. Please come with me." The Master was extremely pleased to see Purna. He said: "I have brought sandesh for you. Please eat it." The Master fed Purna with his own hands. Overwhelmed with emotion, Purna began to cry. The three of them then went to M.'s house, where the Master gave Purna some instructions on spiritual disciplines.[32] This is a scene for meditation on the Master's service.

Latu, Yogin, Rakhal, Baburam, and Senior Gopal were the Master's regular attendants; other disciples served him occasionally. The Master took their personal service, and he gave them service mentally and spiritually. He provided them a little food at night and sent them to different temples and the Panchavati to practise japa and meditation. In the early morning, the Master would pace back and forth in his room and chant the Divine Mother's name. At that time, he could see the obstacles in his disciples' spiritual journey, and he would use his divine power to remove them. Swamiji described to Nivedita how the disciples passed nights with the Master in Dakshineswar: "Oh, what weird scenes things bring before me, the weirdest scenes of my whole life! Perfect silence, broken only by the cries of the jackals, in the darkness under the great tree at Dakshineswar. Night after night we sat there, the whole night through, and He [Ramakrishna] talked to me, when I was a boy."[33] This is a picture for meditation.

Swami Vijnanananda described how the Master made others his own through love: "Although the Master was not a so-called educated person, he had a wonderful sense of etiquette. I walked a long distance in the sun and when I reached his room, he asked me to sit down and relax. I was thirsty, and the Master gave me a glass of drinking water. Then he sat on the small cot and asked me if I had any questions. I asked, 'Does God exist?' 'Yes, He does exist,' he replied. 'Is God with form or without form?' He said: 'He is both with form and formless. No one can express what He is.'"[34]

Ramakrishna was a wonderful teacher as were his disciples. When Latu was staying at Dakshineswar to attend the Master, he never saw anyone's face in the morning until he had seen the face of the Master. He began each day by seeing Ramakrishna and saluting him. One morning for some reason he did not see the Master when he woke up, so he shouted, "Where are you?"

"Wait a minute — I am coming," Ramakrishna answered. Latu kept his hands tightly pressed to his eyes until the Master came. Then he took away his hands and bowed down to his feet.

Another morning when he did not see the Master right away, Latu again called for him to come to the room. But this time the Master answered by asking Latu to come outside. Latu walked out on the western veranda and saw the Master in the flower garden. Latu asked him, "Sir, what are you doing?" "Yesterday a devotee brought a pair of sandals for you," answered the Master, "and I can find only one of them. A jackal may have taken the other, so I am looking for it." Latu said in a plaintive tone: "Sir, please come here. Don't search for that sandal." "But I shall feel sorry if you can't wear these new sandals," replied the Master, "since it was only yesterday that the devotee brought them." Latu anxiously said: "Sir, please stop. If you keep looking for my sandal, it will be harmful for me. My whole day will be spent in vain." (The disciple is expected to serve the guru. The reverse is not only unusual, but is even considered inauspicious for the disciple.) Ramakrishna responded: "Do you know what day is really spent in vain? That day when the Lord's name is not chanted."[35]

These are beautiful scenes for our meditation on Ramakrishna's service to his disciples. Swami Advaitananda narrated two more scenes:

One day Latu was meditating on the bank of the Ganges. He used to choose a seat above the level to which the water rose during flood tide. However, that day the water rose unusually high, up to where he was sitting in meditation, and continued rising. Latu was so absorbed that he did not feel the water. I anxiously reported the matter to the Master. He came hurriedly, waded out to where Latu was, and brought him back to normal consciousness.

Another day during meditation, Latu lost outer consciousness, fell flat on his face, and began to make a noise. I noticed this and immediately informed the Master. Sri Ramakrishna rushed to Latu and helped him to lie down on his back. He then put his knee on his chest and began to massage him. Gradually Latu returned to a normal state of consciousness. The Master asked: "Haven't you seen Mother Kali today? Don't talk about it. If you speak out, people will create a furore here." Latu kept quiet. From then on, whenever Latu meditated, his eyes, face, and chest turned red.[36]

Ramakrishna knew the tendencies of his disciples and would send them to different temples or spots in the temple garden of Dakshineswar to practise meditation. Ramlal told the following story:

One day at noon the Master sent Latu to one of the Shiva temples to med-itate. Late afternoon came and Latu still had not appeared, so the Master sent me to see about him. When I entered the temple, I saw Latu sitting motionless, deep in meditation and bathed in perspiration. When I told the Master what I had seen, he himself went to the temple, taking a fan with him. He asked me to bring a glass of water. When I entered, I saw the Master fanning Latu. Latu began to tremble. The Master said: "My boy, it is twilight. When will you set the lamps and light them?" At the sound of the Master's voice, Latu slowly began to regain consciousness. He opened his eyes and seemed puzzled to see the Master before him. "You have perspired a great deal," the Master said. "Rest a bit more before you leave your seat." By this time Latu was fully conscious of what was going on. "What are you doing, sir!" he cried. "Won't this disgrace me? It is I who should be serving you." With great affection the Master said: "No, my boy, it is not you I am serving, but the Lord Shiva inside you. He was uncomfortable in such unbearable heat. Did you know that He had entered you?" Latu replied: "No, I knew nothing. I was gazing at the *lingam* [the image of Shiva] and saw a wonderful light. I remember only that the light flooded the whole temple. After that I lost consciousness."[37]

Ramakrishna poured his fountain of love into his disciples and capti-vated them forever. It was winter when the Master arrived at the Cossipore garden house. Once, in the middle of a cold night, Shashi left the Master's room to clean the commode; he wore only a thin cloth. On his return he saw that Ramakrishna, who was very sick, had somehow crawled across the room and was reaching up for a shawl that was hanging on a clothes-horse. At this painful sight Shashi thought to himself: "Alas! In my hurry I forgot to cover him sufficiently, so perhaps he is cold and is trying to get a shawl." "What are you doing, sir?" Shashi asked him in a scolding tone. "The air is very chilly, and you should not be up. Why did you not ask me for the shawl?" Filled with love and concern, the Master held out his shawl, and then said in a feeble voice: "I felt cold as you went out almost bare bodied on such a cold night, so I picked up this shawl for you. Please take this."[38] Shashi was overwhelmed.

This reciprocal service of the guru and the disciple can be an object for meditation. We can visualize the Master in the dead hours of a winter night at Cossipore garden house, crawling across the floor to get a shawl for his disciple in the dim light of a kerosene lantern.

The young disciples took turns serving the Master around the clock. Moreover, they were practising spiritual disciplines under his instruction. They renounced hearth and home and surrendered themselves to the Master. Holy Mother narrated the following incident to Nistarini Ghosh:

One evening Niranjan and a few other disciples decided to get juice from a date palm near the southern boundary of the garden. The Master was told nothing about this. When it was dark, Niranjan and others walked towards the tree. A short time later, Holy Mother saw the Master running down the steps and through the door. She wondered: "How is this possible? How can one who needs help even to change his position in bed run like an arrow?" She could not believe her eyes, so she went to the Master's room to see if he was there. He was not. In great consternation she looked all around, but could not find him. With much apprehension, Holy Mother returned to her room.

After a while Holy Mother saw the Master running swiftly back to his room. She then went to him and asked about what she had seen. He replied: "Oh, you noticed that. You see, the boys who have come here are all young. They were proceeding merrily to drink the juice of a date palm in the garden. I saw a black cobra there. It is ferocious and it might have bitten them all. The boys did not know this. So I went there by a different route to drive it away. I told the snake, 'Don't come here again.'" The Master asked her not to tell the others about this.[39]

Girish Ghosh recalled how Ramakrishna transformed his disciple through unselfish love and service:

One day when I arrived at Dakshineswar, Sri Ramakrishna was just finishing his noonday meal. He offered me his dessert, but as I was about to eat it, he said: "Wait. Let me feed you myself." Then he put the rice-pudding into my mouth with his own fingers, and I ate as hungrily and unself-consciously as a small baby. I forgot that I was an adult. I felt I was a child of the mother and the mother was feeding me. But now when I remember how these lips of mine had touched many impure lips, and how Sri Ramakrishna fed me, touching them with his holy hand, I am overwhelmed with emotion and say to myself: "Did this actually happen? Or was it only a dream?"[40]

On 16 April 1886, Girish went to see Ramakrishna at the Cossipore garden house. It is always a joy to see loved ones when one is ill. In the *Gospel* M. described a fascinating scene that took place depicting Ramakrishna's love in action:

That evening Sri Ramakrishna was somewhat better. The devotees saluted the Master and sat down on the floor. The Master asked M. to bring the lamp near him. He greeted Girish cordially.

Master (*to Girish*): "Are you quite well? (*to Latu*) Prepare a smoke for him and give him a betel-leaf."

A few minutes afterwards he asked Latu to give Girish some refreshments. Latu said that they had been sent for.

Sri Ramakrishna was sitting up. A devotee offered him some garlands of flowers. Sri Ramakrishna put them around his neck one by one. Was he thus worshipping God who dwelt in his heart? The devotees looked at him wonderingly. He took two garlands from his neck and gave them to Girish.

Every now and then Sri Ramakrishna asked whether the refreshments had been brought.

Girish was given the refreshments on a tray. Sri Ramakrishna took a grain and Girish accepted the rest as prasad. He sat in front of the Master and began to eat. He needed water to drink. There was an earthen jug in the southeast corner of the room. It was the month of April, and the day was hot. Sri Ramakrishna said, "There is some nice water here."

The Master was so ill that he had not enough strength even to stand up. And what did the disciples see to their utter amazement? They saw him leave the bed, completely naked, and move toward the jug! He himself was going to pour the water into a tumbler. The devotees were almost frozen with fear. The Master poured the water into a glass. He poured a drop or two into his hand to see whether it was cool. He found that it was not very cool; but since nothing better could be found, he reluctantly gave it to Girish.

Girish was eating the sweets. The devotees were sitting about, and M. was fanning Sri Ramakrishna.[41]

This is a dynamic scene for meditation. We visualize the Master, his human behaviour, and his service to the devotees. We see crispy *kachuri* and *luchi*, sweets from Fagu's famous shop. We see a glass of water in Ramakrishna's hand and his satisfaction in serving a devotee.

In his biography of Ramakrishna, Romain Rolland described how the Master sacrificed himself to serve others till the end of his life:

The end was approaching. His feeble body was almost daily consumed in the fire of ecstasy and worn out by his constant gift of himself to the famished crowds. Sometimes like a sulky child he complained to the Mother of the flood of visitors devouring him day and night.

But he never turned anybody away. He said: "Let me be condemned to be born over and over again even in the form of a dog, if so I can be of help to a single soul!"

And again: "I will give up twenty thousand such bodies to help one man. It is glorious to help even one man!"[42]

Ever active with phenomenal deeds

Swami Vivekananda wrote in a vesper hymn on Ramakrishna:

"Bhanjana-dukhaganjana karuāghana karma-kathor — O destroyer of the mass of suffering! O embodiment of compassion! O tremendous performer of deeds!" He again mentioned in a hymn on Ramakrishna: *"Karma-kalevaram adbhuta-cheshtam* — You were ever active [for the good of humanity] and you performed phenomenal activities."

At first glance, we do not see Ramakrishna involved with many activities of importance. He was first a priest of the Vishnu temple and then of the Kali temple of Dakshineswar, where his monthly salary was five rupees. Later, when he reached an ecstatic state and dove into the ocean of sadhana, he could no longer perform his priestly duties. He said to Mathur: "From today Hriday will perform the worship. Mother says that She will accept his worship as She would my own."[43] The devout Mathur accepted the Master's words as a command from the Mother.

We generally evaluate someone's karma (actions) through his or her accomplishments, such as building a big temple or a monastery; establishing a school, a college, or a hospital; or writing books, articles, and lecturing to vast audiences. Ramakrishna did not do any such things although Swamiji described him as a "tremendous performer of deeds" and said that he "performed phenomenal activities"! Ramakrishna lived in a nice, spacious room at the Dakshineswar temple garden near the Ganges, and he received his meals from the temple prasad. For the last five years of his life, he talked to the devotees about God and spiritual life. Although he was married, he did not own a house; nor did he go to the market to buy groceries or clothes. The temple authorities supplied him with dhotis and towels, and the devotees brought him shirts and shoes. When he moved to Calcutta and Cossipore for cancer treatment, Surendra paid the rent for the houses, while Balaram supplied his food, and the doctors treated him at no charge. It is amazing how the Master lived in this world for 50 years, but he was not involved in the typical activities of family life.

We work and earn money, buy or rent a home, maintain our families, and do our duties towards our relatives. Everyone performs these mundane tasks, but Ramakrishna's work was unusual and extremely difficult — it was work that ordinary people could not do. He took away his devotees' bad karma and sin, transformed their lives from the worldly to the spiritual, and destroyed their ignorance or maya. That is the reason Swamiji used the phrases "tremendous performer of deeds" and "ever active [for the good of humanity] and performing phenomenal activities."

We know that Ramakrishna practised superhuman austerities for 12 years beginning in 1856 and that he attained unprecedented spiritual power after God-realization. The Master recalled:

I had no sleep at all for six long years. My eyes lost the ability to blink. Despite repeated efforts, I could not close my eyelids. I had no idea of time. I almost forgot that I needed to maintain my body. When at rare intervals my attention would fall on the body a little, I was frightened by its condition. I thought, "Am I on the verge of insanity?" Standing in front of a mirror, I tried to close my eyelids with my fingers — and I couldn't! I became frightened and tearfully said to the Mother: "Mother, is this the result of praying and wholly surrendering myself to You? Now You have given me this terrible disease!" But the next moment I would say: "Let it be as You wish. Let this body go to pieces, but don't leave me. Reveal Yourself to me; bestow Your mercy on me. I have taken refuge at Your lotus feet alone. I have none else but You." I would shed tears, then suddenly be filled with ecstasy.[44]

We are amazed when we hear the stories of his Tantra and Vedanta sadhana and how he attained spiritual, occult, and divine powers through superhuman efforts and actions. When the devotees began to arrive, he distributed his spiritual treasures to them freely. When flowers bloom, bees come of their own accord. News spread and gradually many people began to flock to Dakshineswar. He talked to them only about God and how to realize God. M. recorded in the *Gospel* how the Master created a wonderful atmosphere through his conversations, singing, dancing, and samadhi. He slept only a couple of hours at night and spent the remaining time chanting the Divine Mother's name. The source of the Master's karma was his compassion, so he was *karuna-ghana,* the embodiment of compassion. Out of compassion for suffering humanity, he worked day and night and gave his life for all.

Towards the end of his life many people were attracted to the manifestation of Ramakrishna's spirituality. Observing the tremendous crowd in Dakshineswar, the Master talked to the Divine Mother in ecstasy: "What are You doing? Why are You bringing such large crowds here? I have no time to bathe or eat. (*Pointing to his own body*) This is nothing but a broken drum. (*The Master had recently developed throat cancer.*) If it's beaten too much, it will be perforated. What will You do then?"[45]

When we are heavily burdened with work, we complain to our boss. Similarly, the Master would sometimes complain to the Divine Mother and say: "Why do You bring such hopeless people here? (*After a brief silence*) I can't do so much. Let one seer of milk be diluted with a quarter-seer of water, but here You have five seers of water and one seer of milk! I'm pushing firewood into the oven to boil this milk; now my eyes are burning with smoke. If You want them to have it, You give them spirituality. I can't push enough fuel into the fire. Don't bring that type of person here anymore."[46]

We learn from these statements that the Master was urged by compassion to light the lamp of wisdom in the hearts of ordinary people and destroy the gloom of dark ignorance. Ramakrishna once told his attendant Latu, who was drowsy: "Everyone in the world sleeps, but God does not; for if God slept, the universe would be plunged into darkness and dissolve. God must remain awake day and night taking care of his creatures, so that they can sleep without fear."[47]

In fact, God is free from ignorance, which means He has no desire and no action; still God is always engaged in action. Krishna said in the Gita: "I have, O Partha, no duty; there is nothing in the three worlds that I have not gained and nothing that I have to gain. Yet I continue to work. For should I not ever engage, unwearied, in action, O Partha, men would in every way follow in My wake. If I should cease to work, these worlds would perish: I should cause the mixture of castes and destroy all these creatures."[48]

This statement in the Gita indicates that the avatar Ramakrishna was always engaged in action. He could not take a vacation like we do. Ramakrishna's power is now working behind the philanthropic activities of the Ramakrishna Mission. The Master transmitted this power to Vivekananda at the Cossipore garden house and said: "Today, giving you my all, I have become a beggar. With this power you are to do much work for the good of the world before you return."[49]

Swami Vivekananda described how hard Ramakrishna worked for the good of humanity in his lecture "My Master" in New York in 1896:

> Men came in crowds to hear him, and he would talk twenty hours out of twenty-four, and that not for one day, but for months and months until at last the body broke down under the pressure of this tremendous strain. His intense love for mankind would not let him refuse to help even the humblest of the thousands who sought his aid. Gradually, there developed a fatal throat disorder and yet he could not be persuaded to refrain from these exertions. As soon as he heard that people were asking to see him, he would insist upon having them admitted and would answer all their questions. When expostulated with, he replied: "I do not care. I will give up twenty thousand such bodies to help one man. It is glorious to help even one man." There was no rest for him. Once a man asked him: "Sir, you are a great yogi. Why do you not put your mind a little on your body and cure your disease?" At first he did not answer, but when the question had been repeated, he gently said, "My friend, I thought you

were a sage, but you talk like other men of the world. This mind has been given to the Lord. Do you mean to say that I should take it back and put it upon the body, which is but a mere cage of the soul?"[50]

Anybody who meditates on Ramakrishna's unselfish service to humankind will develop a desire to serve others, and that person's ego and selfishness will be uprooted. That, in fact, is the goal of meditation on *seva* or service to others.

6

Meditation on the Places of Ramakrishna's Lila

India is a holy land. The Himalayas, the abode of gods, stand to her north and three oceans encircle her shores. The snowclad Himalayas seem to be the motionless Shiva immersed in meditation, and the constantly churning oceans represent the vigorously active Shakti, the Divine Mother. The play of Shiva and Shakti fill India with a spiritual atmosphere. Thus, throughout the land we find innumerable holy places, temples of gods and goddesses, caves and hermitages of sages and rishis, and ashramas and monasteries. In addition there are holy spots where illumined souls practised sadhana and attained perfection, and where avatars performed their divine plays. The scriptures list seven holy cities — Kashi, Kanchi, Maya, Ayodhya, Dwaravati, Mathura, and Avanti — that are considered to be places where one can attain freedom from the cycle of death and rebirth after death.

In the Hindu scriptures, three kinds of pilgrimage sites (*tirthas*) are mentioned: immobile, mobile, and mental. An immobile tirtha refers to the holy and purifying waters of the Ganges, Yamuna, Saraswati, Godavari, Narmada, Sindhu, and Kaveri rivers and their banks where the sages have practised austerities since ancient times. Mobile tirthas are the knowers of Brahman, great devotees, and illumined yogis, who transmit spirituality wherever they travel. Mental tirthas include character traits such as truthfulness, forgiveness, self-control, compassion, simplicity, contentment, charity, celibacy, austerity, knowledge, patience, and sweetness. Each one of the tirthas has a holy influence, because it purifies the mind.

"Tirthi kurvanti tirthāni — Pilgrims make a place holy."* Pilgrims sanctify and awaken the spirituality of a place through japa and meditation, austerities and spiritual practices, fasting and vigils, tears and longing, service and prayer, singing and glorifying God. For that reason, whenever people visit holy places their minds automatically feel peace, joy, and longing for God. The benefit of undertaking a pilgrimage is self-evident. Those who dwell in holy places attain devotion and are blessed by the company of holy sadhus and saints. That is why most Indians cherish a desire to go on pilgrimage at least once in their lifetime.

Blessed are the places where incarnations of God were born and raised, where they lived, travelled, and passed away. Those spots become holy, and they attract pilgrims, historians, writers, poets, artists, and tourists throughout the ages. One of the most wonderful gifts of God is that of inquisitiveness, the desire to know. When children begin to talk, they ask questions: Who? Why? When? How? Where? What? Similarly, when we visit those holy places, we ask a guide to tell us every detail of the stories connected with those divine beings. Thus we try to visualize the divine play of the avatars through the guide's descriptions.

Of course, there is a gulf of difference between tourists and pilgrims when they visit a holy place. Tourists bring cameras, take pictures of themselves with a temple in the background, buy souvenirs and mementos, shop for loved ones, eat in good restaurants, and tell their stories to friends upon returning home. Pilgrims fast and bathe in holy rivers or springs, buy flowers and fruits as offerings to the deity, and engage a priest-guide to perform worship of the deity and teach them about the significance of that vibrant place. Pilgrims practise austerities, pray and meditate for some days, and finally return home with a deep impression of God.

In the Ramayana, we come across a few places connected with Ramachandra: he was born in Ayodhya; he married in Mithila; and during his 14-year banishment he lived in Chitrakut, Dandakaranya, Panchavati, Rameswaram, and Sri Lanka. In the Bhagavata, we learn that Krishna was born in Mathura, raised in Gokula and Vrindaban, and spent his adult life in Mathura and Dwaraka. But we also find him in other places such as Hastinapur, Kurukshetra, and Prabhas. In the Bible, we learn that Jesus was born in Bethlehem and raised in Nazareth, and that he travelled through Judea, Samaria, Galilee, and Jerusalem. The scriptures, however, give us no detailed description of those holy places. Again, when we visit holy places, the priests or tour guides tell us things about those places that may be only partly true; they often embellish or distort history, or concoct stories about the avatars, and describe miracles that they performed.

In *Sri Ramakrishna and His Divine Play*, Swami Saradananda described how Chaitanya discovered the sacred places in Vrindaban:

> It is said that Chaitanya was the first to experience a manifestation of the divine presence in Vrindaban. Long before his advent, the holy spots of Vraja were almost forgotten. When Chaitanya travelled in those places, he ascended to the higher plane of consciousness and experienced whatever Krishna's lila [divine play] had occurred there. In fact, Bhagavan Krishna enacted the same lila long before in the same place. Chaitanya's disciples — Rupa, Sanatan, and others — were the first to accept these revelations, and later all Indians believed what the disciples told them.[1]

Places of Ramakrishna's early lila

Kamarpukur, the birthplace of Ramakrishna, is 60 miles northwest of Calcutta. It is now an important place of pilgrimage. Swami Vidyatmananda, an American monk, called Kamarpukur the "Bengal Bethlehem." Jayrambati, the birthplace of Holy Mother Sarada Devi, is situated four miles away from Kamarpukur. Now guide books with maps are available for both Kamarpukur and Jayrambati, so devotees and pilgrims can see those places of Ramakrishna's early lila and meditate on the episodes connected with them.

Kamarpukur detail map locations:
1. Mango orchard of Manik-raja. Now various educational institutions have been built there.
2. Bhuti's canal
3. Bhuti's cremation ground
4. Lakshmi Jala (paddy field)
5. Haldar pond. Ramakrishna bathed there.
6. Yogi Shiva temple is situated in front of Ramakrishna's family home. A light emanated from the Shiva lingam and entered the womb of Chandramani. Thus Ramakrishna was conceived.
7. Srinivas (Chinu) Shankari's house
8. Budhui Moral's cremation ground
9. Kshudiram's house
   a. Ramakrishna's bedroom (a thatched hut with mud walls and a mud floor)

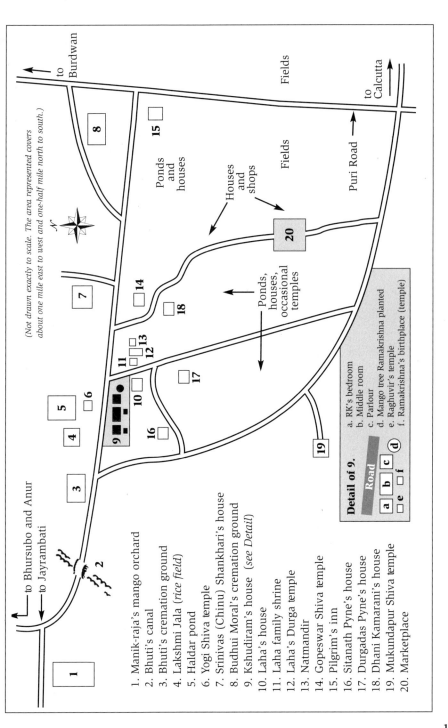

(Not drawn exactly to scale. The area represented covers about one mile east to west and one-half mile north to south.)

to Burdwan

to Calcutta

Fields

Puri Road

Fields

Ponds and houses

Houses and shops

Ponds, houses, occasional temples

20

8

15

7

14

18

13

12

11

5

6

4

3

10

17

16

9

19

1

to Bhursubo and Anur

to Jayrambati

2

1. Manik-raja's mango orchard
2. Bhuti's canal
3. Bhuti's cremation ground
4. Lakshmi Jala (*rice field*)
5. Haldar pond
6. Yogi Shiva temple
7. Srinivas (Chinu) Shankhari's house
8. Budhui Moral's cremation ground
9. Kshudiram's house (*see Detail*)
10. Laha's house
11. Laha family shrine
12. Laha's Durga temple
13. Natmandir
14. Gopeswar Shiva temple
15. Pilgrim's inn
16. Sitanath Pyne's house
17. Durgadas Pyne's house
18. Dhani Kamarani's house
19. Mukundapur Shiva temple
20. Marketplace

Detail of 9.

Road

a. RK's bedroom
b. Middle room
c. Parlour
d. Mango tree Ramakrishna planted
e. Raghuvir's temple
f. Ramakrishna's birthplace (temple)

a b c (d)
e f

Map of Kamarpukur and the places connected with Ramakrishna as there were during his lifetime.

135

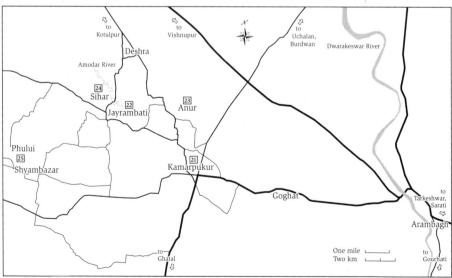

Above: Site of the threshing shed where Ramakrishna was born on 18 February 1836.
Below: Kamarpukur area map.

b. Middle room

c. Parlour

d. A mango tree planted by Ramakrishna when he was a boy is still alive and bearing mangoes.

e. Raghuvir's temple. Ramakrishna's family deities — a stone emblem of Raghuvir Ramachandra, the Rameswar Shiva lingam, and an earthen pot representing Goddess Shitala — are worshipped every day.

f. Ramakrishna's birthplace. Previously it was a thatched roof shed, which was used to husk paddy. In 1951 a temple was built on that spot with a marble image of Ramakrishna.

10. Laha's family home and the kindergarten school under a tin roof shed, which Ramakrishna briefly attended.

11. Laha family shrine

12. Laha's Durga temple

13. Natmandir

14. Gopeswar Shiva temple

15. Pilgrim's inn

16. Sitanath Pyne's house

17. Durgadas Pyne's house

18. Dhani Kamarani's house

19. Shiva temple at Mukundapur

20. Marketplace

Kamarpukur area map locations:

21. Kamarpukur

22. Jayrambati (birthplace of Sarada Devi)

23. Anur temple

24. Sihar (birthplace of Hriday)

25. Phului-Shyambazar

These sites of Ramakrishna's lila can be objects of our meditation. If any devotee came to M. after visiting Kamarpukur, M. would excitedly say to the other devotees present, "He is coming from the Holy Land — Jerusalem." When one such devotee visited, M. joyfully served him refreshments. He then reminisced: "When I first went to Kamarpukur, I asked the villagers and farmers all about the Master. I wanted to embrace them because they were my own people. I considered the birds, beasts, and trees of Kamarpukur as blessed because they had seen and touched the Master. When someone told me anything about the Master, I bowed down to him. The Master had changed my outlook!"[2]

Places of Ramakrishna's adult lila

Undoubtedly, a person's environment has a great impact on his or her mind. The temple garden of Dakshineswar created a favourable atmosphere for Ramakrishna's spiritual journey. The Kali temple, the natmandir, the Vishnu temple, the 12 Shiva temples, the spacious courtyard surrounded by buildings, the beautiful flower gardens, the quiet and densely wooded areas, the Panchavati, the murmuring sound of the Ganges, the songs of birds, and the melodious music from the nahabat created a mystical abode wherein Ramakrishna lived for 30 years and practised his sadhana.

Ramakrishna spent the most of his life (from 1855 to 1885) in the temple garden of Dakshineswar, where he enacted his main divine play. In the beginning of the Bengali *Kathamrita*, M. (the recorder of *The Gospel of Sri Ramakrishna*) vividly described the Dakshineswar temple garden and its surroundings. He also carefully recorded its daily programme. During the early morning services, the temple garden would reverberate with music from one of the two nahabats (concert towers). The priests of the Kali temple, Krishna temple, and Shiva temples performed their worship, loudly chanting mantras as they rang brass bells. During the evening vesper service in all of the temples, priests waved oil lamps to the deities to the accompaniment of conches, bells, and drums, as well as music from the nahabat. Rani Rasmani's Kali temple was well known for its hospitality, and many wandering monks would stop there for a few days to have prasad and rest. Ramakrishna lived in this divine atmosphere and made that place an abode of bliss through his sadhana and spirituality.

The Master usually taught his devotees as he sat on the small wooden cot in his room. Sometimes he even played games with his young disciples in the Panchavati during the day, and at night he taught them meditation there.

Swami Vivekananda reminisced:

The solitude of the Panchavati, associated with the various realizations of the Master, was also the most suitable place for our meditation. Besides meditation and spiritual exercises, we used to spend a good deal of time there in sheer fun and merrymaking. Sri Ramakrishna also joined in with us, and by taking part, enhanced our innocent pleasure. We used to run and skip about, climb on the trees, swing from the creepers [*vines*], and at times hold merry picnics. On the first day that we picnicked the Master noticed that I had cooked the food myself, and he partook of it. I

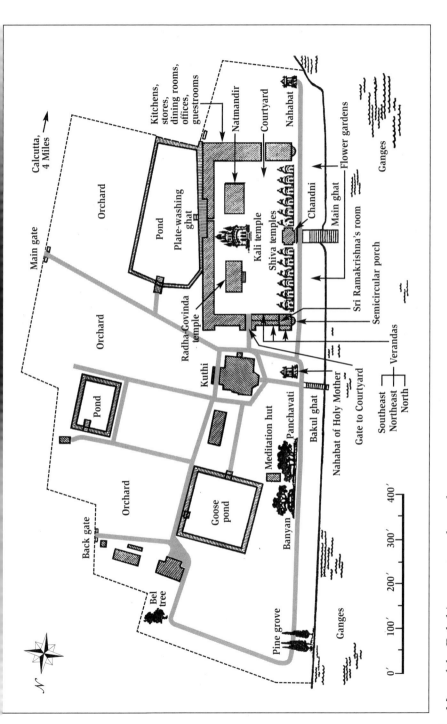

Map of the Dakshineswar temple garden.

knew that he could not take food unless it was cooked by brahmins, and therefore I had arranged for his meal at the Kali temple. But he said, "It won't be wrong for me to take food from such a pure soul as you." In spite of my repeated remonstrations, he enjoyed the food I had cooked that day.[3]

Roughly 130 years have passed since Ramakrishna lived in the temple garden of Dakshineswar. When we visit Dakshineswar even now we can see the same image of the Divine Mother Kali that Ramakrishna worshipped; the same image of Krishna that he worshipped, and which he repaired; the same image of Shiva that he embraced. We can enter Ramakrishna's room and see the cots on which he sat and slept; his collection of pictures still hang on the walls. We can bathe at the Chandni ghat, where he used to bathe; we can sit in the Panchavati and under the bel tree where he practised severe disciplines. When we walk over the tiles of the courtyard, we know that God in human form once walked over them. How blessed are those tiles! Now we try to remember Ramakrishna through japa and meditation; how wonderful it would be if we could have lived there with him, even for a few days!

In the *Gospel*, M. immortalized many persons and places connected with Ramakrishna; if he had not done this, they would have passed into oblivion. M. lived for 46 years after the Master passed away. During this period, he visited Dakshineswar and Cossipore many times and acted as a guide to devotees and distinguished guests. He always encouraged the devotees to visit Dakshineswar. His eyewitness accounts of the Master penetrated deeply into the hearts of those visitors, and they still have a profound effect on all of us.

M. had tremendous passion for truth, a love for history, and an objective mind. He did not dilute the freshness of the original story, like a pharmacist who dilutes medicine to reduce its potency. M. told visitors, "The avatar has just come, so here everything is fresh."[4]

M. as a guide for the Dakshineswar temple garden

Swami Nityatmananda, the author of *Srima Darshan* (in 16 volumes), paid seven visits to Dakshineswar and Cossipore with M., and in *Srima Darshan* he recorded his experiences in detail. M. pointed out the areas in those two holy places that were connected with the Master. These records are extremely precious to devotees and admirers of Ramakrishna. While reading them they can visualize what happened in these locations that were so important in the Master's life. Using these accurate records, pilgrims will not have to depend on a priest or on tour guides. I compiled and translated entries from *Srima Darshan** in this section, so we can see those holy places through M.'s eyes.

Swami Nityatmananda wrote that after Ramakrishna's passing away, the devotees sometimes held picnics in the Dakshineswar temple garden as they had done during his lifetime. One such occasion was on 18 October 1923 during the Durga Puja celebrations. M. joined the devotees at the temple, arriving at 11:30 a.m. with Dr. Durgapada Ghosh. He removed his shoes and went to the Master's room, where he sat on a doormat near the north side of the small cot, just where he used to sit during the Master's lifetime. From that spot, one can see the Ganges through the western door. M. sat there and meditated along with the devotees. Then he moved to the west side of the big cot where the Master used to sleep and put his hands under the mattress. The Master used to sit in the centre of the smaller cot, facing the east. So M. touched his head to that spot, in the same way he used to bow down to the Master.[5]

Swami Dharmeshananda recalled an important story that M. told him:

> Probably in 1882 or 1883 one afternoon after lunch the Master was resting on his bed in Dakshineswar. Sitting on the doormat, I was gently stroking his feet and thinking: "He eats, sleeps, walks, and deals with people like an ordinary human being. How can he be the creator, preserver, and destroyer of the universe? Has he come to this world to bestow grace and save humankind? How is it possible? He is an embodied human being." I was thinking in this way. Suddenly the Master sat up and asked: "Master [M.], what are you thinking?" Then the Master put his hand on his chest and said: "Everything exists here. One will achieve everything by thinking of this place [himself]. One will achieve everything by thinking of this place. One will achieve everything by thinking of this place." After saying this three times, he went into samadhi.
>
> After sometime, he came down from samadhi and began to talk to the Divine Mother: "Mother, I don't know anything. I said what you made me say. I am your child. Mother, did I do anything wrong? You spoke through my mouth." This made me convinced that the Master was God. The Divine Mother and the Master are one.[6]

Swami Nityatmananda continued: Someone asked M., "Which are the pictures that were here during the Master's time?"

M. pointed out the pictures of Rama and Sita, Prahlada, Dhruva, Jesus,

*1. 1 December 1923, vol.4:61-70; 2. 18 October 1923, vol. 3:235-244; 3. 14 January 1924, vol. 8:18-29; 4. 21 March 1924, vol.4:78-85; 5. 30 March 1924, vol. 5:109-124; 6. 30 November 1924, vol. 10: 166-193; 7. 28 January 1926, vol. 13:220-227.

and Chaitanya singing Sankirtan. M. left the Master's room and went to the northern veranda. Jagabandhu (Swami Nityatmananda) asked him, "Where did the Master go into samadhi while listening to Swamiji sing?"* M. pointed out the southeastern corner of the veranda and bowed down to that spot.

M. said: "The Master stood here, leaning his back against the wall. His eyes became still and a divine bliss spread over his face. His form was an embodiment of peace and love....This was the first time I saw samadhi — a state of uninterrupted bliss beyond happiness and misery."[7] He then pointed to the upper step of the veranda's northeast corner and said: "The Master would stand there and say good-bye to the devotees."

M. then came to the southeast veranda of the Master's room and pointed out where Hazra would sit on his asana. During this visit, there was a mat where the Master's nephews would sit and talk to devotees.

Next, M. went to the Radhakanta temple and received sanctified water from the priest.

Readers of Ramakrishna's life know the story of the broken foot of Krishna's image and how the Master repaired it. Nirmal Kumar Roy supplied an important piece of information about that image in his book *Dakshineswar Kali Mandirer Itivritta*:

> The present image of Krishna is made of black stone and its height is 21½ inches, and Radha's image is made of eight metals and its height is 16 inches. These two images are now on the main altar and worshipped daily. This image of Krishna was made during Rani Rasmani's time but was kept in a separate room, because the Master advised her to continue worshipping the broken Krishna. Now that original broken Krishna is in the north room of the Krishna temple, and it was worshipped until 1929. Then while the image was being refurbished, the foot again broke and it was temporarily repaired. Finally in 1930, the trustees of the Kali temple decided to install the spare image on the main altar and replace the broken one.[8]

Swami Nityatmananda continued: M. accompanied the devotees to the Krishna temple and bowed down to the deity; then he bowed down

*Nityatmananda was referring to the occasion on which Swamiji sang the following song:
Meditate, O my mind, on the Lord Hari,
The Stainless One, Pure Spirit through and through.
Ever more beauteous in fresh-blossoming love
That shames the splendour of a million moons,
Like lightning gleams the glory of His form,
Raising erect the hair for very joy.

to Lord Shiva from the courtyard, and then went to the Kali temple. He bowed down to the Divine Mother, sat down at the left end of the veranda, and meditated in front of Her. Nakul, Ramlal's son, gave sanctified water to M. and put a vermillion mark on his forehead.

When M. was in the natmandir, Amrita asked, "Where was the Master when you asked him if there would be any more singing on that evening during your fourth visit?" M. showed him the spot in the middle of the natmandir. Pointing to the second pillar on the left from the north, M. said: "As he listened to Nilkantha's Yatra performance, the Master embraced this pillar and wept." M. then embraced the pillar.

M. was a wonderful guide. He took visitors to important spots in the temple garden, as well as to those that were less significant, so they could get a complete picture of that holy place. He took devotees to the kitchen where Mother Kali's food was cooked and to the room where food staples are stored. He also showed them the western ghat of the Gazi-tala pond, east of the Kali temple, where the Mother's puja utensils were washed. From the ghat, he pointed out Jadu Mallick's garden house where the Master would go for a walk. The Master was fond of Jadu Mallick, and the caretaker of his garden house was very devoted to the Master.

Mr. Jinwala said to M.: "It is said that Ramakrishna tried to kill himself with Kali's sword when he did not have the vision of the Divine Mother. Have you heard this from the Master?"

M.: "No, I didn't hear that."

Dr. De Mello: "Is it in the *Gospel* that you recorded?"

M.: "No, it is not in the *Gospel*. Someone might have written about it, but I didn't."

Dr. De Mello: "The Master himself was God. Then why did he try to kill himself in order to see God?"

M.: "The Master said that the Divine Mother had taken the cosmic form. She Herself was manifest in the Master's body. The goddess said to him that his form was a special manifestation among all forms. Out of longing for Mother, as a devotee, the Master tried to kill himself. He himself was a devotee and also God."[9]

M. crossed the courtyard to the Chandni ghat and then walked down the steps to the Ganges. He sprinkled the holy Ganges water on his head, bowed down to Mother Ganges, and repeated a mantra. On his way to the nahabat, he touched his head to the semicircular veranda of the Master's room. Pointing to the northwest corner of the northern veranda, M. said: "One day I saw the Master himself sweeping this place with a broom. Seeing me, he said, 'The Divine Mother walks here.' He used to see the

Mother's divine play with his open eyes."[10]

Next M. bowed down to the front step of the nahabat, saying:

Holy Mother, the Master, and the devotees walked on these steps while entering the room. This nahabat is the new Shakti-pith [a holy place consecrated to the Divine Mother]. It was Holy Mother's place of tapasya, austerities. She lived here for a long time. She was extremely shy. There were bamboo curtains all around the veranda, and she lived here like a bird in a cage. Setting aside her personal comfort, she served the Master. In this small room, she lived with Golap-ma, Yogin-ma, Sister Lakshmi, and sometimes with Gauri-ma. Here also she stored the Master's groceries and other necessities. Once a day at 3 o'clock in the morning she would go to the jungle to answer the call of nature and then bathe in the Ganges. She would practise japa and meditation, and then cook for the Master. What superhuman patience, forbearance, self-control, renunciation, and self-sacrifice she had![11]

M. bowed down to the first step of the stairs leading to the upper floor of the nahabat and remarked: "Holy Mother used to sit here and repeat her mantra. Sitting here for long hours caused her to develop rheumatism, which continued throughout her life."

M. then went to the bakul-tala ghat and pointed to a cement platform at the west of the path leading to the Panchavati. He said: "I saw the Master seated here 41 years ago. I vividly remember it now, and it feels like it happened yesterday."

M. touched his head to the middle of the bakul-tala ghat and said: "Just before Chandramani passed away, her body was brought here. She was lying on a rope cot. Two legs of the cot were in the Ganges and the other two legs were on the cement ghat. Holding his mother's feet, the Master said tearfully: 'Mother, who are you that carried me in your womb?' He meant that she was not an ordinary mother. She must be like Kaushalya, Devaki, Mayadevi, Mary, and Shachi — who were mothers of Rama, Krishna, Buddha, Jesus, and Chaitanya respectively."[12]

M. said that Narendra once sat on the south embankment of this ghat and sang for the Master an Agamani song [a special song sung inviting Mother Durga to come for Her worship] that he had learned shortly before." M. bowed down to that spot.[13]

Seeing a Shiva image inside the Sadhan-kutir, M. remarked: "During the Master's time, this brick building and the Shiva image were not here. There was only a thatched hut with a mud floor."

M. circumambulated the altar that surrounded the banyan tree in the Panchavati; then he touched the second, third, and fourth steps of its

southern stairs and bowed down. He said: "The Master used to sit here
and put his feet on the lower step. He would talk about God with Keshab
Sen, Vijaykrishna Goswami, and other devotees." Standing at the northwest corner of the Panchavati, M. related one of his sweetest memories:
"One day from here I saw the Master coming from the pine grove. There
was a thick dark cloud behind him and it was reflected on the Ganges."[14]

M. touched and bowed down to the ashwatha tree in the Panchavati,
which the Master had planted himself. He then went under the madhavi
vine, which was nearly 50 feet long and connects the banyan and the ashwatha trees. The Master brought the vine from Vrindaban and planted it
there himself. M. bowed down to it and said: "This madhavi is very dear
to us. The Master took care of it like a mother and helped it grow. The
divine touch of his hand lives within this vine. Blessed is this plant! Perhaps this vine is a great soul, living incognito like the Yamala and Arjuna
trees who were Jaya and Vijaya, the gatekeepers of Vishnu, but were
cursed and became trees."[15] Pointing to the southwest step of the Panchavati, M. said: "On his birthday, the Master sat on this step and gave advice
to Vijaykrishna Goswami and Kedar Chattopadhyay, who were seated on
his left. Tota Puri lived in the open space of the Panchavati and the Master
visited him there quite often."[16]

On the way to the bel-tala from the Panchavati, M. pointed out a spot
on the east side of the path and said: "There was a fence here in which one
of the Master's feet became stuck. He fell down and broke his right arm.
He was in ecstasy and had no body-consciousness."

M. then went to the bel-tala, where the Master had practised Tantric
sadhana. Around the bel tree is a circular altar that is two feet high. M.
circumambulated it, keeping the altar to his right.

Pointing to a spot on the east side of the altar, M. said: "One day
according to the instruction of the Master, a devotee [M. himself] was
meditating facing the east. A few hours passed. The Master came to see
the devotee and stood in front of him. Seeing the Master, the devotee was
overwhelmed with joy and bowed down to him. He saw his Chosen Deity
on whom he had been meditating in his heart."[17] M. bowed down to that
spot where he had once seen the Master standing. He then sat on the altar
to meditate and asked the devotees to do the same.

Later M. pointed to the embankment next to the Ganges and said, "At
midnight the Master would pace back and forth here and listen to the *anahata* [the music of the spheres]."

M. went to the kuthi (Mathur's mansion) and entered the southwest
room. He bowed down and said: "The Master lived in this room for 16

years. His mother also lived here. He had many visions and spiritual experiences in this room. Trailokya, Mathur's son, used to live upstairs when he visited Dakshineswar. The Master's nephew Akshay died here in 1869, and in 1871 the Master moved to the room in the northwest corner of the temple complex and his mother moved to the upper floor of the nahabat."

Nirmal Kumar Roy wrote in *Dakshineswar Kali Mandirer Itivritta*:

> In the early days, Rani Rasmani and Mathur arranged for the Master to stay in the kuthi; but when Akshay died, the Master did not want to stay there anymore. However, an opportunity soon came for the Master to move from the kuthi, as Mathur wanted to repair and paint the building. So it was arranged for the Master to move temporarily to the northwest corner room of the temple complex, which had been used as the storeroom for the Vishnu temple, while his mother would move to the upper room of the nahabat. When the repairs and painting were done, the Master said that he did not want to return to the kuthi. Mathur granted the Master's request and moved the Vishnu temple supplies to one of the rooms in the eastern complex.[18]

Swami Nityatmananda continued: M. stood on the southern ghat of the goose pond, located just east of the Panchavati. M. said: As the Master could not touch metal, someone would fill his brass water pot at this pond, and then pour water for him to wash himself after he had answered the call of nature. He never used holy Ganges water for this purpose. He returned to his room after washing his hands and feet and changing his cloth. Once the Master stood on this ghat and said to Narendra: "Look here. Come a little more often. You are a newcomer. On first acquaintance people visit each other quite often, as is the case with a lover and his sweetheart."[19]

A picnic was arranged at the Gazi-tala, because the temple manager would not allow the devotees to have it in the Panchavati. M. was a little hurt. A devotee then talked about this to Kiran Chandra Datta, the receiver* of the Dakshineswar temple. He immediately wrote a strong memo to the temple manager: "Please allow Revered M. and the devotees to have a picnic wherever they want. And clean that place."

M. was very pleased and remarked:

> You see, every spot of Dakshineswar is holy. But God himself had picnics there with the devotees, so that place is saturated with joy. If we have our picnic there, then that joy will be awakened in our minds. One can experience bliss by imitating a particular lila enacted by God. The Master experienced the bliss of Brahman while sitting under that banyan tree,

---

*A person appointed by a court administrator to take into custody the property or funds of others, pending litigation.

and it still bears witness to those events. The memory of the Master's joyful picnic in that place will intensify the joy of our own picnic. Thus one can connect oneself with God. Otherwise, mere eating is nothing but worldly enjoyment.[20]

According to Swami Nityatmananda, M. had picnics with the devotees in the Panchavati on 14 January 1924, 30 November 1924, and 28 January 1926.

On 30 November 1924, M. made a comment about the picnic:

It is a joyful function. We shall be able to stay at Dakshineswar for a long time because of this picnic. The minds of the devotees will get deep impressions of the trees, garden, ponds, ghats, temples, and so on. Later these will remind them of Mother Kali and the Master. Sometimes the Master would encourage devotees to arrange picnics in the temple garden. An impression becomes deeper if it is connected with good food. The Master would adopt many methods to direct the devotees' minds towards God. Whenever any devotee would come, the Master served him with prasad or gave him something to eat. It would serve two purposes: First, that devotee would remember the food he had eaten; people generally forget verbal advice. Second, the devotee would develop love for the Master unconsciously. His mind would think of the Master's affection because he had given him some food to eat. Eventually this memory will protect him, and give him strength when he struggles for breath in the ocean of maya, almost drowning. Every one of the Master's actions was meant to set an example for others.[21]

While M. and the devotees were returning to Calcutta, M. remarked: "Every particle of that dust of the Panchavati is holy and vibrant because it was touched by the feet of God. The trees, plants, and vines of Dakshineswar are gods, ancient rishis, and devotees who are still seeing and enjoying the divine play of God. Truly, they are the witnesses of the avatar's lila." Whenever M. visited Dakshineswar, he always embraced and bowed down to some old trees.[22]

In the eyes of a lover, everything related to the beloved is sweet and precious. M. tried to imprint his experiences with the Master on the minds of his visitors, thus giving them a taste of the divine bliss that M. had enjoyed. Everything in Dakshineswar — the dust, brick, tiles, wood, stones, temples, images, trees, plants — was made living by the touch of a God-man, so they were holy to M. Dakshineswar is heaven on earth. All deities are living, because the Master brought life to them. The Master tested the image of the Mother with a piece of cotton and felt the Mother breathing. He repaired the broken foot of Krishna's image as a surgeon repairs the broken foot of a man. In fact, M. expanded the horizon of our imagination. The same sun and moon that witnessed the divine plays of Rama, Krishna, Buddha, Jesus, and Chaitanya also witnessed Ramakrishna's divine play.

M.'s farsightedness

M. was a farsighted rishi: By the Master's grace he sensed what would happen in the future. On 9 December 1883, M. wrote in the *Gospel:*

> The Master started for the Panchavati accompanied by M. No one else was with them. Sri Ramakrishna with a smile narrated to him various incidents of the past years of his life.
>
> Master: "You see, one day I saw a supernatural figure covering the whole space from the Kali temple to the Panchavati. Do you believe this?"
>
> M. remained silent with wonder. He plucked one or two leaves from a branch in the Panchavati and put them in his pocket.
>
> Master: "See there — that branch has been broken. I used to sit under it."
>
> M.: "I took a young twig from that tree — I have it at home."
>
> Master (*with a smile*): "Why?"
>
> M.: "I feel happy when I look at it. After all this is over, this place will be considered very holy."[23]

M.'s *Gospel* has made Dakshineswar a place of pilgrimage like Ayodhya, Vrindaban, Varanasi, and Rameswaram. His vivid descriptions have drawn people from all over the world to visit Dakshineswar and to learn more about Ramakrishna. Moreover, inspired by the *Gospel,* many young people have left home and joined the Ramakrishna Order. Thirty-five years after that conversation he recorded in the *Gospel,* M. witnessed the remarkable results of his detailed chronicle.

In October 1918, M. told devotees about the following incident: "Lord Ronaldshey, the present governor of Bengal, read *The Gospel of Sri Ramakrishna,* and then went to Dakshineswar with his wife and secretaries. He saw those places which had been mentioned in the Gospel. He also greeted Ramlal, knowing that he was the Master's nephew."[24]

The world is always changing, but truth never changes. Dakshineswar is very different now from what it was during Ramakrishna's time, yet M.'s chronicle of the Master's message is for all times and will remain vital as long as the sun and moon exist.

Briefly, here are the important places to see in Dakshineswar: Chandni (porch), Bhavatarini Kali, Natmandir, Krishna temple and the courtyard, the 12 Shiva temples, Ramakrishna's room, Nahabat, Bakul-tala ghat, Panchavati, Sadhan Kutir, Bel-tala (Panchamundi), Gazi-tala, and Kuthi. The stories of these places and their connection with Ramakrishna have been elaborately described in *How to Live with God: In the Company of Ramakrishna* (see the chapter "Stage for Ramakrishna's Divine Play").

M. made a wonderful comment about Dakshineswar: "The spiritual fire is blazing intensely there, and whoever goes there will be purified. The body does not burn, but mental impurities are consumed in no time. Then a person can attain immortality. God himself, in a physical form, lived there for 30 years! One can tangibly feel the spirituality at Dakshineswar."[25]

Ramakrishna's pilgrimage

In 1868, Ramakrishna went on a pilgrimage with Mathur and his family. There is a difference between our pilgrimage and Ramakrishna's. We see the temples and images, but the Master saw the living deities. It was not necessary for the Master to attain virtue from his pilgrimage; rather, he visited the holy places to enhance the glory of those places. Regarding an avatar going on pilgrimage, Swami Saradananda wrote in *Sri Ramakrishna and His Divine Play*:

> When mentioning holy places, the Master told us many times in his simple language: "Look, know for certain that there is a special manifestation of God where for a long time many people have practised austerities, concentration, meditation, japa, prayer, and worship in order to attain His vision. Their devotion has caused a spiritual atmosphere to solidify in that place, so one can easily become spiritually awakened and have a vision of God there. Throughout the ages many monks, devotees, and perfected souls have visited sacred places to see God and call on Him wholeheartedly, shunning all other desires. That's why there is a special manifestation of God in those places. However, God exists everywhere equally. If one digs deeply enough, one can find water in any place. But one doesn't need to dig for water where there is a well, a pool, a pond, or a lake. One can get water there at any time. It is like that."[26]

When one visits a holy place and worships the deities there, one's mind is purified, and one develops a longing to hear more about God. M. said:

> According to the scriptures, one should circumambulate a holy place at least three times because that makes an indelible impression on the mind of the pilgrim. But once is enough for those who have a good memory and a strong power of observation.
> What should one do in a holy place? First, drink a little of the deity's sanctified water. Second, sit in front of the deity for a while. Third, sing or

chant the glories of God. Fourth, feed the holy people. Fifth, bring some fruits and sweets to offer. Sixth, don't be stingy or cheat anybody.[27]

During that pilgrimage, Ramakrishna first went to Vaidyanath. Here he asked Mathur to feed and clothe the poor people because he saw God in them. When he visited Varanasi, he saw in a vision that the city of Shiva was truly made of gold. At the Manikarnika cremation ground he witnessed how Shiva gives liberation to those who passed away in Varanasi. According to the custom, Ramakrishna bathed at the confluence of the Ganges and Yamuna in Prayag.

At the Dhruva ghat in Mathura, he saw Vasudeva carrying Krishna while crossing the Yamuna. Absorbed in an ecstatic mood, he visited Shyamkunda, Radhakunda, Govardhan, and other places connected with Krishna's divine play. While staying in Vrindaban, he stayed at Faujdari Kunja, near the Nidhuban. Hriday accompanied him to bathe at the Kaliya-daman ghat on the Yamuna in Vrindaban. He went into samadhi in front of the Banki Bihari temple in Vrindaban. A few years later, he went to Navadwip with Mathur by boat and had a vision of Gauranga and Nityananda.

When we visit these holy places, various incidents of Ramakrishna's life come to our minds. Chaitanya, Ramakrishna, and other illumined souls made the holy places vibrant through their spiritual powers, visions, and experiences. We become blessed then hearing the stories of their divine play.

Places of Ramakrishna's final lila

Ramakrishna's final lila began on 25 September 1885 at Shyampukur house in Calcutta and ended at Cossipore garden house on 16 August 1886. In the middle of 1885, the Master developed cancer in his throat, so the devotees moved him to Calcutta for treatment. Dr. Mahendralal Sarkar was his physician and his conversations with the Master have been wonderfully recorded by M. in the *Gospel*. Holy Mother prepared the Master's meals and the young disciples took responsibility for nursing him. At Shyampukur on Kali Puja night, the devotees worshipped the Master as an embodiment of the Divine Mother. As the polluted atmosphere of Calcutta was not good for the Master, following the doctor's advice, the devotees moved the Master to Cossipore garden house on 11 December 1885.

M. as a guide for the Cossipore garden house

On 30 March 1924, M. visited Dakshineswar and the Cossipore garden house with Dr. De Mello, Mr. Jinwalla and his wife (a Parsi couple), and

some other devotees. In the car on the way to Cossipore, Swami Nityatmananda pointed out to Dr. De Mello in a whisper the Cossipore cremation ground where the Master's body had been cremated. The doctor then
asked M., who was in the back seat, "Shall we stop at the Cossipore cremation ground?" Hearing the words "Cossipore cremation ground" M.
felt deep pain as if he had been stung by a scorpion. His face turned grave.
Nityatmananda asked De Mello not to raise that topic again because this
would cause M. great pain.[28]

The car stopped at the western side of the Cossipore house. M. bowed
down at the entrance. An Armenian Christian family was renting the
house at the time. They were very hospitable and allowed people to visit
the home where the Master had lived.

While waiting for permission to enter the main house, M. showed
them the kitchen, the servant's quarters, and the room where Holy Mother
had lived in the northeastern corner of the first floor. He pointed out three
rooms that had previously been the stable where the young attendants of
the Master had stayed. M. removed his shoes, entered one of the rooms,
and said: "One morning here the young disciples of the Master, who later
became monks, sang this song about Shiva: 'Lord Shiva is adorned with
the crescent moon on his forehead, the Ganges in his matted hair, and a
trident in his hand. His body is besmeared with the ashes, a garland hangs
around his neck.' The all-renouncing Shiva was their ideal. This was the
training place for future teachers."

M. then walked to the pond, which was to the east of the house. He
went to the southern ghat and said, "Sometimes we used to sit here." He
then pointed to a mango tree south of the ghat and said: "Narendra would
sit under that tree, light a dhuni fire, and practise meditation. During the
summer, the devotees would meditate at this ghat. It has been 37 years
since I last visited this place."

M. walked to that holy mango tree and embraced it, and then bowed
down. When he arose, he continued: "One night Narendra was meditating near the dhuni fire. His body was covered with mosquitoes, but he had
no body-consciousness. His mind was absorbed in Brahman."

When the group reached the garden path to the east of the house, M.
pointed out a pine tree and said, "This is our old friend." M. and his companions thus circumambulated the Cossipore house where the Master
lived during his last days.

When M. and his companions received permission to enter the house,
they climbed the steps to the Master's second-floor room and entered it.
M. prostrated on the floor at the southwest corner, where the Master had

rested while he was alive. There is a door on the south wall of the room and a shuttered window on the west. M. pointed to an area two yards from the western window and said, "The Master's bed was here." The Master would lie on a mattress with his head near the southern wall and feet towards the north. M. sat near where the Master's feet would have been and meditated for some time.

He then went out the door on the south side of the room and walked out onto the flat porch overlooking the garden compound; he stood near the western railing and held on to it. Then he and the devotees went downstairs to thank the host. After that, the party and M. left for his Calcutta residence at the Morton Institution.

In the evening gathering, Dr. Bakshi asked: "Why didn't the Master sleep on a bed?"

M.: "It was convenient for the Master to sleep on the floor. His body was weak. There was a mat on the cement floor, then on top of that a cotton carpet, and over that a mattress."

Jagabandhu: "Did the Master ever walk on the porch?"

M.: "Seldom."

Jagabandhu: "Did he go for walk in the garden?"

M.: "A few times. He walked on 1 January 1886, of course. The Master fulfilled his wish.[29]

On 1 January 1886, Sri Ramakrishna became the wish-fulfilling tree. He walked in the garden and blessed the devotees, saying, "Be illumined."

On 30 November 1924, M. revisited Cossipore with Dr. Bakshi, Binay, and Jagabandhu, but this time he was not allowed to enter the house. The Christian gentleman was a patient of Dr. Bakshi, who presented him with a picture of Ramakrishna and asked him to hang it on the wall of the Master's room. The man later did so, but his pastor objected and asked him to remove the picture. Moreover, the man did not want to do anything that would upset his Christian community. However, M. gave the Christian gentleman a copy of *The Gospel of Sri Ramakrishna — Part 1*, and asked, "May we have a look around the garden?"

"Of course," he replied.

The devotees were upset because they were not allowed to see the Master's room. With a heavy heart, M. said to Dr. Bakshi: "Here one should come as a student and not as a preacher."

As they walked around the garden surrounding the house, M. said: "Every particle of dust in Dakshineswar and Cossipore is pure. These trees are gods and rishis incognito. They are hiding their true form to watch and enjoy the divine play of the avatar." M. pointed out an old tree at the southeast corner of the garden near a bend in the path and remarked: "This tree felt the same air that touched Sri Ramakrishna's body." M. then embraced that tree.

M. stopped near the bend in the path. All of a sudden he became indrawn and his eyes became moist. He said: "What a great event took place on this spot! It was 1 January 1886, a holiday. Girish and other devotees were visiting from Calcutta. The Master felt a little better, so he came down from his room and walked in the garden. It was 3 o'clock in the afternoon. The devotees followed the Master. When the Master stopped at this spot, the devotees bowed down to him one after another. He blessed them, saying, 'May you be illumined.' This blessing awakened their inner consciousness and they each had a vision of their Ishta [Chosen Deity]. Everyone was overwhelmed with bliss."

M. then became quiet and still. When he regained his normal mood, he prostrated himself on the garden path where the Master had become the kalpataru, the wish-fulfilling tree, and put some dust from the path on his head. He slowly got up and walked to the car, giving the garden one last and lingering look.[30]

In the footsteps of Ramakrishna

Throughout the world there are many holy places frequented by people on pilgrimage who desire to draw closer to God. The life of Ramakrishna is made more real and immediate when it is visualized against the landscape that was its setting. Goethe said: "If you want to understand the poet you must visit his country."

Following the footsteps of Ramakrishna, in 1997, Nirmal Kumar Roy wrote a book in Bengali called *Charan Chinha Dhare* (*Following the Footsteps of Ramakrishna*). In this book he wrote a history of the places that Ramakrishna visited, their present condition, and how to reach them. He described Calcutta, North 24-Parganas, Howrah, Hooghly, Bankura, Burdwan, Nadia, Khulna in East Bengal, Vaidyanath, Varanasi, Prayag, Mathura, and Vrindaban. In 1979, he wrote another important book in Bengali called *Sri Sri Ramakrishna Samsparshe* (*People Who Came in Contact with Ramakrishna*). The main source for these two books is M.'s *Sri Sri Ramakrishna Kathamrita*.

After closely associating with M. for a number of years, Swami Nityatmananda wanted to visit the places in and around Calcutta and its environs where Ramakrishna had gone. He considered them to be modern places of pilgrimage. When he first approached M. with his plan, M. discouraged him. But later, observing Nityatmananda's enthusiasm for seeing the holy places connected with the Master, M. joyfully encouraged him and offered guidance. When Nityatmananda asked where he should start, M. replied: "Be quick! Please start from this area [central Calcutta]."

On 27 May 1932 (eight days before he passed away) M. dictated a list of places that Nityatmananda recorded:

1. Rajendra Mitra's house on Bechu Chatterjee Street, which Ramakrishna visited. Keshab Sen came there to meet the Master.
2. Thanthania Kali Temple: When the Master was 16 years old, he used to sing there for the Divine Mother.
3. The Sanskrit Tol (school) belonging to Ramakrishna's brother Ramkumar was located on Bechu Chatterjee Street. Later the school building housed a shop selling puffed rice. At present, a Radha-Krishna [Shyamsundar] temple is there.
4. The Master and Ramkumar lived in a hut with a tiled roof just four buildings from the Sanskrit school, on the same side of Bechu Chatterjee Street. The hut [belonged to Govinda Chatterjee] was just opposite a house belonging to the Lahas. The Hare Press presently occupies the place where the hut was.
5. Digambar Mitra's house on Jhamapukur Lane, where the Master performed rituals for the family shrine.
6. Vijaykrishna Goswami's residence at 27 Mechua Bazar Street. When Goswami became ill, the Master visited him there.
7. The Navavidhan Brahmo Samaj at Mechua Bazar, which the Master visited. He also went to Ishan Mukhopadhyay's house on the same street and had lunch there.
8. Keshab Sen's Lily Cottage, at the junction of Mechuabazar Street and Circular Road [now Acharya Prafulla Chandra Roy Road], which Ramakrishna visited many times. Keshab worshipped the feet of the Master in the shrine on the upper floor.
9. Badurbagan, where the Master went to visit Ishwar Chandra Vidyasagar.
10. The Sadharan Brahmo Samaj on Cornwallis Street [now Bidhan Sarani], where the Master went to meet Narendra.
11. Narendra's house in Simulia [Simla].
12. Ram's house behind the Oxford Mission. [It has since been demolished to make way for a road.]
13. Manomohan's house on Simla Street.
14. Kashi Mallick's temple on Harrison Road [now Mahatma Gandhi Road], where the Master went to visit Mother Simhabahini.
15. Mani Mallick's house at Sinduriapatti, where Ramakrishna attended a Brahmo festival. It has since been replaced by a Jain temple.

16. Sutapatti, Barabazar, where the Master visited Lakshminarayan Marwari.
17. Chaitanya Sabha and Navin Sen's house at Coolootola.
18. Rani Rasmani's house at Jan Bazar.
19. The Methodist Church in Taltala, where the Master attended a service.
20. Kalighat, South Calcutta.
21. Museum.
22. Alipore Zoo.
23. Jagannath Ghat.
24. Koila Ghat.
25. The Maidan, where the Master saw a circus perform.
26. The Viceroy's palace. The Master stood outside and made a remark: "The Mother revealed to me that the palace was merely clay bricks laid one on top of another."
27. Jaygopal Sen's house at Ratan Sarkar Square at Barabazar.
28. Jadu Mallick's house at Pathuriaghata.
29. The Adi Brahmo Samaj at Chitpur.
30. Devendra Nath Tagore's house at Jorasanko.
31. The Harisabha at Jorasanko.
32. A devotee's house at Haritaki-bagan.
33. Ram's garden and Suresh's garden at Kankurgachi.
34. Dr. Kali's house at Shyambazar.
35. The house in Shyampukur where Ramakrishna received treatment.
36. The houses of the following devotees at Baghbazar: Nanda Basu, Golap-ma, Yogin-ma, Balaram Basu, and Girish Chandra Ghosh.
37. The following temples at Baghbazar: Siddheswari Kali, Madanmohan.
38. The Master came to our [M.'s] rented house at Kambuliatola at Shyampukur.
39. Vishwanath Upadhyay's house at Shyampukur.
40. Deven Majumdar's house on Nimu Goswami Lane, North Calcutta.
41. The Star Theatre on Beadon Street, where the Master saw Chaitanya Lila performed.
42. Adhar Sen's house at Shobhabazar.
43. Dinanath Mukhopadhyay's house near the Baghbazar bridge, which Ramakrishna visited with Mathur.
44. Kashi Mitra's house in Nandan-bagan, where the Master attended the festival of the Brahmo Samaj.
45. Mahendra Goswami's house in Simulia.

That very day Swami Nityatmananda visited several places in the morning, afternoon, and evening. He reported his experiences to M. in detail the next day so that M. could visualize those places that had been touched by the feet of Sri Ramakrishna.

On 28 May 1932, M. told Nityatmananda about some other places connected with the Master. These are located in various Calcutta suburbs.

1. Cossipore garden house.
2. Beni Pal's garden house in Sinthi.
3. Sarvamangala temple in Cossipore.
4. Cossipore cremation ground.
5. Dasha Mahavidya temple in Baranagore.
6. The house of Thakur-dada (Narayandas Bandyopadhyay), who was a narrator of the scriptures in Baranagore.
7. Joy Mukhopadhyay's shrine and the Ganges ghat at Baranagore.
8. Two houses in Baranagore belonging to Haramohan and Mani Mallick.
9. Patbari of Bhagavat Acharya (a Vaishnava Ashrama) in Baranagore.
10. Natabar Panja's oil mill at Alambazar.
11. Two garden houses in Dakshineswar owned by Shambhu Mallick and Jadu Mallick.
12. Dakshineswar temple garden, the playground of Sri Ramakrishna.
13. Swami Yogananda's house in Dakshineswar.
14. The house of Rasik, who was a sweeper of the Dakshineswar temple. This is where the Master secretly cleaned the privy with his own hair and prayed to the Divine Mother, "Mother, destroy the ego of my brahminical caste."
15. Krishnakishore's house in Ariadaha.
16. Gadadhar's Patbari at Ariadaha.
17. Mati Sil's Thakur-bari and lake in Belgharia. To demonstrate how to meditate on the formless God, the Master showed a devotee [M.] big fish swimming freely in the lake. One can imagine the fish as human souls playing in the ocean of Satchidananda.
18. Panihati: Mani Sen's house, the festival grounds, and Raghav Pandit's Thakur-bari.
19. Kamarhati: Krishna temple and Gopal-ma's house.
20. Kalna, where the Master visited Bhagavandas Babaji.
21. A garden house in Sinthi, where the Master met Dayananda Saraswati.
22. Navachaitanya Mitra's house in Konnagar.
23. The timber yard of Vishwanath Upadhyay in Belur, which became the present Belur Math.[31]*

Although Swami Nityatmananda had already visited many of the places listed with M., he began to revisit those places and report back to

---

*This list of Swami Nityatmananda is not complete. Those who want to know the complete list of the places connected with Ramakrishna, should consult Nirmal Kumar Roy's *Charan Chinha Dhare* (in Bengali).

M. During those visits, M. would relate many anecdotes about the Master in which those places played a part. The swami observed that M.'s health was failing day by day, so he tried to collect information from M. about those holy places and anecdotes about the Master concerning them. Nityatmananda also wanted to list their old and new addresses but could not complete the project. M., the unique guide, chronicler, and custodian of Ramakrishna's life and message, left this world on 4 June 1932, a week after Nityatmananda began his project.

The places where Ramakrishna lived and visited still exist and they hold the memory of him. People from all over the world visit Ayodhya (Rama's birthplace), Mathura (Krishna's birthplace) Bethlehem (Christ's birthplace), and Kamarpukur (Ramakrishna's birthplace), and they bring back with them the memory of those avatars. Memory is precious: one cannot think of or understand anything without memory. So the memories of the places connected with the avatars are useful objects for our meditation. Blessed is that memory which connects our minds with God.

The Chandogya Upanishad reminds us how important it is to cultivate firm memory or constant recollectedness of Brahman, God, or holy objects: "When one gathers pure things through the senses within, the mind becomes pure. When the mind is pure, memory becomes firm. When one attains firm memory, one is released from all bonds or knots of maya" (7:26:2).

7

Ramakrishna's Teachings on Meditation

W hy should I meditate?" asked a teenaged Japanese girl in a Catholic retreat in St. Louis.

"Why do you eat three times a day?" replied a monk.

"I eat to nourish and strengthen my body."

"The monk replied, "Meditation nourishes and strengthens the mind. We seek peace and happiness, and we experience those things in the mind. Moreover, meditation helps to change our life and character. Finally it is a tool for God-realization, which is the goal of human life."

The Sanskrit word *dhyana* (meditation) originates from the root verb *dhai*, and it refers to deep thinking or reflecting on a particular object without interruption. Meditation has been defined and described in various Vedanta scriptures. In the Chandogya Upanishad it is said that Narada read all the scriptures but had no knowledge of the Self, and as a result he was overwhelmed with grief. He sought advice from the sage Sanatkumara, who told him that the purpose of meditation is to eradicate sorrow and mentioned its greatness: "Earth meditates, as it were. The mid-region meditates, as it were. Heaven meditates, as it were. The waters meditate, as it were. The mountains meditate, as it were. The gods meditate, as it were. Men meditate, as it were. Therefore he who, among men, attains greatness here on earth seems to have obtained a share of meditation. Thus while small people are quarrelsome, abusive, and slandering, great men appear to have obtained a share of meditation. Meditate on meditation."[1]

Panchavati at Dakshineswar where Ramakrishna practised sadhana. Photo taken 1896.

There are many instructions on meditation in the Upanishads, Bhagavata, Gita, and other scriptures, and those have been described through analogy. Their results also have been explained. All great human achievements come through deep meditation or deep thinking. Similarly, one can liberate oneself through meditation on God or the Atman. *"Yādrishi bhāvanā yasya; siddhir bhavati tādrishi* — Whatever are one's thoughts, so will be the outcome." If the means are perfect, a successful end is bound to come. Through meditation people achieve peace, bliss, and liberation, which cannot be bought from the market.

The descriptions of meditation in the Upanishads are beautiful and poetic. The Shvetashvatara Upanishad uses a simile to explain what meditation is: "By making the body the lower piece of wood, and Om the upper piece, and through the practice of the friction of meditation, one perceives the luminous Self, hidden like the fire in the wood. As oil [exists] in sesame seeds, butter in milk, water in river-beds, and fire in wood, so the Self is realized [as existing] within the self, when a man looks for It by means of truthfulness and austerity."[2] The Mundaka Upanishad says the following: "Om is the bow; the Atman is the arrow; Brahman is said to be the mark. It is to be struck by an undistracted mind. Then the Atman becomes one with Brahman, as the arrow with the target."[3] The Katha Upanishad says: "The self-existent Supreme Lord inflicted an injury upon the sense-organs in creating them with outgoing tendencies; therefore a man perceives only outer objects with them, and not the inner Self. But a calm person, wishing for Immortality, beholds the inner Self with his eyes closed."[4]

In the Bhagavata, Krishna clearly and methodically instructed Uddhava, who was a *jnani*, in meditation:

1. Concentrate the mind on the whole beautiful form of your Chosen Deity.
2. Focus your entire mind on the Ishta's face only and stop all other thoughts. Meditate on his smiling joyful face.
3. Carry that smiling face into the infinite akasha (space) and merge with it.
4. Forget the space and think no more. Be absorbed only in pure Brahman.[5]

In the Gita, Krishna described the sign of meditation: "As a lamp in a windless place does not flicker — that is the simile used for the disciplined mind of a yogi practising concentration on the Self."[6]

Patanjali, author of the Yoga philosophy, described eight limbs of yoga. Meditation is the seventh limb, and he defines it as follows: "*Dharana* or concentration is the holding of the mind on some particular object. An unbroken flow of knowledge about that object is *dhyana* or meditation."[7] There is a difference between concentration and meditation: When a bee rapidly vibrates its wings and makes a *gun-gun* sound before sitting on a flower, that is concentration; but when it sits motionless on the flower and begins to sip honey, that is meditation. During meditation, the aspirant becomes absorbed in the thought of the Ishta (Chosen Deity) and merges into the blissful ocean of Consciousness. The noble sage Patanjali explained that one can meditate on anything that appeals to one as good.[8] One has full freedom to choose any deity or avatar — such as Rama, Krishna, Kali, Buddha, or Jesus — for meditation. But one should be very careful about meditation on sensual objects, because that could ruin one's spiritual life.

What is meditation? We carry in our hearts the person whom we love. We want to offer our best to our beloved. This is a gospel truth. The more we think of our beloved the more our love for that person increases and gradually the relationship deepens. Thus the nature of the beloved enters the mind of the lover. By meditating on God we develop a divine nature, and this is the significance of meditation.

The necessity of meditation

Meditation is necessary in day-to-day life. It gives rest to the body and fills the mind with joy. Moreover, it improves physical health and reduces disease.

During initiation, the guru instructs the devotee in methods of japa and meditation. What does one gain from meditation? One imbibes some qualities of the Ishta. Ramakrishna said: "If you meditate on an ideal you will acquire its nature. If you think of God day and night, you will acquire the nature of God. A salt-doll went into the ocean to measure its depth. It became one with the ocean."[9]

Regarding the necessity of meditation, Swami Vijnanananda said: "The first quality of God is His lordliness. Meditating on God we develop full control over the senses. We must be the lord of ourselves. Second, all actions take effect by the mere wish of God. Similarly, we must turn our wishes into action. Third, God's infinite unconditional love. We must love all like Him. Thus one's meditation develops in proportion to the qualities of God one imbibes."[10]

Most people practise meditation on someone or something. Some meditate on lust and gold and forget space and time. Others think day and night about how to become famous. Some study books rather than practising meditation. Study develops intellectual knowledge but meditation gives experience and conviction. During intellectual reasoning, thought waves vibrate, whereas spiritual experience stops those thought waves and thus leads to samadhi.

Some people practise meditation mechanically and do not taste any joy. As a result, they give it up. Patanjali explained: "*Sa tu dirgha kāla nairantarya satkārasevito dridhabhumih* — Practice becomes firmly established when it has been cultivated uninterruptedly and with devotion over a prolonged period of time."[11] One should not give up good habits, such as study and spiritual disciplines, which form a strong character. One buys a sitar or guitar, plays it for a couple of days, and then hangs it on the wall. How can such a person become a musician? Inspired by a friend, a person buys weights for exercise, practises weightlifting for a few days, and then gives it up. People are not motivated to exert themselves. If a person does not follow the instructions of the guru, how can that person expect the results of meditation? God-realization depends on purity of heart and that comes from practising meditation and renunciation.

Ramakrishna's meditation practice

It is said that only a good student can be a good teacher. From Ramakrishna's very birth, his mind was pure, sinless, and free from worldly desires. As a result, whenever he would focus his concentrated mind on any object, he became fully absorbed in that. He was born with a phenomenal memory. Because of his intense spiritual moods, he attained samadhi at least three times during his boyhood. He experienced his first samadhi as he watched a flock of white cranes flying against a dark cloud. His second experience occurred when he entered ecstasy and lost consciousness on the way to the Vishalakshi temple at Anur. His third happened during the spring festival of Shiva (Shiva-ratri) when he was supposed to act in the role of Shiva. Instead, when he came on stage dressed as Shiva he went into samadhi.

Although Ramakrishna was perfect in meditation from his very birth, in later life, when he was a temple priest in Dakshineswar, he learned various methods of meditation from his gurus Bhairavi Brahmani, Tota Puri, and others. In addition, he practised various paths of sadhana and gained many experiences, which he taught to his disciples and devotees.

We are dumbfounded when we consider the Master's unique methods of meditation. When he was the priest of the Dakshineswar Kali temple, he would practise meditation under an amalaki tree in the jungle near the Panchavati. Previously the area had been a burial ground and people seldom went there, kept away by their fear of ghosts. The Divine Mother brought Ramakrishna's nephew Hriday to look after him during this period of his sadhana. One night, Hriday did not see the Master in his room, so he looked for him and found him in the jungle near the Panchavati. He later asked the Master, "Uncle, what do you do at night in the jungle?" The Master replied: "I meditate under an amalaki tree there. The scriptures say that if a person meditates under an amalaki tree, whatever he desires is fulfilled." Hriday was concerned and tried to dissuade his uncle from going to the jungle at night and tried to frighten him:

> For the next few nights, Hriday continued throwing stones and creating all sorts of disturbances while the Master was sitting for meditation under the amalaki tree. The Master realized this was Hriday's mischief and did not say anything to him. When he realized that the Master could not be frightened away, Hriday could restrain himself no longer. One evening after the Master had gone to that spot, Hriday silently entered the jungle and saw from a distance that the Master had discarded his clothes and sacred thread and was immersed in meditation. Immediately he thought: "Has my uncle gone mad? Only a crazy person behaves like this. It is all right if he meditates, but why does he sit naked?"
>
> Pondering thus Hriday appeared before the Master suddenly and asked: "What is this? Why are you sitting naked, having discarded your cloth and sacred thread?" After being addressed several times, the Master slowly regained his normal consciousness. Then he listened to Hriday's question and replied: "What do you know? One should meditate by becoming free from all ties. From their very birth human beings are tied with eight fetters: hatred, shame, family status, good conduct, fear, fame, pride of caste, and ego. This sacred thread is a fetter because it signifies vainglory: 'I am a brahmin and superior to all.' One should call on Mother with a one-pointed mind, shunning all bondage. That is why I took off those things. When I return after meditation I shall put them on again." Hriday was dumbfounded; he had never before heard such words. Unable to say anything in reply, Hriday left the place.[12]

Ramakrishna's method of teaching meditation

No one can measure Ramakrishna's experiences in the spiritual realm, as there appears to be no limit to them. The Master had no education and had never formally studied the scriptures. How then was it possible for him to acquire so much wisdom? Ramakrishna was omniscient. As an expert and experienced physician diagnoses a disease, prescribes a medicine, and cures the patient; similarly, the experienced, prudent, and omniscient Master knew each individual's nature, tendencies, and his or her past, present, and future. With his subtle vision he could clearly see the disciple's exact problem and suggest a method to get rid of it. His instruction was extremely effective and infallible. There was no mistake in his diagnoses.

The Master was a doctor of worldly maladies, a specialist in the disease of ignorance. The reputation of a good doctor spreads by word of mouth; he or she does not need to advertise. Similarly, people who were disturbed, unhappy, confused, doubtful, lustful, greedy, or grief-stricken would come to Ramakrishna from afar. In addition, hypocrites, atheists, agnostics, and sincere seekers also came. Truly, Dakshineswar was a hospital for those suffering from ignorance.

In an entry dated 23 March 1884, M. mentioned Thakur-dada (Narayandas Bandyopadhyay) of Baranagore, who was a religious storyteller. Tormented with family problems, he came to the Master.

Dada: "I have come here to visit you. I pray to God. But why do I suffer now and then from worries? For a few days I feel very happy. Why do I feel restless afterwards?"

Master: "I see. Things have not been fitted quite exactly. The machine works smoothly if the mechanic fits the cogs of the wheels correctly. In your case there is an obstruction somewhere."[13]

What a beautiful example! If one's teeth are not properly positioned, the formation of one's face is affected and one cannot achieve a good bite. This is uncomfortable. Like an expert orthodontist, the Master was able to alleviate the situation.

The Master continued:

"Pleasure and pain are inevitable in the life of the world. One suffers now and then from a little worry and trouble. A man living in a room full of soot cannot avoid being a little stained."
Dada: "Please tell me what I should do now."
Master: "Chant the name of Hari morning and evening, clapping your hands. Come once more when my arm is healed a bit."[14]

In another entry of 12 April 1885, the Master gave instructions to Mahendra Mukherji:

Master: "Hello! Why haven't you visited Dakshineswar for so long?"
Mahendra: "Sir, I have been away from Calcutta. I was at Kedeti."
Master: "You have no children. You don't serve anybody. And still you have no leisure! Goodness gracious!"

The devotees remained silent. Mahendra was a little embarrassed.

Master (*to Mahendra*): "Why am I saying all this to you? You are sincere and generous. You have love for God."

Mahendra: "You are saying these words for my good."

Master (*to Mahendra*): "Do you practise meditation?"

Mahendra: "Yes, sir. A little."

Master: "Come to Dakshineswar now and then."

Mahendra (*smiling*): "Yes, sir. I will. You know where my knots and twists are. You will straighten them out."

Master (*smiling*): "First come to Dakshineswar; then I shall press your limbs to see where your twists are. Why don't you come?"[15]

Reading this dialogue, it seems that the Master was an orthopedic doctor or a chiropractor. He knew how to break the *chit-jada granthi* (the knot of the Spirit and matter or consciousness and maya). One can break this knot through unbroken meditation, just as a hunter's unerring arrow hits a target.

M. once described the Master's method of meditation to a monk: "During meditation one should focus on the Ishta and visualize him as living. When the Master would meditate, the Divine Mother appeared before his mental eye like a living person. He would talk to her as I am talking to you. I had an opportunity many times to witness the Master's meditation and his dialogue with the Divine Mother....Most people meditate focussing on the lifeless picture of the Ishta, which makes meditation dry and dull, but the Master's meditation was vibrant, sweet, and joyful."[16]

Ramakrishna's instructions on meditation are scattered throughout the pages of *The Gospel of Ramakrishna* and *Sri Ramakrishna and His Divine Play*. It is important to know to whom, where, and when those instructions were given because the Master would adjust his instructions according to the temperament of each individual. The same instruction is not applicable to all. The methods of dualistic meditation and nondualistic meditation are different. The wrong meditation might do more harm than good, just as the wrong medicine can kill a patient. That is why it is not wise to try to learn meditation and japa by reading books. Just as a patient should visit a doctor to cure his or her disease, so a spiritual aspirant should go to a guru or a teacher and follow his or her instructions. The westernized Brahmos could not understand properly the Master's advice, so he told them: "I have said whatever came into my head. Take as much of it as you wish. You may leave off the head and the tail."[17]

What do we need for meditation? A one-pointed and pure mind.

During deep meditation, the aspirant forgets space and time. In this connection the Master said to Dr. Mahendralal Sarkar at the Shyampukur house in Calcutta on 30 October 1885:

> When the mind is united with God, one sees Him very near, in one's own heart. But you must remember one thing. The more you realize this unity, the farther your mind is withdrawn from worldly things. There is the story of Vilwamangal in the *Bhaktamala*. He used to visit a prostitute. One night he was very late in going to her house. He had been detained at home by the shrāddha ceremony of his father and mother. In his hands he was carrying the food offered in the ceremony to feed his mistress. His whole soul was so set upon the woman that he was not at all conscious of his movements. He didn't even know how he was walking. There was a yogi seated on the path, meditating on God with eyes closed. Vilwamangal stepped on him. The yogi became angry, and cried out: 'What? Are you blind? I have been thinking of God, and you step on my body!' 'I beg your pardon,' said Vilwamangal, 'but may I ask you something? I have been unconscious, thinking of a prostitute, and you are conscious of the outer world though thinking of God. What kind of meditation is that?' In the end Vilwamangal renounced the world and went away in order to worship God. He said to the prostitute: 'You are my guru. You have taught me how one should yearn for God.' He addressed the prostitute as his mother and gave her up.[18]

In an entry dated 9 March 1884, M. described the Master's conversation as he was seated with devotees in his room at Dakshineswar.

> Manilal (*to the Master*): "Well, what is the rule for concentration? Where should one concentrate?"
> Master: "The heart is a splendid place. One can meditate there or in the Sahasrara. These are rules for meditation given in the scriptures. But you may meditate wherever you like. Every place is filled with Brahman-Consciousness. Is there any place where It does not exist? Narayana, in Vali's presence, covered with two steps the heavens, the earth, and the interspaces. Is there then any place left uncovered by God? A dirty place is as holy as the bank of the Ganges. It is said that the whole creation is the Virat, the Universal Form of God.
> "There are two kinds of meditation, one on the formless God and the other on God with form. But meditation on the formless God is extremely difficult. In that meditation you must wipe out all that you see or hear. You contemplate only the nature of your Inner Self. Meditating on His Inner Self, Shiva dances about. He exclaims, 'What am I! What am I!' This is called the 'Shiva yoga'. While practising this form of meditation, one directs one's look to the forehead. It is meditation on the nature of

one's Inner Self after negating the world, following the Vedantic method of 'neti, neti'.

"There is another form of meditation, known as the 'Vishnu yoga.' The eyes are fixed on the tip of the nose. Half the look is directed inward and the other half outward. This is how one meditates on God with form. Sometimes Shiva meditates on God with form, and dances. At that time he exclaims, 'Rama! Rama!' and dances about."

Sri Ramakrishna then explained the sacred Word "Om" and the true Knowledge of Brahman and the state of mind after the attainment of Brahmajnana.

Master: "The sound Om is Brahman. The rishis and sages practised austerity to realize that Sound-Brahman. After attaining perfection one hears the sound of this eternal Word rising spontaneously from the navel.

"'What will you gain', some sages ask, 'by merely hearing this sound?' You hear the roar of the ocean from a distance. By following the roar you can reach the ocean. As long as there is the roar, there must also be the ocean. By following the trail of Om you attain Brahman, of which the Word is the symbol. That Brahman has been described by the Vedas as the ultimate goal. But such vision is not possible as long as you are conscious of your ego. A man realizes Brahman only when he feels neither 'I' nor 'you', neither 'one' nor 'many'.

"Think of the sun and of ten jars filled with water. The sun is reflected in each jar. At first you see one real sun and ten reflected ones. If you break nine of the jars, there will remain only the real sun and one reflection. Each jar represents a jiva. Following the reflection one can find the real sun. Through the individual soul one can reach the Supreme Soul. Through spiritual discipline the individual soul can get the vision of the Supreme Soul. What remains when the last jar is broken cannot be described."[19]

In an entry dated 12 April 1885, M. described a visit to Balaram's house in Calcutta when Ramakrishna related to the devotees his meditation practices and visions, so that they could learn from his experiences. The Master told them how a guardian angel would protect his meditation: "During my *sadhana*, when I meditated, I would actually see a person sitting near me with a trident in his hand. He would threaten to strike me with the weapon unless I fixed my mind on the Lotus Feet of God, warning me that it would pierce my breast if my mind strayed from God."[20]

In *Sri Ramakrishna and His Divine Play*, Saradananda wrote about similar experiences of the Master, which are unprecedented:

During the Master's sadhana, when he sat for meditation he felt all the joints of his body lock, making the sound *"khat khat."* It was as if someone within himself were locking those joints with a key to keep him in that sitting position for a long time. And until that inner being unlocked them, he could not move from the spot despite his efforts, or change his position, or use his limbs as he wished, as we can. Sometimes he would see a person seated near him with a trident in hand, saying, "If you think about anything other than God, I will stab your chest with this trident.[21]

While reading about the Master's unique experience, we wish that a guardian angel would protect our meditation by locking our joints and sitting in front of us with a trident. One trident was enough to calm the Master's pure mind, but we would need four guards with a trident, mace, gun, and bomb to control our restless, mischievous minds. A spiritual aspirant can win in spiritual warfare only through the grace of the guru and God.

In the *Gospel* and the *Divine Play*, we find descriptions of vivid visions that the Master experienced during his meditations. The simple and truthful Master did not hide any aspect of those visions from his disciples, and shared with them freely for their spiritual benefit. The Master's mind and speech were united, whereas we hide our weaknesses to protect ourselves from embarrassment. In an entry dated 12 April 1885, M. quotes the Master as saying:

> During my *sadhana* period I had all kinds of amazing visions. I distinctly perceived the communion of Atman. A person exactly resembling me entered my body and began to commune with each one of the six lotuses. The petals of these lotuses had been closed; but as each of them experienced the communion, the drooping flower bloomed and turned itself upward. Thus blossomed forth the lotuses at the centres of Muladhara, Swadhisthana, Anahata, Vishuddha, Ajna, and Sahasrara. The drooping flowers turned upward. I perceived all these things directly.
>
> When I meditated during my *sadhana*, I used to think of the unflickering flame of a lamp set in a windless place.
>
> In deep meditation a man is not at all conscious of the outer world. A hunter was aiming at a bird. A bridal procession passed along beside him, with the groom's relatives and friends, music, carriages, and horses. It took a long time for the procession to pass the hunter, but he was not at all conscious of it. He did not know that the bridegroom had gone by.
>
> A man was angling in a lake all by himself. After a long while the float began to move. Now and then its tip touched the water. The angler was holding the rod tight in his hands, ready to pull it up, when a passer-by stopped and said, "Sir, can you tell me where Mr. Bannerji lives?" There was no reply from the angler, who was just on the point of pulling up the rod. Again and again the stranger said to him in a loud voice, "Sir, can you tell me where Mr. Bannerji lives?" But the angler was unconscious of

everything around him. His hands were trembling, his eyes fixed on the float. The stranger was annoyed and went on. When he had gone quite a way, the angler's float sank under water and with one pull of the rod he landed the fish. He wiped the sweat from his face with his towel and shouted after the stranger. "Hey!" he said. "Come here! Listen!" But the man would not turn his face. After much shouting, however, he came back and said to the angler, "Why are you shouting at me?" "What did you ask me about?" said the angler. The stranger said, "I repeated the question so many times and now you are asking me to repeat it once more!" The angler replied, "At that time my float was about to sink; so I didn't hear a word of what you said."

A person can achieve such single-mindedness in meditation that he will see nothing, hear nothing. He will not be conscious even of touch. A snake may crawl over his body, but he will not know it. Neither of them will be aware of the other.

In deep meditation the sense-organs stop functioning; the mind does not look outward. It is like closing the gate of the outer court in a house. There are five objects of the senses: form, taste, smell, touch, and sound. They are all left outside.

At the beginning of meditation the objects of the senses appear before the aspirant. But when the meditation becomes deep, they no longer bother him. They are left outside. How many things I saw during meditation! I vividly perceived before me a heap of rupees, a shawl, a plate of sweets, and two women with rings in their noses. "What do you want?" I asked my mind. "Do you want to enjoy any of these things?" "No," replied the mind, "I don't want any of them. I don't want anything but the Lotus Feet of God." I saw the inside and the outside of the women, as one sees from outside the articles in a glass room.[22]

In Vyasa's commentary on the Yoga Sutra (3:51), four classes of yogis are described:

1. *Prathama-kalpika* — beginners who have just begun to develop powers by practising yoga.
2. *Madhu-bhumika* — those who have attained knowledge and are established in truth. At this stage they face all kinds of temptations.
3. *Prajñā-jyoti* — those who have mastered all elements as well as the sense organs.
4. *Atikrānta-bhāvaniya* — those who have renounced all powers and are waiting for liberation.

Ramakrishna faced all kinds of temptations, as he explains here:

How many other visions I saw while meditating during my *sadhana*!

Once I was meditating under the bel-tree when 'Sin' appeared before me and tempted me in various ways. He came to me in the form of an English soldier. He wanted to give me wealth, honour, sex pleasure, various occult powers, and such things. I began to pray to the Divine Mother. Now I am telling you something very secret. The Mother appeared. I said to Her, "Kill him, Mother!" I still remember that form of the Mother, Her world-bewitching beauty. She came to me taking the form of Krishna-mayi*. But it was as if her glance moved the world.

Sri Ramakrishna became silent. Resuming his reminiscences, he said: "How many other visions I saw! But I am not permitted to tell them. Someone is shutting my mouth, as it were. I used to find no distinction between the sacred tulsi and the insignificant sajina leaf. The feeling of distinction was entirely destroyed. Once I was meditating under the banyan when I was shown a Mussalman with a long beard. He came to me with rice in an earthen plate. He fed some other Mussalmans with the rice and also gave me a few grains to eat. The Mother showed me that there exists only One, and not two. It is Satchidananda alone that has taken all these various forms; He alone has become the world and its living beings. Again, it is He who has become food."[23]

In an entry dated 11 October 1884, M. quotes Ramakrishna describing various signs and methods of meditation:

I used to meditate on the flame of a light. I thought of the red part as gross, the white part inside the red as subtle, and the stick-like black part, which is the innermost of all, as the causal.

By certain signs you can tell when meditation is being rightly practised. One of them is that a bird will sit on your head, thinking you are an inert thing.

One can meditate even with eyes open. One can meditate even while talking. Take the case of a man with toothache....Yes, even when his teeth ache he does all his duties, but his mind is on the pain. Likewise one can meditate with eyes open and while talking to others as well.[24]

Again, in an entry dated 26 September 1884, M. described Ramakrishna telling Vijaykrishna Goswami the following: "There was a time when I too would meditate on God with my eyes closed. Then I said to myself: 'Does God exist only when I think of Him with my eyes closed? Doesn't He exist when I look around with my eyes open?' Now, when I look around with my eyes open, I see that God dwells in all beings. He is the Indwelling Spirit of all men, animals and other living beings, trees and plants, sun and moon, land and water."[25]

*A young daughter of Balaram Basu.

Instruction on formless meditation to M.

Meditation on the formless aspect of God is full of mystery because the human mind is capable only of thinking about objects that have a form or a quality. Brahman is devoid of form and qualities. So how can one meditate on Brahman? Vidyaranya Muni described *Nirguna-upasana* in the *Panchadashi* by explaining that when the mind takes the vritti or thought-wave "I am Brahman," that is *Nirguna-upasana*. This ends in the merging of the universe with consciousness, which is simultaneous with the direct perception that the Atman is Brahman. In the Chandogya Upanishad, the Shandilya Vidya also indicates how to meditate on the attributeless Brahman: "All this is Brahman. From It the universe comes forth, in It the universe merges, and in It the universe breathes. Therefore one should meditate on Brahman with a calm mind."[26]

Once the Master described how form remains in formlessness: "Look, during my sadhana I used to look upon God as if He had completely covered the universe like the water of the ocean, and like a fish I was diving, floating, and swimming in that ocean of Satchidananda. Again, sometimes I considered myself to be a pitcher immersed in the water of that indivisible Satchidananda, which pervaded me through and through."[27]

The theological system of *acintya-bheda-abheda-tattva* (inconceivable, simultaneous oneness and difference) reconciles the mystery that God is simultaneously "one with and different from His creation." Lord Chaitanya taught that as souls we are part of God and thus not different from Him in quality; yet at the same time we are different from Him in quantity. This is called *acintya-bheda-abheda-tattva*.

In the entry dated 18 June 1883, M. narrated what happened when the Master attended the Vaishnava Festival at Panihati. On the way back to Dakshineswar, his carriage stopped at Mati Seal's temple garden in Belgharia. M. wrote:

> For a long time the Master had been asking M. to take him to the reservoir in the garden in order that he might teach him how to meditate on the formless God. There were tame fish in the reservoir. Nobody harmed them. Visitors threw puffed rice and other bits of food into the water, and the big fish came in swarms to eat the food. Fearlessly the fish swam in the water and sported there joyously.
>
> Coming to the reservoir, the Master said to M.: "Look at the fish. Meditating on the formless God is like swimming joyfully like these fish, in the Ocean of Bliss and Consciousness."[28]

Meditate in the mind, in a corner of a room, or in the forest

During his second visit to Dakshineswar, M. asked this question: "How, sir, may we fix our minds on God?"

The Master answered:

> Repeat God's name and sing His glories, and keep holy company; and now and then visit God's devotees and holy men. The mind cannot dwell on God if it is immersed day and night in worldliness, in worldly duties and responsibilities; it is most necessary to go into solitude now and then and think of God. To fix the mind on God is very difficult in the beginning, unless one practises meditation in solitude. When a tree is young it should be fenced all around; otherwise it may be destroyed by cattle. To meditate, you should withdraw within yourself or retire to a secluded corner or to the forest.[29]

There are several interpretations regarding the ideal place for meditation. Ramakrishna mentioned three places: *mane*, in the mind; *kone*, in a corner; and *bane*, in the forest. Swami Vijnanananda interpreted *bane* to mean the mind, which is a jungle filled with lust, anger, jealousy, greed, and so on. One should clear away those enemies and then meditate on God. Mane also means heart, so this could mean that one should meditate in the inner chamber of the heart.

Ram Chandra Datta mentioned that *mane* and *kone* are for householders, and *bane* is for monks. Householders should practise meditation in the mind and also in a solitary corner of the house, whereas monks can meditate in the forest away from society.

Swami Virajananda wrote: "Sri Ramakrishna has said, 'You should meditate in a corner, or in the forest, or in the mind.' In a corner means in a private, secluded spot. Spiritual practices should be done in privacy. In the forest means in a solitary spot far away from the noise of people and cities. Meditation in the mind is the essential thing. Wherever you may meditate, install the Chosen Ideal in the inmost recess of your heart."[30]

As Ramakrishna gave this instruction to a householder, we may reverse these instructions: First, it is not possible for a householder to go every day to the forest (*bane*) for meditation. Second, if a person does not have any separate room for a shrine at home, he or she may meditate in the corner (*kone*) of a bedroom or living room. Third, if a person cannot go to the forest or does not have any private space in the home, he or she may meditate within the mind (*mane*).

It is amazing how M. implemented this teaching in his life. After visiting the Master, M.'s mind was imbued with Ramakrishna. He had a very small house, which he named "Thakur Bari" (the Master's House). He had a wife and several children, and there was no privacy or secluded corner for spiritual disciplines. He built a shrine room on the roof of the third floor and practised meditation there. He also planted several flowers in tubs on the roof to create a miniature forest. Later, the monastic disciples of the Master would sometimes meditate with him there. Thus M. fulfilled the Master's instructions.

The Master did not care for any special religious marks or outward display of meditation. He said: "Do you know how a man of sattvic [pure] nature meditates? He meditates in the night, seated upon his bed under the mosquito curtain. The people of his house think that he is asleep. A pure-hearted devotee never makes any outward show of his devotion."[31]

Ramakrishna heard that Ishan was building a big hut on the bank of the Ganges at Bhatpara for the practice of a particular spiritual discipline (*purashcharana*). He asked Ishan eagerly: "Has the hut been built? Let me tell you that the less people know of your spiritual life, the better it will be for you. Devotees endowed with sattva meditate in a secluded corner or in a forest or withdraw into the mind. Sometimes they meditate inside the mosquito net."[32]

Meditation on God with form

The Master taught meditation according to each disciple's temperament. For those who wanted to meditate on a form of a god or goddess, he had these instructions:

> During meditation, think that your mind has been tied to the feet of your Chosen Deity with a silk thread, so that He cannot run away. Why do I say a silk thread? Because those feet are extremely soft and delicate. It would hurt the deity if a different type of string were used." Again, he said: "Should one think of the Chosen Deity during meditation only and then forget Him? Always try to keep part of your mind towards the deity. You have seen how a vigil lamp is kept burning during Durga Puja. One should always keep a lamp near the deity; it should not be allowed to go out. It is inauspicious if a householder's lamp goes out. Likewise, after placing the Chosen Deity in the lotus of the heart, one's meditation should be like the flame of a vigil lamp. While performing household duties one should look inside from time to time to see if the lamp is still burning.[33]

Another time, the Master candidly related his experience: "During my sadhana, before starting meditation on the Chosen Deity I would first imagine that I was washing the mind thoroughly. You see, there are various kinds of dirt and dross [bad thoughts and desires] in the mind. I would imagine that I was flushing out all impurities and placing the Chosen Deity there. Adopt this method."[34]

Meditation on God without form

Many Brahmo devotees who did not believe in God with form (especially Hindu gods and goddesses) would come to see the Master. The Master taught them meditation on God without form. He said to them: "When you sit in meditation, be wholly absorbed in God. During a perfect meditation one would not know if a bird were to perch upon one. When I used to sit in meditation in the theatre-hall of the Kali temple, sparrows and other little birds would perch upon my body and move about in play. People said so."[35]

In a *Gospel* entry dated 26 December 1883, M. narrates the following event:

> Sri Ramakrishna, accompanied by Manilal Mallick, M., and several other devotees, was in a carriage on his way to Ram's new garden.
>
> The garden, which Ram had recently purchased, was next to Surendra's. Ram adored the Master as an Incarnation of God. He visited Sri Ramakrishna frequently at Dakshineswar. Manilal Mallick was a member of the Brahmo Samaj. The Brahmos do not believe in Divine Incarnations.
>
> Master (*to Manilal*): "In order to meditate on God, one should try at first to think of Him as free from upadhis, limitations. God is beyond upadhis. He is beyond speech and mind. But it is very difficult to achieve perfection in this form of meditation.
>
> "But it is easy to meditate on an Incarnation — God born as man. Yes, God in man. The body is a mere covering. It is like a lantern with a light burning inside, or like a glass case in which one sees precious things."
>
> On the way to Surendra's garden, the Master met a monk who believed in God without form.
>
> The Master: "That is good. God is both formless and endowed with form. He is many things more. The Absolute and the Relative belong to one and the same Reality. What is beyond speech and mind is born in the flesh, assuming various forms and engaging in various activities. From that one Om have sprung 'Om Shiva', 'Om Kali', and 'Om Krishna'"[36]

M. writes that on 27 December 1883, Ishan Mukhopadhyay invited the Master for lunch in his Calcutta house. He went with M. and Baburam. He had a wonderful conversation with Shrish, one of Ishan's sons, who was practising law in Calcutta.

> Master (*to Shrish*): "Well, what suits your taste — God with form or the formless Reality? But to tell you the truth, He who is formless is also

endowed with form. To His bhaktas He reveals Himself as having a form. It is like a great ocean, an infinite expanse of water, without any trace of shore. Here and there some of the water has been frozen. Intense cold has turned it into ice. Just so, under the cooling influence, so to speak, of the bhakta's love, the Infinite appears to take a form. Again, the ice melts when the sun rises; it becomes water as before. Just so, one who follows the path of knowledge — the path of discrimination — does not see the form of God anymore. To him everything is formless. The ice melts into formless water with the rise of the Sun of Knowledge. But mark this: form and formlessness belong to one and the same Reality."[37]

Experience of Brahman during meditation

Brahman is beyond the mind and speech. It cannot be expressed by words. But sometimes the Master hinted at his experiences of Brahman:

One day I had the vision of Consciousness, non-dual and indivisible. At first it had been revealed to me that there were innumerable men, animals, and other creatures. Among them there were aristocrats, the English, the Mussalmans, myself, scavengers, dogs, and also a bearded Mussalman with an earthenware tray of rice in his hand. He put a few grains of rice into everybody's mouth. I too tasted a little.

Another day I saw rice, vegetables, and other food-stuff, and filth and dirt as well, lying around. Suddenly the soul came out of my body and, like a flame, touched everything. It was like a protruding tongue of fire and tasted everything once, even the excreta. It was revealed to me that all these are one Substance, the non-dual and indivisible Consciousness.[38]

I was meditating inside the net. It occurred to me that meditation, after all, was nothing but the imagining of a form, and so I did not enjoy it. One gets satisfaction if God reveals Himself in a flash. Again, I said to myself, "Who is it that meditates, and on whom does he meditate?"

Like the Akasha (space), Brahman is without any modification. It has become manifold because of Shakti. Again, Brahman is like fire, which itself has no colour. The fire appears white if you throw a white substance into it, red if you throw a red, black if you throw a black. The three gunas — sattva, rajas, and tamas — belong to Shakti alone. Brahman Itself is beyond the three gunas. What Brahman is cannot be described. It is beyond words. That which remains after everything is eliminated by the Vedantic process of "Not this, not this," and which is of the nature of Bliss, is Brahman.

Suppose the husband of a young girl has come to his father-in-law's house and is seated in the drawing-room with other young men of his age. The girl and her friends are looking at them through the window. Her friends do not know her husband and ask her, pointing to one young man, 'Is that your husband?' 'No', she answers, smiling. They point to another young man and ask if he is her husband. Again she answers no. They repeat the question, referring to a third, and she gives the same answer. At last they point to her husband and ask, 'Is he the one?' She says neither yes nor no, but only smiles and keeps quiet. Her friends realize that he is her husband.

One becomes silent on realizing the true nature of Brahman.[39]

Atman cannot be realized through this mind; Atman is realized through Atman alone. Pure Mind, Pure Buddhi, Pure Atman — all these are one and the same.

Just think how many things you need to perceive an object. You need eyes; you need light; you need mind. You cannot perceive the object if you leave out anyone of these three. As long as the mind functions how can you say that the universe and the "I" do not exist?

When the mind is annihilated, when it stops deliberating pro and con, then one goes into samadhi, one attains the Knowledge of Brahman. You know the seven notes of the scale: sa, re, ga, ma, pa, dha, ni. One cannot keep one's voice on "ni" very long.[40]

What Tota Puri taught

Ramakrishna said, "As long as I live, so long do I learn." He continually learned from his gurus, pandits, sadhus, hypocrites, nature, and even birds and beasts. In his teachings we find fascinating stories, wonderful analogies and similes, apt examples, humour, singing, and samadhi. As a result his audience always found something new. The ordinary guru gives instructions on only one kind of meditation, but the Master taught various kinds.

Tota Puri was a *Naga* (naked) sannyasi who came to Dakshineswar and taught Advaita sadhana to the Master. He stayed in the Panchavati and made a *dhuni* fire there. His only belongings were a brass water pot, a pair of tongs, a leather seat for meditation, and a thick chadar that he used to cover himself when he slept. Saradananda wrote:

> Every day Tota polished his water pot and tongs until they glittered. Observing his regular habit of meditation, the Master once asked him: "You have realized Brahman and have become perfect. Why then do you meditate every day?" Tota looked at the Master calmly and pointed to the water pot. "See how bright it is," he said. "But will it not lose its lustre if I don't polish it regularly? The mind is like that. It gets tarnished if it isn't kept clean with daily meditation." The keen-sighted Master admitted the truth of this statement but remarked: "Suppose the water pot were made of gold. It wouldn't get tarnished even if it was not polished every day."

"Yes, that is true," Tota admitted with a smile. All his life the Master remembered Tota's words regarding the importance of daily meditation and would often mention that teaching to us.[41]

There are some gurus and teachers who take others' teachings and use them as their own. The Master never did that. When he gave advice to his disciples, he always mentioned who had given that teaching to him. On 30 October 1885, the Master mentioned the jnani's method of meditation:

Nangta [Tota Puri] used to tell me how a *jnani* meditates. Everywhere is water; all the regions above and below are filled with water; man, like a fish, is swimming joyously in that water. In real meditation you will actually see all this.

Take the case of the infinite ocean. There is no limit to its water: Suppose a pot is immersed in it: there is water both inside and outside the pot. The *jnani* sees that both inside and outside there is nothing but Paramatman. Then what is this pot? It is "I-consciousness". Because of the pot the water appears to be divided into two parts; because of the pot you seem to perceive an inside and an outside. One feels that way as long as this pot of "I" exists. When the 'I' disappears, what *is* remains. That cannot be described in words.

Do you know another way a *jnani* meditates? Think of infinite Akasha and a bird flying there, joyfully spreading its wings. There is the Chidakasha, and Atman is the bird. The bird is not imprisoned in a cage; it flies in the Chidakasha. Its joy is limitless.[42]

Ramakrishna's guru Tota Puri told him how the monks of his order were trained in meditation. Saradananda wrote:

Tota lived with his guru for a long time, studied Vedanta, and learned the mystery of sadhana. He told the Master that there were seven hundred monks in his community who meditated upon the truths of Vedanta every day under the guidance of their guru. He said further that their monastery had an excellent method of training monks to meditate. The Master told us many times what he had heard from Tota on this subject: "The Naked One mentioned that there were seven hundred Naga monks in their monastery. The beginners were taught to meditate while sitting on thick cushions, for a hard seat would be uncomfortable and the pain would divert their minds from God to the body. As they progressed in meditation, they were given less and less comfortable seats, and finally only an animal skin or the bare ground sufficed. In food and other matters also the same gradation was observed. In dress, for instance, they were trained by degrees to go without clothes. People from their very birth are fettered with the eightfold ties of shame, hatred, fear, pride of caste, good conduct, honour, and so on, so these monks were taught to renounce them one by one. After they were well-grounded in meditation, they were asked to roam from one holy place to another, first in the company of other monks and subsequently alone. Such was the method of training among the Nagas."[43]

Teaching meditation through humour

Ramakrishna was not a dry monk; he was a humorous paramahamsa. As a guru, he taught his disciples and devotees spiritual disciplines and meditation, sometimes using humour and light talk. Once the Master went to attend a service of the Brahmos. After observing their method of meditation, he remarked:

> I went to Keshab's place and watched their prayer service. After speaking at length about the glories of God, Keshab announced, "Let us now meditate on God." I wondered how long they would meditate. But, oh dear, they'd scarcely shut their eyes for two minutes before it was all over! How can one know God by meditating like that? While they were meditating, I was watching their faces. Afterwards I said to Keshab: "I've seen a lot of you meditate, and do you know what it reminded me of? Troops of monkeys sometimes sit quietly under the pine trees at Dakshineswar, just as if they were perfect gentlemen, quite innocent. But they aren't. As they sit there, they're thinking about all the gourds and pumpkins that householders train to grow over their roofs, and about all the gardens full of plantains and eggplants. After a little while, they'll jump up with a yell and rush away to the gardens to stuff their stomachs. I saw many of you meditating like that." And when the Brahmos heard that, they laughed.[44]

Ramakrishna's mind and speech were united, and this he taught to his disciples. One day he humorously corrected Vivekananda. Saradananda describes the incident:

> Sometimes the Master would also use humour to teach us. We remember one day when Swami Vivekananda was singing a devotional song. At that time Swamiji was visiting the Brahmo Samaj regularly and practising prayer and meditation in the morning and evening, according to the Brahmo tradition. Absorbed, Swamiji began to passionately sing this song on Brahman, "Concentrate your mind on that One, ancient, and stainless Purusha." There is a line in that song, "Pray to and meditate on God continuously." To imprint those words deeply in Swamiji's mind, the Master said suddenly: "No, no, don't say that. You'd better say, 'Pray to and meditate on God twice a day.' Why vainly repeat something that you don't actually intend to do?" All laughed loudly, and Swamiji was a little embarrassed.[45]

Various instructions on meditation

Those who think that we can attain the knowledge of Brahman or learn meditation without a guru or teacher should remember how many teachers they had from kindergarten to the university level. Swami Brahmananda said that even if you want to be a pickpocket, you need a teacher; similarly, it is essential to have a perfected guru to attain God. A disciple should practise spiritual disciplines according to the guru's instructions. During meditation our minds encounter more distraction than at other times; this is normal, and one should not be discouraged. During the waking state a person relates to the mind as a friend, so he or she cannot recognize those worldly thoughts. But during meditation, that person considers worldly thoughts to be enemies of the mind, so he or she sees them clearly and wants to drive them away. As a result, those worldly thoughts vehemently fight with the mind. This struggle is an indication of a pure mind.

Ramakrishna taught different kinds of meditation to different people at different times:

"During meditation if a dog, cat, monkey, prostitute, cheat, rakshasa, or demon appears before you, don't be afraid or give up your meditation. Think that they are various forms of God. If any worldly desire pops up in the mind, know that it is an obstacle to your meditation. At that time, stop your meditation and pray to God, "Lord, let this desire not be fulfilled."[46]

"Higher than worship is japa, higher than japa is meditation, higher than meditation is bhava, and higher than bhava are mahabhava and prema. Chaitanyadeva had prema. When one attains prema one has the rope to tie God."[47]

"The mind of the yogi is always fixed on God, always absorbed in the Self. You can recognize such a man by merely looking at him. His eyes are wide open, with an aimless look, like the eyes of the mother bird hatching her eggs. Her entire mind is fixed on the eggs, and there is a vacant look in her eyes. Can you [to M.] show me such a picture?"[48]

"In the course of his meditation an aspirant sometimes falls into a kind of sleep that goes by the name of *yoga-nidra*. On such occasions many aspirants see some kind of divine vision."[49] ... "It is good to meditate in the small hours of the morning and at dawn. One should also meditate daily after dusk."[50]

A Brahmo Devotee: "It is very difficult to bring the mind under control.

Master: "If you let the elephant move freely, he will break all trees around. One must strike the elephant on the head with the goad; that is the elephant's most sensitive spot. And thus the elephant becomes calm. Similarly, if you let the mind run freely, it will think all worldly thoughts. At that time one should hit the mind with discrimination, and that will calm the mind. To achieve concentration for meditation, first one should chant God's name clapping the hands for some time....All the sins of the body fly away if one chants the name of God and sings His glories. The birds of sin dwell in the tree of the body. Singing the name of God is like clapping your hands. As, at a clap of the hands, the birds in the tree fly away, so do our sins disappear at the chanting of God's name and glories."[51]

16 December 1883: Master: "Maya is nothing but 'lust' and 'gold'. A man attains yoga when he has freed his mind from these two. The Self — the Supreme Self — is the magnet; the individual self is the needle. The individual self experiences the state of yoga when it is attracted by the Supreme Self to Itself. But the magnet cannot attract the needle if the needle is covered with clay; it can draw the needle only when the clay is removed. The clay of 'lust' and 'gold' must be removed."

Mukherji: "How can one remove it?"

Master: "Weep for God with a longing heart. Tears shed for Him will wash away the clay. When you have thus freed yourself from impurity, you will be attracted by the magnet. Only then will you attain yoga."

Mukherji: "Priceless words!"

Master: "If a man is able to weep for God, he will see Him. He will go into samadhi. Perfection in yoga is samadhi. A man achieves kumbhaka without any yogic exercise if he but weeps for God. The next stage is samadhi."[52]

2 February 1884: A Devotee: "Sir, what is the way?"

Master: "Discrimination between the Real and the unreal. One should always discriminate to the effect that God alone is real and the world unreal. And one should pray with sincere longing."

Devotee: "But, sir, where is our leisure for these things?"

Master: "Those who have the time must meditate and worship. But those who cannot possibly do so must bow down wholeheartedly to God twice a day. He abides in the hearts of all; He knows that worldly people have many things to do. What else is possible for them? You don't have time to pray to God; therefore give Him the power of attorney. But all is in vain unless you attain God and see Him."[53]

In an entry dated 18 October 1885, M. describes one afternoon in which Dr. Sarkar visited, accompanied by his sons Amrita and Hem. Narendra and other devotees were present. Ramakrishna was talking to Amrita. He asked him, "Do you meditate?" He further said to him: "Do you know what one feels in meditation? The mind becomes like a continuous flow of oil — it thinks of one object only, and that is God. It does not think of anything else."[54]

In an entry dated 16 December 1883, M. quotes the Master:

> There is another method — that of meditation. In the Sahasrara, Shiva manifests Himself in a special manner. The aspirant should meditate on Him. The body is like a tray; the mind and buddhi are like water. The Sun of Satchidananda is reflected in this water. Meditating on the reflected sun, one sees the Real Sun through the grace of God.[55]

Ramakrishna's advice to meditate on his own form

Ramakrishna was egoless. His individual ego had completely become one with the cosmic ego of the Divine Mother. When one begins to practise meditation, the aspirant finds it difficult or impossible to meditate on the invisible, incomprehensible, infinite, formless God. The avatar Ramakrishna suggested that his devotees and disciples meditate on him:

> Look, before you begin meditating, think of this (*pointing to himself*) for a while. Do you know why I say this? Because you have faith in this place (*me*). If you think of this place, that will remind you of God. It is like when one sees a herd of cows, one remembers a cowherd; seeing a son, the father; seeing a lawyer, the court. Do you understand? Look, your mind is scattered among various places. If you think of this (*me*), it will be gathered in one spot. And if you think of God with that concentrated mind you will truly get deep meditation. That is why I am telling you all this.
>
> The Master continued: "Whatever form of God or spiritual mood you like, hold onto that firmly; only then will you get steadfast devotion. 'God can be reached through devotion. Can anyone attain Him without that?' One needs *bhava* [spiritual mood]. One should adopt a particular attitude and call on Him. 'As is a man's meditation, so is his feeling of love. As is a man's feeling of love, so is his gain; and faith is the root of all.' One should cultivate a spiritual attitude and faith, and hold onto Him firmly. Only then can one succeed. Do you know what bhava means? It means establishment of a relationship with God and then remembering it all the time: for example, I am a servant of God; I am a child of God; I am a part of God. This is the ripe ego, the ego of Knowledge. Always remember this — even while you are eating, sitting, and resting. Again, I am a brahmin, I am a kshatriya, I am the son of so-and-so, I am the father of so-and-so — these are all examples of the unripe ego, the ego of Ignorance. One should shun these moods because they increase vanity and pride and bring bondage. One should practise the constant recollectedness of God. Part of the mind should be directed towards Him always. Only then will you succeed. Establish a particular spiritual relationship

with God and make Him your own. Only then can you force your demands on Him. Look at human relationships: In the beginning of intimacy, one addresses the other, *apani*; as it deepens, *tumi*; and when it reaches the final state, tui.* One should make God one's very own. Only then will you succeed.

"Take for example an adulterous woman. When she first begins to love her paramour, there is so much secrecy, fear, and bashfulness! Then as intimacy deepens, all emotional barriers disappear. She leaves her family and appears in front of everyone holding her lover's hand. If at that time the man does not take care of her or wants to leave her, she throws a cloth around his neck and pulls him, saying: 'You wretch, I have left everything and everybody for you, and now you want to drop me on the street! Tell me — will you maintain me or not?' Likewise, a man who has renounced everything for God and made Him his very own forces his demands on Him and says: 'I have renounced everything for You. Now tell me — will You reveal Yourself to me or not?'"[56]

Once the Master sent M. to a devotee at Haritaki Bagan with this message: "Please tell that person in Calcutta to meditate on me. Then he will not have to do anything else." M. recalled: "Actually he was indirectly saying that to me. At night the Master asked the Mother: 'Well, Mother, did I do anything wrong in sending that message to the devotee? I see, Mother, that you have become everything — the five elements, mind, intellect, mind-stuff, ego — all the twenty-four principles.' He was aware of his Divine nature. Who else could speak like this except God?"[57]

On 12 February 1919, M. told a devotee: "Even now if anyone meditates on the Master's form and his ideas, that person will attain the same result as we did when the Master was in his physical form."[58]

In a *Gospel* entry dated 9 December 1883, M. describes an incident that happened when he was meditating on the western veranda of the nahabat. While returning from the pine grove, the Master saw M. there and said: "Hello! You are here? You will get results very soon. If you practise a little, then someone will come forward to help you."[59]

In the early 1900s Swami Vishuddhananda met a gardener in the Dakshineswar temple garden who had once had a vision of the Master's luminous form. The swami wrote:

> I met a gardener of seventy-six or seventy-seven years who had worked in the temple garden during Mathur's time. I first saw him cleaning, very carefully, the path from the Master's room to the Panchavati with a spud

*In the Bengali language there are three forms of the second personal pronoun. When addressing a stranger or a respected elder person, *apani* is used; to a known person of equal rank, *tumi*; and an extremely familiar or a socially inferior person, *tui*.

[a spade-like instrument]. He was a little bent because of his age. I observed that he steadfastly cleaned that path up to the pine grove and the bel tree. I was a little curious because I saw him do the same work every day. One day I asked him, "Have you seen the Master?" He laid the spud on the ground, then looked at me in wonder and said: "I am following his order. The Master told me that many of his devotees would come. So I am cleaning this path for them." He was reluctant to say anything more. When I pressed him to say something more, he told me this wonderful story: "One summer night I could not sleep, so I went for a walk in the garden. I saw a light coming from the Panchamundi area. I went there and found the Master immersed in samadhi under the bel tree; a light emanated from his body. I was so scared, I could not stay there long. The next morning I went to him, fell at his feet, and burst into tears. He asked: 'What is the matter? Why do you have so much overflowing devotion today?' I only said, 'Master, please bless me.' He realized what was in my mind. He lifted me up and said: 'Meditate on the form that you saw last night. Clean the path to the Panchavati. Many devotees will come in the future.' I meditate on that luminous form of the Master and clean this path every day."[60]

Blessed was that old gardener of Dakshineswar, who was instructed in meditation and karma yoga by the Master. The vision and grace he received came from his full surrender to the Master.

Instructions on meditation for monastic disciples

Devotees like Ram Chandra Datta and Girish Chandra Ghosh believed that Ramakrishna was God Himself. At first they considered japa and meditation to be necessary for God-realization. However, after they had seen, touched, talked, served, and lived with the living God in human form, they felt that they no longer needed to practise japa, meditation, or austerities.

However, the Master encouraged his monastic disciples to practise japa, meditation, and austerities. When the householder devotees were not at Dakshineswar, the Master would take his young disciples into his room and teach them brahmacharya, meditation, and the mysteries of different sadhanas. The disciples did not record these teachings. Swamiji wanted that the Master's teachings to each disciple be preserved in Belur Math, but this was not done. Later, some disciples would occasionally recount some of the Master's teachings to the monks and devotees. These are published in *Ramakrishna as We Saw Him* and in the reminiscences of the disciples in Bengali and English. In this section, a few instructions of the Master to his monastic disciples are presented.

In fact, Ramakrishna was the lord of the realm of ideas. He was a ruler of all human minds. He could take away the samskaras and karma of his disciples that had accumulated throughout many lives, and then reshape their minds. In this connection, Swami Vivekananda remarked: "It is no great matter to control external material powers by some means and to perform miracles. But I have never seen a greater miracle than the way that 'mad brahmin'* would handle human minds like a lump of clay. He would pound those minds, beat them into shape, develop them, and then with a mere touch he would cast them into a new mould, with new thoughts."[61]

O **Swami Vivekananda**. Swamiji was a great soul, perfect in meditation. Nonetheless, if he had any difficulties in practising meditation, he would ask for the Master's advice. He recalled:

> Once I felt that I could not practise deep concentration during meditation. I told him of it and sought his advice and direction. He told me his personal experiences in the matter and gave me instructions. I remember that as I sat down to meditate during the early hours of the morning, my mind would be disturbed and diverted by the shrill note of the whistle of a neighbouring jute mill. I told him about it, and he advised me to concentrate my mind on the sound of the whistle itself. I followed his advice and derived much benefit from it.
>
> On another occasion, I felt difficulty in totally forgetting my body during meditation and concentrating the mind wholly on the ideal. I went to him for counsel, and he gave me the very instruction which he himself had received from Tota Puri [*his guru*] while practising samadhi according to Vedantic disciplines. He sharply pressed between my eyebrows with his fingernail and said, "Now concentrate your mind on this painful sensation!" I found I could concentrate easily on that sensation as long as I liked, and during that period I completely let go the consciousness of the other parts of my body, not to speak of their causing any distraction hindering my meditation. The solitude of the Panchavati, associated with the various spiritual realizations of the Master, was also the most suitable place for our meditation.[62]
>
> One day in the Cossipore garden, I expressed my prayer [*for nirvikalpa samadhi*] to Sri Ramakrishna with great earnestness. Then in the evening, at the hour of meditation, I lost consciousness of the body and felt that it was absolutely nonexistent. I felt that the sun, moon, space, time, ether, and all had been reduced to a homogeneous mass and then melted far away into the unknown. Body-consciousness almost vanished, and I nearly merged in the Supreme. But I had just a trace of the feeling of ego

*Swami Vivekananda endearingly referred to Sri Ramakrishna in this way.

so I could again return to the world of relativity from samadhi. In this state of samadhi all difference between "I" and "Brahman" goes away, everything is reduced to unity, like the water of the Infinite Ocean — water everywhere, nothing else exists. Language and thought, all fail there. Then only is the state "beyond mind and speech" realized in its actuality. Otherwise, as long as the religious aspirant thinks or says, "I am Brahman" — "I" and "Brahman," these two entities persist — there is the involved semblance of duality. After that experience, even after trying repeatedly, I failed to bring back the state of samadhi. On informing Sri Ramakrishna about it, he said: "If you remain day and night in that state, the work of the Divine Mother will not be accomplished. Therefore you won't be able to induce that state again. When your work is finished, it will come again."[63]

O **Swami Brahmananda**. Swami Brahmananda was the spiritual son of Ramakrishna, who taught him various sadhanas and intricate mysteries of spiritual life. As a result, the swami became a spiritual dynamo. Once in Dakshineswar he complained to the Master that he was not having spiritual visions or experiences. The Master told him: "Look, that kind of experience comes when one practises meditation and prayer regularly and systematically. Wait. You will get it eventually." Brahmananda recalled:

> A couple of days later, in the evening, the young disciple [Brahmananda] saw the Master walking towards the Divine Mother's temple, and he followed him. Sri Ramakrishna entered the temple, but the disciple did not dare go inside, so he sat in the natmandir [*the hall in front of the temple*] and began to meditate. After a while he suddenly saw a brilliant light, like that of a million suns, rushing towards him from the shrine of the Divine Mother. He was frightened and ran to the Master's room. A little later Sri Ramakrishna returned from the shrine. When he saw the young disciple in his room, he said: "Hello! Did you sit for meditation this evening?" "Yes, I did," answered the young disciple, and he told the Master what had happened.
>
> Then the Master told him: "You complain that you don't experience anything. You ask, 'What is the use of practising meditation?' So why did you run away when you had an experience?"

Another time Brahmananda was experiencing a dry spell, which is common in spiritual life. He was in the temple, contemplating whether to leave Dakshineswar. He then returned to the Master's room. He recalled:

> The Master was then walking on the veranda, and he entered the room when he saw me. It was customary after returning from the shrine to

salute the Master and then eat a light breakfast. As soon as I saluted the Master, he said, "Look, when you returned from the shrine, I saw that your mind seemed to be covered with a thick net." I realized that he knew everything, so I said, "Sir, you know the bad condition of my mind." He then wrote something on my tongue. Immediately I forgot all my painful depression and was overwhelmed with an inexpressible joy.

As long as I lived with him I had spontaneous recollection and contemplation of God. An ecstatic joy filled me all the time. That is why one requires a powerful guru — one who has realized God.[64]

Swami Brahmananda described how the Master gave spiritual instructions:

The Master seldom slept at night. He did not allow the boys who lived with him to sleep either. When others had gone to bed he would wake up his disciples, saying: "What is this? Have you come here to sleep?" Then he would instruct each disciple and send him for meditation to the Panchavati, Kali temple, or Shiva temple, according to his inclination. After practising japa and meditation as directed, each would return to the room and sleep. Thus the Master made his disciples work hard. Often he would say: "Three classes of people stay awake at night: the yogi, one who seeks pleasure (*bhogi*), and the sick person (*rogi*). You are all yogis, so sleeping at night is not meant for you."

Sri Ramakrishna used to say, "Eat as much as you like during the day, but eat sparingly at night." The idea is that the full meal taken at noon will be easily digested. If you eat lightly at night, your body will remain light and you can easily concentrate the mind. A heavy meal at night produces laziness and sleep.

Sri Ramakrishna used to encourage everybody to practise meditation. A person falls from spiritual life if he does not practise meditation regularly. The Master asked his guru Tota Puri, "You have attained perfection, so why do you still practise meditation?"

Tota Puri pointed to his shining brass pot and replied, "If you do not clean brass every day, it will be covered with stains."

The Master used to say: "The sign of true meditation is that one forgets one's surroundings and body. One will not feel even a crow sitting on one's head." Sri Ramakrishna attained that state. Once while he was meditating in the natmandir, a crow sat on his head.[65]

O **Swami Adbhutananda.** Latu Maharaj was a longtime attendant of Ramakrishna. He was the first of the monastic disciples to join the Master. He was simple and pure, but completely illiterate. The Master was very fond of this innocent disciple, and he demonstrated through Latu that one can be a knower of Brahman without any education. One evening the

Master found Latu sleeping, so he scolded him and asked him to leave. Thereafter, Latu struggled to keep himself from sleeping at night and eventually succeeded: for the rest of his life, he never again slept at night.

Brahmananda narrated how the Master roused Latu's spiritual consciousness:

> Following the Master's instructions, Latu woke us one particular morning for meditation. It was not yet dawn. After washing quickly, we sat down to do japam. The Master said to us, "Dive deep today — repeating the Lord's name with devotion." Then he began to sing, "Wake up, O Mother Kundalini, wake up," and walked around and around us. He continued as we did our japam. All of a sudden, without any apparent cause, my whole body shook violently. At the same time, Latu uttered a cry. The Master placed his hands on Latu's shoulders and held him, saying: "Don't get up. Stay where you are." I could see that Latu was feeling great pain, but the Master refused to let him get up. After some time, I saw that Latu had lost normal consciousness. The Master was still singing the same song and continued singing it for more than an hour. Thus even through songs he would transmit spiritual power to us.[66]

During the spiritual journey a perfected guru protects his or her disciples. As soon as Latu sat for meditation he would see an effulgent light. Once he was meditating in the bel-tala in the temple garden and lost outer consciousness. When the Master noticed that Latu had not returned, he went in search of him and found him seated in the Panchamundi guarded by two dogs as he meditated. Slowly Latu regained consciousness, saw the Master in front of him, and bowed down to him. While returning to his room, the Master said to him: "I saw two *bhairavas* [guardian spirits] protecting you disguised as two dogs. You are very fortunate! The Divine Mother sent those spirits to protect you."

In this connection Swami Yogananda told this story about Latu:

> While he was in the temple one evening, Latu found that he could not meditate; he returned to the Master's room feeling discouraged. The Master asked, "Why have you come back so soon?" "I couldn't concentrate my mind on japam." "Why not?" "I don't know," answered Latu. "On other days when I sit for japam and meditation, I see something and the mind gets concentrated. But today nothing appeared. I tried hard to concentrate, but I failed." He added: "On my way to the temple the thought came to me — if Mother would appear to me and offer a boon, what should I ask for?"
>
> Immediately the Master said: "There's the trouble. Can one do japam with the mind full of desires? Never let that happen again. When sitting

to meditate one should not ask for anything....If Mother ever insists on giving you something, then ask only for devotion to Her. Never ask for wealth, power, sense pleasures, or anything else."[67]

O **Swami Shivananda.** Swami Shivananda was married but nonetheless had unbroken chastity: Ramakrishna had taught him how to conquer lust even in married life. Later, he one day mentioned to Vivekananda that the Master had touched his body and taken away his lust. Immediately, Swamiji said, "Then you are a 'Mahapurush'— a great soul." From then on Shivananda was known as "Mahapurush Maharaj." When we read stories of the disciples' living with the Master, our minds long to have his divine association. Not only are his instructions for meditation objects for our own meditation, but also his way of living and activities inspire us. Swami Shivananda recalled:

Once the Master said, "In the future many white-complexioned devotees will come here." God is all-merciful. He is not limited by time, place, or person. Blessed we are! We had the opportunity to serve the Master, making betel rolls and preparing tobacco for him. How fortunate we are! We served the Master and we received so much love and affection from him! His compassion and love for us were infinite.

In those days we used to sleep on the floor of his room. At bedtime the Master would tell us how to lie down. He would say that if we were to lie flat on our backs and visualize the Mother in our hearts while falling asleep, then we would have spiritual dreams. He asked us to think of spiritual things while going to sleep. During the summer we used to sleep on the veranda and were bothered by mosquitoes.

The Master looked upon Swami Brahmananda as Gopala [*the boy Krishna*]. Occasionally he would send him to visit his relatives at home, but when Swami Brahmananda was not with him the Master had great difficulty managing himself. One night at 1:00 a.m. the Master came out to the veranda where I was sleeping and asked, "Could you chant the name of Gopala for me?" I chanted for an hour. Some nights when he did not have anybody around him, he would call the night guard to chant the name of Rama for him. What love the Master had for the name of God!

We saw how little the Master slept. Now and then he might get an hour or half an hour of sleep at the most. Most of the time he was absorbed in samadhi, and the remaining time he spent in spiritual moods. These moods became very pronounced at night. He would spend the whole night repeating the name of Mother or Hari. When we stayed with the Master at Dakshineswar we were filled with awe. He had no sleep at all. Whenever we awoke we would hear him talking with the Divine

Mother in a state of spiritual inebriation. He would pace back and forth in the room, all the while muttering something inaudibly. Sometimes he would wake us in the middle of the night and say: "Hello, my dear boys! Have you come here to sleep? If you spend the whole night in sleep, when will you call on God?" As soon as we heard his voice, we would quickly sit up and start to meditate.[68]

O Swami Premananda. Ramakrishna taught not only meditation and other spiritual disciplines to his disciples but also how to perform daily activities to perfection. Swami Premananda recalled:

> We sometimes find people wasting time by sitting idle in the name of japa and meditation. This is a sign of *tamas* [*inertia*]. The Master did much work. We saw him working in the garden, and he also swept his room. He could not tolerate work done in a slipshod manner. He himself did everything precisely and gracefully, and he taught us to do the same. He would scold us if we did not put tools and other things back in their proper places. Once he taught me how to prepare betel rolls. He did all these things, and yet how inward his mind was all the time! If any of us were cheated when buying something, he would ridicule us, saying, "I asked you to be pious but not to be fools." We heard him say many times, "Yoga is skill in action."[69]
>
> He used to tell us, "I can stand everything except egotism." That is why when he wanted to meet someone, he would send Hriday beforehand to see if that person was proud. He has left a mould for us. We now have to knead the clay of the mind, remove all stones and rubbish from it, and cast it in the mould. A beautiful form will then emerge. The Master came for the whole world.
>
> One night I was sleeping in the Master's room. At dead of night I woke up and found him pacing from one end of his room to the other, saying: "Mother, I do not want this. Do not bring me honour from men. Don't, Mother, don't. I spit on it!" Saying this, he paced back and forth like a madman. I was filled with wonder. I thought: "How strange! People are so eager for name and fame, and he is pleading with the Mother not to give it to him! Why is this happening before me? Is it to instruct me?"[70]
>
> Once the Master assured a devotee: "Have you committed a sin? Don't be afraid. Take a vow, 'I will not sin anymore.' I shall swallow all of your sins."[71]

O Swami Niranjanananda. The Master recognized Swami Niranjana-nanda as one of the *Ishwarakotis*. Before coming to the Master, Swami Niranjanananda was acting as a medium for a group of spiritualists. One day the Master said to him: "My boy, if you allow your mind to dwell on ghosts, you will become a ghost yourself. If you fix your mind on God, your life will be filled with God. Now, which of these are you going to choose?" "Well, of course, the latter," replied Niranjan. Ramakrishna advised him to sever his connection with the spiritualists, and Niranjan agreed to this.

The Master also said to Niranjan: "Look here, my boy, if you do ninety-nine good deeds for a person and one bad, he will remember the bad one and won't care for you anymore. On the other hand, if you commit sins ninety-nine times but do one thing to God's satisfaction, He will forgive all your wrongdoing. This is the difference between the love of man and the love of God. Remember this."[72]

Swami Niranjanananda recalled:

> I was then working in an office. One day I went to visit Sri Ramakrishna at Dakshineswar. He wrote a mantram on my tongue and asked me to repeat it. What an experience! After returning home, even when my eyes were closed, I began to see innumerable fireflies in my room. The mantram was vibrating in my head and in every limb of my body. I wanted to sleep, but I could not stop the repetition of japam. I had previously been unaware of this phenomenon. I became scared and thought that I would go out of my mind. After three days I returned to Dakshineswar and said to the Master, "Sir, what have you done to me?" After listening to my story, he laughed and withdrew the power of the mantram. He then said, "It is called *ajapa japam* [the repetition of japam effortlessly and unceasingly]."[73]

O **Swami Ramakrishnananda**. Ramakrishna was a born teacher. His life was his message. His words were easy and simple, but their meaning was deep and profound. Sometimes he used to teach his disciples in a lighter vein. Ramakrishnananda recalled:

> Sometimes the Master would wake at four in the morning, and he would call the disciples who were sleeping in his room, saying: "What are you all doing? Snoring? Get up, sit on your mat, and meditate." Sometimes he would wake up at midnight, call them, and make them spend the whole night singing and praising the name of the Lord. All the disciples were still at a malleable age, in their teens or early twenties — two were scarcely sixteen — and the Master played with them as if they were little children. He was very fun loving and was discovered near the Panchavati one day by a visitor having a game of leap-frog with his boys. Sometimes he would send them into peals of laughter by his mimicry. Then again he would be grave and wake them long before the dawn and make them sit in meditation on the mats on which they had been sleeping. Again at the

evening hour he would tell them to go to the banyan tree and meditate.

The Master said, "If you will practise even one-sixteenth part of what I have practised, you will surely reach the goal." That sixteenth part of individual striving, however, was essential. He could not impose realization as one pastes a picture on a page. Someone said to him once, "You have the power by a touch to make a man perfect, so why do you not do it?" "Because if I did," he answered, "the person would not be able to keep perfection. He must grow to it and be ready to take it."[74]

O **Swami Saradananda**. Ramakrishna had infinite power. He could transmit spiritual power by a touch or wish and change a person's life at any time. One day in Dakshineswar he sat on Saradananda's lap in an ecstatic mood. Later, he explained to the curious devotees, "I was testing how much weight he could bear."[75]

Saradananda recalled how the Master taught him meditation:

One day the Master showed a young disciple [Saradananda] postures and gestures that are appropriate for meditation on God with form and without form. Seated in the lotus position, the Master placed the back of his right hand on the palm of his left and then raised both to chest level. With his eyes closed, he said, "This is the best posture for all kinds of meditation on God with form." Then, seated in the same position, he placed his right and left hands, palms upward, on his right and left knees respectively, and brought the tips of the thumb and the index finger of each hand together, keeping the other fingers straight. Fixing his gaze between his eyebrows, he said, "This is an excellent posture for meditation on the formless God." As he said that, the Master went into samadhi. He soon forced his mind back to the normal plane of consciousness, and continued: "I couldn't show you more. As soon as I sit in that position, my mind is stimulated and becomes absorbed in samadhi, making an air current move upward and hit the wound in my throat. That's why the doctor advised me to avoid going into samadhi." The young disciple said humbly: "Sir, why did you show me those techniques? I didn't ask you to." The Master replied: "That's true. But it's hard for me to remain quiet and refrain from teaching and demonstrating some spiritual techniques to you all." The young disciple was touched by the Master's infinite compassion and amazed by his natural inclination towards samadhi.[76]

O **Swami Yogananda**. Swami Yogananda was a native of Dakshineswar and met Ramakrishna when he was a young boy. He began practising brahmacharya (celibacy), so that he could have good concentration and meditation. His parents forced him to marry but he had no physical relationship with his wife. The Master turned both of their minds to God, and his wife lived like a nun. Swami Saradananda wrote:

192 O See God with Open Eyes

One day at Dakshineswar, Yogananda asked the Master a question, how to conquer lust. He was then young, about fourteen or fifteen years old, and had been visiting the Master for a short while. At that time, Narayana, a hatha yogi, lived in the hut of the Panchavati at Dakshineswar and was attracting some people by performing *neti-dhauti*.* Swami Yogananda said that he had been among those visitors. As he observed those performances, he thought that perhaps unless one practised these disciplines one could not overcome lust and see God. So after asking that question, he expected the Master to prescribe for him a particular yogic posture, or advise him to eat a *myrobalan* or some other thing, or to teach him a pranayama technique.

Yogananda later said: "In answer to my question the Master said, 'Go on repeating the name of Hari, then lust will go away.' This answer was not at all to my liking. I thought: 'He does not know any technique so he just said something to pacify me. Does lust go away by chanting the name of Hari? So many people do that. Are they free from lust?' Then one day I came to the temple garden and instead of going to the Master I went to the Panchavati and eagerly began to listen to the hatha yogi talk. In the meantime, the Master arrived there. As soon as he saw me, he called me over and took my hand. While we were walking towards his room, he said: 'Why did you go there? Don't go there anymore. If you learn and practise those techniques of hatha yoga, your mind will dwell on the body and will never turn towards God.' At this, I thought: 'He is telling me this lest I stop visiting him.' I always considered myself to be highly intelligent, so my inflated intellect made me think that. It did not occur to me even once that it mattered very little to the Master whether I visited him or not. What a mean and doubtful mind I had! There was no limit to the Master's grace. In spite of my harbouring such erroneous notions in my mind, he gave me shelter. Then I thought: 'Why don't I do what he tells me and see what happens?' So resolved, I took the name of Hari with a concentrated mind. And as a matter of fact, within a few days I began to experience the tangible result that the Master had referred to."[77]

O **Swami Turiyananda.** Swami Turiyananda was a yogi and an austere Vedanta monk. He reminisced: "When I used to meditate in the Master's presence, I would experience a sensation in my spine and feel energy rising. The body was like a desert. Then the guru provided the holy name of

Neti is to gradually swallow a piece of wet cloth ten or fifteen cubits long and an inch wide and then to pull it out from the stomach. Dhauti is to drink two or three seers [one seer equals about two cups] of water and then expel it. Sucking water through the anus and forcing it back out is also called *dhauti*. Hatha yogis thus clean out all mucus, phlegmatic humours, and other such substances from the body. They say these techniques prevent disease and make the body strong.

God, and through its power the desert was transformed into a beautiful flower garden. My life had previously been aimless, but after I received the touch of my guru, I gained my life's ideal.

"Sri Ramakrishna used to pray, 'Mother, may these children of mine surpass me in spirituality.' There is a saying, 'Welcome defeat at the hands of the son or disciple.'"[78]

Swami Turiyananda recalled:

The Master instructed some in different kinds of sadhana. To me, however, he said only to practise meditation and japa. But he told me to meditate at midnight, completely naked. The Master was never satisfied with merely instructing us. He would keenly observe each disciple to see how well his instructions were being executed.

A few days after giving me that particular instruction, he asked me, "Well, do you meditate at midnight, naked?"

"Yes, sir, I do," I replied.

"How do you feel?"

"Sir, I feel as if I am free of all bondage."

"Yes, go on with this practice. You will be greatly benefitted."

On another occasion he told me that sadhana was nothing but "making the mind and speech one." In those days I was intensely studying the Vedanta of Shankara. The Master said to me: "Well, what is the use of merely saying that the world is false? Naren can say that. For if he says that the world is unreal, at once it becomes unreal. If he says there is no thorny plant for him, the thorny plant cannot affect his body. But if you touch the thorns, you will at once feel their pricks."[79]

Sri Ramakrishna said that a man's physiognomy was the index to his character. He used to examine us thoroughly, measure the proportion of our limbs and weigh our hands. He could easily detect a person's nature from his physical characteristics. He had a way of classifying aspirants into grades, but there was room for all.

Sri Ramakrishna used to say: "A fingerprint is clear when the ink is all right, but if the ink is bad, the impression is also bad. Spiritual instructions make a lasting impression on the mind possessed of discrimination and renunciation, but when there is a deficiency in these the impression produced is proportionately small."[80]

O **Swami Abhedananda**. Swami Abhedananda wanted to be a yogi when he was a teenager, so he went to see Ramakrishna in Dakshineswar. In his autobiography he wrote:

The Master took me to the northern veranda. He asked me to sit on a cot. When I was seated in the lotus posture, the Master asked me to stick out my tongue. As soon as I did that, he wrote a mantra on it with the middle finger of his right hand and advised me to meditate on Kali, the Divine Mother. I did what he said. Gradually I lost outer consciousness and sat in deep meditation. I felt an unspeakable joy. I don't know how long I stayed in that condition. After some time the Master touched my chest and brought me back to outer consciousness. He then asked me what had happened, and I told him about my blissful experience during meditation. He was very pleased. Afterwards the Master instructed me on meditation and sang these lines of a mystical song:

> When will you sleep in the divine chamber
> With the clean [*good*] and the unclean [*evil*]?
> When these two wives are friendly to each other,
> Mother Shyama will be within your reach.

The Master further told me to meditate every morning and again at night and to report to him my visions and spiritual experiences. Then the Master asked me to go to the Kali temple and meditate there. When I returned from the temple the Master gave me prasad and asked me to visit him again. He even offered to provide my fare if I could not get it from home.

Sri Ramakrishna taught us to practise japa and meditation every morning and evening. About meditation, he sometimes referred to his naked guru Tota Puri's illustration, telling us, "Tota used to say that if a brass water pot is not cleaned every day, stains accumulate on it. Likewise, if the mind is not cleansed by meditation every day, impurities accumulate in it."

Sometimes while teaching us, the Master would tell us about his own sadhana. He said: "When I meditated I became like a motionless stone image. Sometimes birds sat on my head, but I could not feel them." In fact, during deep meditation, when the mind becomes still and motionless, one does not notice if flies or mosquitoes sit on the body. The Master used to say that this is a sign of a concentrated mind.[81]

O **Swami Subodhananda**. Swami Subodhananda was a schoolboy when he first heard about the Master. One day after school, he and his friend Kshirod went to the Master at Dakshineswar without informing their parents. The Master received the two teenagers warmly and then took the boys to the stairs leading to the Shiva temples to the south of his room. He sat cross-legged on the steps, and asked the boys to sit down also. He then asked them to unbutton their shirts and stick out their tongues. The Master wrote something with his finger on Kshirod's tongue and stroked his body from the navel to the throat. He did the same to Subodh, saying, "Awake, Mother, awake!" Then he told them to meditate.

The Master's magic touch awakened Subodh's latent spirituality. No sooner had he begun to meditate than his whole body trembled, and he felt a current rushing along his spinal column to his brain. An ineffable joy overwhelmed him, and he saw a strange light within him in which the forms of numerous gods and goddesses flashed. His meditation deepened, and he lost all sense of personal identity. When he regained consciousness he found the Master stroking his body in the reverse direction from the head downwards. "Well," he said, "have you practised meditation at home?" "Very little, sir," replied the boy. "I used to think a little of gods and goddesses since I heard of them from my mother." "Ah," said the Master, "that's why you could concentrate so easily." Then he asked Kshirod if he had seen or felt anything. When he replied in the negative, the Master said, "All right, you will do so later on."[82]

Subodh recalled:

One day I went to the Cossipore garden house to see the Master and found him alone in his room. The Master advised me to practise meditation. I said to him: "Sir, I can't do spiritual disciplines such as practising pranayama by pressing the nostrils, japa, or meditation, and sitting in a particular posture. Please bless me so that I can have God realization quickly. If I have to practise meditation, why should I come to you? I may as well go to some other guru."

Smiling, the Master said: "All right, you will not have to do all those things. But think of me in the morning and evening."

I replied: "I shall try. I think of you as the veritable manifestation of God. Please bless me so that I can have direct experience."

Smiling, the Master tapped my back three times and said: "Yes, yes, you will realize God. Afterwards, many people will learn by seeing you."[83]

O **Swami Akhandananda.** When Swami Akhandananda was a teenager, he was already practising brahmacharya and austerities. He later narrated his meeting with the Master:

I went to Sri Ramakrishna for the second time on a Saturday, and I was again made to stay overnight. In the evening, after the vesper service was over, the Master handed me a mat and asked me to spread it on the western veranda. He took his pillow and sat down on the mat. He then asked me to sit in a comfortable posture and meditate. "It is not good to sit leaning forward or to hold the body too straight," he said.

That evening the Master initiated me by writing a mantra on my tongue. He then lay down and put his feet on my lap, then asked me to give them a little massage. I was quite strong as I practised wrestling. No sooner had I begun to press his feet than he cried out: "What are you doing? The legs will be crushed! Press them gently." Immediately I realized how soft and tender the Master's body was, as if his bones were covered with butter. I was embarrassed, and I asked with some fear, "How then should I massage?"

"Pass your hands over them gently," he replied. "Niranjan [*Swami Niranjanananda*] also did like you at first."[84]

Once I spent a night at Dakshineswar with several other disciples, and the Master had us all sit for meditation. While communing with our Chosen Deities, we often laughed and wept in ecstasy. The pure joy we experienced in those boyhood days cannot be expressed in words. Whenever I approached the Master he would invariably ask me, "Did you shed tears at the time of prayer or meditation?" And one day when I answered yes to this, how happy he was! "Tears of repentance or sorrow flow from the corners of the eyes nearest the nose," he said, "and those of joy from the outer corners of the eyes."

O **Swami Vijnanananda.** As a college student, Swami Vijnanananda met Ramakrishna in Dakshineswar, but he could not visit him as frequently as did the other disciples. However, like a good shepherd, the Master kept track of his disciples. During a long absence, the Master sent for him. Swami Vijnanananda recalled:

I went to Dakshineswar, and that day not too many people were around him. As I entered his room he asked in a complaining but affectionate tone: "Hello, how are you? What is the matter? Why haven't I seen you for so long?"

I replied truthfully, "I did not feel like coming."

"That's all right," the Master said, smiling. "But I hope you have continued your practice of meditation."

I said, "I try to meditate, sir, but I find I can't."

The Master seemed surprised at my reply and exclaimed: "What do you mean you cannot meditate? Surely you can." He remained silent for a few moments. I was looking at him, waiting for him to say something more. Soon I noticed a change coming over his face and eyes. He looked at me intently. After a little while he said, "Come near me." As I approached the Master, he asked me to stick out my tongue. When I did, he drew a figure on it with his finger. My whole body began to tremble, and I felt an unspeakable bliss within. Then the Master said, "Go to the Panchavati and meditate there." Following his instruction, I slowly moved towards the Panchavati. I walked with difficulty, intoxicated with joy from the Master's touch. Somehow, I reached there and sat for meditation. Then I lost all outward consciousness. When I regained my ordinary state of mind, I saw the Master seated by me. He was rubbing my body with his hands. His face shone with a heavenly smile. I was still in an intoxicated mood. He asked me, "Well, how was your meditation?"

"It was very good, sir," I replied.

Then the Master said, "From now on you will always have deep meditation."[85]

We meditate in front of a picture of Ramakrishna and think, perhaps, our lives will pass only gazing at the picture of the Master. At that time if we remember this advice of the Master to Vijnanananda, we may feel some faith, hope, and joy:

> Once the Master told me, pointing to his own picture: "Look, I dwell in this picture. Meditate on me."
>
> "Yes, I will," I told him.
>
> All the forms of gods and goddesses are within Sri Ramakrishna's form. His photograph symbolizes the piercing of the six centres of the kundalini. When I look at his luminous form, it seems to me that the Master is immersed in the blissful ocean of Satchidananda transcending the six centres of the kundalini. I see many wonderful things in the Master's picture. Sri Ramakrishna manifests himself to those people who are pure in heart.[86]

Realization comes from meditation

Ramakrishna came in this present age to make religion simple and vibrant. He transmitted spiritual experiences, visions, and even samadhi with a glance or a touch. Realization of God is the essence of religion. Though we were not fortunate enough to be in the company of Ramakrishna, we can learn his method of meditation and the other spiritual practices that he taught his disciples and devotees. As the teachings of the Upanishads and Gita are universal, for all times, and for all people, so are the teachings of Ramakrishna. These teachings originated from truth, and truth never becomes old.

People carry in their hearts those whom they love. They think of their beloved day and night: that is the nature of love. If we love Ramakrishna, he must appear in our hearts all the time — if not continuously, at least at the time of meditation. M. quoted Ramakrishna's promise to humankind: "You will achieve everything just by thinking of me." And again, "As children inherit the wealth of their parents, so those who meditate on me will inherit my treasures." Ramakrishna's treasures are discrimination, renunciation, knowledge, devotion, unselfish love, and samadhi.[87]

Ramakrishna's Prayer

The word prayer means asking, wanting, begging, desiring, wishing, imploring, soliciting, appealing, requesting, and so on. Human beings pray to God, or to a powerful ruler, or a person to fulfill their wants and desires. When an empty pitcher is full of water, it no longer makes a *bhak bhak* sound; similarly, when a person's heart is full, no prayer comes out of his or her mouth. Then the senses become calm, the mouth becomes silent, and the thought waves of the mind stop. When all wishes of illumined souls are fulfilled, they become without desire, free from desires, their desires are satisfied, and their only object of desire is the Self.

The Brihadaranyaka Upanishad says: Human beings are identified with desire alone. As is a man's desire, so is his resolution; as is his resolution, so is his deed; and whatever deed he does, that he reaps (4:4:5). Vedanta scriptures state that God is the dispenser of the results of action and is the kalpataru, or the wish-fulfilling tree. Whatever one asks from the kalpataru, one receives. Based on this belief, the sages composed innumerable prayers to gods and goddesses, which we find in the Vedas, Puranas, and other literature. Our rishis and saints also composed prayers according to their own aptitudes: some prayers are with desire and some without desire; some are for prosperity and some for liberation; some are worldly and some spiritual.

In the Chandi, we find a prayer to the Divine Mother for fulfilling the worldly selfish desires: "O Devi, give us beauty, victory, fame, and kill our enemies. Give us fortune, happiness, wealth, diseaseless bodies, and even beautiful brides." However, there are also unselfish prayers in

Dakshineswar temple compound, sanctified by Ramakrishna's footsteps and prayerful life.

our scriptures: "May all be happy. May all be free from disease. May all realize what is good. May none be subject to misery. May all the wicked become virtuous. May the virtuous attain tranquility. May the tranquil be free from bonds. May the free make others free." While facing the east, west, north, and south, Buddha would pray: "Let all beings be happy. Let all beings be peaceful. Let all beings be blissful."

Krishna said in the Gita that four kinds of people worship or pray to God. The first type of person prays during distress, such as Draupadi prayed to Krishna at the court of the Kurus when she was threatened with humiliation. The second type of person prays for an answer to a question, such as when Uddhava prayed to Krishna in the Bhagavata. The third type of person prays for wealth, as did King Surath in the Chandi and Dhruva in the Bhagavata. The fourth type of person is a jnani, such as Narada and Sukadeva, who desires only to be united with God. It is the nature of desire to bind the soul, but desire for God is not considered to be desire because it releases the soul (*akāmo vishnu-kāmo vā*).

God is the source of bliss and happiness. Yet, unaware of this, human beings run here and there after bliss because no one can live without it. The Upanishads tell us: Bliss is Brahman. All beings are born from bliss, live in bliss, and merge into bliss. All creatures live on a particle of this supreme bliss. In an attempt to obtain this bliss, people marry, procreate, earn money, and pray for objects of enjoyment. If all the desires of restless people were fulfilled, then this world would be topsy-turvy. Human moods and whims change continuously. In this connection Ramakrishna told the story of a weary traveller who was unknowingly resting under a kalpataru tree. He first desired food and water, then a soft bed, and finally a young woman to massage him. He immediately received everything he wished for. Then he started thinking about what would happen if a tiger came there — and immediately a tiger appeared and ate him.

A person is full of desires, but God has full control over whether or not to grant these wishes. Saint Ramprasad sang:

> O Mother, all is done after Thine own sweet will;
> Thou art in truth self-willed, Redeemer of mankind!
> Thou workest Thine own work; men only call it theirs....
> On some Thou dost bestow the bliss of Brahmanhood;
> Yet others Thou dost hurl into this world below.[1]

God plays with created human beings. God pushes some children away by offering them plenty of wealth, a luxurious home, a fancy car, and other worldly objects. God sees how happy his children are with transitory sense objects, and how they suffer from worries and anxieties, disease and death. They don't listen to God's voice: "Having come into this transitory, joyless world, worship Me" (Gita, 9:33). Again, God takes away from some devotees their objects of attachment, and gradually bestows on them peace and bliss. It seems God whimsically plays with His children.

Our scriptures and folklore contain some wonderful episodes regarding various kinds of prayers and their fulfillment. It is narrated in the Mahabharata that Yayati, a decrepit and infirm king, exchanged his old age with the youth of his youngest son Puru so that he could enjoy the pleasures of the senses. After fulfilling his desires for 1,000 years, he expressed his experience: "Lust is never satisfied through enjoyment of sex-pleasure. It only multiplies, just as fire flares up when one tries to put it out with clarified butter."[2] Finally, he returned his youth to his son, took back his old age, and began to practise spiritual disciplines.

Sometimes God protects devotees by fulfilling their desires. Sage Narada and Sage Parvat were both charmed by the beauty of a young princess, Srimati, the daughter of Ambarisa. Both wanted to marry her. The day before Srimati's *swayamvara*, a ceremony in which a woman selects her bridegroom, Narada secretly went to Vaikuntha (heaven) and prayed to Vishnu: "Lord, I want to marry Srimati. Let her see Parvat as a monkey in tomorrow's ceremony." Vishnu said, "Let it be so." Parvat also secretly went to Vishnu and prayed, "Lord, may Srimati see Narada as Hanuman in tomorrow's ceremony." Vishnu said, "Let it be so." Vishnu fulfilled both prayers. So during the *swayamvara*, Srimati did not see Narada or Parvat; instead she saw a monkey and Hanuman standing there. Thus God protected both sages from maya. In fact, God's lila is inscrutable.

God sometimes even fulfills prayers that harm others. The demon king, Brikasur, practised severe austerities for many years to attain a vision of Shiva. Pleased, Shiva appeared and offered him a boon. Brikasur prayed, "Lord, give me this boon: if I put my hand on a person's head, that head will vanish then and there." Shiva said, "Let it be so." Brikasur then tried to put his hand on Shiva's head, but Shiva ran away. Brikasur chased him. Shiva began to run around heaven, earth, and the netherworld. To protect Shiva, Vishnu took the form of a handsome young boy, appeared before Brikasur, and asked, "O king, why are you running so fast?" After listening to the story, Vishnu deluded the demon with his maya, and humbly said: "O king of the demons, you are a wise person, but you trusted the words of Shiva! Don't you know he lives in a cremation ground, besmeared with ashes, with ghosts and hobgoblins as his companions? He smokes marijuana. Why don't you check yourself to see whether his words are true? This way, you will not have to run all over." After listening to that boy's pleasing words, Brikasur put his hand on his own head and it instantly vanished. In this world, those who try to destroy others are destroyed themselves.

Of course, not everyone prays for objects of enjoyment. For example, in the Mahabharata Queen Kunti prayed to Krishna for dangers and troubles: "O teacher of the world, let calamities always overtake us because we would then always have Thy sight, which prevents rebirth."

A real devotee may suffer from various problems, but he or she does not pray for worldly happiness. God tests the devotees' genuine love and faith through trials and tribulations. Tulasidas prayed: "Lord, let lightening fall on my happiness, and let misery be with me always." Happiness takes the mind away from God, but we think of God more at the time of misery.

Most people pray to God for happiness, comfort, health, money, heaven, and so on, but a true devotee prays to have the vision of God. We are encouraged when we listen to stories of the mystics' spiritual adventures. Their pain and agony, struggles and obstacles generate faith and enthusiasm in our hearts. Saint Teresa of Avila travelled by horse carriage to Toledo in Spain to establish a convent. During her journey, a wheel came off of the carriage, and it tumbled into a ditch. Teresa plaintively prayed to Jesus: "Lord, is this your true judgement? I am going to do work for you and now you have put me in this peril. You know, all through my life I have suffered from heart trouble, and still I am working for you. I don't understand your ways, Lord." Jesus answered, "Teresa, this is how I test my devotees." Teresa replied, "And that is why your devotees are very few."

Henry Suso, a German mystic, was a disciple of Meister Eckhart. He was very charismatic, and many young men and women of Germany became monks and nuns under his influence. Once during his visit to a convent, he told the nuns that God had forgotten him. When the nuns asked him the cause, Suso answered: "Sisters, my life is now going on smoothly and happily. No one is attacking or slandering me." At that moment, a monk arrived outside the convent with an urgent message and asked for Suso. He told Suso: "The baron is searching for you. He has threatened to kill you because his only daughter has become a nun and joined the convent."

"Thanks be to God," said Suso. He asked the monk to wait for him.

He returned to the nuns and told them: "Sisters, you see, God is now thinking of me. He did not forget me." He told them what had happened and said good-bye, and then left with the monk. An easy-going life is a great obstacle to spiritual life.

Prayer has been emphasized in every religion. During prayer, a devotee gets a chance to talk to God. Prayer manifests in four stages: 1. The devotee talks, God listens. 2. God talks, the devotee listens. 3. Neither talks, both listen. 4. Neither talks, neither listens: Silence. This silence is samadhi. The deeper the prayer becomes, the fewer words are needed, until one can hear the voice of the Indwelling God in silence.

Street beggars beg from people they do not know; this is not prayer. The main element of prayer is love. On 22 April 1883 Sri Ramakrishna attended the Brahmo festival at Sinthi.

A Brahmo devotee asked, "Sir, what is the way?"

Master: "Attachment to God, or, in other words, love for Him. And secondly, prayer."

Brahmo Devotee: "Which one is the way — love or prayer?"

Master: "First love, and then prayer."

The Master sang: "Cry to your Mother Shyama with a real cry, O mind!/ And how can She hold Herself from you?/ How can Shyama stay away?"...

Continuing, the Master said: "And one must always chant the name and glories of God and pray to Him. An old metal pot must be scrubbed every day. What is the use of cleaning it only once? Further, one must practise discrimination and renunciation; one must be conscious of the unreality of the world."[3]

Christ told his devotees, "Watch and pray." Saint Paul said passionately, "Pray without ceasing." Sri Ramakrishna praised the way Muslims pray five times a day and remarked: "The Mussalmans put aside all activities and say their prayers at the appointed times."[4] According to the Hindu tradition, one should repeat the Gayatri mantra three times a day and pray to God.

Is it possible to attain God while living a family life? Ramakrishna answered this question:

Certainly. But as I said just now, one must live in holy company and pray unceasingly. One should weep for God. When the impurities of the mind are thus washed away, one realizes God....Those who have the time must meditate and worship. But those who cannot possibly do so must bow down whole-heartedly to God twice a day. He abides in the hearts of all; He knows that worldly people have many things to do. What else is possible for them? You don't have time to pray to God; therefore give Him the power of attorney.[5]

Sometimes we pray and wonder if our prayers reach God. If our prayers are not fulfilled, we teasingly say to Sri Ramakrishna: "Master, you are now too old. Perhaps you do not hear well. Please use a hearing aid and kindly listen to our prayers."

On 19 September 1884, Hazra asked the Master: "Does God listen to our prayer for bhakti?"

Master: "Surely. I can assure you of that a hundred times. But the prayer must be genuine and earnest."[6]

Our worldly desires scatter our minds; as a result, our prayers are not one-pointed. On 11 October 1884, Ramakrishna made a remark on insincere prayer:

> You ask me why you don't feel stern renunciation. There is a reason for it. You have desires and tendencies within you. The same is true of Hazra. In our part of the country, I have seen peasants bringing water into their paddy-fields. The fields have low ridges on all sides to prevent the water from leaking out; but these are made of mud and often have holes here and there. The peasants work themselves to death to bring the water, which, however, leaks out through the holes. Desires are the holes. You practise japa and austerities, no doubt, but they all leak out through the holes of your desires.[7]

Prayer is a sincere, sensible, affectionate pouring out of the soul to God. A real prayer is not eloquent, nor is it a mere muttering of some words. It originates from the bottom of the heart with deep feeling. Genuine prayer is sincere, simple, direct, and frank; it manifests with passion through the body, senses, prana, and mind. Saint Ambrose said: "Prayer is the wing wherewith the soul flies to heaven, and meditation the eye wherewith we see God."[8] God definitely responds if the prayer is offered with one-pointed love and sincerity.

Once Ramakrishna taught Gangadhar (Swami Akhandananda) how to pray sincerely, which the swami recorded in his reminiscences:

> Whenever I approached the Master he would invariably ask me, "Did you shed tears at the time of prayer or meditation?" And one day when I answered yes to this, how happy he was! "Tears of repentance or sorrow flow from the corners of the eyes nearest the nose," he said, "and those of joy from the outer corners of the eyes." Suddenly the Master asked me, "Do you know how to pray?" Saying this he flung his hands and feet about restlessly — like a little child impatient for its mother. Then he

cried out: "Mother dear, grant me knowledge and devotion. I don't want anything else. I can't live without you." While teaching us how to pray in this way, he looked just like a small boy. Profuse tears rolled down his chest, and he passed into deep samadhi. I was convinced that the Master did that for my sake.[9]

Sincere prayer arises from deep love within the inmost heart. One day the Master complained to the Divine Mother: "Mother, you will listen only if I speak through the mouth; my heart is wrung like a wet towel. Can't you see that?" If one has sincere love for God, one can force one's demands on Him. There is a line in Ramprasad's song: "I can buy the Divine Mother's property by the force of my devotion."

When people pray to God, they think of Him as compassionate. Once some Sikh devotees came to see the Master at Dakshineswar. They said, "God is compassionate." The Master asked, "Why compassionate?" They said, "Why, revered sir, He constantly looks after us, gives us righteousness and wealth, and provides us with our food." "Suppose," I said, "a man has children. Who will look after them and provide them with food — their own father, or a man from another village?"

Sub-Judge: "Is not God, then, compassionate, sir?"

Master: "Why should you think that? I just made a remark. What I mean to say is that God is our very own. We can exert force on Him. With one's own people one can even go so far as to say, 'You rascal! Won't you give it to me?'"[10]

We are glad that God is not a human being. Otherwise, his ears would have long ago been burned by our loud prayers and demands for money, name and fame, good health, car, home and so on. God would be disgusted with his children. However, God is compassionate and the creator of the universe and all beings, so He looks at us with an eye of grace. Moreover, God fulfills only those prayers that are good for us. In this respect there is a beautiful teaching of Chaitanya in the *Sri Sri Chaitanya-charitamrita*:

If somebody has material desires but worships Krishna,
Krishna gives them His lotus feet, even though they do not ask for it.
Krishna says: "They worship Me desiring material happiness,
"Leaving aside nectar, they ask for poison.
"They are great fools.
"I am wise. Why will I give these fools poison?
"I will give them the nectar of My lotus feet —
"Then they will forget about the poison!"

True devotees do not pray for worldly objects. They are fully devoted to the Chosen Deity. They forget themselves and do not bother God about their needs and sufferings. In the Sunya Purana, a staunch and loving devotee of Shiva prayed: "O Lord, why do you live on alms? Begging is a lowly occupation. Some days you get alms and some days, nothing. Why don't you grow some rice; then you will not suffer from hunger. O Lord, you live in this cold place of the Himalayas. You have no clothes, except a tiger skin around your waist. Why don't you grow some cotton and make your own cloth that will protect you from cold?" This is indeed a wonderful prayer. The devotee is seeking nothing for himself except the welfare of God. This prayer is selfless, desireless, sincere, and full of love for the beloved Lord. God takes responsibility for such devotees and supplies their needs.

Mira Bai, a medieval mystic, worshipped Giridhari Gopala (Krishna). Her Ishta-mantra was: *Chakor rakho ji*, "O Lord, keep me as your servant." She prayed to be able to take care of his garden in Vrindaban, the abode of his divine activities, without any pay. While working, she would sing his glories, and as a result, she was able to see the Lord every day, remember Him always, and attain love and devotion. This is a wonderful way to approach God. A true servant effaces his or her ego. This attitude of self-less service brings love and grace from the Lord.

Ramakrishna's life was full of prayer, meditation, and samadhi. After descending from samadhi, he would talk to gods and goddesses, pray for the welfare of the devotees, and teach them how to pray to God.

Necessity of prayer

People love to talk with others about their thoughts, moods, and emotions. Only the rishis and saints can live alone and pass their days in silence. Of course, they also commune with God. A friendless life is sad and painful. If one does not have a companion with whom one can talk freely, then it is good to make God your companion. God is faithful, loving, compassionate, forgiving, and merciful. During prayer, when we express our pent-up sorrows and sufferings, and our various needs and problems, the indwelling Lord listens and relieves the pressure and heaviness of our hearts. If one can establish a relationship with God through candid, sincere prayer, spiritual life becomes more smooth and easy.

Regarding the necessity of prayer, Ramakrishna said: "Those who lead a householder's life should practise spiritual discipline; they should pray eagerly to God in solitude."[11]

"Too much reasoning throws the mind into confusion. You get clear water if you drink from the surface of a pool. But if you put your hand deeper and stir the water, it becomes muddy. Therefore, pray to God for devotion."[12]

"Shambhu Mallick once talked about establishing hospitals, dispensaries, and schools, making roads, digging public reservoirs, and so forth.... Therefore I said to Shambhu, 'Suppose God appears before you; then will you ask Him to build hospitals and dispensaries for you?' (*Laughter*.) A lover of God never says that. He will rather say: 'O Lord, give me a place at Thy Lotus Feet. Keep me always in Thy company. Give me sincere and pure love for Thee.'... In the kaliyuga the best way is bhaktiyoga, the path of devotion — singing the praises of the Lord, and prayer. The path of devotion alone is the religion for this age."[13]

Intense prayer for God-vision

It is impossible to describe Ramakrishna's longing for God-vision. His intense passion and yearning for God would manifest in his body, senses, and mind, and propel him towards God like a tornado. Here we shall follow the description of his longing from his own lips.

Seeing the setting sun over the Ganges, he would piteously cry:

"Mother, another day is gone in vain, still Thou art not revealed unto me."

"Sometimes the pain of my separation from God would make me rub my face desperately on the ground until it was cut and bleeding in some places. I was completely oblivious to how the entire day would slip away in meditation, devotional practices, prayer, and self-surrender. At the advent of evening when the temple garden reverberated with the sound of conch shells and bells, I would be reminded: 'Another day is gone in vain; still I have not seen the Mother.' Then such a frenzy of despair would seize my soul that I could bear no more. I would throw myself down and shout, 'Mother, still You haven't revealed Yourself to me.' I would cry bitterly, tormented with pain. People would say, 'He is suffering from colic; that is why he is crying so terribly.'"[14]

Another day while singing to the Divine Mother in the Kali temple at Dakshineswar, he prayed:

Mother, I have been praying to You so long! Why don't You listen to me? You showed Yourself to Ramprasad. Why won't You show Yourself to me?... There was an unbearable pain in my heart because I could not have a vision of Mother. Just as a man wrings out a towel with all his strength to get the water out of it, so I felt as if my heart were being wrung out. I began to think I should never see Mother. I was dying of despair. In my agony, I asked myself: 'What's the use of living this life?'

Suddenly my eyes fell on the sword that hangs in the Mother's shrine. I decided to end my life then and there. Like a madman, I ran to the sword and seized it. Then I had a marvelous vision of the Mother and fell down unconscious. Afterwards what happened in the external world, or how that day and the next passed, I don't know. But within me there was a steady flow of undiluted bliss that I had never before experienced, and I felt the immediate presence of the Divine Mother."[15]

It is not so easy to handle God-vision. Some get confused and some even lose their minds. In fact, when God possesses a soul, that person's ego cannot function. He becomes an instrument in the hands of God. Ramakrishna's testimony is a great help to illumined souls. The Master related his experience and described how he handled the situation through prayer:

When I sat to meditate, at first I would see particles of light like swarms of fireflies. Sometimes I would see masses of light on all sides, covering everything like a mist; at other times I would see that everything was pervaded by bright waves of light like molten silver. I would see those things sometimes with eyes closed and sometimes with eyes open. I didn't understand what I saw, nor did I know if it was good or bad to be having such visions. So I prayed anxiously to Mother: "I don't understand what's happening to me. I don't know any mantras and incantations to call You. Please teach me how to know You. Mother, if You won't teach me, who will? I have no refuge or guide except You." Thus I used to pray with a one-pointed mind and cry profusely with a longing heart.[16]

There is a similarity between Ramakrishna's longing for God-vision and the gopis' longing for Krishna. During the Raslila, when Krishna danced with the gopis, he observed their vanity and self-importance, so he suddenly disappeared to purify them through suffering. Sukadeva described to King Parikshit the condition of the gopis then: "O King, the gopis wailed at the top of their lungs, singing and raving in their intense longing to meet Krishna."[17]

Ramakrishna's prayer for devotion

M. said: "Every word of the Master's is a great mantra. Repetition of any one of them leads to perfection. His prayer too is a mantra. Is it necessary that all mantras be in Sanskrit? A mantra can be in Bengali too." The Master prayed to the Divine Mother only for pure devotion. He offered flowers at Her lotus feet and said with folded hands:

Mother, here is Thy virtue, here is Thy vice; take them both and grant me only pure love for Thee.

Here is Thy knowledge, here is Thy ignorance; take them both and grant
me only pure love for Thee.
Here is Thy purity, here is Thy impurity; take them both and grant me
only pure love for Thee.
Here is Thy good and here is Thy evil; take them both and grant me only
pure love for Thee.
Here is Thy dharma, here is Thy adharma; take them both and grant me
only pure love for Thee.[18]

The Master continued: "You see, I didn't ask even for knowledge
or public recognition. When one renounces both dharma and adharma,
there remains only pure love of God — love that is stainless, motiveless,
and that one feels only for the sake of love. I mentioned all these, but I
could not say: 'Mother, here is Thy truth and here is Thy falsehood. Take
them both.' I gave up everything at Her feet but could not bring myself to
give up truth.... Truthfulness in speech is the tapasya of the kaliyuga. By
adhering to truth, one attains God."[19]

One can pray in a positive way and in a negative way, but one should
pray in a way that is conducive to spiritual life. Ramakrishna taught the
seekers of God to pray in both ways:

Mother, I don't want any physical enjoyment;
Mother, I don't want name and fame;
Mother, I don't want the eight occult powers;
Mother, I don't want the other hundred powers;
Mother, give me pure, unchanging, selfless devotion to You.
Mother, may I never be deluded by Your bewitching maya.[20]

After the Master attained illumination, a spiritual tempest blew
through his mind and he had various spiritual experiences. Finally, his
guru's guidance, and his own devotion and sincere prayer sustained him:

I vowed to the Divine Mother that I would kill myself if I did not see God.
I said to Her: "O Mother, I am a fool. Please teach me what is contained in
the Vedas, the Puranas, the Tantras, and the other scriptures." The Mother
said to me, "The essence of the Vedanta is that Brahman alone is real and
the world illusory." The Satchidananda Brahman described in the Vedas
is the Satchidananda Siva of the Tantra and the Satchidananda Krishna
of the Purana.... I saw the visions described in the scriptures. Sometimes
I saw the universe filled with sparks of fire. Sometimes I saw all the quarters glittering with light, as if the world were a lake of mercury. Sometimes I saw the world as if made of liquid silver. Sometimes, again, I saw
all the quarters illumined as if with the light of Roman candles. So you
see my experiences tally with those described in the scriptures.[21]

One can attain everything through bhakti yoga. I wept before the Mother and prayed, "O Mother, please tell me, please reveal to me what the yogis have realized through yoga and the jnanis through discrimination." And the Mother has revealed everything to me. She reveals everything if the devotee cries to Her with a yearning heart. She has shown me everything that is in the Vedas, the Vedanta, the Puranas, and the Tantra.[22]

God is the Kalpataru

Ramakrishna always encouraged the devotees to pray to God, yet at the same time he cautioned them not to pray for worldly things. Worldly objects are like poison and worldly enjoyments tie human beings with the bondage of maya.

I pray to the Divine Mother, "Mother, do not give me Brahmajnana. Formerly believers in God with form used to visit me a great deal. Then the modern Brahmajnanis [Brahmos] began to arrive. During that period I used to remain unconscious in samadhi most of the time. Whenever I regained consciousness, I would say to the Divine Mother, "O Mother, please don't give me Brahmajnana."

Pandit: "Does God listen to our prayers?"

Master: "God is the Kalpataru, the Wish-fulfilling Tree. You will certainly get whatever you ask of Him. But you must pray standing near the Kalpataru. Only then will your prayer be fulfilled. But you must remember another thing. God knows our inner feeling. A man gets the fulfillment of the desire he cherishes while practising sadhana. As one thinks, so one receives. A magician was showing his tricks before a king. Now and then he exclaimed: 'Come confusion! Come delusion! O King, give me money! Give me clothes!' Suddenly his tongue turned upward and clove to the roof of his mouth. He experienced *kumbhaka*. He could utter neither word nor sound and became motionless. People thought he was dead. They built a vault of bricks and buried him there in that posture. After a thousand years someone dug into the vault. Inside it people found a man seated in samadhi. They took him for a holy man and worshipped him. When they shook him his tongue was loosened and regained its normal position. The magician became conscious of the outer world and cried, as he had a thousand years before: 'Come confusion! Come delusion! O King, give me money! Give me clothes!'

"I used to weep, praying to the Divine Mother, 'O Mother, destroy with Thy thunderbolt my inclination to reason.'"

Pandit: "Then you too had an inclination to reason?"

Master : "Yes, once."

Pandit: "Then please assure us that we shall get rid of that inclination too. How did you get rid of yours?"

Master: "Oh, somehow or other."

Sri Ramakrishna was silent awhile. Then he went on with his conversation.

Master: "God is the Kalpataru. One should pray standing near It. Then one will get whatever one desires.

"How many things God has created! Infinite is His universe. But what need have I to know about His infinite splendours? If I must know these, let me first realize Him. Then God Himself will tell me all about them. What need have I to know how many houses and how many government securities Jadu Mallick possesses? All that I need is somehow to converse with Jadu Mallick. I may succeed in seeing him by jumping over a ditch or through a petition or after being pushed about by his gatekeeper. Once I get a chance to talk to him, then he himself will tell me all about his possessions if I ask him. If one becomes acquainted with the Master, then one is respected by his officers too. (*All laugh.*) "There are some who do not care to know the splendours of God. What do I care about knowing how many gallons of wine there are in the tavern? One bottle is enough for me. Why should I desire the knowledge of God's splendours? I am intoxicated with the little wine I have swallowed."[23]

Result of praying for occult powers

Occult powers often appear in the life of a yogi or a true spiritual aspirant when he or she attains perfection in yoga-sadhana. These powers inflate some yogis' egos and turn their minds from God to name and fame. Saradananda wrote:

Once the Master called Narendra into the Panchavati and said: "Look, as a result of practising austerities, I have long since possessed all the supernatural powers. But what would a person like me do with such powers? I can't even keep a wearing-cloth tied around my own waist! So I'm thinking of asking Mother to transfer them all to you. She has told me that you will have to do much work for Her. So if these powers are transmitted to you, you can use them when necessary. What do you say?"

Narendra had seen various divine powers in the Master since their first meeting, so he had no reason to doubt him. But his deeply rooted love of God did not allow him to accept those powers without careful consideration. After serious thought, Narendra asked, "Sir, will they help me to realize God?" The Master replied: "No, they won't help you to do that. But they might be very useful once you have realized God and have started doing His work." To this, Narendra said: "Sir, I don't need them. Let me realize God first; after that, there will be time enough to decide whether I need them. If I get these marvellous powers now, I might forget the whole purpose of my life and use them to gratify worldly desires.

Then they would only become my ruin." The Master was extremely pleased when Narendra refused his offer.[24]

Ramakrishna abhorred occult powers because he knew that they divert aspirants in a wrong direction. Regarding occult powers, the Master remarked:

> People of small intellect seek occult powers — powers to cure disease, win a lawsuit, walk on water and such things. But the genuine devotees of God don't want anything except His Lotus Feet. One day Hriday said to me, "Uncle, please ask the Mother for some powers, some occult powers." I have the nature of a child. While I was practising japa in the Kali temple, I said to Kali, "Mother, Hriday asked me to pray to You for some occult powers." The Divine Mother at once showed me a vision. A middle-aged prostitute, about forty years old, appeared and sat with her back to me. She had large hips and wore a black-bordered sari. Soon she was covered with filth. The Mother showed me that occult powers are as abominable as the filth of that prostitute. Thereupon I went to Hriday and scolded him, saying: "Why did you teach me such a prayer? It is because of you that I had such an experience."
>
> People with a little occult power gain such things as name and fame. Many of them want to follow the profession of guru, gain people's recognition, and make disciples and devotees. Men say of such a guru: "Ah! He is having a wonderful time. How many people visit him! He has many disciples and followers. His house is overflowing with furniture and other things. People give him presents. He has such power that he can feed many people if he so desires."[25]

Conversation with the Divine Mother

Knowers of Brahman see Brahman in every being and everything. They do not see good and bad as ordinary human beings do. One day the Master descended from the realm of samadhi and began to talk in a semi-ecstatic state: "Mother, You are the embodiment of fifty letters.* Those letters of Yours that constitute the Vedas and Vedanta also compose filthy words and obscene songs. The *ka* and *kha*** of Your Vedas and Vedanta are no different from those of the obscene songs. Mother, You are verily the Vedas and Vedanta as well as obscene words and songs." With that the Master again entered into samadhi.[26]

One day the Master sang this song in the natmandir of Dakshineswar:

O Mother, Consort of Shiva, You have deluded this world.

*The Sanskrit alphabet consists of fifty letters.
** *Ka* and *kha* are the first two consonants in the Sanskrit alphabet.

You entertain Yourself by playing the vina in the great lotus of the muladhara.

Your music vibrates through the great mantra in three scales, taking the form of the three gunas.

Your music strikes the three cords — sushumna, ida, and pingala — of that musical instrument, the body.

You play with melody, rhythm, and tempo at the six centres of kundalini.

After singing that song, the Master's kundalini awakened and he was overwhelmed with that power and lost control. Swami Saradananda described the scene:

In this condition the Master crawled down the steps of the northern side of the natmandir to the temple courtyard. He was then speaking like a little child, saying: "Mother, I will not fall. Will I fall?" In truth, when watching the Master at that time one felt that he was a boy of three or four years. He was saying those words as he gazed at the Mother, depending on Her as he confidently made his way down the steps. Shall we ever see anywhere else such wonderful reliance on God, even in such small matters?

After crossing the courtyard, the Master reached his own room and went to the western semicircular veranda to sit. He was still in ecstasy; the mood possessed him. Sometimes it lessened a little, but would increase again and he would almost lose consciousness. After being in this condition for some time, the Master — still in that condition — said to the devotees: "Have you seen the Snake? It is giving me so much trouble!" Forgetting the devotees, he addressed the snake-like kundalini (for he was then experiencing the Serpent Power): "Please go now. Madam, move away. I shall smoke tobacco and wash my mouth. I have not yet brushed my teeth." Thus, he spoke with the devotees at times and sometimes addressed the divine form seen in ecstasy. Gradually he returned to the normal plane of consciousness.[27]

M. said that he had seen at least one person in his life who would talk with God in front of everyone. One day while in ecstasy, Ramakrishna began to talk with the Divine Mother:

Mother, that I should first speak and You then act — oh, that's nonsense! What is the meaning of talk? It is nothing but a sign. One man says, "I shall eat." Again, another says, "No! I won't hear of it." Well, Mother, suppose I had said I would not eat; wouldn't I still feel hungry? Is it ever possible that You should listen only when one prays aloud and not when one feels an inner longing? You are what You are. Then why do I speak? Why do I pray? I do as You make me do. Oh, what confusion! Why do You make me reason?

As Sri Ramakrishna was thus talking to God, the devotees listened wonder-struck to his words.[28]

In many places in *The Gospel of Sri Ramakrishna*, we come across the Master's conversations with the Divine Mother. Even in trifling matters, the Master would act according to the behest of the Divine Mother, such as "Mother, shall I go?" "Mother, shall I eat?" "Mother, what shall I say?" "Mother, tell me what shall I do?" If someone caused him pain or trouble, that also he would put to the Divine Mother. Once Hazra contradicted the Master's words, "Brahman and Its power are one; power and the possessor of power are one."

Then the Master prayed to the Divine Mother: "O Mother! Hazra is trying to upset the views of this place [himself]. Either give him right understanding or take him from here." The Master mentioned: "The next day he came to me and said, 'Yes, I agree with you.' He said that God exists everywhere as All-pervading Consciousness."[29]

Prayer for self-concealment

There is a saying: The more hidden it is, the stronger and more fruitful it becomes; the more it is expressed, the weaker and more superficial it becomes. Some preachers proclaim their own messages by beating their own drums. They might have food for five people but they invite five thousand through advertisement and publicity. The result will be that the remaining people will leave without food. In this respect, the Master said: "When the flowers bloom, bees come of their own accord." The flowers do not advertise that they have honey. Be spiritual first. First earn spirituality, and then distribute it. Some modern yogis write their autobiographies for publicity, or they ask their followers to spread their names through Wikipedia, YouTube, Facebook, and other media. In response to this type of preacher, Rabindranath Tagore wrote in *Gitanjali*:

O Lord, bow my head under the dust of your feet.
Submerge all my vanity under my tears.
While glorifying myself, I only humiliate myself.
May I never preach myself in my actions,
Let your wish be fulfilled in my life
O Lord, submerge all my vanity under my tears.

When Ramakrishna was practising spiritual disciplines, a light manifested around his divine body. He said to his disciples: "At that time my beauty became manifest in such a way that people would stare at me. My face and chest were always crimson, and a lustre emanated from my body.

Because people stared at me, I would cover myself with a thick *chadar*. I would pray to the Divine Mother, 'Take away my external beauty, O Mother, and give me inner beauty.' I used to pass my hand over the body and slap it again and again, saying, 'Go within, go within.' After some days my skin turned pale, as you see it now."[30]

Swami Saradananda narrated an incident:

Once while the Master was in Kamarpukur, arrangements were made for his visits to Jayrambati and Sihar. Because the Master was constantly in bhava samadhi, his limbs were as delicate as those of a boy or a woman. He could not walk even a short distance and needed a palanquin or a carriage to convey him. A palanquin had been brought for the trip to Sihar via Jayrambati. Hriday was also ready to go. After lunch the Master put on a scarlet silk cloth and fastened his gold amulet around his arm. His lips were crimson from chewing betel. As he was about to get into the palanquin, he noticed that a large crowd had gathered on the street nearby. Seeing so many men and women around, the Master asked Hriday in wonder, "Hriday, what is the reason for this crowd?"

Hriday: "For what else? You are going away, and they *(pointing to the crowd)* won't see you for some days. So they have come to have a parting look at you."

The Master: "But they see me every day. What new feature has attracted them in such large numbers today?"

Hriday: "You look so handsome in that silken cloth, and your lips shine with crimson colour. That is why they want to see you."

As soon as the Master heard that those people were attracted to his physical beauty, an unusual mood filled his mind. He thought: "Alas! These people are preoccupied by this external, ephemeral, physical beauty. No one wants to see God, who is within."

He had abhorred physical beauty beforehand, but this incident increased that aversion a thousandfold. "What!" he exclaimed. "People are gathering just to look at a man! I won't go. Wherever I go, people will crowd about like this!" In utter disgust the Master returned to his room and took off the silk cloth. Filled with humility, the Master did not go to Jayrambati and Sihar that day.[31]

It is extremely difficult to crush the ego, which is the barrier between God and humanity. The Master demonstrated how to wipe out the ego all through his life; as a result he could not utter "I" and "my." These "I" and "my" are the warp and woof of maya. Saradananda wrote:

He had completely burnt his ego and vanity to ashes and consigned them forever to the Ganges. When beggars were fed in the Kali temple, he carried their dirty leaf-plates on his head, dumped them outside, and cleaned the place where they had eaten. Once he even ate the food left by those beggars, considering them to be Narayana. He washed the outhouse that the servants and workers of the Kali temple used. While wiping that place with his hair, he prayed, "Mother, may I never feel that I am superior to them."[32]

Prayer to cure disease

The human body inevitably encounters birth, disease, and death. This is the nature of the body. Because it decays day by day it is called *sharira* in Sanskrit. Each human body passes through six stages: it is born, exists, grows, modifies, decays, and dies. As a human, Ramakrishna also occasionally suffered from various kinds of ailments, such as fever, dysentery, cough, and cancer. M. recorded in the *Gospel:*

> Sri Ramakrishna had been conversing with Rakhal, Mahimacharan, Hazra, and other devotees, when M. entered the room and saluted him. He brought with him splint, pad, and lint to bandage the Master's injured arm.
>
> One day, while going toward the pine-grove, Sri Ramakrishna had fallen near the railing and dislocated a bone in his left arm. He had been in an ecstatic mood at the time and no one had been with him.
>
> Master (*to M.*): "Hello! What was ailing you? Are you quite well now?"
>
> M: "Yes, sir, I am all right now."
>
> Master (*to Mahima*): "Well, if I am the machine and God is its operator, then why should this have happened to me?"
>
> Weeping like a child, he said to the Divine Mother: "O Brahmamayi! O Mother! Why hast Thou done this to me? My arm is badly hurt. (*To the devotees*) Will I be all right again?" They consoled him, as one would a child, and said: "Surely. You will be quite well again."
>
> Master (*to Rakhal*): "You aren't to blame for it though you are living here to look after me; for even if you had accompanied me, you certainly wouldn't have gone up to the railing."
>
> The Master again went into a spiritual mood and said: "Om! Om! Om! Mother, what is this that I am saying? Don't make me unconscious, Mother, with the Knowledge of Brahman. Don't give me Brahmajnana. I am but Thy child. I am easily worried and frightened. I want a Mother. A million salutations to the Knowledge of Brahman! Give it to those who seek it. O Anandamayi! O Blissful Mother!"
>
> Uttering loudly the word "Anandamayi", he burst into tears and said:
> "Mother, this is the grief that sorely grieves my heart,
> That even with Thee for Mother, and though I am wide awake,
> There should be robbery in my house."

Again he said to the Divine Mother: "What wrong have I done, Mother? Do I ever do anything? It is Thou, Mother, who doest everything. I am the machine and Thou art its Operator."

(*To Rakhal, smiling*) "See that you don't fall! Don't be piqued and cheat yourself."

Again addressing the Mother, Sri Ramakrishna said: "Do I weep because I am hurt? Not at all.

Mother, this is the grief that sorely grieves my heart,
That even with Thee for Mother, and though I am wide awake,
There should be robbery in my house."[33]

Most of the time an avatar or an illumined soul transcends the body idea and dwells in the Atman. But as long as avatars live in the body, they experience pain and suffering like other human beings. We know from our own experience that whenever we have a stomachache or headache, we cannot meditate; our minds go straight to the physical plane. During his sickness or when he suffered from an accident, the Master would discriminate and pray:

"The body has, indeed, only a momentary existence. God alone is real. Now the body exists, and now it does not. Years ago, when I had been suffering terribly from indigestion, Hriday said to me, 'Do ask the Mother to cure you.' I felt ashamed to speak to Her about my illness. I said to Her: 'Mother, I saw a skeleton in the Asiatic Society Museum. It was pieced together with wires into a human form. O Mother, please keep my body together a little, like that, so that I may sing Thy name and glories.'

"Why this desire to live? After Ravana's death Rama and Lakshmana entered his capital and saw Nikasha, his old mother, running away. Lakshmana was surprised at this and said to Rama, 'All her children are dead, but still life attracts her so much!' Rama called Nikasha to His side and said: 'Don't be afraid. Why are you running away?' She replied: 'Rama, it was not fear that made me flee from You. I have been able to see all these wondrous actions of Yours simply because I am alive. I shall see many more things like these if I continue to live. Hence I desire to live.'

"Without desires the body cannot live. (*Smiling*) I had one or two desires. I prayed to the Mother, 'O Mother, give me the company of those who have renounced "woman and gold".' I said further: 'I should like to enjoy the society of Thy jnanis and bhaktas. So give me a little strength that I may walk hither and thither and visit those people.' But She did not give me the strength to walk."

Trailokya (*smiling*): "Have all the desires been fulfilled?"

Master (*smiling*): "No, there are still a few left. (*All laugh.*)

"The body is really impermanent. When my arm was broken I said to the Mother, 'Mother, it hurts me very much.' At once She revealed to me a carriage and its driver. Here and there a few screws were loose. The carriage moved as the driver directed it. It had no power of its own.

"Why then do I take care of the body? It is to enjoy God, to sing His name and glories, and to go about visiting His jnanis and bhaktas."[34]

As long as one has a body, one becomes ill and also may have an accident. Although Ramakrishna was an avatar, he could not escape this reality. One experiences pain and happiness by means of the mind and not by the body. Ramakrishna was an expert in samadhi, so he could withdraw his mind from the body at any moment. When his mind was in the physical plane, he would express his pain, uttering "Ah, Uh"; the next moment, he would raise his mind into the divine plane and laugh joyfully.

Master (*to the devotees*): "Well, people ask why, if I am such a holy person, I should be ill."

Tarak: "Bhagavan Das Babaji, too, was ill and bed-ridden a long time."

Master: "But look at Dr. Madhu. At the age of sixty he carries food to the house of his mistress; and he has no illness."

Goswami: "Sir, your illness is for the sake of others. You take upon yourself the sins of those who come to you. You fall ill because you accept their sins."

A Devotee: "You will soon be cured if only you say to the Divine Mother, 'Mother, please make me well.'"

Master: "I cannot ask God to cure my disease. The attitude of the servant-Master relationship is nowadays less strong in me. Once in a while, I say, 'O Mother, please mend the sheath [his body] of the sword a little.' But such prayers are also becoming less frequent. Nowadays I do not find my 'I'; I see that it is God alone who resides in this sheath....Every now and then I think that the body is a mere pillow-case. The only real substance is the Indivisible Satchidananda. When I go into divine ecstasy this illness of the throat remains away from me. I am now somewhat in that mood and so I feel like laughing."[35]

Pandit Shashadhar had great love and respect for Sri Ramakrishna. One day he came to see the Master at Cossipore when his cancer was in an advanced stage. Shashadhar said to the Master, "Sir, if you put your mind on your throat a little, your cancer will surely be cured." The Master answered, "How can the mind that I have already offered to the Lord be diverted again to this body of flesh and blood?" But still Shashadhar pleaded, "Sir, when you talk to the Divine Mother, please ask Her to cure your cancer." Then the Master replied: "When I see the Mother of the Universe, I forget my body and the universe. So, how can I tell the Mother about this insignificant body of flesh and blood?" The pandit was dumbfounded.[36]

A prayer to conquer lust

Generally people hide their weaknesses because they are afraid to be snubbed or humiliated by society. Shameful acts are always embarrassing. There is a saying: dark deeds are better done in the dark. Ramakrishna did not have that problem. He was an embodiment of purity, and his mind and mouth were one. Ordinary people cannot express what is in their minds because their impure thoughts and feelings will expose them and put them in an embarrassing situation. Saradananda wrote:

> A young man came and sadly asked the Master: "Sir, how can I get rid of lust? I strive so hard, still I suffer from restlessness due to passion and bad thoughts."
>
> The Master: "Look, lust does not completely go away even when one realizes God. As long as the body lasts, a little lust remains even after God-vision — but it cannot raise its head. Do you think I am free from it? At one time I believed that I had conquered lust. Then one day when I was seated in the Panchavati, I suddenly had such an onrush of lust that it was hard for me to maintain control! Immediately I began crying, rubbing my face in the dust and saying to the Divine Mother: 'I have made a big mistake, Mother. I shall never again think that I have conquered lust.' Only then did it subside. Do you know that you boys are now passing through a flood tide of adolescence. You cannot stop it. Can an embankment or a breakwater stop a tidal wave? The overflowing water breaks through and rushes forward, and then the water stands as high as a bamboo over the paddy fields. There is a saying, 'Mental sin is not considered to be a sin in this kaliyuga.' If a bad thought happens to arise once or twice in the mind, why should you go on brooding about it? Sometimes those feelings come and go. That is natural to the body; consider them to be physical functions like the call of nature. Do people worry when they have an urge for the call of nature? Similarly, consider those feelings to be insignificant, trifling, and worthless, and don't think of them anymore. Pray to God intensely, chant His name, and meditate on Him. Don't pay any heed to whether those feelings come or go. Gradually they will come under control." It was as if the Master had become a youth while talking to that young man.[37]

Sometimes the omniscient Master would behave like a child and discuss his mental condition with others. Saradananda wrote:

Although Mathur's Chosen Deity was the Father [Ramakrishna], who was established in bhavamukha and identified with Kali, sometimes he had to console the Father in various ways because he was an embodiment of childlike simplicity and dependence. Mathur's genuine love gave him the ingenuity to answer all sorts of questions. One day while talking with Mathur, the Father suddenly left. He returned with a sad face and asked Mathur: "Can you tell me what kind of disease this is? I saw a worm coming out of my body with the urine. I have never heard that such a worm dwells in the human body. Now what has happened to me?"

Shortly before, this very Father had been charming everyone by explaining hidden spiritual truths in simple language, and now the same Father was extremely anxious, like a boy thinking of the unknown, and he was depending on Mathur's intelligence and consoling words. Mathur quickly reassured the Master: "It is good, Father, that it happened. Everyone has a worm in his body that generates lust. It is this lust-worm that creates various bad thoughts in the mind and forces one to commit evil. It is the grace of the Mother that the lust-worm has left your body. Why are you so worried about it?" The Father was greatly relieved by this and said: "You are right. It is fortunate that I asked you about it." He was then as joyful as a child.[38]

The Bhagavata says: "Kamam hridrogam — Lust is a disease of the mind." Lustful feeling is natural to all human bodies. Ramakrishna said, "I have never enjoyed a woman, even in a dream."[39] Despite his pristine purity, a bad thought once appeared in his mind, which he candidly told his devotees to encourage and assure them.

> Master: Is it an easy matter to get rid of lust? I myself felt a queer sensation in my heart six months after I had begun my spiritual practice. Then I threw myself on the ground under a tree and wept bitterly. I said to the Divine Mother, 'Mother, if it comes to that, I shall certainly cut my throat with a knife!'
>
> (To the devotees) "If the mind is free from 'woman and gold', then what else can obstruct a man? He enjoys then only the Bliss of Brahman."[40]

Prayer prompted by fear

When God comes to this world as a human being, He behaves like a human. Hunger and thirst, anger and fear, worries and anxieties, impatience and grief, and other feelings more or less appear in His mind. It is amusing to hear Ramakrishna list his weaknesses.

Once Ramakrishna was going from Burdwan to Kamarpukur in a

bullock-cart, when a great storm arose. Some people gathered near the cart. His companions said they were robbers. So out of fear he began to repeat the names of God.

Sometimes the Master was very impatient like a boy, and the devotees would console him.

Master: "Well, where then is my faith in God? Once I was going to Kamarpukur in a bullock-cart, when several persons came up to the cart with clubs in their hands. They looked like highwaymen. I began to chant the names of the gods. Sometimes I repeated the names of Rama and Durga, and sometimes 'Om Tat Sat', so that in case one failed another would work.

(*To M.*) "Can you tell me why I am so impatient?"

M: "Your mind, sir, is always absorbed in samadhi. You have kept a fraction of it on your body for the welfare of the devotees. Therefore, you feel impatient now and then for your body's safety."

Master: "That is true. A little of the mind is attached to the body. It wants to enjoy the love of God and the company of the devotees."[41]

It is fun to watch the avatar's divine and human play going on simultaneously. As there was no secrecy, duplicity, or clandestine activities in Ramakrishna's life, we marvel seeing his childlike simplicity and guilelessness, frankness and naturalness. Saradananda wrote:

Master: "Look, there is no book-learning here. I am an unlettered man. I was terribly afraid when I heard that the pandit [Shashadhar] was coming to see me. You see, I am not even aware of my clothing. I was extremely nervous that I might say something improper. I prayed to the Divine Mother: 'Look after me, Mother. I don't know any scriptures except You. Please protect me.' I told some people around me: 'You all be present when the pandit arrives. I shall feel confident if I see you near me.' When the pandit arrived, I was not entirely rid of my nervousness; I kept looking at him and listening to his words. Suddenly, the Mother revealed Shashadhar's inner self to me. I saw that scriptural erudition was of no avail without discrimination and renunciation. Then I felt a current rush towards my head, and the last trace of fear vanished from my mind. I was completely overwhelmed. My face turned upward and out of my mouth came an incessant torrent of words. The more I talked, the more I felt that a fresh supply was coming from within, just as when a man in Kamarpukur measures paddy, another person pushes forward a fresh supply. I was entirely unaware of what I was saying. When I regained a little consciousness, I found the pandit in tears, completely overwhelmed.

Occasionally, I have this experience. One day Keshab sent word that he would take me for a boat trip on the Ganges and bring with him a Westerner [Reverend Joseph Cook, who was visiting India]. I was nervous that day also and had to go to the pine grove again and again to answer the call of nature. When they arrived and I got into the boat, I had the same experience that I did when the pandit came. I said many things unconsciously. Later, they (*pointing to us*) said, 'You gave much wonderful advice.' But you see, I was completely unaware of it."[42]

Prayer for the monastic disciples

It is really amazing that Ramakrishna had to wait nearly 25 years after he attained God-realization for his monastic disciples to arrive. When the disciples finally came to him, the Master trained them and they carried his message all over the world. His disciples were not ordinary human beings; some of them had been companions of previous divine incarnations. The Master told them how he had waited and prayed for them:

In those days there was no limit to my yearning to see you all. My heart was wrung like a wet towel, and I was restless with pain. I wanted to weep loudly, but I couldn't cry in public or people would misunderstand me. I could just manage to keep my grief under control during the daytime. But when evening came and the vesper music resounded from the temples of the Mother and of Vishnu, I could master my feelings no longer; I was overcome by the thought that another day had gone and still you were not here. I would climb onto the roof of the kuthi and cry out at the top of my voice: "Come to me, my boys! Where are you? I can't bear to live without you!" I thought that I would go mad. Then after some days, you began to come one after another, and I calmed down. As I had seen you all earlier in my vision, I immediately recognized you when you came, one by one. After Purna came, the Mother said: "You had visions about those who were to come. It is now complete with Purna's arrival. No others belonging to this class of devotee will come in the future." The Mother showed you all to me and said, "These devotees are your inner circle."[43]

We think that only human beings pray to God, but God as an avatar also prays for human beings. On 23 December 1885, M. recorded the Master's prayer for the devotees: "At the hour of the evening worship in the Kali temple, I would climb to the roof of the kuthi and cry out: 'O devotees, where are you all? Come to me soon! I shall die of the company of worldly people!' I told all this to the 'Englishmen'. They said it was all an illusion of my mind. 'Perhaps it is', I said to myself and became calm. But now it is all coming true; the devotees are coming."[44]

The disciples knew that the Master had the power to impart God-vision, spiritual experience, and samadhi with a mere wish. Saradananda recorded:

Baburam (Swami Premananda) wanted to have bhava samadhi. With tearful eyes he implored the Master, saying, "Please help me to have samadhi." The Master consoled him, saying: "All right, I shall ask the Divine Mother about it. Does anything happen by my will, my child?" But who would listen to him? Baburam kept on, saying, "Please let me have that experience." A few days after this request, Baburam had to go to his country home at Antpur on some business. It was 1884. The Master was extremely anxious about how Baburam could have samadhi. He expressed his concern to others: "You see, Baburam wept much and asked for samadhi before he left. What will happen? If he does not have it, he will have no regard for the words of this place (*meaning himself*)." He then prayed to the Mother: "Mother, please grant that Baburam may have a little ecstasy or some other spiritual experience." The Mother replied, "He will not have ecstasy, but he will have knowledge." Even with the Mother's assurance, the Master remained anxious. He told some of us: "Well, I prayed to the Mother for Baburam, but She said, 'He will not have ecstasy; he will have knowledge.' At any rate, let him have something at least so that he can have peace. I am anxious for him. He wept bitterly before he left." Ah, how anxious the Master was that Baburam might have some kind of spiritual experience! Expressing his concern, he repeated, "If he does not have a spiritual experience, he will not respect me anymore." It was as if the Master's life and all depended on Baburam's regard or disregard![45]

The Master prayed for all his disciples, removed the obstacles in their spiritual journeys, and bestowed his infallible blessings upon them. He trained his disciples, especially Narendra, to carry out the work of the Divine Mother. The Master related:

I have had many amazing visions. I had a vision of the Indivisible Satchidananda. Inside It, I saw two groups with a fence between them. On one side were Kedar, Chuni, and other devotees who believe in the Personal God. On the other side was a luminous space like a heap of red brick-dust. Inside it was seated Narendra immersed in samadhi. Seeing him absorbed in meditation, I called aloud, "Oh, Narendra!" He opened his eyes a little. I came to realize that he had been born, in another form, in Simla in a kayastha family. At once I said to the Divine Mother, "Mother, entangle him in maya; otherwise he will give up his body in samadhi....Mother, please put a little maya in him, otherwise it will not be possible for him to do your work.[46]

When the Master heard that Narendra's marriage had been arranged, he went to the Kali temple. Holding the feet of the Divine Mother, he tearfully prayed: "O Mother, please upset the whole thing! Don't let Narendra be drowned."[47] In fact, that is what happened. The marriage did not take place.

When Narendra's father died, a cloud of poverty descended on his family. Narendra applied for jobs in many places but failed to acquire one. When self-effort fails, people seek help from God. Narendra knew the Master's divine power and that the Divine Mother listened to him. Finally he came to Dakshineswar and requested the Master to pray to the Divine Mother for him. The Master answered:

> "My boy, I can't make such demands. But why don't you go and ask the Mother yourself? All your sufferings are due to your disregard of Her."
> Narendra said, "I do not know the Mother; you please speak to Her on my behalf. You must."
> The Master replied tenderly: "My dear boy, I have done so again and again. But you do not accept Her, so She does not grant my prayer. All right, it is Tuesday — go to the Kali temple tonight, prostrate yourself before the Mother, and ask of Her any boon you like. It shall be granted. She is Knowledge Absolute, the Inscrutable Power of Brahman. By Her mere will She has given birth to this world. Everything is in Her power to give."[48]

Narendra went to the temple three times but could not ask for money or worldly prosperity. He prayed for only five things: "Mother, give me knowledge, devotion, discrimination, renunciation, and uninterrupted vision."

When Narendra failed to pray to relieve his family's poverty, the Master finally blessed him, saying: "All right, your people at home will never be in want of plain food and clothing." From this point, Narendra's family had their needs met.

Prayer for the householder devotees

In front of the Krishna temple in Dakshineswar, Ramakrishna had a wonderful vision that firmly convinced him that God, devotees, and the scriptures are in reality one and the same, though they appear to be distinct entities. The Master used to say, "The Bhagavata, the devotee, and God — these three are one and the One manifests as three." That is why the Master loved and served the devotees, became their helpmate during their happiness and misery, and prayed for their welfare and spiritual unfoldment.

Ramakrishna prayed for M.: One day the Master took M. to the Kali temple and began to dance and sing, "O Mother, you are the destroyer of danger and obstacles." He knew the main obstacles in spiritual life are body-consciousness and attachment to sense objects. One should pray to the Mother to remove those obstacles. He prayed to the Mother on behalf of M. and taught him how to pray.

Another day, the Master went to the Panchavati, accompanied by M. He bowed down to the old banyan tree, where a big branch had broken off and was down on the ground. He said to M.: "I had so many divine visions here. You bow down here." Like a loving Mother, the Master was trying to instill faith and devotion in M.'s rational mind.

On another occasion the Master prayed for M.: "Mother, this devotee is very simple and quiet. I am asking you fervently, please attract him."

Sometimes the Master instructed M. in secret spiritual practices, which M. later related to the devotees: "The kundalini lies in the lotus of the muladhara. That lotus has four petals. The Primordial Energy resides in all bodies as kundalini. She is like a sleeping snake coiled up.... Kundalini is speedily awakened if one follows the path of bhakti. God cannot be seen unless She is awakened. Sing earnestly and secretly in solitude: Waken, O Mother! O kundalini, whose nature is Bliss Eternal! Thou art the serpent coiled in sleep, in the lotus of the muladhara."[49]

M. recorded another event in the *Gospel*. At dusk Ramakrishna went to the Kali temple; he was pleased to see M. meditating there. M. described the scene:

> The evening worship was over in the temples. The Master returned to his room and sat on the couch absorbed in meditation on the Divine Mother. M. sat on the floor. There was no one else in the room.
>
> The Master was weeping and praying to the Mother with a voice choked with emotion: "Mother, may those who come to You have all their desires fulfilled! If you keep them in the world, Mother, then please reveal Yourself to them now and then. Otherwise, how will they live?"[50]

Devotees' love for God has been recorded in the scriptures and books, but God's love for the devotees is seldom found in the scriptures because God's infinite love cannot be described.

The Master's heart would melt out of compassion for the devotees as M. described:

> The Master used to pray to the Divine Mother for the devotees, "Mother, fulfill their desires." Tears fell from his eyes. He had so much compassion for the devotees! They could not serve him to their heart's content while he was ill because of their family obligations, so he prayed to the Mother

on their behalf: "Mother, they are very busy and have so many problems at home. Don't consider their shortcomings. Bless them, Mother."

Soldiers of the Dum Dum cantonment would sometimes take a few hours of leave to visit the Master. The Master used to pray for them: "Mother, be kind to them. They come to you after undergoing so many difficulties."

Once some ornaments were stolen from the Radhakanta temple of Dakshineswar. Haladhari, a cousin of the Master, was then the priest of that temple, and the police arrested him as a suspect. The Master prayed: "Mother, your name is Durga [*One who saves devotees from danger*]. Your name will be tarnished if misfortune befalls your child. Mother, remove all obstacles." [*As far as we know Haladhari was released.*]

A man came to the Master and said: "Sir, I am incapable of practising spiritual disciplines. If you wish, give me an experience." Immediately the Master went into samadhi. After some time he began to talk to the Divine Mother, saying: "Mother, this person does not want to do anything. Do I have to make curd from milk, butter from curd, and then put the butter into his mouth?" This attitude towards spiritual practice is prevalent in the modern age.[51]

When we are sick, injured, or in pain, we pray to God for recovery. Ramakrishna had an accident and injured his arm, but despite his pain he kept his mind in God. M. recorded:

The Master was again talking and laughing, like a child who, though ailing, sometimes forgets his illness and laughs and plays about.

Master (*to the devotees*): "It will avail you nothing unless you realize Satchidananda. There is nothing like discrimination and renunciation. The worldly man's devotion to God is momentary — like a drop of water on a red-hot frying pan. Perchance he looks at a flower and exclaims, 'Ah, what a wonderful creation of God!'

"One must be restless for God. If a son clamours persistently for his share of the property, his parents consult with each other and give it to him even though he is a minor. God will certainly listen to your prayers if you feel restless for Him. Since He has begotten us, surely we can claim our inheritance from Him. He is our own Father, our own Mother. We can force our demand on Him. We can say to him, 'Reveal Thyself to me or I shall cut my throat with a knife!'"

Sri Ramakrishna taught the devotees how to call on the Divine Mother.

Master: "I used to pray to Her in this way: 'O Mother! O Blissful One! Reveal Thyself to me. Thou must!' Again, I would say to Her: 'O Lord of the lowly! O Lord of the universe! Surely I am not outside Thy universe. I am bereft of knowledge. I am without discipline. I have no devotion. I know nothing. Thou must be gracious and reveal Thyself to me.'"[52]

God does not hesitate to give knowledge and liberation to the devotees, but He is reluctant to bestow devotion. Devotees bind God with
their love and devotion, and as a result God comes at their beck and call
and is always ready to fulfill their prayers. We find the Master praying to
cure Mathur's wife, Jagadamba, of a life-threatening illness. On another
occasion, Balaram and his family were returning from Dakshineswar to
Calcutta during a storm, and their boat was in danger. The Master prayed
to the Mother for its safety. Later, the Master prayed to the Mother for
his devotee Adhar, so he could get the position of vice-chairman of the
Calcutta Corporation. He also asked Jadu Mallick to recommend Adhar.

Master: "Hazra said to me, 'Please pray to the Divine Mother for
Adhar, that he may secure the job.' Adhar made the same request to me.
I said to the Mother: 'O Mother, Adhar has been visiting You. May he get
the job if it pleases You.' But at the same time I said to Her: 'How small-
minded he is! He is praying to You for things like that and not for Knowledge and Devotion.'"[53]

It is common to pray for dear ones when they are sick or passing
through difficult times. The Master was very human. Although he could
not help the devotees physically or financially, he helped them spiritually
through prayer. Ramakrishna said to Keshab Chandra Sen: "Whenever
I hear that you are ill, I become extremely restless. After hearing of your
last illness, I wept to the Divine Mother in the small hours of the morning.
I prayed to Her, 'O Mother, if anything happens to Keshab, with whom,
then, shall I talk in Calcutta?' Coming to Calcutta, I offered fruits and
sweets to the Divine Mother with a prayer for your well-being."[54]

Petitionary prayers

When we listen to Ramakrishna's petitionary prayers, we feel how
he had established a true relationship with the Divine Mother that was
so close, deep, candid, strong, and sweet. He was the child of the Mother
completely and wholeheartedly. Every step of his life was guided by Her.
His whole life was a continuous prayer. He realized that there is no substance in this world, so he wanted to be a monk. M. recorded:

Master (*to M.*): "There is no substance whatsoever in the worldly life. The
members of Ishan's family are good; so he has some peace here. Suppose
his sons had been lewd, disobedient, and addicted to drink and other
vices. Then there would have been no end to his troubles. One very seldom comes across such a religious family, in which all the members are
devoted to God. I have seen only two or three such families. Generally one finds quarrels, misunderstanding, jealousy, and friction. Besides,

there are disease, grief, and poverty in the world. Seeing this condition, I prayed to the Divine Mother, 'O Mother, turn my mind at once from the world to God.'

"Look at Narendra's troubles. His father is dead and the members of his family are starving. He has been trying his utmost to secure a position, but he has not yet found one. Just see how unsettled his mind is!

(*To M.*) "You used to come to Dakshineswar very frequently. But why have you become such a rare visitor? Perhaps you have become particularly friendly with your wife. Is it true? Why should I blame you? The influence of 'woman and gold' is everywhere. Therefore I pray, 'O Divine Mother, please don't make me a worldly man if I am to be born again in a human body.'"[55]

Generally people think that a monk's life is dry and austere, antisocial and joyless. During his sadhana, the Master prayed to the Divine Mother, "Mother, don't make me a dry monk; allow me to enjoy the fun in life."[56]

It is sweet to hear how the Divine Mother fulfilled the prayers of the Master. She always fulfilled his needs so that he could fulfill his mission.

Master: You must have noticed that when I see certain people I jump up with a start. Do you know why? A man feels that way when he sees his own people after a long time.

I used to pray to the Mother, crying: "Mother, if I do not find the devotees I'll surely die. Please bring them to me immediately." In those days whatever desire arose in my mind would come to pass. I planted a tulsi-grove in the Panchavati in order to practise japa and meditation. I wanted very much to fence it around with bamboo sticks. Soon afterwards a bundle of bamboo sticks and some string were carried by the flood-tide of the Ganges right in front of the Panchavati. A temple servant noticed them and joyfully told me.

In that state of divine exaltation I could no longer perform the formal worship. "Mother," I said, "who will look after me? I haven't the power to take care of myself. I want to listen only to talk about Thee. I want to feed Thy devotees. I want to give a little help to those whom I chance to meet. How will all that be possible, Mother? Give me a rich man to stand by me." That is why Mathur Babu did so much to serve me.

I said further, "Certainly I shall not have any children, Mother. But it is my desire that a boy with sincere love for God should always remain with me. Give me such a boy." That is the reason Rakhal came here. Those whom I think of as my own are part and parcel of me.[57]

Krishna declared in the Gita (9:22): "Those who worship me, meditating on their identity with me and ever devoted to me — to them I carry what they lack and preserve what they have." This is God's promise to humankind. Ramakrishna related how the Mother took care of him: "The Divine Mother also showed me in a vision the five suppliers of my needs: first, Mathur Babu, and second, Shambhu Mallick, whom I had not then met. I had a vision of a fair-skinned man with a cap on his head. Many days later, when I first met Shambhu, I recalled that vision; I realized that it was he whom I had seen in that ecstatic state. I haven't yet found out the three other suppliers of my wants. But they were all of a fair complexion. Surendra looks like one of them."[58]

"I cherished a desire. I said to the Mother, 'O Mother, I shall be the king of the devotees.'"[59]

"O Mother, make me like Sita, completely forgetful of every-thing — body and limbs, totally unconscious of hands, feet, and sense-organs — only the one thought in her mind, 'Where is Rama?'"[60]

Pique and complaint

We release our wounded feelings and complaints to the person whom we love. In this way, we lighten the heaviness and depression of the heart. We are not ashamed or afraid to quarrel with our beloved because that person is our very own and our dearest one. Saradananda wrote:

> Recalling his divine ecstasy of this period, the Master used to tell us: "An ordinary man could not have borne a quarter of that tremendous spiritu-al fervour; it would have burnt him up. I could forget my indescribable pangs only by seeing the Mother in some form or other for the greater part of the day and night. Otherwise this body could not have survived. I had no sleep at all for six long years. My eyes lost the ability to blink. Despite repeated efforts, I could not close my eyelids. I had no idea of time. I almost forgot that I needed to maintain my body. When at rare intervals my attention would fall on the body a little, I was frightened by its condition. I thought, 'Am I on the verge of insanity?' Standing in front of a mirror, I tried to close my eyelids with my fingers — and I couldn't! I became frightened and tearfully said to the Mother: 'Mother, is this the result of praying and wholly surrendering myself to You? Now You have given me this terrible disease!' But the next moment I would say: 'Let it be as You wish. Let this body go to pieces, but don't leave me. Reveal Yourself to me; bestow Your mercy on me. I have taken refuge at Your lotus feet alone. I have none else but You.' I would shed tears, then suddenly be filled with ecstasy. I would feel my body to be a trifling thing. I was comforted when I saw the Mother and heard Her reassuring voice."[61]

We suffer from worries and anxieties regarding our work and our problems, but the Master was so detached that his mind was not affected by good and bad. Saradananda wrote:

> "Mother does Her own work. Who am I to work for the world and teach all of humanity?" We cannot even imagine how deeply this attitude was rooted in the Master's mind throughout his life. The Master's self-abnegation made him a true instrument for the Mother's work.
>
> It was completely impossible for the Master to assume the role of a teacher to serve his ego, as we learned by witnessing his many boyish quarrels with the Divine Mother during ecstasy. As bees swarm to a full-blown hundred-petalled lotus, attracted by its fragrance, so large crowds began to visit Dakshineswar, drawn there by the Master's spirituality. When we arrived one day, we heard the Master saying to the Divine Mother in ecstasy: "What are You doing? Why are You bringing such large crowds here? I have no time to bathe or eat. (*Pointing to his own body*) This is nothing but a broken drum. (The Master had recently developed throat cancer.) If it's beaten too much, it will be perforated. What will You do then?"[62]

Ramakrishna gathered spirituality in the first half of his life and distributed it till his death. When he was suffering from cancer, he prayed to the Divine Mother to impart some power to his disciples and devotees.

> The Master told his devotees: "Today I prayed to the Mother: 'Please give a little power to Vijay, Girish, Kedar, Ram, and Master [M.], so that they can prepare newcomers to a certain extent before they come to me.'" In regard to providing people with spiritual direction, he once said to a woman devotee, "I shall pour water and let you knead the mud."
>
> One day in October 1884, we were seated with the Master at Dakshineswar. Some days previously we had been present when we learned about the illness of Pratap Hazra's mother, and the Master persuaded Pratap to go home to serve her. On this day news reached us that Pratap had gone to Vaidyanath instead of going home. The Master was a little annoyed by this. After a brief conversation, the Master asked us to sing a song, and a little later he went into ecstasy. While he was in ecstasy, the Master began to quarrel with the Mother like a little boy. He said: "Why do You bring such hopeless people here? (*After a brief silence*) I can't do so much. Let one seer of milk be diluted with a quarter-seer of water, but here you have five seers of water and one seer of milk! I'm pushing firewood into the oven to boil this milk; now my eyes are burning with smoke. If You want them to have it, You give them spirituality. I can't push enough fuel into the fire. Don't bring that type of person here anymore." Overwhelmed with awe and wonder, we sat there quietly and wondered whom the Master was talking about to the Divine Mother and

how unfortunate that person was. Quite often he would quarrel with the Mother in this manner. This proves that the Master considered the honourable position of a teacher — which others so coveted — to be trivial, and repeatedly asked the Mother to relieve him of it.[63]

The Divine Mother was the Master's High Court. Whenever he encountered any problem or confusion, he approached the Mother for a solution. Saradananda wrote:

Confused by Haladhari's scholarly arguments, the childlike Master would sometimes rush to the Divine Mother for guidance about what he should do. We heard that Haladhari once raised a terrible doubt in the Master's mind: He tried to prove as false the Master's experiences of God that occurred during ecstasy by pointing out with the help of the scriptures that God is beyond existence and nonexistence. The Master said later: "I thought that the divine visions I had had during ecstasy and the commands I had received were all false. The Mother must have cheated me! I was extremely upset. Piqued, I cried to the Mother: 'Mother, I am unlettered and ignorant. Why have You cheated me in this way?' I couldn't control myself, and kept crying. I was in a room of the kuthi [bungalow]. After awhile a smoke-like mist arose from the floor and covered some space before me. Then I saw within it a golden-complexioned, living, calm face with long flowing beard. That figure looked at me intently and said in a deep voice: 'My child, you remain in bhavamukha. You remain in bhavamukha. You remain in bhavamukha!' After repeating this three times, the form slowly dissolved into the mist, then that mist also disappeared. This vision reassured me." Much later, the Master himself related this incident to Swami Premananda. On another occasion the Master said: "Haladhari's words raised doubt in my mind at another time. So while performing worship in the temple, I cried and pressed the Mother to solve that matter. At that time the Mother, in the guise of a woman known as 'Rati's mother,' appeared beside the consecrated pitcher [installed in front of the image] and told me: 'You remain in bhavamukha!'" Later, when the itinerant monk Tota Puri left Dakshineswar after teaching Vedanta to the Master, Sri Ramakrishna remained continuously in the nirvikalpa state for six months. Towards the end of that period, he heard the Divine Mother's voice again commanding: "You remain in bhavamukha!"[64]

When news of Adhar's death reached the Master, he immediately went into samadhi. Regaining normal consciousness, he wept and said to the Divine Mother: "Mother, You asked me to stay in the world with the devotees, cherishing devotion. Now look, how much pain I have!" It is something to think about — that an Incarnation of God would cry for his devotee. It is said that out of grief, Ramakrishna remained in bed for three days, covering himself with a cloth.[65]

On the prayer of the Brahmo Samaj

The Brahmo Samaj was a nineteenth-century Indian socio-religious reform movement devoted to the formless Brahman with attributes. The Brahmos used to visit the Master at Dakshineswar and the Master would also attend their congregation. During their prayer services, the Brahmos eulogized the glories and powers of God. Ramakrishna told them:

> "Why do you talk so much about the various powers of God? Does a child, sitting in front of his father, keep thinking about how many horses, cows, houses, and estates his father has? Isn't he simply happy knowing how much he loves his father and how much his father loves him? Is it any wonder that the father feeds and clothes his child? We are all God's children. Is it so extraordinary that He looks after us? Instead of dwelling on that, a real devotee makes God his very own by loving Him. He begs importunately, demanding that his prayer be answered and that God reveal Himself to him. If you dwell too much on God's powers, you can't think of Him as your nearest and dearest, and you can't feel free to demand things of Him. Thinking about His greatness makes Him seem distant from us. Think of Him as your very own. That's the only way to realize Him."[66]

> Master (to the Brahmos): "Dive deep. Learn to love God. Plunge into divine love. You see, I have heard how you pray. Why do you Brahmos dwell so much on the glories of God? Is there such great need of your saying over and over again, 'O God, You have created the sky, the great oceans, the lunar world, the solar world, and the stellar world?'

> "Everybody is wonder-struck at the mere sight of a rich man's garden house. People become speechless at the sight of the trees, the flowers, the ponds, the drawing-room, the pictures. But alas, how few are they who seek the owner of all these! Only one or two inquire after him. He who seeks God with a longing heart can see Him, talk to Him as I am talking to you. Believe my words when I say that God can be seen.[67]

Prayers that Ramakrishna quoted

The writers of The Gospel of Ramakrishna and Sri Ramakrishna and His Divine Play shared the wonderful prayers of Ramakrishna. However, Ramakrishna also taught his devotees prayers from the scriptures and from holy people, to create hunger for God in their minds.

Ahalya said to Rama, "O Rama, it doesn't matter if I am born as a pig or any other being; only bless me that my mind may dwell on Thy Lotus

Feet and be filled with real devotion to Thee."[68]

Narada said to Rama: "O Rama, I want from Thee no other favour. Please give me real love for Thee; and please bless me, that I may not come under the spell of Thy world-bewitching maya."[69]

When Draupadi's clothes were being taken off, she cried earnestly, praying to God. God revealed Himself to her and said: "Try to remember whether you have ever made a gift of a cloth to anyone. Then your modesty will be preserved." Draupadi replied: "Yes, I remember now. Once a rishi was taking his bath when his loin-cloth was carried away by the current. I tore off half my cloth and gave it to him." Thereupon the Lord said, "Then you have nothing to fear."[70]

Hanuman once said to Rama: "O Rama, I have taken refuge in Thee. Bless me that I may have pure devotion to Thy Lotus Feet and that I may not be caught in the spell of Thy world-bewitching maya."[71]

God keeps in many people the "ego of a jnani" or the "ego of a bhakta" even after they have attained Brahmajnana. Hanuman, after realizing God in both His Personal and His Impersonal aspect, cherished toward God the attitude of a servant, a devotee. He said to Rama: "O Rama, sometimes I think that You are the whole and I am a part of You. Sometimes I think that You are the Master and I am Your servant. And sometimes, Rama, when I contemplate the Absolute, I see that I am You and You are I."[72]

Yashoda became grief-stricken at being separated from Krishna and called on Radha. Radha saw Yashoda's suffering and revealed herself to her as the divine Shakti, which was her real nature. She said to Yashoda: "Krishna is Chidatma, Absolute Consciousness, and I am Chitshakti, the Primal Power. Ask a boon of Me." Yashoda said: "I don't want Brahmajnana. Please grant me only this: that I may see the form of Gopala in my meditation; that I may always have the company of Krishna's devotees; that I may always serve the devotees of God; that I may always chant God's name and glories."

Once the gopis felt a great desire to see the forms of the Lord. So Krishna asked them to dive into the water of the Yamuna. No sooner did they dive into the water than they all arrived at Vaikuntha. There they saw the form of the Lord endowed with His six celestial splendours. But they did not like it. They said to Krishna: "We want to see Gopala and serve Him. Please grant us that boon alone. We don't want anything else."[73]

Therefore I say to Hazra, "Never think that you alone have true understanding and that others are fools." One must love all. No one is a stranger. It is Hari alone who dwells in all beings. Nothing exists without Him.

The Lord said to Prahlada, "Ask a boon of Me." "I have seen You," replied Prahlada. "That is enough. I don't need anything else." But the

Lord insisted. Thereupon Prahlada said, "If You must give me a boon, let it be that those who have tortured me may not have to suffer punishment." The meaning of those words is that it was God who tortured Prahlada in the form of his persecutors, and, if they suffered punishment, it would really be God who suffered.[74]

God's sole desire is love. God loves His children and is pleased when the children return that love by thinking of Him, working for Him, and surrendering themselves to Him. This is the path of liberation from maya. This maya binds us, and bondage is always painful. How does one get rid of maya? Krishna clearly said in the Gita (7:14): "Those who take refuge in me alone, shall cross over this maya."

Ramakrishna taught the devotees to pray for pure unselfish love. As M. narrated in the *Gospel*: Master (*to Dr. Sarkar*): "There is such a thing as love for love's sake. It is very good if one can grow such love. Prahlada loved God for the sake of love. A devotee like Prahlada says: 'O God, I do not want wealth, fame, creature comforts, or any such thing. Please grant me the boon that I may have genuine love for Thy Lotus Feet.'"[75]

God always listens

Even those who know Bengali do not always understand Ramakrishna's patois, the form of Bengali used in his native village. In the Bengali *Gospel* we find some of the Master's words and usages from the Hooghly and Bankura districts that are not found in the dictionary: for example, *vishālākshir da* (a deep ditch filled with mud and water on the road to the Vishālākshi temple); *kānkharke* (to prick up one's ears). The Master always said that God listens to everything, even the footsteps of a tiny ant, and he always pricks up his ears to listen to the prayers of the devotees. However, if our prayers are not answered immediately, we are disappointed and lose faith in God. Saradananda wrote:

> When the devotees were despondent because their japa, prayer, and meditation seemed to have no results, the Master would encourage them by saying: "If you want to catch fish, first throw some spiced bait into the water. You may sit there for a long time holding a line and a rod without any sign of fish. You may think perhaps there are no fish in the pond. Then perhaps one day you may see a big fish jumping with a splash, and immediately you know there are fish in the pond. Another day perhaps the float on the line moves, and you believe a fish has come near the hook. Some days later when the float sinks, you lift the line and find the fish has eaten the bait and fled. Again you put bait on the hook and watch carefully after dropping the line. Then one day when the fish swallows

the bait, you pull the line and the fish is landed."

Sometimes the Master would say: "God is quick of hearing. He listens to everything. He has heard everything you have prayed for. Some day He will certainly reveal Himself to you — at least at the time of death." He told someone: "If you cannot ascertain whether God has form or is formless, pray in this way: 'O Lord, I don't know whether You are with form or formless. Whatever You may be, please bestow grace on me and reveal Yourself to me.'" Again he said to some others: "Truly one can see God. As we are sitting here together and talking, so one can see God and talk to Him. I am speaking the truth — I swear to you."[76]

The soul of prayer is love and faith

This chapter presented only a few of Ramakrishna's prayers. Innumerable prayers are scattered throughout *The Gospel of Sri Ramakrishna* and *Sri Ramakrishna and His Divine Play*. A person may be learned, intelligent, wealthy, and powerful but sometimes he or she feels helpless and cannot find a solution to a problem. Suppose a man has terminal cancer and the doctor has given him three months to live. He knows that no amount of money or human effort will save his life. He then seeks help from God and prays for his life. Ramakrishna even taught atheists how to pray: "O God, I do not know if Thou existeth or not. If Thou art, reveal Thyself to me."[77] "O Lord, I don't know whether You are with form or formless. Whatever You may be, please bestow grace on me and reveal Yourself to me."[78]

Here are the differences between our prayers and those of Ramakrishna:

1. We pray to an invisible God, yet Ramakrishna prayed to the visible living Divine Mother and other deities.
2. Most of our prayers come from our lips and not from our hearts. The Master's mind and speech were united, so his prayers originated from the inner recess of his heart.
3. Most of our prayers are directed towards maya, which means that we pray for worldly things. When we suffer, we pray, "God, we want you." Again when we feel better, we pray, "O Lord, we bought a lottery ticket in the name of 'Ma Kali.' May we win the lottery." The Master jokingly said to his rich devotee Jadu Mallick: "I now understand your nature. You are like the stone at Ramjivanpur — half-warm and half-cold. You are devoted to God and also to the world."[79] Ramakrishna prayed only for God and not for wealth or powers.

4. Most of our prayers are self-motivated; the Master's prayers were unselfish and for the welfare of others.

5. Our prayers lack devotion, and for that reason God will not fulfill them. We see children force their parents to fulfill their demands because of the parents' love for and dependence on them. When our prayers are not fulfilled quickly, we scold God: "You are deaf. Please get a hearing aid." We lose faith and enroll our names on the list of atheists. The soul of prayer is love and faith. Ramakrishna's prayers became living through his love and faith.

Swami Premananda witnessed how Ramakrishna's love and faith vividly manifested during prayer, and he described this to Swami Vishuddhananda. At Varanasi on 21 October 1951, Swami Vishuddhananda reminisced:

One day, Baburam Maharaj [Swami Premananda] arrived at Dakshineswar. The Master was seated on his small cot. Suddenly, out of ecstasy he began to sing:

"If only I can pass away repeating Durga's name,
How canst Thou then, O Blessed One,
Withhold from me deliverance, wretched though I may be?"

While singing that song, his ecstasy went deeper and deeper. Gradually he became excited and left his cot. He stood up, took off his cloth, and began to roll it like a rope. He then tied it around his waist tightly and continued that song. He was mad with ecstasy.

Baburam Maharaj remarked: "That day I realized that Faith embodied itself and appeared in Ramakrishna's form."[80]

God in the form of Ramakrishna taught human beings how to pray to God. God is completely free from desires and is the ruler of maya. Does God need to pray for anything? The whole world and all beings move at God's command. All the prayers in this chapter are part of the Master's divine play. Ramakrishna said: "My experiences are for others to refer to."[81]

9

Ramakrishna Scripture

*S*hastra and *Shāstra*: These two Sanskrit words are similar in spelling and pronunciation, but completely different in meaning. *Shastra* (with the initial *a* pronounced as *o* in *son*) means "weapon," while *shāstra* (with the initial *ā* pronounced as *ah*) means "scripture." Both words imply destruction, with the former aiming towards the destruction of a person and the latter aiming towards the destruction of ignorance. According to the *Hitopadesha*: "Knowledge of the weapons and of scriptures are two types of knowledge for proper living: the first is a matter for laughter in old age, and the second is always respected."[1]

The derivative meaning of *shāstra* is to discipline, advise, admonish, or rule. Scriptures are the teachings of God and saints; they guide human beings to the path of blessedness. Bhamati, an authority on the scriptures, said that shruti, or the eternal Veda, and smriti, or scriptures written by human beings, guide people to follow the path of action (*pravritti*) and the path of renunciation (*nivritti*). The purpose of the scriptures is to make the unknown known. We receive knowledge through the five organs of knowledge: That is, we see through the eyes, hear through the ears, taste through the tongue, smell through the nose, and touch through the skin. But the scriptures help us to achieve transcendental knowledge. The scriptures teach us what Brahman is, what the Atman is, and who God is. Moreover, they try to answer the fundamental questions of life: What relationship should we have with God? What is the way to know God, and why is this necessary? How were the world and all beings within it created? What is this world we live in? What is our true nature? What is

The symbol Om is called Nada-Brahman, the Sound-Brahman. The three letters A, U, and M, pronounced in combination as Om, are the generalized symbol of all possible sounds. It is the most sacred word of the Vedas.

the true purpose of human life? What are bondage and liberation? What is the mystery of birth and death?

According to the *Hitopadesha*, "The person who does not know the scriptures, which remove various doubts, bring transcendental knowledge, and bring clarity to our vision, is truly blind." Deluded people cannot differentiate between dharma and adharma, righteousness and unrighteousness. However, one can ascertain dharma and adharma by observing the mandates of the scriptures. Krishna said in the Gita: "Let the scriptures be your authority in determining what ought to be done and what ought not to be done. Having learnt the injunctions of the scriptures, you should do your work in the world."[2]

Shortsighted and egotistic people do not listen to the words of the saints and scriptures, and as a result they make mistakes and suffer from their wrong deeds. Those who are farsighted and wise follow the teachings of the saints and the scriptures, and they enjoy peace and happiness. Some modern, educated people, who are blown up with egotism, love to break the rules and traditions of the scriptures, criticize holy people, and reform societies according to their own self-interest. The ego invariably brings one's downfall. The scriptures help human beings to develop patience, self-control, compassion, truthfulness, simplicity, detachment, and other divine qualities. The Mahabharata says: "The activities of eating, sleeping, mating, and defending are common to animals and human beings. But the human beings are considered superior only when they inquire about the Absolute Truth; otherwise they are considered no better than animals."

Hindu scriptures

Hindu scriptures are vast and more numerous than any other religion in the world. Each religion in the world is guided by its own scripture, such as Buddhism by the Tripitakas, Zoroastrianism by the Zend Avesta, Judaism by the Torah, Christianity by the Bible, and Islam by the Koran. But Hinduism is a little different. It does not derive from any particular founder or a single book. The list of Hindu scriptures is so vast that it makes us dizzy.

Hinduism is an ancient religion. Many avatars, saints, and sages first realized God and then pointed out the various paths to God-realization from their experiences. There have been many seers of truth in the holy land of India and they all discovered various paths to reach the same goal — God. That is the reason the Hindu scriptures are many and not one as with other religions.

The Vedas are the source books of the Hindu religion, and they are based on the experiences of the rishis, the seers of truth. In ancient times there were no books, so the wisdom of the Vedic tradition was passed down orally from guru to disciple in succession, so it is called the *shruti*, meaning "what is heard."

O   Four Vedas. The Vedas are comprised of the Rig, Sama, Yajur, and Atharva. In his great commentary on the Vedas, Patanjali wrote that there were 101 branches of Yajur Veda, 1,000 branches of Sama Veda, 21 branches of Rig Veda, and 9 branches of Atharva Veda, for a total of 1,131 branches in all. The first section of each Veda is *karmakanda* (Vedic rituals and sacrifices), and the last part is *jnanakanda* (Upanishadic knowledge and philosophy). In the course of time, many Upanishads have been lost. The names of 108 Upanishads have been mentioned in the Muktika Upanishad.

O   Six Vedangas — Shiksha (phonetics), Chhandas (prosody), Vyakarana (grammar), Nirukta (etymology), Jyotisha (astronomy), and Kalpa (ritual instructions).

O   Four Upavedas — Dhanurveda (Archery), Āyurveda (Medicine), Gāndharvaveda (Music and Dance), and Sthapatyaveda (Architecture). Another school mentioned Artha-shastra (Economy) instead of Sthapatyaveda.

O   Smriti-shastra or Dharma-shastra — The number of Smriti scriptures are many. Manu, Vashishtha, Yajnavalkya, Daksha, Parashara, Gautama, Harita, Vyasa, Katyayana and other sages prescribed rules and guidelines regarding the Hindu way of life, as well as dharma according to each caste and ashrama, and their duties.

O   Eighteen Puranas — There are five signs or characteristics of the Puranas. Each Purana includes discussions on creation, destruction and re-creation, plus stories of gods and goddesses, the periods of Manus, and stories of the kings of the Sun and Moon dynasties. Some Puranas deal with stories of gods and goddesses and the glory of certain holy places of India. Scholars have divided the 18 Puranas into three categories: six Brahma Puranas, six Vishnu Puranas, and six Shiva Puranas.

Brahma Puranas: Brahmanda Purana, 12,000 verses; Brahmavaivarta, 18,000 verses; Markandeya, 9,000 verses; Bhavishya, 14,500 verses; Vamana, 10,000 verses; and Brahma, 10,000 verses.

Vishnu Puranas: Vishnu Purana, 23,000 verses; Naradiya, 25,000 verses; Bhagavata, 18,000 verses; Garuda, 19,000 verses; Padma, 55,000 verses; and Varaha, 24,000 verses.

Shiva Puranas: Matsya Purana, 14,000 verses; Kurma, 17,000 verses; Linga, 11,000 verses; Vayu, 24,000 verses; Skanda, 81,100 verses; and Agni, 15,400 verses.

The total verses of 18 Puranas are 400,000. Over and above the 18 Puranas, there are 18 Upa-puranas, or subsidiary puranas, which contain mythological stories of the Hindu tradition.

O **Six darshanas, or philosophical schools** — As the scenes of the world manifest in our eyes, so meditation on and study of abstruse philosophical thoughts manifest clearly in the mind. Thus, various philosophical schools originated in India in different times.

The Nyaya philosophy (logic) was founded by the Sage Gautama with 528 sutras or aphorisms.

The Vaisheshika philosophy was founded by the Sage Kanada with 370 sutras.

The Sankhya philosophy was founded by the Sage Kapila with 521 sutras.

The Patanjala Yoga philosophy was founded by the Sage Patanjali with 195 sutras.

The Purva Mimamsa philosophy was founded by the Sage Jaimini with 2500 sutras.

The Uttara Mimamsa philosophy was founded by the Sage Vyasa with 555 sutras. It is also called Brahma Sutras, Vedanta Sutras, or Shariraka Sutras.

O **Two epics: Ramayana and Mahabharata** — Sage Valmiki composed the Ramayana in 24,000 verses, and Sage Vyasa composed the Mahabharata in 100,000 verses. These two great epics can be placed in the category of history. The touching stories on morality, ethics, dharma, and adharma in these two epics provide the great lessons of the Hindu tradition.

O **Bhagavad Gita and Chandi** — The Gita and the Chandi are the two most popular Hindu scriptures. The Gita is embedded in the Mahabharata and it contains 700 verses. The Chandi is in the Markandeya Purana and it contains 700 verses.

O **Prasthana-trayi** — This term literally means the *three sources*, and refers to the three canonical texts of Vedanta philosophy. It consists of the Upanishads (revealed truth), the Brahma Sutras (reasoned truth), and the Bhagavad Gita (practical truth).

O **Tantra** — Tantra is an important, practical, and popular religious path of Hinduism. The word *Tantra* is derived from the Sanskrit root *tan* (*tanyate*), meaning "to spread." Tantra means the scripture by which the light of knowledge is spread.

The Tantric scriptures are in question-and-answer form so that ordinary people can easily understand them. There are two branches in Tantric teachings: *agama* and *nigama*. *Agama* means the great teachings that come from the lips of the teacher. In the *agamas*, we find Shiva as the teacher and Parvati, his wife, as the student. She asks questions and Shiva answers them. However, *nigama* is just the reverse: Parvati, the Divine Mother, is the teacher, and Shiva is the student.

There are three divisions of Tantra: Vishnukranta, Ashvakranta, and Rathakranta. Each branch of Tantra, called a *kranta*, has 64 sadhanas or spiritual disciplines — for a total of 192. Tantric sadhanas and spiritual instructions are recorded in these small treatises.

Ramakrishna practised the 64 sadhanas of Vishnukranta. (A list of the Tantra sadhanas of the Vishnukranta has been mentioned in *Principles of Tantra* by Arthur Avalon; Introduction, lxv.) This is an amazing accomplishment. An ordinary person would spend his or her whole life — even life after life — to attain perfection in even one sadhana. Sri Ramakrishna practised all 64 sadhanas in just two years.

There are five schools of Tantra, each devoted to a different deity: Shaiva Tantra (Shiva), Shakta Tantra (Shakti, the Divine Mother), Vaishnava Tantra (Vishnu), Saurya Tantra (the Sun deity), and Ganapatya Tantra (Ganesha). When we speak of Tantric scriptures, we think primarily of the sacred books of the Shaktas, worshippers of Shakti, the Divine Mother. Some important books on Tantra include the Mahanirvana Tantra, Kularnava, Kulasara, Prapanchasara, Tantraraj, Rudrajamal, Brahmajamal, Vishnujamal, and Toraltantra.

O **Pancharatra Samhita and Shaivagama** — Pancharatra Samhita of the Vaishnavas and Shaivagama of the Shaivas are in the category of Tantra-shastra. The instructions in these scriptures are easy to practise in this kaliyuga, and all men and women can practise these sadhanas after initiation. The numbers of Pancharatra Samhita are 215, and Shaivagama are 28.

O **Shrauta-sutra, Grihya-sutra, and Dharma-sutra** — The Shrauta-sutra prescribes the methods of performing Vedic sacrifices; the Grihya-sutra prescribes the duties of householders and discusses brahminical initiation; and the Dharma-sutra prescribes daily obligatory duties and occasional ritualistic duties.

O **Ashtadhyayi Grammar** — This scripture helps people to purify and correct their language. Using the right word and framing sentences correctly are vital for human communication. Sage Panini wrote the Ashtadhyayi Grammar in Sanskrit in 3,863 sutras.

O **Dharma-shastra, Artha-shastra, Kama-shastra, and Moksha-shastra** — In Hinduism four ideals of life are described: Dharma (righteousness) is the law of inner growth and the basis of human action. Artha (wealth) is a legitimate goal of pursuit to live in this world. Kama is the fulfilment of sensuous and aesthetic desire. Moksha is the desire for liberation. The first three ideals belong to the material world and the last one to the spiritual realm. The authors of the Hindu scriptures wrote books on each of the four subjects. Manu, Yajnavalkya, and other sages wrote scriptures on the dharma or Smriti shastra. Brihaspati, Sukracharya, and Chanakya wrote the *Artha-shastra*. Sage Vatsayana wrote the *Kama-sutra*. According to the Hindu view of life, the ultimate goal of life is moksha, or liberation. The Upanishads, Gita, and various other treatises and commentaries on Vedanta literature are in the category of Moksha-shastra.

This long list of Hindu scriptures has been presented in order to indicate the position of the Ramakrishna scriptures in this tradition. In every age the smriti scriptures, customs and practices, conduct and behaviour change, but the eternal religion does not change. In the Satya-yuga, truth was emphasised; in Treta-yuga, sacrifice; in Dwapara-yuga, austerity; and in this Kali-yuga, charity is emphasised. Ramakrishna fulfils the need of this age. He came to establish the harmony of all religions and to make religion simple, practical, and universal.

Quarrels concerning the scriptures

There are zealots in every religion. They believe their religion, their prophet, and their scripture to be the best, or even the only true ones. In the Hindu religion some bigoted followers of Vishnu, Shiva, and the Divine Mother (Shakti) consider their scriptures and their path to be the best. Once there was a quarrel between the followers of Vishnu and Shiva. Each group claimed that its deity was the greatest. Pandit Padmalochan became the umpire. He asked a Shaivite, "Have you seen Shiva?"

"No."

"Has your father or grandfather seen Shiva?"

"No."

Padmalochan asked the same questions of a Vaishnavite and got the same answers. He then asked them both: "Then how can you say who is greatest?" Finally, he commented that Vaishnava scriptures glorify the greatness of Vishnu and the Shaiva scriptures glorify the greatness of Shiva. Those who have not seen God, only quarrel.

Other world religions — Judaism, Christianity, Islam, and Buddhism — also have some fanatics such as these. Many have not read the scriptures of other religions, yet they consider their religion to be the greatest. In 2015 a Christian minister in the United States burned a Koran, and Muslims in Afghanistan took revenge by burning some Bibles. Another time, one Muslim sect burned the mosque of another Muslim sect in Iraq. God laughs while watching the foolishness of these children.

Chandrakanta Tarkalankar narrated in a lecture on philosophy that many Hindu scriptures were destroyed during the Buddhistic period:

> Probably Bhojadeva, the king of Dhareswar, compiled the first book on the Smriti-scriptures, namely *"Kamadhenu"*. The following story had been mentioned in the introduction to that book: Mataditya was a son of the famous king Vikramaditya and the grandson of the King Bhojadeva. He was the king of Ujjain but died at an early age. When his body was taken for cremation to the cremation ground, a Buddhist yogi desiring a wish entered Mataditya's body through yogic power. When the king rose from death, there was great joy all over his kingdom. After some time Mataditya expressed a desire to perform a sacrifice and his ministers approved it. He then commanded that all pandits of India should come with all their scriptures to Ujjain to attend the great sacrifice, and decide which sacrifice was the greatest after consulting their scriptures. The king's order was executed and a big pavilion was set up on the bank of the Shipra river. Several sacrificial altars were set up and the date was fixed for the sacrifice. Meanwhile, Mataditya arranged a short pilgrimage trip for the pandits and sent them away for a few days. Then the king gave the order to set fire to the sacrificial altar and burn all the scriptures brought by the pandits. The pandits returned to the kingdom, heard the sad news, and then returned to their homes.
>
> Mataditya started to torture the Hindus with a view to spreading Buddhism. Gradually this news reached King Bhojaraj, who wondered why his grandson had this kind of evil intention! He was sad and engaged an astrologer to find the cause of this disaster. The astrologer found through his calculations that Mataditya was not alive, and that a Buddhist yogi had entered his body and was making all this mischief. Immediately a 'Vighatak' sacrifice was arranged in Dhara city to counter the power of entering another's body. The moment this sacrifice ended, Mataditya died.
>
> Then King Bhojaraj collected the remaining scriptures of India and asked the pandits to record the scriptures from their memory. Thus, he composed the 'Kamadhenu' scripture and mentioned the sources in a list at the beginning of this vast scripture.[3]

Shankara's first disciple, Padmapada, once went on a pilgrimage to

South India, where he stayed for a few days with his maternal uncle at Shrirangam. This uncle was a follower of the Mimamsa philosophy, and he believed in Vedic sacrifice. Padmapada had written *Vijay Dindima*, a commentary on Shankara's Brahma Sutra commentary. The only manuscript of this book was with him. His uncle read the commentary and became angry because it used reason to refute the dualistic school. The uncle said to Padmapada: "You are going to Rameswaram for a pilgrimage. Please leave this book with me and take it back when you return." Padmapada was unaware of his uncle's evil intention. One evening when he was gone, his uncle set fire to the thatched hut where that manuscript lay. When Padmapada returned and found his uncle's cottage and the manuscript burnt, he was broken-hearted. He went to his guru, Shankara, and reported the incident. Shankara said: "Don't be upset. You read that manuscript to me once, and I remember everything. Let me dictate and you write down your lost commentary." Thus, that valuable scripture was restored.

Quarrel and debate among the philosophical schools of India

It is said that each sage has his own opinion. The friction, rivalry, opposition, and disagreement among different Indian schools of philosophy developed into competing doctrines in the philosophical systems. Every philosopher or rishi used his knowledge and intellect to comprehend the truth. In the fourth chapter of the Brihadaranyaka Upanishad, we find that six sages described Brahman in six different ways. Each one of these described Brahman as: the organ of speech (*vak*), the vital breath (*prana*), the eyes (*cakshu*), the organ of hearing (*shrotra*), the mind (*manas*), and the heart (*hriday*). These sages each had a partial experience. In this connection, Ramakrishna told the parable of four blind men who touched four different parts of an elephant and described the elephant differently.

It is amazing how differences of opinion created 10 commentaries on the Brahma Sutra: Shankara's *Advaitavāda*, Bhaskara's *Brahma-parināmavāda*, Nilkantha's *Shivādvaitavāda*, Ramanuja's *Vishishtādvaitavāda*, Nimbarka's *Dvaitādvaitavāda*, Ballabha's *Shuddhādvaitavāda*, Madhva's *Dvaitavāda*, Vijnanabhikshu's *Dvaitavā*da, Baladeva's *Achintya-bhedābhedavāda*, and Panchanan's *Shaktivāda*.

Each of the commentators on the Brahma Sutra tried to establish his own view by refuting the others' philosophy. Earlier Buddha fought against Vedic rituals and sacrifices. In the eighth century, Shankara refuted 75 schools of thought and established his own philosophy of Advaita. In the 11th century, Ramanuja established Vishishtadvaitavada, and in the

13th century, Madhva established Dvaitavada. Later, the teachers who followed these three schools attacked others through debate, or wrote the commentaries, and in this way they established their own schools of thought.

In the 12th century, the great poet and logician Sriharsha wrote *Khandakhanda-khādyam*, using reason to refute the Nyaya and Vaisheshika philosophies and establish Advaita Vedanta. As medicine can cure a disease and improve physical and mental health, so Sriharsha's book establishes the supreme bliss of Brahman by refuting the views of others.

Then in the 13th and 14th centuries, Venkatanath (Vedantadeshika) wrote a book called *Shatadushani* and refuted Advaitavada. He supported Ramanuja's *Vishishtadvaitavada* (which is a counter-argument to Sriharsha's *Khandakhanda-khādyam*). In the 16th century, Vyasaraj Swami wrote *Nyayamrita*, which established Swatantraswantravada. He was a follower of Madhva and he refuted the views of Ramanuja and Shankara. Again, in the 17th century, Madhusudan Saraswati wrote *Advaita-siddhi*, which refuted Vyasaraj's *Nyayamrita*. *Advaita-siddhi* refuted all the arguments of the dualists with the help of Navyanyaya. This book covered all aspects of Advaita Vedanta and revealed its mysteries. Thus, over a period of many centuries, through attack and counter-attack, the philosophers developed the wonderful systems of Indian philosophy.

Now the question is: Where is Ramakrishna's position in the Indian philosophical traditions? What is Ramakrishna's philosophy? Ramakrishna's teachings constitute his philosophy. His teachings never criticized anyone's else's religious path. Once Girish Ghosh said that he would write a book against the left-handed Tantra sadhana of the Kartabhaja sect. Immediately, Ramakrishna gravely said: "That is also a path. Some people made progress following that path." He could not bear any criticism against anyone's religious faith.

Ramakrishna's philosophy

When I was in Hollywood in 1971, Swami Prabhavananda told me about this incident: "In 1919 I was a Brahmachari at the Madras Math, and Swami Sharvananda would give a class on the scriptures. One day we had a heated discussion in our class regarding Ramakrishna's philosophy. Finally, we decided we must find out this important point from Swami Turiyananda, who was an authority on the scriptures. Swami Sharvananda wrote a letter asking our question [What is Ramakrishna's philosophy?] to Swami Turiyananda, who was then living in Varanasi. Swami Turiyananda wrote us back."

The following letter from Swami Turiyananda is a valuable document regarding Ramakrishna's philosophy. The solution to the wrangling and arguments among philosophical pandits can be found in this letter. The Master used to say: "You have come to this world to eat mangoes. Enjoy them. You will not have to count the leaves and mangoes of the trees."

Varanasi
18 April 1919
Dear Sharvananda,

I received your letter some time ago, but I could not write to you until now because I was ill. Though the subject [What is Sri Ramakrishna's philosophy?] is extremely difficult, with the Lord's grace, I will try my best to answer your question.

It is not so easy to speak about Sri Ramakrishna's philosophy. It seems to me that to encourage the followers of all religions, he declared, "As many faiths, so many paths." He made this statement after he himself practised disciplines of various religious paths and experienced that their paths lead to the same Truth.

The ultimate Truth is one and nondual. It is called by various names: Brahman, Paramatman, Bhagavan, God, and so on. Whoever has realized that Truth has tried to express it according to his own temperament and understanding by giving it a particular name. But nobody has been able to express the *whole* truth. "What he is, he is" — that is the final conclusion of those who have realized Him.

From different standpoints, Gaudapada's doctrine of no creation, Shankara's doctrine of superimposition, Ramanuja's doctrine of transformation, and [Sri Kantha's] doctrine of Shivadvaita — each one of these is true. Apart from all these doctrines, He [God] is beyond all human expression and beyond cognition. The founders of all these philosophical systems practised austerities and, having received God's grace, they preached the various doctrines at His command. God is the subject from which these doctrines evolved, but He Himself is beyond them. To express this truth is the philosophy of Sri Ramakrishna. That is what I think.

Hanuman said to Rama: "O Lord, when I identify myself with the body I am Your servant. When I consider myself as an individual soul, I am a part of You. And when I look upon myself as the Atman, I am one with You — this is my firm conviction." Sri Ramakrishna referred to this statement as the best conclusion of the different phases of spiritual experience.

Why should it not be possible to see the worship vessels as Brahman, saturated with consciousness? [This is a reference to Sri Ramakrishna's vision in the Kali temple, where it was revealed to him that everything is Pure Spirit.] "Throughout the universe He exists, pervading every being and thing, animate and inanimate." There is nothing but He. He verily is all. Because we cannot see Him we see objects instead, but the fact is that He is everything. Names and forms originate from Him and remain in Him. The waves, the foam, the bubbles — they are all nothing but water. Who cares if your doctrine of superimposition stands or falls? One who has known this truth [that Brahman is all] cannot be content with a lesser standpoint.

The Master used to experience a state beyond all thought and ideas. That state transcends name and form, words and mind. There exists only One without a second, beyond the realm of *Prakriti* [that is, beyond relativity]. Where is the doctrine of superimposition or the doctrine of no creation in that realm of Oneness? And yet again, all doctrines — whether of superimposition, or of no creation, or of transformation, and so on — originate from Him.

He alone is the Reality, the Truth. And again, He is the source of all individual beings and of the universe. This manifestation is also true if He is not forgotten. Name and form become unreal if we forget God, because they cannot exist without Him.* But if He dwells in our thoughts, only then can we understand the truth that "the pith belongs to the sheaths and the sheaths belong to the pith."** At that time one can understand these sayings of the Gita: "All things in this universe are pervaded by Me" (9:4); "All is strung on Me as a row of gems on a thread" (7:7).

The *main thing* is we must see Him. When we see Him, everything else disappears. One experiences Him as everything. Before we see Him, we have doubts and confusion, and all sorts of theories and controversies. But these cease to exist as soon as we see Him. Then one experiences uninterrupted peace and bliss.

Sri Ramakrishna's philosophy therefore is: We must attain God by any means necessary, and at any cost. The Master said, "Tie nondual knowledge in the corner of your cloth and then do as you please." This means that once you attain Him, it does not matter which doctrine your temperament bids you to uphold. Liberation is assured when you know Him. Then there is no more bondage. After death, whether you take another body or not depends upon your wish.

The seekers of nirvana consider this world to be a dream. They merge their minds in the impersonal aspect of Brahman and become one with It. And devotees who are attached to the Personal God consider this world to be a manifestation of God's power. They attach themselves to the Lord,

*Sri Ramakrishna said: "Zeros added together amount to zero. Place the digit one before them, and they add in value." The digit one is God.
**A reference to Sri Ramakrishna's saying that as long as the plantain tree contains sheaths, it also contains pith. He was illustrating the point that while God keeps the "ego of a devotee" in a person, the Relative (the sheaths) is real as well as the Absolute (the pith).

who is Existence-Knowledge-Bliss Absolute. They are not afraid to be born again and again. They consider themselves to be playmates of God, and they come to the world to join His divine play.

They delight in the Atman and at the same time remain devoted to God. They covet nothing in this world. They even refuse to accept nirvana if it is offered to them. That is enough for today.

Turiyananda[4]

Swami Vivekananda on Ramakrishna-shāstra

Swami Vivekananda was the main expounder and commentator on Ramakrishna's life and message. He was the person who best understood the infinite nature of Ramakrishna. He heard from the Master: Do not limit God. Narrow and bigoted people form sects like snails in stagnant water.

Sharat Chandra Chakrabarty, a disciple of Swamiji, asked him: "Why do you not preach Sri Ramakrishna as an avatara? You have, indeed, power, eloquence, and everything else needed to do it."

Swamiji: Truly, I tell you, I have understood him very little. He appears to me to have been so great that, whenever I have to speak anything of him, I am afraid lest I ignore or explain away the truth, lest my little power does not suffice, lest in trying to extol him I present his picture by painting him according to my lights and belittle him thereby!"[5]

Swamiji was a seer. He knew that in the future monks and devotees would form many sects based on the life and teachings of Ramakrishna, according to their limited intellect and understanding. With a view to preventing this, he elaborately explained the views of Ramakrishna in the Belur Math rule book:

1. If we compile the sayings of Sri Ramakrishna and make them the sole scriptures, the only outcome of His broad ideas and ideals and our life-long labour will be that we shall be creating a small and narrow sect and making this society, already divided into many quarrelling factions, still more tumultuous.
2. Therefore, our eternal scripture, the Vedas, will be accepted and preached as the sole scriptures. And even as the Gita was in the ancient times, so will Sri Ramakrishna's sayings be the most modern and perfect commentary on the Vedic doctrines.
3. In other words, Shankara and all other commentators made a tremendous mistake in thinking that the whole of the Vedas presented only a single doctrine. Therefore, they are guilty of torturing those of the apparently conflicting Vedic texts which go against their own doctrines into ideas of their particular schools.
4. Even as in ancient times it was only the Lord, the deliverer of the

message of the Gita, who partially harmonized the apparently conflicting views, so also to settle once and for all the same dispute which assumed immense proportions in the course of time. He Himself has come as Sri Ramakrishna.

5. Therefore, no one has the power to understand the Vedas and Vedanta, unless they are read in the light of His utterances and seen through the medium of His life. In other words, it was Sri Ramakrishna who for the first time taught and exemplified in His life that the scriptural statements which appear at first sight to be contradictory, were meant for different types of aspirants, and arranged in the order of gradual development. That the whole world will, in consequence of these teachings, forget its disputes and disagreements and be united in a fraternal bond in religious and other matters, is inferred from the ever-widening sphere of influence which radiates from the very centre.

6. That is to say, the Vedas and other scriptures were long hidden in the darkness of ignorance, but the light of Sri Ramakrishna has revealed them again.

7. Hence it is clearly understood that new scriptures are necessary. New light is coming from the ancient, eternal Shastras. We shall have to gather their significance through the microscope on the life of Sri Ramakrishna.

8. Sri Ramakrishna's utterances, well compiled and accepted by his constant attendants will be honoured as commentaries of the Vedas.

9. The Vedas are to be interpreted in the light of Sri Ramakrishna's ideas and ideals. Above all, it should be always borne in mind that all his teachings are for the good of the world. If ever anyone heard from Him anything that was harmful, it should be understood that it was meant for a particular individual, and that, though it might be harmful when followed by others, it was beneficial to that particular individual.[6]

Ramakrishna's life and his message are intertwined with the eternal religion. Swamiji wrote about it elaborately in his article "Hinduism and Sri Ramakrishna." This was Swamiji's last article published in *Udbodhan* magazine during his lifetime. In it he indicated that the followers of Ramakrishna should not form any new sects in the future. After Buddha's passing away, his followers were divided into 18 groups, just as Christ's followers ultimately divided into many denominations. Now, there are 296 Christian denominations mentioned in the *Yearbook of American and Canadian Churches.*

Hindus have different ideas regarding the true Hindu religion. There are many branches of Hinduism in India. In 1897, Swamiji gave a lecture in Lahore, "The Common Bases of Hinduism," in which he pointed out that all Hindus believe in these things: Vedas, God, Theory of Creation,

Atman, and the Doctrine of Reincarnation. In his article "Hinduism and Sri Ramakrishna," Swamiji introduced the life and teachings of the Master as a "teacher of harmony" and "the embodiment of the Vedas." Swamiji said: "This new religion of the age will benefit the whole world, but most especially India. Bhagavan Sri Ramakrishna, the founder of this new religion, is the reconstructed manifestation of the earlier founders of religions. O human beings, have faith in this and realize it."[7]

In some of his letters, Swamiji hinted at the position of Ramakrishna's teachings in Hinduism and Hindu scriptures. In 1894, Swamiji wrote to Swami Shivananda from the United States: "Without studying Ramakrishna Paramahamsa first, one can never understand the real import of the Vedas, the Vedanta, or the Bhagavata and the other Puranas. His life is a searchlight of infinite power thrown upon the whole mass of Indian religious thought. He was the living commentary to the Vedas and to their aim. He lived in one life the whole cycle of the national religious existence in India."[8]

On 30 November 1894, Swamiji wrote to Alasinga from the United States:

The life of Sri Ramakrishna was an extraordinary searchlight under whose illumination one is able to really understand the whole scope of Hindu religion. He was the object-lesson of all the theoretical knowledge given in the Shastras [scriptures]. He showed by his life what the rishis and avataras really wanted to teach. The books were theories, he was the realization. This man had in fiftyone years lived the five thousand years of national spiritual life and so raised himself to be an object-lesson for future generations. The Vedas can only be explained and the Shastras reconciled by his theory of *Avastha* or stages — that we must not only tolerate others, but positively embrace them, and that truth is the basis of all religions. Now on these lines a most impressive and beautiful life can be written.[9]

On 30 May 1897, Swamiji wrote to Pramadadas Mitra from Almora:

Such a God I have seen in my life, and his commands I live to follow. The Smritis and the Puranas are productions of men of limited intelligence and are full of fallacies, errors, the feelings of class and malice. Only parts of them breathing broadness of spirit and love are acceptable, the rest are to be rejected. The Upanishads and the Gita are the true scriptures; Rama, Krishna, Buddha, Chaitanya, Nanak, Kabir, and so on are the true avataras, for they had their hearts broad as the sky — and above all, Ramakrishna. Ramanuja, Shankara etc., seem to have been mere pandits with much narrowness of heart. Where is that love, that weeping heart at the sorrow of others? — Dry pedantry of the pandit — and the feeling of only oneself getting to salvation hurryscurry! But is that going to be possible, sir? Was it ever likely or will it ever be so? Can anything be attained with any shred of "I" left anyhow?[10]

The Brihadaranyaka Upanishad tells us that the source of all scriptures is Brahman (God): "As from a fire kindled with wet fuel various kinds of smoke issue forth, even so, the Rig Veda, Yajur Veda, Sama Veda, Atharvangirasa, history, mythology, arts, Upanishads, verses, aphorisms, elucidations, and explanations are like the breath of this infinite Reality. From this Supreme Self are all these, indeed, breathed forth."[11]

Swamiji saw with his own eyes the true nature of Ramakrishna. That is why he forcefully expressed that Ramakrishna was a "father of God," and "foremost among the avataras." Swamiji said: "Certain fishermen and illiterate people called Jesus Christ a God, but the literate people killed him. Buddha was honoured in his lifetime by a number of merchants and cowherds. But Ramakrishna has been worshipped in his lifetime — towards the end of this nineteenth century — by the demons and giants of the university as God incarnate."[12]

Finally, Swamiji glorified Ramakrishna with this salutation mantra: "Constant salutation be to Sri Ramakrishna, the Free, the Ishvara, the Shiva-form, by whose power we and the whole world are blessed."[13]

According to Swamiji, the teachings of Ramakrishna themselves comprise a scripture. His words surpassed the teachings of the Vedas and Vedanta. On 28 January 1900, Swamiji gave a lecture in California entitled "The Way to the Realization of a Universal Religion," in which he said: "Is God's book finished? Or is it still a continuous revelation going on? It is a marvellous book — these spiritual revelations of the world. The Bible, the Vedas, the Koran, and all other sacred books are but so many pages, and an infinite number of pages remain yet to be unfolded. I would leave it open for all of them. We stand in the present, but open ourselves to the infinite future."[14]

According to Swamiji, the Vedic scriptures are without beginning and without end. In this context, Sri Ramakrishna appeared as an embodiment of the Vedas and manifested the ancient Vedas in a new form.

Ramakrishna-shastra: *Sri Sri Ramakrishna Lilaprasanga* and *Sri Sri Ramakrishna Kathamrita*

Swami Saradananda wrote *Sri Sri Ramakrishna Lilaprasanga* (*Sri Ramakrishna and His Divine Play*) in five parts, and M. originally published *Sri Sri Ramakrishna Kathamrita* (*The Gospel of Sri Ramakrishna*) in five parts. We consider these two books to be the Ramakrishna-shastra. The goal of the shastras or scriptures is to show people how to reach God, how to practise spirituality in day-to-day life, how to determine the goal of human life, how to attain liberation from bondage, and how to determine dharma [righteousness] and adharma [unrighteousness]. From the scriptures we learn morality and ethics, rules of conduct and our duties in every station of life, as well as the effects of good and bad karma. Moreover, the stories and teachings of gods and saints help us to appreciate holy company, make us understand the impermanency and emptiness of this world of maya, and bring peace and bliss to our minds. When we study and reflect upon the *Lilaprasanga* and the *Kathamrita*, we feel Ramakrishna's presence. We listen to his instructions and teachings, and visualize his divine play. This book [*See God with Open Eyes*] contains two chapters — Chapter 10 on the *Lilaprasanga* and Chapter 11 on the *Kathamrita* — pointing out their depth, vastness, significance, and history.

It is amazing that neither the *Lilaprasanga* nor the *Kathamrita* is complete. Swami Saradananda did not write about the last days of the Master in Cossipore, nor did he include accounts of his death even though he was an eyewitness to those events. In addition, he wrote only about the Master's relationship with Swamiji and Gopal-ma, and not about other disciples and devotees. M. visited the Master over a period of four and a half years, but he recorded the Master's conversations and gave descriptions of various events for only 177 days. The last entry of the *Kathamrita* is dated 24 April 1886. Afterwards, M. continued to write about the Master in his diary but did not develop or publish this material. We do not know why Saradananda and M. did not complete these two important scriptures. Perhaps it was not the will of the Master or the decree of Divine Providence. We shall be content with whatever we have received by the Master's grace, and we shall use our imagination to meditate on his infinite forms and messages.

The Ramakrishna-shastra did not end with the *Lilaprasanga* and *Kathamrita*. Several other chroniclers recorded Ramakrishna's immortal teachings in Bengali: Girish Chandra Sen recorded "*Adi Kathamrita* — 184 teachings"; Suresh Chandra Datta, "*Sri Sri Ramakrishnadever Upadesh* — 950 teachings"; Ram Chandra Datta, "*Tattva-Prakashika* — 300 teachings"; Swami Brahmananda, "*Sri Ramakrishner Upadesh* — 248 teachings." Later, several subsidiary scriptures on Ramakrishna were written:

1. *Sri Sri Ramakrishna Punthi* — Akshay Kumar Sen
2. *Sri Ramakrishna Mahima* — Akshay Kumar Sen

3. *Tattwasara* — Ram Chandra Datta
4. *Sri Sri Ramakrishna Lilamrita* — Vaikuntha Nath Sanyal
5. *Sri Ramakrishna Bhagavatam* — Ramendrasundar Bhaktitirtha
6. *Sri Sri Ramakrishna Bhagavat* — Rajendranath Roy
7. *Ramakrishna as We Saw Him* — Compiled by Swami Chetanananda
8. *Sri Ramakrishna Upanishad* — Chakrabarty Rajagopalachari
9. *Sri Sri Ramakrishna Upanishad* — Swami Ramananda
10. *Sri Ramakrishna Karnamritam* — Ottur Nambudripad
11. *Sri Ramakrishna Panchali* — Sharat Chandra Chakrabarty
12. *Parables of Sri Ramakrishna* — Ramakrishna Math, Chennai
13. *Upama Ramakrishnashya* — Vishnupada Chakrabarty
14. *Ramakrishna Bhaktisutra* — Swami Yatishananda
15. *Sri Ramakrishna Namamrita* — Devendranath Chakrabarty
16. *Sri Ramakrishna Katha O Kavya* — Sankariprasad Basu
17. *Sri Sri Ramakrishna Stotraratnakar* — Swami Abhedananda
18. *Kathamrite Gita* — Biswanath Das

Apart from these books, many others have been written and will be written on the life and teachings of Ramakrishna in various languages in India and abroad. Moreover, many hymns and songs on Ramakrishna have been composed in Sanskrit and other languages. Swami Bhuteshananda produced *Sri Ramakrishna Kathamrita-prasanga* in seven volumes in Bengali, a wonderful commentary based on his sayings in the *Kathamrita*. Swami Prajnanananda wrote *Vani O Vichar* in six volumes, and Swami Lokeswarananda wrote *Tava Kathamritam* — both of which are commentaries on the *Kathamrita* in Bengali. In the future, many more scholars and writers will write commentaries, notes, annotations, theses, philosophies and reviews based on the life and teachings of Ramakrishna.

Language of the Ramakrishna-shāstra

The popular Hindu scriptures — the Gita, Chandi, Bhagavata, Ramayana, Mahabharata, Purana, Tantra, Manusamhita and others — are in Sanskrit shlokas (verses). But *Sri Sri Ramakrishna Lilaprasanga* and *Sri Sri Ramakrishna Kathamrita* are in Bengali prose. How can they be scriptures?

Scriptures can be composed in any language, such as the Buddhist Tripitaka in Pali, the Christian New Testament in Greek, the Jewish Torah in Hebrew, and the Muslim Koran in Arabic. Similarly, many Hindu scriptures have been written in Hindi, Tamil, Marathi, and other regional Indian languages. Nishchaldas wrote *Vichar-sagar* (*The Ocean of Discrimination*), a beautiful and important book on Vedanta, in Hindi;

Tulasidas wrote *Ramacharitmanas* in Hindi; and the teachings of Kabir and Dadu are in Hindi verses. These are all popular and inspiring scriptures. The lives and songs of the Alwars were written in Tamil, and the *Gita-Jnaneswari* by Sant Jnaneswar was written in Marathi. These books are also scriptures, because they inspire and guide innumerable people on the spiritual path.

Again, there is no rule that scriptures must be in verse. The Brihadaranyaka, Chandogya, Prashna, Taittiriya, Aitareya, and other Upanishads are written in prose.

We call Sanskrit *deva-bhasa*, or the divine language. The thoughts and experiences of India's ancient sages were expressed in Sanskrit. The source of most Indian languages is Sanskrit. In the present age, however, Sanskrit is very much neglected. As a result, there is poverty in our thoughts and languages. Most people nowadays get a technical or scientific education so they can make money and they consider Sanskrit to be a dead language. Although Sanskrit is not a normally spoken language, a handful of Indian people still speak in Sanskrit. Our ancient scriptures — the Vedas, Upanishads, Puranas, Ramayana, Mahabharata, Gita, Bhagavata, and other important scriptures have been translated into regional languages so that common people can read them.

Ramakrishna once said that he was "*murkhotama* — a foremost illiterate person," as he had not had much formal education. Nonetheless, all the greatest truths of the scriptures came from his lips. On 23 March 1884, the Master said to the devotees: "During my boyhood I could understand what the sadhus read at the Lahas' house at Kamarpukur although I would miss a little here and there. If a pandit speaks to me in Sanskrit, I can follow him, but I cannot speak it myself. The realization of God is enough for me. What does it matter if I don't know Sanskrit?"[15]

Scripture is a testimony of truth

Scriptures are tested truths that originated from the experiences of the avatars, prophets, sages, and rishis. Truth is also of two kinds: relative and absolute. Relative truths such as hunger and thirst, happiness and misery, constantly change. But the absolute truth — Brahman, or God — does not change. Brahman is the unchanging Reality that exists in the past, exists in the present, and will continue to exist in the future. According to the Brihadaranyaka Upanishad, it is "*Satyasay satyam* — the Truth of truth." The Mundaka Upanishad says, "Truth alone triumphs, and not untruth." When we study the Yoga Sutras of Patanjali, we should remember that those teachings were tested truths. As scientific truths come from experimentation, observation, and verification, so spiritual truths were discovered through experiment, were verified, and then recorded: they work.

Before teaching humanity, Ramakrishna himself tested the truth of the existence of God. Swami Turiyananda said, "Sri Ramakrishna practised everything three times."[16] Ramakrishna's life was based on truth, so every one of his words was true. He said that the Divine Mother had never allowed an untruth to pass through his lips. That is the reason his words are scripture. It is amazing how he established the veracity of his visions and words. Swami Vijnanananda reminisced:

> When the Master was blessed for the first time with the vision of the Divine Mother, he thought: "If this vision of mine is true, then let this big stone [*which was in front of the nahabat*] jump up thrice." What he thought immediately happened, and seeing that, the Master was fully convinced of the genuineness of his vision.
>
> The Master had passionate love for truth. He always kept his word....Once he said, "If one word of mine is untrue, then whatever I have said is untrue." What a great statement! It is unprecedented. Can anybody speak such words if his life is not firmly established in truth?[17]

Ramakrishna's words are tested truth, so they are scriptures. His disciples verified his words and found them true. The Master also tested his disciples and advised them:

> "Whoever holds to truth in word, thought, and action is blessed by the vision of God, who is Truth Itself" and "One who observes truth in thought, word, and deed for twelve years reaches a state in which whatever he resolves comes to pass."

Swami Saradananda related this event, how the Master would verify the veracity of his disciple's words:

> We remember an amusing incident concerning the Master's firm belief in Narendra's truthfulness. Once in a conversation the Master explained that the nature of a devotee is like a chataka bird. He said: "As the chataka bird drinks only rainwater, it is always looking to the clouds to quench its thirst. It depends completely on them. Similarly, devotees depend on God alone to appease their spiritual thirst and to fulfill other needs as well." Narendra said suddenly: "Sir, although it's a common belief that the chataka bird drinks only rainwater, it isn't true. I've seen these birds drink water from rivers and ponds like the others." The Master said: "What? Does the chataka bird drink water like other birds? Then this longstanding conviction of mine is proven false. But because you've seen

this, I have no doubt about it." The childlike Master became anxious, thinking: "If this conviction of mine happens to be false, others may be the same." This made him very sad. After a few days Narendra called to the Master and said: "Sir, look! A chataka bird is drinking Ganges water." The Master rushed out of the room and asked, "Where?" But where Narendra was pointing the Master saw a small bat drinking water. He laughed and said: "That's a bat. You rascal! You mistook a bat for a chataka and made me anxious. I won't believe everything you say anymore."[18]

"The spiritual experiences of this place [*meaning himself*] have surpassed even the Vedas and Vedanta"

Swami Saradananda wrote in the introduction to the third part of *Lilaprasanga*: "The Master told us explicitly again and again: 'He who was born as Rama and as Krishna in previous ages is now in this sheath,' as he pointed to his own body. 'The spiritual experiences of this place [*meaning himself*] have surpassed even the Vedas and Vedanta.'"[19]

After experiencing Brahman, Ramakrishna saw that Cosmic Consciousness in every being and everything. He saw the stone image of Mother Kali to be breathing and the worship utensils as conscious. Here are some examples of how the Master's nondual experience manifested: One day someone was walking on the green lawn of the Kali temple garden, and Ramakrishna felt pain in his chest. He said: "At that time I felt that kind of sharp pain that would be felt if someone trampled on one's chest. This kind of ecstasy is extremely painful. I had it for six hours only, but still that pain was too much for me."[20]

Swami Abhedananda related a similar incident which took place in the Cossipore garden house: "One afternoon, while the Master was lying on his bed, a man was pacing back and forth outside on the green lawn of the garden house. The Master said to me: "Please ask that man not to walk on the grass. I am in great pain, as if he were walking on my chest." I was amazed when I heard his words and actually saw this. I hurriedly went and asked the man not to walk on the grass. Then the Master was relieved."[21]

One day at Dakshineswar, the Master was in an ecstatic mood as he stood on the spacious ghat of the main porch watching the Ganges. Two boats were anchored there, and the boatmen were quarreling with each other. Gradually the quarrel grew intense, and the stronger man slapped the weaker one sharply on the back. At this, the Master cried out loudly in pain. The sound of his distressed cry reached Hriday, who was inside the Kali temple. He hurriedly came to the ghat and saw that the Master's back was red and swollen. Impatient with anger, Hriday asked repeatedly: "Uncle, show me the person who hit you. I will chop off his head." When the Master regained his composure, he told Hriday what had happened. Hriday was dumbfounded by this and asked himself, "How is this possible?"[22]

The Chandogya Upanishad states that whatever objects a knower of Brahman desires, by his mere thought all these things come to him. Swami Abhedananda reminisced:

> Pandit Shashadhar had great love and respect for Sri Ramakrishna. One day he came to see the Master at Cossipore when the cancer was in an advanced stage. Shashadhar said to the Master, "Sir, if you put your mind on your throat a little, your cancer will surely be cured." The Master answered, "How can the mind that I have already offered to the Lord be diverted again to this body of flesh and blood?" But still Shashadhar pleaded, "Sir, when you talk to the Divine Mother, please ask her to cure your cancer." Then the Master replied: "When I see the Mother of the Universe, I forget my body and the universe. So, how can I tell the Mother about this insignificant body of flesh and blood?" The pandit was dumbfounded. We too remained still. No one spoke a word.[23]

In the scriptures, we find various descriptions of the nondual experience, but we do not find elsewhere such vivid descriptions and examples as in the Master's life. There was no limit to Ramakrishna's spiritual experiences. Later, on various occasions, he narrated some of his experiences to devotees:

> I vowed to the Divine Mother that I would kill myself if I did not see God. I said to Her: "O Mother, I am a fool. Please teach me what is contained in the Vedas, the Puranas, the Tantras, and the other scriptures." The Mother said to me, "The essence of the Vedanta is that Brahman alone is real and the world illusory." The Satchidananda Brahman described in the Vedas is the Satchidananda Siva of the Tantra and the Satchidananda Krishna of the Purana.
>
> After the realization of God, how far below lie the Vedas, the Vedanta, the Purana, the Tantra! (*To Hazra*) I cannot utter the word "Om" in samadhi. Why is that? I cannot say "Om" unless I come down very far from the state of samadhi.
>
> I had all the experiences that one should have, according to the scriptures, after one's direct perception of God. I behaved like a child, like a madman, like a ghoul, and like an inert thing.
>
> I saw the visions described in the scriptures. Sometimes I saw the universe filled with sparks of fire. Sometimes I saw all the quarters glittering

with light as if the world were a lake of mercury. Sometimes I saw the world as if made of liquid silver. Sometimes, again, I saw all the quarters illumined as if with the light of Raman candles. So you see my experiences tally with those described in the scriptures.

It was revealed to me further that God Himself has become the universe and all its living beings and the twenty-four cosmic principles. It is like the process of evolution and involution.*

Oh, what a state God kept me in at that time! One experience would hardly be over before another overcame me. It was like the movement of the husking-machine: no sooner is one end down than the other goes up.

I would see God in meditation, in the state of samadhi, and I would see the same God when my mind came back to the outer world. When looking at this side of the mirror I would see Him alone, and when looking at the reverse side, I saw the same God.[24]

But lila is by no means the last word. Passing through all these states, I said to the Divine Mother: "Mother, in these states there is separation. Give me a state where there is no separation." Then I remained for some time absorbed in the Indivisible Satchidananda. I removed the pictures of the gods and goddesses from my room. I began to perceive God in all beings. Formal worship dropped away. You see that bel-tree. I used to go there to pluck its leaves. One day, as I plucked a leaf, a bit of the bark came off. I found the tree full of Consciousness. I felt grieved because I had hurt the tree. One day I tried to pluck some durva grass, but I found I couldn't do it very well. Then I forced myself to pluck it.

I cannot cut a lemon. The other day I managed to cut one only with great difficulty; I chanted the name of Kali and cut the fruit as they slaughter an animal before the Goddess. One day I was about to gather some flowers. They were everywhere on the trees. At once I had a vision of Virat; it appeared that His worship was just over. The flowers looked like a bouquet placed on the head of the Deity. I could not pluck them.[25]

God talked to me. It was not merely His vision. Yes, He talked to me. Under the banyan-tree I saw Him coming from the Ganges. Then we laughed so much! By way of playing with me He cracked my fingers. Then He talked. Yes, He talked to me.

For three days I wept continuously. And He revealed to me what is in the Vedas, the Puranas, the Tantras, and the other scriptures.

One day He showed me the maya of Mahamaya. A small light inside a room began to grow, and at last it enveloped the whole universe.

Further, He revealed to me a huge reservoir of water covered with green scum. The wind moved a little of the scum and immediately the water became visible; but in the twinkling of an eye, scum from all sides

---

*That is to say, God Himself evolves as the universe, at the time of creation, and names and forms are involved back into God, at the time of dissolution.

came dancing in and again covered the water. He revealed to me that the water was like Satchidananda, and the scum like maya. On account of maya, Satchidananda is not seen. Though now and then one may get a glimpse of It, again maya covers It.[26]

Formal worship drops away after the vision of God. It was thus that my worship in the temple came to an end. I used to worship the Deity in the Kali temple. It was suddenly revealed to me that everything is Pure Spirit. The utensils of worship, the altar, the door-frame — all Pure Spirit. Men, animals, and other living beings — all Pure Spirit. Then like a madman I began to shower flowers in all directions. Whatever I saw I worshipped.

One day, while worshipping Siva, I was about to offer a bel-leaf on the head of the image, when it was revealed to me that this Virat, this Universe, itself is Siva. After that my worship of Siva through the image came to an end. Another day I had been plucking flowers when it was revealed to me that the flowering plants were so many bouquets.

It was revealed to me in a flash. I didn't calculate about it. It was shown to me that each plant was a bouquet adorning the Universal Form of God. That was the end of my plucking flowers. I look on man in just the same way. When I see a man, I see that it is God Himself who walks on earth, as it were, rocking to and fro, like a pillow floating on the waves. The pillow moves with the waves. It bobs up and down.[27]

These visions and experiences of Ramakrishna are so clear, vivid, explicit, and distinct with minute details that they do not need any explanation. We can only imagine his visions with wonder, listen to his spontaneous words with breathless adoration, and imagine with astonishment the divine realm in which Ramakrishna lived. The scriptures say that the person who treads on the path of Nirguna Brahman cannot be touched by any injunction or prohibition of the scriptures. Most of the time the Master lived in the realm of Advaita, which is beyond the gunas of maya; and other times he lived in this world to help human beings and to enact his divine play. A monk from Rishikesh saw five kinds of samadhi in the Master — like an ant, frog, monkey, bird, and snake. Ramakrishna himself described this, how the Kundalini Shakti moves during samadhi through the sushumna channel:

"Look," he would say, "that which rises to the brain with a tingling sensation does not always move in the same way. The scriptures speak of its five kinds of motion. First, it moves like an ant: One feels a slow creeping sensation from the feet upwards, like a row of ants crawling along with food in their mouths. When it reaches the brain, the aspirant merges into samadhi. Second, it moves like a frog: Just as a frog makes two or three short jumps in quick succession, stops for a while, then proceeds again in the same way, so something is felt advancing from the feet to the brain. When it reaches the brain, the aspirant goes into samadhi. Third, it moves like a serpent: As a snake lies quietly, straight or coiled up, but moves in a zigzag motion when it sees prey or is frightened, so does the kundalini move upward to the head. When it reaches the brain, the aspirant goes into samadhi. Fourth, it moves like a bird: Birds in their flight from one place to another sometimes fly a little high and sometimes low, but never stop till they reach their destination. Likewise, something is felt moving towards the head; when it reaches the brain, samadhi ensues. Fifth, it moves like a monkey: As a monkey goes from one tree to another, leaping from branch to branch and clearing the distance in two or three bounds, so the yogi feels the kundalini power go to the brain, and samadhi follows."[28]

In Vedanta, there are seven stages of spiritual unfoldment:

1. *Subhechcha* — One has an auspicious resolve to know the Self.
2. *Vicharana* — After initiation from the guru, one reflects on the *Mahavakya* (the great Vedic dictum, such as "I am Brahman").
3. *Tanumanasa* — While meditating on the Atman, the mind becomes light.
4. *Sattvapatti* — The light of knowledge dawns when one is full of sattva.
5. *Asangsakti* — While meditating on the Atman, one transcends the body idea.
6. *Padartha-abhavana* — Absorbed in the Atman, the mind becomes objectless.
7. *Turyaga* — In this transcendent experience, one merges into Brahman.

Ramakrishna's mind used to pass through all these seven stages.

One day the Master described the visions and experiences that take place when the kundalini shakti rises through every chakra, or centre, of the Sushumna channel:

Vedanta speaks of seven planes, in each of which the aspirant has a particular kind of vision. The human mind has a natural tendency to confine its activities to the three lower centres — the regions of the anus, the genitals, and the navel — and therefore is content with the satisfaction of eating, dressing, coition, and so forth. If the mind transcends those three centres and reaches the fourth, the one near the heart, the aspirant sees a divine light. The mind may sometimes reach the heart centre but then descend to the three lower centres. However, when the mind comes to the fifth centre, near the throat, the aspirant cannot speak of mundane things: He or she talks about God only. While I was in this state, if anybody spoke of worldly things before me I would feel as though I were being struck violently on the head. I would run away to the Panchavati, just to avoid hearing secular talk. I would hide fearfully at the sight of worldly-minded people. Relatives appeared to me to be on the edge of a yawning chasm, trying to push me down into it, and there would be no escape if I once fell. In their presence I felt suffocated — almost to the point of death — and found relief only when I fled from them. Even from this throat centre a person may slip down to the three lower centres; so one should remain vigilant. But if one's mind reaches the sixth centre, between the eyebrows, there is no more fear of falling. The aspirant then attains the vision of the Paramatman, the Supreme Self, and remains always in samadhi. There is only a thin veil, as transparent as glass, between this centre and the *sahasrara*, the thousand-petalled lotus at the crown of the head. The Supreme Self is then so close that one can imagine oneself merged in It. But that is not the case. From this state the mind can come down to the fifth, or at the most to the fourth centre, but not below that. However, ordinary aspirants, classed as jivas, cannot return from this state. After remaining constantly in samadhi for twenty-one days, they break that thin veil and become one with Brahman forever. This eternal union of the jiva and Brahman in the sahasrara is known as reaching the seventh plane.[29]

Swami Saradananda wrote:

Sometimes as we listened to the Master discuss the Vedas, Vedanta, and the science of yoga, some of us would ask him: "Sir, you have never cared for reading books. How do you know all these things?" This strange question did not disturb the wonderful Master. He would reply with a smile: "It is true that I have not read them myself. But I have heard a lot, and I remember everything. I have heard the Vedas, Vedanta, Puranas, and philosophy from good and scholarly pandits. After hearing them and learning all they contained, I made a garland of the scriptures, put it around my neck, and offered it to the Divine Mother, saying, 'Please take Your scriptures and Puranas; grant me pure devotion.'"[30]

The six centres of the kundalini in the human body have been mentioned in the Tantra scriptures. But the scriptures do not describe how that power moves. The kundalini moved the Master like a leaf in a gale, and he would talk inspired by that Conscious-energy (chaitanya-vayu). In 1885 the Master went to attend the Chariot Festival at Balaram's Calcutta house. When he returned to Dakshineswar by boat, he went to the Kali temple and sang this enigmatic song on the kundalini:

O Mother, Consort of Shiva, You have deluded this world.
You entertain Yourself by playing the vina in the great lotus of the
muladhara.
Your music vibrates through the great mantra in three scales, taking the
form of the three gunas.
Your music strikes the three cords — sushumna, ida, and pingala — of
that musical instrument, the body.
You play with melody, rhythm, and tempo at the six centres of the
kundalini:
Bhairava-raga in muladhara, Sri-raga in swadhisthana, Mallara-raga
In manipura, Vasanta-raga in anahata, Hindola-raga in vishuddha, and
Karnataka-raga in ajna.
Again, O Mother, You transcend all sound by crossing the three octaves.
O Mother, Sri Nandakumar* says that one cannot realize the Supreme
Truth unless You remove the veil of Your three gunas, which covers the
face of Brahman.[31]

Swami Saradananda wrote:

While singing, the Master suddenly stood up and went into ecstasy. The
Master remained in that state for some time and only gradually regained
his normal consciousness after hearing the name of God. But he could
still not stand in a normal way because of that divine intoxication. His
legs were wobbling excessively.

In this condition, the Master crawled down the steps of the northern
side of the natmandir to the temple courtyard. He was then speaking like
a little child, saying: "Mother, I will not fall. Will I fall?" In truth, when
watching the Master at that time one felt that he was a boy of three or
four years. He was saying those words as he gazed at the Mother, depending on Her as he confidently made his way down the steps. Shall
we ever see anywhere else such wonderful reliance on God, even in such
small matters?

After crossing the courtyard, the Master reached his own room and
went to the western semicircular veranda to sit. He was still in ecstasy; the mood possessed him. Sometimes it lessened a little, but would
increase again and he would almost lose consciousness. After being in
this condition for some time, the Master — still in that condition — said
to the devotees: "Have you seen the Snake? It is giving me so much
trouble!" Forgetting the devotees, he addressed the snake-like kundalini (for he was then experiencing the Serpent Power): "Please go now.
Madam, move away. I shall smoke tobacco and wash my mouth. I have
not yet brushed my teeth." Thus, he spoke with the devotees at times

*The composer.

and sometimes addressed the divine form seen in ecstasy. Gradually he returned to the normal plane of consciousness.[32]

We may study and memorize the Gita, but the Master experienced the truths contained in that scripture. Once he commented: "It isn't necessary to read all of the Gita. One can get the essence of the Gita by repeating the word ten times. It becomes reversed and is then 'tagi', which indicates renunciation. The essence of the book is: 'O man, renounce everything and worship God.'"[33] Referring to the Master's comment on the Gita, a great scholar remarked that he had studied 50 commentaries on the Gita but Ramakrishna's was the best.

Swami Basudevananda described the similarity between Krishna's Bhagavad Gita and Ramakrishna's *Kathamrita:*

> Gita is a wonderful conclusion of various philosophical schools of India and Ramakrishna was its paradigm. Gita explained various spiritual paths according to the temperament of different individuals. Ramakrishna practised the sadhanas of those paths and, reaching the culmination, demonstrated that the goal of all paths is the same. He was the living Gita scripture. That is why he did not care for bookish education. We find very little of his teachings in the *Kathamrita, Lilaprasanga,* and *Punthi.* Many of his teachings are lost. In this scientific age, his exemplary life of sadhana preaches spirituality more than his teachings. Who would believe in Gita's teaching "a clod, a stone, and gold are the same," if people had not seen it in Ramakrishna's life? Observing the manifestation of nirvikalpa samadhi, the signs of mahabhava, and jivanmukta in the Master's life, people are understanding the veracity of Gita's teachings. Holding on to the dry doctrines and dogmas of religions, people quarrel among themselves instead of practising spiritual sadhana; as a result, religions have become lifeless mockeries. Ramakrishna rediscovered the spiritual experiences of innumerable saints' and rishis' lifelong sadhanas in his single lifetime. We wonder what a colossal spiritual power manifested in his life. It takes so many lives for a person to attain perfection in one sadhana, whereas Ramakrishna studied those sadhanas, practised them, attained perfection in them, and finally pointed out their unity. God in His Krishna-body taught the Gita to Arjuna, and again He in His Ramakrishna-body demonstrated the Gita.[34]

While talking with the novelist Bankim Chandra Chattopadhyay about the relationship between the scriptures and God-realization, Ramakrishna said:

> "Some people think that God cannot be realized without the study of books and scriptures. They think that first of all one should learn of this

world and its creatures; that first of all one should study 'science.' They think that one cannot realize God without first understanding His creation. Which come first, 'science' or God? What do you say?"

Bankim: "I too think that we should first of all know about the different things of the world. How can we know of God without knowing something of this world? We should first learn from books."

Master: "That's the one cry from all of you. But God comes first and then the creation. After attaining God, you can know everything else, if it is necessary. If you can somehow get yourself introduced to Jadu Mallick, then you will be able to learn, if you want to, the number of his houses and gardens, and the amount of his money invested in government securities. Jadu Mallick himself will tell you all about them."[35]

Ramakrishna always emphasized that one should actually have knowledge of the scriptures rather than talking and boasting about them. In the *Gospel*, M. recorded this beautiful story about a pandit and his erudition of the scripture.

Master (*To Manilal*): "Please tell them that little story of yours."

Manilal (*smiling*): "Once several men were crossing the Ganges in a boat. One of them, a pandit, was making a great display of his erudition, saying that he had studied various books — the Vedas, the Vedanta, and the six systems of philosophy. He asked a fellow passenger, 'Do you know the Vedanta?' 'No, revered sir.' 'The Samkhya and the Patanjala?' 'No, revered sir.' 'Have you read no philosophy whatsoever?' 'No, revered sir.' The pandit was talking in this vain way and the passenger sitting in silence, when a great storm arose and the boat was about to sink. The passenger said to the pandit, 'Sir, can you swim?' 'No,' replied the pandit. The passenger said, 'I don't know the Samkhya or the Patanjala, but I can swim.'"

Master (*smiling*): "What will a man gain by knowing many scriptures? The one thing needful is to know how to cross the river of the world."[36]

Many people consider scriptures to be dry and difficult, somber and serious; some think they are boring, unpractical, antique, and out-of-date. Some believe the scriptures have no use in modern day-to-day life, and therefore, it is meaningless to spend time and energy studying and practising the ancient teachings of the scriptures. But when we study the Ramakrishna-shastra, we find something new and magnetic, inspiring and intriguing, comforting and joyful, simple and practical, rational and universal. For example, his broad outlook and message of harmony are essential for us all to live together in this global village. Ramakrishna learned what was contained in the scriptures from the Divine Mother, the creator of the universe and the source of all knowledge. Then he taught from his experience and with authority. He demonstrated in this age that, without much education and without studying any scriptures, one could know the essence of the scriptures. This is a new and a unique characteristic of Ramakrishna, whereas avatars like Ramachandra, Krishna, Buddha, and Chaitanya were great scholars.

God is infinite; so are his message and scriptures. The scriptures of all the world's religions are different pages of God's infinite scripture, and Ramakrishna's *Lilaprasanga* and *Kathamrita* are two pages in that infinite scripture.

It is mentioned in the *Kashikhanda* of the *Skandapurana* that if anyone dies in Varanasi, Lord Vishwanath bestows liberation on that person. But how Lord Viswanath does this is not mentioned in the Purana. In 1868 Ramakrishna went to Varanasi with Mathur. One day he went on a boat trip on the Ganges. Seeing several funeral pyres of the Manikarnika cremation ground from the boat, he went into samadhi. He then described his vision to Mathur and the others:

> I saw a tall white figure with tawny matted hair steadily approach each funeral pyre in turn, carefully raise each individual soul from its cast-off body, and whisper into its ear the particular name of Brahman that liberates a soul. Seated on the opposite side of the pyre, the all-powerful Divine Mother Kali untied the gross, subtle, and causal knots of bondage created by each individual soul, thus sending the soul to the Absolute by opening the gate of liberation. Lord Vishwanath was blessing those souls by bestowing in an instant the experience of nondual, infinite bliss that people can attain only after ages of concentration and austerity.[37]

The pandits who were with Mathur verified this vision from their knowledge of the scriptures. They said to the Master: "The *Kashikhanda* mentions that Shiva confers nirvana on those who die at Varanasi, but does not explicitly state how. Your vision clearly elucidates how this is accomplished. Your visions and experiences have surpassed even the scriptural records."[38]

Only a few visions and experiences of Ramakrishna have been described in this chapter. It is said that no painter or sculptor has ever been born to portray or give shape to the image of Kali envisioned by Ramprasad. Similarly, no human being is capable of describing Ramakrishna's bhava (ecstasy), darshan (vision), and samadhi. He was the emperor in the realm of samadhi. He continually travelled through various kinds of samadhi — savikalpa-nirvikalpa, samprajnata-asamprajnata, vitarka-vichar-ananda-asmita, bhava-sahaja, sthita-unmana, jada-chetan, and so on. These states are beyond the reach of ordinary people. Seeing the Master in samadhi, a pandit told him, "Sir, I have read about samadhi in the scriptures, but I have never witnessed it except now in you." The Master would come down from the transcendental plane to teach people, and he loved to live with people who had pure sattva. One day he said to M.: "Look, God speaks though my mouth." This proves that Ramakrishna's words are the scriptures.

Ramakrishna's life, teachings, visions, and experiences are his shastra (scriptures), and many of them were recorded in the *Lilaprasanga* and *Kathamrita*. The Master said: Know the essence of the scriptures and then dive deep to realize God. In this age *Sri Ramakrishna and His Divine Play* (*Lilaprasanga*) and *The Gospel of Sri Ramakrishna* (*Kathamrita*) are new additions to the Hindu scriptures and the religious literature of the world.

10

History of *Sri Sri Ramakrishna Lilaprasanga*

Sri Ramakrishna and His Divine Play is a new translation of *Sri Sri Ramakrishna Lilaprasanga*, which was written in Bengali by Swami Saradananda, a monastic disciple of Sri Ramakrishna. This is an authentic, factual, descriptive, interpretive, and comprehensive biography of Sri Ramakrishna, the spiritual phenomenon of our age.

According to Indian tradition, the word "Sri" is used before the title of the scriptures, such as *Srimad Bhagavad Gita, Sri Chandi, Srimad Bhagavata, Sri Sri Chaitanya-charitamrita, Sri Sri Ramakrishna Kathamrita*, and *Sri Sri Ramakrishna Lilaprasanga*. "Sri" is also used before the name of an avatar, such as Sri Ramachandra, Sri Krishna, Sri Chaitanya, and Sri Ramakrishna. The word "Sri" has many meanings, including beauty, fortune, wealth, splendour, lustre, light, virtue, excellence, majesty, glory, and superhuman power. When "Sri" is placed before a name, it indicates respect, and before a scripture it indicates sanctity. In the *Kathamrita* and the *Lilaprasanga*, Sri Ramakrishna declared his true divine nature both directly and indirectly. The word *Lilaprasanga* is very significant. In Bengali, when human beings play it is called *khela*, and when divine beings play it is called *lila*. Thus in the title of the book Saradananda indicated that this book is about the lila of an incarnation of God.

Once a devotee asked Swami Saradananda: "Does God really descend as an avatar?"

"Of course He does," replied Saradananda. "We have heard the Master say: 'He who was Rama and Krishna is now Ramakrishna.' In other

Swami Saradananda in 1920s at Udbodhan house, Calcutta. He wrote *Sri Sri Ramakrishna Lilaprasanga* (*Sri Ramakrishna and His Divine Play*) sitting in this room.

words, the same power manifests according to the need of the age. He further said, 'I will be born again in the northwest after two hundred years.' You see, this universe and all beings are nothing but His manifestation. But at some times and in some places one can see His special manifestation according to need."[1]

A couple of days before the Master's passing away, Swamiji was sitting by his bedside, mentally saying to the Master, "Well, now if you can declare that you are God, then only will I believe you are really God Himself." Immediately the Master looked at Swamiji and said, "He who was Rama, he who was Krishna, verily is he now Ramakrishna in this body."[2]

Avatars do not write their autobiographies. The sages or their disciples write the story of their lives and record their message. Sage Narada requested Sage Valmiki to write the life story of Ramachandra. Valmiki inquired: "O great sage, is there any person in this world at present, who is endowed with all the divine qualities and a pure character, who is all-powerful, virtuous, humble, truthful, steady, and a benefactor to all beings? Is there any person who is learned, skillful, handsome, calm, luminous, and free from anger and jealousy? Is there any man whom even the gods are scared of when he becomes angry? Do you know any such person on this earth? Please satisfy my curiosity."[3] Narada mentioned Ramachandra, a son of King Dasharatha. Afterwards, Valmiki began to compose the Ramayana.

Sage Vyasa compiled the Vedas and Upanishads, and wrote the Brahma Sutras, the Mahabharata, and many Puranas. He wrote the Gita — the quintessence of Vedanta — and incorporated it into the Mahabharata. Despite writing these colossal Hindu scriptures, Vyasa did not have mental peace. Sage Narada understood and said to him: "O great sage Vyasa, it is true that you have recorded all these great scriptures, but you have not written the life of that person in whom all those scriptures were manifested. You did not write the detailed story of the divine play of that person whose words are the living scriptures. You recorded Krishna's message in the Gita, but you have not written the Srimad Bhagavata, the stories of his divine play. When you complete Krishna's life story, you will find peace and all beings will attain peace, by hearing it."[4] Then Narada imparted to Vyasa the famous *Vasudeva mantra* and the gist of the Bhagavata Purana in four verses. After receiving the mantra and the verses, Vyasa became absorbed in meditation and visualized the entire lila of Krishna. He then spontaneously wrote the Bhagavata — the story of Krishna's divine play.

In this present age, Swami Saradananda wrote the story of Sri Ramakrishna's divine play in his immortal magnum opus *Sri Sri*

Ramakrishna Lilaprasanga. Only by God's grace is it possible to depict the divine life of an avatar, God in human form. Valmiki and Vyasa were two great rishi-poets, who narrated the life stories of two great avatars — Rama and Krishna — in Sanskrit verse. In this regard Saradananda did not follow in their footsteps. He wrote Ramakrishna's life story in simple, elegant, fluent Bengali prose.

Suren Roy wrote in his Bengali article, *"Swami Saradananda, the author of the Ramakrishna-Veda"* that the task of Valmiki and Vyasa was easier than that of Saradananda. Those ancient rishi-poets gave shape to the avatars' life stories using their imagination, whereas Saradananda was an eyewitness to Ramakrishna's life and lived with him day after day, month after month. He heard the Master's immortal words and saw his expressions and gestures. It is easier to use paint and a brush to create an imaginary portrait, but Saradananda did not have that opportunity. Instead, he presented to his readers the minute, detailed events of Ramakrishna's real life. He published the stories of Ramakrishna's human play along with the unique interpretation of his immortal message in such simple, lucid language that ordinary people could understand it.[5]

On the Kalpataru Day (1 January 1886), Girish Ghosh said to Ramakrishna: "What more can I say of Him? Even the sages Vyasa and Valmiki could find no words to measure His glory!" This statement is absolutely true. Despite writing voluminous books on Krishna and Rama, Vyasa and Valmiki could not express their glory fully. They portrayed only a little of the infinite nature of those avatars. In fact, those two rishi-poets were bewildered by the vast characters of Krishna and Rama, so they described only one aspect of those avatars: Valmiki wrote only about Rama, and Vyasa, only about Krishna. But in this present age, those two avatars appeared as Ramakrishna, so Saradananda faced the serious challenge of depicting two characters in one.

To perform this serious and difficult task, Saradananda received his guru Ramakrishna's grace, Holy Mother's blessings, and inspiration from his brother disciples and devotees of the Master. Endowed with all these, Saradananda wrote the mystery of Ramakrishna's divine play. Put simply, the *Lilaprasanga* is the philosophy, biography, and message of Ramakrishna's life. Yet Ramakrishna was no other than Satchidananda Brahman. In that case, the *Lilaprasanga* is the philosophy of nondual Brahman.

Ramakrishna's biographies before the *Lilaprasanga*

Swami Saradananda started to write the *Lilaprasanga* in 1909 and finished it in 1919. A few biographies of Ramakrishna had already been written before this exhaustive work by Saradananda. If we briefly discuss those earlier biographies, we shall understand the uniqueness of the *Lilaprasanga*.

In 1879, Pratap Chandra Mujumdar, a disciple of the Brahmo leader Keshab Chandra Sen, wrote *"Ramakrishna Paramahamsa,"* a short (12 pages) biographical sketch in English, which was published in the *Theistic Quarterly Review*. Impressed by Ramakrishna's life and message, Mujumdar wrote: "If all his utterances could be recorded they would form a volume of strange and wonderful wisdom. If all his observations on men and things could be reproduced, people might think that the days of prophecy, of primeval, unlearned wisdom had returned. But it is most difficult to render his sayings in English. This good and holy man is living evidence of the depth and sweetness of the Hindu religion."[6]

In 1878, Girish Chandra Sen, a follower of Keshab Chandra Sen, wrote *Adi Kathamrita* in Bengali, collecting 184 teachings of Ramakrishna. In 1886, Girish Sen was present when Ramakrishna's body was cremated at the Cossipore cremation ground. He wrote a long account, actually a short biography of Ramakrishna (21 pages), which was published in the magazine of the Navabidhan Brahmo Samaj. It contains new material, but also has some mistakes. In 1883, Shyamal Basu edited *Adi Kathamrita* and published it through Ananya Prakashan, in Calcutta.

In May 1885, Ram Chandra Datta compiled some of Sri Ramakrishna's important teachings that he had noted down, and he published them in a Bengali book entitled *Tattvasara*. A few of the devotees, however, objected to this, and they reported it to the Master. Sri Ramakrishna called Ram aside one day and said: "Look here, some devotees informed me that you were publishing a book. What have you written?" Ram replied that he had collected some of his (Ramakrishna's) teachings and put them together in a book. Ram then read some of it to the Master, who said: "Oh, you have written those teachings? Very good. Listen, if you think that you have written them, you will get very little response from others; but if you think that the Lord is working through you, then it will be in great demand." Ramakrishna further cautioned Ram: "Do not publish my biography now. If you do, my body will not last long."[7] Ram obeyed. In 1890, after the Master had passed away, he wrote the first biography, *Sri Sri Ramakrishna Paramahamsadever Jivanvrittanta*. Later he enlarged *Tattvasara* and published it as *Tattva-Prakashika (The Teachings of Sri Ramakrishna)*. He also began to publish a Bengali magazine, *Tattvamanjari*, to spread the Master's teachings.

In the late 1800s, Akshay Kumar Sen wrote the life of Ramakrishna in Bengali verse following the style of Krittivasa's Ramayana and Kashiram Das's Mahabharata. The book was first published in four parts between 1894 and 1901 under the title *Bhagavan Sri Sri Ramakrishna Paramahamsadever Charitamrita*. Later, on 25 November 1901, all four parts were published in one volume under the title *Sri Sri Ramakrishna Punthi*. Swami Vivekananda praised this book and appreciated the author's effort. However, it is not a complete biography. Moreover, it contains some hyperbole, including stories of miracles. Later, the author read the *Lilaprasanga* and corrected some mistakes in his book. In 1998, the Bengali poem was translated into English and published by the Ramakrishna Mission Institute of Culture, Calcutta, under the title *A Portrait of Sri Ramakrishna*.

In 1897, Satyacharan Mitra wrote *Sri Sri Ramakrishna Paramahamsa* (192 pages) in Bengali. The author said that he collected half of the information in the book from Mahimacharan·Avadhuta. I have not seen this book.

In 1898, Frederick Max Müller wrote *Ramakrishna: His Life and Sayings* in English. The biographical portion of the book was actually written by Swami Saradananda and approved by Swami Vivekananda.

In 1901, Bhuban Chandra Mukhopadhyay wrote *Ramakrishna Charitamrita va Bhagavan Sri Sri Ramakrishnadever Jivani* in Bengali (89 pages). Recently this book was reprinted by Bibhas Chanda. Many incidents in this book are full of errors; for example, Mukhopadhyay describes the Shodashi worship of Holy Mother as taking place in Jayrambati.

Sri Sri Ramakrishna Kathamrita by Mahendra Nath Gupta (M.) was published in four parts from 1902 to 1910. (A fifth part was published in 1932.) This is a unique book in the religious literature of the world (see Chapter 11 in this volume). The *Kathamrita* is not a biography; instead it is based on M.'s diary, in which he recorded conversations of the Master with the devotees.

In 1908, Suresh Chandra Datta published *Srimat Ramakrishna Paramahamsadever Samkshipta Jivani O Upadesh*. The author collected various incidents of the Master's life and wrote a beautiful, short biography that includes 950 teachings.

In 1910, Priyanath Sinha, a classmate and disciple of Swami Vivekananda, wrote *Sri Sri Ramakrishna Charit* under his pen name, Gurudas Barman. He began by publishing the Master's biography serially in the *Udbodhan* magazine. He collected the materials for the book from the Master's disciples at Baranagore Math and also from the Master's nephew Hriday. He wrote in the introduction:

Hriday would sometimes come to Baranagore Math and stay a few days. He would charm the audience describing the wonderful episodes of the Master's god-intoxicated life. Hriday would imitate his uncle's gestures and manners, his bearing and deportment, and his voice beautifully and perfectly, and act accordingly. Sitting around Hriday, the disciples requested him to tell the wonderful and inspiring stories of the Master. [Hriday is the only person who lived with the Master for 25 years. He was also the witness of the Master's sadhanas long before the disciples arrived.] Swami Abhedananda and Swami Ramakrishnananda would record those stories in a notebook, and they also recorded in it what they had heard directly from the Master. The main source of this book is that notebook. Moreover, I collected materials from Ramakrishna's life by Ram Chandra Datta and Satyacharan Mitra, *Ramakrishna Punthi* by Akshay Kumar Sen, and the *Kathamrita* by M. In addition, the monastic and householder disciples of the Master shared with me how they had lived with the Master and received his grace. Girish Chandra Ghosh himself wrote his reminiscences about the Master and gave them to me.[8]

Although Gurudas Barman's book was based on those wonderful sources, it had many factual mistakes. Before publishing the installments in the *Udbodhan*, Saradananda corrected them.

The ten books discussed here were all written before the *Lilaprasanga*. Each book has its own characteristics, but none is a complete biography of Sri Ramakrishna, and they cannot even come near the *Lilaprasanga* in depth and scholarship.

Swami Saradananda's preparation

God selects a person through whom He will perform a particular work and determines how long He will work through that person. In 1883, Sharat (Swami Saradananda) met Sri Ramakrishna when he was a student at St. Xavier's College, and he was closely associated with the Master for the next three years. He was a witness to many incidents in Ramakrishna's divine life. After the Master's passing away in 1886, Sharat joined the Ramakrishna Math at Baranagore, where he practised sadhana and studied Vedanta scriptures and Western philosophy. Latu Maharaj (Swami Adbhutananda) recalled:

> I noticed that everyone at the Math was studying hard. One day I asked Brother Sharat: "Why do you read so many books? All of you are finished with school, yet you study so hard! Are you to appear for an examination?"
>
> Brother Sharat replied, "Brother, without serious study how are we to understand the subtle matters of religion?"

I rejoined that the Master had talked so much about these matters, and I had never seen him reading books. Sharat said: "His case is completely different. He himself said that the Divine Mother used to provide him with heaps of knowledge. Have we reached that stage, or can we ever hope to reach it? We have to read in order to acquire such knowledge."

I did not leave the matter there, but replied, "The Master said that we get one conception of the Truth through studying books and quite another by spiritual experience." Then Sharat said, "But didn't he say that those who would be teachers will have to study the scriptures as well?"

Then I realized that men understand differently according to their mental constitutions and that the Master taught each one according to his own nature. So from then on, I kept quiet.[9]

From 1890 to 1895, Saradananda travelled to many holy places in India and practised austerities in the Himalayas. The disciples knew that the Master was an embodiment of austerity, and one cannot comprehend him properly without practising austerities and renunciation. Then in 1896, Saradananda left for the West at the behest of Swami Vivekananda to preach Vedanta. He reached London on 1 April. Saradananda wrote:

At the invitation of Max Müller, Swamiji went to Oxford and stayed in his home as a guest. Max Müller wrote an article in the *Nineteenth Century* on Sri Ramakrishna entitled "*A Real Mahatman.*" He asked Swamiji to furnish him with enough material for a book so he could write about Sri Ramakrishna in greater detail. Swamiji agreed to help. When he returned, he asked me to undertake the job forthwith. I worked hard and gathered all the incidents in the life of the Master and the teachings of the Master and showed the manuscript to Swamiji. I thought Swamiji would edit it and make extensive corrections. He didn't do that. He simply changed a few words for fear of exaggeration and sent the whole manuscript to Professor Müller. As I remember, Professor Müller incorporated the complete manuscript in his book [*The Life and Sayings of Sri Ramakrishna*] and published it without making any alterations.[10]

Saradananda stayed in the West for two years and then Swamiji asked him to return to India. In 1897, Swamiji established the Ramakrishna Mission, and in 1901 he made Saradananda the General Secretary (the executive head). It is a very demanding and responsible position. Then in 1898, Swamiji began publishing the *Udbodhan*, a Bengali magazine, and made Trigunatita editor. In September 1902, Trigunatita left for America to preach Vedanta, and the responsibility for publishing the magazine fell on Saradananda. Sometimes he acted as the editor and at other times he helped others write important articles. In 1909, Saradananda arranged to build a house in Baghbazar, Calcutta, for the magazine and to serve also as Holy Mother's residence when she was in Calcutta.

Saradananda was well versed in Bengali, English, and Sanskrit. He also lectured in Hindi in the northern and western areas of India and guided the *Samanwaya*, a Hindi magazine published by Advaita Ashrama in Mayavati. He also helped to edit *The Complete Works of Swami Vivekananda* and *The Life of Swami Vivekananda* by His Eastern and Western Disciples.

Saradananda knew that learning and intelligence were not enough to write the life of Ramakrishna. Ramakrishna's character, sadhana, spiritual experiences, frame of mind, and behaviour were beyond the reach of the ordinary human intellect. He taught through *bhavamukha*, a mysterious spiritual state. Saradananda explained *bhavamukha*: "The Cosmic I-ness that exists between the Nirguna and the Saguna aspects of Brahman is called *bhavamukha*, and because of it, innumerable ideas arise in the Cosmic Mind. This Cosmic I is the 'I' of God, or the Divine Mother."[11]

Ramakrishna said to the spiritual aspirants: "Dive deep. Is it possible to realize the Truth floating over the surface? One should listen to the Vedas and Puranas, and practise the sadhanas of the Tantras methodically according to the tradition."[12] Remembering that teaching, Saradananda dove deep in the realm of sadhana. To understand the mystery of Tantra sadhana, he took initiation from his uncle Ishwar Chandra Chakrabarty on 25 November 1900. Before starting this sadhana, he received permission from Holy Mother and Swami Brahmananda. By their grace, he made rapid progress. The first step of Tantra sadhana is to experience all women as mother, and then perceive the Divine Mother in all of them. Soon he succeeded in this sadhana. Saradananda dedicated his beautiful Bengali book *Bharate Shaktipuja* (*Mother Worship in India*) to the Holy Mother: "By whose gracious glance the author has been able to realize the revelation of Divine Motherhood in every woman — to her lotus feet the work is dedicated in all humility and devotion."[13]

Swami Vijnanananda said, "Every day Sharat Maharaj used to practise japa and meditation for a long time and then he would start writing the *Lilaprasanga*."[14]

Divine command and personal experience

Ramakrishna would ask preachers, "Well, have you received a command from God to preach?" Without this command from God, there is no authority in a preacher's sermons and the audience is not inspired. Swami Bhumananda described how Swami Saradananda spoke about the Master's command to write the *Lilaprasanga*:

One day at Udbodhan house, Golap-ma said to Sharat Maharaj, "Jnan [Bhumananda] wrote about the Master." Sharat Maharaj said to me: "Jnan, what have you written? Please show me." I said: "I wrote about the Master's miraculous power in verse. It is not worthwhile seeing it." Sharat Maharaj insisted, "Bring your manuscript, let me see." I presented my notebook to the swami. My handwriting was not good, so the swami said, "You read. Let me hear." I began to read. After listening to a couple of incidents, the swami said: "Swamiji said that the Master manifested those powers for the good of some individuals, so it is not necessary to write those things. Rather, if you describe those miracles, people will think that we are biased and preaching a dogmatic view." I kept quiet. The swami asked me to prepare tobacco for his hubble-bubble.

When the swami began to smoke, I said to him, "Maharaj, why don't you write a biography of Sri Ramakrishna, where people could get all stories about him?"

Sharat Maharaj: "Is it so easy to write about the Master? One should not undertake such work without having his command. If I get his command, I shall try." Then he continued: "Swamiji himself did not dare to write about the Master. If somebody would ask him to write, he answered, 'Shall I make the image of a monkey while trying to make the image of Shiva?' Without having any command, one should not undertake this task; otherwise that writing does not bear any result."

In that year [1909] Sharat Maharaj began to write *Lilaprasanga*. I did not forget that word "command". Some years later, I asked Sharat Maharaj, "Maharaj, did you start writing the *Lilaprasanga* after receiving the command of the Master?" "That is none of your business," replied the swami. I could not say anything more.[15]

One day, Asitananda, an attendant of Saradananda, worked up the courage to ask the swami if he had experienced nirvikalpa samadhi. "Did I waste my time cutting grass [i.e., living meaninglessly] when I lived in the company of Sri Ramakrishna?" Saradananda replied. When the attendant pressed him for details, the swami said: "Read the chapter on samadhi in *Sri Ramakrishna and His Divine Play*. I have not written anything about samadhi without experiencing it myself."[16]

Christopher Isherwood, the author of *Ramakrishna and His Disciples*, wrote:

Although Saradananda did not begin his work until more than twenty years after Ramakrishna's death, there is no doubt of its authenticity. Many of those who had known Ramakrishna were then still alive, and Saradananda carefully compared his memories with theirs. *The Great Master* has also the value of having been written by a monastic disciple, who has actually shared the extraordinary experiences he describes. "Nothing beyond my spiritual experience has been recorded in the book," Saradananda once told a questioner. This seemingly cautious answer is in fact a claim so tremendous that it silences all suspicion of boastfulness; a man like Saradananda could not have made it unless it was literally true.[17]

Swami Jagadananda, a disciple of Holy Mother and a great scholar, said: "I have not heard whether Sharat Maharaj had nirvikalpa samadhi or not; but after studying the *Lilaprasanga* I am convinced that only a person with experience could write about samadhi in that way. Now it irritates me when someone says that Sharat Maharaj had not experienced nirvikalpa samadhi."[18]

The necessity of writing the *Lilaprasanga*

Not verbally, but through action, Saradananda proved that he had started to write the *Lilaprasanga* at the behest of Providence. Girish and the other devotees and disciples of the Master felt it necessary to have a complete biography of Sri Ramakrishna. Once when Girish requested Swamiji to write a biography of the Master, he replied: "G.C., if you ask me to overturn the world, I will do it; but I will not be able to write the biography of the Master. Shall I make the image of a monkey while trying to make that of Shiva?" On another occasion Swamiji said, "Sharat will write."

Later, after Swamiji's passing, Girish asked Saradananda to write about Ramakrishna's divine life, his sadhana, and his message. Girish feared that in the future some less adept people might present the Master in a narrow, incorrect way. This might eventually lead to the creation of a cult, and defeat the purpose of his incarnation. There was cause for such apprehension: It was well known that Girish had given his power of attorney to the Master, who took complete responsibility for him. Some people had started imitating him, saying, "O Ramakrishna, here I give you my power of attorney." They deceived themselves because they did not understand the true purport of the power of attorney. God takes responsibility for that person who wholeheartedly surrenders to Him.

Saradananda first wrote *Sri Ramakrishna as a Guru – Part 1* (which is now *Lilaprasanga*, volume 3); its first chapter is "Sri Ramakrishna in Bhavamukha." In this chapter, he wrote a detailed version of the story of Girish's "power of attorney" and showed it to him. Brahmachari Akshay Chaitanya wrote: "We heard from Sharat Maharaj that he read out the story of Girish giving the power attorney to the Master, and Girish commented that it was correctly written."[19]

Saradananda explained his reasons for writing the *Lilaprasanga* as follows:

First, while he was an editor for the *Udbodhan*, Saradananda mentioned this concern: "Various articles about Sri Ramakrishna would come for publication in Udbodhan magazine. Those articles were full of mistakes. I had to cut them at random and rewrite the whole thing. Then I would often think even during our lifetime such misinformation about the Master is spreading among people!"[20]

Second, by 1909, several books had been published about Ramakrishna, including *Sri Sri Ramakrishna Paramahamsadever Jivanvrittanta* by Ram Chandra Datta, *Sri Ramakrishna Punthi* and *Sri Ramakrishna Mahima* by Akshay Kumar Sen, *Sri Ramakrishna Charit* by Gurudas Barman, and *Sri Sri Ramakrishna Kathamrita* by M. Some of these writers' records were not accurate and some focussed on the miracles that the Master had performed — which he himself had despised. With the goal of presenting an accurate biography of Ramakrishna, Saradananda began to write the *Lilaprasanga*. He appealed to the Master's devotees to send him or the president of the Order their authentic stories and other incidents concerning the Master.[21]

Third, when Holy Mother would come to Calcutta, the disciples had to rent a house for her. Swami Saradananda wanted Holy Mother to have her own house in Calcutta and also wanted the *Udbodhan* publication department to have a permanent location. He took out a loan from devotees to build Udbodhan House. To repay the loan, he began to write the *Lilaprasanga*. He explained: "I took a loan of 11,000 rupees for building the Mother's house. It was a heavy burden on my shoulders. I paid off the debt by selling books. Udbodhan House was built to keep Mother in Calcutta. She was our focal point, and centred on her, I did all my work in a joyful mood."[22]

Fourth, Saradananda tried to justify the philanthropic activities of the Ramakrishna Mission and to remove misunderstandings about Ramakrishna's teaching, "Serve human beings as God." M., the recorder of *The Gospel of Sri Ramakrishna*, had commented that the monastic disciples had changed the focus of the Master's teaching, which according to M. was God-realization and not social service. This hurt Saradananda. Of course, later M. revised his opinion when the Holy Mother visited the Ramakrishna Mission Home of Service in Varanasi in 1912 and said, "The Master is ever-present in this place, and Mother Lakshmi always casts Her benign glance upon it."[23]

Fifth, Saradananda wrote in the preface to Volume 3: "When Swami Vivekananda, the foremost disciple of Sri Ramakrishna, came to the West to preach religion, people became eager to know more about the Master's life. As a result, many people have written many things about the Master, but until now no one has clearly indicated that his extraordinary life was deeply connected to the eternal Hindu, or Vedic, religion. While reading those other books one might come to the opposite conclusion: that Sri Ramakrishna was an individual, separated from the eternal Hindu religion, who had created a particular religious sect."[24] He also reproduced Swamiji's article on "Hinduism and Sri Ramakrishna" at the beginning of the third volume as testimony that the Master's life was the meeting point of all sects and that his message harmonized all religions.

Vaikuntha Nath Sanyal, an eyewitness, wrote in his *Sri Sri Ramakrishna Lilamrita* that the straw merchant Kedarnath Das donated a small piece of land for Mother's house and a little money for *Udbodhan* magazine. Saradananda took out a loan to complete the house. To repay the loan, Saradananda began to write the *Lilaprasanga*. He spent five to six hours writing every day for several years and always sat in one place as he wrote. He did not care for his health, but rather sacrificed his life with joy in order to pay the debt on the Mother's House.[25]

Collecting materials for the *Lilaprasanga*

Swami Saradananda was a great karmayogi and a man of steady wisdom; he did not write the *Lilaprasanga* for name and fame. He considered that 23 years had elapsed since the Master's passing away. Swamiji and some monastic and householder disciples of the Master had left the world. A few disciples — such as Holy Mother, Swami Brahmananda, and Girish Chandra Ghosh — were still living. If he did not collect the materials about the Master's life soon, then all would be lost. He received tremendous inspiration from within, Holy Mother's blessings, and help and encouragement from monks and devotees.

Swami Saradananda's first article, titled "Sri Ramakrishna Jivanalochana," was published in the *Udbodhan* (Chaitra 1311: year 7, issue 3). He read this paper on Sunday, 6 Chaitra 1311 (March 1905), at Belur Math on the occasion of Ramakrishna's birth anniversary. Later, this paper was added as an appendix to Volume 4 of the *Lilaprasanga* under the title "*Thakurer Manushbhava.*" Gurudas Barman published "*Sri Ramakrishna's Sadhana and Sri Ramakrishna Charit*" serially in the *Udbodhan* from Year 8 to Year 11. Then Saradananda began to publish the *Lilaprasanga* serially in the Udbodhan beginning with Year 11, Issue 11; and in the last two issues (i.e., Issues 11 and 12 of Year 11), he presented the marvelous stories about Gopal-ma. In Issue 11 of Year 11 (Agrahayan 1316), Saradananda published an appeal to the disciples and devotees of the Master to supply their accounts and stories of the Master.

> The editor's appeal: Some people have published Sri Ramakrishna's wonderful life stories partially at present, which have created curiosity among many people. Apart from curiosity, whatever little information people learned, that made them convinced that such a wonderful personality had not appeared in India for the last 400 years. So nowadays many people are eager to shape their lives following the footsteps of this extraordinary great teacher. Now people are inquiring where they can get a complete, elaborate, and flawless biography of the avatar Sri Ramakrishna with the play of his close companions. So far, whatever books have been published about him bring only partial satisfaction. Moreover, most of the books have mistakes and are not authentic, so one reads them with hesitation and reservation.

> Because of such problems of the readers, the Udbodhan publication wants to be extremely careful to collect as far as possible authentic stories and events of Bhagavan Sri Ramakrishna and his disciples and devotees, especially after studying Swami Vivekananda's life stories. Henceforth, the *Udbodhan* will publish regularly *Sri Sri Ramakrishna Lilaprasanga* and *Sri Swami Vivekananda Prasanga.*

> It is the fervent request of the *Udbodhan* editor to Sri Ramakrishna's disciples and devotees to collect stories and accounts of the Master and send them to the president of Belur Math or to us. These will greatly benefit the public. It is to be mentioned that all these years the *Udbodhan* published serially Gurudas Barman's articles under the title "*Sri Sri Ramakrishna Charit.*" Its life portion was collected from Hridayram Mukhopadhyay, a nephew of Sri Ramakrishna. Hriday was an attendant of the Master for a long period, so his accounts were published in the *Udbodhan.* But those accounts were not flawless, and some discrepancies were found in his statements. We are happy that Gurudas Barman is now correcting those passages and trying to publish them in a book form.[26]

From October 1883 to August 1886, Swami Saradananda was an eyewitness to various episodes of Ramakrishna's life. From September 1885 till the Master's last day, he was one of his attendants and lived with him in Shyampukur and Cossipore. Twenty-three years after the Master's passing away, Saradananda collected materials for the *Lilaprasanga* from Holy Mother, Hriday, Ramlal, and the Master's monastic and householder disciples. They provided Saradananda with information on all the major and minor incidents and episodes in the Master's life that they could remember. Saradananda also went to Kamarpukur and collected stories and incidents of the Master's childhood days from people who had known him at that time. Since Hriday was the only eyewitness to the Master's sadhana in Dakshineswar, Saradananda obtained that information from him. Saradananda also got information about the Master's days of sadhana from disciples who had heard stories of that period from Hriday. After the Master's passing away, Hriday became a hawker and sold clothes and chadars from door to door in Calcutta, and sometimes he would have lunch with the disciples at Baranagore and Alambazar Math. At that time he would relate many stories of the Master's early days in Dakshineswar, and the disciples recorded them in a notebook.

Brahmachari Akshay Chaitanya wrote: "Holy Mother Sarada Devi was very fond of the *Lilaprasanga* written by Saradananda. When she lived in Calcutta, Sharat Maharaj would read the manuscript to her, and Yogin-ma also would listen attentively, sitting next to the Mother. When the Mother was in Jayrambati, someone would read to her the latest chapter of the *Lilaprasanga* that was published in *Udbodhan* magazine. Holy Mother remarked: "All of the information that Sharat has written in his book is correct."[27]

Some pages from Saradananda's diary

On 10 August 1982, I (the present author) was in Udbodhan House and Swami Niramayananda showed me Swami Saradananda's diary. I was moved by how the swami collected various incidents concerning the Master and noted them in Bengali in his diary. After having prasad, I took the diary into my room and copied it into my notebook. I shall present that valuable information here to help the reader understand how Saradananda wrote page after page of the *Lilaprasanga* after reflecting and meditating on these brief words and short notes. A literal translation of the original Bengali words is not possible because it would not be understandable to readers, so I shall present a free translation. Ordinary readers might find it difficult to understand these brief notes, but serious readers of *Sri Ramakrishna and His Divine Play* will understand the references.

O   O   O

Victory to Sri Ramakrishna

Father: 1. Daughter's house and bel leaves, 2. Evening meditation and tears, 3. Mother and brother, scolding the mother (Raghuvir Ramachandra is at home), 4. Going for bath, 5. Attaining the image of Raghuvir in the bushes, 6. Serving the guests, 7. Visiting Gaya and vision in dream.

Mother: Simple and free from greed (Mathur Babu and tobacco leaf), vision of the Goddess Lakshmi.

Uncle: Ram-yatra and Kaikeyi (wretched woman).

8. Making image — Painting pictures — selling in market, 9. Raghuvir image in hand and on the altar, 10. Pyne's house and dressed as a woman, 11. Women's affection, 12. Women in Kamarpukur, 13. Srinivas and garland, 14. Manik Bandyopadhya's house and accepting invitation, 15. Sacred thread ceremony and receiving alms from Dhani Kamarani (against the wishes of his brother), 16. Shrimp curry (Dhani's house) — you won't forget its taste if you eat, 17. Living at home, 18. Service to Raghuvir.

Jhamapukur (Calcutta)

1. Brother's tol (Sanskrit school in Jhamapukur, Calcutta), 2. Worshipping in some householders' homes and living at Gopal Bhattacharya's house at Bechu Chatterjee Street, 3. Bhulu Mitra and Digambar Mitra's houses — visiting Siddheswari.

Dakshineswar

1. Temple dedication and eating one pice worth of puffed rice, 2. Dresser of Kali and sometimes performed worship and arati (very beautiful), 3. Marriage (difficult to be a monk having a wife) — Checking Holy Mother's horoscope and selection, 4. Curse of the brother, 5. Brother, don't sleep [with your wife] — disease, 6. Started worship (Mother, you revealed yourself to Ramprasad, etc.), 7. Vision of ocean at natmandir, 8. Ate naivedya, 9. Long time singing after worship, 10. Worshipping himself and long time arati, 11. Receiving mantra and stood on the altar of the image, 12. Feeding naivedya to a cat, 13. Letter came to the temple officials, 14. Mathur Babu (Mother, engage a rich man), 15. Worship, 16. Rasmani and slap, 17. Panchavati and tulsi grove — japa — flower decoration — fence and gardener, 18. Shouting and crying, 19. Meditation seeing the image on the natmandir, 20. Burning sensation in the body — took amulet (Kanai Ghoshal), 21. A bamboo on the shoulder — Pandit "He is mad", 22. First vision — Vision of Sita blue sari — ivory necklace — entered the body — a monkey came with a "hup hup" sound, 23. Ram mantra — Ramait monk — garb for three days, 24. Ramlala image — Mother of that monk's image, 25. Haladhari's conviction (Brahmadaitya), 26. Mother [Chandramani] thought (possessed by a fairy), 27. Treatment — Gangaprasad — Hriday, what does he say? Two and a half months giving up water and drinking only milk (Ram Kaviraj), 28. Mahimnah hymn, 29. Giving up worship, making Shiva's image — walking over the grass — bel leaves (let knowledge and ignorance go — give me pure devotion — renouncing the ritual for the manes), 30. Mental worship — mad, 31. Upturned the eyes (like Shiva) from sunrise to sunset, 32. Palate and blood, 33. Looking at the sun for one year.

Brahmani

1. Mother, please come and teach, 2. Brahmani at Chandni ghat (cried and said that she saw three persons), 3. Lived at Deva Mandal ghat — near the women of Dakshineswar — preaching — explain the spiritual mood comparing the scriptures — Gauranga experienced it — food according to Brahmani's suggestion, 4. Tantra sadhana — Feeding rice and fish from a skull — Father eat — Panchamundi — Sadhana — Four makara [*madya* (wine) *māmsa* (meat) *matsya* (fish) *mudrā* (parched grain)]. Inhaled the smoke from the burning corpse at the cremation of Ariadaha and Bali — Ananda seat — Yoni worship at natmandir with hibiscus and naivedya — offering one rupee four annas. Achalananda and Dharani — wine for them. Repeating yoni yoni — samadhi. 5. Cleaning the nerves of the body to make them new, 6. Bathing linga at Panchavati, 7. Meditation — bird on the head, 8. Hearing the anahata sound, 9. Bakultala and lust — Divine message (after rubbing the mouth), 10. Cleaning the toilet, 11. Sadhu's arrival (in subtle body), 12. Seedling from the matted hair, 13. Tears made mud, 14. Encircle the Panchavati clapping hands (could not stop), 15. Heavy rain on the head, 16. Vision of Maya-form at Panchavati, 17. Stayed as Mother Kali's confidante, 18. Calling Krishna in the mood of Balaram — and Balaram in the mood of Krishna, 19. Tasted excreta — rupee clay, 20. Story of shawl 21. Taking the defiled leaf-plates of the beggar on the head prayed — quarrel (with oneself because of anger) — monastic ego if big, so gave up external sign [ochre cloth] — root like a Aswatha tree — Tuhun (Thou), 22. Garland of books — Bhagavata-Purana-Charitamrita, etc. — Renounced, 23. Carrying pudding and butter in a plate — "Where is Gopala?" — Brahmani, 24. Searching for Brahmani in the bushes during her absence, 25. Appearance of Chaitanya in Nityananda's form, 26. You have 19 bhavas [moods], 27. Pouring poison in the name of Chaitanya — but Brahmani — suggesting — vision — Balaram Babu and other devotees, 28. Brahmani — Drank one cup blood of goat after sacrifice.

Other episodes

1. Study…, 2. Festival at Dakshineswar, 3. Feeding the monks at Janbazar, 4. Visited Bhutananda, 5. Ecstasy at Navadwip, 6. Visiting Mathur's guru, 7. Mathur's guru's wife at Dakshineswar. 8. Ashananda Dhenki's son Ambika Bhut, 9. Hriday's stealing, 10. Hriday's ecstasy, 11. Mathur's ecstasy, 12. His riding on an elephant, 13. Kon hisebe harahride — Rasmani's favourite song, 14. Slap to Jaynarayan Mukhopadhyay, 15. Mokshada [a woman] in Varanasi, 16. Waving incense to a woman, 17. Govinda Teli and Gopal in Baranagore, 18. Mother's death, 19. Went to attend kirtani in city.[28]

O   O   O

The triumphal march of the *Lilaprasanga*

From 1909 to 1919, Swami Saradananda churned the ocean of

Ramakrishna's lila and produced his magnum opus, *Sri Sri Ramakrishna Lilaprasanga*. The entire *Lilaprasanga* was not published in *Udbodhan* magazine, and he did not write the entire work chronologically. First, he finished Volume 3 in August 1911 (*Sri Ramakrishna as a Guru – Part 1*), then Volume 4 in October 1911 (*Sri Ramakrishna as a Guru – Part 2*), Volume 2 in March 1913 (*Sri Ramakrishna as a Spiritual Aspirant*), Volume 1 in March 1914 (*Introduction and Early Life*), and finally Volume 5 in March 1919 (*The Master's Divine Mood and Narendranath*). The last three chapters ("The Cossipore Garden House," "The Vow of Service to the Master at Cossipore," and "The Master Bestows Fearlessness through Self-Revelation") of Volume 5 were published in the Shravan, Bhadra, and Aswin issues of *Udbodhan's* 21st year. These chapters were not incorporated into the *Lilaprasanga* during Saradananda's lifetime. In 1935, they were added as an appendix to the fourth edition of Volume 5.

It is extremely important to read the introduction to each volume of the *Lilaprasanga* because they give the reader a clear picture of the author's mind, explaining why Saradananda wrote the *Lilaprasanga* and why he did not write the volumes chronologically.

O Volume 1. Saradananda collected the stories of Ramakrishna's early life from Hriday, Ramlal, and from some people of the Kamarpukur village who knew him. Saradananda also included some incidents that he had heard from the Master himself. Ramakrishna's horoscope could not be located, so the swami engaged famous astrologers to ascertain the exact birth date of the Master by comparing his statements and calculating the zodiac signs.

Saradananda wrote in the introduction: "Many incidents in this book were told to us by the Master himself. When we began writing of Sri Ramakrishna's divine play, we could not have believed that we would be able to record the events of his childhood and youth in such a detailed and connected way. But by the grace of the Lord — who makes the dumb eloquent and the lame scale mountains — we were able to do so."[29]

O Volume 2. Saradananda wrote: "By God's grace, the unique spiritual practices of Sri Ramakrishna have been recorded in this volume. We have tried not only to communicate his unprecedented passion for these spiritual practices and the philosophical truths of sadhana, but also to chronologically narrate the main events of his life from his 17th to his 40th year. This volume may be regarded as a history of the Master's life as a spiritual aspirant until the time just before the arrival of Swami Vivekananda and the other disciples."[30]

O **Volume 3**. Saradananda wrote in the introduction:

> In many places in this volume we have discussed Sri Ramakrishna's divine life in light of the scriptures. We have also done a study of his unique mental states, experiences, and activities, comparing them with those of other great souls, such as Krishna, Buddha, Shankara, and Chaitanya of India, and Jesus and others in other countries. The Master told us explicitly again and again: "He who was born as Rama and as Krishna in previous ages is now in this sheath," as he pointed to his own body. "The spiritual experiences of this place (*meaning himself*) have surpassed even the Vedas and Vedanta." In fact, while discussing as impartially as possible the biography of Sri Ramakrishna, who was established in bhavamukha, we were forced to admit that such an extraordinary life had never before been seen in the spiritual world.[31]

O **Volume 4**. In the introduction to this volume Saradananda explained why he wrote the third and fourth volumes first and then the other volumes:

> First — We did not start writing the life of this extraordinary man with a plan in mind. We never dared to cherish the ambition that it would ever be possible for insignificant persons such as ourselves to properly write the story of his great life. It so happened that we undertook this project to inform the *Udbodhan* [magazine] readers about some events in Sri Ramakrishna's life. We did not then know that we would come so far. Under such circumstances, it is not surprising that some later events [of the Master's life] have been described before earlier ones.
>
> Second — Unless people understand how the Master remained in bhavamukha and how the mood of a guru was natural to him, they will not be able to comprehend the Master's wonderful character, unprecedented mental state, and extraordinary activities. That is why we tried to make the reader understand this subject at the outset.[32]

O **Volume 5**. In this volume, Saradananda described the period when the Master stayed mostly in a divine mood and enacted his lila with Narendra and other intimate disciples and devotees. Saradananda also recorded the events of the Master's life, as much as possible, from the time of his first meeting with the Brahmo devotees until his stay in Shyampukur, Calcutta, where he went to undergo treatment for his throat cancer. The three chapters on Cossipore were added later.

Finally, Saradananda wrote: "When we first started writing of the divine play of the Master, we never imagined that we would proceed so far. It was possible only by his inconceivable grace. We bow down to the Master again and again and offer this volume to the reader."[33]

Extra information about *Lilaprasanga*

In 1945, Swami Nirlepananda, a grandson of Yogin-ma, published a booklet entitled *Bhagavan Sri Sri Ramakrishnadev* that was written by Swami Saradananda. In 1968, that pamphlet was incorporated into Swami Nirlepananda's book *Ramakrishna-Saradamrita* as "Extra Information about *Lilaprasanga*."* In the introduction, Swami Nirlepananda wrote:

> A wish to write the sixth volume of *Lilaprasanga* arose in Swami Saradananda's mind. The monks and devotees now and then were asking him to start this undertaking. He gave his two small notebooks to us. It was written in one of them "Reference to be made in the 6th part *Lilaprasanga* or Sri Ramakrishna at Cossipore." This wish was not fulfilled. In that connection he wrote three articles, which are now incorporated in the 5th volume of *Lilaprasanga* as an appendix. It seems that most of the information from those two notebooks has already been published. The remaining information which he recorded but did not use (no one can say whether he planned to use it in the future), I selected and rearranged in this section. One should remember these facts are the materials or rough sketches for the articles but not their full living account. The swami's hand-written notes have been preserved in the original as far as possible.
>
> The readers of Ramakrishna literature know that the Master clearly saw that the young Sharatchandra in his previous birth was a companion of the great teacher Jesus Christ. In fact, Swami Saradananda was a rishi and a seer of truth. Externally he was a serious, grave, and reserved person. Nevertheless, he was a great soul endowed with the ancient Aryan wisdom, and a strong body and mind. His limitless forbearance and sweet motherly heart was hidden behind the form of this luminous steady yogi. He left the field of tapasya and action suddenly — the great Order started and nourished by Ramakrishna and Vivekananda — to make us understand who he was, and how precious was he.[34]

Swami Saradananda said that he had covered only the Master's relationship with Gopal-ma and Swami Vivekananda in the *Lilaprasanga*. He wanted to write details of the Master's relationship with other disciples and devotees, and for that reason he began to write notes in his diary. But his plan never materialized.

Eyewitness accounts of Saradananda's method of work

It is natural for readers to be curious about Saradananda's daily life and the place, time, and environment in which he undertook this great

---

*This unpublished material has been translated into English and published in *Ramakrishna as We Saw Him* by Swami Chetanananda as "Sri Ramakrishna: Some New Findings" in Appendix A.

work. We want to know about his struggles and disciplines, his obstacles and hardships, and how he completed the project. A great undertaking demands great sacrifice. In fact, stories of great writers inspire us. Here we present some eyewitness accounts.

From Swami Bhumananda's reminiscences:

Getting up at daybreak, Swami Saradananda took his morning bath from a bucket of water, which he carried himself to the bathroom. [Some days he bathed in the Ganges.] He always washed his own clothes after his bath. He then went to his room upstairs, changed his clothes, and spread his washed clothes in the sun on the roof. He would not accept any help from anybody. Then he went to the shrine and bowed down to the Master [and the Mother, if she was in Calcutta]. After that, he went downstairs to his small office and reception room to the left of the entrance to Udbodhan House, and sat on a cotton mattress. He then arranged his official things. He put a blotting pad on a small low wooden desk; and to the right of the desk on the mattress different stacks of letters, a container of cigarettes with a matchbox on its top, plus two small inkpots — one with ink and the other with clean water. He would wash the nib of his pen in the water pot and dry it with a piece of torn rag. Every day he would clean his desk and the stacks of letters with a dusting cloth. He kept a towel for wiping his perspiration. At his left, he had a hubble-bubble, which was presented to him by Swami Brahmananda. All this I visualize vividly even today.

Sitting calmly, he wrote the *Lilaprasanga* for hours together, and from time to time rubbed his chin slowly with the back of his left hand. Sometimes he stretched his legs on the mattress but without leaving his seat. As a result, in later years the circulation in his legs was greatly impaired, and they would sometimes tremble. Between writing sessions, he drank tea and smoked his hubble-bubble. This was his method of giving himself a break to think and rest. During teatime in Udbodhan, he took tea with others.

Swami Saradananda never took his lunch before 1:30 p.m. As he was so busy with writing, he did not have his lunch with others. After lunch, he would take a little rest for an hour and a half on the mattress in his office. In the afternoon, he washed his mouth and again started to write *Lilaprasanga*. Again during teatime, he took tea with us.

Before the vesper service, Swami Saradananda would wind up his office. He arranged his files and letters in such a beautiful way, it seemed his every action was perfect. Then the devotees would arrive and they would discuss various topics. We observed in those gatherings that everyone was a speaker, but Swami Saradananda was mainly a listener. Sometimes he would answer questions of the devotees. Occasionally he would go to Belur Math and stay for a couple of days.

He spoke calmly. He could write English and Bengali correctly and his pronunciation of Sanskrit, English, and Bengali was perfect. His life and actions reminded us that his very nature was perfect.[35]

From Swami Asitananda's reminiscences:

Swami Saradananda's office was on the left side of the entrance of the Udbodhan House. The room was neatly and methodically arranged. Here *Sri Sri Ramakrishna Lilaprasanga*, the magnum opus of the religious classics, came into existence. Swami Saradananda had a small low wooden table; he wrote on it the vast life story of Sri Ramakrishna, the new Mahabharata of the present age. After lunch, when he would take rest, that table would become his side pillow. In this room, Swami Saradananda, the gatekeeper of the Mother's house, would meet many famous people of the world and devotees.[36]

In 1925, during the Chariot Festival in Puri, Saradananda lived for some days in Sashi Niketan, accompanied by his disciple Gurudas Gupta. Once by-the-by the swami talked to him about the adverse conditions in which he wrote the *Lilaprasanga* in the Udbodhan House:

Holy Mother was living upstairs along with Radhu; I was surrounded by devotees and I had to keep the accounts also; the burden of the loan for the house was on me. I used to write the *Lilaprasanga* sitting in the small room downstairs. Then nobody dared to talk to me, as I had no time to chat for a long time. If anybody would ask anything, I would say, "Be quick," and finish the talk briefly. People would think that I was egotistic. I could not write much about the devotees [except Gopal-ma and Vivekananda], because there was so much material to write about the Master. When the mind was ready, only then could I write.[37]

Years earlier at Sashi Niketan in Puri, Saradananda wrote "The Quintessence of Madhurabhava," Chapter 13 of Volume 2, which he considered the most well-written chapter of the *Lilaprasanga*. Sometimes he told the spiritual seekers to read Chapter 2 of Volume 3, "A Discourse on Bhava, Samadhi, and Darshana," to learn what true spiritual experience is.

Saradananda was a yogi; if he had not been, he could not have written such a challenging book in the chaotic environment of Udbodhan House. In addition to writing the *Lilaprasanga*, he edited *Udbodhan* magazine and other publications, lectured here and there, and carried the heavy responsibility as general secretary of the Ramakrishna Order. Like the waves

of the ocean, waves of activity would inundate him, but he would perform his duties calmly and boldly. Fatigue could not overwhelm him. The
Bhagavad Gita (4:18) says, "He who finds action in inaction, and inaction
in action, he is a perfect yogi."

Monks who could not adjust in other centres of the Order would take
shelter with Holy Mother and Saradananda in the Udbodhan House.
There was not enough room to accommodate them comfortably. However, Mother and the swami would keep those rowdy monks under control through their love and affection. Amidst the hectic surroundings and
among crowds of devotees and monks, Saradananda steadily worked on
his important project. One day some young monks were talking loudly
and laughing in the Udbodhan office, adjacent to the swami's room.
Golap-ma, an attendant of Holy Mother, scolded them: "Shame on you!
Mother is upstairs and Sharat is doing serious work, and you boys are
making such loud noise!"

Overhearing Golap-ma's loud voice, the swami said to her: "Well,
Golap-ma, please don't give your ears to them. It is the nature of the boys
to behave like that. I am so close to them, but I don't listen to what they
are talking about. I have told my ears, 'Don't listen to anything that is
unnecessary.' So my ears do not hear them."[38]

Such control over the senses is a sign of a *sthitaprajna*, a person of
steady wisdom. When we read the last part of the second chapter of the
Gita, we find the description of a *sthitaprajna* — that is to say, we learn
how a person of steady wisdom, or an illumined soul, lives in this world.
Although all of the disciples of Ramakrishna demonstrated this quality, each one was unique.

The language of the *Lilaprasanga*

Language is the carrier of ideas. Readers will abandon a book if its
language is difficult to understand, cryptic, archaic, or bombastic. For
example, Swami Nikhilananda's translation of the *Kathamrita* is faithful
and beautiful. But Swami Jagadananda's translation of the *Lilaprasanga* is
in a Victorian style and not very easy to understand. Language evolves,
changing every forty years. We can observe the evolution of the English
language: there is Chaucer's English, Biblical English, Shakespearean
English, Carlyle's English, Somerset Maugham's English, Christopher
Isherwood's English, and now we find the English of the *Reader's Digest*.
We see distinct changes. Similarly, we know that the Bengali language
has changed over the years. According to a modern survey, the Bengali
language is the sweetest language in the world. Conducted by UNESCO,

the survey ranked Spanish and Dutch as the second and third sweetest tongues respectively. There are two standard styles in Bengali: the *Sadhubhasa* (elegant or genteel speech) and the *Chaltibhasa* (colloquial speech). The former is an archaic, written form of Bengali and the latter is the current spoken language.

Authors such as Kali Prasanna Singha and Pandit Ishwar Chandra Vidyasagar wrote in an archaic and Sanskritized Bengali that is not current today. The Bengali of Bankim Chandra, as in his novels *Durgeshnandini, Devi Chaudhurani, Ananda Math,* and others, is no longer used. However, the more standard language of Rabindranath Tagore and of Sharat Chandra Chattopadhyay is beautiful and will not change for ages to come.

Swami Saradananda's Bengali is somewhat different from that of previous Bengali writers. His language is neither colloquial and light, nor serious and grave. It is not flowery, full of adjectives, Sanskritized, cumbersome, or awkward. On the contrary, Saradananda's Bengali is very elegant, literary, and dignified. Nevertheless, it is not modern Bengali, so ordinary Bengalis sometimes stumble while reading the *Lilaprasanga.* Although Saradananda's language is elegant and literary, he tried to use a more colloquial language in the dialogue of Ramakrishna. His uniqueness lies in how he balanced these aspects. He reconciled the language of the heart and the language of the intellect in the *Lilaprasanga.* He wrote the biography of his guru in a simple, understandable, and elegant language. His ideas and language marched together. In conclusion, Saradananda's language is deep and lively, clear and flowing, original and easy, sweet and inspiring. Above all, one feels that the *Lilaprasanga* originated from the author's love, wisdom, and experience, and not from his ego.

Brahmachari Akshay Chaitanya wrote: "The style of language in *Lilaprasanga* is somehow original to the author. Where the subject matter is complicated and difficult to understand, his language is thoughtful and decisive; where the description is of the Master's lila, there the language is simple and light. When he described the highest spiritual truth or experience, his language flowed and did not become sluggish or ambiguous. It seems that he is describing the events as an eyewitness. The style of *Lilaprasanga's* language was his own; it was powerful as well as beautiful."[39]

Surendranath Roy wrote in his article "*Swami Saradananda — the Author of the Ramakrishna-Veda*":

Saradananda's language is not modern like Rabindranath's language. During that period, written language and spoken language were not united, so Saradananda used the style of written language. That is why

Lilaprasanga has become forceful and vibrant. If the philosophy of Brahman and the Vedas were written in spoken language, it might not have preserved the gravity of the text. As Saradananda was a perfect soul and loving devotee, his language was simple and thoughtful, and at the same time his expression was charming and beautiful. It has rhythm and flow. There was not a single extra word; and he used the appropriate word in each place. He did not keep any option to replace a word with another word. *Lilaprasanga* is unique in language, rhythm, thought, and expression. I felt joy in my first reading, and my second reading brought more joy. The more I read the more my passion to read increases. It never becomes distasteful. It is like the Ishta-mantra — one never gets tired repeating it.[40]

In the *Kathamrita*, M. tried to preserve the Master's language as much as possible, but he did not preserve the Master's usage of verbs. The verbs that M. used are typical of the Hooghly district. Similarly, Saradananda tried to preserve in the *Lilaprasanga* the Master's dialogue as he heard it from his lips. Both are the recorders, carriers, and distributors of Ramakrishna's message.

Sankariprasad Basu, a renowned writer, wrote in his book, *Sri Ramakrishna: Katha O Kavya*:

Ramakrishna was a rishi-poet. Ramakrishna's words, undoubtedly, are the new Upanishads in Bengali. It is greatly fortunate for Bengali literature that it preserved directly the words of a great spiritual personality. The tremendous power of the colloquial Bengali language was able to express easily a serious and deep subject. We wonder who was that unique genius who impregnated that power in the colloquial Bengali language! This theme is found to some extent in the writings of two illumined poets — Chandidas and Ramprasad. Its indication can be found in the songs of Sahajiya and Baul songs, but it reached its perfection and culmination in Ramakrishna.[41]

Before we discuss the charm of Ramakrishna's language, it is important to understand the difference between the colloquial mother tongue and literary language. Children learn their mother tongue spontaneously from their parents, friends, and relatives, but they learn literary language from teachers in school.

As a child, Ramakrishna learned the alphabet, reading, and writing at the Lahas' school in Kamarpukur and then stopped attending. Therefore, he knew his native mother tongue, Bengali, but he never learned literary language, or "proper language," at school. In fact, Bengalis enjoy the freshness and liveliness of Ramakrishna's colloquial village language.

His language is simple and sweet; his words are clear and charming; his examples are apt and beautiful; his descriptions are poetic and graphic; his ideas are profound and meaningful; his style of conversation is original and captivating; his gestures and mimicry are joyful and entertaining. Ramakrishna used similes and examples, short and simple sentences to communicate his profound teachings, so his powerful statements would remain in his listeners' minds. Even the great savants of India sat spellbound, listening to this uneducated temple priest.

Poetic description in the *Lilaprasanga*

Although Saradananda wrote the *Lilaprasanga* in elegant prose (*sadhu-bhasa*), his poetical imagination and talent are apparent in various places. His original descriptions in some passages are so beautiful, poetic, rhythmic, graphic, graceful, and flowing with alliteration that they overwhelm us. It is not possible to translate them into English; however, in this section some passages from *Sri Ramakrishna and His Divine Play* are reproduced.

Regarding the scriptural testimony of the advent of an avatar, Saradananda wrote in one sentence (which was broken into six sentences in English):

> They [the authors of the Puranas] said that the eternal, universal religion declines with the passage of time. Infatuated by the inscrutable power of maya, people lead their lives in the belief that this world and its mundane enjoyments are their all in all; they consider the Atman, God, liberation, and other eternal transcendental realities to be a poet's fancy — an illusory dream. They achieve wealth and worldly pleasures one way or another, but still they cannot satisfy their hearts' desires. Carried away by a dark, endless, terrible current of despair, they cry out in agony and seek deliverance. Under such circumstances, the all-powerful God makes the eternal religion luminous, like the moon when it has emerged from an eclipse. Out of compassion for human weakness, He takes a human form and again puts humanity on the spiritual path.[42]

While describing Ramakrishna receiving his monastic vow from Tota Puri, Saradananda employed his poetic faculty to present a vivid picture of the environment:

> At the end of the night, the auspicious *brahma muhurta* [48 minutes before sunrise] arrived. Guru and disciple entered the hut. After they completed the preliminary rituals, they ignited the *homa* fire. The Panchavati and the surrounding groves reverberated with the holy and profound sound of the mantras chanted prior to the monastic vows. From ancient times

these vows to renounce everything for God have been passed along in succession from guru to disciple, making India a land of knowers of Brahman. When that sweet sound touched the gentle undulating surface of the holy river Ganges, it seemed that She came to life. She flowed joyfully with a sweet murmuring sound as if carrying this message in all directions: after a long time, here in this age an extraordinary aspirant is taking the all-renouncing monastic vows for the good of all people in the world.[43]

This is a theme for meditation: In the darkness under the Panchavati of Dakshineswar burns a sacred dhuni fire. We see the faces of Tota Puri, a *naga* (naked) monk with matted hair, his body besmeared with ashes, and the young Ramakrishna with shaven head. The guru Tota Puri recites the sannyasa mantras and the disciple Ramakrishna repeats them.

In the *Kathamrita*, M. sometimes passionately described the environment, place, people, time, and the season in poetic language. Similarly, in the *Lilaprasanga*, Saradananda beautifully and vividly described some incidents that we can visualize clearly. Gopal-ma, a woman devotee of Ramakrishna, had a vision of Gopala (the Child Krishna) after repeating the mantra 16 hours a day for 30 years. This passage touches the reader's heart:

The winter of 1884 passed, and the pleasant spring of 1885 arrived. The whole world was alive with birdsong, and plants and trees were adorned with new leaves and blossoms. In the external awakening of the natural world, there is no distinction between good and bad, except the tendencies of human beings. Nature manifests itself to people according to their good and bad habits and past impressions. The holy are awake to the spiritual side of nature and the unholy to worldly matters. That is the difference.

It was 3:00 one spring morning when Aghoremani started to practise her japa. After finishing, she began pranayama and was about to offer the result of her practices to her Chosen Deity when she noticed Sri Ramakrishna seated at her left, his right fist clenched. She saw the Master vividly — as alive as she saw him in Dakshineswar. She wondered: "What is this? How did he get here at such an odd hour?" Gopal-ma later described it thus: "I looked at him in amazement and thought, 'How did he get here?' Meanwhile, Gopala (*as she called Sri Ramakrishna*) kept smiling sweetly. I gathered my courage and grasped his left hand—and Sri Ramakrishna's form disappeared. In its place appeared the real Gopala — a large baby of ten months old. His beauty and appearance beggars' description! He crawled towards me and, raising one hand, said, 'Mother, give me butter.' I was overwhelmed and bewildered by this amazing experience! I cried out so loudly that if there had been men around the house they would have rushed there. With tearful eyes, I said: 'My son, I am a poor, helpless widow. What shall I feed you? Where shall I get butter and cream, my child?' But that wonderful Gopala did not listen to me. 'Give me something to eat,' he kept saying. What could I do? Sobbing, I got up and took some dry coconut balls from a hanging basket. Placing them in his hand, I said, 'Gopala, my darling, I offer you these wretched things; but please don't give me such poor food in return.'

"I could not perform japa at all. Gopala sat on my lap, snatched away my rosary, jumped on my shoulders, and crawled around the room. At daybreak, I rushed to Dakshineswar on foot like a crazy woman. Gopala accompanied me. I held his buttocks with one hand and his back with the other while his head rested on my shoulder. I distinctly saw Gopala's two tiny, rosy feet dangling over my bosom."[44]

This wonderful vision of Gopal-ma is an object of our meditation. In the dim light of the early dawn, we see Gopal-ma walking the five miles to Dakshineswar hurriedly, filled with exuberant joy, to inform Ramakrishna the news of her vision of Gopala and carrying Gopala as a witness.

Saradananda also carefully described Gopal-ma's last moments in such a vivid way that the reader could visualize the death of this illumined woman saint and great devotee of Ramakrishna: "On 8 July 1906 as the rising sun painted the eastern horizon with a reddish hue, a few dim stars in the blue sky were still twinkling as they looked downward towards the earth. When the high tide of the Ganges, the daughter of the Himalayas, flooded both banks with white waves and the river flowed with a gentle and sweet murmur, Gopal-ma's body was immersed halfway into that holy water. The five vital forces of her pure life merged into the Divine, and she attained the eternal abode of fearlessness."[45]

What a glorious death! During Gopal-ma's last moments, a monk recited this mantra into her ear: "Om Ganga Narayana! Om Ganga Narayana Brahma!" As she listened to that holy name, she merged with her beloved Ishta.

Saradananda used the Master's own analogy — "When a flower blooms, bees come of their own accord" — to describe how Ramakrishna gathered spiritual honey and distributed it to humanity:

The flower blossomed and the bees came flying from countries far and near to taste the intoxicating honey. As the sun's touch makes the lotus open its petals and allows bees to sip honey, so spiritual illumination revealed the spiritual honey in Sri Ramakrishna's heart, allowing him to share it with devotees without reservation, satisfying them completely. Sri Ramakrishna's life was built on the so-called superstitious religious tradition of India with no influence from Western education. But as for the spiritual honey that he distributed to the world in this modern age, has anyone ever tasted its equal?

As the wind blows from one flower to another, so human beings travel from truth to truth. Gradually and steadily they are moving towards the unchanging nondual Truth; surely one day they will attain perfection by realizing the infinite, boundless Truth beyond mind and speech. Has such a gospel of fearlessness and hope ever before been proclaimed in this world?[46]

In this age, the advent of Ramakrishna is spreading the light of Dharma across world, removing the darkness of ignorance in worldly-minded people, and illumining the great spiritual paths. Religion is no longer dull and dreary, boring and uninspiring; rather it is dynamic and glowing, joyful and comforting. Ramakrishna's life and message testified to this truth.

The small waves of the ocean create a huge tidal wave; it breaks and becomes many small waves. Again, they create another tidal wave and move forward. Swami Saradananda witnessed this phenomenon in Ramakrishna's ecstatic dance with the devotees on 26 November 1883, during the Brahmo festival at Mani Mallick's house. He depicted that scene in his wonderful language:

We remember vividly that it was the fall season. After enduring the torments of a hot summer, Nature was enjoying bathing in the rains and adorning herself with the beauties of autumn, and was now pulling her veil around her as the chill of winter drew near. It was the last quarter of the season.

We saw a wonderful scene. High waves of heavenly bliss seemed to be flowing in the room. Everyone there was laughing, crying, and dancing — they had become completely lost in the kirtan. Some people fell on the ground, unable to control themselves. Others were overwhelmed with emotion and acted like lunatics. The Master was dancing in the centre of that god-intoxicated group, rapidly moving forward and backward with rhythmic steps. In whatever direction he moved the crowd made room for him, as if enchanted.

An extraordinary combination of tenderness, sweetness, and leonine strength was visible in every one of the Master's limbs. His face shone with a divine smile. What a superb dance! There was no artificiality or affectation in it — no jumping, no unnatural gestures or acrobatics. Nor was any absence of control apparent. Rather, one saw in the Master's dancing a rhythm of natural gestures and movements that sprang from his overwhelming bliss, sweetness, and zeal. His phenomenal dance was like that of a big fish that swims freely and joyfully throughout a vast clear lake, sometimes slowly and sometimes quickly. Absorbed in the ocean of blissful Brahman, the Master used his body to express his inner feelings. At times he lost consciousness of his surroundings as he danced, and sometimes his cloth fell from his body. When that happened, someone fastened it tightly around his waist. And if he saw anyone become overwhelmed with spiritual emotions and lose consciousness, he touched that man's chest, bringing him back to a normal state.

A current of divine bliss emanated from the Master and spread in all directions, allowing the devotees to see God face to face. Those of a lukewarm temperament found their fervour intensified; those with idle minds began to enthusiastically progress in the realm of spirituality; and those who were attached to the world became, for a while, free from their attachment.[47]

This kind of eyewitness account helps the reader to visualize and experience Ramakrishna's divine play. We are forever indebted to Saradananda for his writing skill and poetic faculty along with his deep love and devotion for his guru. All this made Ramakrishna living to us.

The translation of the *Lilaprasanga*

Swami Saradananda himself began to translate the first volume of the *Lilaprasanga* into English. This translation was published in *Prabuddha Bharata*, in the April, May, June, August, September, October, and December issues of 1915 and in the April issue of 1916. (I saw his handwritten English manuscript.) However, he was unable to finish his translation of the first volume. Swami Sharvananda later completed the translation and published it in 1920 as *Sri Ramakrishna, the Great Master*. Swami Saradananda wrote to him: "I am glad you have taken up the translation of the Bengali life of the Master to satisfy the eagerness of the English-knowing general public, [who want] to learn all that is possible of that towering personality. And I wish you every success in your undertaking. I wish I could do it myself but I have not yet been permitted — and who knows whether I shall ever be in a position to do so or not?"[48] In 1921, Swami Sharvananda translated part of the second volume. In 1952, Swami Jagadananda translated the entire *Lilaprasanga*. This version was published by the Ramakrishna Math, Chennai.

In 1996, I began work on a new translation of the *Lilaprasanga* and finished it in 2003. The translation was published as *Sri Ramakrishna and His Divine Play*. I must express my indebtedness to the previous translators because I had the opportunity to compare my translation with theirs. I worked directly from the most recently published *Lilaprasanga, 22*nd edition (1996). I tried to translate Swami Saradananda's words as literally as possible, and at the same time I made a sincere effort to make the translation readable and understandable, faithful and beautiful. Of course, no translation can do full justice to the original. I followed the original format of the Bengali *Lilaprasanga*, wherein the author listed the contents in detail and used them as subtitles in boxes in the body of the book.

Characteristics of the *Lilaprasanga*

We described the origin, history, importance, and magnitude of Swami Saradananda's magnum opus, *Sri Sri Ramakrishna Lilaprasanga*. Here are some characteristics of this great biography:

> In addition to an account of the god-intoxicated life of Sri Ramakrishna, the reader will find in this book glimpses of mysticism, discussions of various religious and philosophical traditions of India, accounts of different religious leaders, and descriptions of the social customs, the educational system, and the socio-religious movements of nineteenth-century India. It is really astounding how Sri Ramakrishna, who had no formal education, overwhelmed the great savants and religious leaders of India with his spiritual power. In this book the reader will see how Sri Ramakrishna, the avatar of our modern age, lived and behaved, how he practised sadhana and taught spirituality, how he evaluated and trained his disciples by observing their physical characteristics and reading their minds as one would a book, how he used parables and folktales in his teachings, how he laughed and cried, sang and danced, made jokes like an ordinary human being, and at the same time frequently experienced spiritual visions and samadhi. It is important to see how Sri Ramakrishna's divine life reflected his phenomenal renunciation, passion for truth, childlike simplicity, complete lack of egotism, longing for God, and love for humanity.
>
> This book bears witness to Sri Ramakrishna's testimony that all religions are equally valid. He found a place for each one in his own life. He first realized God by following Hindu practices, and then by following the Christian and Muslim paths. Such a journey is unique in the religious history of the world. He afterwards proclaimed, "As many faiths, so many paths," thus establishing an ideal harmony of religions for our present age in which religions are in conflict, and hatred and violence are rampant. He taught a religion so badly needed today — a religion that is constructive and not destructive, scientific and not fanatical, practical and not theoretical, rational and not superstitious, universal and not parochial. Truly, Sri Ramakrishna worked to create unity in our time and he

repeatedly stated that the goal of human life is to realize God.

In Sri Ramakrishna's life can be found a synthesis of four yogas: karma, jnana, bhakti, and raja. In addition, the philosophies of the three main schools of Vedanta — dualism, qualified nondualism, and nondualism — were blended in his teachings. He lived his life at the crossroads where many religious sects of India met. He never spoke a harsh word against anyone's faith. He was so all-embracing that members of every sect thought that he was one of them. His all-encompassing love and compassion transcended all sectarian narrowness and bigotry. Truly, Sri Ramakrishna's life is a bridge between the ancient and the modern, between the East and the West. [49]

Generally, a biographer writes the stories and events of a person chronologically. But in the *Lilaprasanga*, Saradananda described Ramakrishna's human and superhuman aspects — such as his ecstasies, visions, samadhi, bhavamukha, guru-bhava, divya-bhava, manush-bhava — through question and answer. This is very helpful for explaining those abstruse subjects, and we seldom find this technique used in biographies.

Saradananda mentioned another interesting characteristic of the *Lilaprasanga* that is not clearly shown in the lives of other avatars:

During the ancient Puranic [Epic] Age, the avatars' human characteristics were kept hidden and only their divine aspects were discussed. In our sceptical modern age, however, the human aspects of the avatars have been stressed and their divine natures have been completely disregarded. In this present context, while discussing the avatars' lives we shall try to explain to the reader how both aspects exist simultaneously in them. It is no exaggeration to say that we would never be able to understand the life of an avatar in that way if we had not seen the godman Sri Ramakrishna.[50]

Lilaprasanga — an incomplete biography

God's will is beyond the human intellect. Saradananda wrote the life stories of Ramakrishna thoroughly and painstakingly over a period of ten years to produce the *Lilaprasanga*. He described Ramakrishna's life from his birth on 18 February 1836 to his move to the Cossipore house on 11 December 1885 — and then he stopped writing. Saradananda had been one of the Master's attendants during his stay at Cossipore from 11 December 1885 to 16 August 1886. He was a witness to the Master's *antyalila* (last days). Why did he stop writing? This is mysterious. We can only offer the following possible explanations: 1. Perhaps he did not want to give pain to the devotees and himself by remembering the Master's suffering from cancer. 2. Perhaps he thought that the Master was God himself and he developed that terrible terminal cancer after absorbing sins from some of his devotees. So, if Saradananda discussed the cause of the Master's cancer in detail, those devotees would have felt guilty. 3. Perhaps he did not write of the Master's passing away because he experienced the continuing presence of the Master. 4. Perhaps he did not receive any command from the Master to finish the book.

After many requests, Saradananda wrote three articles on Cossipore. There are no incidents concerning the Master in those articles except for a brief description of the Master's becoming kalpataru (the wish-fulfilling tree). Nonetheless, Saradananda was witness to many important incidents that took place in the Master's life in those last eight months.

Many monks and devotees asked Saradananda to complete the *Lilaprasanga*. Swami Nikhilananda recalled:

> Before we left for Varanasi [in 1925], Swami Shuddhananda asked Swami Saradananda in front of me to finish the Cossipore chapter of the *Lilaprasanga* [which would describe Sri Ramakrishna's last days]. He said that he had some notes but he was not well enough to write the article. Swami Shuddhananda then said: "You can dictate it and Nikhilananda will write it." He said he would see what could be done. I believe he took his notebook with him. He did not feel well in Varanasi, so nothing was done. When we were leaving for Puri, Swami Shuddhananda reminded him about the article and again asked him to dictate the whole thing to me. Then the swami made the following significant remark: "When the Holy Mother was alive I felt a great deal of inner strength and began to write the *Lilaprasanga*. She died and I felt as if my powers were gone. Then I saw Swami Brahmananda and began to feel strong again. When he died, I felt as if my brain were completely paralyzed. I simply cannot finish the book." Then he added: "When I began to write the *Lilaprasanga* I thought I understood the Master. But now I clearly see that the life of the Master was very deep. I was merely hovering over the top branches; the root is far beneath the ground."[51]

Neither M. nor Saradananda recorded the last days of Ramakrishna. Perhaps it was not the will of the Master. Brahmachari Akshay Chaitanya wrote: "In the beginning of 1925, Swami Saradananda was at Varanasi. One day, Burobaba [Swami Satchidananda], a disciple of the swami, said to him, 'Maharaj, please complete the *Lilaprasanga*.' Saradananda answered humbly: 'Perhaps it will never be completed. I am not getting any inspiration from within. The Master made me write whatever he wanted. Now when I read the *Lilaprasanga*, I wonder, have I written all these things? I have no more inclination to do anything. It seems that the Master is doing everything.'"[52]

Swami Nirlepananda reminisced:

Swami Saradananda, an extraordinary great soul, after long deliberation and meditation month after month, wrote the life stories of Sri Rama-krishna. He published those stories in the *Udbodhan* magazine and people benefited from his work. As a new form of the ancient Sage Vyasa, he acted as a wonderful interpreter of the Master's life and message.

Towards the end of his life, when Saradananda was requested to write the last days of the Master (the events that took place in the Cossipore garden house) and complete the immortal *Lilaprasanga*, he said: "Look, now I see that I understood very little about the Master. If he wishes, then I shall write."[53]

Brahmagopal Datta wrote in his memoir: "Many years after the publication of *Lilaprasanga*, someone asked Sharat Maharaj, 'You have written almost all the episodes of the Master, why did you not write about his passing away?' Sharat Maharaj replied, 'Whatever I was commanded to write, I wrote that much. If I again get a further command, I will write.' In the divine play of Ramakrishna, Saradananda acted like Vyasa and Valmiki, and behind his writing *Lilaprasanga* was the Master's com-mand — who can deny it?"[54]

Swami Saradananda was a votary of truth. To make the *Lilaprasanga* free from mistakes, he reviewed each event before writing it down. Akshay Chaitanya wrote:

Each part of *Lilaprasanga* went into three or four editions during Sarada-nanda's lifetime. Later he intended to change or add something in some parts, but due to inadvertence of the manager, his wish did not material-ize. During his last visit in Varanasi, he commented: 'I don't know when the book goes out of print and when it is reprinted.' He referred to one incident that he wanted to add: During the sadhana of dasya-bhava (ser-vant attitude), the Master saw Mother Sita in his normal state with open eyes. He remarked that because he saw first the all-suffering Sita, his life was also full of sufferings. He further said that he imbibed the sweet smile of Sita because of that vision. The story of having that sweet smile is not in *Lilaprasanga*.[55]

In the *Lilaprasanga*, Saradananda did not describe the details of the Master's relationship with any of the disciples except for Swamiji and Gopal-ma. The *Lilaprasanga* would have been much longer if the Master's divine play with all his disciples and devotees had been included. In this connection, Swami Bhumananda wrote:

In May 1915, Swami Saradananda contemplated writing a section about

302 O See God with Open Eyes

Raja Maharaj (Swami Brahmananda), but stopped because Swami Premananda forbade him. We heard this news, but we did not know the topic. I asked him: "Maharaj, when you went to Puri to see Raja Maharaj, Baburam Maharaj asked you not to publish that story about him. What is it?"

Observing Swami Saradananda's face, I understood that he did not understand my question. Without saying any more, I looked at him. After a while he said, "Kamale Krishna* — that topic?" I said, "I don't know." After some reflection he said, "Baburam Maharaj forbade me to write "Kamale Krishna." I asked, "Maharaj, what is 'Kamale Krishna'?"

Sharat Maharaj continued: "Once the Master had a wish to know his relationship with Raja Maharaj. The Divine Mother showed him — Krishna standing on a lotus holding the hand of a boy. The form of that boy was also like Krishna. The Master told us about this vision and cautioned us not to mention this to Rakhal Maharaj. I forgot that caution. So I thought I would write about 'Kamale Krishna' in *Lilaprasanga*. It was the Master's wish that when I related my intention to Baburam Maharaj, he reminded me of the Master's forbidding words. That is the reason that portion has not been written in the *Lilaprasanga*."[56]

In 1921, Swami Nikhilananda went to Mayavati, where Swami Madhavananda asked him to write a biography of Ramakrishna. Swami Nikhilananda wrote in his reminiscences:

I drafted the manuscript, which was thoroughly revised by Swami Madhavanandaji. Most of the material of the manuscript was taken from Swami Saradanandaji's classic work, the *Ramakrishna Lilaprasanga*, which did not contain, however, the Master's life at Cossipore Garden. I collected the material from several Bengali books. The manuscript was completed in 1923, I believe. I came down to Calcutta in order to read the last chapter to Swami Saradanandaji for any necessary corrections. Two things I recall in this connection. In one place I had mentioned that the Master referred to Swami Saradanandaji as the embodiment of Ganesha. I think this was due to my pure imagination because of the fact of the swami's having written his classic *Lilaprasanga*, a true landmark in the Bengali literature. The swami corrected me. He said that Sri Ramakrishna had asked him to regard himself as Sri Ramakrishna's Shakti.

The other incident was about the dying moments of the Master. I wrote that the disciples present in the room were plunged into a sea of sorrow. The Master's body was a mere skeleton covered with skin. Sanyal Mahashay (Vaikuntha Nath Sanyal) said that when the Master breathed his last the whole room was filled with a celestial light. The swami, who was also a matter-of-fact man and disliked any unnecessary emotion, said that they did not see any light as all of them were grief-stricken.

*Krishna on the Lotus.

I remember another incident he told me. On the Kalpataru Day, many of the disciples who were in the Cossipore Garden were in ecstasy as the Master bestowed upon them his blessings. I asked Swami Saradanandaji what he was doing at that time and whether he had witnessed the great event. He said in a matter of fact way that he was tidying the Master's room and saw the incident through the window but he did not feel like going there because such an experience was not at all new to him.[57]

Regarding the history of the *Lilaprasanga*, Swami Saradananda's own statements are valuable. Gurudas Gupta, one of his disciples, wrote in his memoir:

The history of Swami Saradananda's *Lilaprasanga* is wonderful. *The Life of Sri Ramakrishna* [foreword by Mahatma Gandhi] has been published by Mayavati Advaita Ashrama. This biography will be helpful to those who have started to develop devotion for Ramakrishna, but not of much help to Westerners. A discussion took place on this subject in Swami Saradananda's small office room in Udbodhan. The swami commented: "I had a desire to write an English biography of the Master. While writing *Lilaprasanga*, I wrote a few chapters in English. One should write the events chronologically so that Western readers would be drawn to read it. But my wish did not materialize."[58]

Concluding Remarks

In 1919, the writing of *Sri Sri Ramakrishna Lilaprasanga* was completed. Holy Mother passed away in 1920, and Swami Brahmananda followed in 1922. Saradananda realized that the Master, the director of his drama, was giving him a signal to wind up his own role. He began to pack his belongings and prepare to depart to the other world. Swami Bhumananda wrote: "While writing *Lilaprasanga*, the swami would write hour after hour holding his pen; and toward the end he would continue to repeat the mantra from morning to noon holding the rosary in the same hand."[59]

Swamiji had made Saradananda the General Secretary of the Ramakrishna Math and Mission, and he carried out that heavy responsibility till his last day. In his office in Udbodhan House, he had no table or chair. There was a wall-to-wall mattress and a low wooden desk over it. The swami wrote the *Lilaprasanga* on that wooden desk and also performed his secretarial work. In addition, he was the "gatekeeper (*dwaroan*) of the Mother's house," and he was proud of this post.

Later in his life, as he sat on his mattress, monks and devotees would come and ask him questions about the *Lilaprasanga* and the Master, and he would answer them. Once he told the following story:

Once Bhavanath asked the Master to take away his maya. The Master told him to come to Dakshineswar on a Tuesday or a Saturday. When Bhavanath arrived, the Master tried to give him a little prasad, but he could not lift his hand. He tried several times, then said, "Mother is not allowing me to do it." Swami Saradananda later explained this mystery: "The Master had two moods — human and divine. When he was in the human plane, he had infinite compassion for the suffering humanity. He was eager to remove the sufferings of those who came to him. But when he ascended to the divine plane to remove their suffering, he would see the time had not yet come and it was not the will of the Mother."[60]

One day, Swami Nirvanananda asked Swami Saradananda: "Maharaj, you have written the sannyasa mantras in the second volume of *Lilaprasanga* (Sri Ramakrishna as a Spiritual Aspirant). Did you hear those mantras from the Master?" Saradananda replied: "No, the Master did not repeat those mantras to us in that way. But he told us that he took sannyasa from Tota Puri according to the system of one of the Dashnami Sannyasi sects. I wrote the mantras the way they were recited by the Puri sect of Shankara during sannyasa."[61]

There is no beginning or end to an avatar's life because he is God in human form. The human mind cannot limit the infinite God. Thus the avatar's life always remains incomplete and unfinished. Saradananda wrote Ramakrishna's biography up to 11 December 1885. Similarly, when M. published his diary, he included entries up to 24 April 1886 only. Many stories and sayings of the Master have been lost. However, the all-auspicious and omniscient Master allowed these men to publish enough material about his life to be of benefit to humanity. Sometimes we think if there had been tape recorders and DVDs at that time, we could have preserved the Master's voice, words, and pictures. Now he is in the abode of meditation. Saradananda said: "Meditate on Sri Ramakrishna. Manifest his divine qualities in your life. Then he will reveal his divine nature within you."[62]

After reading the *Lilaprasanga* and *Kathamrita* many times, it is my firm faith and conviction that Ramakrishna himself is the author of these books. He first made Saradananda and M. egoless and then made them suitable instruments to write his life and message. M. could not find his own ego; he experienced the Master within and without. His whole being was saturated with Ramakrishna. Saradananda said that it is not possible to understand the Master as long as a person's ego exists. An eyewitness in Barisal (now in Bangladesh) remembered how Saradananda's mind was full of Ramakrishna: "While talking about the Master, the swami's voice choked, his body became motionless, his eyes were a little open and turned upward, a couple of tears trickled from the corner of his eyes, and his breath stopped. A divine glow lighted his face. After some time, his external consciousness slightly returned. Again, after a while he regained his normal consciousness uttering indistinctly 'Ramakrishna, Ramakrishna.'"[63]

Sarada Devi approved both the *Lilaprasanga* and the *Kathamrita*, and said: "Sharat's book is the correct record of the Master. The *Kathamrita* by M. is also very nice. This is because he has put down the exact words of the Master. How sweet are those words!"[64] As the Ramayana and Bhagavata are source books for Rama's and Krishna's life stories, so the *Lilaprasanga* is the source book for Ramakrishna's biography. Writers of Ramakrishna's biography in the past, present, and future are indebted to Saradananda's *Lilaprasanga*. As long as the sun and moon exist, the Ramayana, Bhagavata, and *Lilaprasanga* will also exist.

History of *Sri Sri Ramakrishna Kathamrita*

S ri Sri Ramakrishna Kathamrita is known all over the world as *The Gospel of Sri Ramakrishna*. The word gospel comes from godspell or goodspell, which means glad tidings or good news. This good news uplifts human minds. Innumerable people from all over the world read *The Gospel of Sri Ramakrishna* every day and get peace and joy from the divine life and teachings of Ramakrishna. But very few people know the life of the recorder and the history of the *Gospel*. In this chapter, the background, environment, and the history of M.'s *Kathamrita* are discussed.

Some of Ramakrishna's teachings have been recorded differently by different writers. Although each of his teachings bears the same truth, the wording and language he used are sometimes different. Stories have been recorded in more or less detail, depending on the writer. When we read the Bible, we find the same thing: the teachings or stories of Jesus were recorded differently by Matthew, Mark, Luke, and John. The wording of each gospel is different; some stories provide more details than others. It is quite natural for two persons to see and hear the same thing at the same time and yet describe the event differently.

The first gospel of Ramakrishna was published in 1878 by Girish Chandra Sen, a disciple of the Brahmo leader Keshab Chandra Sen; it consists of 184 of the Master's teachings. The second gospel was published in 1884 by Suresh Chandra Datta, a householder devotee of Ramakrishna, and comprises 950 teachings of the Master. The third gospel was published in 1885 by Ram Chandra Datta, a householder devotee of Ramakrishna. It

M. at bel-tala in Dakshineswar on 23 February 1927.

consists of 300 teachings of the Master. The fourth gospel was recorded in diary form by M. (Mahendra Nath Gupta) from 1882 to 1886. Published in five volumes between 1902 and 1932, it has 177 entries. The fifth and last gospel was recorded by Swami Brahmananda, a monastic disciple of Ramakrishna. It was published serially from 1898 to 1900 in the *Udbodhan* magazine. Then in 1905 these teachings were collected in a book, *Sri Sri Ramakrishna Upadesh*, containing 248 teachings of the Master.

All of these gospels were recorded in Bengali, Ramakrishna's mother tongue. The first three of these gospels have not yet been translated into English in their entirety. M.'s record was published in five volumes and appeared in English in one volume in 1942 as *The Gospel of Sri Ramakrishna*. Swami Nikhilananda of the Ramakrishna-Vivekananda Center in New York translated this huge work and Aldous Huxley wrote the foreword. The gospel according to Swami Brahmananda was translated into English and edited by Jnanendra Nath Mukhopadhyay and F.J. Alexander as *Words of the Master* and published by Udbodhan Publication Office, Calcutta, in 1924.

The Master's teachings were so impressive and instructive that Swami Shivananda, as a young disciple, felt a desire to take notes. He recalled:

> One day at Dakshineswar, I was listening to the Master and looking intently at his face. He was explaining many beautiful things. Noticing my keen interest, the Master suddenly said: "Look here! Why are you listening so attentively?" I was taken by surprise. He then added: "You don't have to do that. Your life is different." I felt as if the Master had divined my intention to keep notes and did not approve of it, and that was why he had spoken in that way. From that time on I gave up the idea of taking notes of his conversations, and whatever notes I already had I threw into the Ganges.[1]

Ramakrishna advised his young monastic disciples to renounce both externally and internally; and he advised his householder disciples to renounce internally. Many years later Swami Premananda related how the Master taught the monastic disciples: "Very little of the Master's teachings are recorded in the *Gospel*," he said. "M. used to visit the Master occasionally and would note down his teachings as he heard them....His teachings to the monastic disciples were given in private. As soon as the householder devotees would leave the room, he would get up and lock the door and then speak to us living words of renunciation. He would try to impress upon our young minds the emptiness and vanity of worldly enjoyments."[2]

The origin of *The Gospel of Sri Ramakrishna*

M. based his *Sri Sri Ramakrishna Kathamrita* (*The Gospel of Sri Rama-krishna*) on his diary entries recorded from 26 February 1882 to 10 May 1887. Within a couple of years after the Master's passing away, he began to develop his diaries for publication but he did not make all of the entries public. On 11 July 1888, M. read a chapter of the *Kathamrita* to Holy Mother, who was then living in Nilambar Babu's garden house in Belur. After she heard this reading from the manuscript, she praised M. and encouraged him to write more. On 15 March 1890, M. read another chapter to Holy Mother and received her blessing and approval to pub-lish it.

In 1892, a small pamphlet of 20 pages was released under the title *"Paramahamsadever Ukti — Part 3"* by "Satchidananda Gitaratna," col-lected by "Sadhu Mahindranath Gupta."[3] Swami Vivekananda read this pamphlet[*] and wrote to M. from Antpur on 7 February 1889: "Thanks! 100,000 times, Master! You have hit Ramkristo in the right point. Few alas, few understand him!!

"My heart leaps in joy — and it is a wonder that I do not go mad when I find anybody thoroughly launched into the midst of the doctrine which is to show peace on earth hereafter."[4]

M. was busy with family duties, so he could not always concentrate on developing his diaries for publication. On 26 November 1895, Holy Mother wrote to M. from Kamarpukur: "Please preserve those teachings of the Master which he left with you." M. was inspired by her letter to publish *"Leaves from the Gospel of the Lord Sri Ramakrishna,"* which came out serially in the English-language *Brahmavadin* magazine starting on 15 October 1897.

Swami Vivekananda read the series and wrote to M. from Rawalpindi in October 1897: "Dear M., C'est bon, mon ami — Now you are doing just the thing. Come out man. No sleeping all life. Time is flying. Bravo! That is the way.

"Many many thanks for your publication. Only I am afraid it will not pay its way in a pamphlet form....Never mind — pay or no pay. Let it see the blaze of daylight. You will have many blessings on you and many more curses but that is always the way of the world, sir. This is the time."[5]

*Sunil Behari Ghosh, a researcher and librarian, presumed that *Paramahamsadever Ukti* — Part 1 was compiled and published by Keshab Chandra Sen in 1878, and Part 2 was collected and published by Girish Chandra Sen in 1887, and Part 3 by M. in 1892. Behind his guess is that none could ever find Parts 1 and 2 made by M. (Adapted from *Sri Ramakrishna O Tar Kathamrita*, 219.)

Swami Vivekananda wrote to M. again on 24 November 1897, this time from Dehra Dun:

> My dear M., Many many thanks for your second leaflet. It is indeed wonderful. The move is quite original and never was the life of a great teacher brought before the public untarnished by the writer's mind as you are doing. The language also is beyond all praise — so fresh, so pointed and withal so plain and easy. I cannot express in adequate terms how I have enjoyed the leaflets. I am really in a transport when I read them. Strange, isn't it? Our teacher and Lord was so original and each one of us will have to be original or nothing. I now understand why none of us attempted his life before. It has been reserved for you — this great work. He is with you evidently.
>
> P.S. The Socratic dialogues are Plato all over. You are entirely hidden. Moreover, the dramatic part is infinitely beautiful. Everybody likes it, here and in the West.[6]

After M. began publishing the Master's teachings in English in pamphlet form, a critic wrote in the *Tattwamanjari* magazine: "We have a request to Mr. Gupta to publish these teachings in a big book form instead of in small pamphlets that will benefit the masses. Again, we wonder, why did he publish it in English instead of Bengali? It is needless to remind him that sometimes the spirit of such deep spiritual truths diminishes while translating them into English. It would be difficult for our people to understand these teachings."[7] M. later acquiesced to the critic's request.

This criticism, however, was nothing compared to the appreciation that M. received from many distinguished reviewers. The English-language pamphlets created a tremendous stir because readers found Ramakrishna's teachings new and exciting. But M. eventually decided to publish *The Gospel of Sri Ramakrishna* in Bengali, so that readers could taste the original beauty of the Master's mother tongue. Again, he sought Holy Mother's blessing.

On 4 July 1897, Holy Mother wrote to M. from Jayrambati: "My dear child, whatever you heard from the Master was true. You should not feel any fear in publishing them. At one time he left those teachings in your custody, and now he is bringing them to light through you. Know for certain that people's spiritual consciousness will not be awakened without bringing out those teachings. Whatever words of the Master you collected are true. One day while I was listening to your manuscript, I felt as if the Master was saying all those things."[8]

With this encouragement from Holy Mother, M. began in earnest to develop *Sri Sri Ramakrishna Kathamrita*. He published chapters from the

book in many Bengali magazines and newspapers such as the *Udbodhan,*
Tattwamanjari, Anusandhan, Arati, Alochana, Utsaha, Rishi, Janmabhumi,
Navya Bharat, Punya, Pradip, Prabasi, Prayas, Bamabodhini, Sahitya, Sahitya
Samhita, and *Hindu Patrika.*[9] M. then arranged those chapters in chrono-
logical order and published them as *Sri Sri Ramakrishna Kathamrita* — Volume I, which was published on 11 March 1902 by Udbodhan Press under
Swami Trigunatitananda's supervision. Volume II was published in 1904,
Volume III in 1908, Volume IV in 1910, and Volume V in 1932. In its
entirety, *Sri Sri Ramakrishna Kathamrita* contains nearly 177 diary entries
that M. recorded during Ramakrishna's lifetime and eight entries that
he added after the Master passed away. In addition, M. collected a few
entries and a letter from other sources that he included in appendices to
those volumes.

Swami Nityatmananda described how M. wrote notes to himself in
his diary. On Sunday, 1 January 1882,* Ramakrishna attended the Brahmo
Festival at Jnan Chaudhury's house in Simla, Calcutta. On this occasion
M. wrote only two words in his diary entry for that day: *kamārshālār lohā,*
meaning "iron in a smithy." Prompted by those two words, M. wrote the
words of the Master as he remembered them:

> Why shouldn't it be possible for a householder to give his mind to God?
> But the truth is that he no longer has his mind with him. If he had it,
> then he could certainly offer it to God. But, alas, the mind has been mort-
> gaged — mortgaged to "woman and gold." So it is necessary for him con-
> stantly to live in the company of holy men. Either he should think of God
> in solitude day and night, or he should live with holy men. The mind left
> to itself gradually dries up. Take a jar of water, for instance. If the jar is set
> aside, the water dries up little by little. But that will not happen if the jar
> is kept immersed in the Ganges.
>
> The iron becomes red in the forge of a smithy. Take it out and it be-
> comes black as before. Therefore, the iron must be heated in the forge
> every now and then.[10]

On 21 February 1924, a devotee asked M.: "Why did you assume
three names — Master, Srima, Mani — in the *Kathamrita* instead of one?"

M.: "Where there is a private conversation, I put 'Mani'; because it
is not necessary for the reader to know the person. It is enough to know
what the Master said to him. What is the necessity for others to know
whether the Master scolded or praised him?"

*This event took place before M. met Sri Ramakrishna. M. collected the information
from a reliable source and recorded it in his diary. He later developed and added it in
the *Kathamrita* as an appendix.

The devotee: "Will readers understand if your diary is printed as it is?"

M.: "No, people won't understand it. It is recorded in a very concise way. Some parts are in my mind and some are in the diary, such as a subtitle in the chapter, 'The Brahmachari and the Snake.'"[11]

On 16 July 1925, Swami Vireswarananda asked M. how he wrote the wonderful *Kathamrita* from such meagre sketches. M. humbly replied: "By the Master's grace alone. People take these incidents to have occurred over forty years ago. But I see them happening this very moment before my very eyes. In meditation the distance of time vanishes. In love and devotion everything is ever-present — there is no past or future."[12]

On 3 November 1927, a devotee asked M.: "Is it true that the Master forbade anyone to record his words, except you?"

M.: "The Master did not allow people to record his words in his presence. No one knew that I was recording the Master's sayings. I habitually maintained a diary, so I went on recording his words accordingly. When the Master was ill at the Cossipore garden house, others learned [somehow] that I was recording his conversations, and he did not forbid it."[13]

M. would listen attentively and become absorbed in the words of the Master, and then return home and write in his diary, sometimes the entire night. On 13 September 1924, M. described the stress this caused: "One day on Badurbagan Street, in front of Vidyasagar's house, I fell unconscious on the sidewalk. Then someone took me home in a horse carriage. When the Master heard about this incident, he said: 'Please sleep more and drink milk. And stop writing for some days.'"[14]

Ramakrishna's contribution to M.'s work

Ramakrishna's life was based on truth, so every one of his words was true. He said that the Divine Mother had never allowed an untruth to pass through his lips. The omniscient Master knew that M. was preserving his message, so from time to time he corrected M.'s ideas to make sure they were accurate. The following conversation took place between Ramakrishna and M. on 9 November 1884:

Master: "How did you like today's conversation?"
M.: "Very much indeed."
Master (*smiling*): "How I spoke about the Emperor Akbar!"
M.: "It was very good."
Master: "Repeat it to me."
M.: "A fakir came to visit Akbar. The Emperor was saying his prayers.
In his prayers, he was asking God to give him wealth and riches.

Copy of M.'s diary, p. 1 (first and second visit, 26 and 28 February 1882)

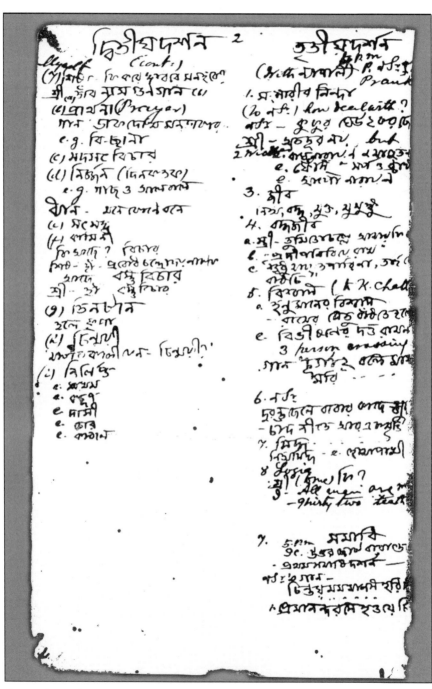

Copy of M.'s diary, p. 2 (second and third visit, 28 February and 5 March 1882)

314

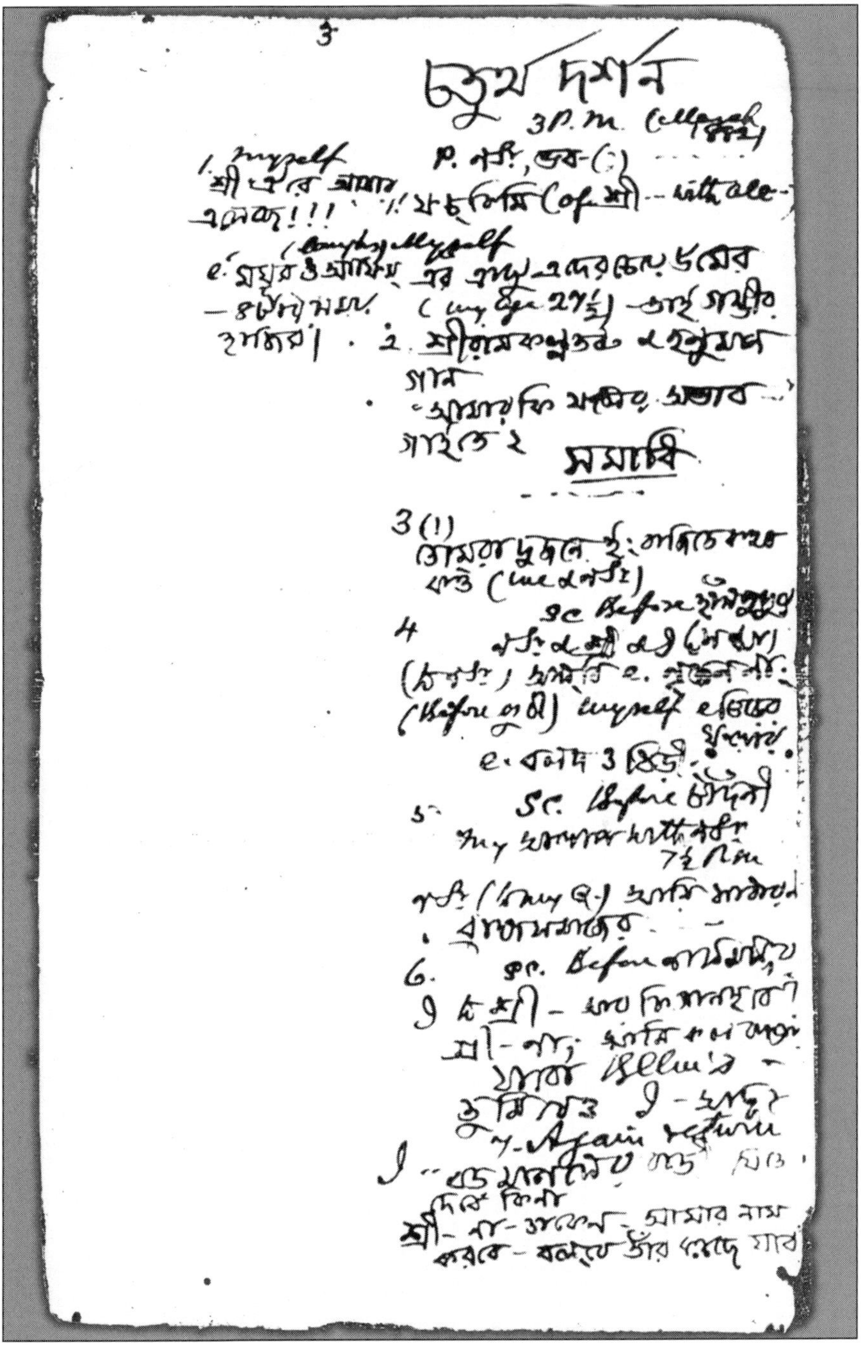

Copy of M.'s diary, p. 3 (fourth visit, 6 March 1882)

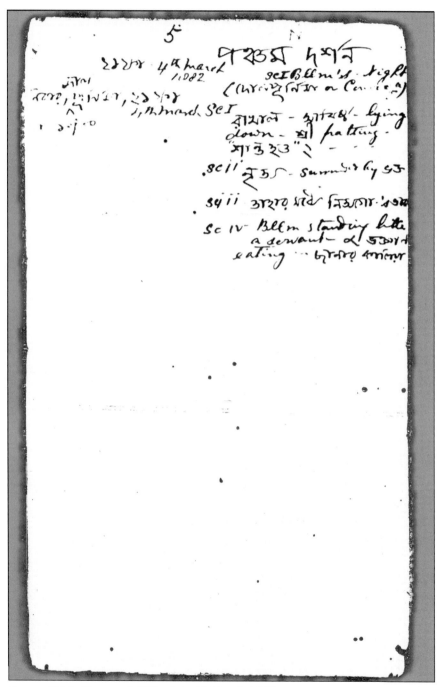

Copy of M.'s diary, p. 4 (fifth visit, 11 March 1882)

Visit to Vidyasagar 1882 /12

5th aug. 82, Sat.; ঠা. ৫.5

Scp. Myself, Hazra; চন্ডি

SC I বাসুর গাহাঁগ- before রাম-
যাত্রা গায়ের বাড়ী
M- reminding of রামযেয়ন
শ্রী "দুধ র আমি এবং অন্যান্ডু
গুনীর না"

SC II
(গহীহেতবামাবণর, সিন্ধু বৈতরণ্য আলে)

শ্রী (to me) "আমার যেতায় কি
দেবা ?"

৯ - তার দরকার নাই- আপনার
বিণ্ডু দরকার নাই।

SC III upstairs
(গ্রন্থ ব্যর দান্চ্যমীয়া সহযমী)

শ্রী - looks at Vidyas.
Who stands don't receive:

SC IV
শ্রী (আবিষ্') আমি কল (ময়ময়ু)
প্রায়।

বিদ্যা - goes in a bring সিদ্ধ
te (from বঙ্গ গ্রাম).
(সিদ্ধাই being offered time)

বিদ্যা - ও ঘরের ছেলে
Myself

শ্রী (ছবিতায়) সহ ওগন্তু সার
যেমন যাহ্নু নদী "

2. Est. of বিদ্যাসাগর

শ্রী- আম সায়ার এস সিনিময়-
প্রতিদিন যাহ্নবিহি নদী হুদি দেখেদি

বি- "সোমাকুল নিবেধন"

শ্রী- নানা ভুমিতা। প্রবিদার সাগর
নও ভুমিশ্রীর সমুদ্র-বিভাগ মহায়

বি - ও বিকণ্ডও পাবেন   (a)
....

শ্রী - তোমার মাঠের রচা- দানাদি
দ্যেনাই- দয়া   (1)

Copy of M.'s diary, p. 5 (visit to Vidyasagar, 5 August 1882)

317

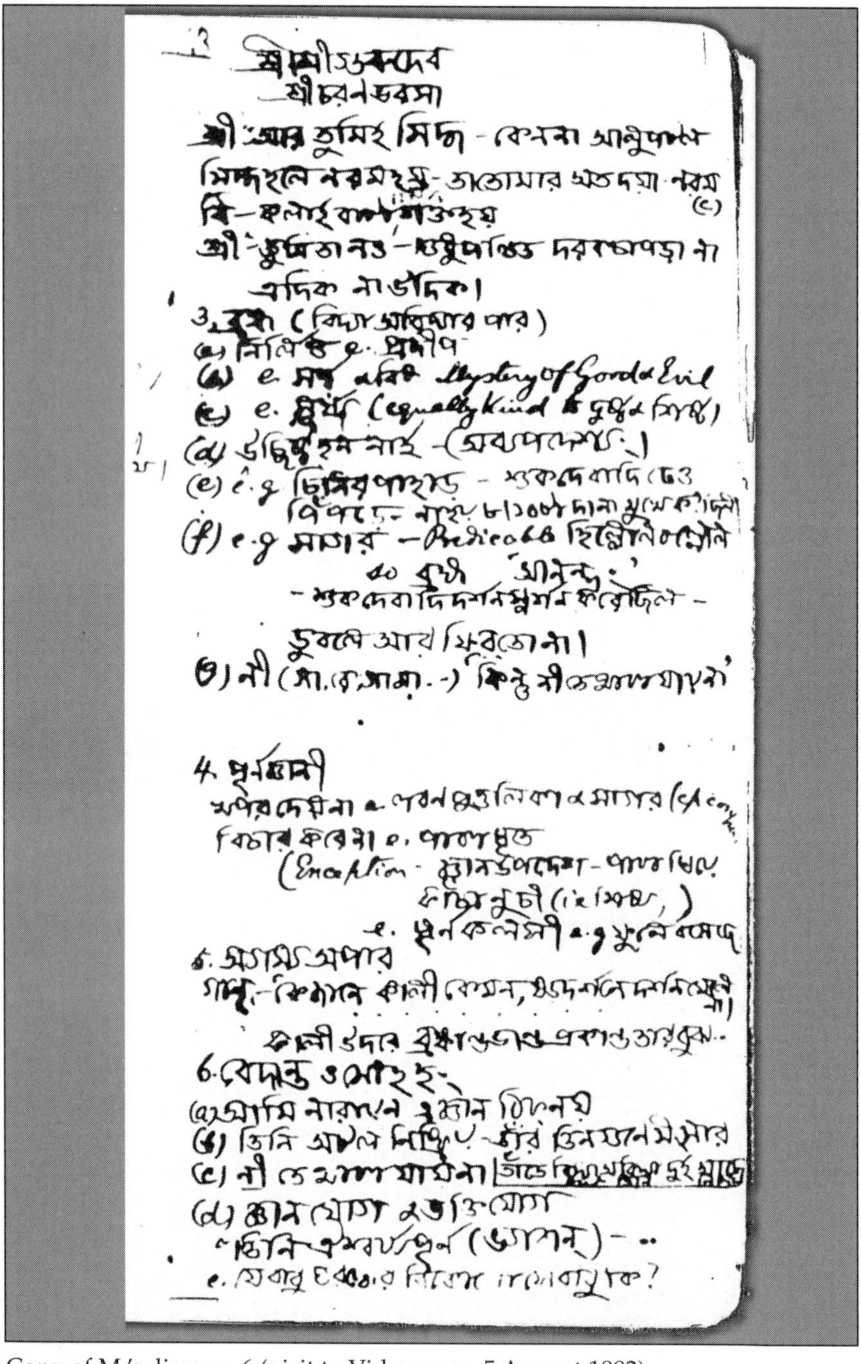

Copy of M.'s diary, p. 6 (visit to Vidyasagar, 5 August 1882)

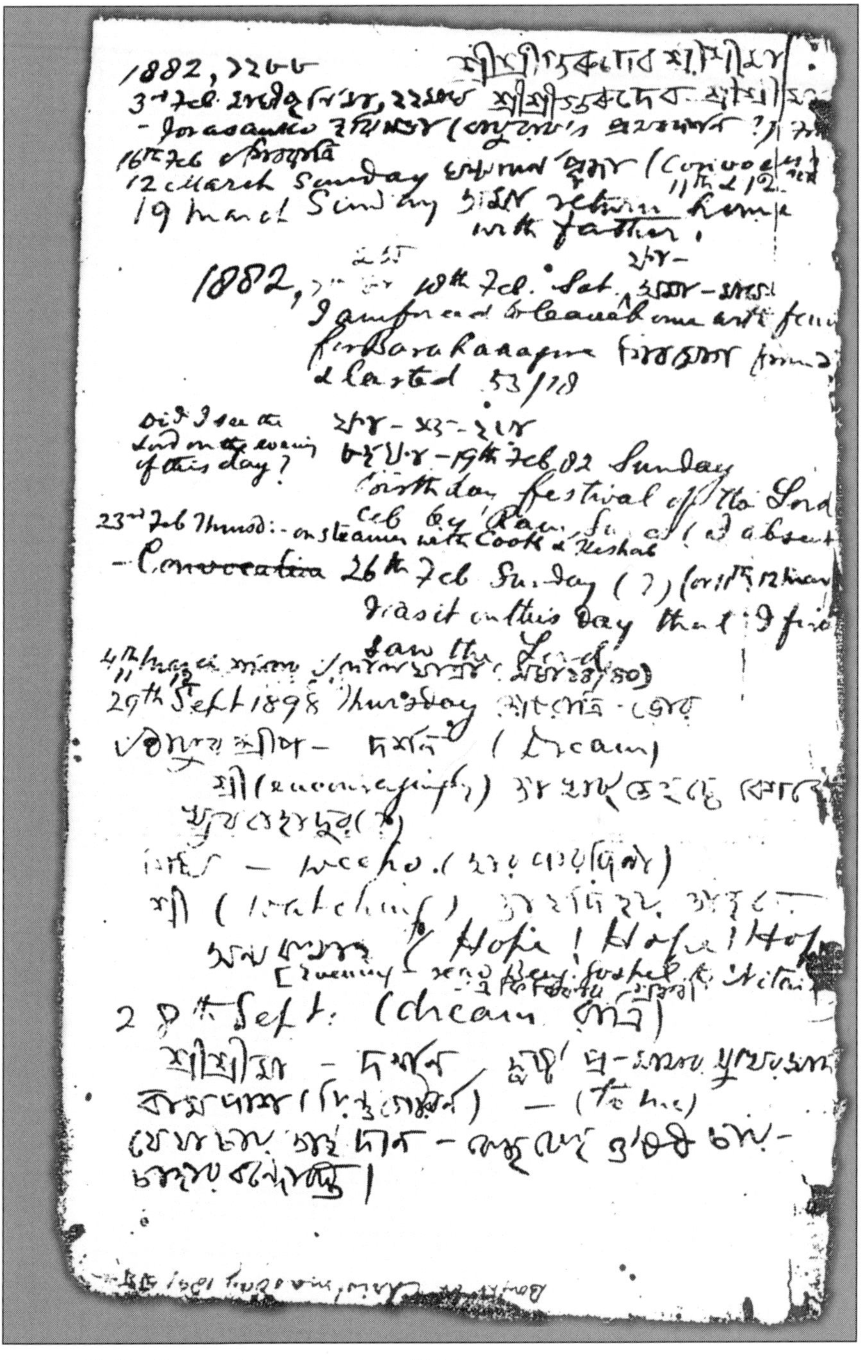

Copy of M.'s diary, p. 7 (some notes of M.)

Thereupon the fakir was about to leave the room quietly. Later, when the Emperor asked him about it, the fakir said, 'If I must beg, why I should beg of a beggar?'"

Master: "What else did we talk about?"

M.: "You told us a great deal about saving up for the future."

Master (*smiling*): "What did I say?"

M.: "As long as a man feels that he must try, he should make an effort. How well you told us about it at Sinthi!"

Master: "What did I say?"

M.: "God takes upon Himself complete responsibility for one who totally depends upon Him. It is like a guardian taking charge of a minor. You also told us that at a feast a child cannot by himself find a place to eat his meal; someone finds a place for him."

Master: "No, that is not quite to the point. I said that the child doesn't fall if the father leads him and holds his hand."

M.: "You also described the three classes of sadhus. The best sadhu does not move about to get his food; he lives in one place and gets his food there. You told us about that young sadhu who said, when he saw the breasts of a young girl, 'Why has she those abscesses?' You told us many other things."

Master (*smiling*): "What else?"

M.: "About the crow of Pampa Lake. He repeated the name of Rama day and night. That is why he couldn't drink the water though he went to its edge. And about the holy man in whose book was written only 'Om Rama.' And what Hanuman said to Rama."

Master: "What did he say?"

M.: "Hanuman said to Rama: 'I saw Sita in Ceylon; but it was only her body. Her mind and soul were lying at Your feet.'

"And about the chataka bird. He will not drink anything but rainwater. And about jnana yoga and bhakti yoga."

Master: "What did I say about them?"

M.: "As long as one is conscious of the 'jar', the ego will certainly remain. As long as one is conscious of 'I', one cannot get rid of the idea, 'I am the devotee and Thou art God.'"

Master: "No, it is not that; the 'jar' doesn't disappear whether one is conscious of it or not. One cannot get rid of the 'I'. You may reason a thousand times; still it will not go."

M. remained silent a few moments.

M.: "You had that talk with Ishan Mukhopadhyay in the Kali temple. We were very lucky to be there."

Master (*smiling*): "Yes, yes. Tell me, what did I say?"

M.: "You said that work is only the first step. You told us that you said to

Shambhu Mallick, 'If God appears before you, will you ask Him for a number of hospitals and dispensaries?'

"You said another thing: 'God does not reveal Himself to a person as long as he is attached to work.' You said that to Keshab Sen."

Master: "What did I say?"

M.: "As long as the baby plays with the toy and forgets everything else, its mother looks after her cooking and other household duties; but when the baby throws away the toy and cries, then the mother puts down the rice-pot and comes to the baby.

"You said another thing that day: Lakshmana asked Rama where one could find God; after a great deal of explanation, Rama said to him, 'Brother, I dwell in the man in whom you find ecstatic love — a love which makes him laugh and weep and dance and sing.'"

Master: "Ah me! Ah me!"

Sri Ramakrishna sat in silence a few minutes.

M.: "That day you spoke only words of renunciation to Ishan. Since then many of us have come to our senses. Now we are eager to reduce our duties. You said that day, 'Ravana died in Ceylon and Behula wept bitterly for him.'"

Sri Ramakrishna laughed aloud.

M. (*humbly*): "Sir, isn't it desirable to reduce the number of one's duties and entanglements?"

Master: "Yes. But it is a different thing if you happen to come across a sadhu or a poor man. Then you should serve him."

M.: "And that day you spoke very rightly to Ishan about flatterers. They are like vultures on a carcass. You once said that to Padmalochan also."

Master: "No, to Vamandas of Ulo."[15]

Sometimes Ramakrishna tested M.'s understanding of specific terms that he used. On 3 August 1884, the Master talked about false and real renunciation. Because M. was a family man, it was not possible for him to renounce completely, so the Master asked him to renounce mentally.

M.: "I now desire that my activities may be much reduced and that I may devote myself greatly to God."

Master: "Ah! Certainly your desire will be fulfilled. But a jnani can live unattached in the world."

M.: "True, sir. But one needs special power to lead an unattached life."

Master: "That is also true. But perhaps you wanted the worldly life. Now you should pray to God that your worldly duties may be reduced. And you will achieve the goal if you renounce mentally."

M.: "Mental renunciation is prescribed for those who cannot give up the world outwardly. For superior devotees, total renunciation is enjoined — both outer and inner."

Ramakrishna was silent for a few minutes and then resumed the conversation.

Master: "How did you like what I said about renunciation a little while ago?"

M.: "Very much, sir."

Master: "Tell me, what is the meaning of renunciation?"

M.: "Renunciation does not mean simply dispassion for the world. It means dispassion for the world and also longing for God."

Master: "You are right. You no doubt need money for your worldly life; but don't worry too much about it. Those who surrender their hearts and souls to God, those who are devoted to Him and have taken refuge in Him do not worry much about money. As they earn so they spend. This is what the Gita describes as 'accepting what comes of its own accord.'"[16]

The story of M. and his chronicle

Every avatar or divine incarnation comes with a chronicler who records the avatar's life and teachings. Valmiki wrote Ramachandra's life and teachings in the Ramayana; Vyasa wrote Krishna's life and message in the Bhagavata and the Mahabharata. Buddha's and Christ's lives and messages were recorded by their disciples. According to a divine plan, M. was earmarked to record *The Gospel of Sri Ramakrishna*, the avatar of this present age.

Observing Ramakrishna, sometimes 24 hours a day for a number of years, M. recorded in the pages of his diary the Master's daily routine, conversations, and way of life. He presented the divine drama of Ramakrishna, showing how an avatar eats and sleeps, talks and behaves, laughs and cries, sings and dances, worships and prays, meditates and goes into samadhi. Such minute details and vivid descriptions of an avatar are unique in religious history. For his contributions, M. deserves not only respect and appreciation, but also humanity's adoration.

Once a famous writer expressed to me his doubt about the authenticity of the *Kathamrita*: "How was it possible to write five volumes of the *Kathamrita* [*The Gospel of Sri Ramakrishna* consists of 1063 pages] based on a diary? How could M. develop long conversations, songs, and stories so elaborately and vividly after many years? It seems to me that some words belong to Ramakrishna and some M. supplied in the *Gospel*."

I answered: "Well, do you have any doubt about the Gita, Bhagavata, or Ramayana? When Krishna was teaching the Gita to Arjuna, Vyasa was not there. Ugrasrava Sauti was present when Shukadeva narrated 18,000 verses of the Bhagavata to Parikshit and later he recited them to the rishis at Naimisharanya from his memory. Valmiki wrote Ramayana without being an eyewitness to Rama's life. No Hindus have any doubt about the Gita, Bhagavata, or Ramayana. Regarding the Bible, Matthew recorded Christ's life and teachings in Hebrew 30 years after his passing away. Mark recorded the story from Peter, and Luke's recording came from Paul. John emphasized Christ's philosophy and message rather than his life. No true Christians doubt the Bible. Muhammad recited Allah's message as told by the Angel Gabriel, and thus the Koran was recorded. No Muslims doubt the Koran." This is how I tried to remove the doubt of the writer.

As the rishis of the Vedic age discovered the truths of the Upanishads, in the same way M. practised truth wholeheartedly so that he could establish the *Kathamrita* on truth. In the Ramakrishna incarnation he played the role of the sage Vyasa. It is true that without divine grace no human being could have written the *Kathamrita*. During M.'s second visit the Master smashed his ego and possessed him, so that he could perform the job of a chronicler. The Master also empowered him, saying this prayer: "Mother, I cannot speak anymore. Please give some power to Ram, Mahendra (M.), Vijay, and others. Let them now work for you."[17]

On 22 July 1883, the Master was talking with the Divine Mother in an ecstatic mood: "O Mother, why hast Thou given him [M.] only a particle?" Remaining silent a few moments, he added: "I understand it, Mother. That little bit will be enough for him and will serve Thy purpose. That little bit will enable him to teach people."[18]

On 6 February 1919, a devotee asked M.: "When did you write the *Kathamrita*? Did you write at night after working all day? It must have been exhausting."

M. replied: "Is it possible to achieve anything without hard labour? Yes, I used to write at night. Sometimes I listened to the Master's conversation and then wrote it down in my diary the next day after meditation." Then he opened a page from the Chandi (4:11) and recited, "'O Devi, you are the intelligence by which the essence of all scriptures is comprehended.' Have I done this work? It was the Master's work; he did it. He appeared in me as *medha* [the power of memory]. He is the doer and makes others act. We may or may not realize this.

"What a wonderful thing the Master produced! Such a thing does not exist for other avatars. The *Kathamrita* is like a photograph, an exact reproduction. It depicts the place, time, *tithi* or lunar day, even the high and low tides of the Ganges. If someone reads this book after visiting Dakshineswar, he or she will experience deep meditation."[19]

On different occasions, M. later related the genesis or the birth story of the *Gospel* to the monks and devotees:

Once the Master said to me: "The Divine Mother has told me that you have to do a little work for her. You will have to teach the Bhagavata, the word of God, to humanity. God binds the Bhagavata pandit to the world with one tie; otherwise, who would remain to explain the sacred book? He keeps the pandit bound for the good of men. That is why the Divine Mother has kept you in the world."

To what extent can we foresee God's plan? The Master made me start keeping a diary in 1867 when I was a student of class seven at Hare School. Since then I recorded in my journal my daily activities, the places I had visited, and so on. I met the Master in the later part of February 1882. That is when my habit of maintaining a diary really became fruitful. When we look back on our past, we realize that God is making us do everything. God determines beforehand what he will do through a particular person and then gets it done through him. There were many people around the Master, but he made me write the chronicle. As a result, *The Gospel of Sri Ramakrishna* came into existence. I was an apprentice for fifteen years. The hard discipline greatly helped me. It sharpened my memory and increased my skill in writing. I could recall the sequence of all of the incidents that had occurred during the day after I returned home at night. I would try to remember the first lines of the songs I had heard. This is the way the Master worked through me.

I was involved in worldly activities, bound to my work, and could not visit the Master whenever I wished. Therefore, I used to note down his words so that I could think over what he had said between my visits to him. In this way the impressions made on my mind might not be counteracted by the stress of worldly work and responsibilities. It was thus for my own benefit that I first took notes, so that I might realize his teachings more perfectly.

I used to memorize the Master's words, and then after returning home I would write brief notes in my diary. Sometimes I would spend the whole night in completing my record. Later I would fill in all the details from memory. Sometimes I would spend seven days completing the record of one day's happenings. Thus, *The Gospel of Sri Ramakrishna* appeared in book form from the notes of my diary. Sometimes I had to wait for a word of the Master's to come to my mind as a chataka bird waits for a drop of rainwater to fall. Sometimes I meditated on one scene over a thousand times. As a result, I could vividly visualize the Master's divine play, though it had happened long before. By the grace of the Master I used to feel that his play had just happened. Therefore, one can say that it was written in the Master's presence. At times I would not be satisfied with a particular description of an episode, so I would get absorbed in meditation on the Master. Then the correct picture would vividly appear in my mind. Therefore, from a human standpoint there was a great distance of time, but in my thought world I felt that it had happened just before I recorded it. My account is not culled from other sources. I recorded whatever I heard from the Master's lips with my own ears and whatever I saw of his life with my own eyes.

The Gospel of Sri Ramakrishna is the world's only firsthand record of the life and teachings of an avatar. One can collect materials about Sri Ramakrishna in three ways: First, direct observation recorded on the same day; second, direct observation but unrecorded during the lifetime of the Master; and third, hearsay, also unrecorded during the lifetime of the Master. *The Gospel of Sri Ramakrishna* belongs to the first category. I was present during each scene of the *Gospel*. A few entries and Aswini Datta's letter I added in the appendix and not in the main text.

I have published my diary very carefully. If there is any mistake in it, then its value will diminish. People do not realize that at one time I had to study the Law of Evidence. If a witness makes a single mistake, the entire case becomes nullified. Addressing the judge, the lawyer says, "My Lord, this witness is not reliable." I used to visit the court and observe all these details. The evidence of an eyewitness is very valuable. For that reason the judge asks, "Did you see this yourself?" If a person has seen and heard something himself, his words carry weight. I checked all the facts and details before I published *The Gospel of Sri Ramakrishna*.[20]

When somebody asked M. to remove some of the repetitions from the *Gospel*, he replied:

I cannot do that. The Master told the same parable to different people. If I remove a particular section, the train of the conversation will be broken. Moreover, you won't be able to see the effect of the *Gospel* on a particular person's life. The Master gave the same teaching to five different people in five different places. What he said to Bankim, he said to others also; and whatever conversation he had with Vivekananda, he had with others too.

You see, sometimes the brilliance of a diamond is enhanced by changing its setting. Putting it on the dusty ground produces one effect, and putting it on a green lawn produces another. But putting it in a casket lined with blue velvet produces the most brilliant effect of all. The same is true of the words in the *Gospel*. The rays of the sun look different when they fall on water, on the earth, and on glass, but the maximum brilliance is produced when the sun is reflected on glass. So I cannot avoid the repetitions in the *Gospel*, because removing them would disturb the Master's dialogue.

Once Hriday said to the Master: "Uncle, please reserve some of your best teachings. Otherwise, if you say everything all at once, and then repeat the same thing again and again, people will not come to you anymore." The Master replied: "You rascal! I shall repeat my words fifty times. What does it matter to you?"[21]

M. added the *Kathamrita* to the curriculum of his school. When M. was accused by some people of trying to sell his books to the students, he calmly replied:

> The students will understand the effect of reading the *Gospel* when they enter family life. The Master used to say, "The world is a burning fire." And I fully realized it. After the boys enter the world and are tormented by sorrows and sufferings, the Master's immortal words will save them, like a loving mother. If they remember at least one of the Master's teachings, that will be like a boat to ferry them across the turbulent ocean of maya and it will bring peace to their lives.[22]

In spite of illness, M. read the proofs of the last part of the *Kathamrita* at 1 o'clock in the morning by the light of a kerosene lantern. When lovingly chastised by Swami Nityatmananda, he said:

> People are finding peace by reading this book, the Master's immortal message. It is inevitable that the body will meet its end, so it is better that it be used for spreading peace to others. We are in the world and have fully experienced how much pain there is in it, yet I have forgotten that pain through *The Gospel of Sri Ramakrishna*. I am hurrying so that the book may come out soon.[23]

Ramakrishna's language in the *Kathamrita*

The teachings of Buddha and Christ spread quickly among the masses because they spoke in the language of the people. Buddha used Pali, while Christ taught in Aramaic. Language is the carrier of ideas, and those great teachers explained their ideas through tales and parables that were very effective. Even people who had no formal education could understand their message.

The tenth chapter of the *Lalita-vistara* describes Prince Siddhartha's education under Vishwamitra. Siddhartha (later Buddha) learned 64 lipis — that is, dialects or languages, such as Anga lipi, Banga lipi, Magadh lipi, Shakari lipi, Dravir lipi, Chin lipi, and Brahmavali lipi. He also studied the Vedas in Sanskrit.

Halley's Bible Handbook describes Christ's use of language: "Aramaic was the common language of the people. This was the language Jesus used. He was instructed in Hebrew, the language of the Old Testament

Scriptures. He must have known Greek, for it was the language of a large part of the population, and the universal language of the time. Jesus was familiar with both the Hebrew and Septuagint Old Testament. His own language is superb."[24] Before his crucifixion Jesus talked to Pilate, who was a Roman ruler, which indicates he might have known Latin.

Like Buddha and Christ, Ramakrishna taught in the language of the people. His mother tongue was Bengali, but he also knew some English words, including *friend, refine, like, honorary, science, society, under, tax, cheque,* and *thank you.* Although he had no formal education, he could read and write Bengali. Once he humorously said: "Narendra considers me to be illiterate, but I know the alphabet." He copied some scriptures by hand, and these copies are now in the Belur Math archives. Ramakrishna spoke Hindi with his guru Tota Puri and with monks from western India. He also studied Sanskrit "a little" at his brother's Sanskrit school in Calcutta. He once said: "If a pandit speaks to me in Sanskrit, I can follow him, but I cannot speak it myself."[25]

Before we discuss the charm of Ramakrishna's language and how M. recorded it almost verbatim in the *Kathamrita,* it is important to understand the difference between the colloquial mother tongue and literary language. Children learn their mother tongue spontaneously from their parents, friends, and relatives, but they learn literary language from teachers in school.

As a child, Ramakrishna learned his native mother tongue, which was Bengali, but he never learned the literary language or "language proper," from his school. Thus, when we read the *Kathamrita,* we enjoy the freshness and liveliness of Ramakrishna's colloquial village language. His language is simple and sweet; his words are clear and charming; his examples are apt and beautiful; his descriptions are poetic and graphic; his ideas are profound and meaningful; his style of conversation is original and captivating; his gestures and mimicry are joyful and entertaining. Ramakrishna used short and simple sentences to communicate his profound teachings, so his powerful statements remained in the minds of his listeners. Even the great savants of India sat spellbound, listening to this uneducated temple priest.

On 28 March 1875, *The Indian Mirror* wrote about Ramakrishna: "We met one (a sincere Hindu devotee) not long ago and were charmed by the depth, penetration, and simplicity of his spirit. The never-ceasing metaphors and analogies in which he indulged, are most of them as apt as they are beautiful."[26] On 19 August 1886, *The Indian Mirror* wrote again: "He [Ramakrishna] was an unlettered man, but his commonsense was strong and his power of observation keen. He had [a] facility for expressing his ideas in such homely language that he could make himself easily understood by all on intricate points of religion and morality. His childlike simplicity and outspokenness, his deep religious fervour and self-denial, his genial and sympathetic nature and his meek and unassuming manners won the hearts of those who came in contact with him, and music from his lips had a peculiar charm on those who heard him sing."[27]

Swami Vivekananda said: "My ideal of language is my Master's language, most colloquial and yet most expressive. It must express the thought which is intended to be conveyed."[28]

When flowers bloom, bees come of their own accord. On 23 February 1896 in New York, Vivekananda gave a lecture entitled "My Master" in which he said:

> People came by thousands to see and hear this wonderful man who spoke in a *patois*, every word of which was forceful and instinct with light. For it is not what is spoken, much less the language in which it is spoken, but the personality of the speaker, which dwells in everything he says that carries weight. Every one of us feels this at times. We hear most splendid orations, most wonderfully reasonedout discourses, and we go home and forget everything. At other times we hear a few words in the simplest of language, and they remain with us all the rest of our lives, become part and parcel of ourselves and produce lasting results. The words of a man who can put his personality into them take effect, but he must have tremendous personality. All teaching means giving and taking: the teacher gives and the taught receives, but the one must have something to give, and the other must be open to receive.[29]

It is true that Ramakrishna did not have much formal education, but his words had the force of scripture and he spoke only truth. Vivekananda later said: "The Vedas and other scriptures were so long hidden in the darkness of ignorance, and the light of Sri Ramakrishna has revealed them again."[30] While in America, Vivekananda reminisced to his disciples: "When I think of that man [Ramakrishna], I feel like a fool, because I want to read books and he never did. He never wanted to lick the plates after other people had eaten. That is why he was his own book."[31]

Observing the Master's encyclopedic knowledge of religion and philosophy, a disciple asked him how he came to have such deep and broad knowledge.

Ramakrishna answered: "I have not read; I have listened and learned. I have made a garland of their knowledge and put it round my neck, and I have offered it at the feet of the Mother."[32]

On 2 January 1884, Ramakrishna said to M.: "At Kamarpukur I have seen grain-dealers measuring paddy. As one heap is measured away another heap is pushed forward to be measured. The Mother supplies devotees with the 'heap' of Knowledge.... Weeping, I prayed to the Mother: 'O Mother, reveal to me what is contained in the Vedas and Vedanta. Reveal to me what is in the Purana and the Tantra.' One by one She has revealed all these to me."[33] Ramakrishna used to say that the Divine Mother spoke through his mouth.

M. was blessed with the opportunity to record Ramakrishna's divine language in the pages of the *Kathamrita*. He did not vitiate that wonderful language by paraphrasing it or rewriting the Master's words. Like a skilled craftsman, M. set those divine jewels of the Master's words in the pages of the *Kathamrita*. He re-created Ramakrishna's speech by reviewing his diary entries and notes, and meditating upon them. I had the opportunity to see some pages of M.'s diary — and from those I could understand that without divine grace, no one could have accurately recorded those divine dialogues with Ramakrishna.

M. emphatically said, "Every word of the Master is a mantra." By this he meant that reflecting upon those words connects individual souls with God. Here I present some of the Master's words as M. recorded them in the *Kathamrita*.

- *Manav jivaner uddeshya iswarlabh*: The goal of human life is to realize God.
- *Kamini kanchan maya*: Lust and gold are maya.
- *Satya-katha kalir tapasya*: Practising truthfulness is the austerity in this kaliyuga.
- *Bhagavata-bhakta-bhagavan — tine ek*: The scripture, the devotee, and God are all one.
- *Ami mole ghuchibe janjal*: All troubles will cease when the "I" dies.
- *Ami jantra tumi jantri*: I am the instrument and You are the operator.
- *Naham naham, tuhun tuhun*: Not I, not I, but Thou, Thou.
- *Yato mat tato path*: As many faiths, so many paths.
- *Advaita-jnan anchale bendhe ja ichha tai karo*: Tie nondual knowledge in the corner of your cloth and then do whatever you like.
- *Bhakta hobi to boka hobi kena*: Be a devotee, but don't be foolish.
- *Ishwar kalpataru*: God is the wish-fulfilling tree.
- *Brahma ar shakti abhed*: Brahman and His power are identical.
- *Vedanter sar — brahma satya jagat mithya*: The essence of Vedanta is: Brahman is real and the world is impermanent.

- *Gitar sar — tyagi tyagi*: The essence of the Gita is this: Renounce, renounce.
- *Bishay-asakta mon bhije deshlai*: The attached mind is like a box of wet matches.
- *Nirakaro satya avar sakaro satya*: God without form and with form — both are true.
- *Jeman bhav temni labh*: As is a man's feeling of love, so is his gain.
- *Dhyan korbe mone, bone, o kone*: Meditate in your mind, in the forest, or in the corner of your room.
- *Dub dao*: Dive deep.
- *Satchidanandai guru*: Satchidananda alone is the guru.
- *Ishwarke tushta karo, sakalai thushta hobe*: Please God, then everyone will be pleased.
- *Tini sab hoyechen tabe manushai tini beshi prakash*: God has become everything, but He is manifested to the utmost in human beings.
- *Ishwarer iti karata hina buddhi*: It is petty to limit God.
- *Mon mukh ek karai dharma*: True religion is the union of mind and speech.
- *Bhaver ghare churi koro na:* Let there be no theft [hypocrisy] in the chamber of your heart (i.e., shun hypocrisy).

Translating *Sri Ramakrishna Kathamrita*

M. wrote his first drafts of the *Kathamrita* in Bengali so that he could read them to Holy Mother. In 1888, he expanded four entries from his diary: (1) 15 June 1884, Surendra's Garden, Calcutta; (2) 25 June 1884, visit to a Hindu Pandit and Preacher (Shashadhar), Calcutta; (3) 5 August 1882, Visit to Pandit Ishwar Chandra Vidyasagar, Calcutta, (4) 3 August 1884, Dakshineswar Thakurbari. M. then translated these entries into English under the heading *Leaves from the Gospel of the Lord Sri Ramakrishna*, and they were published serially in the *Brahmavadin* magazine (which was started by Swami Vivekananda in 1895) on 15 October 1897, 16 November 1897, 1 February 1898, and 16 May 1898. He wrote these articles under his pen name: "According to M., a son of the Lord and servant." He also added a footnote below the title: "Translated by M. from original records kept in Bengali by M. These records are based on notes put down from memory by M. on the very day of the meeting, shortly after the meeting was over, and purport to be an attempt to give the *Lord's own words* as far as possible."[34] Later these four entries were published in two pamphlets in English.

Enthusiastic readers were not satisfied with these pamphlets and demanded that the entire *Gospel* be published in book form. M. worked diligently to develop his diary entries, writing first in Bengali and then translating them into English. In 1907, M. took the four chapters from the Brahmavadin, added ten more chapters, and produced a book entitled *"The Gospel of Sri Ramakrishna* (According to M., a son of the Lord and disciple)." M. added a subtitle: "or The Ideal Man for India and for the World." This publication, part one of the *Gospel*, was published by the Brahmavadin Office, Madras. It consists of 386 pages. In the first edition of the *Gospel*, M. wrote: "It is no sentence by sentence translation but M.'s own rendering of his thoughts rather than language, directly into English with many elaborations and elucidating repetitions."[35] In 1912, Swami Trigunatitananda of the Vedanta Society of San Francisco published this first edition of the *Gospel*.

The English of the first edition was archaic, a kind of evangelical language: Thou thinkest, thou comest, thou askest, thou art, and so on. When M. made revisions for the second edition, he freed it of its biblical turns of expression. In its second edition, the word 'Mahendra' and the entire subtitle was deleted. This edition was published in 1911 by Ramakrishna Math, Madras. The Madras Math published several more editions, and this work was in circulation until 1942, when the complete translation of *The Gospel of Sri Ramakrishna* (which contained all five volumes of the original *Kathamrita*) by Swami Nikhilananda came out. In 1978, the Madras Math reprinted M.'s version under the title *The Condensed Gospel of Sri Ramakrishna*.

In 1907, Swami Abhedananda of the Vedanta Society of New York published another version, the *Gospel of Ramakrishna*. In the preface, Swami Abhedananda wrote:

> This is the authorized English edition of the *Gospel of Ramakrishna*. For the first time in the history of the world's Great Saviours, the exact words of the Master were recorded verbatim by one of his devoted disciples. These words were originally spoken in the Bengali language of India. They were taken down in the form of diary notes by a householder disciple, M.
>
> M. wrote to me letters authorizing me to edit and publish the English translation of his notes, and sent me the manuscript in English which he himself translated. At the request of M., I have edited and remodeled the larger portion of his English manuscript, while the remaining portions I have translated directly from the Bengali edition of his notes.[36]

Although Swami Abhedananda's edited version of the *Gospel* received many favourable reviews from the U.S. papers and was translated into

Spanish, Portuguese, Danish, Scandinavian, and Czech, it lacks the flavour and style of M.'s original. M. later remarked that Swami Abhedananda had added his own reminiscences to the book.[37] In 1939, Ramakrishna Vedanta Math republished this book as *The Memoirs of Ramakrishna*. In 1947, the Vedanta Society of New York reprinted this book with a foreword by Christopher Isherwood.

In 1922, Ramakrishna Math, Madras, published an English translation of Volume II of *Sri Sri Ramakrishna Kathamrita*, without consulting M., who was still alive. The material of this volume first came out serially in *Vedanta Kesari*. M. disapproved of this and asked Swami Shivananda, the president of the Ramakrishna Order, to stop the publication. The *Vedanta Kesari* discontinued the series, but the Madras Math published this material as Volume II of the *Gospel*. This volume was edited by a Westerner, and the second edition was published in 1928. Then it was withdrawn as it did not meet M.'s approval.

Regarding the translation of Volume II, M. commented:

Even a student of eighth grade translates from Bengali into English. Translation is not an easy thing. One should transmit the idea and mood. A literal translation is not enough. Western people do not understand the Bengali language.... While talking, the Master would express an idea with a living feeling. In my translation I have tried my best to convey the same spirit by preserving his words as far as possible. The primary importance is the sense or meaning; words or the language are only secondary. Moreover, I have tried to express it in a simple language. In translation, the meaning changes if one overlooks the viewpoint of the Master's saying.[38]

M. was very particular about his record of the Master's words. It was extremely painful for him if his work was translated in a distorted form. Swami Avyaktananda began to publish the translation of other volumes of *Kathamrita* in *Morning Star*, a magazine in Patna.

On 17 May 1930, M. wrote to him:

Dear Avyakta Babaji, My love and salutations to you all. The translation of the *Gospel* in the Morning Star, is, I regret to say, not satisfactory to me. Being an eyewitness, I naturally want the spirit to be kept up in the translation. Moreover, the report of a meeting should not appear in a mutilated form. The translation should be done by myself. You may do the work after my passing, which is by no means a distant contingency. I am 76 and my health is not at all good. It is painful to see the *Gospel* presented in this way. I do not approve of the translation which has appeared as Vol. II from Madras. — M.[39]

In 1942, Swami Nikhilananda of the Ramakrishna-Vivekananda Center, New York, translated all five volumes of M.'s *Kathamrita* into English and published the work in one chronologically arranged volume. He did not translate the entire *Kathamrita*. As he writes in the preface: "I have made a literal translation, omitting only a few pages of no particular interest to English-speaking readers." He wrote a long biographical introduction on Ramakrishna, replacing the sketch that M. had written. On the whole, Swami Nikhilananda's translation is superb and elegant. The swami's manuscript was edited by Margaret Woodrow Wilson (a daughter of President Woodrow Wilson) and Joseph Campbell (a famous scholar and orientalist). John Moffitt, Jr. (a poet and scholar) used his poetical talent on the mystical and spiritual songs of *The Gospel of Sri Ramakrishna*, which enhanced their beauty. Aldous Huxley wrote the foreword to this work. This translation drew the attention of the literary world of the East and the West. Dr. S. Radhakrishnan wrote: "Swami Nikhilananda has done an excellent piece of work. His very readable English translation of the *Ramakrishna-Kathamrita* will enable Western readers to understand the deep spiritual life of Sri Ramakrishna and the homely way in which profound truths are conveyed to ordinary mortals, and I hope that the book will have wide publicity."[40]

M.'s Bengali *Kathamrita* has been translated into the following Indian languages: Sanskrit, Hindi, Marathi, Gujarati, Telugu, Tamil, Malayalam, Kannada, and some selected portions in Sindhi, and probably in Gurumukhi and Khasi. Swami Nikhilananda's translation of *The Gospel of Sri Ramakrishna* has been translated into German, Italian, Spanish, Dutch, Swedish, Portuguese, Chinese (Mandarin), Bulgarian, Polish, Serbo-Croatian (Yugoslavia), Greek, and Hebrew. There may be more translations in Japanese, and French.

M.'s diary: lost and found

Now and then M. would visit Gadadhar Ashrama (a branch of the Ramakrishna Order) in South Calcutta as he loved to stay with the monks in the monastery. Wherever he went, he carried his diary, which reminded him of the Master. Sometimes he would open it to an entry, meditate on a particular scene, and then talk about it to the monks and devotees. On 16 January 1924, M. was returning by tram from Gadadhar Ashrama to his home in Central Calcutta. Absorbed in thoughts of the Master, he accidentally left his diary next to his seat while changing trams at the Esplanade Station. The diary was found two days later.

On 18 January, M. described his agony to the devotees:

What terrible distress I have gone through! It was worse than losing a son. I felt I should not live anymore; otherwise why had the Master taken away his words from me? When I got back my diary, I realized that this body would remain a few days more. Last Tuesday while returning from Gadadhar Ashrama, I left my diary in the tramcar. It struck me when I returned home. It was then 11:00 a.m. Immediately I rushed to the Kali temple of Thanthania. I had visited the Divine Mother after getting down from the tram. I thought that I had left the diary there. Some pandits were reading the holy scriptures in front of the temple. I asked them but no one gave me a positive answer. Then I tried to locate my tram ticket, which I had torn and discarded on the sidewalk. It took me 45 minutes to collect those pieces of the ticket and then bring them home. I pasted them on a piece of paper with flour gum and discovered the number of the ticket.

Immediately I went to the Gadadhar Ashrama. In the afternoon, the devotees took the ticket and went to the Kalighat tram depot. They discovered the name of the conductor who was on that tram. On Wednesday morning news came that the diary had been found. The conductor had deposited it with the overseer of the tram depot. This overseer was a devotee. He saw the name 'Jayrambati' on the cover of the diary, so he carefully saved it.

In the evening, I fervently prayed to the Master. My fear did not go away even after I learned that the diary had been found. I was worried that it might be lost again before picking it up. Oh, how much fear and anxiety I went through for that diary! How sincerely I prayed to the Master for that! What joy I felt when it came to my hand!

Again, another thought arose in my mind: It is not a big deal. I left the diary in the tramcar and the conductor deposited it in the office. That is the normal procedure. After receiving the diary, I felt that it had not been necessary to say so many prayers. Such are the vagaries of our minds! It behaved in quite another way once the diary was retrieved. You see, many things could have happened: There could have been a tram accident, or someone could have been run over, or the conductor might not have taken proper care of it.

A Devotee: "It also might have fallen into the hands of the sweeper of the car."

M.: "Yes, that could have been, or someone could have taken it and thrown it away on the street. But as soon as I got the diary back, I forgot all those possibilities. What irony! And we live with this mind, which plays tricks on us all the time. So we should always pray: May we not deviate from our goal. May we not forget God when something has been accomplished."

M. presented a copy of the *Kathamrita* to the overseer as a token of his gratefulness.[41]

An interview with M. at Morton School on 20 March 1924

Swami Madhavananda, the president of Advaita Ashrama in Mayavati, was working on a biography of Ramakrishna. He found some discrepancies between the *Kathamrita* by M. and the *Lilaprasanga* by Swami Saradananda, so he went to M. to verify those facts. Furthermore, he wanted to ask M. how he had recorded the *Kathamrita* and gathered some other information about the Master.

Swami Madhavananda (*to M.*): "How many times did Sri Ramakrishna go on pilgrimage? You have mentioned two times."

M.: "Yes, twice. First, the Master went with Mathur; then he went with Mathur's sons. At that time, one could go to Varanasi by train. I corresponded with the Railway Company with reference and compared its record of the dates and of who went with him, and they were the same. Moreover, there is some circumstantial evidence. I visited Janbazar and Barrackpore and collected information from the descendants of Rani Rasmani."

Swami Madhavananda: "Did you write in your diary immediately after listening to the Master?"

M.: "No, I didn't write on the spot. After I returned home I wrote from memory. Sometimes I spent the whole night completing an entry. My record [*The Gospel of Sri Ramakrishna*] is not a collection from other sources. I wrote down whatever I heard with my own ears from the lips of the Master and whatever I saw of his life with my own eyes. I didn't collect materials like historians or write like the antiquarians."

Swami Madhavananda: "It is amazing that within such a short period there are so many different versions of the Master's life and teachings!"

M.: "This is nothing to wonder at. It happens that way. Look at the Bible: there is little similarity among the four gospels recorded by Matthew, Mark, Luke, and John. The same thing will happen in the case of the Master. Sometimes I spent seven days recording from memory the events of one day — arranging chronologically the songs, stories, samadhi, and so on."

Swami Madhavananda: "To whom did the Master offer the articles during the night of Kali Puja at Shyampukur house?"

M.: "He offered them to himself."

Swami Madhavananda: "Did he offer them to himself or to Mother Kali?"

M.: "In fact, he offered them to himself. As soon as all of the devotees had offered flowers to the Master, his hands assumed the gestures symbolizing fearlessness and the bestowal of boons [that are seen in images of Kali]. Thus — (saying so, M. demonstrated those two gestures with his own hands). Then everyone realized who the Master was."

Swami Madhavananda: "What do you know about the name 'Ramakrishna'?"

M.: "I didn't hear anything from the Master about his name. Probably 'Ramakrishna' was the name given by his family, because the prefix of his brothers' names was 'Rama' (such as Ramkumar and Rameswar). They were all devotees of Ramachandra, and Raghuvir was their household deity. The village people called him 'Gadai.' We did not know that he was called Gadadhar. We learned it later. Tota Puri didn't give him the name 'Ramakrishna,' because long before Tota Puri arrived the name 'Ramakrishna Bhattacharya' was registered in Rani Rasmani's documents."*

Swami Madhavananda: "A knower of Brahman came to Dakshineswar who shared food with the dogs. Who followed that knower of Brahman? Was it Hriday or Haladhari?"

M.: "Haladhari."**

Swami Madhavananda: "Who returned with bel leaves instead of visiting his daughter's house? You have written 'Haladhari's father,' and Swami Saradananda has written 'the Master's father.'"

M.: "I know that way [that is, the version I have written]."

Swami Madhavananda: "Akshay Sen [the author of *Sri Ramakrishna Punthi*] has written about a pandit who sat on the Master's bed with his shoes on. What is your opinion about that?"

M.: "No, that is not correct. I was present. The pandit sat on the floor. As soon as the Master touched his chest with his feet, the pandit exclaimed, 'O guru, please awaken my consciousness.' That man had a very devotional temperament."

Swami Madhavananda: "How many years did the Master go through a spiritual tempest?"

M.: "Seven years. The Master said that his family members then took him back to Kamarpukur for his wedding."

Swami Madhavananda: "Whom did the Master send to Bankim Chattopadhyay?"

M.: "The Master sent Girish Babu and myself to Bankim, saying, 'Please go to Bankim and invite him to come here.' Bankim also invited the Master to visit him, but he could not go."

Swami Madhavananda: "Did Krishnadas Pal [a national leader and the editor of *Hindu Patriot*] visit the Master?"

M.: "Yes, he did. The Master said about him, 'Krishnadas observed the Hindu custom. He entered my room after leaving his shoes outside. I asked him: "What is the goal of human life?" He replied, "It is to do good to the world." I told him: "You see this world? Have you seen

*Vide Deed of Endowment by Rani Rasmani 1861, 18 February. Tota Puri came to Dakshineswar in 1864.
** It was Hriday, according to the *Lilaprasanga* by Swami Saradananda.

innumerable crab eggs floating in the Ganges during the rainy season? As many eggs so many worlds. They are numberless. Who are you to do good to the world? You better try to help yourself. God dwells in every being. Be blessed by serving Him in all beings. The owner of the world will look after his own affairs. You look to your own path."'"

Swami Madhavananda: "When did the Master meet Keshab Sen?"

M.: "In 1875."*

Swami Madhavananda: "Will you publish the fifth part of *Sri Sri Ramakrishna Kathamrita*? It would be nice if you would publish the Master and Bankim's meeting in it."

M.: "I want to do that. The *Basumati* publishing house sent a person to me. They are eager to publish it."

Senior Jiten: "Swami Madhavananda and others are writing a biography of the Master."

M.: "Who else will write it? They have practised so much austerity and lived with the disciples of the Master. Moreover, they live in the Himalayas [Advaita Ashrama, Mayavati]."

M. continued: "Mayavati Ashrama is doing a marvellous job. It has published many important books. The monks are doing *nishkam* karma (unselfish action) without any personal motive."

Swami Madhavananda left after having some refreshments.[42]

Characteristics of *The Gospel of Sri Ramakrishna*

M. had a photographic memory, artistic talent, and, above all, a poetic imagination. Though one can challenge the historicity of Christ, Buddha, or Krishna, one cannot challenge the existence of Ramakrishna. M. meticulously documented his conversations with the Master, carefully noting the dates and times, the places, and the people who were present, and even any songs that were sung.

Did Ramakrishna say anything new? Not really. He reinterpreted the same ancient Truth. He said, "The money which is used at the time of a Nawab [a Muslim king] becomes outdated with the rule of a Badshah [Muslim emperor]." The coins change according to the rule of different dynasties. Similarly, the ancient avatars brought the message that was needed for their particular age and the conditions in which they lived. Now a new avatar has preached according to the need of our age. One hundred years ago people did not know much about modern medicine. They treated their diseases with herbs and natural medicines. Now we use antibiotics. Herbs and antibiotics are both medicines, but their usage

---

*Sri Ramakrishna first met Keshab Sen in 1864 at the Adi Brahmo Samaj, but became closely acquainted with him only in 1875 at Jaygopal Sen's garden house in Belgharia.

changes with the times. Krishna said in the Gita, "Arjuna, I am speaking to you the same Truth again."[43] Tautology is a weakness in logic, but it is not a weak point in scripture. The scriptures never tire of declaring the same truth again and again in different languages in different ages.

In the *Gospel* we find that M. not only preserved the teachings of Ramakrishna, but also described the settings in order to make a deeper impression on the reader's mind. Here is an example of a description from the *Gospel*, dated 22 July 1883: "Sri Ramakrishna had enjoyed a little rest after his midday meal. The room had an atmosphere of purity and holiness. On the walls hung pictures of gods and goddesses, among them being one of Christ rescuing the drowning Peter. Outside the room were plants laden with fragrant flowers, and the Ganges could be seen flowing towards the south. It was the rainy season; the exuberant Ganges was hurrying to meet the ocean and was happy to touch and to see the holy ground where the great saint of Dakshineswar resided."[44]

Here, M. was comparing the spiritual seekers who were coming to meet Ramakrishna to rivers merging in the infinite ocean of Satchidananda.

Swami Ritajananda once wrote:

The Gospel of Sri Ramakrishna begins like a novel with a little bit of description of the surroundings in picturesque language, so that the reader can visualize everything around the Master: the large property of the Dakshineswar temple with its gardens, tanks, temples, etc. If anyone desires to make a film, he will find all the directions necessary in the masterly descriptions one reads in the *Gospel*. The place and times, the people present, the positions they took in the room where they met, the songs, and finally every movement of Sri Ramakrishna — these are all presented so vividly that it becomes a special attraction. We have no such presentation of anyone else's life.

In the *Gospel*, we find plenty of information about Sri Ramakrishna and how he lived in the world. With him there was plenty of laughter, and it was really fortunate for so many to be near him and feel that the world is really a mansion of mirth in spite of their many painful experiences. Sri Ramakrishna also talked of suffering, the suffering of others and even his own. His health was not perfect and he eventually got cancer of the throat, which entailed extreme physical pain. Many who were dear to him left this world, and those who lived with him were not always kind and respectful. Yet he was above all these things. The Divine Mother was constantly near Her beloved son, answering his questions. M. ignored nothing that took place in the small room of Sri Ramakrishna. He tells us how Ramakrishna ate, how he spoke, how he imitated people and amused the youngsters. Never trying to idolize

Sri Ramakrishna, never judging his actions or his words, M. presents a picture of his Master in the most natural way possible. This makes us understand that a highly evolved spiritual person can also be a human being.[45]

The Gospel of Sri Ramakrishna is an authentic record of Ramakrishna's life and teachings. M. testified that whatever he saw and heard from the Master on that particular day, he recorded on the same day or night in his diary, including year, month, date, day and *tithi* (lunar day).

Ramakrishna's teachings are profound and yet very simple and appealing. Moreover, his language and the expressions he used are fascinating. Many people learn Bengali so that they can read this wonderful piece of literature in its original form and get a taste of how Ramakrishna actually spoke.

When we read the *Gospel*, its vivid descriptions help us visualize Ramakrishna as he moved through his environment. We see the places he saw and the people he came in contact with. This vivid and artistic depiction of an avatar's life is unique. As we read the *Gospel*, we enjoy the holy company of the Master. In the *Gospel*, festivities are always going on with Ramakrishna at their centre. We enjoy the theatre, music, singing, dancing, humour, worship, meditation, and samadhi. Reading the *Gospel* drives away loneliness and boredom. The *Gospel* presents to us the divine drama of Ramakrishna with various characters representing all types of people: intellectuals, devotees, hypocrites, drunkards, householders, monks, actors, actresses, musicians, and so on. We visualize and enjoy the Master's superb acting with Keshab, Vijay, Ram, Narendra, Balaram, M. and others in different places, such as Dakshineswar, the Brahmo Temple, Balaram's house, Shyampukur, and Cossipore.

Swami Bhajanananda once wrote: "Every great religion has its own scripture. There are several scriptures already existing in the world, including the Vedas, Zend-Avesta, Tripitaka, the Bible, and the Koran. Do we need one more? Yes, precisely because there are several scriptures: We need just one more to show the validity of every one of them and to establish their overall harmony. *The Gospel of Sri Ramakrishna* compiled by M. serves this purpose admirably well."[46]

M.'s chronicle of Ramakrishna's life is fascinating, in part because he himself played a vital role. Sometimes he was a silent witness to the divine drama of Ramakrishna; at other times, he was an active participant in the play. In addition, M.'s love for the Master was extraordinary. His I-consciousness was saturated with Ramakrishna-consciousness. If this were not so, he never could have produced *The Gospel of Sri Ramakrishna*, which is unique among the world's religious literature. Faithfully and vividly, M. chronicled the Master's samadhi and meditation, his prayer and worship, his dreams and visions, actions and devotion, purity and renunciation, singing and dancing, humour and mimicry, sadhana and pilgrimage, behaviour and psychology, religion and philosophy, and his social and scientific outlook. But most important, M. preserved Ramakrishna's conversations with God, as well as his discussions with the people who came to him, his love and empathy for others, and his fervent concern for his devotees.

M. writes in the *Gospel*: "The Master was weeping and praying to the Mother. In a voice choked with emotion, he prayed to Her with tearful eyes for the welfare of the devotees: 'Mother, may those who come to You have all their desires fulfilled. But please don't make them give up everything at once, Mother. Well, You may do whatever You like in the end. If You keep them in the world, Mother, then please reveal Yourself to them now and then. Otherwise, how will they live? How will they be encouraged if they don't see You once in a while?' "[47]

Christopher Wood wrote about *The Gospel of Sri Ramakrishna*: "It is a fascinating piece of biography, quite extraordinarily honest. And as for its being long, the truth about anyone is never dull. Try it. I don't think you will be disappointed."[48]

Hundreds of people came to Ramakrishna with their questions and problems. Some came out of curiosity. Scholars came, and so did scientists, doctors, lawyers, teachers, professors, and students. Spiritual leaders and social reformers visited him, as did actors, actresses, dramatists, singers, and dancers. Hypocrites, drunkards, ruffians, and villains also came. *The Gospel of Sri Ramakrishna* is the firsthand account of the conversations that these various characters had with Ramakrishna. Each person can find his or her own personality reflected in a character in the *Gospel*.

Sitting on his wooden cot in the temple garden of Dakshineswar, Ramakrishna offered solutions to the problems of those who came to him because his own life was free from problems. Only a person whose life is trouble-free can solve another's problems. Ramakrishna also boosted the spirits of his visitors. As he himself said: "One man makes a fire and others enjoy the heat. I have cooked food for you; you need only come and eat it."

On another occasion he said: "I am the destroyer of karma. I am the French colony."[49] At that time India was divided among three colonial powers: British, French, and Portuguese. If one did something wrong in British India, that person could take shelter in the French colony where the British had no jurisdiction. "I am the French colony" means that whatever sins one may be guilty of, one need only take shelter in Ramakrishna to be free from fear of punishment for them. No worldly rules can bind such a person. Only a saviour has the power to protect people from the consequences of their actions.

The subject of *The Gospel of Sri Ramakrishna* is God and God *alone*. It is concerned with how to realize Him and nothing else. Ramakrishna frequently made this simple statement: "I know only God and nothing else." In the beginning, in the middle, and in the end of the *Gospel*, you will find only one thing: God.

Ordinary people *preach* religion, but Divine Incarnations like Buddha, Christ, Krishna, and Ramakrishna can *give* religion. Religion means realization. A touch, a glance, or a word from one of the Incarnations can spark a life-altering transformation in a human being. Ramakrishna was a tremendous spiritual force that could awaken God-consciousness in an instant. He was a spiritual phenomenon! In the *Gospel,* we find him in samadhi one moment, while the next he is making fun and cutting jokes. He was that prince who could travel through all seven stories of the royal palace (the seven levels of consciousness) without any restriction. Ordinary people live on the first floor and do not know what is on the other six floors. Even Ramakrishna's jokes and frivolities were connected with God.

Some people consider religious talk to be dry, dull, difficult, disgusting, and distasteful. That is the reason that during classes, some doze or yawn, and some leave to go out and chat with their friends. Ramakrishna's conversations in the *Gospel* are so captivating, uplifting, and inspiring that everyone in the audience remained spellbound. It is amazing how he presented the highest truths through simple stories, folklore, parables, and even humour. On 19 September 1884, the Master told a Vaishnava devotee about various tendencies of human beings. During a religious festival, each sect — Vaishnavas, Shaktas, Kartabhajas — has its own booth. The followers of each sect assemble their respective booth and gaze at images of Radha-Krishna, Shiva-Durga, Sita-Rama. "But," Ramakrishna said, "it is quite different with those who are not spiritually minded at all. In the *Baroari* (public festival) one sees another image also — a prostitute beating her paramour with a broomstick. Those people stand there with gaping mouths and cry to their friends: 'What are you looking at over there? Come here! Look at this.'"[50] All laughed. He further said: "I don't give the youngsters a pure vegetarian dish: now and then I give them a little water smelling of fish. Otherwise, why should they come?"[51]

Christopher Isherwood wrote: "Another side of Ramakrishna which seems to me important is that he had a sense of fun and that he was joyous. It is a tragic mistake that the popular idea of a good person is so often that of someone rather dull and somber, someone who rarely laughs. Whereas in actual fact it seems that the joy, the sheer pleasure even, of approaching God surpasses anything we know."[52] In the *Gospel*, M. notes in many places: "All laugh," or "Laughter."

Traditional Vaishnavas observe the annual festival of the Bhagavata scripture. A devotee suggested to M. that he observe the birth-anniversary of the *Kathamrita*. M. said: "The Master's words are the Vedas. He himself said that 'the Bhakta (devotee), Bhagavata (scripture), and Bhagavan (God) are one.' The Bhagavata is nothing but the words of God. The *Kathamrita* consists of His words, so it is Bhagavata. It reminds me of an episode. One day the Master was seated on his small cot and told me, "Look, God speaks through my mouth."

A devotee said to M.: "Reading the *Kathamrita* it seems that you were with the Master all the time." M. replied: "No, I did not live with him all the time. But he used to say, 'One becomes immortal, whether one drinks one drop or one pitcher of the nectar from the ocean of Immortality.' That is my only hope. I tried to preserve a very small portion of the Master's words in the *Kathamrita*. No one can write his entire words."[53]

The invocation of *The Gospel of Sri Ramakrishna*

According to Indian tradition, the author of a scripture is supposed to introduce the text with an invocation consisting of an auspicious verse or a salutation mantra. Following that custom, M. placed the following verse on the title page of each of the five volumes of his original Bengali *Kathamrita*.

Tava kathāmritam tapta jivanam kavibhir-iditam kalmasāpaham;
Shravana-mangalam shrimad-ātatam bhuvi grnanti ye bhuridā janāh.
— Bhagavata 10:31:9
"O Lord, your nectar-like words relieve the burning misery of afflicted souls. Your words, which poets have sung in verses, destroy the sins of worldly people forever. Blessed are they who hear of your vast glory. Blessed indeed are those who speak of you. How unparalleled is their bounty!"

The above-quoted invocation is taken from the *Gopi-Gita* of the Bhagavata. Krishna promised to meet the gopis, the milkmaids of Vrindaban, on a full-moon night in autumn. That night, the gopis came to meet Krishna on the bank of the Yamuna River, and he played affectionately with them. But he sensed that they had become proud and egotistic due to this rare privilege, so he suddenly disappeared from them. Grief-stricken, the gopis wept and prayed to him to return. The above verse is from that prayer.

Tava kathāmritam: "Your words, O Lord, are like nectar." We sometimes say, "Oh, your words are so sweet!" But having no nectar ourselves, we do not know how to speak nectar-like words. The Divine Incarnations have this nectar within and so their words are full of sweetness.

Amrita means "nectar" and also "immortality." According to Hindu mythology, the gods and the demons churned the ocean in order to obtain the nectar of immortality. After a hard struggle, they extracted a jar of it. But the gods deceived the demons and drank it all, becoming immortal. This immortality, however, was relative: Absolute immortality comes only from the knowledge of Brahman. That nectar is within all beings. Jesus said, "The Kingdom of Heaven is within you." Dive deep inside. There you will find that nectar and attain immortality.

God is the ocean of *amrita*, nectar. Once Ramakrishna asked Swami Vivekananda: "Suppose there were a cup of syrup and you were a fly. Where would you sit to drink the syrup?"

Vivekananda replied: "I would sit on the edge of the cup and stretch out my neck to drink it."

"Why?" Ramakrishna asked. "What's the harm in plunging into the middle of the cup and drinking the syrup?"

Vivekananda answered: "Then I should stick in the syrup and die."

"My child," Ramakrishna said to him, "that isn't the nature of the Nectar of Satchidananda. It is the Nectar of Immortality. Man does not die from diving into it. On the contrary, he becomes immortal."[54]

We say that human beings are mortal, but this is not true. The body is mortal. The Atman, our real nature, is immortal. It is this immortality that human beings are always searching for. The Brihadaranyaka Upanishad says that when Yajnavalkya offered wealth to his beloved wife, Maitreyi, she replied: "*Yenāham nāmritasyām, kimaham tena kuryām* — What should I do with that wealth which would not make me immortal?"[55] This is the bold message of Vedanta to modern people. If you want immortality, give up whatever you have. Christ also said the same thing: "Sell what you have and then follow me. Ye cannot serve God and mammon."

The Bengali title of *The Gospel of Sri Ramakrishna* is *Sri Sri Ramakrishna Kathamrita*, which means "Sri Ramakrishna's immortal (or nectar-like) words." We hear the *Gospel*; we read the *Gospel*; we speak about the *Gospel*; but we do not "drink" the *Gospel*. It does not matter if we drink a drop, a glass, a jar, or a barrel of amrita. Any amount will make us immortal. It is not a matter of quantity, but of the substance itself. If we could actually absorb the *Gospel*, all our worldly desires would quickly dissipate. But it is not easy. We like to hold on to our desires: that is our problem.

Ramakrishna told this beautiful parable:

> Once a fishwife was a guest in the house of a gardener who raised flowers. She came there with her empty fish-basket after selling fish in the market, and was given a place to sleep in a room where flowers were kept. But because of the fragrance of the flowers, she couldn't get to sleep for a long time. Her hostess saw her condition and said: "Hello! Why are you tossing from side to side so restlessly?" The fishwife said: "I don't know, friend. Perhaps the smell of the flowers is disturbing my sleep. Can you give me my fish-basket? Perhaps that will put me to sleep." The basket was brought to her. She sprinkled water on it and set it near her nose. Then she fell sound asleep and snored all night.[56]

Worldly people like the smell of fish. They cannot stand a beautiful divine fragrance. Mere speaking, mere talking, mere hearing won't help us. We may repeat the word "wine" a thousand times but that will not make us intoxicated. We must drink the wine. Christ said, "Whosoever heareth these sayings of mine and doeth them, I will liken him unto a wise man, who built his house upon a rock."

Tapta jivanam: "Your words relieve the burning misery of worldly life." The world is burning with misery. When we talk about life we heave a deep sigh. I remember that once when I was a young student of Vedanta I heard a vivid description of this world. Our teacher was expounding the concept of maya. He said: "Do you know what this world is? A traveller was passing through a desert. The sun was scorching hot. He was dead tired, thirsty, hungry, and exhausted. He was trying to find shelter, a shady place where he could take a little rest. At last he found a place where he laid down his head and slept, not knowing that the spot was made shady by the shadow of a poisonous cobra's hood! A single hiss and one drop of poison from that cobra would finish his life. So that is this world." We do not know how the mysterious maya traps, binds, and enslaves us.

Human beings are tormented by desire, doubt, disease, death, passion, jealousy, hatred, anger, and so many other things. This is truly Hell. The word of the Lord alone rescues us from this awful situation. The gospel of the Lord carries solace and succour for suffering humanity. It soothes our nerves and brings us peace and joy. Just as water extinguishes fire, the words of the Lord extinguish the burning misery caused by worldly desires and our enjoyment of them.

Krishna said in the Gita: "Having come into this transitory, joyless world, worship me." Jesus said: "Come to me, all who labour and are heavy laden, and I will give you rest." Similarly, we see how Ramakrishna showered peace and bliss to suffering humanity by his stories and immortal words. In fact, the words of *Kathamrita* act like mantras for forgetting the world.

Kavibhir-iditam: "Poets eulogize the words of the Lord in many ways." A renaissance begins with the advent of each avatar. Many books and dramas are written, songs and music are composed, and artwork and sculptures are created. Ramakrishna spoke but a few words, and Swami Vivekananda expounded that message of the harmony of religions and the divinity of human beings, spreading it throughout the world. M. recorded the Master's immortal gospel, while the actor-dramatist Girish Chandra Ghosh wrote several dramas that incorporated the ideas of Ramakrishna. Again, many poets composed songs based on the teachings of the Master. But Ramakrishna himself had no formal education. His knowledge came straight from God. One day he said: "If you want to understand in one sentence, come to me. If you want to understand the same thing in a thousand words, go to Keshab."[57] Keshab Chandra Sen, the Brahmo Samaj leader, was a famous orator. It was he who first wrote about Ramakrishna, in his Brahmo newspapers and magazines. When the Master came to know about it, he said, "Keshab, by writing about me, you want to make me famous? Don't try. He whom Mother makes famous, becomes famous."

Kalmasāpaham: The words of God "destroy all kinds of sins and their results." God's name purifies our bodies and minds. Try to visualize the world as a room freshly painted with black paint. You are there, dressed in white clothes. You may be extremely cautious, but you cannot be alert all the time. In one moment of forgetfulness, you may spoil your clothes. So it happens in this world: Desire, doubt, pride, anger, jealousy, greed, and lust are continually polluting our minds. Human beings stumble and fall, overcome by temptations. But they should not yield helplessly; they must fight. The Atman manifests in a human being through three powers: *jnana-shakti* — wisdom, *ichha-shakti* — will, and *kriya-shakti* — action. Life is a struggle. Only two groups of people do not have to struggle: the illumined and the dead. *The Gospel of Sri Ramakrishna* helps us develop a strong discriminative faculty and protects us from weakness and temptation.

Ramakrishna did not care for the Christian doctrine of sin. He said: "He who says day and night, 'I am a sinner, I am a sinner' verily becomes a sinner....All the sins of the body fly away if one chants the name of

God and sings His glories. The birds of sin dwell in the tree of the body. Singing the name of God is like clapping your hands. As, at a clap of the hands, the birds in the tree fly away, so do our sins disappear at the chanting of God's name and glories."[58] What a gospel of hope!

Shravana-mangalam: Anybody who "hears the words of God will undoubtedly be benefited". If one eats a hot chili, knowingly or unknowingly, one's tongue will burn. It can't be helped. Similarly, these words of the Lord definitely do people good. One may think that just hearing the *Gospel* will not give one the flavour of it, but it will.

Shrimad: Beautiful. The words of the Lord are beautiful; they are truly enchanting and delightful. *The Gospel of Sri Ramakrishna* draws us irresistibly to God.

Ātatam: "Vast and easily available." Just as we do not need to search for space and air because they surround us, so the words of God are easily accessible. Those who are spiritual aspirants feel divine inebriation from the *Gospel*, but it comes gradually and slowly, as the *Gospel* reveals its truths according to the aspirant's spiritual development and understanding. The *Gospel* has an intoxicating effect. We may read it a thousand times, yet it remains an endless source of inspiration. Truth never becomes old — it is always fresh. There is no end to spiritual experience, and *The Gospel of Sri Ramakrishna* is a unique chronicle of the highest immeasurable realizations. Once a disciple of Holy Mother said that he had read the *Kathamrita* 50 times and still he was finding new light in it. The message of God is endless. An American student read the *Gospel* and remarked: "There is one defect in this book: it has an end."

Bhuvi grnanti ye bhuridā janāh: You may "perform charity in various forms, but the best charity is to distribute the word of God to humanity." This final Sanskrit phrase has another meaning: Those who are spiritual seekers, those who have done spiritual practices in previous lives and also in this very life, get bliss, which is the flavour of spirituality.

Despite the cancer in his throat, Ramakrishna taught whoever came to him. He never turned anyone away. He said: "Let me be condemned to be born over and over again, even in the form of a dog, if by doing so I can be of help to a single soul. I will give up twenty thousand such bodies to help one man."[59]

Ramakrishna's teachings in the *Gospel*

The qualifications for studying Vedanta are extremely difficult to meet. A Vedanta student should practise discrimination, renunciation, and control of the senses; and he or she should have a burning desire for

liberation. But if you want to read *The Gospel of Sri Ramakrishna,* no qualifications are necessary; no commentator is necessary; no teacher is necessary. It is simple. Simplicity was Ramakrishna's style, so his sentences are
seldom complicated. Simplicity is holiness.

Aldous Huxley wrote in the foreword to Swami Nikhilananda's
translation of the *Gospel*: "What a scholastic philosopher would call the
'accidents' of Ramakrishna's life were intensely Hindu and therefore, so
far as we in the West are concerned, unfamiliar and hard to understand:
its 'essence,' however, was intensely mystical and therefore universal."[60]

Though the background and plots of Ramakrishna's stories and parables are Indian in origin, they are so vivid and simple, so enchanting, that
even a child can understand them. A man once came to Ramakrishna and
asked, "Sir, how can I realize God?" He answered: "You may see God if
your love for Him is as strong as these three attachments put together,
namely, the attachment of a worldly man to the things of the world, the
attachment of a mother to her child, and the attachment of a chaste and
devoted wife to her husband."[61]

Ramakrishna's stories and parables are very positive, instructive, and
uplifting. He was always inspiring. His parable of the woodcutter is typical: A holy man told a poor woodcutter, "Go forward." The woodcutter
took his advice, advanced further into the forest, and found a sandalwood
forest. He sold the sandalwood and became very rich. Then one day he
thought to himself: "That holy man told me to go forward. He did not ask
me to be satisfied." So he went even further into the forest and found a
copper mine. Going further still, he found a silver mine, and then a gold
mine. Finally, he found a diamond mine with which he became exceed-
ingly wealthy. Ramakrishna said that there was no end to spiritual bliss,
spiritual illumination.

Ramakrishna's teachings are also practical: "To meditate, you should
withdraw within yourself or retire to a secluded corner or to the forest."

"Sir, I cannot go to the forest."

"All right. Meditate in the corner of a room."

"Sir, my house is full of people. I cannot get a corner of a room."

"Meditate in the inner chamber of your heart."

There are many alternatives. If you cannot do anything at all, surrender to the Lord and He will do everything for you. "Give me the power of
attorney," said Ramakrishna. Only an avatar like Ramakrishna could say
that. Ramakrishna gave the example of kittens being carried by a mother
cat. The kitten completely surrenders itself.

Another beautiful metaphor that Ramakrishna used concerns three men who were curious to know what was on the other side of a high wall. The first man climbed up a ladder and found Infinite Bliss on the other side. He immediately laughed and jumped into it. The second man did the same thing. The third man also climbed up and saw what was there, but he came back down to tell others of that Infinite Bliss behind the wall, behind maya. That third man is Ramakrishna. In the evening when the sound of the vesper bells reverberated throughout the Dakshineswar temple compound, Ramakrishna would climb up onto the roof of the kuthi [mansion] and call out for his future devotees: "Come to me, my children! Where are you? I can't bear to live without you!"

In 1916, at a railway station in East Bengal, Swami Brahmananda told a young girl who asked for advice from him: "Daughter, the train is coming. I don't have much time, but I will give you knowledge in one sentence: Read *The Gospel of Sri Ramakrishna* regularly every day. That is enough. You will find in this book the truth of all religions."[62]

In 1924, at Belur Math Swami Vijnanananda said to M.: "Master Mahashay, the Master is unique, and so is the recorder of his gospel. Every time I read the *Gospel*, it appears new to me. What an excellent book you have produced! On inquiry I learned that ninety percent of the monks in the Ramakrishna monastery joined after reading *The Gospel of Sri Ramakrishna*."[63]

The Gospel of Sri Ramakrishna is a large volume, and it is expensive. But whatever the price may be, no price can be put on the value of those words. Ramakrishna had a householder disciple, an *ishwarakoti* (godlike soul), whose name was Purna Chandra Ghosh. Long after Ramakrishna passed away, there was trouble in Purna's family and he wanted to commit suicide. He decided to bathe first, and then pay his respects to his guru before killing himself. He took a bath, then went to the shrine and bowed down to the Master. But then he thought: "Let me read a little bit of the *Kathamrita*. Taking the beautiful message of the Master, I shall depart from this world." He opened the book at random and his eyes fell on this sentence: "*Purna balak bhakta. Thakur Purner mangal chinta karitechen.*" (Purna is a young devotee. The Master was thinking of his welfare.) "What?" cried Purna. "The Master is thinking of me and I shall commit suicide? Impossible! He is thinking of my welfare and I am contemplating killing myself. It cannot be."[64] He gave up the idea and thus his life was saved. Such is the power of the words of *The Gospel of Sri Ramakrishna*!

A blessing from Holy Mother

Holy Mother had a great appreciation for *The Gospel of Sri Ramakrishna*. On 2 April 1905, Holy Mother, Golap-ma, and Nikunja Devi (M.'s wife) were listening to a reading of the *Gospel*. When the reading was over, Holy Mother commented: "It is not a small thing to remember the Master's words and ideas, and then write them. I wholeheartedly bless M.: Let his books spread everywhere and let all people know him."

Another day when someone was reading the *Gospel*, Holy Mother was listening with deep absorption. Golap-ma, Nikunja Devi, and some other women were seated there. After some time Holy Mother exclaimed: "How wonderful! How Master Mahashay kept these teachings in his mind! Did he go to the Master with paper and pencil?"

Nikunja Devi: "No, Mother. He would write these things from his memory."

Holy Mother: "What a powerful brain he has! He wrote all these things from memory."

Golap-ma: "Naren also had a powerful mind."

Holy Mother: "He had a different kind of power — for lecturing, writing books, and so on. M. has another kind of power. [Addressing Nikunja Devi] My daughter, give your husband more milk [which is supposed to increase mental power]. May he attain more power. Ah, what a great service he is giving to the world!"

The reading continued.

"The Master said to Mani: 'You are all my relatives.'"

Holy Mother commented: "Of course, everyone is in his inner circle."

Another section was read: "Keshab was coughing."

To this, the crazy aunt [Radhu's mother] said, "Why did M. write such a thing?" Holy Mother replied with a smile: "What do you know? It has a purpose."

The reader was reading a passage about the Master's ecstasy: "M. was thinking: Is the Master describing his own state?"

Holy Mother commented: "Yes, M.'s thinking was correct." After a while Holy Mother said to Nikunja Devi: "My daughter, tell your husband that I am blessing him wholeheartedly."[65]

Appreciations

M. tried to hide himself in the pages of *The Gospel of Sri Ramakrishna* by using several pseudonyms, such as Mani, Master, Mohinimohan, a Devotee, a Servant, an Englishman, and so on; but readers quickly discovered him. While intending to make his guru well known, he became famous himself. Truly, *The Gospel of Sri Ramakrishna* made M. immortal. Here are a few appreciations of his great work.

Swami Premananda wrote to M. on 28 September 1897:

Two copies of your *Gospel* are just at hand, also a p.c. (post card). I am just going to send one copy to Swami Vivekananda. How are you doing now? We are very anxious to see you and hear from you "the *Gospel* of our Lord," so carefully kept by yourself. Not only I, but all of us, especially our boys — sannyasins and brahmacharins — are anxious to have your holy company and hear from your *Gospel*.[66]

Girish Chandra Ghosh wrote on 22 March 1909:

If my humble opinion goes for anything I not only fully endorse the opinion of the great Swami Vivekananda but add in a loud voice that the *Kathamrita* has been my very existence during my protracted illness for the last three years.... You deserve the gratitude of the whole human race to the end of days.[67]

Swami Ramakrishnananda wrote on 27 October 1904:

You have left the whole of humanity in debt by publishing these invaluable pages fraught with the best wisdom of the greatest avatar of God.[68]

In December 1897, Satish Chandra Mukhopadhyay wrote in the journal *Dawn*:

We are extremely thankful to our friend M., whom we may introduce to the reader as an unassuming gentleman of high spiritual attainments, and a devoted servant of his Lord and Master, Sri Ramakrishna, for having given us an opportunity of presenting to our readers what we may most appropriately call 'A Modern Gospel' — which breathes throughout a deep catholicity in reference to all forms of religious discipline and is therefore at war with not *one* of them.[69]

Mr. N. Ghosh wrote in the *Indian Nation on 19 May 1902:*

Ramakrishna Kathamrita by M. (Part I) is a work of singular value and interest. He has done a kind of work which no Bengalee had ever done before, which so far as we are aware no native of India had ever done. It has been done only once in history namely by Boswell.... What a treasure would it have been to the world if all the sayings of Sri Krishna, Buddha, Jesus, Muhammad, Nanak, and Chaitanya could have been thus preserved.[70]

Nagendra Nath Gupta, who personally knew Ramakrishna, wrote in *Ramakrishna-Vivekananda* in 1933:

The Gospel of Ramakrishna Paramahamsa is a record taken at first hand. The words were taken down as they came fresh from the lips of the Master. They were frequently read over to him and he suggested alterations and corrections. There is no room for imagination or exaggeration in anything that concerns Ramakrishna Paramahamsa. Much about the earlier prophets is wrapped in uncertainty and speculation. There are no real likenesses of Buddha, Christ, and Chaitanya. Ramakrishna's photographs are available everywhere. His spoken words are available to all almost just as he uttered them.[71]

The *Brahmavadin* published a review in April 1902:

The life of no prophet has ever been written in the way in which M. has done it in the book under review. Even Boswell's life of Johnson falls into shade before this magnificent record of the Paramahamsa's sayings and doings during the last two years of his life. To the student of psychology and psychic research these conversations are of immense value. They give us a peep into the workings of an extraordinary mind which has risen above the din and incessant devouring activity of this work-a-day world to the eternal presence of the music of the higher spheres. They point out how a Godman who has attained spiritual oneness and realized universal harmony becomes the interpreter of God to man. The dialogues of Socrates resemble to some extent these conversations but without the sublime and tranquil ecstasies of the oriental saint.[72]

Romain Rolland, a French writer and Nobel prize winner, wrote to M.:

The Gospel of Sri Ramakrishna is valuable for it is the faithful account by M. of the discourses with the Master, either his own or those which he actually heard for the next four years. Their exactitude is almost stenographic. The book containing the conversations (*The Gospel of Sri Ramakrishna*) recalls at every turn the setting and the atmosphere. Thanks for having disseminated the radiance of the beautiful Smile of your Master.[73]

Aldous Huxley, an English novelist and essayist, wrote in his foreword to *The Gospel of Sri Ramakrishna*:

M., as the author modestly styles himself, was peculiarly qualified for his task. To a reverent love for his Master, to a deep and experiential knowledge of that master's teaching, he added a prodigious memory for the small happenings of each day and a happy gift for recording them in an interesting and realistic way. Making good use of his natural gifts and of the circumstances in which he found himself, M. produced a book unique, so far as my knowledge goes, in the literature of hagiography. No other saint has had so able and indefatigable a Boswell. Never have the small events of a contemplative's daily life been described with such a wealth of intimate detail. Never have the casual and unstudied utterances of a great religious teacher been set down with so minute a fidelity.[74]

Muhammad Daud Rahbar, a writer and professor of Boston University, wrote:

I have read some delightful portions of the one-thousand-page *Gospel of Sri Ramakrishna*. This marvellous volume has extraordinary revelations. Immediately one recognizes a cherishable friend in Sri Ramakrishna. His open, passionate, and transparent devotion humbles and chastens us. He is no common mortal. He is a man of phenomenal gifts. His presence is a haven. His conversations, recorded abundantly in *The Gospel of Sri Ramakrishna* by his disciple M., are charming, inspired. Their literary merit is due to the inspired goodness of Sri Ramakrishna.[75]

Christopher Isherwood, an English novelist, wrote:

M. shows us Ramakrishna by day and by night, chiefly at Dakshineswar but also at the houses of Balaram and other devotees, on river-boats with Keshab Sen, or driving in a carriage through the streets. Usually, there are quite a lot of people present: disciples, householder devotees and casual visitors. Naturally, they tend to ask Ramakrishna the same questions and so Ramakrishna's answers often repeat or paraphrase themselves. M. records these repetitions, as well as the words of all the songs Ramakrishna sings. A newcomer to the *Gospel* may find this tiresome at first. But, if he reads the book straight through from beginning to end, instead of merely dipping into it, he will probably agree that it is these very repetitions which give the narrative its continuity and its sense of life actually being lived from day to day. In any case, a teacher who never repeats himself is a creation of art and editorship rather than a live being!

The most important function of Ramakrishna as a teacher was available to householder devotee and monastic disciple alike. Both had the opportunity of watching him in the silence of samadhi, in the incoherent mutterings of ecstasy, in the radiant joy of devotional dancing and song. And it was in these manifestations that even some casual visitors to Dakshineswar caught a glimpse of Ramakrishna's true nature. To those who were not utterly insensitive, this was a demonstration, more convincing than the Master's most eloquent words, of the reality of God's presence.

The service M. has rendered us and future generations can hardly be exaggerated. Even the vainest of authors might well have been humbled, finding himself entrusted with such a task. M. was the least vain. M. embodies Ramakrishna's ideal of the householder devotee.[76]

N. Bangarayya, a journalist, wrote in his reminiscences of M:

I became fully convinced that it is impossible for anybody to add to the charm of Ramakrishna. M. spoke beautifully; but there was a distinct and ineffaceable barrier between the two styles, the style of the Master as the disciple has recorded and the style of the disciple himself. The originality, suggestiveness, simplicity, and directness of the former are all its own. It soars far above the reach of any human intellect, be it ever so great. It is not possible for anyone to have invented for the world 'The Ramakrishna Art.' It is greatness enough to have been preserved.[77]

Sarala Devi (later Pravrajika Bharatiprana) recalled:

Revered M. presented me a copy of the *Kathamrita* and asked me to read it. He also told me that he would give me other volumes in the future if I liked them. He later gave me the other three volumes. Seeing my set of the *Kathamrita*, the Holy Mother remarked: 'M. is very fond of Sarala and he has presented her his wonderful books. Well, Sarala, please read a little to me from them.' I used to read the *Kathamrita* to the Mother. She would listen very attentively and joyfully tell us the stories of olden days. Recounting the stories of the Master in Dakshineswar, the Mother said: "M. is so clever that he has recorded the Master's words just as they were. Truly, the Master would speak in that way. Now he is publishing those teachings in book form. Thus so many people are able to know of the Master. I also heard so many things from the Master. I would have recorded them if I had known that these teachings would be published. Well, my child, who could guess that such things would happen."[78]

As long as the sun and moon exist, so long will Ramakrishna's name and his gospel exist — and so will the name of M., a humble householder who recorded *The Gospel of Sri Ramakrishna.*

12

Krishna and Ramakrishna on Meditation

rom the 1960s onward, people in Western countries have been using meditation, japa, and hatha yoga to relieve restlessness and mental illness. People are now using hatha yoga to counteract blood pressure problems, diabetes, heart issues, arthritis, and other ailments, and even to preserve youth. Organizations in the West are teaching Transcendental Meditation, Zen meditation, Vipasanna meditation, Yoga meditation, Kundalini Yoga, Integral Yoga, Ashtanga Yoga, and Vikram Yoga. Many books and articles have been published, and instructions in various techniques of meditation are available on the Internet. Many yogis, gurus, and teachers are teaching meditation as they understand it, and some are even selling mantras and meditation techniques to students.

In fact, nowadays most people are beginning to understand that meditation has an intrinsic value. Previously people believed that meditation was only for yogis, to use for God-realization. Now many people use meditation in the field of action, and scientists apply it in their research. Even ordinary people understand that one cannot attain success in any field without concentration. Many great thinkers have acknowledged the value and necessity of meditation in daily life. Yogis say that one can realize God through meditation, and that it also helps the body to rest and to experience joy. Meditation not only brings mental peace, but it also enhances physical health and reduces disease.

In ancient times, our Indian sages taught meditation and through it their students achieved the goal. The Upanishadic meditations are very

354

Krishna as a charioteer of Arjuna on the battlefield, painted by Nandalal Basu.

poetic and their similes are vivid. The goal of human life is to experience the Atman, which exists within all of us. The Atman is the true nature of all beings. It is our Ishta (Chosen Deity), dearest to us. None can live in this world without the Atman, which is pure consciousness. Sage Yajnavalkya said in the Brihadaranyaka Upanishad that the Atman can be realized through hearing, reflection, and meditation. Although these instructions are thousands of years old, still they are very effective.

Mental restlessness existed in the past, it exists at present, and it will continue to exist in the future. Human beings have no peace of mind because of this restlessness. Repetition of practice and nonattachment are two important means for stopping restlessness. Both Krishna and Ramakrishna unequivocally stated this. Three thousand years ago Krishna taught meditation to Arjuna in the Gita and to Uddhava in the Bhagavata. Now in this present age Ramakrishna instructed his disciples in meditation. We are amazed by the similarities between the advice given by these two avatars. In the sixth chapter of the Gita, Krishna briefly instructed Arjuna in meditation, whereas Ramakrishna elaborately taught meditation with examples and from his own experience according to the need of the age. The teachings of these avatars are universal, and they are applicable to all people, in all countries, and all times.

Regular practice of meditation

"A yogi should always try to concentrate his mind" (Gita, 6:10), said Krishna. This is the first instruction of Krishna to Arjuna. He advised us to practise always — daily and regularly — but he did not mention mornings and evenings in particular.

In contrast, Ramakrishna advised his devotees to chant God's name in the morning and evening: "It is good to meditate in the small hours of the morning and at dawn. One should also meditate daily after dusk."[1] He further said: "If anybody meditates day and night, he can see God all around and he even imbibes His nature."

He knew that it is not possible for ordinary human beings to meditate all the time. Swami Saradananda wrote:

> Sometimes the Master would also use humour to teach us. We remember one day when Swami Vivekananda was singing a devotional song. At that time Swamiji was visiting the Brahmo Samaj regularly and practising prayer and meditation in the morning and evening, according to the Brahmo tradition. Absorbed, Swamiji began to passionately sing this song on Brahman, "Concentrate your mind on that One, ancient, and stainless Purusha." There is a line in that song, "Pray to and meditate on

God continuously." To imprint those words deeply in Swamiji's mind, the Master said suddenly: "No, no, don't say that. You'd better say, 'Pray to and meditate on God twice a day.' Why vainly repeat something that you don't actually intend to do?" All laughed loudly, and Swamiji was a little embarrassed.[2]

Observing his [Tota Puri's] regular habit of meditation, the Master once asked him: "You have realized Brahman and have become perfect. Why then do you meditate every day?" Tota looked at the Master calmly and pointed to the water pot. "See how bright it is," he said. "But will it not lose its lustre if I don't polish it regularly? The mind is like that. It gets tarnished if it isn't kept clean with daily meditation." The keen-sighted Master admitted the truth of this statement but remarked: "Suppose the water pot were made of gold. It wouldn't get tarnished even if it was not polished every day." "Yes, that is true," Tota admitted with a smile. All his life the Master remembered Tota's words regarding the importance of daily meditation and would often mention that teaching to us.[3]

The Master further said: "Those who have the time must meditate and worship. But those who cannot possibly do so must bow down whole-heartedly to God twice a day. He abides in the hearts of all; He knows that worldly people have many things to do. What else is possible for them?"[4]

The Master appreciated how Muslims prayed at regular times throughout the day: "At dusk put aside all duties and pray to God. One is reminded of Him by darkness. At the approach of darkness one thinks: 'I could see everything a moment ago. Who has brought about this change?' The Mussalmans put aside all activities and say their prayers at the appointed times."[5]

The place of meditation

Where shall we meditate? Krishna's answer was "Retiring in solitude" (6:10).

Ramakrishna said: "Meditate inside the heart, in the corner of the room, and in the forest." These words have great significance. The best meditation is to place the Ishta in the mind or heart and focus on him or her. The Master further said: "The heart is a splendid place. One can meditate there or in the sahasrara [crown of the head]. These are rules for meditation given in the scriptures." "In the corner of the room" means in a secluded corner of the house. One should practise spiritual disciplines alone, in secret. Those who do not have any separate shrine in their house should set up a small shrine with pictures of gods and goddesses in one of their rooms and practise japa and meditation there. "The forest" means in a solitary place away from noise and distractions.

Meditate in solitude

Krishna specifies that one should meditate alone and not in a group (6:10). Ramakrishna said: "You will not be able to think of God and meditate on Him in this confusion of the world. A little solitude is necessary for you; otherwise your mind will not be steady. Therefore, you must fix a place for meditation at least half a mile away from your house."[6] He also specified that one should be discreet: "A devotee who possesses sattva guna meditates on God in absolute secret, perhaps inside his mosquito net. Others think he is asleep. Since he is late in getting up, they think perhaps he has not slept well during the night."[7] Finally, he said that one should depend entirely on God: "During your sadhana in solitude, please think that you have none else in this world and God is your all in all."

The Master emphasized these two words: *nirjane*, in solitude; and *gopane*, secretly. When the Master heard that Ishan Mukhopadhyay was building a huge hall for practising *purascharana* (performing japa a certain number of times a day), he told him, "Let me tell you that the less people know of your spiritual life, the better it will be for you." He said to Balaram's father: "There are many kinds of spiritual aspirants. Those endowed with sattva perform their spiritual practices secretly. They look like ordinary people, but they meditate inside the mosquito net. Aspirants endowed with rajas exhibit outward pomp — a string of beads around the neck, a mark on the forehead, an ochre robe, a silk cloth, a rosary with a gold bead, and so on. They are like stall-keepers advertising their wares with signboards."[8]

Exercise self-control

Krishna said that a person should meditate after "Having subdued his mind and body and got rid of desires and possessions" (6:10). Desires and possessions make the mind scattered and restless, pulling it away from God. Meditation is not possible for a person whose body and mind are not under control. A wealthy man may go to a cave in the Himalayas or to a retreat to practise meditation, but his mind will dwell on his possessions.

The Master demonstrated how to control the body and mind. He described his experiences:

> There is an image of Bhairava [a form of Shiva] in meditation on the parapet of the natmandir in front of the Kali temple. While going to the temple to meditate, I would point to that image and tell my mind, "You must meditate on the Mother like that motionless statue." No sooner did I sit down to meditate than I would hear clattering sounds in all of my joints,

beginning in my legs. It was as if someone inside me were turning keys to lock me up, joint by joint. I was powerless to move my body or change my posture, even slightly. I couldn't stop meditating, or leave the temple, or do anything else I wanted. I was forced to sit in that posture until my joints began clattering again and were unlocked, this time beginning at my neck and ending in my legs.[9]

This description of the Master's meditation is incomparable. When we sit for meditation, we generally feel aches and pains in the knees, back, and neck, and our minds begin to wander. In addition, desires and doubts, hopes and aspirations ruin our meditation.

One day in Dakshineswar, Latu went to meditate in the temple, but soon after he returned to the Master. When the Master asked him why he returned so quickly, he replied:

"On other days when I sit for japam and meditation, I see something and the mind gets concentrated. But today nothing appeared. I tried hard to concentrate, but I failed." He added: "On my way to the temple the thought came to me — if Mother would appear to me and offer a boon, what should I ask for?"

Immediately the Master said: "There's the trouble. Can one do japam with the mind full of desires? Never let that happen again. When sitting to meditate one should not ask for anything. If Mother ever insists on giving you something, then ask only for devotion to Her. Never ask for wealth, power, sense pleasures, or anything else."[10]

A clean, comfortable place for meditation

Krishna describes the place where one should meditate: "In a clean spot having fixed his seat — a firm seat, neither too high nor too low — and having spread over it kusa-grass, and then a deer skin, and then a cloth" (6:11).

The shrine or the place for meditation must be clean; a nice view is also preferable. It is important to create a spiritual atmosphere with beautiful pictures of deities and saints, flowers, and incense. The Master himself created one of his meditation places by planting plants such as madhavi and tulsi in the Panchavati grove. He had another place for meditation in the jungle under the bel tree. He used to send his disciples to meditate in the different temples in Dakshineswar and also in the Panchavati. He said: "You may meditate wherever you like. Every place is filled with Brahman-Consciousness. Is there any place where It does not exist? Narayana, in Vali's presence, covered with two steps the heavens, the earth, and the interspaces. Is there then any place left uncovered by God? A dirty place is as holy as the bank of the Ganges."[11]

As far as we know, the Master used a wooden seat while taking his food and a carpet seat while performing worship in the temple. He meditated on his bed, and also on the altars in the Panchavati and bel-tala. He might have also sat on a folded blanket laid on kusa grass. Various kinds of asanas (seats) are mentioned in the scriptures. Yogi Yajnavalkya said: "Spread the kusa-grass on the ground and then a deer skin on top of it." Patanjali said that the asana should be stable and comfortable. Vyasa mentioned that meditation is possible in a sitting posture only and not lying or standing. Moreover, one can achieve results from meditation quickly if one sits on one's own asana on the same spot and at the same time every day.

Gathering one's thoughts

Krishna specifies that "There, seated on that seat, he should practise yoga for the purification of the self, restraining the activities of his mind and senses, and bringing his thoughts to a point" (6:12).

Ramakrishna taught meditation from his own experience:

Do you know what one feels in meditation? The mind becomes like a continuous flow of oil — it thinks of one object only, and that is God. It does not think of anything else....In deep meditation a man is not at all conscious of the outer world. A person can achieve such single-mindedness in meditation that he will see nothing, hear nothing. He will not be conscious even of touch. A snake may crawl over his body, but he will not know it. Neither of them will be aware of the other. In deep meditation the sense-organs stop functioning: the mind does not look outward. It is like closing the gate of the outer court in a house. There are five objects of the senses: form, taste, smell, touch, and sound. They are left outside.[12]

During my sadhana, before starting meditation on the Chosen Deity I would first imagine that I was washing the mind thoroughly. You see, there are various kinds of dirt and dross (bad thoughts and desires) in the mind. I would imagine that I was flushing out all impurities and placing the Chosen Deity there. Adopt this method.[13]

According to the yoga scriptures, one is supposed to withdraw the mind from sense objects prior to meditation on the Ishta. This is called *pratyahara*. Bees gather together where the queen bee dwells. Similarly, the mind is the king of the senses; where the mind is absorbed, the senses become still along with the mind. Ramakrishna said: "The mind is like a packet of mustard seeds: once they are scattered, it's almost impossible to gather them up."

Correct posture for meditation

Krishna describes the correct posture for meditation: "He should sit firm, holding his body, neck, and head erect and still" (6:13).

Swami Brahmananda said that the Master always sat with his back upright. Swami Akhandananda mentioned how the Master instructed him to sit for meditation: "One morning Sri Ramakrishna asked me to accompany him to the Panchavati, and there he told me to meditate facing the east. He left for a while, and when he came back he set my body straight. He remarked, 'You become a bit bent during meditation.'"[14]

Saradananda wrote how the Master taught him how to sit for meditation:

> One day the Master showed a young disciple [Saradananda] postures and gestures that are appropriate for meditation on God with form and without form. Seated in the lotus position, the Master placed the back of his right hand on the palm of his left and then raised both to chest level. With his eyes closed, he said, "This is the best posture for all kinds of meditation on God with form." Then, seated in the same position, he placed his right and left hands, palms upward, on his right and left knees respectively, and brought the tips of the thumb and the index finger of each hand together, keeping the other fingers straight. Fixing his gaze between his eyebrows, he said, "This is an excellent posture for meditation on the formless God."[15]

Forms of meditation

Krishna continued his description of meditation: "Gaze steadily at the tip of his nose, without looking around" (6:13).

Regarding various kinds of meditation, Ramakrishna said:

> There are two kinds of meditation, one on the formless God and the other on God with form. But meditation on the formless God is extremely difficult. In that meditation you must wipe out all that you see or hear. You contemplate only the nature of your Inner Self. Meditating on His Inner Self, Siva dances about. He exclaims, "What am I! What am I!" This is called the "Shiva yoga." While practising this form of meditation, one directs one's look to the forehead. It is meditation on the nature of one's Inner Self after negating the world, following the Vedantic method of "neti, neti."
>
> There is another form of meditation known as the "Vishnu yoga." The eyes are fixed on the tip of the nose. Half the look is directed inward and the other half outward. This is how one meditates on God with form.[16]
>
> In deep meditation a man is not at all conscious of the outer world.

A hunter was aiming at a bird. A bridal procession passed along beside him, with the groom's relatives and friends, music, carriages, and horses. It took a long time for the procession to pass the hunter, but he was not at all conscious of it.[17]

Most people close their eyes to meditate. In that connection, the Master said: "There was a time when I too would meditate on God with my eyes closed. Then I said to myself: 'Does God exist only when I think of Him with my eyes closed? Doesn't He exist when I look around with my eyes open?' Now, when I look around with my eyes open, I see that God dwells in all beings. He is the Indwelling Spirit of all — men, animals and other living beings, trees and plants, sun and moon, land and water."[18]

Moderation in all things

According to Krishna, "For him who is temperate in his food and recreation, temperate in his exertion at work, temperate in sleep and waking, yoga puts an end to all sorrows" (6:17).

Regarding food, work, and sleep, Ramakrishna fully accepted Krishna's view. The Master did not like fasting because one cannot concentrate on God when one is hungry. However, because overeating can also hinder one's meditation, he even allocated the number of chapatis to be served to each disciple at night and instructed Holy Mother accordingly. Once the Master said to M.: "It is best to take only sattvic food. Haven't you read about it in the Gita?"

M. replied: "Yes, sir. The Gita speaks of temperance in eating. Sattvic food, rajasic food, tamasic food — all these are described in the Gita."[19]

Ramakrishna considered the Gita to contain the essence of all the scriptures.

Ramakrishna taught individually, according to each person's aptitude and capacity. For example, he did not put any food restrictions on Vivekananda, but he forbade Niranjanananda to eat ghee. One day the Master asked Jogin (later, Yogananda), "What do you eat at night?" "Bread made from one pound of flour, and one half pound of potato curry," replied Jogin. Immediately the Master said: "My goodness! I don't need your service. I cannot afford to provide such a large quantity of food every day. You had better eat at home before coming here."[20] When Latu overheard this, he cut back the amount of food that he ate, and as a result suffered from hunger. The omniscient Master observed this and told him: "Look, you have gone to the other extreme. Please eat the amount that will keep your body in fit condition. Otherwise, if you eat too little you won't be able to focus your mind during meditation."

On another day, Latu ate a large quantity of food in a devotee's house, and that devotee praised his appetite. The Master said to Latu: "Look, it is not good to eat excessively by competing with others. During lunch, you may eat as much as you wish; but at night, don't eat too much."[21]

Our scriptures offer wonderful advice on eating: *hitabhuk*, eat nutritious food; *mitabhuk*, eat moderately; *ritabhuk*, eat at the right time. The Master's general advice for food: eat what you can digest. He advised M. to eat rice with a little ghee and drink a little milk at the end of a meal.

Along with advice on controlling what they ate, the Master advised his disciples to control their sleeping habits. Latu used to wrestle, so he slept a little more than the other disciples. One evening, the Master noticed his disciple sleeping and not only woke him, but also rebuked him sharply: "If you sleep in the evening, when will you meditate? You should meditate so deeply that the night passes unnoticed. Instead, your eyelids are heavy with sleep at this auspicious time. Did you come here only to sleep?"[22] Latu struggled for two years to conquer sleep and thereafter he never slept at night.

Swami Shivananda recalled: "In those days we used to sleep on the floor of the Master's room. At bedtime the Master would tell us how to lie down. He would say that if we were to lie flat on our backs and visualize the Mother in our hearts while falling asleep, then we would have spiritual dreams. He asked us to think of spiritual things while going to sleep."[23]

The Master did not like laziness at all. Apart from japa and meditation, he exhorted his disciples to always to do some work.

A lamp in a windless place

In a famous description of meditation, Krishna said: "'As a lamp in a windless place does not flicker' — that is the simile used for the disciplined mind of a yogi practising concentration on the Self" (6:13).

The Master used this wonderful illustration while teaching his disciples. He said: "When I meditated during my sadhana, I used to think of the unflickering flame of a lamp set in a windless place."[24] He further said: "What will you gain by floating on the surface? Dive a little under the water. The gems lie deep under the water. They do not float. To get the real gem you must dive deep."[25]

Another day the Master talked about the cause of restlessness and the remedy for it:

The mind is bent down toward the world. If there are no desires, the mind naturally looks up toward God. Do you know what it is like? It is like the needles of a balance. On account of the weight of "lust and gold" the two needles are not in line. It is "lust and gold" that makes a man stray from the path of yoga. Haven't you noticed the flame of a candle? The slightest wind makes it waver. The state of yoga is like the candle-flame in a windless place. The mind is dispersed. Part of it has gone to Dhaka, part to Delhi, and another part to Coochbehar. That mind is to be gathered in; it must be concentrated on one object.[26]

In order to make meditation attractive and sweet, the Master said: "During meditation, think that your mind has been tied to the feet of your Chosen Deity with a silk thread, so that He cannot run away. Why do I say a silk thread? Because those feet are extremely soft and delicate. It would hurt the deity if a different type of string were used." He also said:

Should one think of the Chosen Deity during meditation only and then forget Him? Always try to keep part of your mind towards the deity. You have seen how a vigil lamp is kept burning during Durga Puja. One should always keep a lamp near the deity; it should not be allowed to go out. It is inauspicious if a householder's lamp goes out. Likewise, after placing the Chosen Deity in the lotus of the heart, one's meditation should be like the flame of a vigil lamp. While performing household duties one should look inside from time to time to see if the lamp is still burning.[27]

Renounce desires for sense objects

Krishna said, "Renounce entirely all the desires born of the will, drawing back the senses from every direction by strength of mind" (6:24).

Bad thoughts may arise when we are awake, but we do not feel their intensity too strongly. Those bad thoughts exist like friends, mixing with the impurities of the mind. But during meditation we consider those bad thoughts to be enemies. When we try to uproot them forcefully, they vigorously fight back. This is a sign of the purification of the mind. One can see the enemies in the mirror of the mind.

Renunciation of sense objects is indispensable at the time of meditation. Ramakrishna explained how renunciation and discrimination work side by side:

At the beginning of meditation, the objects of the senses appear before the aspirant. But when meditation becomes deep, they no longer bother him. They are left outside. How many things I saw during meditation! I vividly perceived before me a heap of rupees, a shawl, a plate of sweets, and two women with rings in their noses. "What do you want?" I asked my mind. "Do you want to enjoy any of these things?" "No," replied the mind, "I don't want any of them. I don't want anything but the Lotus Feet of God." I saw the inside and the outside of the women as one sees from outside the articles in a glass room. I saw what is in them: entrails, blood, filth, worms, phlegm, and such things."[28]

The ever-pure Master assured us, "In this kaliyuga, mental sin is not considered as sin." But if anybody physically performs a sinful act, it makes a deep impression in the mind that is extremely difficult to erase. Many bad and good thoughts pass over the mind, consciously and unconsciously, like footmarks on a sandy beach — but then a big wave comes and wipes them all away. Every day we experience this phenomenon. Good impressions bury bad impressions. Meditation helps us to create good impressions. Worldly desires are the enemies of meditation. The Master said: "The truth is that you cannot attain God if you have even a trace of desire. Subtle is the way of dharma. If you are trying to thread a needle, you will not succeed if the thread has even a slight fibre sticking out."[29]

How to attain tranquility

Krishna said, "Let a man little by little attain tranquility with the help of the buddhi [intellect] armed with fortitude" (6:25).

One cannot become spiritual overnight. The Master once told someone that there is a time factor. The mother bird does not break the shell of the egg until the right time comes. Develop your power by practising spiritual disciplines. A sapling needs to be protected with a fence, but when it becomes a tree, then even an elephant cannot harm it. The Master explained that the mind is like a white cloth; it will take the colour you dye it with. He also advised us:

Just as you practise much in order to sing, dance, and play on instruments, so one should practise the art of fixing the mind on God. One should practise regularly such disciplines as worship, japa, and meditation....*Abhayasayoga*, the yoga of practice. You should practise calling on God every day. It is not possible to succeed in one day; through daily prayer you will come to long for God.[30]

You cannot achieve anything by moving at such a slow pace. You need stern renunciation. Can you achieve anything by counting fifteen months as a year? You seem to have no strength, no grit. You are as mushy as flattened rice soaked in milk. Be up and doing! Gird your loins. I don't like that song: "Brother, joyfully cling to God; thus striving, some day you may attain Him." I don't care for that line. "Thus striving, some day you may attain Him."[31]

If the Master noticed that a devotee's love for God had waned, he would say: "Why do you say, 'I shall realize God in the next life, if not in this?' You should not have that kind of lukewarm devotion. 'By His grace I will realize Him in this life and right now' — one should maintain such determination and faith."[32]

Focus the mind on the Self

Krishna said, "Once the mind is established in the Self, he should think of nothing else" (6:25).

As in the Gita, Krishna instructed Arjuna in meditation, so in the Bhagavata, he instructed Uddhava (11:14:32-46):

> First step: Concentrate the mind on the whole beautiful form of your Chosen Deity.
>
> Second step: Focus your entire mind on the Ishta's face only and stop all other thoughts. Meditate on His smiling, joyful face.
>
> Third step: Carry that smiling face to the infinite akasha (space) and merge into it.
>
> Fourth step: Forget the space and think no more. Be absorbed only in pure Brahman.

Here the meditator, meditation, and the object of meditation become one. This is the culmination of meditation. But this type of meditation is difficult. The Master suggested: "In order to meditate on God, one should try at first to think of Him as free from *upadhis*, limitations. God is beyond upadhis. He is beyond speech and mind. It is very difficult to achieve perfection in this form of meditation. But it is easy to meditate on an Incarnation — God born as man. Yes, God in man. The body is a mere covering. It is like a lantern with a light burning inside, or like a glass case in which one sees precious things."[33]

Ramakrishna gave this advice to those who practise nondualistic meditation: "Look, during my sadhana I used to look upon God as if He had completely covered the universe like the water of the ocean, and like a fish, I was diving, floating, and swimming in that ocean of Satchidananda. Again, sometimes I considered myself to be a pitcher immersed in the water of that indivisible Satchidananda, which pervaded me through and through."[34]

Thinking is the faculty of the mind. Thoughts exist as long as the mind exists. The mind dissolves during samadhi as well as in deep sleep. Human minds are generally occupied with worldly thoughts, but when those thoughts stop, one can see the Ishta. Patanjali said: "*Tadā drashtuh swarupe avasthānam* — At that time [when the thought-waves stop] the Seer [Purusha] rests in his own [unmodified] state" (1:3).

This type of meditation and samadhi is beyond the reach of ordinary people. For this reason, Krishna gave some simple alternatives to us: "I am easily attainable by that ever-steadfast yogi who remembers me constantly and daily with a single mind, O son of Pritha" (8:14); also, "Fix your mind on me alone and surrender your intellect to me. Thereupon, you will always live in me. Of this, there is no doubt" (12:8).

Ramakrishna said: "If you meditate on an ideal you will acquire its nature. If you think of God day and night, you will acquire the nature of God."[35]

Ramakrishna's divine life, immortal message, and divine play are now objects of meditation for innumerable people all over the world. He reminded us:

> Look, before you begin meditating, think of this (*pointing to himself*) for a while. Do you know why I say this? Because you have faith in this place (*me*). If you think of this place, that will remind you of God. It is like when one sees a herd of cows, one remembers a cowherd; seeing a son, the father; seeing a lawyer, the court. Do you understand? Look, your mind is scattered among various places. If you think of this (me), it will be gathered in one spot. And if you think of God with that concentrated mind you will truly get deep meditation. That is why I am telling you all this.[36]

13

Dakshineswar: An Abode of Bliss

A divine plan
Providence may have decreed that a certain pilgrimage of a devout woman should not be successfully carried out, but this failed pilgrimage found fulfillment instead in the Divine Mother's form in the Dakshineswar temple garden. A great woman, Rani Rasmani (1793-1861), had long desired to make a grand pilgrimage to Varanasi by boat, as there was no railway at that time. Elaborate preparations had been made, but on the night before she was to embark, Rani Rasmani saw in a dream the Divine Mother, who said to her: "You need not go to Varanasi. Install my image in a beautiful spot along the bank of the Ganges and arrange for my worship and offerings there. In this image I shall be present constantly and shall ever accept your worship." (In another version of this incident it is said that Rasmani started her journey, and halted on the first night near Dakshineswar, where she had the dream.)[1]

The construction of the Dakshineswar temple complex began in 1847 and required more than eight years to complete. In addition to the main temple, dedicated to the Divine Mother Kali, twelve small temples are dedicated to Shiva and one temple is dedicated to Krishna. Rasmani spent 50,000 rupees for the land, 160,000 rupees to build an embankment along the river, and 900,000 rupees for the construction of the temple complex. In addition, she spent 226,000 rupees for property that was meant to be used as an endowment for the maintenance of the temple.

Rani Rasmani was not an ordinary woman. Sri Ramakrishna said:

Dakshineswar temple garden (playground of Ramakrishna and an abode of bliss) from the Ganges.

"Rani Rasmani was one of the eight *nāyikās* [attendant goddesses] of the Divine Mother. She came down to the world to spread the worship of the Divine Mother."[2] Before Ramakrishna's arrival in Calcutta, Rasmani began to set the stage where the coming avatar would enact his divine play for thirty years. Shiva and Shakti traditionally remain side by side, so temples to Kali and Shiva are generally built close to one another. But Rani Rasmani included a Radha-Krishna temple in the same compound with her Kali temple and twelve shrines to Shiva. This was something new. Perhaps Rasmani was inspired by the Divine Mother to thus symbolize the harmony of faiths in concrete form for Ramakrishna, who was the embodiment of all religions.

It is amazing that in the nineteenth century it was a woman who formed the main backdrop for the Master's divine play. Swami Vivekananda's disciple Sister Nivedita put it nicely: "Humanly speaking, without the Temple of Dakshineswar there [would have] been no Ramakrishna; without Ramakrishna, no Vivekananda; and without Vivekananda, no Western mission [of Vedanta]."[3]

My first visit to Dakshineswar

It was probably in June 1950 that I made my first visit to Dakshineswar. I was 14 years old. I vividly remember how I took the bus, route number 78, from Barrackpore to Dunlop Bridge; from there I took bus number 32B to Dakshineswar. When I arrived at about 2:30 p.m. the temples were closed, so my elder brother and I waited in the Panchavati until 4:00 p.m. My brother told me that Ramakrishna used to sit under those trees and talk to the Divine Mother. My young mind began to picture this holy place as it must have looked during the time of Ramakrishna's austerities and divine play.

When I first visited Dakshineswar, there was no barbed-wire fence around the Panchavati. Between the Panchavati and the Panchamundi where Ramakrishna practised Tantra, there were some old pine trees and some mango, lichi, and other fruit trees. There was a bamboo fence around the Panchamundi, and anyone could sit on its circular cement platform. The Dakshineswar temple garden was like a beautiful ancient hermitage.

When I visited Dakshineswar in 1997, a brick wall had been built between the Panchavati and the Panchamundi and a meditation cottage had been constructed near the pine grove. These additions have ruined the beautiful atmosphere of Rasmani's temple garden. But nonetheless, Dakshineswar still holds a powerful attraction for me.

From 1950 onward I visited Dakshineswar regularly. Almost every Sunday, I would go to Udbodhan House, where Holy Mother had lived, in North Calcutta. From there, I would go to Dakshineswar in the evening. First I would visit the temples, then I would go to Sri Ramakrishna's room and sit for meditation between the western wall and his bed. I would imagine that the Master was seated on his bed with his legs hanging over the side; I would touch my head to his feet. This was how I daydreamed as a boy. At that time there was no wooden barricade around the Master's bed. Even though the caretaker burned a lot of incense, the room was infested with healthy mosquitoes that lived on the pure blood of the Master's devotees.

There was a red cement floor in the Master's room then, the same as in his time. Photos that the Master had collected — Jagannath, Dhruva, Prahlada, Chaitanya and the kirtan party, Jesus rescuing Peter, and so on — hung on the walls. In 1955, during the centenary of Dakshineswar, the temple authorities built a temple to Rani Rasmani between the Master's room and the nahabat, and they replaced the red cement floor of the Master's room with a mosaic. In India our sense of history is very poor. How wonderful it would have been if the temple authorities had installed a museum in the kuthi (bungalow) where Rasmani and Mathur lived, instead of building a temple obstructing the path to the nahabat. Ramakrishna lived in that kuthi for 16 years. A good museum would have tremendous educational value and would attract pilgrims and visitors [now a museum has been installed]. There is no shortage of Kali temples in Bengal, but the Dakshineswar Kali temple is unique because of Ramakrishna.

M. has left us a vivid description of the Kali temple of Dakshineswar in the first part of *Sri Sri Ramakrishna Kathamrita*, which has been fully translated in the appendix of *Ramakrishna As We Saw Him*. This wonderful historical document will help future generations to visualize the playground of Ramakrishna and to meditate on his divine play. I have some pictures of old Dakshineswar in which one can see beautiful flower gardens on the bank of the Ganges, a dense forest in the Panchavati area, pilgrims bathing at the chandni and bakul-tala ghats, and the domed temples between the two nahabats. This panoramic view reflected on the Ganges makes us think that the heavenly palace of Indra has descended on Dakshineswar.

Every particle of dust at Dakshineswar is holy; every bit of ground there is precious to the devotees of Ramakrishna. Ramakrishna lived there for thirty years, practised various sadhanas, taught his devotees and disciples, and enacted his divine play. This temple garden of Dakshineswar is now an object of meditation for innumerable people from all over the world. There are many people who have never been to Dakshineswar, but they have read *The Gospel of Sri Ramakrishna* and *Sri Ramakrishna and His Divine Play*. They try to visualize the playground of Ramakrishna, imagining various scenes in the Master's life: how he tested the image of Kali by putting cotton near Her nostrils to see if She breathed; how he repaired the broken foot of Krishna; how he tearfully embraced the image of Shiva and glorified the Lord. These devotees also picture in their minds the places where Ramakrishna practised Tantra, Vedanta, and Islam; the chandni ghat where Ramakrishna bathed; and the room in which he slept. These visualizations are helpful for meditation.

Two sweet memories

Ramlal, a nephew of Ramakrishna, recalled:

I was young at the time, and it was winter. The Master used to go for a walk in the morning, covering himself with a shawl and wearing a cap on his head. I used to cut a twig for the Master to use as a toothbrush. We would go to the main road through the northeast gate of the temple garden and then walk up to Barrackpore Trunk Road, which was broad and straight. Standing on the road one day, the Master said: "Look, this broad and straight road is like the mind of a sadhu. It is not crooked." One could see the pinnacle of the temple from that road. As he looked at the curved structure of the temple's pinnacle one day, the Master said: "The temple is overflowing with joy because the Divine Mother is in its inner sanctuary. The temple is having goose bumps out of joy." The Master said so many wonderful things. On our way back, he would stop in our [Ramlal's] house near the temple garden to inquire about the family members and their welfare. Sometimes he would say: "Give me some puffed rice. Let me have my breakfast here." Afterwards, he would slowly return to the temple.

I remember another incident. Mathur presented a beautiful necklace to the Divine Mother. Later, Mathur's son Trailokya became the custodian of the Dakshineswar temple. The Master told him: "Your father gave a necklace to the Divine Mother. Will you not present anything to Her?" Trailokya had anklets made for the Divine Mother. She looked beautiful when She was dressed with those anklets. One day the Master was seated on the southeast veranda of his room. All of a sudden, he saw the Divine Mother standing on the top of the temple. She was wearing those anklets, and was about to step forward towards the courtyard. Immediately the Master cried out and waved for Her to stop, shouting: "Don't — don't go farther! You will fall." As he did this he went into samadhi.[4]

At Dakshineswar with Swami Subodhananda

The following account was recorded by Swami Subodhananda's attendant:

At 3:00 p.m. [in November 1929 (6 Paush 1336)] we left for Dakshineswar from Udbodhan House by car with Swami Subodhananda. As we passed Baranagore, the swami said: "When the Master was alive, I walked through this street many times to see him at Dakshineswar. The Master said to M. and other devotees, 'Please pay this boy's carriage fare or boat fare whenever he comes.' I was afraid to travel by boat because I did not know how to swim."

When the car reached Dakshineswar, the swami first took us to the bel-tala [the Panchamundi, where the Master had practised Tantra]. Seeing the bamboo fence around the bel tree and its cement platform, the swami said: "This fence was not here during the Master's time. The place where the Master sat for sadhana is now within that fence."

When we arrived at the Panchavati, the swami bowed down to the platform. Pointing to the brick cottage where the Master had attained nirvikalpa samadhi, the swami said, "During the Master's time this room was a thatched hut with a mud floor."

While we were passing near the nahabat, the swami said, "The Holy Mother lived in the small room in the nahabat." Reaching the Master's room, the swami bowed down on the floor. We also bowed down. The swami recalled: "Oh, what a crowd was here during the Master's time!" The swami sat there for a while.

He then left the room to visit the Divine Mother in the temple. We followed him. He came down the steps of the southeastern veranda and walked through the courtyard. He stopped in front of the steps of the Shiva temples on the north side. He said: "One day I came to Dakshineswar and the Master's room was full of people. Meanwhile, the Master left his room accompanying me. We sat on the steps of these temples. The Master then gave me spiritual instructions and passed his hand over my head and body. Shortly something [kundalini power] arose in my head and overwhelmed me and made me almost unconscious. After a while, the Master again passed his hand over my head and I became normal again."[5]

An abode of bliss

Dakshineswar, the playground of Ramakrishna, is an abode of bliss for innumerable people of the East and the West. Those who have not seen Dakshineswar try to imagine and meditate on various places in the temple garden where the Master lived for thirty years. The devotees of Krishna strongly believe that even now Krishna plays with the gopis every night in Nidhuban (which is in Vrindaban). In the same way, Ramakrishna's devotees visualize his divine play in Dakshineswar even now.

M. made a wonderful comment about Dakshineswar: "The spiritual fire is blazing intensely there, and whoever goes there will be purified. The body does not burn, but mental impurities are consumed in no time. Then a person can attain immortality. God himself, in a physical form, lived there for thirty years! One can tangibly feel the spirituality at Dakshineswar."[6]

There is a beautiful verse in *Sri Sri Chaitanya-charitamrita*: "*Adyāpiha sei lilā kare gorā rāi, kono kono bhāgyavāne dekhibāre pāi.* — Chaitanya is still performing his divine play; only the fortunate ones can see it." Let us pray to Ramakrishna to grant us the good fortune to be able to visualize his divine play.

Ramakrishna enacted the first part of his divine play in Kamarpukur, the second part in Dakshineswar, and the last part in Shyampukur and Cossipore. In an ecstatic mood, the Master once said to Mathur, "As long as you are alive, I shall be in Dakshineswar." This startled Mathur and made him apprehensive because he knew that the Divine Mother was protecting him and his family through the Master. So when he heard the Master's words, he thought that the Master would forsake his family after he died. He then humbly said to the Master: "What are you saying, Father? My wife and son Dwaraka are very much devoted to you." Observing Mathur's distress, the Master replied, "All right, I shall remain as long as your wife and Dwaraka live." It indeed came to pass that the Master left Dakshineswar for good after both Jagadamba and Dwaraka had passed away. Dwaraka died in 1878 and Jagadamba in 1881. The Master remained in Dakshineswar until September 1885.

Krishna left Vrindaban and went to Mathura, which is only seven or eight miles away. He was so unattached that he never returned to see his dear ones in Vrindaban. The Master left for Calcutta and Cossipore to enact the last part of his divine play, and he never returned to Dakshineswar. However, he sometimes sent his disciples to practise sadhana there. Swamiji would go to Dakshineswar with a few brother disciples and spend the whole night in the Panchavati in meditation. Later, Swamiji reminisced: "Oh, what weird scenes things bring before me, the weirdest scenes of my whole life! Perfect silence, broken only by the cries of the jackals, in the darkness under the great tree at Dakshineswar. Night after night we sat there, the whole night through, and He [Ramakrishna] talked to me, when I was a boy."[7] Later, M. took devotees to Dakshineswar and pointed out the spots connected with various events of the Master's life.

In 1897, Swami Vivekananda returned to India from the West and celebrated the birth anniversary of Ramakrishna at Dakshineswar. In 1898, the Dakshineswar temple authorities did not give permission to observe Ramakrishna's birth anniversary there, so it was held at Daw's temple complex in Belur. Ramakrishna Monastery was then at Nilambar's garden house in Belur and Belur Math was under construction.

Swami Akhandananda depicted Swamiji's mental condition at that time in one of his letters:

> Standing on the bank of the Ganges in the southern side of Belur Math Swamiji told me: "Look, the frontage (the bank of the Ganges) of Belur Math is longer than the frontage of the Dakshineswar temple garden. When the embankment is constructed then it will surpass the Dakshineswar temple in length. Don't you think so?" I agreed. Then he said: "You see, they did not allow us to observe the Master's festival there this year. It seems that the Master did the right thing for us. You know — there are some among you who might raise various objections in the future to observing the Master's festival in Belur Math. Truly speaking, the Dakshineswar authorities in a way did good to us."[8]

This indicates that the Master wanted his disciples to stand on their own feet.

However, the monks of the Ramakrishna Order have a special love and attraction for Dakshineswar, the playground of Ramakrishna. Swami Satprakashananda told me about a visit he paid to Dakshineswar on Jagaddhatri Puja Day in 1917. Swamis Brahmananda, Saradananda, and Akhandananda made the trip, along with many devotees. Swami Akhandananda loudly chanted various hymns in the Mother's temple in his melodious voice. In an ecstatic mood, Swami Brahmananda went to all the temples, the Master's room, the Panchavati, and the Panchamundi. The monks and devotees expected that Brahmananda would say something about the Master, but he remained silent. He was absorbed in the thought of his guru.

Swami Nirvanananda, an attendant of Brahmananda, recalled:

> It was a hot summer day in June at 3:00 p.m. There was a flat roof adjacent to the room of Swami Brahmananda at Belur Math. The swami got up from his rest and walked barefoot to the northeast corner of the roof. Barefoot, I carried water for the swami so that he could rinse his mouth. The roof was so hot that it was very painful to stand there. I was continually shifting from foot to foot. I noticed that the swami was in an ecstatic mood gazing at Dakshineswar across the Ganges. His feet were very soft,

but he stood motionless on that hot roof. After a while, he came back to the normal plane.[9]

Blessed is the holy land of Dakshineswar — an object of meditation for devotees of the Master.

14

The Magnitude of Ramakrishna's Life and Message

One of my friends used to tease me by saying, "Hinduism is a weak religion because God has to incarnate again and again to rejuvenate that religion, but Buddhism, Christianity, and Islam have only one prophet." I jokingly replied: "God is afraid to be born in Christian communities or any other religion, because He might be crucified or murdered again. So He goes to India and takes birth among the Hindus. The Hindus love God in many forms and they will not kill Him. Moreover, the Christians and followers of other religions would not accept or recognize another incarnation or prophet. So God does not want to be born among them anymore."

Raimon Panikkar, a Jesuit theologian, once told me that there is a Buddhist canon: "If you see Buddha on the street, kill him." This means Buddha is not a person; Buddha is a state of enlightenment. According to this theologian, there is a similar saying in the Christian tradition: "If you see Jesus on the street, crucify him." He explained that Christians believe that Christ is resurrected in heaven and will not be seen as a human in this world.

I told my Jesuit friend: "If you see Ramakrishna on the street, have a nice time with him. Enjoy his stories and his jokes along with his samadhi."

According to the Vishnu Purana: "Some people neither do their duties nor practise religion, but repeat, 'God, God.' They are enemies of

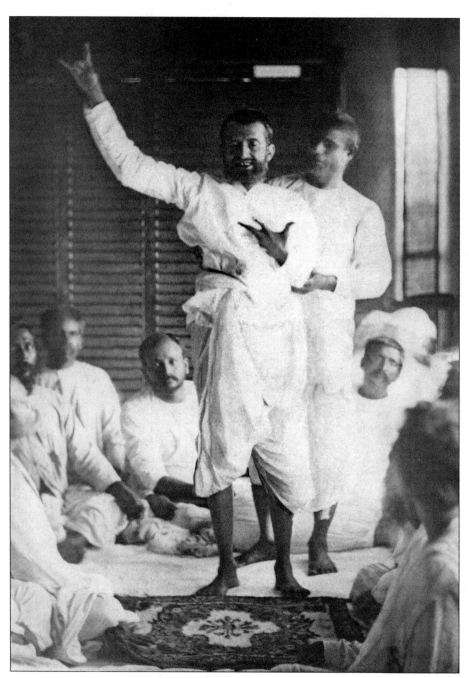

Ramakrishna in samadhi during a kirtan at Keshab Sen's house in Calcutta, 21 September 1879. His nephew, Hriday holds him. Brahmo devotees sit on the carpet.

378

God because God has to take a human form to demonstrate true religion to them." Moreover, Krishna said in the Gita that when religion declines and irreligion prevails, God incarnates in every age to protect the virtuous and punish the wicked. That is why we find many avatars (divine incarnations) in Hinduism. As the same moon rises in the sky again and again, so the same God descends to earth as a human being in different places and at different times to fulfill the need of the age and to lead us to the goal of human life. This is not a fantasy: the lives of Rama, Krishna, Buddha, Moses, Christ, Muhammad, Chaitanya, and Ramakrishna attest to the Gita's statement.

On 6 February 1898, Swami Vivekananda composed the following salutation mantra to Ramakrishna: "O Ramakrishna, establisher of righteousness, embodiment of all religions, the greatest of the avatars, salutations to Thee." The word "greatest" created some controversy. Here are some explanations: Of course, each avatar is God in human form and they are all endowed with equal powers, but each one does not release the entirety of his or her power. Think of a golfer who has sufficient strength to hit a ball a long distance but strikes the ball only as hard as necessary to reach the next hole. Similarly, avatars release only enough power to fulfill their mission in a particular age. For example, Rama killed Ravana and other demons who were disrupting the peace; Krishna destroyed Kamsa, Shishupala, and many unrighteous beings who were killing and torturing innocent people; Buddha fought against animal sacrifice, ritualism, and priestcraft; Christ wanted to establish the religion of love and compassion by trying to remove hypocrisy and injustice. We also find that all the past avatars emphasized the virtues of truth, righteousness, justice, good conduct, devotion, and detachment.

In this modern age, Ramakrishna did not kill any demons, nor did he fight any person. Rather, he destroyed the greatest demon that plagues the human mind: doubt regarding God's existence. It is easier to kill a demon or an unrighteous person than to eradicate doubt. Ramakrishna's ecstasies, visions, and experiences of samadhi proved that God exists; thus, he removed all doubts about God in this age. Moreover, he demonstrated how one can realize God, and he even imparted spiritual experiences to many with a touch.

On 1 March 1885, Ramakrishna told M. about one of his experiences: "I saw Satchidananda come out of this sheath [his body]. It said, 'I incarnate myself in every age.'...I saw that it is the fullest manifestation of Satchidananda; but this time the Divine Power is manifested through the glory of sattva."[1] It is due to the preponderance of the sattva quality in

Ramakrishna that he experienced samadhi many times a day. This has not been seen in other avatars, to our knowledge.

As all rivers lead to the ocean, so all religions are different paths to God. Among avatars, only Ramakrishna practised different religions. He proclaimed, "As many faiths, so many paths." In this way he established an ideal harmony of religions for our present age — in which religions are in conflict, and hatred and violence are rampant. Ramakrishna also repeatedly stated that the goal of human life is to realize God. He taught a religion badly needed today, a religion that is constructive and not destructive, scientific and not fanatical, practical and not theoretical, rational and not superstitious, universal and not parochial. Truly, Ramakrishna worked to create unity in our time.

Some followers in every religion think that their prophet is the greatest. Once Sariputra said to Buddha, "You are the manifestation of supreme knowledge, and none is greater than you."

Buddha replied, "Do you have knowledge of the past arhats?"

"No, I do not, Lord."

"Are you aware of the knowledge of the present Buddha?"

"No, Lord."

"Then how do you dare make such a bold statement?"

"I made this statement based on the limits of human understanding and by accepting the standard of the highest ideal of Buddhahood."[2]

Similarly, Vivekananda used the phrase "the greatest of the avatars" based on his understanding of Ramakrishna and his own spiritual experience. Vivekananda himself admitted that he understood very little of the infinite Ramakrishna. He said: "To remove all corruption in religion, the Lord has incarnated himself on earth in the present age in the person of Sri Ramakrishna. The universal teachings that he offered, if spread all over the world, will do good to humanity and the world."[3] Some of Ramakrishna's Westernized disciples were amazed when they saw how their Master faced agnostics, atheists, sceptics, and materialists, silencing them through his infallible logic, apt and convincing illustrations, magnanimous personality, and spiritual power — even though he had very little formal education.

It is not proper to judge the greatness of avatars with our limited understanding, yet from a worldly standpoint we do see a difference in the manifestation of each avatar. God smiles at the ignorance of His children when Hindus, Christians, Buddhists, Muslims, and others quarrel among themselves about the greatness of their religion and their respective prophets. But all quarrels and hatred will stop when they realize that

God is One without a second and that they all are His children. This is the attitude that Ramakrishna taught humanity in the modern age.

The extent of Ramakrishna's activity

All avatars travelled to some extent to fulfill their mission and spread their message. Ramachandra's activities were carried out in Ayodhya, Chitrakut, Dandakaranya, Panchavati, Rameswaram, and Sri Lanka; Krishna's movements and activities took place in Mathura, Gokula, Vrindaban, Dwaraka, and Kurukshetra; Buddha carried his message to Nepal, Uttar Pradesh, and Bihar during his lifetime; Jesus preached in Galilee, Samaria, Judea, and Idumea. At that time the population of the world was not as large as it is now and many regions were undiscovered. People now call the world a global village. Although Ramakrishna went on pilgrimage to Deoghar, Varanasi, Mathura, Vrindaban, Prayag, and Navadwip, he did not travel very much to spread his message. He mainly stayed at the Dakshineswar temple garden and now and then visited nearby Calcutta by horse carriage.

It was once said that the sun never set on the British Empire. During Ramakrishna's time, Calcutta was the capital of British India, the citadel of materialistic civilization. (Delhi became the capital in 1912.) Many people in Calcutta imitated the English lifestyle and were carried away by the current of Western culture. When the Master referred to "Calcutta people," he meant the city's Westernized and worldly inhabitants. They were slaves of the British, beggars in search of name and fame, and their main goal was the enjoyment of lust and gold. They were bound souls and atheists. When he referred to "Calcutta people," the Master meant all the atheistic hedonists of the world. "Calcutta people" can also be found in Europe, America, and other parts of the globe. Ramakrishna remarked: "It is not in England alone that one sees attachment to worldly things. You see it everywhere."[4]

With his sharp, discriminating intellect, Ramakrishna understood that a life based on worldly enjoyment cannot bring permanent peace and happiness. He knew that by confronting the materialistic milieu of Calcutta, he could resist the sway of materialistic culture throughout the world. If the capital is conquered, then it is not necessary to conquer the entire country.

In various ways, Ramakrishna devoted his life to helping the people of Calcutta. But he especially tried to build up their spiritual life, the source of eternal peace and happiness. In fact, most people of the world run after lust and gold. Ramakrishna conquered those two invisible enemies of spiritual life, saying, "*Kamini kanchan maya* — lust and gold are maya. They cannot make people happy permanently." The world was in need of Ramakrishna, who was fully capable of giving a fitting answer to the hedonistic and capitalistic philosophers of the West.

Once Ramakrishna went to see Fort William, the British fort in Calcutta. Just as he arrived by carriage, a Sikh regiment was marching there. When the soldiers saw him, they dropped their rifles on the ground and bowed down to him, shouting, "Victory to the guru!" The British commander-in-chief was nonplussed. When he asked the Sikh soldiers about their unusual behaviour, they replied that it was the custom of their religion to show respect for their guru in that manner. Thus Ramakrishna conquered the British fort by merely sitting in his carriage. It was not even necessary for him to step out of the vehicle. This was truly amazing! The Master later compared the road to Fort William with the path to perdition. He said: "Men do not realize how far they are dragged down by women. Once I went to the Fort in a carriage, feeling all the while that I was going along a level road. At last I found that I had gone four storeys down. It was a sloping road. A man possessed by a ghost does not know he is under the ghost's control. He thinks he is quite normal."[5]

Dynamism of Ramakrishna's message

It takes time for the message of an avatar to spread. Ramachandra's and Krishna's eternal messages of truth and righteousness were recorded by Valmiki and Vyasa in Sanskrit, and they are still spreading throughout the world. Buddha's disciples recorded 84,000 of his teachings in the Tripitakas. After 400 years, his message spread during Emperor Ashoka's reign in 250 BCE. Christ's teachings were recorded by Matthew, Mark, Luke, and John in the New Testament. It takes only two and an half to three hours to read what Christ said in the Bible, but those immortal teachings are still spreading. In 597 CE, during the time of Pope Gregory the Great, Augustine brought Christianity to England. At that time, it was easy to proselytize: if the king and queen were converted to a particular religion, all of their subjects would accept that religion. But those days are gone.

Science and technology have made the world smaller. Ramakrishna's message encircled the globe within seven years of his passing away. His main disciple Swami Vivekananda presented his guru's message of universal religion at the Parliament of Religions in Chicago in 1893. Yet even now the spiritual current of Ramakrishna has not become fully manifest. The Master himself said: "I have seen big steamers going by on the

Ganges, at the time hardly noticing their passing. But oh, my! What a terrific noise is heard after a while, when the waves splash against the banks!"[6] Similarly, people cannot recognize the avatar when he comes. His life and mission become more apparent after some time has passed.

Religion is supposed to bring peace and bliss. The Golden Rule is the same in all religions.

- Buddhism: "Hurt not others in ways that you yourself would find hurtful."[7]
- Christianity: "Do to others what you want them to do to you; this is the meaning of the Laws of Moses and the teaching of the prophets."[8]
- Hinduism: "Whatever you consider injurious to yourself, never do to others. This is the essence of dharma [righteousness]."[9]
- Islam: "No one of you is a believer until he desires for his brother that which he desires for himself."[10]
- Judaism: "What is hateful to you, do not do to your fellowman. That is the entire Law; all the rest is commentary."[11]

Despite all these wonderful teachings, there is so much intolerance, narrowness, bigotry, fanaticism, unrest, and mistrust among people of various religions, and the result is bloodshed.

Once an old rabbi from New York told me that he wondered what Moses, Jesus, Muhammad, Krishna, and Buddha think of all the hatred and animosity between followers of their religions. He thought they must be ashamed by the foolishness of their children, to whom they never taught such things.

A professor of world religions at Harvard Divinity School once asked this question of his students: "How can we solve the problem of religious intolerance and bloodshed in this world?"

A Muslim student replied: "This problem will be solved if all people in the world become Muslims."

A Christian student said that there would be no more problems if all people become Christians.

The professor replied: "But I see sectarian fighting among the Muslims. See how the Shias and Sunnis are fighting among themselves." Then, calling the students' attention to the fighting between the Catholics and Protestants in Ireland, the professor told this story:

"Once there was a peace conference that included a Catholic priest, a Protestant minister, and a Jewish rabbi. An angel appeared before them and asked how peace could be restored in Ireland.

The minister said: 'Peace will reign supreme if all Catholics leave Ireland.'

The priest said: 'There will be permanent peace if there is not a single Protestant here.'

The angel then asked the rabbi for his opinion, who said: "I have no personal opinion. Just attend to the wishes of these two gentlemen. Then there will be peace in Ireland."

Ramakrishna was born at a critical time of religious history. Referring to the significance of Ramakrishna's message for the modern world, Vivekananda said:

This is the message of Sri Ramakrishna to the modern world. "Do not care for doctrines, do not care for dogmas, or sects, or churches or temples; they count for little compared with the essence of existence in each man, which is spirituality; and the more that this is developed in a man, the more powerful is he for good. Earn that first, acquire that, and criticize no one, for all doctrines and creeds have some good in them. Show by your lives that religion does not mean words, or names, or sects, but that it means spiritual realization. Only those can understand who have felt. Only those who have attained to spirituality can communicate it to others, can be great teachers of mankind. They alone are the powers of light."

The more such men are produced in a country, the more that country will be raised; and that country where such men absolutely do not exist is simply doomed, nothing can save it. Therefore, my Master's message to mankind is: "Be spiritual and realize truth for yourself." He would have you give up for the sake of your fellow beings. He would have you cease talking about love for your brother, and set to work to prove your words. The time has come for renunciation, for realization; and then you will see the harmony in all the religions of the world. You will know that there is no need of any quarrel, and then only will you be ready to help humanity. To proclaim and make clear the fundamental unity underlying all religions was the mission of my Master. Other teachers have taught special religions which bear their names, but this great teacher of the nineteenth century made no claim for himself. He left every religion undisturbed because he had realized that in reality, they are all part and parcel of one eternal religion.[12]

In Ramakrishna's life can be found a synthesis of four yogas: karma, jnana, bhakti, and raja. Moreover, the philosophies of the three main schools of Vedanta — dualism, qualified nondualism, and nondualism — were blended in his teachings. He lived his life at the crossroads where many religious sects of India met. He never spoke a harsh word against any faith. He was so all-embracing that members of every sect thought that he was one of them. His all-encompassing love and compassion transcended sectarian narrowness and bigotry. Truly, Ramakrishna's life is a bridge between the ancient and the modern, between the East and the West.

Ramakrishna came to make religion simple. He knew that human beings in this age have complex personalities and little time to practise spiritual disciplines and think of God. Peace and bliss cannot be bought at the market; they can be acquired only through leading a spiritual life. For this reason, Ramakrishna's teachings are practical and universal, free from doctrines and dogmas. They do not need any commentary. Ramakrishna incorporated into his teachings parables, symbols, songs, stories, folklore, myths, scientific reasoning, anecdotes from ordinary life, and examples from nature as well as the behaviour of humans and animals. He seldom quoted the scriptures. He taught from his personal experience and explained the deep truths of spiritual life in an utterly simple way. Here are some examples of Ramakrishna's teachings, which suit all kinds of temperament.

1. You see many stars in the sky at night, but not when the sun rises. Can you therefore say that there are no stars in the heavens during the day? O human beings, because you do not find God in your ignorance, say not that there is no God.

2. God dwells in all beings, but all beings do not identify themselves with God, so they suffer.

3. Some people shed a jugful of tears to have children; some cry for money and property; but who longs to see God? Those who want God, find Him.

4. In this kaliyuga, a human being can attain perfection in three days. Those who cry with a longing heart for God day and night see Him.

5. Question: "How can one ascertain the state of perfection?"
   Answer: "As potatoes and eggplants become soft when they are boiled, so people become very soft or humble when they attain perfection. Their egos dissolve completely."

6. A room may be dark for a thousand years, but it is lighted instantly as soon as a lamp is lit. Similarly, one glance of God's grace can wipe away sins accumulated in thousands of births.

7. If one drops a salt doll, a cloth doll, and a stone doll in the ocean, the salt doll melts instantly and loses its individual existence. The cloth doll becomes soaked with water: It does not become one with it, and it maintains its own separate existence. Water does not enter into the stone doll at all. A free soul is like the salt doll, a worldly soul is like the cloth doll, and a bound soul is like the stone doll.

8. The sun may shine equally everywhere, but it reflects more clearly in clean water, mirrors, and other transparent objects. Similarly, God may dwell in every heart, but He manifests more completely in the hearts of holy people.

9. Tears of repentance and tears of joy come out from opposite corners of the eyes: the former from the inner corner and the latter from the outer corner.

10. Question: "Nowadays many preachers are preaching religion. What do you think of them?"
Answer: "It is like a man who has food for one person, but he has invited one hundred. After practising a little sadhana, he has started to make money by initiating disciples like a professional guru."

11. Question: "What is real preaching?"
Answer: "Real preaching requires that one be absorbed in God before preaching spirituality to others. He who tries to make himself free, preaches well. Hundreds of people from all directions come to one who is free and they ask for instruction. When the flowers bloom, bees come of their own accord."

12. Let the boat be in the water, but let not water be in the boat. Let a spiritual aspirant live in the world, but not let worldliness enter inside him.

13. The same God manifested here as Krishna and manifested there as Jesus.

14. God laughs twice. When two brothers divide the land, saying, "This part is mine and that part is yours," God laughs. He says to Himself, "The whole universe belongs to Me, but they say they own this portion or that portion." When the physician says to a patient's mother, "Don't be afraid, mother; I shall certainly cure your boy," God laughs. He says to Himself, "I am going to take his life, and this man says he will save it!"

15. When shall I be free? When "I" ceases to be. If "I" wants to remain, let it stay as a servant-I of God.

16. Neither sin nor mercury can be hidden.

17. One who eats radish belches radish; one who eats cucumber belches cucumber. What is inside of a person comes out through his or her speech.

18. One cannot see God without renouncing lust and gold.

19. Question: "What should I do with bad thoughts?"
Answer: "Let bad thoughts arise in the mind; they cannot do any harm until you do something wrong."

20. "If you want to understand after hearing one sentence, come to me. And if you want to understand after hearing a thousand sentences, go to Keshab Chandra Sen." A man asked him, "Please give me knowledge in one sentence." He said, "*Jagat mithyā Brahma satya* — This world is impermanent and Brahman is real."

21. One cannot achieve anything if there is any theft in the chamber of the heart [meaning hypocrisy].

22. Friend, as long as I live so long do I learn.

23. As many faiths, so many paths. Have steadfast devotion to your path, but never hate or criticize the paths of others.

24. God loves simplicity. Call on Him with a simple and pure mind. You will then surely find Him.[13]

Ramakrishna lived for only fifty years, but the impact of his life and message is immense. It is not possible for ordinary people to comprehend the greatness of avatars, so we try to have some understanding of them through the words of great thinkers and savants of the world.

Romain Rolland, a French writer and Nobel Prize winner, wrote: "I am bringing to Europe, as yet unaware of it, the fruit of a new autumn, a new message of the Soul, the symphony of India, bearing the name of Ramakrishna. The man whose image I here evoke was the consummation of two thousand years of the spiritual life of three hundred million people."[14]

The famous English historian Arnold J. Toynbee wrote: "Sri Ramakrishna's testimony to the harmony of religions...can make it possible for the human race to grow together into a single family — and, in the Atomic Age, this is the only alternative to destroying ourselves."[15]

Joseph Campbell, an American writer and Orientalist, wrote: "Sri Ramakrishna cut the hinges of the heavens and released the fountains of divine bliss."[16]

The Russian novelist and social reformer Leo Tolstoy said: "Wonderful sayings! Ramakrishna...a remarkable sage."[17]

The Indian nationalist leader Mahatma Gandhi wrote: "The story of Ramakrishna's life is a story of religion in practice. His life enables us to see God face to face."[18]

It is said that we have enough religion to hate one another, but not enough to love one another. Religious sects are not bad, but sectarianism is horrible: it teaches people to hate others. This world would be an awfully boring place if all people looked alike, thought alike, ate alike, dressed alike, drove the same type of car, prayed the same prayer, learned the same things, and died from the same kind of disease.

Vivekananda once said: "It is the clash of thought, the differentiation of thought, that awakens thought. Now, if we all thought alike, we would be like Egyptian mummies in a museum, looking vacantly at one another's faces."[19]

In this diverse world, if we cannot live together in peace, we shall die together by killing each other. Love unites and hatred separates. Hatred cannot be conquered by hatred; it can be conquered only by love. All avatars teach us to love one another, but religious bigotry, narrowness, and superstition separate us from one another.

Variety is the spice of life. A restaurant that lists various kinds of food on its menu attracts many people because people get bored if they eat the same food every day. Ramakrishna did not care for one-sidedness. He used to say, "In order not to become monotonous, I eat a variety of dishes."[20] Again, he said: "One player is producing only a monotone on his flute, while another is creating waves of melodies in different ragas and raginis. That is my attitude. Why should I produce only a monotone when I have an instrument with seven holes?"[21]

In this present age, Ramakrishna played a variety of notes on his divine flute and created a symphony to blend all the 'isms' of the world. He taught humanity to listen to the splendid symphony of the Soul and realize the divine unity in the diversity of this world.

15

Meditation on the New Year

There is a custom in every country of the world to welcome the New Year. On the first day of the New Year we try to feel a new impetus or motivation towards life. A desire for newness is hidden in every human heart, so human beings always aspire to see something new, to hear something new, to do or say something new. We look at the activities of the previous year and begin to reckon the profit and loss. What did we achieve last year? What did we lose? What did we learn? To retrieve whatever we lost, or could not achieve or learn, we make New Year's resolutions. We start our New Year with new enthusiasm and zeal. We pray to God to give us patience and perseverance to carry out our resolution.

Welcoming the New Year is a cultural tradition. On New Year's Day, ancient Babylonians would take a vow to repay their debt to God. The ancient Romans would make various solemn resolves to their God Janus — which is why the name of the first month is January in the Julian Calendar. On New Year's Day, many Christians pray to God to preserve their resolutions. Among the Jews, it is customary to beg forgiveness for any wrongdoings committed during the previous year. On New Year's Day, Hindu merchants go to temples with new account books and offer worship for the success of their businesses.

Although there is no connection with the New Year to religion in most cultures, it is a day of festivity. In India, on the first day of the year people go to parks, seaside resorts, or gardens to picnic. Some go to the zoo with their children. Some visit their friends and families, and some go to Belur Math, Dakshineswar, and other temples to worship. On New Year's Day thousands of people go to the Cossipore garden house, where

Cossipore garden house. Ramakrishna became the kalpataru (a wish-fulfilling tree) on 1 January 1886, near the curve of the mango tree.
(*Photo illustration by Diane Marshall.*)

Sri Ramakrishna became the kalpataru (the wish-fulfilling tree) on 1 January 1886 and blessed the devotees.

In the United States, New Year's Day is generally observed with parties, parades, and picnics. Some people go to church to pray, and some make New Year's resolutions like these for self-improvement:

1. Improve physical well-being: eat healthy food, lose weight, exercise more, eat better, quit drinking alcohol and smoking, get rid of bad habits.
2. Improve mental well-being: think positively, laugh more often, enjoy life.
3. Improve finances: get out of debt, save money.
4. Improve career: perform better at one's current job, or get a better job.
5. Improve education: get a better education, learn something new, read more books.
6. Improve self: become more organized, reduce stress, be less grumpy, watch less television, get along with people.

Our Vedanta centres in the United States observe New Year's Day in various ways: Some centres start with midnight meditation and prayer. Some centres observe a vigil from six o'clock in the morning to six o'clock in the evening; during this time, monks and devotees take turns each hour in silently repeating their Ishta-mantra. Some centres conduct retreats where they discuss the episode of Ramakrishna as the kalpataru.

Although more than 130 years have passed, people from all over the world have not forgotten that memorable day: 1 January 1886. One proof of this is the Kalpataru Festival that is held at Cossipore every year. On that day nearly a million people stand in line from morning to night to bow down to Ramakrishna's picture in his room, and they pray to him to fulfil their wishes. That day is now the object of our meditation.

Meditation has infinite power. It is not limited by time. One can turn a past event into a present event in the mind through meditation. We can imagine that it is New Year's Day and visualize Ramakrishna lying on his bed in the southwest corner of his room at the Cossipore garden house. There was no cot in his room: his bed was a mattress placed on a carpet and a mat. It was convenient for him to sleep that way, because his body was weak from cancer. The Master is chanting the Divine Mother's name and praying for the welfare of the devotees.

During the Master's stay in Dakshineswar, he used to pace his room in the late hours of the night and pray to God. He could see then the spiritual progress of his devotees and remove their obstacles if there were any. Truly, he loved the devotees, because he had experience that the Bhakta (devotee), Bhagavata (scripture), and Bhagavan (God) are one. If there were no devotees, then with whom would God play? If there are no companions, God cannot enact his divine play.

In Cossipore, the Master continued to observe his daily routine. Sashi Maharaj would help the Master with his morning ablutions. The Master would brush his teeth with a twig and scrape his tongue. He always kept his mouth clean because he used it for chanting God's name and talking about Him to the devotees. He then drank a little fruit juice or milk. He could not eat solid food because of the cancer in his throat. Holy Mother would prepare farina or tapioca pudding for his lunch. After lunch, he would take some rest. After his noon rest on 1 January 1886, he felt better than usual. At 3 p.m. he told his nephew: "Ramlal, I feel good today. Let us go for a walk in the garden." Ramlal replied: "Yes, uncle. You look good. Let us go for a walk."

The Master put on a red-bordered dhoti, a shirt, a coat, a broad red-bordered chadar, a cap that covered his ears, and sandals. He took his walking stick. Latu Maharaj and Ramlal helped him go down the wooden steps to the ground floor. He then came out of the house through the western door and began to walk on the garden path. Because it was a holiday, more than 30 people had come from Calcutta to see the Master. Some were waiting inside the house and some were under the trees in the garden. They were talking amongst themselves about the Master. When they saw him, they all stood up reverently and bowed down. They were delighted to see him in the garden, and they followed him as he walked.

When Latu Maharaj saw that the Master was walking with the devotees, he returned to the Master's room. He and Sharat Maharaj then took the opportunity to clean his bed and room thoroughly. They quickly removed the Master's cotton mattress, quilt, and pillow and placed them in the sun on the southern roof to air them out. In the winter season, having a warm mattress and pillow are very comfortable. The disciples' love, feeling, and thoughtful service for their guru overwhelm us. People always try to make the person whom they love happy and comfortable.

It was a pleasant and sunny afternoon. The red brick-dust garden path went from the main house to the south and then turned right towards the gate. The Master proceeded slowly southward to the gate. The devotees followed him at a little distance. When he reached the midpoint of the path between the house and the gate, the Master saw Girish, Ram, Atul, and a few others under a tree on the west side of the path. They bowed down and came over to him joyfully.

Before anyone had spoken a word, the Master addressed Girish, asking him: "Girish, what have you seen and understood [about me] that makes you say all these things [that I am an avatar and so on] to everyone, wherever you go?" Girish responded by kneeling down at the Master's feet, folding his hands before his raised face, and saying in a voice choked with emotion: "What more can I say of Him? Even the sages Vyasa and Valmiki could find no words to measure His glory!"[1]

Ramakrishna was deeply moved by Girish's words and his conviction. He stood still on the red brick-dust garden path, his whole body covered in goosebumps as his mind ascended into ecstasy. His whole face beamed with divine bliss. Seeing that wonderful form of the Master, the devotees' joy knew no bounds. Exultant, they began to shout, "Jai Sri Ramakrishna, Jai Sri Ramakrishna — Victory to Sri Ramakrishna!" Some collected flowers from the garden and offered them to him, and some took the dust of his feet. This scene reminds us of a couplet from devotional Vaishnava literature: "O Radhanath, Krishna, please give us the dust of your feet. Let us smear some dust on our bodies, and some we shall keep with us. O Krishna, give us the dust of your feet. May we have unflinching devotion at your blessed feet birth after birth. O Radhanath, the beloved of Radha, please give us the dust of your feet."

We regret that there was nobody there with a camera to take a picture of the Master in samadhi on the garden path. How wonderful it would be to have such a photograph! However, if we did have such a picture, we would be deprived of the bliss that our limitless imagination can bring.

After some time, the Master came down from deep samadhi (*antar-dashā*) to a half-ecstatic state (*ardhya-bāhya-dashā*). Smiling, he said three sentences: "What more need I tell you? I bless you all. May you all be illumined!"[2] After uttering those words, he became overwhelmed with love and compassion for his devotees, and went into ecstasy. Please remember that this auspicious occasion was the last time that he appeared outside the house to a group of devotees, blessing them collectively. On this day he expressed his last message to all. (Of course, later he blessed and advised some devotees individually.)

Swami Saradananda wrote:

That selfless and profound blessing touched the devotees deep within their hearts and they became mad with joy. They forgot time and space; they forgot the Master's illness; they forgot that they had vowed not to touch the Master until his recovery. They saw that a wonderous divine being had come down to them from heaven and was calling to them affectionately; they also felt that their suffering grieved him and that he was carrying in his heart an infinite pain and compassion for them and offering them shelter as selflessly as a loving mother. They became anxious to bow down to him and take the dust of his feet. Their cries of "Victory to Ramakrishna" resounded in all directions as one by one they bowed down to him. As they touched his feet, the ocean of the Master's compassion burst through all bounds and created an astonishing phenomenon. Almost every day in Dakshineswar we had seen the Master become overwhelmed with compassion and grace and bless some devotees with his powerful divine touch. On this day, remaining in a semiecstatic state, he began to touch each devotee present in a similar way, and their joy was boundless.

The devotees understood that from this day on, the Master would no longer conceal his divinity from them or from anyone else in the world. They had no doubt that from now on all sinners and sufferers — despite their shortcomings, lack of spirituality, or feelings of inadequacy — would find shelter at his blessed feet. Seeing the Master in that unique and exalted state, some became speechless and could only watch him as if bewitched. Some called out loudly to everyone inside the house to come and be blessed by the Master's grace. Others picked flowers from the garden and began to worship him, uttering mantras and showering him with flowers.[3]

On Easter some devout Christians meditate on the last seven utterances of Christ: 1. Father, forgive them, for they know not what they're doing. 2. (*To the thief*): I assure you, today you will be with me in paradise. 3. (*To his mother*): Dear woman, here is your son. 4. My God, my God, why have you forsaken me? 5. I am thirsty. 6. It is finished! 7. Father, I entrust my spirit into your hands.

Now we shall meditate on the last three public sentences of Ramakrishna:

1. *"Tomāder ār ki balba* — What more need I tell you?" From 1879 to 1885 the devotees and disciples visited the Master and listened to his message. The blessed M. recorded 177 days of the Master's conversations in the *Kathamrita* (*Gospel*). Still there is no limit to how many incidents and talks of the Master we have lost.

According to an ancient Greek legend, swans sing a beautiful song just before dying. This is the origin of the phrase "swan song." Like that legendary Rajahamsa (swan), Paramahamsa Ramakrishna was in essence saying to his devotees: "Look, I have been giving my message to you continually for the last seven or eight years. Now my throat has developed cancer due to speaking for long periods day after day, and also due to taking upon myself the sins of others. I have no more strength to speak. I am now at the end of my life, and I am telling you the most important thing. Listen carefully."

The Master used to teach according to the needs of each individual. Once a man came and said, "Sir, give me knowledge in one sentence." The Master replied: "Brahman alone is real and the world is unreal." On another occasion he told someone: "If you want to know in a thousand words, go to Keshab Sen. And if you want to know in one sentence, come here."

2. *"Asirbād kori — I bless you all."* In Bengali, the word "I" does not appear. It is implied by the verb "kori." The Master meant to say, "I bless you all," but he could not utter the word "I" and "mine." His ego was completely uprooted, and his "I" was merged with God's "I".

On 28 November 1883, the Master went to see Keshab Sen, who was then very ill. Keshab's mother requested the Master to bless her son so that he would recover. The Master gravely said: "What can I do? God alone blesses all. Please pray to the Divine Mother, who is the bestower of all bliss. She will take away your troubles." When he was asked to bless Keshab's eldest son, the Master said, "It is not given to me to bless any-one." With a sweet smile he stroked the boy's body gently.[4]

Ramakrishna's mysterious "I" played out in different planes at differ-ent times. Swami Saradananda wrote:

> It is evident that after he attained nirvikalpa samadhi, the Master's lit-tle, or unripe, "I" completely disappeared. And whatever I-ness was left saw itself as ever connected with the Cosmic, or ripe, "I". Sometimes it would feel itself to be a limb or a part of the Cosmic "I", and sometimes it would ascend gradually to the level of the Cosmic "I" and merge in It. The Master could therefore grasp all ideas within all minds because all ideas of all minds in the world spring from that Cosmic "I". Because the Master was always identified with that all-pervading "I", he was able to know and understand any ideas that arose in the Cosmic Mind. In that exalted state, the Master's feeling "I am a part of God" would gradual-ly vanish and the Cosmic "I" or the Divine Mother's "I" would become manifest through him, and he would act as a guru, possessing the power of bestowing grace and inflicting punishment. At that time the Master would not appear to be humbler than the humblest: His demeanour, be-haviour with others, and other actions took a different form. Becoming like the mythical wish-fulfilling tree, he would ask a devotee, "What do you want?" as if he was ready to use his superhuman power to fulfill the devotee's desire immediately.[5]

When the Master became the kalpataru on that auspicious New Year's Day, he blessed his devotees. This blessing was infallible. It is not true that the Master became kalpataru only on that day; he had fulfilled the wishes of his disciples and devotees many times on different occasions earlier. Swamiji once said: "He is actually distributing love. Love, devotion, knowledge, liberation, and whatever one desires — Gora [Sri Ramakrishna] is bestowing upon us whatever he wishes. What wonderful power!"[6] Even now the Master listens to his devotees' prayers and fulfills them.

3. *"Tomāder sakaler chaitanya hok* — May you all be illumined!" This was Ramakrishna's last public utterance. The phrase is similar to the word *"Tattwamasi* — thou art that," a great Vedic dictum. In the Chandogya Upanishad, the sage Aruni instructed his son Svetaketu nine times using the phrase "Tattwamasi — That thou art." *Tat* = Brahman; *twam* = you; *asi* = are. Through this, Svetaketu attained Self-knowledge. Aruni told his son: "You have always been Brahman, but due to ignorance you were unaware of it. One attains the bliss of Brahman when ignorance disappears."

On that New Year's Day in Cossipore, many devotees were present, so the Master said, "May you all be illumined," meaning "Let your hidden Brahman-consciousness be awakened." The difference between *"Tattwamasi"* and *"Tomar chaitanya hok"* is the wording and not the meaning. But on that day the Master did not stop at saying "May you all be illumined"; he touched each devotee's chest, one by one, with the palm of his hand and transmitted spiritual power to them instantly. In Tantra, awakening someone's spiritual consciousness by touch is called *Shāmbhavi* initiation.

What is this consciousness? Spiritual consciousness is the *chit* aspect of *Sat-chit-ananda* Brahman. All kinds of knowledge come from this consciousness. This question arose in the Mundaka Upanishad: "What is that by knowing which all this becomes known?" That is Satchidananda Brahman. It is the light of all lights. When It shines, everything shines. Stars, moon, sun, lightning, and fire are lighted by the light of Brahman.

The Master once said: "One cannot know that Consciousness without awakening one's own spiritual consciousness. Futile is the human birth without the awakening of spiritual consciousness." For this reason the Master awakened spiritual consciousness in the hearts of his devotees on this New Year's Day.

Spiritual consciousness is knowledge. The Master further said: "It is to know one's own Self and keep the mind in It. One must light the lamp of Knowledge in one's heart to see the Divine Mother. After attaining knowledge, when a man lives in this world, he can see clearly the difference between good and bad, real and unreal. The sign of knowledge is passion for God, the awakening of the kundalini, a peaceful nature, and the absence of pride."

The Master came to lead human beings from darkness to light, bondage to liberation. So he blessed the devotees, saying, "Be illumined." He knew the mind goes up and down in the dualistic plane, so there is no permanent peace and happiness there. The nondualistic experience is the final goal in spiritual life. The Master said, "First tie the knowledge of nonduality in a corner of your cloth, then do as you please. Consciousness is awakened after the knowledge of the nondual Brahman. After this realization comes eternal bliss." On that New Year's Day, the Master bestowed his supreme blessing not only upon those 30 devotees, but also for future human beings. Among the four goals of human life — dharma (righteousness), artha (wealth), kama (esthetic desire), and moksha (liberation) — moksha is the supreme or ultimate goal. The scriptures say "*Jnānāt moksha* — liberation comes from Self-knowledge."

The main intention of the Master's blessing was to impart the knowledge of Brahman to devotees by destroying the fetters binding their hearts. The Brihadaranyaka Upanishad says: "This Brahman is the supreme goal, supreme glory, supreme abode, and supreme bliss. On a particle of this bliss other creatures live" (4:3:32).

On this auspicious New Year's Day, the Master broke the jar of bliss in front of everybody assembled in that garden. Akshay Kumar Sen wrote in *Ramakrishna Punthi*: "Sri Ramakrishna promised that before he left the world he would break the earthen jar in the market place. Let me tell you how the Master broke the jar." Then the author described the events of 1 January 1886. Ram Chandra Datta also wrote what the Master had said: "When I leave the world, I shall break the jar of love publicly."

The meaning of "breaking the jar in the market place" is "to reveal a mystery in front of all." However, this also implies that if the earthen jar is broken in the marketplace, its contents (generally sweets) come out and can no longer be sold. The treasure within the jar is gathered up by the public to enjoy — as during a festival when sweets are scattered in honour of Lord Hari for the devotees to collect.

On that New Year's Day, standing on the red brick-dust path at the Cossipore garden house, the Master became the kalpataru and broke the jar of love in front of his devotees. Tasting that supreme divine love, some became intoxicated, some peaceful, and some completely immersed in the bliss of the Atman. Out of exuberant joy they began to call others to partake of that joy. This is the sign of supreme love. The Master used to say, "Pure knowledge and pure love are the same."

Ram Datta wrote:

> On that day there was no limit to the devotees' joy. But, alas, who knew that it was his last act? Who knew that Ramakrishna would not distribute love anymore? At that time we had not an iota of knowledge, or it did not arise in our minds, that it was the day of breaking the jar of love which he had promised. We did not have the slightest inkling that the Master brought an end to his divine play. We had so much hope and expectation to see more of his lila, but he fulfilled everything with that single blessing, which was beyond our imagaination. We attained peace and bliss and fulfilled our self-interest. On that day a curtain dropped on his divine drama.[7]

Ramlal also provided information about what happened after that event. The Master returned to his room after blessing the devotees. As Lord Shiva drank the poison of this world to protect the creation, so the Master absorbed the poisonous sins of the devotees whom he had touched and began to suffer from a burning sensation. Ramlal recalled:

> The Master said to me, "Ramlal, my hands and feet are burning. Please bring some Ganga water and sprinkle it on me." He was extremely restless. I asked, "What happened?" He replied: "I came into this world secretly with a few close devotees, and now Ram [Ram Chandra Datta] is spreading my name. He brings all sorts of people here and asks me to touch and bless them. How much burden can I carry? I got this disease by taking the sins of these people upon myself. Look, I shall not stay in this world any longer." I consoled him: "No, no. You will not have to receive any visitors or touch anybody." Then I brought the Ganga water and washed his hands and feet, and gradually he calmed down.[8]

From then on, to protect the Master's body, Swami Niranjanananda would sit on the staircase leading to the Master's room holding a stick to prevent new visitors and sometimes even familiar devotees from entering.

The Master's *kalpataru-lila* and last public message are the objects of our meditation. On this day, the Master bestowed fearlessness to the devotees through Self-revelation, fulfilled their wishes, and lighted the lamp of wisdom in their hearts. However, God does not become the kalpataru only on one day; God is always the kalpataru. If we meditate daily on this lila of the Master, then he will appear before us every day as the kalpataru.

16

Blessed Meditation

People in this world seek positive results from their actions. Some expect good results even when they perform bad actions. We sometimes wonder what we shall achieve if we go to the shrine and close our eyes to meditate? Once in Madras a monk said to Swami Brahmananda, "Maharaj, I am practising japa and meditation but getting no *phal* (fruit or result)."* Maharaj listened but kept quiet. In the evening, when that monk went to the shrine to practise spiritual disciplines, Maharaj said to his attendant, "Please put this apple in front of that monk." When the monk later came to bow down to Maharaj, he asked, "Have you received the *phal* (fruit) of your meditation?"

Most of the time people are trying to fulfill their desires and self-interest. Krishna mentioned in the Gita: "To work alone you are entitled, never to its fruit. Wretched are they who work for results." We are so selfish that we even make demands on our beloved in exchange for our love. What shall we get if we love our beloved Lord? If we bargain for love the result is extremely inferior.

Rabindranath Tagore wrote: "In the Bengali language, there are two words indicating love: *bhalo laga* or liking and *bhalobasa* or love. The meaning of these two words is poles apart. *Bhalo laga* means I like it; and *bhalobasa* means I love someone. When love is directed towards myself that is *bhalo laga* and when it is towards someone else, that is *bhalobasa*. The former yields the satisfaction of enjoyment and the latter, the joy of renunciation."

We think day and night of that person whom we love. We wish to

*In Bengali, *phal* means fruit or result.

offer our body, mind, and everything else to that person; and we wish for that person's eternal welfare. In family life, mutual love and service bring peace and happiness — and in spiritual life, love for God brings peace, joy, and liberation.

What shall we get from meditation? If one meditates regularly every day, it will bring auspicious results to one and others will also benefit. In *Bhatti Kāvyam*, a famous Sanskrit literature, King Dasharatha said to Sage Vishwamitra: "O Sage, you are practising meditation to end rebirth. This helped you to withdraw your mind from the sense world and to enter into the mysterious realm of the truth. Is that meditation propitious?" God is all-auspicious. Meditation helps us to understand that what God does is good for us.

Our ancient sages gave us unrestricted freedom regarding meditation. Patanjali said: "One can meditate on any object one likes. It will calm the mind." What a wonderful advice! There is no narrowness, no restriction, no diffidence. The sage gave us freedom to practise meditation with the understanding that we are seekers of God. However, if anyone tries to meditate on lust and gold it will be disastrous.

Some people think that concentration and meditation are the same; that is not correct. There is a difference between the two. An analogy: when a bee rapidly vibrates its wings and makes a *"gun-gun"* sound before sitting on a flower, that is concentration. When it sits on the flower motionlessly and begins to sip honey, that is meditation. To meditate is to fix the mind on the Chosen Deity uninterruptedly for an extended period. During meditation the aspirant becomes absorbed in the thought of the Ishta (Chosen Deity) and merges into the blissful ocean of Consciousness. The Garuda Purana discusses the timing of concentration, meditation, and samadhi: One unit of concentration is 12 units of the time spent doing pranayama; one unit of meditation is 12 units of the time spent in concentration multiplied by 12; and one unit of samadhi is 12 units of the time spent in meditation multiplied by 12.

A spiritual aspirant should practise japa and meditation according to the instruction of his or her guru. Later, when one becomes steadfast in this, one may experiment and try new methods of sadhana if one wishes. Ramakrishna himself demonstrated this in his life. After attaining illumination, the Master received the Divine Mother's command to stay in *Bhavamukha* — an exalted state in which the spiritual aspirant keeps his or her mind on the border between the Absolute and the Relative planes of consciousness. Concerning his spiritual adventures, Ramakrishna said: "One who lives near the sea sometimes has a desire to find out how many pearls are hidden in the ocean depths. Similarly, after realizing the Divine Mother and being constantly near Her, I thought that I should see Her multiple forms." As the Master saw his Divine Mother in manifold forms and in various moods, we shall try to see the Master in his various forms and moods. We practise japa and meditation in front of the Master's picture and ask ourselves: Will we spend our lives simply looking at a picture? Our minds oscillate between disbelief and doubt, and we experience dejection and monotony, disgust and lethargy. At this point, some aspirants stop their spiritual practices. At that time, one needs patience, holy company, the study of holy and inspiring books, pilgrimage, and above all, faith in the words of the guru.

A monk who went for tapasya (spiritual discipline) was suffering from restlessness and depression. Swami Turiyananda wrote to him on 11 July 1915:

> Never forget this adage of Swami Vivekananda: "Make your own fair — whether you have a companion or not." To whom else should you look for help? The Master used to say, "I am and my Mother is." That is all. Whom else do you want? The main thing is to adhere to the ideal with patience. If you can do that, gradually everything will be favourable. Hold on to the Master; you will be surprised at the result that will follow. The Master used to say, "An imitation custard-apple reminds one of the real fruit." Similarly, the Master's photograph will remind you of the Master. Feel his presence in his photograph and devote yourself to his service and worship. You will surely be imbued with his spirit.
>
> Just make up your mind to engage yourself in the Lord's work. Let others go wherever they please; you calmly stay in your place with your beloved Master. Let your body and mind be absorbed in him. What will you gain by running around? Days are passing by, never to return.[1]

We want to achieve spiritual experience and divine inebriation through meditation. There are two kinds of meditation on a Personal God: active and still. Still meditation is when a devotee is seated in front of the Master's picture in the shrine. The devotee is intently focusing on the Master's feet, knees, hands, chest, face, nose, eyes, ears, head, and entire body, and then closes his or her eyes and visualizes the Master's form in his or her heart. In active meditation, the devotee is not actually in motion, but instead uses his or her imagination to imagine that the Master is living and moving. For instance, he is worshipping the Mother Kali in the Dakshineswar temple, singing to her, offering food to her, or performing vespers. To visualize each of the Master's actions is also meditation. Thus we can create various themes for meditation on the Master in Dakshineswar, in Calcutta, and in other places. For example, we could visualize the Master listening to the Bhagavata in front of the Krishna temple in Dakshineswar. A light emanates from Krishna, touches the Master, and then touches the Bhagavata. The Master realizes then that Bhagavata (scripture), Bhakta (devotee), and Bhagavan (God) are one. We can visualize the Master crying in the Shiva temple, embracing Lord Shiva and saying, "O Mahadeva, there is no limit to the glory of your divine qualities." We can also visualize the Master sitting under the Panchavati tree facing the Ganges, talking to the Divine Mother. Scenes to be used for active meditation can be found throughout the pages of *The Gospel of Sri Ramakrishna* and *Sri Ramakrishna and His Divine Play*.

We can also use our imagination to meditate thus: In his room at Dakshineswar, the Master is seated on his small cot, with his feet dangling, facing east. A devotee is seated on the floor with his head on the Master's knees. He holds the Master's feet to his chest and begins to sing this song:

> Thou art my All in All, O Lord! — the Life of my life, the Essence of essence;
> In the three worlds I have none else but Thee to call my own.
> Thou art my peace, my joy, my hope; Thou my support, my wealth, my glory;
> Thou my wisdom and my strength.
> Thou art my home, my place of rest; my dearest friend, my next of kin;
> My present and my future, Thou; my heaven and my salvation.
> Thou art my scriptures, my commandments; Thou art my ever-gracious guru;
> Thou the Spring of my boundless bliss.
> Thou art the Way, and Thou the Goal; Thou the adorable One, O Lord!
> Thou art the Mother tender-hearted; Thou the chastising Father;
> Thou the Creator and Protector; Thou the Helmsman who dost steer
> My craft across the sea of life.[2]

Ramakrishna (*to the devotee*): "Aha, what a song! *Nātha tumi sarvaswa āmār* — Thou art my all in all, O Lord" — saying this the Master blessed the devotee, putting his hands on his head.

This is a wonderful example of an active meditation on the Master's lila.

According to the Bhagavata, "One should unite the mind with Krishna in whatever way possible" (7:1:31). Ramakrishna demonstrated how one can unite the mind with God through karma, bhakti, jnana, and yoga.

This union brings peace, while separation from God brings misery. A devotee went to his guru and said, "Swami, I have no peace of mind."

The guru answered, "I can tell you how to get peace."

"How?"

"Give up all desires."

"We live in this world with families. It is not possible to give up all desires."

"Well, then live with worry and anxiety," replied the guru.

The mind becomes calm and tranquil when one meditates on Brahman or the Ishta — and when the mind becomes calm, the world becomes calm. It is a great blessing to realize God in this present life; otherwise, it is a terrible disaster and one continues to go round on the wheel of birth and death.

Nowadays, few people understand the depth of and importance of meditation. In this world — especially in Western countries — some techniques of meditation are taught to calm the mind. Our scriptures have mentioned various methods of meditation. But meditation is not possible without purity of mind. For that reason, self-control is necessary. Every person in this world invariably meditates on someone or something, which is normal and natural. A tamasic man meditates on his enemy; a rajasic man meditates on objects of lust and gold; and a sattvic man meditates on God.

In the Bhagavata, while instructing Uddhava on meditation, Krishna used the phrase *"dhyāna mangalam"* (11:14:37), which means one should meditate on that object which will bring goodness, welfare, well-being, prosperity, liberation, and God-realization. Krishna taught meditation clearly and methodically to Uddhava, who was a jnani (Bhagavata, 11:14:32-46):

> First step: Concentrate the mind on the whole beautiful form of your Chosen Deity.
> Second step: Focus your entire mind on the Ishta's face and stop all other thoughts. Meditate on his smiling joyful face.
> Third step: Carry that smiling face into the infinite akasha (space) and merge into it.
> Fourth step: Forget the space and think no more. Be absorbed only in pure Brahman.

As light merges into light, so the Atman will be united with the Paramatman. By practising this meditation, one can transcend the threefold division of the mind: that is, the meditator, meditation, and the object of meditation; the seer, seeing, and the seen; the knower, knowledge, and the knowable. When this division dissolves, one attains supreme peace, nirvana.

Some people repeat their mantra mechanically but do not think of its meaning, so they do not get joy. Patanjali clearly stated: *Tat japah tat artha bhavanam* — Repetition of the mantra (Om) and meditating on its meaning [is the way to calm the mind] (1:28). When we repeat our Ishta-mantra and visualize the Ishta simultaneously, we get a taste of bliss and that calms the mind. How can one meditate on the Ishta and at the same time repeat his name? It is like a dancing girl who sings and dances simultaneously. How can one live in this world and think of God? Ramakrishna answered: "You must have noticed that a man with a carbuncle on his back speaks to others in his usual way; perhaps he attends to his daily duties also; but his mind is always on the carbuncle. It is like that. Live in the world like an immoral woman. Though she performs her household duties, her mind is fixed on her sweetheart."[3]

While repeating the mantra, one can meditate on one's Ishta in this way. Suppose a devotee of Rama is repeating the Rama-mantra and visualizing the following scene: his Ishta Rama is going to be the king of Ayodhya and a big festival is going on. The devotee becomes very happy. Then he becomes unhappy as he sees Rama, Sita, and Lakshmana banished to the forest. He becomes angry when he sees Ravana kidnapping Sita. Then he is joyful when Ravana is killed. Finally, he becomes very happy when Rama ascends to the throne of Ayodhya. Thus while repeating the mantra, the devotee's mind was absorbed in Rama.

Our minds are restless — there is no doubt about this. We experience this restlessness every moment. People love to watch movies because pictures flash on the screen continuously; there is a relationship between the mind and the movie because both are restless. Yet we can make this very restless mind travel to 11 different places connected with Ramakrishna and Holy Mother on a kind of spiritual adventure. One can practise japa, meditation, and prayer simultaneously and can affix the mind to the Ishta by visualizing the following scenes.

First place — Kamarpukur: Suppose that we repeat a mantra on Ramakrishna. Mentally we can go to Kamarpukur, sit in front of the Master's image, and repeat the Ishta-mantra 100 times. With each repetition of the mantra, we pray, "Master, please remove all our sufferings (*dukha*)." Thus we repeat the mantra, meditate on the form of the Ishta, and say the prayer. This practice will alleviate the mechanical feeling of mantra sadhana, enhance longing, and bring closeness with the Ishta through prayer. Truly, prayer is nothing but a dialogue between a devotee and God. Hazra asked the Master, "Does God listen to our prayers?" The Master replied: "Surely. I can assure you of that a hundred times. But the prayer must be genuine and earnest. Do worldly minded people weep for God as they do for wife and children?"[4]

Second place — Jayrambati: Human thought travels faster than anything in this world. Now we are in front of Holy Mother's image at Jayrambati. We shall again repeat the mantra 100 times, visualize the Mother's image, and connect this prayer with each mantra: "Mother, please remove our worldly desires (*bhog-vāsanā*)." As a result of 100 repetitions, we shall be able to meditate slowly and comfortably. The Master and Mother are not separate — the same consciousness took two different forms. Moreover, Ramakrishna is the embodiment of all gods and goddesses.

Third place — Udbodhan House: We are now at the Mother's shrine at Udbodhan, in Calcutta. We shall follow our practice of japa-meditation-prayer. As usual we shall repeat the mantra 100 times and the object of meditation will be the deity of each place. Here we shall pray, "Mother, please remove our delusion (*moha*)."

Fourth place — Dakshineswar Kali temple: In front of Mother Kali, we shall pray, "Mother, please destroy our egos (*ahamkāra*)." The format of japa-meditation-prayer will remain the same in all other places.

Fifth place — Dakshineswar Krishna temple: We shall pray in front of Krishna, "Lord, please make us pure (*pavitra*) and give us longing (*vyākulatā*) for God."

Sixth place — Dakshineswar Shiva temple: There are 12 Shiva temples in Dakshineswar. The Master embraced the image that is at the end of the north one, next to his room. We shall pray in front of that image: "O Lord Shiva, please accept our service (*sevā*)."

Seventh place — Ramakrishna's room in Dakshineswar: We shall visualize the Master seated on his small cot facing east. We shall pray to him, "Master, please give us pure love and devotion (*bhāva-bhakti*)."

Eighth place — The nahabat in Dakshineswar: We shall pray to the Mother, "Mother, be gracious and reveal yourself to us (*darshan*)."

Ninth place — Ramakrishna's room in Cossipore: We shall pray in front of his picture, "Master, may we never forget you (*tomāi jena nā bhuli*)."

Tenth place — The Ramakrishna temple in Belur Math: We shall prostrate ourselves at full length and pray to the Master, "*Sharanāgata, Sharanāgata, Sharanāgata* — we fully surrender to you."

Eleventh place — Holy Mother's temple in Belur Math: So far, we have completed 1,000 japa. We shall now finish the remaining eight times in front of the Mother's picture. She is the giver of knowledge, happiness, boons, and peace. We shall pray to her: "Mother, you are *Sarvamangalā* — all-auspicious. Bestow your grace on us (*kripā karo*). Do good to all. Bless all beings."

As there is no end to God's forms and qualities, so there is no end to his methods of meditation. Ramakrishna said: "The heart is a splendid place. Meditate on God there." During initiation, our gurus instruct us to meditate on the Ishta in the heart. Our scriptures say: "Those who carry the all-auspicious Lord in their hearts, they enjoy festivity every day, and attain always wealth and goodness." This is the benefit of meditation.

Left: 1. Ramakrishna's marble image in the Kamarpukur temple, installed in 1951 during the temple dedication.
Right: 2. Marble image of Sarada Devi in Jayrambati, installed in 1953 during her centenary.

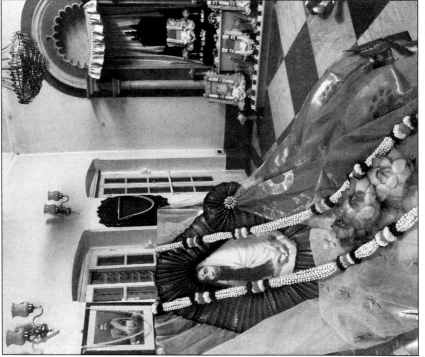

Left: 3. Sarada Devi's room and shrine at Udbodhan House, Calcutta.
Right: 4. Image of Bhavatarini Kali at Dakshineswar that Ramakrishna worshipped.

Left: 5. Krishna and Radha at Dakshineswar, worshipped by Ramakrishna.
Right: 6. Shiva at Dakshineswar, embraced by Ramakrishna.

409

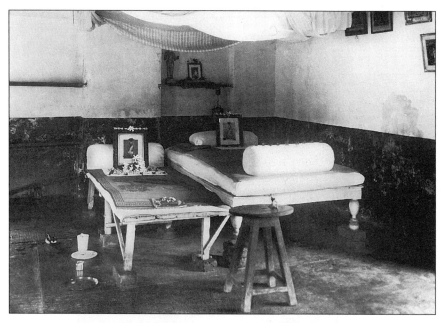

Above: 7. Ramakrishna's room at the northwest corner of the temple complex of Dakshineswar, where he lived for fourteen years.
Below: 8. Holy Mother image at nahabat in Dakshineswar.

Above: 9. Ramakrishna passed away in this room at the Cossipore garden house on 16 August 1886 at 1:02 a.m.
Below: 10. Marble image of Ramakrishna at Belur Math, installed in 1938.

11. Sarada Devi's shrine at Belur Math, built on her cremation site.

17

An Imaginary Interview with Ramakrishna

Reporter: Sir, you are a world-famous spiritual personality. On the occasion of your 175th birth anniversary, we would like to publish an interview with you in our magazine.* I shall ask you a few questions, and our readers will be delighted to hear directly from you. Please introduce yourself.

Ramakrishna: My name is Gadadhar Chattopadhyay; my village friends call me Gadai, but Calcutta people know me as Ramakrishna Paramahamsa. My father's name was Kshudiram Chattopadhyay, and my mother's, Chandramani Devi. I was born in 1836 in Kamarpukur village and lived there for sixteen years. In 1852, my elder brother Ramkumar took me to Calcutta for further education and to help him perform priestly rituals in people's homes. I lived with him in a small apartment on Bechu Chatterjee Street. Following that from 1855 to 1885, I lived at Dakshineswar as a priest of Rani Rasmani's Kali temple, but I performed the ritual for only few years. The last year of my life I lived in Shyampukur and Cossipore.

Reporter: We know that you were a great sādhaka [spiritual aspirant] and you had the vision of Kali. We will be very happy if you can tell us the story of your sadhana and what kind of obstacles you faced.

Ramakrishna: Look, Sharat [Swami Saradananda] wrote about my sadhana in detail in the *Lilaprasanga* [*Sri Ramakrishna and His Divine Play — Part 2*]. I spoke about spiritual disciplines at different times to the

---

*This interview was originally written in Bengali for *Udbodhan* magazine in 2011.

413

Ramakrishna in samadhi. This photo was taken on 10 December 1881, at the studio of Bengal Photographers, Calcutta.

devotees, and this was all recorded by Mohindar Master [M.] in the *Kath-amrita* [*The Gospel of Sri Ramakrishna*]. I don't like to repeat these things. Ask your readers to read those books. However, I will briefly describe the kind of obstacles I had to face. You see, after my vision of the Divine Mother, people of the Kali temple thought that I had gone mad. Mathur engaged a few āyurvedic doctors who prescribed Madhyam Narāyan oil and Vishnu oil. [These are different kinds of medicinal oils that have a cooling effect on the body.] These oils are used by mad people. I put several gallons of those oils on my head and my navel.

But you know, I slapped Rani Rasmani [Mathur's mother-in-law] in the Kali temple because she was thinking of a lawsuit during her time for meditation. On that very day, Mathur thought that I was really crazy, and that the cause of my craziness was my unbroken chastity. To break my chastity Mathur hired a prostitute. When I was performing *ārati* [vesper service] in the Kali temple, that prostitute entered my room and sat on my bed waiting for me. There was an oil lamp flickering in the corner of my room. When I came into my room, I saw a beautiful girl with *dāgar-dāgar chokh* [large, fascinating eyes]. When I saw her I ran out and called Haladhari and Hriday. They and some temple workers came to my room. Seeing a big crowd, that young girl hung her head in shame and left the room.

To tell you the truth, I passed through various ordeals during the time of my sadhana. I suffered from a burning sensation in my body and also from blood dysentery. I was completely oblivious to food and sleep. While I meditated, snakes would crawl over my knees, and birds would sit on my head searching for food in my hair. Moreover, the temple officials ill-treated me. Let me be frank with you, during that time, only one person stood behind me and saved the situation. That was a woman named Bhairavi Brahmani. She was a great yogi and was expert in Tantra scriptures. She saw all the signs of an avatar [divine incarnation] in me. She confronted Mathur, challenging him to bring scholars to the temple so that she could prove to them that these signs in me were the signs of *Maha Bhava* (the great ecstasy). Radha and Chaitanya had those signs.

Mathur was tired of spending money on my treatment. I had no health insurance. Anyhow, he invited Vaishnavcharan, Gauri Pandit, and other scholars to Dakshineswar. In that gathering Bhairavi quoted the scriptures to prove that my divine ecstasy was not madness. The scholars agreed with her, and that convinced Mathur. This was a great relief for me. Afterwards the Divine Mother showed Mathur the forms of Kali and

Shiva in my body, and from that time on Mathur served me with great devotion for fourteen years.

Reporter: Your father died when you were very young. Did your mother and brothers help you in your spiritual life?

Ramakrishna: No, they did not help me much in spiritual life. My eldest brother was 31 years older than me, and the second brother was 10 years older. They loved me and tried to educate me, but I was not interested in a bread-earning education. Then, when I went back for a visit to Kamarpukur, my mother thought that I was possessed by a spirit, so she engaged an exorcist to get rid of it. They could not understand my divine madness. When nothing worked, my mother and second brother thought that if they put the responsibility for a wife on my shoulders, then she would straighten me out. They began to search for a bride for me. Finally, I told them to go to the house of Ram Mukhopadhyay in Jayrambati, as his daughter was earmarked for me. There they located Sarada, a five-year-old girl. The marriage was arranged, my brother took out a loan of 300 rupees to pay the dowry, and I got married.*

Reporter: I know you are a Paramahamsa sannyasi and you have given up "woman and gold." Still, we are eager to know a little more about your married life.

Ramakrishna: I understand that you are curious to know about my married life. Sharat has written elaborately about why I got married in the *Lilaprasanga* [Part 3, Chapter 4]. Ask your readers to read about it there. Listen, Ram, Krishna, Buddha, and Chaitanya were avatars and they were all married. The first three of them had children and the last two left their wives. I married to demonstrate how one can transcend the physical relationship while being a married man. If I had given advice about renunciation without marrying, people would comment: "Well, he is a monk, so he is talking about renunciation. He has no knowledge of family life." Five years after my wedding, I took monastic vows from Tota Puri. Then I attained nirvikalpa samadhi and became absorbed in sadhana.

To tell you the truth, my luck was very good — I had a wonderful wife. Have you noticed that some men's mouths water when they praise their wives? They are so enamoured of their wives! You see, I don't belong to that group. When I married, Sarada was five years old. She was a village girl, very straight-forward, very simple, shy, hardworking,

*In those days, the dowry for a grown-up girl was high. Ramakrishna's family could not afford it, so they got a little girl for less money.

gentle, and extremely intelligent. I am glad that I did not marry a sophisticated city girl, who would demand jewelry, fancy clothes, cosmetics, a big house, a car, and all sorts of gadgets and furniture. They nag day and night for those things. Sarada never demanded anything from me.

Not only that, when she grew up, she never wrote me a letter. You are a modern reporter. You do not know how in the old days a wife would write letters to her husband. I am just giving you an example of how a bride would address her husband:

Sri charan prāyasi — I am ever devoted to your feet;

Sārā divānishi — the whole day and night;

Darshana piyāsi — I am hankering to see you;

Dāsi — I am your maidservant.

And the format of the husband's letter was:

Prānādhikā — You are greater than my heart;

Swadharma-pratipālikā — You maintained your *swadharma* (own duty) that the husband is the guru;

Srimati Mālati-manjari Devi — O Malati-manjari, you are endowed with beauty and fortune like a goddess;

Sāvitri — You are chaste and pure like Savitri in the Puranas;

Dharmāshriteshu — You have taken refuge in dharma, righteousness.

But those days are gone. Nowadays the husband and wife exchange their love through mobile phones, email, WhatsApp, and Skype. And they address each other as "Honey," "Sweetie," "My Dear," and they say "I love you," "I miss you," and so on. Nowadays they call each other by name. My wife was 19 years younger than me, but I respected her so much that I never called her by her name. I used to address her, saying: "Hello," "O Ramlal's aunt."

Observing that I had become a sannyasin, my mother-in-law used to lament that her daughter would not have any children. You see, old ladies all over the world are the same. They hanker for grandchildren. One day I told my mother-in-law: "Listen, mother, please do not worry. Your daughter will have so many children that her ears will burn from constantly being called 'Ma, Ma, Ma — Mother, Mother, Mother.'"

Reporter: The Brahmos say that you ill-treated your wife because you did not have any physical relationship with her.

Ramakrishna: It is not true. I never ill-treated my wife. Don't listen to those Brahmos; they are *bhogis* (enjoyers); they only understand sensual enjoyment. Their minds dwell below the level of the navel. I loved my wife very dearly. I never quarreled with her, and never hurt her even by throwing a flower. I always addressed her with respect, saying, *"tumi"* and not "*tui*."* One evening at Dakshineswar I was in an ecstatic mood. I heard a noise and thought it was my niece Lakshmi, so I said, "Shut the door as you go out," addressing her familiarly as *tui*. When I heard "All right," I realized it was Sarada. I was startled and cried: "Oh, it is you! I thought it was Lakshmi. Please forgive me for addressing you as *tui*." Look, we were married 27 years and not a single day did we have any misunderstanding or disagreement. Could you show me another married couple like us nowadays? I trained my wife in various ways and gave her many spiritual instructions. I even arranged for a teacher to teach her how to read primary books in Bengali. She could read the Ramayana and Mahabharata in Bengali, and she could also write. In the beginning she did not know how to cook properly, but then my sister-in-law, Shakambhari, taught her. She never met my eldest sister-in-law, Sarvajaya, who died in 1849 while giving birth to Akshay. Sarada served me and my old mother with love and great care. I installed a pitcher of bliss in her heart.

Reporter: According to the Hindu tradition, a wife used to consider her husband to be a god and worship his feet. In your case, you did the reverse. You put vermillion on your wife's forehead, applied *āltā* [red paint] on her feet, worshipped her with flowers and sandal paste, and bowed down to her, touching her feet. Is this right?

Ramakrishna: You modern people won't understand the mystery of my worship of her as the goddess Shodashi. Let me tell you frankly, you people consider women as 'second class' citizens and objects of enjoyment. Women all over the world are neglected, ill-treated, humiliated, persecuted, used and abused! By worshipping Sarada as the goddess Shodashi, I gave supreme honour and dignity to womankind. I awakened the Motherhood of God in her and offered the results of all my sadhanas to her so that she could carry my message and demonstrate the Motherhood of God to the world.

Reporter: One hundred and seventy-five years have passed since your birth. What changes do you see in the places where you lived?

Ramakrishna: Look, this world of maya is ever-changing. Only God never changes. Look at Kamarpukur, my birthplace. Now it has changed so much that I cannot recognize it without a guide. Kamarpukur used to be called a "queen of villages." Now it has become an "emperor of cities."

---

*In the Bengali language there are three forms of the second person pronoun. When addressing a revered elder, *apani* is used. To a person of equal rank and age, one says *tumi*. But the familiar form, *tui*, is used only when speaking to juniors or servants. Thus it would have been considered disrespectful had the Master knowingly addressed Holy Mother in this manner.

In fact, it has become a city with electric lights, a cinema house, TVs in most houses and antennas on thatched roofs, restaurants, hotels, photography studios, shops, schools and colleges, paved roads, cars, buses, and so on. People are building condominiums around my village, destroying the green paddy fields. The Ramakrishna Mission has kept only our three thatched huts and the mango tree that I planted, and has changed everything else. The Mission has installed my marble statue in a stone temple on my birthplace, and Raghuvir's thatched hut has been replaced with a brick structure. The Shiva temple of the Pyne family is gone, but the tin roof of the Lahas' school is still standing on some bamboo posts. A couple of *jilipi* [Indian sweet] shops are still there.

You ask about change? I remember when I first went to Calcutta with my brother via the Telo-Bhelo meadow. We had to cross four big rivers — the Dwarakeswar, Mundeswari, Damodar, and Ganges. But now bridges have been constructed over all those rivers. Previously it would take three days to reach Calcutta from Kamarpukur, and now you can reach there in two to three hours by car. You can have your breakfast in Calcutta, lunch in Kamarpukur, and dinner back in Calcutta. There are wonderful guesthouses with running water, electricity, and other modern facilities.

Reporter, look at the irony of fate! The landlord of Dere village evicted my honest father from our parental home because he refused to give false witness in favour of the landlord. Now the landlord's palatial building has been reduced to ruins, and the villagers of Dere have built a temple with a marble statue of me on our old family property. Just see, truth always triumphs.

Reporter: You were present during the dedication ceremony of the Dakshineswar temple in 1855. What changes do you see there?

Ramakrishna: Mother Kali's image in the temple is unchanged, and so is the temple complex. You will have to understand that those buildings are over 150 years old and so they have deteriorated to a great extent. But somehow the descendants of Rasmani are continuing to repair and repaint those buildings. The floor of my room was of red cement; now it has been changed to mosaic. They have kept my cots as they were and put lots of pictures in my room. You see, I collected some pictures and images — Kali, Krishna, Rama, Chaitanya and his kirtan party, Dhruva, Prahlada, Christ extending his hand to Peter, plus a marble image of Buddha, and also an image of Ramlala. They created a spiritual atmosphere in my room. But I am sorry to tell you that some have been stolen, especially my beloved Ramlala.

During Rasmani's time, I repaired the broken foot of the image of Krishna and installed that image on the altar. In 1930, her descendants replaced the old Krishna image with a new one. And the image of Krishna that I repaired is on an altar in the north room of the Krishna temple. Music is no longer played from the northern nahabat and Sarada's marble statue has been installed there. During the centenary of the Dakshineswar temple in 1955, Rani Rasmani's temple was dedicated between my room and the nahabat. My beloved banyan tree in the Panchavati is dead and so also the bel tree. They were witnesses to my sadhana. The sadhan kutir, where I practised Advaita sadhana, was a thatched hut — now it is a brick building. No one can stop the flow of time. The village of Dakshineswar is now part of the city of Calcutta. Two bridges have been constructed over the Ganges near the south side of the Dakshineswar temple. A meditation cottage has been built near the pine grove on the north. The kuthi has become a museum and my statue has been installed in my previous room there. Recently they built a flyover on the previous road towards the temple gate. If you really want to know more about Dakshineswar during my time, then read Mohindar Master's description of the temple garden of Dakshineswar in the *Kathamrita* [see the appendix of *Ramakrishna as We Saw Him*].

Reporter: Sir, Dakshineswar is really a marvelous place and you lived there for thirty years. Now it is a historical as well as holy place, and every day many people visit your playground.

Ramakrishna: I really loved Dakshineswar; it was my sadhan-place and the place of my divine play. Once I wanted to leave Dakshineswar, but Mathur did not let me. I told him that I would stay as long as he was alive. But he said to me: "Father, my wife, Jagadamba, loves you, so please stay." I said: "All right, as long as she lives, I will stay." Again he said, "Father, my son Dwaraka is very fond of you." "All right, as long he lives, I will stay," I said. Mathur knew who I was, so he did not want me to leave Dakshineswar. However, Dwaraka died in 1878 and Jagadamba died in 1881. I left Dakshineswar in 1885 and went to Calcutta for my cancer treatment. I lived in Shyampukur for 70 days. I could not stay there longer because I could not bear the pollution from the coal smoke that came from the kitchens in the neighbourhood. I wanted to return to Dakshineswar, but Mathur's son Trailokya did not allow me to come back. But as it was hard for me to breathe in polluted city of Calcutta, the devotees rented a nice garden house in Cossipore, where I stayed till the end of my life.

Reporter: Sir, please tell us about your disciples.

Ramakrishna: Those stories are all published in many books. Ask your readers to read them. However, I will tell you a few things: My main disciple, Narendra [Swami Vivekananda], used to think that I was an unlettered person. I told him categorically that I knew the alphabet. Perhaps you have seen my signature, "Sri Gadadhar Chattopadhyay," in some printed books. Moreover, I copied some books, such as the stories of Harishchandra, Mahirāvan, Subāhu, and Yogodyā, which you may find now in the Belur Math museum. The Divine Mother taught me the essence of all the scriptures.

Narendra was proud of his learning and intellect. He used to tell me: "Sir, you are illiterate. What can you teach me?" I told him: "Very good, I will not have to talk then. You just come here and enjoy this beautiful temple garden." Afterwards, observing my samadhi and the depth of my spiritual experiences, he was puzzled. One day he finally said to me, "Sir, could you give me some medicine so that I can forget what I have learned?"

Really, I had some wonderful disciples. I trained them and transmitted my spirituality to them so that they could carry my message. Now people are amazed when they learn about their divine lives and achievements. My disciples are now in the pages of history along with me.

Reporter: You are talking about your monastic disciples, but your householder disciples, such as M. [Mahendra Nath Gupta], Girish Chandra Ghosh, Ram Chandra Datta, and others also preached your message.

Ramakrishna: Of course, they did. Their contributions are not insignificant. You see, Mohindar Master was a wonderful devotee, but a shy and tongue-tied person. He was a schoolteacher and used to secretly record my conversations in his diary. Later he developed his diary and published the *Ramakrishna Kathamrita* [*The Gospel of Sri Ramakrishna*], and thus my message spread all over the world. Now you can even find it as an e-book.

Girish was a drunkard and debauchee, but his life was totally changed when he gave me the power of attorney over his life. He incorporated my teachings into his dramas and spread my message in the red-light districts of Calcutta. Ram gave lectures on me in the Star and Minerva theaters in Calcutta and spread my message. Surendra, Balaram, Durgacharan, Kalipada, and others were also wonderful devotees. My women devotees — Jogin, Gauri, Golap, Aghoremani, and Nistarini — were also outstanding.

Reporter: Sir, nowadays some intellectuals are writing books based on your philosophy. There is no dearth of philosophers in India who have been debating and arguing about philosophical ideas over the centuries. Some think that you are a "dualist," some say a "qualified nondualist," and some believe that you are a "nondualist." There is so much confusion about your philosophy. Our readers will be benefitted if you throw some light on this issue.

Ramakrishna: I see that you have raised a very sensitive issue. Look, I practised sadhanas of various sects of Hinduism, and then I practised Christianity and Islam, and I realized God in all those paths. Finally, I declared: "As many faiths, so many paths." I tell people not to fight or quarrel about religion. If you sincerely follow your path and love God, you will attain Him. This is also the view of the Gita.

You see, I enjoy various kinds of dishes — soups, pickles, hot curry, and fried stuff. I love to play a flute with seven holes, as this creates various ragas and raginis [melodies]. I do not like the bagpipe's monotone "poooooo" because it reminds me of the Brahmos, who think of God in only one way. Sometimes I say, "Ma, Ma, Kali, Kali," sometimes, "Krishna-Krishna, Ram-Ram, Shiva-Shiva, Jesus-Jesus, Allah-Allah, Gaur-Gaur." I don't care for dogmatic views about God or monotonous ideas. All gods and goddesses of all religions are my relatives, so I have a large spiritual family. I can joyfully communicate with the people of all religions. I told my disciples to never think their learning has ended: "As long as I live, so long do I learn." I am the meeting point of all faiths, all paths, all yogas, all philosophies, and all doctrines. If someone tries to establish a single school based on my religious thought, that person will be an object of ridicule.

There is a controversy about God — whether He is formless or with form. I explained this mystery to Mohindar and others by citing the example of water and ice, which are not different. God has form and again is formless. Through the cooling influence of bhakti one sees the forms of God in the Ocean of the Absolute. But when the Sun of Knowledge rises, the ice melts, and it becomes the same water it was before. I told this to the Brahmos many times because they only believed that God is formless.

You see, Reporter, my disciple Narendra joined the Brahmo Samaj and did not believe in Mother Kali. Not only that, he used to criticize my Divine Mother. He used to consider my vision of Kali to be a hallucination. One day I angrily told him: "You criticize and ridicule my Mother. Don't come here anymore." He smiled and prepared my smoke. He had deep love for me. Then his father passed away and he was in a dire state of poverty. He could not get a job. One day he came to me and said: "Sir, I can't bear to see my mother, sisters, and brothers starve. I know Mother

Kali answers your prayers. Why don't you pray for me?" I told him: "You don't believe in my Mother and that is why you have all this trouble." "I don't know your Mother, sir," he said. Seeing his pitiable condition, I said: "All right, today is an auspicious day. In the evening go to the Kali temple and She will give you whatever you will ask for." He went to the temple and prayed: "Mother, give me knowledge, devotion, discrimination, renunciation, and uninterrupted vision." He prayed for only those five things and could not ask for money. I sent him to the temple three times but he could not ask for money. You see, he is a great soul. He was not born to lead a worldly life like others. Finally, when he fell at my feet and requested me to do something for his family, I told him, "Your family will not suffer from lack of plain food and plain clothing." I also taught him a song to Kali, *"Ma tvam hi Tara* — Mother, Thou art our soul redeemer." He sang that song the whole night and finally fell asleep on my floor.

I knew Narendra would carry my message of universal religion to the world. My view is: God is both with form and without form. I don't care for narrow, bigoted, and one-sided views about God. Blind people touch different parts of an elephant and express their respective views. In the same way different sects of religion grow and argue over their views because they have not seen the whole elephant. I showed Narendra the whole elephant so that he would not be able to form any narrow sect. I emphatically told him: "Do not limit God. He is infinite." Narendra proclaimed this universal religion all over the world. Soon all religions of the world will be harmonized under that one religion. You see, religions are paths but they are not God.

I remember you were saying something about my philosophy, or *phalajophy*. Look, I have not studied the scriptures, but I listened to many of them. Later I made a garland of those scriptures, put it around my neck, and danced. My Divine Mother made me realize the wisdom of those scriptures. My disciple Harinath [Swami Turiyananda] was well versed in the scriptures and he wrote a letter about my philosophy to Swami Sharvananda on 18 April 1919. Ask your readers to read it [see Ramakrishna Scripture — Chapter 9 of this book]. He raised a host of different views of various schools of philosophy, such as Gaudapada's doctrine of no creation, Shankara's doctrine of superimposition, Ramanuja's doctrine of transformation, and Sri Kantha's doctrine of Shivādvaita. These philosophers expressed their views according to their understanding. Finally, Harinath wrote: "Sri Ramakrishna's philosophy is: In whatever way, and at any cost, we must attain God. The Master said, 'Tie nondual knowledge in the corner of your cloth and then do as you please.' Once you attain God, it does not matter which doctrine your temperament bids you to uphold." However, I just quoted here a little from that letter to satisfy your curiosity. I don't like to prattle about this *phalajophy* [philosophy].

I forgot to tell you one thing: One day Keshab Sen requested me to speak on *nirakara* [the formless God]. I uttered "nirakara, nirakara, nirakara," and went into samadhi. I tried to make him understand that nirakara is beyond the mind and speech. One cannot give a lecture on that subject. I am a dualist, a qualified nondualist, a nondualist, and again beyond all those doctrines. God is unique — devoid of duality and nonduality. The rascal who tries to bind me to any particular doctrine is a fool.

Reporter: Sir, although the Brahmos did not believe in the gods and goddesses of the Hindus, it was Keshab who first preached your teachings and made you known in society. Moreover, most of your disciples were connected with the Brahmo Samaj.

Ramakrishna: You are right. Keshab recognized my divinity and wrote about my life and teachings in his various papers and journals. I first thought that Vaishnavcharan would spread my message, as he was a sadhaka and pandit. But Keshab was so impressed by my samadhi and my teachings that he would often come to me with his group. I also visited them at Keshab's house and at their temples. There was a commotion in Calcutta when the Brahmos wrote about me in the *Indian Mirror, Sulabh Samachar,* and *New Dispensation.* You could ask your readers to read those stories in *Samasamayik Drishtite Sri Ramakrishna Paramahamsa.*

Narendra, Rakhal, Sashi, Sharat, Yogin, Ram, Manomohan, Girish, and others came to know about me by reading those journals of the Brahmo Samaj. Keshab also introduced many of my ideas in his *New Dispensation* magazine, such as the Motherhood of God, devotional singing, and so on. One day, Keshab took me to his meditation room and worshipped my feet with flowers and sandal paste.

I was very fond of Shivanath [a Brahmo leader], but later he cut off all connection with me because he noticed that I mixed with drunkards and fallen people and gave them spiritual instructions. Look, Reporter, Narada and Shukadeva will not come to me for spiritual instructions because they are ever-free. There is no glory in making a good man good; but it is something if one can transform the life of a drunkard or a fallen person. He is truly a real sadhu — a redeemer of the fallen and a changer of people's destiny — who can transform others' lives.

Reporter: Sir, perhaps you are aware that in 1982 when the copyright of M.'s *Ramakrishna Kathamrita* expired, there was an explosion in sales of that book because several publishers published the *Kathamrita* simultaneously and offered it to the public at cheaper prices. In fact, there was a mob scene in the book market on College Street in Calcutta. Thousands and thousands of copies were sold, and thus your message reached almost all Bengali homes.

Ramakrishna: Don't talk about the Bengalis; they are very emotional and sentimental, and their excitement goes up and down like the waves. Most Bengalis buy the *Kathamrita* to keep it in their bookcases. How many actually read it? Nowadays, I see that non-Bengalis and foreigners are studying my life and message seriously. You are talking about the Bengalis! Listen, they used to call me *"Pāglā bāmun"* — mad brahmin. Then when Max Müller, Romain Rolland, Christopher Isherwood, Aldous Huxley, and Gerald Heard praised my life and message, the Bengalis began to give me a little recognition and appreciation.

Reporter: Sir, you are praising only the Western writers, but our Bengali novelist, Achintya Sengupta, wrote four volumes of the *Parama Purush Ramakrishna* and Satyajit Ray, the famous cinema director, made the covers for those books. Moreover, many Bengali writers wrote many books on you, composed songs and poems, and some playwrights wrote dramas on you.

Ramakrishna: You see, Reporter, I see only the good qualities of a person. I agree that Achintya is a wonderful writer. He has a good command of the language and he can write in an attractive way. In the 1950s, when his book was published, it sold very well. Most people would present *Parama Purush Ramakrishna* to newly married couples, but they did not read it. The bride locked me in her glass-covered bookcase to show her friends how spiritual she was. Anyhow, Achintya made a lot of money from that book on me. People used to say: "Prabhu, [O Lord], who would have known you (chinto), if you were not introduced by Achintya?"

You are talking about other writers? Well, they write books on me just to earn money and fame, because I am popular in the market. But I tell you one thing: No one will be able to write a romantic novel about me. The main theme of such a novel is the amorous relationship between a man and a woman. But the smell of lust never came near me. A Western writer tried to write a romantic novel on me, but could not succeed. How could he? He could not connect any woman's character with my life. I worshipped my wife and made her a goddess. I told her: "You, my biological mother in the nahabat, and Mother Kali in the temple are the same to me. I see all women as my Divine Mother, and I am Her son."

Let me tell you my secret: I destroyed all lust and infatuation for women through the mantra *"kāmini-kānchan maya"* — woman and gold are maya, illusion. I uprooted greed for money with the mantra "*tākā māti, māti tākā*" — money is clay, clay is money. I wiped out the morbid desire for name and fame with the mantra "*nām-jash hyāk-thu*" — name and fame are spittle.

You see, Reporter, Mathur engaged Lakshmi-bai, a famous courtesan in Calcutta, to test my character. But the moment I saw her, I cried out "Ma, Ma" and went into samadhi. She realized that it would be a great sin to tempt a holy man. She scolded Mathur for bringing a holy man to her. Embarrassed, Mathur hurriedly brought me back to Dakshineswar in his phaeton. I have never enjoyed a woman even in a dream. If a woman touches me I fall ill. That part of my body aches as if stung by a horned fish. After listening to my story, who would try to write a romance novel about me?

Lakshminarayan Marwari offered 10,000 rupees to me; I refused his offer and asked him not to see me again. The greedy Kali temple officials considered me crazy to the extreme.

People in this world are hankering after name and fame. Mathur looked after me like his Chosen Deity and said, "Father, inside and outside you are nothing but God." Name and fame did not affect me at all.

Reporter: Sir, a modern writer wrote a humorous story about you and some other famous people of Bengal. Are you interested in hearing about it?

Ramakrishna: Of course. Please tell the whole story. I would like to know what modern writers are thinking about me and how they are taking my ideas.

Reporter: The story is quite long, but I will make a long story short. There were two Nanigopals in Calcutta. By mistake, Vishnu's messenger took the wrong one to heaven. Now when the mistake was caught in the computer, Vishnu asked him to go back to earth. Nanigopal said, "Lord, I have no objection to returning to earth, but please give me a guided tour before I go back." Vishnu asked his attendant to show Nanigopal around. Nani saw that Bankim Chandra Chatterjee was deep in concentration, writing something. Nani asked him: "What are you writing?" Bankim told him that many people were getting academic prizes and other awards, but he had never received any award, so he was writing a novel. Nani told him, "You are the emperor of Bengali literature. You should not compete with those writers. They have no originality. They steal others' ideas and make them their own by changing the language." Upon hearing this, Bankim put his pen down and decided not to write.

After that Nani met the great novelist Sharat Chandra Chattopadhyay, who was then counting money. When Nani asked him what he was doing, Sharat replied that most of his stories had been turned into movies, so he was checking his income.

Nani then noticed that Rabindranath Tagore was very unhappy. Being asked, Rabindranath said that people were cursing him because they were not getting any sleep. Young people were playing his songs day and night through loudspeakers during festivals. Nani assured him that the Calcutta Corporation had just made a law that there should be no music after 10:00 p.m.

Finally, Nani met you and saw you reading books with deep concentration. Nani asked: "Master, you never cared for books before and now you are reading books here?" You replied: "Nanigopal, nowadays so many writers are writing books about me. I am really amazed. They are putting words in my mouth that I never said. So I am checking which words are mine and which are the creation of those rascals."

Hearing the story, Sri Ramakrishna laughed and laughed.

Ramakrishna: Nowadays books about me sell very well in the market, so modern writers are writing all sorts of things about me, exaggerating what I say. I have no control over them. They want to make money, and they want name and fame. However, you may tell your readers that these two books about me are authentic: *Ramakrishna Kathamrita* by Mohindar Gupta [M.] and *Ramakrishna Lilaprasanga* by Sharat [Swami Saradananda].

Look, Reporter, now I marvel seeing so many books on me in the market. Here are some publications about me: Rajagopalachari wrote the *Ramakrishna Upanishad*; Ramendra Sundar Bhattacharya wrote the *Ramakrishna Bhagavatam*; Ottur Nambudripad wrote the *Ramakrishna Karnamritam*; Akshay Kumar Sen wrote the *Ramakrishna Punthi*; and Sharat Chakrabarty wrote the *Ramakrishna Panchali*. Afterwards people will write the *Ramakrishna Gita, Ramakrishna Purana, Ramakrishna Sutra, Ramakrishna Shata Nam, Ramakrishna Sahasra Nam*, and so on. In the 1950-60s there were several Bengali movies produced on me, such as *Yugadevata, Pagla Thakur*, and *Sri Ramakrishna*.

This is only my 175th birth anniversary. Wait some more years. Sagar Enterprise and Chopra Enterprise of Mumbai will produce TV serials based on my life, as they did for Rama and Krishna with the Ramayana, Mahabharata, Vishnu Purana, and Krishna TV serials. Then my message will spread all over India. Eventually, when Hollywood and the Western media get interested in me, I will be known all over the world.

Thank you for having me, Reporter!

Appendix

A New Religion Begins*

oday the world is very sick, for it is passing through a crisis of the birth of a new religion,"[1] observed Sarvepalli Radhakrishnan in the 1950s. The term "new religion" in this context signifies the spirit of the age. It does not mean that all religions should come under one banner. What it refers to is a spiritual awakening in the hearts of humanity so that all can realize their spiritual unity.

If somebody were to ask me, "Can you tell me what aspect of religion will play a vital role in the twenty-first century?" my answer would be "mysticism." Mysticism is communion with God — experience of one's own Self through meditation and love. Mysticism does not belong exclusively to Christianity, Judaism, Hinduism, Buddhism, or Islam, yet it exists in all of these.

The modern world is familiar, to some extent, with the theory of evolution. As human beings are evolving, so is religion. "Religion is a growth," said Swami Vivekananda. "Each one must experience it himself.... Religion is the realization of Spirit as Spirit; not Spirit as matter."[2] Only in Spirit are we all one. Both modern science and religion are now moving toward Unity — the mysterious Oneness where there is no space, time, or causation, where there is neither bondage nor liberation, nor any pairs of opposites. This is the realm of mysticism. Knowledge from the senses cannot reach there, nor can the mind. Mystics, through spiritual disciplines, attain the intuitive knowledge that unveils the mystery of life

*This article had been published in the Souvenir edition of the Ramakrishna Math and Mission Convention of 1980.

428

A painting of Ramakrishna by Frank Dvorak, a Czechoslovakian artist.

to them. They experience the truth through and through, and thus they become free. This is the goal of religion.

All religions have two aspects: the external (doctrines, dogmas, symbols, and rituals) and the internal (purity, devotion, renunciation, and unselfishness). The external aspects differ from each other, but the internal aspects are the same. The language of the mystics may be different, but their experiences are identical. The phrases "*Aham Brahmasmi* — I am Brahman" of Hinduism, "I and my Father are one" of Christianity, and "*Anal Haq* — I am God" of Islam mean the same thing. Mystics do not belong to any particular country or race; they are a group unto themselves. All religions of the world have produced these saints, and their lives and teachings have a universal appeal. With their exemplary lives, they not only maintain the spiritual current of their respective religions, but they also boost the spirit of universal religion.

What is happening in America today? Many religious leaders are introducing "Charismatic Services," "Crusades," "Yogas," "Meditation," and "Zen" in an effort to bring revivals into their faiths. In addition to this, Evangelicals are transmitting the message of Christ through the "Electronic Church" to mainland China. According to *Melton's Encyclopedia of American Religions*, there are more than 2,500 religious groups in the United States and Canada. The *Encyclopedia* takes a rigorously objective approach, offering no judgments. The work is a unique reference owing to Melton's material on what he calls the nations' "hidden religions" — groups that lie outside the mainstream and are barely visible to outsiders, such as spiritualists, religious psychics, occultists and assorted "New Age" sects.[3] More books, journals, and articles are published about religion, I believe, than on any other subject.

Nowadays, many Western religious traditions are incorporating some of the practices of Eastern religions, such as meditation, mindfulness, japa, chanting, and also yoga practices such as Hatha Yoga and pranayama.

Dr. Huston Smith, who was a well-known professor of philosophy in the United States, wrote an article on "The Spiritual Heritage of India" in *Vedanta for East and West* (Issue 171), in which he stated: "Around the middle of this century Arnold Toynbee predicted that at its close the world would still be dominated by the West, but that in the twenty-first century 'India will conquer her conquerors.'* Preempting the place that is now held by technology, religion will be restored to its earlier importance and the center of world happenings will wander back from the shores of

*"Culturally, not politically. Toynbee's prediction appeared in an address he gave to The Philosophical Society of Edinburgh University in November 1952."

the Atlantic to the East where civilization originated five or six thousand years ago."[4]

If we study carefully and observe the religious evolution of the world, we shall clearly notice that our modern civilization is indirectly creating an emptiness in the minds of people. It has given the world a plethora of comforts and enjoyments, but people are not happy. They live in fear and tension. Radhakrishnan wrote: The half-religious and the irreligious fight about dogmas and not the truly religious. In the biting words of Jonathan Swift, "We have enough religion to hate one another, but not enough to love one another." The more religious we grow, the more tolerant of diversity shall we become. Today we are earnestly seeking a spiritual renaissance that will remove hatred, intolerance, superstition, narrowness, bigotry, and fanaticism, and install love, sympathy, equality, and universal oneness in our hearts instead.

Modern men and women can forgive or overlook lapses and imperfections in other spheres of life, but hypocrisy in religion is unbearable. Religion promulgates and gives meaning to the basic values of human life by its purity of outlook and its high ideals. If a religion is corrupted or its ideals are lowered, these values are jeopardized and the result is bankruptcy in human life. True religion will always teach God first and then the world.

Surprisingly, atheists are not the real enemies of religion; rather, they keep religion alive through their inquiries and criticisms. Apathy and indifference toward religion are more dangerous than criticism, denial, or contempt. This type of attitude says: "Some think God exists; some think not. It is hard to say. What does it matter?"

Utopians, in contrast, speak of one world, one religion, one humankind, or one government. This sounds wonderful, but it can never be realized. Why? Because unity in variety, and not uniformity, is the pattern of this world order. From the lowest to the highest, in people and in nature, the pattern is the same. No two people are alike, yet the same consciousness pervades all.

We are by nature spiritual beings, so the quest for bliss and freedom is inherent within us. This search for the eternal Spirit, which is within all beings, will eventually lead us to mysticism. We can never be content with the merely hedonistic philosophy of "Eat, drink, and be merry." We are infinite dreamers; we cannot be satisfied with finite dreams. We will seek only that religion which gives us a taste of the infinite, because our true nature is infinite.

"Unity in variety" is the special theme for the New Age, and to realize this is the special challenge to modern civilization. Only this realization will help us to transcend all limitations and shortcomings and give us the taste of infinite bliss. Only this realization can unveil the mystery: "There is One who is the eternal Reality among non-eternal objects, the One [truly] conscious Entity among conscious objects, and who, though non-dual, fulfils the desires of many. Eternal peace belongs to the wise, who perceive Him within themselves — not to others."[5]

The call to the modern world now is that of the highest ideal: to see the underlying spiritual unity in the diversity of all us, and to love and serve one another as different manifestations of that divinity. The New Age will unite the mind of the West with the soul of the East, and the science of the West with the spirituality of the East; it will teach us how to develop the head, heart, and hands simultaneously so that we can all attain perfection in this very life.

Some facets of the new religion

"There is no new thing under the sun,"[6] says the Old Testament. Still we love to see something new, to hear something new. This passion for novelty is inherent in us. When life becomes dull and dreary, stale and stagnant, boring and burdensome, we long for a renaissance; we want to rejuvenate our lives through life-giving principles; we try to revitalize our bodies and minds with spiritual power; we want to breathe the freshness of the Eternal.

Thousands of years ago, a Vedic sage uttered the *Rik mantra*: "O self-luminous One, my eyes are open to see you; my ears are hungry to hear your glory; and the light of my intellect is curious to know you."[7] In order to see something new we must keep our eyes open and our minds free. "As long as I live, so long do I learn," said Ramakrishna.

In this present age, Ramakrishna taught how to breathe the unpolluted air of the spiritual, how to get rid of the monotony of life, how to make life meaningful, and how to be in the world and not of the world. The religion that Ramakrishna presented to the modern world is based on the ancient eternal religion, but he reconstructed it. His renunciation of lust and gold is a glowing example to spiritual seekers; his samadhi, verified by doctors and scientists, was an amazing phenomenon; his spiritual experiences surpassed descriptions in the Vedas and Vedanta; his gospel of the harmony of religions fulfils the need of the age; his synthesis of the four yogas — Jnana, Karma, Bhakti, and Raja — opened a new vista in the field of practical religion; his life was the meeting point of all faiths, all paths, and all sects.

Ramakrishna not only worshipped God as the Divine Mother, but he also accepted a woman as one of his teachers and made his wife his first disciple. Realizing, also, the significance and necessity of the role of women in the field of religion, he empowered his wife to continue the spiritual ministry that he started.

Ramakrishna never claimed that he was the greatest of all. Those who cultivated a feeling of superiority and exclusiveness, he would correct with his sweet epigrams: "Everyone thinks that his watch is correct"; "It is a dogmatic view"; "All jackals howl in the same way."

"In point of character," said Swami Vivekananda, "Paramahamsa Deva [Sri Ramakrishna] beats all previous records; and as regards teaching, he was more liberal, more original, and more progressive than all his predecessors. In other words, the older Teachers were rather one-sided, while the teaching of this new Incarnation or Teacher is that the best point of yoga, devotion, knowledge, and work must be combined now so as to form a new society.... The older ones were no doubt good, but this is the *new religion of this age* — the synthesis of yoga, knowledge, devotion and work."[8]

Swami Vivekananda further said: "Ramakrishna came to teach the religion of today, constructive, not destructive. He had to go afresh to Nature to ask for facts, and he got scientific religion which never says 'believe,' but 'see'; 'I see, and you too can see.' Use the same means and you will reach the same vision."[9]

Once Swami Vivekananda was lecturing in London. When he ended his talk, a well-known philosopher said to him: "You have spoken splendidly, sir, and I thank you heartily, but you have told us nothing new." Immediately came Swamiji's frank reply: "Sir, I have told you the Truth. That, the Truth, is as old as the immemorial hills, as old as humanity, as old as Creation, as old as the Great God. If I have told it in such words as will make you think, make you live up to your thinking, do I not do well in telling it?" The murmurs of "Hear! Hear!" from the audience silenced the philosopher.[10]

Before his passing away, Ramakrishna transmitted his power to Vivekananda and commissioned him to carry the message of the universal religion of Vedanta to the world. In the opening address at the World's Parliament of Religions in Chicago, Swamiji thanked the Western audience "in the name of the mother of religions"; but he never said that he was a representative of the Hindu religion. Some of the audience of that Parliament felt that Vivekananda was a representative of all of the world's religions.

Western people, in general, are very suspicious about cults, but
Vedanta can never be considered as such, as it is based on scientific reasoning, universality, and experience. Ramakrishna and Swami Vivekananda reiterated the ancient religion and philosophy of Vedanta to the
modern world:

As many faiths so many paths.[11]

We believe not only in universal toleration, but we accept all religions
as true.[12]

Man is to become divine by realizing the divine. Idols or temples or
churches or books are only the supports, the helps, of his spiritual childhood: but on and on he must progress.[13]

Do I wish that the Christian would become Hindu? God forbid. Do
I wish that the Hindu or Buddhist would become Christian? God forbid.... Each must assimilate the spirit of the others and yet preserve his
individuality and grow according to his own law of growth.[14]

Holiness, purity and charity are not the exclusive possessions of any
church in the world, and...every system has produced men and women
of the most exalted character.[15]

We reject none, neither theist, nor pantheist, monist, polytheist, agnostic, nor atheist; the only condition of being a disciple is modelling
a character at once the broadest and the most intense. Nor do we insist
upon particular codes of morality as to conduct, or character, or eating
and drinking, except so far as it injures others. We leave everybody free
to know, select, and follow whatever suits and helps him.[16]

We believe that every being is divine, is God. Every soul is a sun covered over with clouds of ignorance; the difference between soul and soul
is owing to the difference in density of these layers of clouds. We believe
that this is the conscious or unconscious basis of all religions....We believe that this is the very essence of the Vedas.[17]

We believe that it is the duty of every soul to treat, think of, and behave to other souls as such, i.e., as Gods, and not hate or despise, or vilify,
or try to injure them by any manner or means.[18]

We believe that nowhere throughout the Vedas, Darshanas, or Puranas, or Tantras, is it ever said that the soul has any sex, creed, or caste.[19]

Social laws were created by economic conditions under the sanction
of religion. The terrible mistake of religion was to interfere in social matters....What we want is that religion should not be a social reformer, but
we insist at the same time that society has no right to become a religious
law-giver.[20]

Religion is the manifestation of the Divinity already in man.[21]

I will tell you my discovery. All of religion is contained in the Vedanta, that is, in the three stages of the Vedanta philosophy, the Dvaita,

Vishishtadvaita and Advaita; one comes after the other. These are the three stages of spiritual growth in man. Each one is necessary. This is the essential of religion: the Vedanta, applied to the various ethnic customs and creeds of India, is Hinduism. The first stage, i.e., Dvaita, applied to the ideals of the ethnic groups of Europe, is Christianity; as applied to the Semitic groups, Mohammedanism. The Advaita, as applied in its Yoga-perception form, is Buddhism etc.[22]

We want to lead mankind to the place where there is neither the Vedas, nor the Bible, nor the Koran; yet this has to be done by harmonizing the Vedas, the Bible, and the Koran. Mankind ought to be taught that religions are but the varied expressions of THE RELIGION, which is Oneness, so that each may choose the path that suits him best.[23]

What I want to propagate is a religion that will be equally acceptable to all minds; it must be equally philosophic, equally emotional, equally mystic, and equally conducive to action.[24]

The old religions said that he was an atheist who did not believe in God. The new religion says that he is the atheist who does not believe in himself.[25]

All that was good in the past must be preserved; and the doors must be kept open for future additions to the already existing store. Religions must also be inclusive, and not look down with contempt upon one another, because their particular ideals of God are different.[26]

These statements depict some facets of the new religion presented by Ramakrishna and Swami Vivekananda. But why is there a need for a new approach to old religious truths, or a need for a "new religion"?

We know that the doctrines or dogma of a particular denomination change, but the Truth proclaimed by an Incarnation of God does not. Two thousand years ago Jesus said, "Blessed are the pure in heart: for they shall see God."[27] This is an eternal Truth that cannot be altered. Due to social pressures and changes, modern reformers change codes of morality and ethics, but this statement of Christ will never change.

Every religion of the world needs three basic things upon which to stand: a Personal God, a prophet, and a book. We cannot think of Christianity without God, Jesus Christ, and the Bible. Vedanta, however, does not accept the view that religion is confined to a particular book or is dependent upon a particular person. The Upanishads testify that not one man or one woman has ever become the exclusive object of worship among Vedantins. Moreover, the Upanishads tell us that if anyone wants to experience the Ultimate Reality, he or she will have to transcend the Vedas and all other scriptures because they are inferior. Just as a cookbook is merely a compilation of various recipes and cannot appease our hunger, so also scriptures are simply testimonies to the spiritual experiences of the sages and cannot by themselves show us God. We might have read all the scriptures in the library but that does not mean we have experienced God.

Vedanta does not subscribe to a Personal God. The God of Vedanta is a democratic God: We are all gods. The same divinity is in all beings, so how can you hate or humiliate or shun others? God is not Hindu, nor Christian, nor Muslim. Though God cannot be described, this much can be asserted: God is Existence-Knowledge-Bliss Absolute.

I think it will not be out of place to share two of my experiences in this connection. In 1976, I was invited to represent Vedanta in a bicentennial religious conference in Southern California. A friend of mine, a Jesuit priest originally from India, was giving a presentation of the Catholic faith. He said, "We have a definite definition of God in Christianity, in Judaism, and in Islam, but in Hinduism there is no such definition of God. If you ask the Hindus about their conception of God, each person will speak of Him differently."

Seated at the back of the room, I enjoyed his talk and was glad that Hindus do not define God. This reminded me of what Swami Vivekananda included in the Belur Math rule book: "If the Master [Sri Ramakrishna] has repeatedly commanded us to renounce anything besides lust and gold, it is the limiting of the infinite aspect of God by saying, 'He is this much only.'"[28]

In the evening session of the conference, I was interviewed by people of various faiths. In a discussion about the role of women in religions, a Catholic nun said some churches felt a need to change the traditional concept of the Trinity, "God the Father, God the Son, and God the Holy Ghost," into "God the Mother, God the Daughter, and God the Holy Ghost" because of the pressure of the women's liberation movement.

I said, "Sister, Vedanta does not have such a problem because Vedanta teaches no doctrine or dogma, only Truth. The Truth is unchanging and unchangeable. Vedanta teaches that the Atman [pure consciousness] is sexless. It is neither he nor she. Sex belongs only to the body. The *Shvetashvatara Upanishad* says: 'You are woman. You are man. You are the youth and the maiden too.... Being born you assume diverse forms.'"[29]

Religion cannot function or spread without organization

All organized religions are human institutions and thus cannot be absolutely perfect. Only God is perfect. Religion is not God: it only points the way to God. Generally, religions are introduced to people through scriptures. But as time goes on, theologians and commentators interpret the simple and sublime teachings of the scriptures according to their own understanding. These scholars make the simple truth complicated. They twist and torture the scriptural texts with a view to establishing their own schools of thought, thus causing confusion. Nowadays many people in the West are very skeptical about organized religion.

Vedanta was never an organized religion and it never will be, as it deals with the knowledge of Oneness, which is not confined to any time, place, or personality. Vedanta proclaims absolute freedom — physical, mental, and spiritual. There is a saying in the Vedanta tradition: "The monastery is for the monks but the monks are not for the monastery." The monks are free souls and therefore no rules or organization can bind them. However, as did Christ and Buddha, Ramakrishna bound his disciples with a chord of love. He made Vivekananda their leader.

After reaching the United States in 1893, Swami Vivekananda saw the power in organization and he felt its necessity. An individual may be very powerful, but it is not possible for one person to do everything on a large scale, and moreover a movement needs a following to carry on its ideals and ideas to posterity. During this time Swamiji was the guest of the Lyon family in Chicago. Cornelia Conger, a grand-daughter of Mrs. John B. Lyon, wrote in her reminiscences: "Once he [Swamiji] said to my grandmother that he had had the greatest temptation of his life in America. She liked to tease him a bit and said, 'Who is she, swami?' He burst out laughing and said, 'Oh, it is not a lady, it is Organization!' He explained how the followers of Ramakrishna had all gone out alone and when they reached a village, would just quietly sit under a tree and wait for those in trouble to come to consult them. But in the [United] States he saw how much could be accomplished by organizing work."[30]

Swami Vivekananda, well-acquainted with religious history, knew the causes of the decline and fall of a religion and also its safeguards. He witnessed how organized religions in the West stifled their adherents and barred them from thinking freely, making them narrow, intolerant, and bigoted. If a person wants to breathe freedom, he or she should be free from superstition.

In the later part of the nineteenth century, Robert G. Ingersoll, a famous agnostic, recognized this need for freedom and tried to clear religious superstition from American society. In one of his famous lectures, he said: "It is far better to have no heaven than to have heaven and hell; better to have no God than God and Devil; better to rest in eternal sleep than to be an angel and know that the ones you love are suffering eternal pain; better to live a free and loving life — a life that ends forever at the grave — than to be an immortal slave."[31]

With firsthand knowledge of both the East and the West, Swami Vivekananda compared the advantages and disadvantages of each. On one hand, he knew that the East had religious freedom but not social freedom. On the other hand, he saw that the West had social freedom but not religious freedom. Americans, great lovers of freedom, enthusiastically accepted and appreciated Swami Vivekananda's message — a gospel of freedom, not a gospel preaching Heaven's celestial joys. Swamiji cautioned his Western listeners:

> If you want to be religious, enter not the gate of any organized religion. They do a hundred times more evil than good, because they stop the growth of each one's individual development. Study everything, but keep your own seat firm. If you take my advice, do not put your neck into the trap. The moment they try to put their noose on you, get your neck out and go somewhere else. [As] the bee culling honey from many flowers remains free, not bound by any flower, be not bound.... Enter not the door of any organized religion. [Religion] is only between you and your God, and no third person must come between you. Think what these organized religions have done! What Napoleon was more terrible than those religious persecutions?... If you and I organize, we begin to hate every person. It is better not to love, if loving only means hating others. That is no love. That is hell! If loving your own people means hating everybody else, it is the quintessence of selfishness and brutality, and the effect is that it will make you brutes.[32]

Swami Vivekananda knew the pros and cons of organized religion. In 1895, when he was at Thousand Island Park, Sister Christine observed him pacing back and forth on the upper veranda, saying over and over: "To organize or not to organize? If I organize, the spirit will diminish. If I do not organize, the message will not spread."[33]

In the autumn of 1895, following his Thousand Island work, Swamiji wrote a letter to Swami Abhayananda (Marie Louise): "We have no organization, nor want to build any. Each one is quite independent to teach, quite free to preach whatever he or she likes. If you have the spirit within, you will never fail to attract others.... Individuality is my motto. I have no ambition beyond training individuals. I know very little; that little I teach without reserve; where I am ignorant I confess it as such.... I am a Sannyasin. As such I hold myself as a servant, not as a master of this world."[34]

In 1897, Swami Vivekananda returned to India after three and a half years in the West. His lectures from Colombo to Almora created a sensation all over India, and he became the undisputed leader of the nation. He pointed out that behind the diverse languages, customs, and cultures of India, there was a unity. As he said at Madras in his lecture, "The Future of India":

> The one common ground that we have is our sacred tradition, our religion. That is the only common ground, and upon that we shall have to build. In Europe, political ideas form the national unity. In Asia, religious ideals form the national unity. The unity in religion, therefore, is absolutely necessary as the first condition of the future of India. There must be the recognition of one religion throughout the length and breadth of this land. What do I mean by one religion? Not in the sense of one religion as held among the Christians, or the Mohammedans, or the Buddhists. We know that our religion has certain common grounds, common to all our sects, however varying their conclusions may be, however different their claims may be. So there are certain common grounds; and within their limitation this religion of ours admits of a marvellous variation, an infinite amount of liberty to think and live our own lives.[35]

Swami Vivekananda foresaw the great awakening of India, and he resolved to reshape modern India with his bold new religious ideas. He noticed the spontaneous response of the masses and the intense fervour and enthusiasm among youth. Addressing a mammoth gathering at Madras, he said: "Friends, I am very much pleased with your enthusiasm. It is marvellous....Only make it permanent; keep it up. Let not the fire die out. We want to work out great things in India."[36]

After arriving in Calcutta, Swamiji decided to implement the mission of Ramakrishna. Based on his experience of the East and the West, the ancient and the modern, he formed an organization with a view to fulfilling the need of the age. On 1 May 1897, Swami Vivekananda founded the Ramakrishna Association at Calcutta. He said in his inaugural address:

> From my travels in various countries I have come to the conclusion that without organization nothing great and permanent can be done....This Association will bear the name of him in whose name we have become Sannyasins [monks], taking whom as your ideal you are leading the life of the householders in the field of activity of this *Samsara* [world], and whose holy name and the influence of whose unique life and teachings have, within twelve years of his passing away spread in such an unthought-of way both in the East and the West. Let this Sangha, or organization, be therefore named the Ramakrishna Mission. We are only the servants of the Master. May you all help us in this work.[37]

His proposal was enthusiastically supported by everyone at that meeting. The aims and ideals of the organization and its methods of action, its Indian work, and its foreign work were all delineated.

In this way the message of Ramakrishna gradually spread all over the world and drew the attention of Western scholars and thinkers. Inspired by the life and teachings of Ramakrishna, Romain Rolland wrote: "I am bringing to Europe, as yet unaware of it, the fruit of a new autumn, a new message of the Soul, the symphony of India, bearing the name of Ramakrishna.... The man whose image I here evoke was the consummation of two thousand years of the spiritual life of three hundred million people."[38]

Too many rules curb the spirit of religion

History shows how rules and regulations inhibit religions. Before Buddha, lawgivers and priests set rules and prescribed religious rites and rituals, and the people observed them mechanically. As a result, the Hindu religion turned into a mere formality. Buddha brought a religion of love and unselfishness that touched the hearts of millions and thus saved India from stark materialism.

Just as we see how life invariably has its ebbs and tides, so also religion rises and falls. All religions, without exception, have to pass through transitions. Sukumar Dutt discussed this phenomenon in his famous book *Buddhist Monks and Monasteries of India*, "From a founder's inspired teachings to a system of doctrinal interpretations made by disciples and followers seems to be a law of the historical development of a religion."[39] A faction soon came also among the disciples and followers of Buddha, and they formed two sects: the Hinayana,* or "small vehicle," and the Mahayana, or "great vehicle." Both of these schools established their doctrines on the teachings of Buddha, but their approaches were different. Originally the religion of Buddha was based on *Dhamma-Vinaya*. Dhamma dealt with the inner life and spirit, and Vinaya with outer life and organization. Gradually the Vinaya aspect became more and more important while the Dhamma aspect almost disappeared. Thus, Buddhism declined in India. After Buddha, India witnessed religious revivals under Shankara, Ramanuja, Madhva, Chaitanya, and Ramakrishna.

Before Christ, there were three main religious sects in Judaism: Sadducees, Pharisees, and Essenes. The Scribes, scholars who were expert in Jewish law and custom, were mainly Pharisees. They taught in

*Hinayana is now called Theravada Buddhism.

synagogues and schools, and held debates on the law in private and in public. They were also the custodians of Jewish law and religious culture. They expanded the Code of Moses into thousands of detailed precepts designed to meet every circumstance, and as a result a pall of stagnation fell on Judaism. Priests exploited the common people in the name of religion. Christ then created a tremendous spiritual current that moved religion out of its stupor and wiped out superficiality and hypocrisy. Will Durant wrote in *The Story of Civilization*: "He [Jesus] transformed everything by the force of his character and his feeling....He brought religion back from ritual to righteousness, and condemned conspicuous prayers, showy charities."[40]

The religion of Christ was organized by his disciples and followers. Doctrines, dogmas, rituals, and ecclesiastical laws and rules gradually constricted Christianity while also creating hundreds of denominations. The *Yearbook of American and Canadian Churches* lists 291 Christian denominations in the United States and Canada alone.

Swami Vivekananda studied the religious history of the world and found that no religious organization can function without some kind of rules or regulations. Yet he felt it necessary to protect the new religion from the evils inherent in organized religion. The spirit of religion must be maintained through rules, not in spite of them. Thus, he emphasized that the Ramakrishna Mission should have no connection with politics; that the men's and women's organizations should be completely separate; and that the wealthy should have no influence on the organization. In this connection he said, "To pay respect to the rich and hang on them for support has been the bane of all the Sannyasin [monastic] communities of our country."[41] The history of Buddhism and Christianity also testifies to this truth. As George Bernard Shaw once wrote, "All religious organizations exist by selling themselves to the rich."[42]

Swamiji also noticed how luxury and wealth weaken religions and diminish their spiritual powers. He stated, "In the absence of renunciation and austerity, luxury takes possession of the organization; hence the spirit of renunciation and austerity should always be kept bright."[43]

Gerald Heard, a great thinker and orator, narrated in *The Creed of Christ* how too much wealth ruins an organization and diminishes its spiritual power:

> The real force — not words or violence, but actual spiritual power, the divine indwelling life — that we lack and we and everyone else know we lack. Some shrewd Oxford dons were discussing one day which personage is the more powerful, a bishop or a Judge. "The bishop," said one

"for the judge can only say, 'You be hanged,' while the bishop can say 'You be damned.'" "Ah," replied the other, "but when the Judge says, 'You be hanged,' you *are* hanged." The same fact, the lack of spiritual power recognized by ecclesiastical authorities, is illustrated by the story of the pope, seated with the great medieval theologian Thomas Aquinas watching the revenues of Europe being carried into the Vatican. He exclaimed, "The time has gone when the church had to say, 'Silver and gold have I none.'" And the theologian replied, "And the time has also gone when she could say to the paralytic, 'But what I have I give thee, Arise and Walk!'"[44]

Although Swami Vivekananda recognized the need for some rules to safeguard the new organization for future generations, he played down their importance and stressed spiritual development instead. "Organization is power," he emphasized, "and the secret of this is obedience."[45] Placing spirituality first, he told the monks: "Look here, we are going to make rules, no doubt; but we must remember the main object thereof. Our main object is to transcend all rules and regulations. We have naturally some bad tendencies which are to be changed by observing good rules and regulations, and finally we have to go beyond all these even, just as we remove one thorn by another and throw both of them away."[46]

It was Swami Shuddhananda, a disciple of Swamiji, who took down the dictation of the rules at Alambazar Math in 1897. His record runs:

The course of discipline and routine decided upon was of this kind: Both mornings and evenings should be devoted to meditation, while the afternoons, after a short rest should be utilized for individual studies, and in the evenings one particular religious book should be read and expounded. It was also provided that each member would take physical exercise both morning and evening. Another rule was to the effect that no intoxicant save tobacco should be allowed. Having dictated the rules, Swamiji asked me to make a fair copy of the rules and instructed me that I should put all the rules in the positive form.[47]

Nearly one year later, when the monastery was moved to Nilambar Babu's garden house in Belur, Swami Vivekananda dictated the general principles of the Ramakrishna Order, which included The Math (monastery), The Message, The Methods of Spiritual Practice, The Shrine Room, The Plan of Work for India, and so on. Swami Basudevananda wrote:

One morning at Belur Math, these rules of the Ramakrishna Order were read aloud in Swami Brahmananda's room. The revered Maharaj [Swami Brahmananda] was seated on his small cot absorbed in deep meditation. Swami Shuddhananda was the reader. When the reading was over,

Maharaj said: "Swamiji did not utter these rules from the physical plane; he raised his mind to a higher realm and then gave dictation and Tarakda [Swami Shivananda] wrote them down. Swamiji did not mean these rules for a particular person or group. He delineated them with a view to spreading the ideas and ideals of Sri Ramakrishna and for the good of humanity. Everyone, whether man or woman, rich or poor, high or low, has an equal right to the spiritual heritage and service of Sri Ramakrishna. Blessed is he who serves the Master and follows his teachings! Accept those instructions of Swamiji with candid faith; practise them in your lives and then spread them in all directions. As a result you will see that the evil influence of the dark age will diminish and the golden age will come in sight."[48]

On another occasion, Swami Brahmananda was asked by Swami Dhirananda to form some rules for the monastics. Swami Brahmananda replied: "Did not Swamiji already frame the rules? Brother, instead of increasing rules, please increase your love."[49]

Most organizations are guided by rules and regulations, but the disciples of Ramakrishna placed far greater emphasis on love for the ideal. Love naturally brings harmony and peace without the stress and sense of bondage often engendered by rules and regulations. Once in Shanti Ashrama the Western students of Swami Turiyananda asked him to make some rules for them. To this, the swami replied:

> Why do you want rules? Is not everything going on nicely and orderly without formal rules? Don't you see how punctual everyone is, how regular we all are? No one ever is absent from the classes or meditations. Mother has made Her own rules, let us be satisfied with that. Why should we make rules of our own? Let there be freedom, but no license, that is Mother's way of ruling. We have no organization, but see how organized we are. This kind of organization is lasting but all other kinds of organizations break up in time. This kind of organization makes free, all other kinds are binding. This is the highest organization; it is based on spiritual laws.[50]

Religion finds its fulfilment in love and freedom

What is lacking in religion today? It is love and freedom. Churches, temples, mosques, and synagogues are reverberating with prayers, music, sermons, and religious discourses, yet there is emptiness in people's minds. Hunger for spirituality is innate in all human beings and this hunger can be satisfied only by practising religion. In the spiritual tradition of Vedanta, religion is based upon three things: scriptures, reason, and experience. Among these, experience is the most important. Those illumined souls who have realized the truth through their own experience are the real custodians of religion and they maintain its inner spirit. Theologians, in contrast, often bind and suffocate the true spirit of religion with their endless quarrels and debates on doctrines and dogma. To those who are illumined, however, God, the embodiment of love and freedom, is real and not a matter of speculation or argument. Moreover, these saints are truly loving, unselfish, and free. As trees and plants bloom at the advent of spring, so spiritual seekers are awakened by the touch of these great souls.

More and more, people are beginning to see the value of the contemplative and mystical aspect of religion. Simply reading books and listening to sermons on Sunday are not enough. People are looking for something that will fill their hearts. One of my American friends wrote to me: "One of the greatest changes occurring in modern life in the United States is the growing numbers of laypersons going to the monasteries for varying periods of time to partake in the work and the contemplation of these monks. I, myself, have on numerous occasions participated in such silent, meditative week-long retreats — and am completely amazed by the dedication, sincerity, and self-imposed rigorous efforts being made by large numbers of unaffiliated young people."

Swami Vivekananda understood from his experience that the West is a grand field for non-dualistic Vedanta, which teaches freedom of the soul. As a messenger of a new religion, Swami Vivekananda said, "I have a message to the West, as Buddha had a message to the East."[51] What was that message?

> Love cannot come through fear, its basis is freedom. When we really begin to love the world, then we understand what is meant by brotherhood or mankind, and not before.... Everything in the universe is yours, stretch out your arms and embrace it with love. If you ever felt you wanted to do that, you have felt God.... When you have that feeling, you have true personality. The whole universe is one person; let go the little things. Give up small enjoyments for infinite bliss. It is all yours, for the Impersonal includes the Personal. So God is Personal and Impersonal at the same time. And Man, the Infinite, Impersonal Man, is manifesting Himself as person. We the infinite have limited ourselves, as it were, into small parts. The Vedanta says that Infinity is our true nature; it will never vanish, it will abide forever. But we are limiting ourselves by our Karma, which, like a chain round our necks has dragged us into this limitation. Break that chain and be free. Trample law under your feet. There is no law in human nature, there is no destiny, no fate. How can there be law in

infinity? Freedom is its watchword. Freedom is its nature, its birthright. Be free.[52]

Humanity has the power to transcend all limitations. We cannot change the world, but we can change ourselves; and when we change ourselves the world begins to change. A forest is nothing but the sum total of individual trees; the existence of the forest depends on them. So the growth or prosperity of a society or a nation depends on the quality of its individuals. "Numbers do not count," said Swamiji, "nor does wealth or poverty; a handful of men can throw the world off its hinges, provided they are united in thought, word, and deed."[53]

Swami Vivekananda once related to Sister Nivedita from his own experience how "tears of sorrow alone bring spiritual vision, never tears of joy. That dependence is fraught with misery, independence alone is happiness. That almost all human love, save sometimes a mother's, is full of dependence."[54] He then mentioned the unflinching love of his brother disciples, who would never leave him, even if he had done something objectionable. To them he would still be the same. "And mind this, Margot," he said. "It is when half a dozen people learn to love like that *a new religion begins*. Not till then."[55]

What he was trying to emphasize was that religion dawns in the heart and not in the brain. One should try to love and to feel religion as did Mary Magdalene. Swamiji continued:

I always remember the woman who went to the sepulchre early in the morning, and as she stood there she heard a voice and she thought it was the gardener, and then Jesus touched her, and she turned round, and all she said was "My Lord and my God!" That was all, "My Lord and my God." The person had gone. Love begins by being brutal, the faith, the body. Then it becomes intellectual, and last of all it reaches the spiritual. Only at the last, "My Lord and my God." Give me half a dozen disciples like that and I will conquer the world.[56]

References

We have provided exhaustive references so that readers can know the sources of incidents and utterances. Following is a list of abbreviations for important sources that have been frequently cited:

Abbr.	Title
Girish	*Girish Chandra Ghosh* by Swami Chetanananda, Vedanta Society: St. Louis, 2009
GLWT	*God Lived with Them* by Swami Chetanananda, Vedanta Society: St. Louis, 2014
Gospel	*The Gospel of Sri Ramakrishna* by M., trans. by Swami Nikhilananda, Ramakrishna-Vivekananda Center: New York, 1969
HLWG	*How to Live with God* by Swami Chetanananda, Vedanta Society: St. Louis, 2008
HMDP	*Sri Sarada Devi and Her Divine Play* by Swami Chetanananda, Vedanta Society: St. Louis, 2016
M.	*Mahendra Nath Gupta (M.)* by Swami Chetanananda, Vedanta Society: St. Louis, 2011
RKASWE	*Ramakrishna as We Saw Him* by Swami Chetanananda, Vedanta Society: St. Louis, 2012
RKDP	*Sri Ramakrishna and His Divine Play* by Swami Saradananda, trans. by Swami Chetanananda, Vedanta Society: St. Louis, 2006
SD	*Srima Darshan* by Swami Nityatmananda, General Printers: Calcutta
TLWG	*They Lived with God* by Swami Chetanananda, Vedanta Society: St. Louis, 2006

Introduction
1. HLWG, 73
2. Ibid., 74
3. Ibid., 74
4. Gospel, 115
5. Ibid., 173
6. Ibid., 561
7. GLWT, 596
8. RKASWE, 43
9. M., 295
10. Matthew, 7:7
11. *Prabuddha Bharata*, May 2007
12. *Spiritual Treasures* by Swami Chetanananda, Vedanta Society: St. Louis, 112

1. Meditation on Ramakrishna's Form
1. *Teachings of Sri Rama-krishna*, Advaita Ashrama: Calcutta, 1994, 5-7
2. *Tomorrow's God* by Neale Donald Walsch, Atria Books: New York, 2004, 3
3. GLWT, 346
4. *Teachings of Sri Rama-krishna*, 48
5. Gospel, 725-26
6. SD, I:333
7. TLWG, 116
8. Ibid., 318
9. GLWT, 80
10. Gospel, 285
11. RKDP, 321
12. GLWT, 251
13. RKDP, 900
14. GLWT, 518-19
15. *Vivekananda: The Yogas and Other Works*, ed., Swami Nikhilan-anda, Ramakrishna-Vivekananda Center: New York, 1953, 708-09
16. Gospel, 542

17. *The Gospel of the Holy Mother Sri Sarada Devi* by Her Devotee-Children, Sri Ramakrishna Math: Chennai, 1984, 100
18. *Sri Ramakrishna Karnam-ritam* by Ottur Bala Bhatta, Sri Ramakrishna Math: Chennai, 1975, 19

2. Meditation on Ramakrishna's Mind
1. *Brihadaranyaka Upani-shad*, 1.3.5
2. *Panchadashi*, 2:12
3. Gospel, 245
4. RKDP, 150
5. Ibid., 163
6. Ibid., 886
7. Ibid., 243
8. Ibid., 175
9. Ibid., 175
10. Ibid., 207-8
11. Gospel, 568
12. RKDP, 200
13. *Ramakrishna Katha O Kavya* by Sankariprasad Basu, Mandal Book House: Calcutta, 1987 (a)
14. RKDP, 218
15. Ibid., 210
16. Ibid., 349
17. Ibid., 214
18. Ibid., 276
19. Ibid., 236-37
20. Ibid., 240
21. Ibid., 295
22. Ibid., 301
23. Ibid., 712
24. Ibid., 398
25. Ibid., 415
26. Ibid., 416
27. Ibid., 438
28. Ibid., 441
29. Ibid., 466-67

30. RKASWE, 362-63
31. RKDP, 607-08
32. Ibid., 630
33. RKASWE, 333
34. Gospel, 538

3. Meditation on Ramakrishna's Divine Qualities
1. Gospel, 657
2. Ibid., 720
3. RKDP, 659
4. *Swami Vijnanananda* by Swami Jagadiswaranan-da,Ramakrishna Math: Allahabad, 1947, 289-90
5. Gospel, 152
6. SD, 8:100,125
7. RKASWE, 271-72
8. Gospel, 92
9. RKASWE, 326
10. Ibid., 109
11. Ibid., 280
12. RKDP, 502
13. RKASWE, 25
14. HLWG, 16
15. Ibid., 16
16. Gospel, 465-66
17. RKDP, 498
18. Ibid., 672
19. Ibid., 671
20. HMDP, 127-28
21. Gospel, 584
22. Ibid., 580
23. RKASWE, 86
24. Gospel, 894-95
25. RKDP, 825
26. Gospel, 296
27. RKASWE, 85-86
28. RKDP, 418
29. RKASWE, 362-63
30. Gospel, 739
31. RKDP, 401-02
32. Ibid., 517-18
33. Gospel, 260
34. RKASWE, 93
35. Gospel, 433

36. RKASWE, 352
37. HLWG, 139-40
38. RKDP, 262-63
39. Ibid., 312
40. Gospel, 568
41. RKDP, 437
42. *Bhakti O Bhakta* by Swami Krishnananda, Kashi Yogashrama, 1936, a and b
43. Gospel, 494
44. Ibid., 202
45. RKDP, 212
46. *Sri Sri Ramakrishna Upadesh* by Swami Brahmananda, Kiran Niketan: Calcutta, 66-67
47. *Kathasar* by Kumar Krishna Nandi, Students' Library: Calcutta, 1948, 86-87
48. RKDP, 496-97
49. Gospel, 220
50. HLWG, 128-29
51. *The Gospel of the Holy Mother*, Ramakrishna Math: Chennai, 2004, 215
52. RKDP, 686
53. Gospel, 540-41
54. TLWG, 254
55. Gospel, 717
56. Ibid., 717-18
57. Ibid., 140-41
58. RKDP, 388-90
59. Gospel, 866
60. RKASWE, 111
61. RKDP, 632
62. *Siva-mahimnah Stotra*, verses, 31-32

4. Meditation on Ramakrishna's Lila
1. RKASWE, 9
2. RKDP, 384-85
3. *The Complete Works of Swami Vivekananda*, Advaita Ashrama: Calcutta, 7:413
4. *Complete Works of Sister Nivedita*, Nivedita Girls' School: Calcutta, 1967, 137
5. *Life of Ramakrishna* by Romain Rolland, Advaita Ashrama: Calcutta, 1931, 23
6. HLWG, 108
7. Gospel, 866
8. HLWG, 317
9. RKDP, 450
10. TLWG, 160
11. Ibid., 295
12. GLWT, 360-61
13. SD, 4:71
14. *Swami Saradananda* by Br. Prakash Chandra, Basumati Sahitya Mandir: Calcutta, 203
15. SSDP, 87
16. HLWG, 502-03
17. Ibid., 503
18. M., 411-12
19. Ibid., 375
20. Ibid., 504
21. Gospel, 175
22. M., 504
23. Ibid., 84
24. Swami Dhireshananda's diary
25. RKASWE, 91
26. Gospel, 943
27. SSDP 102-03
28. M., 318
29. GLWT, 63
30. Gospel, 518 and *Kathamrita*, Udbodhan, 1:529
31. RKDP, 465
32. RKASWE, 256-57
33. Ibid., 112
34. HLWG, 508
35. Ibid., 508
36. Chetanananda's diary
37. Gospel, 118-19
38. *Srima-Katha* by Swami Jagannathananda, Ramakrishna Math: Bhubaneswar, 1953, 2:148
39. Ibid., 148
40. RKDP, 401-02
41. HLWG, 510
42. Ibid., 510
43. *Sri Ramakrishna Punthi* by Akshay Kumar Sen, Udbodhan Office: Calcutta, 626
44. *Srima-Katha*, 2:160, 163, 221
45. Gospel, 973
46. Ibid., 973-74
47. Ibid., 338
48. *Sri Ramakrishner Antyalila* by Swami Prabhananda, Udbodhan Office: Calcutta, 1897, 2:211

5. Meditations on Ramakrishna's Service to Humanity
1. Taittiriya Upanishad, 1:11:2
2. Gita, 4:34
3. Gospel, 289
4. Girish, 375
5. Gospel, 891
6. Ibid., 210-11
7. Ibid., 215-16
8. Ibid., 216-17
9. M., 409
10. Ibid., 118
11. RKDP, 505-06
12. RKASWE, 38-39
13. RKDP, 339
14. Ibid., 400-01
15. Ibid., 614
16. SD, 4:71
17. *Swami Saradananda* by Brahmachari Prakash, Calcutta, 203

18. RKDP, 615
19. Ibid., 150
20. Ibid., 581-82
21. M., 402-03
22. Gospel, 621; SD, 2:158
23. RKDP, 519
24. Ibid., 851-53
25. Ibid., 393
26. Ibid., 867
27. RKASWE, 112
28. SD, 9:142
29. RKASWE, 224
30. Ibid., 92-93
31. Ibid., 112
32. TLWG, 452
33. HLWG, 227
34. *Swami Vijnanananda* by Jagadishwarananda, Allahabad, 150
35. GLWT, 401-02
36. Ibid., 407
37. Ibid., 406
38. Ibid., 271
39. HMDP, 142
40. RKASWE, 380
41. Gospel, 955-56
42. *Life of Ramakrishna* by Romain Rolland, Advaita Ashrama: Calcutta, 1931, 294-95
43. RKDP, 222
44. Ibid., 248
45. Ibid., 648
46. Ibid., 649
47. *How a Shepherd Boy Became a Saint* by Swami Chetanananda, Vedanta Society: St. Louis, 24
48. Gita, 3:22-24
49. GLWT, 37
50. *Vivekananda: The Yogas and Other Works*, ed., Swami Nikhilananda, Ramakrishna-Vivekananda Center: New York, 711

6. Meditation on the Places of Ramakrishna's Lila

1. RKDP, 636
2. M., 508-09
3. RKASWE, 69
4. SD, 3:223
5. Ibid., 4:70
6. Chetanananda's collection from audio tape, 1982
7. SD, 3:240 and 5:118
8. *Dakshineswar Kali Mandirer Itivritta* by Nirmal Kumar Roy, Dakshineswar Temple, 2005, 59
9. SD, 5:116-17
10. Ibid., 4:84
11. Ibid., 10:184-85
12. Ibid., 10:183-84
13. Ibid., 10:184
14. Ibid., 5:113
15. Ibid., 10:179-80
16. Ibid., 5:113
17. Ibid., 5:114-15
18. *Kali Mandirer Itivritta*, 66
19. Gospel, 91
20. SD, 178
21. Ibid., 10:174-75
22. Ibid., 3:235-44
23. Gospel, 332
24. *Srima Samipe*, ed., Swami Chetanananda, Udbodhan Office: Calcutta, 276
25. TLWG, 204
26. RKDP, 605
27. SD, 4:103
28. Ibid., 5:118-19
29. Ibid., 5:119-24
30. Ibid., 10:166-72
31. Ibid., 15:412-36

7. Ramakrishna's Teachings on Meditation

1. Chandogya Upanishad, 7:6:1
2. Shvetashvatara Upanishad, 1:14-15
3. Mundaka Upanishad, 2:2:4
4. Katha Upanishad, 2:1:1
5. Bhagavata, 11:14:32-46
6. Gita, 6:19
7. Patanjala Yoga Sutras, 3:1-2
8. Ibid., 1:39
9. Gospel, 657
10. *Swami Vijnanananda* by Swami Jagadishwarananda, Allahabad, 289-90
11. Yoga Sutras, 1:14
12. RKDP, 207-09
13. Gospel, 409
14. Ibid., 409
15. Ibid., 751-52
16. SD, 14:259
17. RKDP, 723
18. Gospel, 916-17
19. Ibid., 403-04
20. Ibid., 743
21. RKDP, 641
22. Gospel, 744-45
23. Ibid., 746
24. Ibid., 604-05
25. Ibid., 561
26. Chandogya, 3:4:1
27. RKDP, 437
28. Gospel, 256
29. Ibid., 81
30. *Towards the Goal Supreme* by Swami Virajananda, Advaita Ashrama: Calcutta, 135-37
31. *Words of the Master* by Swami Brahmananda, Udbodhan Office: Calcutta, 81
32. Ibid., 292
33. RKDP, 435
34. Ibid., 435-36
35. *Words of the Master*, 81
36. Gospel, 365-66

37. Ibid., 370
38. Ibid., 282
39. Ibid., 280
40. Ibid., 802
41. RKDP, 532
42. Gospel, 915
43. RKDP, 535
44. Ibid., 723-24
45. Ibid., 724
46. *Ramakrishnadever Upadesh*, compiled by Suresh Chandra Dutta, Calcutta, 201
47. Gospel, 588
48. Ibid., 113
49. *Words of the Master*, 81
50. Gospel, 258
51. *Adi Kathamrita* by Girish Chandra Sen, Ananya Prakashan: Calcutta, 1983, 29-30 and Gospel, 181-82
52. Gospel, 343-44
53. Ibid., 385
54. Ibid., 850
55. Ibid., 344
56. RKDP, 437-38
57. M., 413, 477
58. *Srima Samipe*, ed., Swami Chetanananda, Udbodhan Office: Calcutta, 79
59. M., 78
60. HLWG, 64-65
61. RKDP, 441
62. RKASWE, 68-69
63. Ibid., 74-75
64. Ibid., 79
65. Ibid., 82-83
66. GLWT, 406
67. Ibid., 407-08
68. RKASWE, 138
69. Ibid., 118-19
70. Ibid., 109
71. Ibid., 113
72. GLWT, 245
73. Ibid., 246
74. RKASWE, 170

75. GLWT, 309
76. RKDP, 896-97
77. Ibid., 402-03
78. RKASWE, 218
79. Ibid., 221
80. Ibid., 218
81. Ibid., 241, 243
82. GLWT, 533
83. RKASWE, 297
84. Ibid., 255
85. Ibid., 273-74
86. Ibid., 280
87. M., 12, 45

8. Ramakrishna's Prayer

1. Gospel, 818
2. Mahabharata, 1:75:49
3. Gospel, 215
4. Ibid., 588
5. Ibid., 98, 385
6. Ibid., 542
7. Ibid., 612
8. *The New Dictionary of Thoughts*, Doubleday: USA, 1966, 507
9. RKASWE, 259
10. Gospel, 629-30
11. Ibid., 183
12. Ibid., 186
13. Ibid., 142-43
14. RKDP, 227
15. Ibid., 212
16. Ibid., 215
17. Bhagavata, 10:32:1
18. RKASWE, 357-58
19. Gospel, 312, 749
20. RKASWE, 358
21. Ibid., 544
22. Gospel, 579
23. Ibid., 481-82
24. RKDP, 827-28
25. Gospel, 745
26. RKDP, 582
27. Ibid., 668
28. Gospel, 541
29. Ibid., 567

30. RKDP, 501
31. Ibid., 502-04
32. Ibid., 659
33. Gospel, 383-84
34. Ibid., 396-97
35. Ibid., 846-47
36. GLWT, 454
37. RKDP, 401-02
38. Ibid., 516-17
39. Gospel, 832
40. Ibid., 739
41. Ibid., 391
42. RKDP, 671-72
43. Ibid., 850
44. Gospel, 934
45. RKDP, 657-58
46. Gospel, 831 and *Yuganayak Vivekananda* by Swami Gambhirananda, Udbodhan Office: Calcutta, 1:133
47. Gospel, 980
48. *Vivekananda: East meets West* by Swami Chetanananda, Vedanta Society: St. Louis, 2013, 20
49. M., 89
50. Ibid., 94
51. RKASWE, 360-61
52. Gospel, 384
53. Ibid., 518
54. Ibid., 323
55. Ibid., 463
56. RKDP, 686
57. Gospel, 332
58. Ibid., 934
59. Ibid., 832
60. Ibid., 342
61. RKDP, 248
62. Ibid., 648
63. Ibid., 648-49
64. Ibid., 233-34
65. TLWG, 281
66. Ibid., 724
67. Gospel, 625
68. Ibid., 819-20
69. Ibid., 820

70. Ibid., 542
71. Ibid., 176
72. Ibid., 480
73. Ibid., 480-81
74. Ibid., 548
75. Ibid., 866
76. RKDP, 439
77. HLWG, 543
78. RKDP, 439
79. Gospel, 264
80. *Yogakshema* by Swami Vishuddhananda, Calcutta, 50
81. Gospel, 747

9. Ramakrishna Scripture

1. *Hitopadesha*, 7
2. Gita, 16:24
3. *Fellowshiper Lecture* by Chandrakanta Tarkalankar, Calcutta, 1:7
4. RKASWE, 235-37
5. *The Complete Works of Swami Vivekananda*, Advaita Ashrama: Calcutta, 5:390
6. *Belur Math Rule Book*, 8-11
7. RKDP, 385
8. *Complete Works of Vivekananda*, 7:481
9. Ibid., 5:53
10. Ibid., 6:393-94
11. Brihadaranyaka Upanishad, 2:2:10
12. *Complete Works of Vivekananda*, 7:481-82
13. Ibid., 5:132
14. Ibid., 2:374
15. Gospel, 407
16. RKASWE, 222
17. Ibid., 280
18. RKDP, 825-26
19. Ibid., 380
20. Ibid., 321
21. RKASWE, 248
22. RKDP, 321

23. RKASWE, 249
24. Gospel, 544-45
25. Ibid., 687-88
26. Ibid., 830-31
27. Ibid., 396
28. RKDP, 424-25
29. Ibid., 425-26
30. Ibid., 426
31. Ibid., 667
32. Ibid., 668
33. Gospel, 587
34. *Astarage Alapan* by Swami Basudevananda, Calcutta, 1:37-38
35. Gospel, 672
36. Ibid., 392
37. RKDP, 610
38. Ibid., 612

10. History of *Ramakrishna Lilaprasanga*

1. HLWG, 490
2. RKASWE, 75
3. *Ramayaner Charitavali* by Sukhamoy Bhattacharya, Anandadhara Prakashan: Calcutta, ix
4. Bhagavata by Mahanamavrata Brahmachari, Calcutta, I:D-F
5. *Srima Sarada* magazine, Yogeswari Ramakrishna Math: Howrah, 16 year 7 issue
6. RKASWE, 448-49
7. TLWG, 106
8. *Ramakrishna Charit*, Gurudas Barman, 1910, Intro. a-b
9. *How a Shepherd Boy Became a Saint* by Swami Chetanananda, Vedanta Society: St. Louis, 63-64
10. GLWT, 325
11. RKDP, 447
12. *Swami Saradananda* by

Brahmachari Prakash, Calcutta, 139
13. GLWT, 331
14. *Swami Vijnanananda* by Swami Jagadishwarananda, Ramakrishna Math: Allahabad, 251
15. *Swami Saradananda Jeman Dekhiachi* by Swami Bhumananda, Udbodhan: Calcutta, 18-20
16. HLWG, 397
17. *Ramakrishna and His Disciples* by Christopher Isherwood, Methuen & Co Ltd: London, 2
18. *Saradanander Jivani* by Brahmachari Akshay Chaitanya, Model Publishing House: Calcutta, 154
19. Ibid., 147
20. Ibid., 146
21. *Udbodhan*, 11:641
22. HMDP, 560
23. GLWT, 335
24. RKDP, 381
25. *Sri Ramakrishna Lilamrita* by Vaikuntha Nath Sanyal, Calcutta, 398
26. *Udbodhan*, 11 year 11 issue
27. *Saradananda*, Akshay, 150-51
28. Saradananda's Diary copied by Swami Chetanananda
29. RKDP, 68
30. Ibid., 144
31. Ibid., 380
32. Ibid., 544
33. Ibid., 716
34. *Ramakrishna-Saradamrita* by Swami Nirlepananda, Karuna Prakashani: Calcutta, 21-22
35. *Jeman Dekhiachi*, 57-59

36. *Srima Sarada,* 6 year 1 issue
37. GLWT, 336-37
38. Ibid., 337
39. *Saradananda,* Akshay 151-52
40. *Srima Sarada,* 16 year 7 issue
41. *Sri Ramakrishna: Katha O Kavya* by Sankariprasad Basu, Mandal Book House: Calcutta, Introduction, *ka*
42. RKDP, 73
43. Ibid., 309
44. Ibid., 680
45. Ibid., 702
46. Ibid., 712-13
47. Ibid., 734
48. Ibid., 8
49. Ibid., 6-7
50. Ibid., 159
51. Ibid., 945
52. *Saradananda,* Akshay, 148
53. *Ramakrishna-Vivekanander Jivanaloke* by Swami Nirlepananda, Udbodhan: Calcutta, 247
54. *Smritisamchayan* by Brahmagopal Datta, Calcutta, 41
55. *Saradananda,* Akshay, 152
56. *Jeman Dekhiachi,* 289-90
57. *Glimpses of a Great Soul* by Swami Aseshananda, Vedanta Press: Hollywood, 238-39
58. *Swami Saradanander Smritikatha,* ed., Swami Chetanananda, Udbodhan: Calcutta, 287
59. *Jeman Dekhiachi,* 450
60. *Saradananda,* Akshay, 348-49
61. Diary of Swami Chetanananda
62. *Smritikatha,* 61

63. Ibid., 242-43
64. *Sri Sri Mayer Katha* (Undivided Edition), Udbodhan: Calcutta, 39

11. History of *Ramakrishna Kathamrita*

1. RKASWE, 125
2. GLWT, 189
3. *Samasamayik Drishtite Sri Ramakrishna Paramahamsa* by Brajendra Nath Bandyopadhyay & Sajani Kanta Das, General Printers and Publishers: Calcutta, 1968, 122
4. *Sri Sri Ramakrishna Kathamrita* by Srima, Kathamrita Bhavan: Calcutta, 1951, 3:vi
5. Ibid., 3:vii
6. Ibid., 3:vii
7. *Vivekananda O Samakalin Bharatvarsha* by Sankari Prasad Basu, Mandal Book House: Calcutta, 1976, 2:275
8. *Kathamrita,* 3:v
9. *Sri Ramakrishna O Tar Kathamrita* by Anonymous, Ramakrishna Vivekananda Ashrama: Howrah, 1983, 220
10. Gospel, 1019 and *Sri Sri Ramakrishna Kathamrita Centenary Memorial,* ed., D.P. Gupta & D.K. Sengupta, Srima Trust: Chandigarh, 1982, 142
11. *Srima Sarada* magazine, Sri Sri Yogeswari Ramakrishna Math: Howrah, 4:135
12. SD, 13:97
13. *Srima Sarada,* 6:8
14. SD, 13:184

15. Gospel, 662-64
16. Ibid., 506
17. *Srima Samipe,* ed., Swami Chetanananda, Udbodhan Office: Calcutta, 32
18. Gospel, 270
19. M., 467, 469
20. RKASWE, 364-65
21. Ibid., 365
22. Ibid., 365
23. Ibid., 366
24. H.H. Halley, *Halley's Bible Handbook,* Zondervan Publishing House: Grand Rapids, 1965, 493
25. Gospel, 407
26. *Samasamayik Drishtite,* 3
27. Ibid., 46-47
28. *The Complete Works of Swami Vivekananda,* Advaita Ashrama: Calcutta, 1968, 5:259
29. *Vivekananda: Yogas and other works,* ed., Swami Nikhilananda, Ramakrishna- Vivekananda Center: New York,1953, 708
30. *Belur Math Rule Book,* 10
31. *Complete Works of Swami Vivekananda,* 6:64
32. *The Life of Ramakrishna* by Romain Rolland, Advaita Ashrama: Calcutta, 1931, 89-90
33. Gospel, 376
34. *Brahmavadin* magazine, 3:104
35. *Sri Sri Ramakrishna Kathamrita Centenary Memorial,* 147
36. Gospel, preface, vii-ix
37. SD, 5:126
38. Ibid., 3:295-97
39. *Srimar Jivan Darshan* by Abhay Chandra Bhattacharya, Grantha

Bharati: Calcutta, 1990, 351
40. From the back cover of the Gospel
41. SD, 5:55-57 and *Srima Sarada* 1959:251
42. SD, 6:103-110
43. Bhagavad Gita, 10:13
44. *Sri Sri Ramakrishna Kathamrita*, Kathamrita Bhavan: Calcutta, 1957, 1:129 and Gospel, 266
45. *Ramakrishna Kathamrita Centenary Memorial*, 77, 79
46. Ibid., 85
47. Gospel, *381*
48. *Vedanta for the Western World*, ed., Christopher Isherwood, George Allen & Unwin Ltd.: London, 1961, 266
49. *Udbodhan*, 37:359
50. Gospel, 540
51. Ibid., 540-41
52. *Vedanta for the Western World*, 267
53. SD, 2:187
54. Gospel, 675
55. Brihadaranyaka Upanishad, 4:5:4
56. Gospel, 433-34
57. *Sri Sri Ramakrishnadever Upadesh* by Suresh Chandra Datta, Haramohan Publishing: Calcutta, 1968, 162
58. Gospel, 181-82
59. *The Life of Ramakrishna* by Romain Rolland, Advaita Ashrama: Calcutta, 1931, 294-95
60. Gospel, vi
61. Ibid., 83
62. *Vedanta and the West* magazine (Memories of Maharaj), 59

63. SD, 11:130
64. *Swamijir Padaprante* by Swami Abjajananda, Ramakrishna Mission Sarada Pitha: Belur Math, 1972, 37
65. *Amritarup Ramakrishna* by Swami Prabhananda, Udbodhan Office: Calcutta, 1991, 201-02
66. *Jivan Darshan*, 344
67. *Kathamrita*, 3:viii
68. Ibid., 3:viii
69. *Samakalin Bharatvarsha*, 2:302
70. Ibid., 3:viii
71. Ibid., 2:306
72. *Amritarup Ramakrishna*, 184
73. *Kathamrita*, (1st edition), 5:iv
74. Gospel, v
75. *World Thinkers on Ramakrishna Vivekananda*, ed., Swami Lokeswarananda, Ramakrishna Mission Institute of Culture: Calcutta, 1992, 13
76. *Ramakrishna and His Disciples* by Christopher Isherwood, Methuen & Co.: London, 1965, 279-82
77. *Prabuddha Bharata*, 1949:228-29
78. *Udbodhan*, 60:95

12. Krishna and Ramakrishna on Meditation

1. Gospel, 258
2. RKDP, 724
3. Ibid., 732
4. Gospel, 385
5. Ibid., 588
6. Ibid., 911-12
7. Ibid., 146

8. Ibid., 306
9. RKDP, 214
10. GLWT, 407-08
11. Gospel, 403
12. Ibid., 850, 744-45
13. RKDP, 435-36
14. RKASWE, 256
15. RKDP, 896
16. Gospel, 403-04
17. Ibid., 744
18. Ibid., 561
19. Ibid., 849
20. GLWT, 226-27
21. Ibid., 404
22. Ibid., 403
23. RKASWE, 138
24. Gospel, 744
25. Ibid., 674
26. Ibid., 612
27. RKDP, 435
28. Gospel, 745
29. Ibid., 769
30. Ibid., 427, 703
31. Ibid., 612
32. RKDP, 438
33. Gospel, 365
34. RKDP, 437
35. Gospel, 657
36. RKDP, 437

13. Dakshineswar: An Abode of Bliss

1. TLWG, 11
2. Ibid., 1
3. Ibid., 1
4. *Tattwamanjari* magazine, 23:216-17
5. *Swami Subodhananda*, Abani Mohan Gupta, 1:148-49
6. TLWG, 204
7. *Reminiscences of Swami Vivekananda* by His Eastern and Western Admirers, Advaita Ashrama: Calcutta, 1983, 278-79
8. *Udbodhan*, 31:266

9. *Devaloker Katha* by Swami Nirvanananda, Udbodhan Office: Calcutta, 1997, 96-97

14. The Magnitude of Ramakrishna's Life and Message
1. Gospel, 720
2. *Astarage Alapan* by Swami Basudevananda, Sri Ramakrishna Basudevananda Sangha: Calcutta, 1956, 2:99-100
3. *The Complete Works of Swami Vivekananda,* Advaita Ashrama: Calcutta, 1968, 6:465
4. Gospel, 452
5. Ibid., 439
6. Ibid., 322
7. Udana-Varga, 5:18
8. Matthew, 7:12
9. Mahabharata, Udyoga Parvan, 39:71
10. Sunnah
11. Talmud, Shabbat 3id
12. *Complete Works of Vivekananda* (1966), 4:187
13. HLWG, 348-50
14. *The Life of Ramakrishna* by Romain Rolland, Advaita Ashrama: Calcutta, 1931, 14
15. *Great Thinkers on Ramakrishna-Vivekananda,* Ramakrishna Mission Institute of Culture, Calcutta: 2009, 6
16. Ibid., 32
17. Ibid., 33
18. Ibid., 35
19. *Complete Works of Vivekananda* (1968), 2:363
20. Gospel, 782
21. Ibid., 1009-10

15. Meditation on the New Year
1. RKDP, 926
2. Ibid., 926
3. Ibid., 926-27
4. Gospel, 323-24
5. RKDP, 450
6. Ibid., 803
7. *Kalpataru Sri Ramakrishna,* ed., Swami Chetanananda, Udbodhan Office: Calcutta, 2015, 47-48
8. RKASWE, 60

16. Blessed Meditation
1. *Spiritual Treasures,* trans., by Swami Chetanananda, Vedanta Society: St. Louis, 1992, 98–99
2. Gospel, 207
3. Ibid., 903
4. Ibid., 542

Appendix
A New Religion Begins
1. *The Philosophy of Sarvepalli Radhakrishnan* by Paul Arthur Schilpp, Tudor Publ. Co., New York: 1952, 26
2. *The Complete Works of Swami Vivekananda,* Advaita Ashrama: Calcutta, 1979, 4:98
3. *Time* magazine, July 16, 1979, 59
4. "The Spiritual Heritage of India," Huston Smith, *Vedanta for East and West,* Issue 171 (January-February 1980), 10
5. Katha Upanishad, 2:2:13
6. Holy Bible, King James Version, Ecclesiastes 1:9
7. *Rig-Veda,* 6:9:6

8. *Complete Works of Vivekananda,* 7:496
9. Ibid., 7:24
10. *The Life of Swami Vivekananda* by His Eastern and Western Disciples, Advaita Ashrama: Calcutta, 1965, 415
11. *Sri Ramakrishna the Great Master,* Swami Saradananda, trans. by Swami Jagadananda, Sri Ramakrishna Math, Madras:1956, 299
12. *Complete Works of Vivekananda,* 1:1
13. Ibid., 1:16
14. Ibid., 1:24
15. Ibid., 1:24
16. Ibid., 4:356-57
17. Ibid., 4:357
18. Ibid., 4:357
19. Ibid., 4:358
20. Ibid., 4:358
21. Ibid., 4:358
22. Ibid., 5:81-82
23. Ibid., 6:416
24. Ibid., 2:387
25. Ibid., 2:301
26. Ibid., 2:67
27. Holy Bible, Matthew, 5:8
28. Belur Math Rule Book, 15
29. Shvetashvatara Upanishad, 4:3
30. *Reminiscences of Swami Vivekananda* by His Eastern and Western Admirers, Advaita Ashrama: Calcutta, 1964, 144
31. *The Devil: A Lecture* by Robert G. Ingersoll, C. P. Farrell: New York, 1899, 66
32. *Complete Works of Vivekananda,* 1:474

33. "As I Knew Her" by Gertrude Emerson Sen, *Prabuddha Bharata*, Vol. 83, No. 3, March 1978, 125

34. *Life of Vivekananda* by Eastern and Western Disciples, 369

35. *Complete Works of Vivekananda*, 3:286-87

36. Ibid., 3:205

37. *Life of Vivekananda* by Eastern and Western Disciples, 500-501

38. *The Life of Ramakrishna* by Romain Rolland, Advaita Ashrama: Calcutta, 1974, 12-13

39. *Buddhist Monks and Monasteries of India* by Sukumar Dutt, George Allen and Unwin Ltd.: London, 1962, 169

40. *Caesar and Christ, The Story of Civilization Part III* by Will Durant, Simon and Schuster: New York, 1944, 568

41. *Complete Works of Vivekananda*, 5:260-61

42. Bernard Shaw, quoted in *Modern Man in Search of Religion* by Swami Pavitrananda, Advaita Ashrama: Calcutta, 1947, 61

43. Belur Math Rule Book, 2

44. *The Creed of Christ* by Gerald Heard, Harper & Bros.: New York, 1940, 71-72

45. *Complete Works of Vivekananda*, 6:364

46. *Reminiscences of Vivekananda*, 340

47. Ibid., 340

48. *Udbodhan*, 56:43

49. Told by Swami Prabhavananda: From Swami Chetanananda's diary

50. *With the Swamis in America* by Swami Atulananda, Advaita Ashrama: Calcutta, 1938, 77-78

51. *Complete Works of Vivekananda*, 5:314

52. Ibid., 2:322-23

53. Ibid., 7:372

54. *Reminiscences of Vivekananda*, 281

55. Ibid., 282

56. Ibid., 282

Index

Bhagavata Purana, 270
Bhagavata scripture festival, 342
Bhagavat-Sandarva (Goswami, Jiva), 48
bhairava, 34, 187, 358
Bhairavi Brahmani, 33, 66, 162, 284, 415
Bhajanananda, Swami, 339
bhakta(s), 175, 217–218, 233, 342, 392, 402
bhakti: defined, 68–69; bhava-bhakti, 405;
  God, unite mind with, 402; kundalini and,
  225; types, 69, 104, 358
bhakti yoga: importance of, 104, 210; other
  yogas, synthesis with, 299, 384, 402–403;
  religion for this age, 207, 432
Bhaktitirtha, Ramendrasundar, 254
bhalo laga, 399
bhalobasa, 399
Bhamati, 237
Bharate Shaktipuja (Saradananda), 276
Bharatiprana, Pravrajika, 353
Bhattacharya, Kenaram, 33, 109
Bhattacharya, Ramendra Sundar, 427
Bhatti Kāvyam, 400
bhava, 179, 181
bhava samadhi, 40–41, 179, 215, 223
bhāva-bhakti, 405
bhavamukha, 220, 231, 276, 278, 286, 400
Bhavatarini Kali, 148
bhogis, 186, 417
bhog-vāsanā (worldly desires), 186, 405, 417
Bhojadeva, 244
Bhojaraj, 244
Bhumananda, Swami, 276–277, 288, 301–303
Bhuteshananda, Swami, 254
Bhuvi grnanti ye bhuridā janāh, 346
Bible. *see also* Christ; Christianity: burning of,
  244; gospels, 306, 323, 335, 382; as guide,
  239, 252; New Testament, 11, 254, 382; Old
  Testament quote, 432
Binay, 152
Binodini, 76
birth and death, 113, 239, 403
black cobra story, 125–126
blind faith, 67–68
bliss, 48, 73–74, 118, 200, 397–398
body consciousness, 69, 145, 184–185, 225
Boswell, James, 350, 351
brahma muhurta, 293
Brahma Puranas, 240
Brahma Sutras (Vyasa), 241, 245, 270
Brahmajnana, 167, 233
Brahmajnanis, 210–211
Brahman: "... alone is real...", 55, 209, 258, 395;
  with attributes, 232; described, 245, 252,
  255; is bliss, 200, 397; as Ishwara, 15, 44, 47;

knowers of, 41, 47, 176, 258, 343, 397; maha-
  vakya, 261; maya and, 15; meditation and,
  47, 119, 171, 175–176; Nada- Brahman, 238;
  nature/essence of, 43, 44, 47, 255, 257, 396;
  Nirguna, 47, 260, 276; Om as sound of, 167,
  238; Saguna, 47, 276; sarvabhute brahmadarshan, 10; Satchidananda Brahman, 271,
  396; Shakti and, 175; Sound-Brahman, 167,
  238; source of all scripture, 252
Brahmananda, Swami, 20–21; with brother
  disciples, *105*; Dakshineswar and, 375–376;
  death, 303; Divine Mother, vision of, 20–21;
  Kamale Krishna, 302; Madras monk story,
  399; pickpocket comment, 179; RK, fifth
  gospel of, 308; RK, relationship with, 9,
  185, 188, 189, 228, 302; RK, service to, 216–
  217; RK's, observations of, 361; RK's personal instructions, 185–186; "Sri Ramakrishner Upadesh — 248 teachings", 253;
  Swamiji's rules, 442–443; young girl, advice
  to, 348
Brahman-Consciousness, 310, 396
Brahmavadin magazine, 309, 330, 331, 351
brahmins: education, 30; ego/pride of caste,
  34, 64, 112, 159, 181; food restriction, 31, 41,
  61–62, 140; spiritual power, 51; upanayana
  (sacred thread ceremony), 29, 108, 283
Brahmo festival, 71, 203, 296, 311
Brahmo Samaj. *see also* Sen, Keshab Chandra:
  as bhogis, 417; meditation, 10, 174, 179–180;
  as modern/Westernized Brahmajnanis,
  165, 210–211; prayer, 232; publication, 272,
  424; RK and, 71, 232, *378*; Sadharan, 64,
  74–75; schism, 74–75; Sinthi festival, 203;
  Swamiji and, 178, 356–357
Brahmo Samaj prayer, 232
"breaking the jar in the market place", 397–
  398
Brihadaranyaka Upanishad: Atman realization, 356; Brahman described, 245, 252, 255;
  message of, 198, 343, 397
Brihaspati, 243
Brikasur, demon king, 201–202
British rule in India, 76, 84, 340–341, 381–382
Buddha: Buddhahood, 380; disciples, 322; as
  divine incarnation, 83, 377, 379; family, 144,
  416; followers, groups of, 250; honoured,
  252; languages learned, 326; life, recorded
  by followers, 322; meditation, object of,
  161; message of, 13–14, 200, 341, 381, 440,
  444; Pali, 254, 326; scholarly, 250; teachings,
  language of, 326–327; Tripitakas, 11, 239,
  254, 339, 382; Vedic rituals, fights against,
  245

maya (*continued*)
gunas, 43, 47; lust and gold, 180, 363–364, 381–382, 403, 425–426; nature of, 24, 26; Tapta jivanam, 344–345; traveller/cobra story, 344; 'woman and gold', 220, 228, 311, 364–365
Mayadevi, 144
Mayavati, 276, 302, 303, 335, 337
medha, 323. *see also* memory
medicinal oils, 415
meditation. *see also* mantra; Patanjali; pranayama; pure mind; scenes/themes for meditation:
defined, 161, 363–364
alternatives to, 367
bee analogy, 161, 400
benefits of: infinite power of, 391; mental/physical/spiritual, 12–14, 158, 160, 347, 354, 356, 400; realization from, 197; self-control, 34, 358–359
concentration vs., 161, 354, 363, 400
deep meditation, 160, 166–169, 181, 360–362, 367
God-realization, 158, 183, 354, 403
history, 160, 354, 356
instruction, 162–171, 186, 356–357
methods: active and still, 401–402; on Brahman, 47, 174–175; candle flame, 170, 364; on Chosen ideal, 46–47, 173–174; eyes open/eyes closed, 11, 362; focus, 11–13, 78; forms of, 361–362; four steps, 403–404; on God, 27, 173–174, 347, 357, 366–367, 401; on the heart, 406; on holy places, 404–406; on ideal, 46; on Inner Self, 361; know the object of, 68, 165; "neti, neti", 167, 361; nondualistic, 165, 366; places of, 357–360; posture for, 191, 360, 361; on RK's physical body, 20–23; on sahasrara, 357; Shiva yoga, 361; in solitude, 358; various, 179–181, 186; Vipasanna, 354; withdrawing, 360
obstacles, 161–162, 359, 363–364
perspectives, 26–28
pratyahara, 360
samyama, 35–36
seventh limb of yoga, 161
Vishnu yoga, 167, 361
for Westerners, 403, 430
yoga-nidra, 179
Meister Eckhart, 202
Melton's Encyclopedia of American Religions (Melton), 430
Memoirs of Ramakrishna, The (Abhedananda), 331–332

memory, 24, 28–29, 157, 323
mental restlessness, 13, 34, 38, 356, 401, 404
mental sin, 62, 219, 365
mental tirthas, 132
Mimamsa philosophy, 241, 245
mind. *see also* pure mind: body and, 26–28; God, unite mind with, 402; as guru, 35; mindfulness, 430; mind-intellect-memory-ego, 24; nature of, 12, 24, 26–28, 78, 220; restless, 13, 34, 38, 356, 401, 404; withdrawing, 360
mindfulness, 430
mind-intellect-memory-ego, 24
Mira Bai, 104, 206
mitabhuk, 363
Mitra, Manomohan, 20, 52–53
Mitra, Pramadadas, 251–252
Mitra, Satyacharan, 273, 274
mobile tirtha, 132
modern civilization, 431–432
modern yogis, publicity and, 214
moha (delusion), 210, 405
Mohindar Master, 415, 420, 421. *see also* Gupta, Mahendra Nath (M.)
moksha, 243, 397. *see also* liberation
Moksha-shastra, 243
monastic disciples. *see also specific disciples*: arrival of, 222; Brahmo Samaj and, 424; brother disciples, 105; early education, 18–19; japa and meditation, 172, 183, 193–194; RK's service to, 115–116, 120–127; samadhi, 277; vows, 293–294
monastic vows, 293–294, 416
money: aishwarya, 49; desire for, 28; greed, 93, 426; obstacle to God, 33; RK's reaction to, 21, 49, 57, 58, 83; shri, 53
Morning Star magazine, 332
mortality, 343
Moses, 8, 379, 383, 441
Mother Kali. *see* Kali
Mother's house, 279, 280, 289, 303. *see also* Udbodhan
mourning, 101, 113. *see also* grief
Muhammad, 11, 323, 350, 379, 383. *see also* Islam
Mujumdar, Pratap Chandra, 272
Mukherji, Jaya, 51, 99
Mukherji, Mahendra, 164–165, 180
Mukhopadhyay, Bhuban Chandra, 273
Mukhopadhyay, Dinanath, 155
Mukhopadhyay, Hridayram, 281. *see also* Hriday
Mukhopadhyay, Ishan, 154, 173, 174, 227, 320–321, 358

Mukhopadhyay, Jaynarayan, 284
Mukhopadhyay, Jnanendra Nath, 308
Mukhopadhyay, Joy, 156
Mukhopadhyay, Prankrishna, 120
Mukhopadhyay, Ram, 416
Mukhopadhyay, Satish Chandra, 350
Muktika Upanishad, 240
muladhara, 27, 168, 213, 225, 263
Müller, Fredrick Max, 273, 275, 425
Mundaka Upanishad, 9–10, 83, 160, 255, 396
Muni, Vidyaranya, 27, 47, 171
murkhotama (illiterate), 255
Muslims. *see* Islam
Mussalman, 170, 175. *see also* Islam
"My Master" lecture (Vivekananda), 130–131, 328
mysticism/mystics: aspects of, 8, 428, 430, 431; God realization and, 104; religion and, 444; RK and, 347; spiritual adventure, 202, 206

Nada-Brahman, *238*
naga (naked) sannyasi, 176–178, 294. *see also* Tota Puri
nahabat: area map, 139*f*; Chandramani Devi in residence, 146; HM in residence, 60, 95, 143–144, 371, 373, *410*; scenes/themes for meditation, 405
Naimisharanya, 323
Naiyayikas (logicians), 26
Naked One. *see* Tota Puri
Nakul, 143
Nambudripad, Ottur, 254, 427
name and fame: desire for, 28, 52, 53, 189, 205, 426; rajasic meditation and, 46–47; RK shuns, 53, 65, 83, 189, 209, 426
Nandakumar, 263
Nangta. *see* Totapuri
Nanigopal story, 426–427
Nānya panthāh, 103
Narada (sage): on bhakti, 68; meditation, 158; nature of, 67, 200, 424; Ramachandra and, 233; Srimati and, 201; Valmiki and, 270; Vasudeva mantra, 270
nara-lila, 103
Narendra/Naren, 21, 120, 151. *see also* Vivekananda, Swami
Narmada river, 132
Nawab (Muslim King), 337
Nāyikās, 370
negative emotions, 99–100, 220–222, 344. *see also* hatred
neti, 192n
"neti, neti", 167, 361
neti-dhauti, 192, 192n

New Age sects, 430–432
new religion: atheists, 431, 435; evolving, 428, 430–431; facets of, 432–436; fulfilment, 443–445; hidden religion, 430; love and freedom, 443–445; mystics, 428, 430; organization, 436–440; RK and, 79, 251; rules for, 440–443; unity in diversity (variety), 431–432; wealth and, 441–442
New Testament, 11, 254, 382
New Year practices, 389–398
Nidhuban, 150, 374
Nietzsche, Friedrich, 17
nigama, 242
Nikasha, 217
Nikhilananda, Swami: biographer, 302–303; *Gospel* translator, 290, 308, 331, 333; Huxley and, 347; Saradananda and, 300
Nikunja Devi (M.'s wife), 102–103, 348–349
Nilambar Babu's garden house, 309, 375, 442
nirakara, 424
Niramayananda, Swami, 282
Niranjan. *see* Niranjanananda, Swami
Niranjanananda, Swami, 101, *105*, 189–190, 196, 362, 398
Nirguna Brahman, 47, 260, 276
Nirguna- upāsanā, 171
nirjane, 358
Nirlepananda, Swami, 287, 301
nirvana, 248–249, 266, 404
Nirvanananda, Swami, 91, 304, 375–376
nirvikalpa samadhi
  RK and: manifestation, 264; no obstacles to, 38, 373; photograph of, 55; sadhana and, 66–67, 416; six-month duration, 231; unripe "I", disappearance of, 395
  Saradananda and, 277–278
Nishchaldas, 254
nishkam karma, 337
Nityatmananda, Swami, 140–142, 146–147, 151, 153–157, 311
Nivedita, 82, 123, 370, 445
nivritti, 237. *see also* renunciation
nonattachment, 13, 48, 57, 356. *see also* attachment
nondualism: knowledge, 248, 329, 397, 423; meditation, 165, 366; nondualistic experience as goal, 396–397; qualified, 75, 299, 384, 422; ultimate Truth and, 247–248; unity in diversity (variety), 14, 388, 431–432; Vedanta and, 15, 299, 384, 444
Nyaya philosophy, 26, 241, 246
Nyayamrita (Vyasaraj), 246

occult powers, 35–36, 129, 209, 211–212

old gardener story, 182–183
old rabbi story, 383
Old Testament quote, 432
Om: in meditation, 46, 160, 174, 404; RK, unable to utter, 258; Sound-Brahman, 167, 238; symbol (Nada-Brahman), *238*
organized religion, 436–443
organs of knowledge, 26, 237
Oxford dons story, 441–442

padartha-abhavana, 261
Padmalochan (pandit), 29, 55, 243, 321
Padmapada, 244–245
Pagla bamun, 425. *see also* mad brahmin
Pagla Thakur movie, 427
Pal, Krishnadas, 336–337
Pal, Mahendra, 21
Pali, 254, 326
Paltu, 73–74
Panchadashi (Vidyaranya Muni), 27, 47, 171
Panchamundi, 66, 148, 370, 373, 375
Pancharatra Samhita, 242
Panchavati, *159*; amalaki tree, 31, 163; banyan tree, 111, 139*f*, 144–145, 225; creation of, 228; five trees, 111; as holy place, 89–90; M., picnics, 146–147; madhavi plant, 145, 359; meditation in, 359–360; M's devotion to, 146–148; RK, sadhana, 23, 30, 31, 67; RK with disciples, 52, 123, 138, 140, 196–197; 'saturated with joy', 146–147; scenes/themes for meditation, 69, 294; tulsi grove, 228, 359
pandit crossing Ganges story, 265
Pandit Shashadhar, 55, 56–57, 218–219, 221, 258
Panikkar, Raimon, 377
Panini (sage), 243
Parables of Sri Ramakrishna (Ramakrishna Math, Chennai), 254
Parama Purush Ramakrishna (Sengupta), 425
"Paramahamsadever Ukti — Part 3" (M.), 309
Parashara, 240
Parikshit (King), 208, 322
Parliament of Religions, 382, 433
Parvat (sage), 201
Parvati, 86, 242
Patanjali: asana, 360; concentration, 26, 160–162; eight limbs of yoga, 160–161; illumination, what is needed, 65–66; mantra, 404; on meditation, 19, 26, 160–162, 360, 400, 404; nonattachment, 13; renunciation, 57; savikalpa samadhi, 36; the Seer, 366; Vedas, commentary on, 240; yoga philosophy, 160–161, 241; Yoga Sutras, 26, 65–66, 169, 255–256

path of action (pravritti), 237
Paul, Christ's apostle, 203, 323
pavitra (pureness), 405
Pavitrananda, Swami, 99
peace mantra, 38
Peter, Christ's apostle, 90, 323, 338, 371, 419
phalajophy (philosophy), 423, 424
Pharisees, 440–441
philosophical schools (India), 241, 245–246, 264
Phului-Shyambazar, 92, 136*f*, 137
pilgrimage sites (tirthas), 114, 132–134. *see also specific holy sites*
poets, 32–33, 85, 153, 246, 292
Portrait of Sri Ramakrishna, A (Sen, A.K.), 273
"power of attorney", 75–76, 180, 204, 278–279, 347, 421
Prabhavananda, Swami, 246
Practical Vedanta, 117–120
Prahlada, 114, 141, 233–234, 371, 419
Prajnanananda, Swami, 254
Prajnā-jyoti, 169
Prakriti, 43, 44, 46, 73, 248. *see also* Sankhya philosophy
pranayama, 192, 195, 294, 400, 430
Prashna Upanishad, 255
Prasthana-trayi, 241
Prathama-kalpika, 169
pratyahara, 360
pravritti, 237
prayer. *see also* Ramakrishna, prayer: atheists and, 235; of the Brahmo Samaj, 232; to conquer lust, 219–220; to cure disease, 216–219; to deities, 198, 235; devotional, 208–210; fear and, 220–222; God listens, 23, 234–235; for God-vision, 207–208; necessity of, 206–207; for occult powers, 211–212; overview, 198–206; petitionary, 227–229; for self-concealment, 214–216; selfish, 198; sincere/insincere, 204–205; soul of, 235–236; unselfish, 200; when in distress, 202–203; for worldly objects, 205–206
prema, 65, 179
Premananda, Swami: bhava samadhi request, 223; with brother disciples, *105*; *Gospel*, appreciation for, 349; RK, recollections of, 53, 76–77, 97–98, 120, 122; RK as embodiment of faith, 236; RK's personal instructions, 189, 308; samadhi, begs for, 223; story publication issue, 302
premer cakshu, 10
premer karna, 10
premer sharir, 10
Principles of Tantra (Avalon), 242